Berlin

timeout.com/berlin

Published by Time Out Guides Ltd, a wholly owned subsidiary of Time Out Group Ltd.
Time Out and the Time Out logo are trademarks of Time Out Group Ltd.

© **Time Out Group Ltd 2009**
Previous editions 1996, 1998, 2000, 2002, 2004, 2006.

10 9 8 7 6 5 4 3 2 1

This edition first published in Great Britain in 2009 by Ebury Publishing
A Random House Group Company
20 Vauxhall Bridge Road, London SW1V 2SA

Random House UK Limited Reg. No. 954009

Random House Australia Pty Limited 20 Alfred Street, Milsons Point, Sydney, New South Wales 2061, Australia
Random House New Zealand Limited 18 Poland Road, Glenfield, Auckland 10, New Zealand
Random House South Africa (Pty) Limited Isle of Houghton, Corner Boundary Road & Carse O'Gowrie,
Houghton 2198, South Africa

Distributed in the US by Publishers Group West
Distributed in Canada by Publishers Group Canada

For further distribution details, see www.timeout.com

ISBN: 978-1-84670-057-6

A CIP catalogue record for this book is available from the British Library.

Printed and bound by Firmengruppe APPL, aprinta druck, Wemding, Germany.

The Random House Group Limited supports The Forest Stewardship Council (FSC), the leading international forest
certification organisation. All our titles that are printed on Greenpeace approved FSC certified paper carry the FSC
logo. Our paper procurement policy can be found at www.rbooks.co.uk/environment.

Time Out carbon-offsets all its flights with Trees for Cities (www.treesforcities.org).

Time Out Guides Limited
Universal House
251 Tottenham Court Road
London W1T 7AB
Tel + 44 (0)20 7813 3000
Fax + 44 (0)20 7813 6001
Email guides@timeout.com
www.timeout.com

Editorial

Editor Dave Rimmer
Deputy Editor Lesley McCave
Copy Editors Edoardo Albert, Emma Howarth
Researchers John Fitzsimons, Moritz Hauptvogel,
  Mark Reeder
Proofreader Jo Willacy
Indexer Anna Norman

Managing Director Peter Fiennes
Editorial Director Ruth Jarvis
Deputy Series Editor Dominic Earle
Business Manager Dan Allen
Editorial Manager Holly Pick
Assistant Management Accountant Ija Krasnikova

Design

Art Director Scott Moore
Art Editor Pinelope Kourmouzoglou
Senior Designer Henry Elphick
Graphic Designers Gemma Doyle, Kei Ishimaru
Advertising Designer Jodi Sher

Picture Desk

Picture Editor Jael Marschner
Deputy Picture Editor Katie Morris
Picture Researcher Gemma Walters
Picture Desk Assistant Marzena Zoladz
Picture Librarian Christina Theisen

Advertising

Commercial Director Mark Phillips
International Advertising Manager Kasimir Berger
International Sales Executive Charlie Sokol
Advertising Sales (Berlin) In Your Pocket
Advertising Assistant Kate Staddon

Marketing

Marketing Manager Yvonne Poon
Sales & Marketing Director, North America Lisa Levinson
Senior Publishing Brand Manager Luthfa Begum
Marketing Designers Anthony Huggins, Nicola Wilson

Production

Group Production Director Mark Lamond
Production Manager Brendan McKeown
Production Controller Damian Bennett
Production Coordinator Julie Pallot

Time Out Group

Chairman Tony Elliott
Group General Manager/Director Nichola Coulthard
Time Out Communications Ltd MD David Pepper
Time Out International Ltd MD Cathy Runciman
Group IT Director Simon Chappell
Head of Marketing Catherine Demajo

Contributors

Introduction Dave Rimmer. **History** Frederick Studemann (*Truth and spies* Kevin Cote; *False economy* Dave Rimmer; *Making history* Zoe Jewell). **Berlin Today** Don Mac Coitir (*Grounded for good* Dave Rimmer). **Architecture** Michael Lees, Francesca Rogier (*Abstract concrete* Dave Rimmer). **Tower of the Hour** Dave Rimmer. **Where to Stay** Neal Wach. **Sightseeing** Zoe Jewell, Dave Rimmer (*Remember, remember* Dave Rimmer; *Walk: The Wall remembered* Julie Gregson; *The Turkish capital* Edmund Gordon; *Walk: Berlin revived* Dave Rimmer & Zoe Jewell; *Boot trips* Nicky Gardner; *Beats of Berlin* Dave Rimmer). **Restaurants** Kimberly Bradley, Kevin Cote, Andrew Horn, Zoe Jewell, Jenna Krumminga, Dave Rimmer (*The odd history of the Currywurst* Dave Rimmer). **Cafés, Bars & Pubs** Kimberly Bradley, Kevin Cote, Zoe Jewell, Jenna Krumminga, Neale Lytollis, Dave Rimmer (*Breakfast time* Dave Rimmer). **Shops & Services** Jenna Krumminga (*Keep it local* Jenna Krumminga; *Immaculate concepts* Jenna Krumminga; *Chocolate city* Zoe Jewell). **Festivals & Events** Nickolas Woods (*Pop goes Berlin* Dave Rimmer). **Children** Don Mac Coitir (*Children at work* Kevin Cote). **Film** Andrew Horn. **Galleries** Kimberly Bradley. **Gay & Lesbian** Nickolas Woods. **Music: Rock, World & Jazz** Rachel Doyle, Tommy Bell (*Rhythm of the city* Tommy Bell). **Nightlife** Neale Lytollis, Dave Rimmer (*Having a ball* Kimberly Bradley). **Performing Arts** Classical & Opera David Canisius; Theatre, Cabaret, Dance Sarah Lewis (*Palace of pleasures* Sarah Lewis). **Sport & Fitness** Don Mac Coitir (*Brave new World* Don Mac Coitir; *Games without frontiers* Peterjon Cresswell). **Trips Out of Town** Julie Gregson, Dave Rimmer (*Getting nowhere fast* Nicky Gardner). **Directory** Zoe Jewell, Dave Rimmer.

Maps john@jsgraphics.co.uk.

Photography Britta Jaschinski, except: page 14 Stapleton Collection/Bridgeman Art Library; page 16 Stasimuseum Berlin; page 19 Getty Images; page 22 Boening/Zenit/Laif; page 28 Corbis; page 38 www.bauhaus.de; page 127 Uwe Walz/Corbis; page 199 Sandra Wildeman/Messe Berlin; pages 271, 272, 274, 277, 280, 281, 282, 283, 284 Jael Marschner; page 279 Thomas Marschner; page 285 Elan Fleisher. The following images were provided by the featured establishments/artists: pages 57, 263, 266, 267.

The Editor would like to thank Gavin Blackburn, Chris Bohn, Kimberly Bradley, Elke Bruesch, Bianca Donatangelo, John Fitzsimons, Doris Jaud, Volker Hauptvogel, Sandra Portman, Mark Reeder, Martin Rimmer, Silke Sauer, Neil Tennant, Udo Victor, Neal Wach and Nickolas Woods.

Contents

Introduction

Producing one of these guides is like taking stock of a city. What's new, what's still here… what the hell happened in the last couple of years? When we compiled the previous edition of *Time Out Berlin*, Germany's capital of cool and confusion was polishing off the last of its major reunifying construction projects in time for the resounding success that was the FIFA World Cup 2006. The city was finished. Sort of. And it put on a friendly face and smiled at all the visitors and found that, hey, it enjoyed being friendly!

Since then, something new has been in the air, a quality alien to most of this schizoid city's recent selves – confidence. It's with a calm but wholly novel mood of self-assurance that Berlin, now one of Europe's most-visited cities, greets an ever-rising tide of tourists. Once a geographical and cultural backwater, it's now the hub of the north European transport network and a creative hub that's home to literally thousands of artists, writers and musicians. It also hosts arguably the continent's most important film and music industry festivals. The art scene is going international, there's enough classical music for two or three normal cities, and the party of the long Berlin night still pulses right through until dawn.

There are still divisions, of course, but this formerly sliced-up metropolis has found its ways of transcending them. In the new, creatively confident Berlin, cultural collisions are celebrated, rather than avoided. This is a city where football tournaments bring out hybrid German-Turkish flags, where people dance to Beethoven at classical club nights, where tattoo parlours merge with burger bars, where the line between dance and theatre becomes hard to distinguish on the performance cutting-edge, where abstractly themed designer kiosks exist as much to interrogate the very nature of consumption as to sell you some pop art knick-knacks, where gays and lesbians rub shoulders in truly mixed-up cruising areas, and where ancient ideological adversaries face off in new street names.

It's also a city confident enough to fill its new centre with memorials to the victims of its former evil selves. Berlin will never be a place where things are taken lightly. But that's no reason not roll up your sleeves, get involved, have fun, and experience the very model of a modern, multicultural metropolis.

ABOUT TIME OUT CITY GUIDES

This is the eighth edition of *Time Out Berlin*, one of an expanding series of more than 50 Time Out guides produced by the people behind the successful listings magazines in London, New York, Chicago and other cities around the globe. Our guides are all written by resident experts who have striven to provide you with all the most up-to-date information you'll need to explore the city or read up on its background, whether you're a local or a first-time visitor.

THE LOWDOWN ON THE LISTINGS

We've tried to make this book as useful as possible. Addresses, telephone numbers, websites, transport information, opening times, admission prices and credit card details have been included in the listings, as have details of selected other facilities and services. All were checked and correct at press time. However, business owners and managers can change their arrangements at any time, and with little notice. Before you go out of your way, we strongly advise you to phone ahead and check opening times and other relevant particulars. While every effort has been made to ensure the accuracy of the information in this guide, the publishers cannot accept responsibility for any errors it may contain.

PRICES AND PAYMENT

Our listings detail which of the five major credit cards – American Express (AmEx), Diners Club (DC), Discover (Disc), MasterCard (MC) and Visa (V) – are accepted at each venue. Many businesses will also accept other cards, as well as travellers' cheques issued by a major financial institution.

The prices we've listed in this guide should be treated as guidelines, not gospel. Fluctuating exchange rates and inflation can cause prices to change rapidly, especially in shops and restaurants. If prices vary wildly from those we've quoted, ask whether there's a good reason, and then please email us to let us know. We aim to give the best and most up-to-date advice, and we always want to know if you've been badly treated or overcharged.

THE LIE OF THE LAND

Berlin is a big, sprawling city. For ease of use, we've split many chapters of this guide into district. The first page of each Sightseeing chapter contains a small locator map, so you can see how each area relates to those around it. There's a larger overview map of Berlin's *Bezirke*, or boroughs, on page 336.

The back of this book also includes street maps of inner Berlin, which include enlarged maps of those areas that are most densely packed with things to do along with a comprehensive street index. The street maps start on page 316, and pinpoint the locations of hotels (**❶**), restaurants (**❶**), and cafés and bars (**❶**). The majority of addresses fall into the areas we've mapped, and we've given map references to make them easier to find.

TELEPHONE NUMBERS

The code for Berlin is 030, dialled before the relevant number when calling from within Germany. From abroad, you need to dial the international access code followed by 49 for Germany, 30 for Berlin and then the number itself. For more on telephones, *see p299*.

LANGUAGE

Many Berliners, especially younger ones, speak some English, but you shouldn't assume that you'll be understood. A few basic German phrases go a long way; you'll find a few on page 302, along with some help with restaurant menus on page 138.

ESSENTIAL INFORMATION

For practical information on the city, including visa, customs and immigration information, disabled access, emergency phone numbers, useful websites and details of the local transport network, see the Directory, which begins on page 286.

LET US KNOW WHAT YOU THINK

We hope you enjoy *Time Out Berlin*, and we'd like to know what you think of it. We welcome tips for places that you believe we should include in future editions and appreciate your feedback on our choices. Please email us at guides@timeout.com

There is an online version of this guide, along with guides to more than 50 other international cities, at **www.timeout.com**.

In Context

Brandenburger Tor. *See p15.*

History

Despotism, militarism, Nazism, communism – you name it, Berlin's been through it.

Berlin's origins are unremarkable. A settlement emerged sometime in the 12th century on swamplands that German knights had wrested from the Slavs. The name Berlin is believed to come from the Slav *birl*, 'swamp'.

Facing off across the Spree river, Berlin and its twin settlement Cölln (on what is now the Museumsinsel) were founded as trading posts halfway between the older fortress towns of Spandau and Köpenick. Today, the borough of Mitte embraces Cölln and old Berlin, and Spandau and Köpenick are outlying suburbs. The town's existence was first recorded in 1237, when Cölln was mentioned in a church document. In the same century, construction began on the Marienkirche and Nikolaikirche, both of which still stand.

The Ascanian family, as Margraves of Brandenburg, ruled over the twin towns and the surrounding region. To encourage trade, they granted special rights to merchants, with the result that Berlin and Cölln – which were officially united in 1307 – emerged as wealthy trading centres linking east and west.

Early years of prosperity came to an end in 1319 with the death of the last Ascanian ruler, leaving the city at the mercy of robber barons from outlying regions. Yet, despite political upheaval, Berlin's merchants continued business. In 1359 the city joined the Hanseatic League of free-trading northern European cities.

BLOODY BROTHERS

The threat of invasion remained, however. In the late 14th century, two powerful families, the Dukes of Pomerania and the brutal von Quitzow brothers, vied for control of the city.

Salvation came in the guise of Friedrich of Hohenzollern, a southern German nobleman sent by the Holy Roman Emperor in 1411 to bring peace to the region. Initially, Friedrich was well received by the local people. The bells of the Marienkirche were melted down and made into weapons for the fight against the aggressors. (Echoing this, the Marienkirche bells were again transformed into tools of war in 1917, during the reign of Kaiser Wilhelm II, the last ruling Hohenzollern.)

Having defeated the von Quitzow brothers, Friedrich officially became Margrave. In 1416, he took the further title of Elector of Brandenburg, denoting his right to vote in the election of the Holy Roman Emperor – titular head of the German-speaking states.

Gradually, Berlin was transformed from an outlying trading post to a small-sized capital. In 1442, foundations were laid for Berlin Castle and a royal court was established. By 1450, the city's population was 6,000.

With peace and stability came the loss of independent traditions, as Friedrich consolidated power. Disputes rose between the patrician classes (representing trade) and the guilds (which represented crafts). Rising social friction culminated in the 'Berlin Indignation' of 1447-48, when the population rose up in rebellion. Friedrich's son, Friedrich II, and his courtiers were locked out of the city and the foundations of the castle were flooded, but it was only months before the uprising collapsed and the Hohenzollerns returned triumphant. Merchants faced new restrictions and the economy suffered.

UNREFORMED CHARACTERS

The Reformation arrived in Berlin and Brandenburg under the reign of Joachim I Nestor (1535-71), the first Elector to embrace Protestantism. He strove to improve Berlin's cultural standing by inviting artists, architects and theologians to work in the city.

In 1538, Caspar Theyss and Konrad Krebbs, two master builders from Saxony, began work on a Renaissance-style palace. The building took 100 years to complete, and evolved into the bombastic Stadtschloss, which stood on what is now Museumsinsel in the Spree until the East German government demolished it in 1950.

Joachim's studious nature was not reflected in the self-indulgent behaviour of his subjects. Attempts to clamp down on drinking, gambling and loose morals had little effect. Visiting the city, Abbot Trittenheim remarked that 'the people are good, but rough and unpolished; they prefer stuffing themselves to good science'.

After stuffing itself with another 6,000 people, Berlin left the 16th century with a population of 12,000.

THE THIRTY YEARS WAR

The outbreak of the Thirty Years War in 1618 dragged Berlin on to the wider political stage. Although initially unaffected by the conflict between Catholic forces loyal to the Holy Roman Empire and the Swedish-backed Protestant armies, the city was eventually caught up in the war, which left the German-speaking states ravaged and divided for two centuries.

In 1626, imperial troops occupied Berlin and plundered the city. Trade collapsed and the city's hinterland was laid waste. To top it all, there were four serious epidemics between 1626 and 1631, which killed thousands. By the end of the war in 1648, Berlin had lost a third of its housing and the population had fallen to less than 6,000.

LAYING THE FOUNDATIONS

Painstaking reconstruction was carried out under Friedrich Wilhelm, 'the Great Elector'. He succeeded his father in 1640, but sat out the war in exile. Influenced by Dutch ideas on town planning and architecture (he was, after all, married to a Princess of Orange), Wilhelm embarked on a policy that linked urban regeneration, economic expansion and solid defence.

New city fortifications were built and a garrison of 2,000 soldiers established as Friedrich expanded his 'Residenzstadt'. In the centre of town, the Lustgarten was laid out opposite the Stadtschloss. Running west from the palace, the first Lindenallee ('Avenue of Lime Trees' or *Unter den Linden*) was created.

To revive the city's economy, a sales tax replaced housing and property taxes. With the money raised, three new towns were built – Friedrichswerder, Dorotheenstadt and Friedrichstadt. (Together with Berlin and Cölln, these now form the district of Mitte.)

Marienkirche.

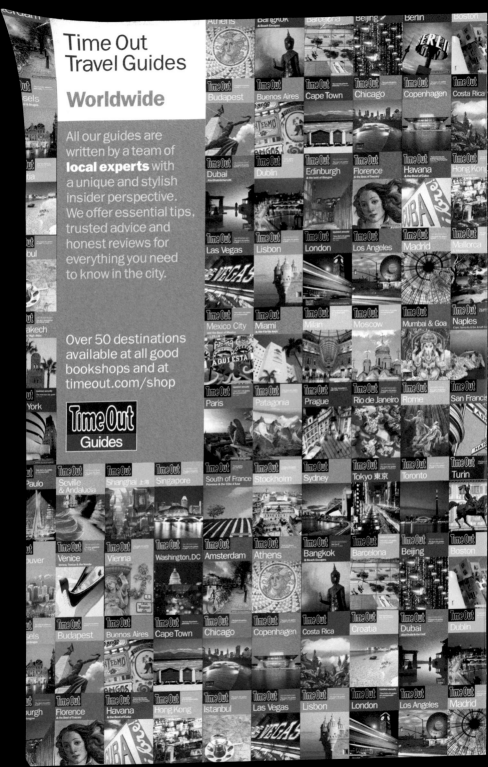

Time Out
Travel Guides

Worldwide

All our guides are
written by a team of
local experts with
a unique and stylish
insider perspective.
We offer essential tips,
trusted advice and
honest reviews for
everything you need
to know in the city.

Over 50 destinations
available at all good
bookshops and at
timeout.com/shop

Time Out
Guides

Friedrich Wilhelm, 'the Great Elector'.

In the 1660s, a canal was constructed linking the Spree and Oder rivers, confirming Berlin as an east-west trading centre.

But Friedrich Wilhelm's most inspired policy was to encourage refugees to settle. First to arrive were over 50 Jewish families from Vienna. In 1672, Huguenot settlers came from France. And both groups brought with them vital new skills.

The growing cosmopolitan mix laid the foundations for a flowering of intellectual and artistic life. By the time the Great Elector's son Friedrich III took the throne in 1688, one in five Berliners spoke French. Today, French words still pepper Berlin dialect, among them *boulette* ('hamburger') and *étage* ('floor').

In 1695, work commenced on Schloss Charlottenburg west of Berlin. A year later the Academy of Arts was founded and, in 1700, the Academy of Sciences. The building of the Französischer Dom and Deutscher Dom at Gendarmenmarkt in 1701 gave Berlin one of its loveliest squares. Five years later the Zeughaus ('Armoury'), now housing the Deutsches Historisches Museum, was completed on Unter den Linden.

In 1701, Elector Friedrich III had himself crowned Prussian King Friedrich I (not to be confused with the earlier Elector).

MILITARY PRECISION

The common association of Prussia with militarism can broadly be traced back to the 18th century and the efforts of two men in particular: King Friedrich Wilhelm I and his son Friedrich II (also known as Frederick the Great). Although father and son hated each other, and had different sensibilities (Friedrich Wilhelm was boorish and mean, Friedrich II sensitive and philosophical), together they launched Prussia as a major military power and gave Berlin the character of a garrison city.

King Friedrich Wilhelm I (1713-40) made parsimony and militarism state policy – and almost succeeded in driving Berlin's economy into the ground. The only thing that grew was the army, which by 1740 numbered 80,000 troops. Many of these were deployed in Berlin and billeted with ordinary citizens.

With a king more interested in keeping the books than reading them, intellectual life suffered. Friedrich Wilhelm had no use for art, so he closed down the Academy of Arts; instead he collected soldiers, and swapped a collection of oriental vases for one of the King of Saxony's regiments. The Tsar received a small gold ship in exchange for 150 Russian giants.

But the obsession with all things military did have some positive effects. The King needed competent soldiers, so he made school compulsory; the army needed doctors, so he set up medical institutes. Berlin's economy also picked up on the back of demand from the military. Skilled immigrants arrived (mostly from Saxony) to meet the increased demand. The result was a population boom – from 60,000 in 1713 to 90,000 in 1740 – and a growth in trade.

FREDERICK THE GREAT

While his father collected soldiers, Frederick the Great (Friedrich II) deployed them – in a series of wars with Austria and Russia (1740-42, 1744-5 and 1756-63; the last known as the Seven Years War) in a bid to win territory in Silesia in the east. Initially, the wars proved disastrous. The Austrians occupied Berlin in 1757, the Russians in 1760. However, thanks to a mixture of good fortune and military genius, Frederick emerged victorious from the Seven Years War.

When not fighting, the King set about forging a modern state apparatus (he styled himself 'first servant of the state'; Berliners called him 'Old Fritz') and transforming Berlin and Potsdam. This was achieved partly through conviction – the King was friends with Voltaire and saw himself as an aesthetically-minded Enlightenment figure – but it was also a political necessity. He needed to convince enemies and subjects that even in times of crisis he was able to afford grand projects.

So Unter den Linden was transformed into a grand boulevard. At the palace end, the Forum Fredericianum, designed and constructed by the architect von Knobelsdorff, comprised the Staatsoper, Sankt-Hedwigs-Kathedrale, Prince Heinrich Palace (now housing Humboldt-Universität) and the Staatsbibliotek. Although it was never completed, the Forum is still one of Berlin's main attractions.

To the west of Berlin, the Tiergarten was landscaped and a new palace, Schloss Bellevue (now the German president's official residence), built. Frederick also replaced a set of barracks at Gendarmenmarkt with a theatre, now called the Konzerthaus.

To encourage manufacturing and industry (particularly textiles), advantageous excise laws were introduced. Businesses such as the KPM (Königliche Porzellan-Manufaktur) porcelain works were nationalised and turned into prestigious and lucrative enterprises.

> **'On 27 October, Napoleon and his army marched through the Brandenburger Tor. Once again, Berlin was an occupied city.'**

There were legal and administrative reforms that saw religious freedom enshrined in law and torture abolished. Berlin also became a centre of the Enlightenment. Cultural and intellectual life blossomed around figures such as philosopher Moses Mendelssohn and poet Gottfried Lessing. By the time Frederick died in 1786, Berlin had a population of 150,000 and was the capital of one of Europe's great powers.

A DEBT TO ARCHITECTURE

The death of Frederick the Great marked the end of the Enlightenment in Prussia. His successor, Friedrich Wilhelm II, was more interested in spending money on classical architecture than wasting time debating the merits of various political philosophies. Censorship was stepped up and the King's extravagance sparked an economic crisis. By 1788, 14,000 Berliners were dependent on state and church aid. The state apparatus crumbled under the weight of greedy administrators. When he died in 1797, Friedrich Wilhelm II left his son with huge debts.

However, the old King's love of classicism gave Berlin its most famous monument: the Brandenburger Tor (Brandenburg Gate). It was built by Karl Gottfried Langhans in 1789, the year of the French Revolution, and modelled on the Propylaea in Athens.

Two years later, Johann Schadow added the Quadriga, a sculpture of Victoria riding a chariot drawn by four horses. Originally one of 14 gates, the Brandenburger Tor is now Berlin's geographical and symbolic centre.

If the King did not care for intellect, then the emerging bourgeoisie did. Towards the turn of the century, Berlin became a centre of German Romanticism. Literary salons flourished; they were to remain a feature of the city's cultural life into the middle of the 19th century.

Despite censorship, Berlin still had a platform for liberal expression. The city's newspapers welcomed the French Revolution so enthusiastically that in the southern German states Jacobins were referred to as 'Berliners'.

THE NAPOLEONIC WARS

In 1806, Berlin came face to face with the effects of revolution in France: following the defeat of the Prussian forces in the battles of Jena and Auerstadt on 14 October, Napoleon's army headed for Berlin. The King and Queen fled to Königsberg and the garrison was removed from the city. On 27 October, Napoleon and his army marched through the Brandenburger Tor. Once again, Berlin was an occupied city.

Napoleon set about changing the political and administrative structure. He called together 2,000 prominent citizens and told them to elect a new administration ('the Comité Administratif'), which ran the city until the French troops left in 1808. Napoleon also ordered the expropriation of property belonging to the state, the Hohenzollerns and many aristocratic families. Priceless works of art were removed from palaces in Berlin and Potsdam and sent to France. Even the Quadriga was taken from the Brandenburg Gate and shipped to Paris, earning Napoleon the nickname *Pferdedieb* – 'horse thief'. At the same time, the city was hit by crippling war reparations.

When the French left, a group of energetic, reform-minded aristocrats, grouped around Baron vom Stein, moved to modernise the moribund Prussian state. One key reform was the clear separation of state and civic responsibility, which gave Berlin independence to manage its own affairs. A new council was elected (though only property owners and the wealthy were entitled to vote). In 1810, the philosopher Wilhelm von Humboldt founded the university. All remaining restrictions on the city's Jews were removed. Meanwhile, Generals Scharnhorst and Gneisenau completely overhauled the army.

Although the French occupied Berlin again in 1812 on their way home from the disastrous Russian campaign, this time they were met with stiff resistance. A year later the Prussian King finally joined the anti-Napoleon coalition and thousands of Berliners signed up to fight. Napoleon was defeated at nearby Grossbeeren. This, together with a subsequent defeat in the Battle of Leipzig, marked the end of Napoleonic rule in Germany.

In August 1814, General Blücher brought the Quadriga back to Berlin, restoring it to the Brandenburg Gate with one symbolic addition: an Iron Cross and Prussian eagle were added to the staff in Victoria's hand.

POLICE AND THINKERS

The burst of reform was, however, fairly short-lived. Following the Congress of Vienna (1814-15), which established a new political and strategic order for post-Napoleonic Europe, King Friedrich Wilhelm III reneged on promises of constitutional reform. Instead of a greater unity among the German states, a loose alliance came into being; dominated by Austria, the German Confederation was distinctly anti-liberal in its tenor.

Truth and spies

Nobody's exactly sure how many unofficial informers were on the payroll of East Germany's Ministerium für Staatssicherheit, better known as the Stasi. There were something like 90,000 full-time agents, and about 175,000 Inoffizielle Mitarbeiter – unofficial informers – otherwise known as IMs. One thing's for sure, however: the secret police apparatus was the most pervasive in the history of state-sponsored repression; in its 1940s heyday, the Gestapo only had about 30,000 members.

Though its grip on everyday life in the DDR was exhaustive, the Stasi must go down in history as a flawed institution. In spite of its secret prisons, hidden cameras and microphones, and burgeoning network of IMs, the Stasi ultimately failed to prevent the peaceful revolution of 1989. Still, only a few weeks after the Wall was breached, crowds fell on the Stasi headquarters at Normannenstrasse, venting anger and frustration at their former tormentors.

In the preceding days, Stasi agents were working overtime, using up to 100 shredding machines to destroy documents. They barely put a dent in the six million or so files, which are now administered by a special authority charged with reviewing them and making

them available to prosecutors and everyday people who are simply curious to know what the Stasi knew about them.

Not surprisingly, the files contained embarrassing revelations for many politicians, journalists, athletes and other folks trying to get on with life in united Germany. Most of the charges involve people being listed as unofficial informers, a status hard to dispute or verify. West German investigative reporter Günther Wallraff and former transport minister Manfred Stolpe are among those who have been implicated in discussions about the Stasi files. Stolpe explained that it was necessary to be a double agent in order to retain his contacts with the dissident movement. Wallraff has flatly denied any Stasi connection at all.

Many could have been falsely implicated by over-ambitious Stasi career types, whose rank and pay were pegged to their success at recruiting spies.

There are thousands of Germans who readily own up to their double lives with the Stasi. They have to, in fact, to get their pensions – one major function of the agency minding the Stasi files is to determine who is eligible for retirement payments. One of those qualifying was Erich Mielke, the Stasi supremo, who collected about €400 a month until his death. Mielke was sentenced to prison in 1993 for murdering two policemen in Berlin in 1931, but was set free a few years later due to senility and declining health. He died in an old-age home in May 2000 at the age of 92. His former office is now the centrepiece of the **Forschungs- und Gedenkstätte Normannenstrasse** (see p129), otherwise known as the Stasi Museum. You can also tour a Stasi prison at the **Gedenkstätte Berlin-Hohenschönhausen** (see p130), and there's **Stasi: Die Ausstellung**, a Stasi exhibition, in Mitte (see p83).

In Prussia state power increased. Alongside the normal police, a secret service and a vice squad were established. The police president even had the power to issue directives to the city council. Censorship increased and the authorities sacked von Humboldt from the university he had created.

With their hopes for change frustrated, the bourgeoisie withdrew to their salons. It is one of the ironies of this time that, although political opposition was quashed, a vibrant cultural movement flourished. Academics like Hegel and Ranke lectured at the university, enhancing Berlin's reputation as an intellectual centre.

The period became known as Biedermeier, after a fictional character embodying bourgeois taste, created by Swabian comic writer Ludwig Eichrodt. Another legacy of this period is the range of neo-classical buildings designed by Schinkel, such as his Altes Museum and the Neue Wache.

For the majority, however, it was a period of frustrated hopes and bitter poverty. Industrialisation swelled the ranks of the working class. Between 1810 and 1840, the city's population doubled to 400,000. But most of the newcomers lived in conditions that would later lead to riot and revolution.

THE INDUSTRIAL REVOLUTION

Prussia was ideally equipped for the industrial age. By the 19th century, it had grown dramatically and boasted one of the greatest abundances of raw materials in Europe.

It was the founding of the Borsig Werke on Chausseestrasse in 1837 that established Berlin as the workshop of continental Europe. August Borsig was Berlin's first big industrialist. His factories turned out locomotives for the new Berlin-to-Potsdam railway, which opened in 1838. Borsig also left his mark through the establishment of a suburb (Borsigwalde) that still carries his name.

The other great pioneering industrialist, Werner Siemens, set up his electrical engineering firm in a house near Anhalter Bahnhof. The first European to produce telegraph equipment, Siemens personified the German industrial ideal, with his mix of technical genius and business savvy. And to house its workers, the Siemens company also added a new suburb, Siemensstadt, to the city.

THE PEOPLE V FRIEDRICH WILHELM

Friedrich Wilhelm IV's accession to the throne in 1840 raised hopes of an end to repression; and, initially, he appeared to share the desire for change. He declared an amnesty for political prisoners, relaxed censorship, sacked the hated justice minister and granted asylum to refugees.

Political debate thrived in coffeehouses and wine bars. The university was another focal point for discussion. In the late 1830s, Karl Marx spent a term there, just missing fellow alumnus Otto von Bismarck. In the early 1840s, Friedrich Engels did his military service in Berlin.

The thaw didn't last. It soon became clear that Friedrich Wilhelm IV shared his father's opposition to constitutional reform. Living and working conditions worsened for most Berliners. Rapid industrialisation brought sweatshops, 17-hour days and child labour. This misery was compounded in 1844 by harvest failure. Food riots broke out on Gendarmenmarkt, when a crowd stormed the market stalls.

'Dissension suppressed, Bismarck turned his mind to German unification.'

Things came to a head in 1848, the year of revolutions. Political meetings were held in beer gardens and in the Tiergarten, and demands made for internal reform and a unification of German-speaking states. After one demonstration in the Tiergarten, there was a running battle between police and demonstrators on Unter den Linden.

On 18 March the King finally conceded to allowing a new parliament, and vaguely promised other reforms. Later that day, the crowd of 10,000 that gathered to celebrate the victory were set upon by soldiers.

Shots were fired and the revolution began. Barricades went up throughout central Berlin and demonstrators fought with police for 14 hours. Finally, the King backed down for a second time. In exchange for the dismantling of barricades, he ordered his troops out of Berlin. Days later, he took part in the funeral service for the 'March Dead' – 183 revolutionaries who had been killed – and promised more freedoms.

Berlin was now ostensibly in the hands of the revolutionaries. A Civil Guard patrolled the city and the King rode through the streets wearing the revolutionary colours (black, red and gold), seeming to embrace liberalism and nationalism. Prussia, he said, should 'merge into Germany'.

But the revolution proved short-lived. When pressed on unification, the King merely suggested that the other German states send representatives to the Prussian National Assembly, an offer that was rebuffed.

Leading liberals instead convened a German National Assembly in Frankfurt in May 1848, while a new Prussian Assembly met in what is now the Konzerthaus to debate a new constitution. At the end of 1848, reforming fervour took over Berlin.

THE BACKLASH

Winter, however, brought a change of mood. Using continuing street violence as the pretext, the King ordered the National Assembly to be moved to Brandenburg. In early November, he brought troops back into Berlin and declared a state of siege. Press freedom was again restricted. The Civil Guard and National Assembly were dissolved. On 5 December the King delivered his final blow by unveiling a new constitution fashioned to his own tastes.

Throughout the winter of 1848-49, thousands of liberals were arrested or expelled. A new city constitution, drawn up in 1850, reduced the number of eligible voters to five per cent of the population. The police president became more powerful than the mayor.

By 1857, Friedrich Wilhelm had gone senile. His brother Wilhelm acted as regent until becoming King on Friedrich's death in 1861.

Once again, the people's hopes were raised: the new monarch began his reign by appointing liberals to the cabinet. The building of the Rotes Rathaus ('Red Town Hall') gave the city council a headquarters to match the size of the royal palace. Completed in 1869, the Rathaus was named for the colour of its bricks, not (yet) the political persuasion of its members.

But by 1861 the King was locked in a dispute with parliament over proposed army reforms. He wanted to strengthen his control of the armed forces. Parliament refused, so the King went over its members' heads and appointed a new prime minister: Otto von Bismarck.

THE IRON CHANCELLOR

An arrogant genius and former diplomat, Bismarck was well able to deal with unruly parliamentarians. Using a constitutional loophole to rule against the majority, he quickly pushed through the army reforms. Extra-parliamentary opposition was dealt with in the usual manner: oppression and censorship. Dissension thus suppressed, Bismarck turned his mind to German unification.

Unlike the bourgeois revolutionaries of 1848, who desired a Germany united by popular will and endowed with political reforms, Bismarck strove to bring the states together under the authoritarian dominance of Prussia. His methods involved astute foreign policy and outright aggression.

Wars against Denmark (1864) and Austria (1866) brought post-Napoleonic order to an abrupt end. Prussia was no longer the smallest Great Power, but an initiator of geopolitical change. Austria's defeat confirmed Prussia's primacy among German-speaking states. Victory on the battlefield boosted Bismarck's popularity across Prussia – but not in Berlin

itself. He was defeated in his constituency in the 1867 election to the new North German League. This was a Prussian-dominated body, linking the northern states, and a stepping stone towards Germany's overall unification.

Bismarck's third war – against France in 1870 – revealed his scope for intrigue and opportunism. Exploiting a dispute over the Spanish succession, he provoked France into declaring war on Prussia. Citing the North German League and treaties signed with the southern German states, Bismarck brought together a united German army under Prussian leadership.

> 'The economic boom fuelled a wave of speculation. Farmers became millionaires overnight as they sold off their fields to developers.'

Following the defeat of the French army on 2 September, Bismarck turned a unified military into the basis for a national nation. The Prussian king would be German emperor: beneath him would be four kings, 18 grand dukes and assorted princes from the German states, which would retain some regional powers. (This arrangement formed the basis for the modern federal system of regional *Länder*.)

On 18 January 1871, King Wilhelm was proclaimed German Kaiser ('Emperor') in the Hall of Mirrors in Versailles. In just nine years, Bismarck had united Germany and forged an empire that dominated central Europe. The political, economic and social centre of this new creation was Berlin.

IMPERIAL BERLIN

The coming of empire threw Berlin into its greatest period of expansion and change. The economic boom (helped by five billion gold francs extracted from France as war reparations) fuelled a wave of speculation. Farmers in Wilmersdorf and Schöneberg became millionaires overnight as they sold off their fields to developers.

During the following decades, Berlin emerged as Europe's most modern metropolis. This period was dubbed the Gründerzeit ('Foundation Years') and was marked by a move away from traditional Prussian values of thrift and modesty towards the gaudy and bombastic. The mood change manifested itself in monuments and buildings. The Reichstag, the Kaiser-Wilhelm-Gedächtniskirche, the Siegessäule ('Victory Column') and the Berliner Dom were all built in this period.

Adolf Hitler surveys a rally in Berlin. *See p21.*

Superficially, the Reichstag (designed by Paul Wallot, and completed in 1894) represented a commitment to parliamentary democracy. But in reality Germany was still in the grip of conservative, backward-looking forces. The Kaiser's authoritarian powers remained, as demonstrated by the decision of Wilhelm II to sack Bismarck in 1890 following policy disagreements.

SEEING RED

When Bismarck began his premiership in 1861, his offices on Wilhelmstrasse overlooked potato fields. By the time he lost his job, they were in the centre of Europe's most congested city. Economic boom and growing political and social importance attracted hundreds of thousands of new inhabitants. At unification in 1871, 820,000 people lived in Berlin; by 1890 this number had nearly doubled.

The working class was shoehorned into tenements – *Mietskasernen*, 'rental barracks' – that sprouted across the city, particularly in Kreuzberg, Wedding and Prenzlauer Berg. Poorly ventilated and overcrowded, the *Mietskasernen* (many of which still stand) became a breeding ground for unrest.

The Social Democratic Party (SPD), founded in 1869, quickly became the voice for the have-nots. In the 1877 general election it won 40 per cent of the Berlin vote. Here was born the left-wing reputation of *Rotes Berlin* ('Red Berlin') that persists to the present day.

In 1878, two assassination attempts on the Kaiser gave Bismarck an excuse to classify socialists as enemies of the state. He introduced restrictive laws to ban the SPD and other progressive parties. The ban lasted until 1890 – the year of Bismarck's sacking – but did not stem support for the SPD. In the 1890 general election, the SPD dominated the vote in Berlin; in 1912 it won more than 70 per cent of the vote, becoming the largest party in the Reichstag.

BUMBLING BILL

Famed for his ridiculous moustache, Kaiser Wilhelm II came to the throne in 1888, and soon came to personify the new Germany: bombastic, awkward and unpredictable. Like his grandmother Queen Victoria, he gave his name to an era. Wilhelm's epoch is associated with showy militarism and foreign policy bungles leading to a world war that cost the Kaiser his throne and Germany its stability.

'Soon dog and cat meat started to appear on the menu in Berlin restaurants.'

The Wilhelmine years were also notable for the explosive growth of Berlin (the population rose to four million by 1914) and a blossoming of cultural and intellectual life. The Bode Museum was built in 1904. In 1912, work began next door on the Pergamonmuseum, while a new Opera House was unveiled in Charlottenburg (later destroyed in World War II; the Deutsche Oper now stands on the site). Expressionism took off in 1910 and the Kurfürstendamm filled with galleries – Paris was still Europe's art capital, but Berlin was catching up. By Wilhelm's abdication in 1918, Berlin had become a centre of scientific and intellectual development. Six Berlin scientists, including Einstein and Max Planck, were awarded the Nobel Prize.

In the years immediately preceding World War I, Berlin appeared to be loosening its stiff collar of pomposity. The tango became all the

False economy

Of all the disasters that befell Berlin, nothing was as mad as the hyperinflation of 1923. It wasn't a sudden catastrophe: the German government had been dallying with inflation for years, funding its war effort by printing bonds. In 1914, a dollar was buying 4.2 marks; by late 1922, it was buying 7,000. And then the French occupied the Ruhr and things got really out of hand. By 20 November 1923, the rate had reached a mind-boggling 4,200,000,000,000 marks to the dollar.

Images from the time are vaguely comic: children using bundles of notes as building blocks, a wheelbarrow of currency for a loaf of bread. At the height of the crisis, over 300 paper mills and 2,000 printing presses worked around the clock to supply the Reichsbank with notes – in denominations of one million, then one billion, then a hundred billion. Some companies paid their employees twice a day, so they could shop at lunch to beat afternoon inflation.

A little hard currency could buy anything – or anyone. Foreign visitors splashed out in an orgy of conspicuous consumption. Entrepreneurs created whole business empires from ever-cheaper marks. And the homes of peasants in nearby villages filled up with Meissen porcelain and fine furniture as Berliners traded valuables for eggs or bread.

Although it was absurd, it wasn't funny. People starved as all their possessions vanished. The suicide rate shot up, as did infant mortality. Teenagers prostituted themselves after school, often with parental approval. Nothing made sense anymore. And as the simple fabric of everyday life was seen to unravel, so did people's faith in government. Among the worst hit were those who had most trusted the idea of Germany: the middle-class patriots who had sunk their money into war bonds, only to be paid back in useless paper.

The crisis was eventually brought under control, but the result had been a mass transfer of wealth to a handful of adventurers, big business and government. And as a pauperised people wondered who to blame, the hard right had found a cause. Nothing prepared the ground for Hitler better than the literal and moral impoverishment of the inflationary period.

Currency issues would continue to rumble through Berlin's 20th century. The formal division of Germany and Berlin followed the introduction of zonal currencies in 1948. The destabilisation of the East mark was one factor behind the later decision to build the Wall. For the rest of the Cold War, foreign visitors whooping it up on hard currency once again became a feature of city life, at least in its Eastern half. The true end of the DDR came on 1 July 1990, when the East mark was absorbed by its Western counterpart – at a one-to-one rate so unrealistic that it promptly caused the collapse of East German industry. These days, of course, everyone's moaning about the euro.

rage in new clubs around Friedrichstrasse – though the Kaiser banned uniformed officers from joining in the fun. Yet, despite the progressive changes, growing militarism and international tension overshadowed the period.

By 1914, Europe was armed to the teeth and ready to tear itself apart. In June, the assassination of Archduke Franz Ferdinand provided the excuse. On 1 August Germany declared war on Russia, and the Kaiser appeared on a balcony of the royal palace to tell a jubilant crowd that from that moment onwards, he would recognise no parties – only Germans. At the Reichstag the deputies, who had near unanimously voted for war, agreed.

WORLD WAR I AND REVOLUTION

No one was prepared for the disaster to come. After Bismarck, the Germans had come to expect quick, sweeping victories. The armies on the Western Front settled into their trenches for a war of attrition that would cost over a million German lives. Meanwhile, the civilian population faced austerity and shortages. After the 1917 harvest failed there were outbreaks of famine. Soon dog and cat meat started to appear on the menu in Berlin restaurants.

The SPD's initial enthusiasm for war evaporated, and in 1916 the party refused to pass the Berlin budget. A year later, members of the party's radical wing broke away to form the Spartacus League. Anti-war feeling was voiced in mass strikes in April 1917 and January 1918. These were brutally suppressed, but, when the Imperial Marines in Kiel mutinied on 2 November 1918, the authorities were no longer able to stop the anti-war movement.

The mutiny spread to Berlin, where members of the Guards Regiment came out against the war. On 9 November the Kaiser was forced into abdication and, later, exile. This date is weirdly layered with significance in German history: it's the anniversary of the establishment of the Weimar Republic (1918), the Kristallnacht pogrom (1938) and the fall of the Wall (1989).

On this day in 1918 Philip Scheidemann, a leading SPD parliamentarian and key proponent of republicanism, broke off his lunch in the second-floor restaurant of the Reichstag. He walked to a window overlooking Königsplatz (now Platz der Republik) where a crowd had massed and declared: 'The old and the rotten have broken down. Long live the new! Long live the German Republic!'

At the other end of Unter den Linden, Karl Liebknecht, who co-led the Spartacus League with Rosa Luxemburg, declared Germany a socialist republic from a balcony of the occupied Stadtschloss. Liebknecht and the Spartacists wanted a communist Germany; Scheidemann and the SPD favoured a parliamentary democracy. Between them stood those still loyal to the vanished monarchy. All were prepared to fight; street battles ensued throughout the city.

It was in this climate of turmoil and violence that the Weimar Republic was born.

THE WEIMAR REPUBLIC

The revolution in Berlin may have brought peace to the Western Front, where hostilities were ended on 11 November, but in Germany it unleashed political terror and instability. Berlin's new masters, the SPD under Friedrich Ebert, ordered renegade battalions returning from the front (known as the Freikorps) to quash the Spartacists, who launched a concerted bid for power in January 1919.

Within days, the uprising was bloodily suppressed. Liebknecht and Luxemburg were arrested on 15 January, interrogated in a hotel near the Zoo, and then murdered by the Freikorps. A plaque marks the spot on the Liechtenstein Bridge from which Luxemburg's body was dumped into the Landwehr Canal.

Four days later, national elections returned the SPD as largest party: the Social Democrats' victory over the far left was complete. Berlin was deemed too dangerous for parliamentary business, so the government decamped to the provincial town of Weimar, which gave its name to the first German republic.

Germany's new constitution ended up being full of good liberal intentions, but riddled with technical flaws, leaving the country wide open to weak coalition government and quasi-dictatorial presidential rule.

Another crippling blow was the Versailles Treaty, which set the terms of peace. Reparation payments (set to run until 1988) blew a hole in an already fragile economy.

Support for the right-wing nationalist lobby was fuelled by the loss of territories in both east and west, and restrictions placed on the military led some on the right to claim that Germany's soldiers had been 'stabbed in the back' by Jews and left-wingers.

In March 1920 a right-wing coup was staged in Berlin under the leadership of Wolfgang Kapp, a civil servant from east Prussia. The recently returned government once again fled the city. For four days Berlin was besieged by roaming Freikorps. Some had taken to adorning their helmets with a new symbol: the *Hakenkreuz* or swastika.

Ultimately, a general strike and the army's refusal to join Kapp ended the putsch. But the political and economic chaos in the city remained. Political assassinations were commonplace, and food shortages lead to bouts of famine. Inflation started to escalate.

> ## 'Hitler's first attempt to seize power came to nothing. Instead of marching on Berlin, he went to prison.'

There were two main reasons for the precipitate devaluation of the Reichsmark. To pay for the war, the desperate imperial government had resorted simply to printing more money, a policy continued by new republican rulers. The burden of reparations also led to an outflow of foreign currency.

In 1923, the French government sent troops into the Ruhr industrial region to take by force reparation goods that the German government said it could no longer afford to pay. The Communists planned an uprising in Berlin for October, but lost their nerve.

In November a young ex-corporal called Adolf Hitler, who led the tiny National Socialist Party (NSDAP or Nazi Party), launched an attempted coup from a Munich beerhall. He called for armed resistance to the French, an end to the 'dictatorship of Versailles' and punishment for those – especially the Jews – who had 'betrayed' Germany at the war's end.

Hitler's first attempt to seize power came to nothing. Instead of marching on Berlin, he went to prison. Inflation was finally brought down with the introduction of a new currency. But the overall decline of moral and social values that had taken place in the five years since 1918 was not so easy to reverse.

THE GOLDEN TWENTIES

Josef Goebbels came to Berlin in 1926 to take charge of the local Nazi Party. On arriving, he noted: 'This city is a melting pot of everything that is evil – prostitution, drinking houses, cinemas, Marxism, Jews, strippers, negroes dancing and all the offshoots of modern art.' Omitting the reference to 'evil', Goebbels' description of 1920s Berlin was not far wrong. During that decade, the city overtook Paris as Europe's arts and entertainment capital, and added its own decadent twist. 'We used to have a first-class army,' mused Klaus Mann, the author of *Mephisto*… 'now we have first-class perversions.'

By 1927, Berlin boasted more than 70 cabarets and nightclubs. While Brecht's *Dreigroschenoper* (*Threepenny Opera*) played at the Theater am Schiffbauerdamm, Dadaists gathered on Tauentzienstrasse at the Romanisches Café (which was later one of the victims of the Allied bombing campaign – the Europa-Center mall now stands on the site). There was a proliferation of avant-garde magazines focusing on these exciting new forms of art and literature.

But the flipside of all the frenetic enjoyment was raw poverty and glaring social tension, reflected in the works of artists like George Grosz and Otto Dix. In the music halls, Brecht and Weill used a popular medium to ram home points about social injustices.

In architecture and design, the revolutionary ideas of the Bauhaus school in Dessau (it moved to Berlin in 1932, but was closed down by the Nazis a year later) were taking concrete form in projects such as the Shell House on the Landwehr Canal, the Siemensstadt new town, and the model housing project Hufeisensiedlung ('Horse Shoe Estate') in Britz.

STREET-FIGHTING YEARS

The Wall Street Crash and the onset of global depression in 1929 ushered in the brutal end of the Weimar Republic. The fractious coalition governments that had clung to power in the prosperous late 1920s were no match for rocketing unemployment and a surge in support for extremist parties.

By the end of 1929, nearly one in four Berliners were out of work. The city's streets became a battleground for clashes between Nazi stormtroopers (the SA), Communists and Social Democrats. Increasingly, the police relied on water cannon, armoured vehicles and guns to quell street fighting. One May Day demonstration left 30 dead and several hundred wounded. Bülowplatz (now Rosa-Luxemburg-Platz), where the Communist Party (KPD) had its headquarters, was a regular scene of street battles, including one in August 1931 that saw two police officers murdered. One of those accused of the murders (and later found guilty, albeit by a Nazi court) was Erich Mielke, a young Communist, later to become the head of East Germany's secret police, the Stasi (*see p16* **Truth and spies**).

In 1932, the violence in Berlin reached crisis level. In one six-week period, 300 street battles resulted in 70 people dead. In the general

Olympiastadion, built for the 1936 Olympics and now home to Hertha BSC. *See p24.*

election in July the Nazis took 40 per cent of the general vote, becoming the largest party in the Reichstag. Hermann Göring, one of Hitler's earliest followers and a wounded veteran of the beerhall putsch, was appointed Reichstag president.

But the prize of government still eluded the Nazis. In November elections they lost two million votes across Germany and 37,000 in Berlin, where the Communists emerged as the strongest party.

The election was held against the backdrop of a strike by some 20,000 transport employees protesting against planned wage cuts. The strike had been called by the Communists and the Nazis, who vied with each other to capture the mass vote and bring the Weimar Republic to an end. Under orders from Moscow, the KPD shunned all co-operation with the SPD, ending any possibility of a broad left-wing front.

As Berlin headed into another winter of depression, almost every third person was out of work. A survey recorded that almost half of Berlin's inhabitants were living four to a room, and that a large proportion of the city's housing stock was unfit for human habitation. Berlin topped the European table of suicides.

The new government of General Kurt von Schleicher ruled by presidential decree. Schleicher had promised President von Hindenburg that he could tame the Nazi Party into a coalition. When he failed, his rival Franz von Papen manoeuvred the Nazi leader into power. On 30 January 1933, Adolf Hitler was named chancellor.

That evening, the SA staged a torchlight parade through the Brandenburg Gate. Watching from the window of his house, the artist Max Liebermann remarked to his dinner guests: 'I cannot eat as much as I'd like to puke.'

HITLER TAKES POWER

Hitler's government was a coalition of Nazis and German nationalists, led by the media magnate Alfred Hugenberg. Together their votes fell just short of a parliamentary majority, so another election was called for March, while Hitler continued to rule by decree.

Weimar's last free election was also its most violent. Open persecution of Communists began. The Nazis banned meetings of the KPD, closed left-wing newspapers and broke up SPD election rallies.

On 27 February a fire broke out in the Reichstag. It was almost certainly started by the Nazis, who used it as an excuse to step up the persecution of opponents. Over 12,000 Communists were arrested. Spelling it out in a speech at the Sportspalast two days before the election, Goebbels said: 'It's not my job to

practise justice, instead I have to destroy and exterminate – nothing else.'

The Nazis still didn't achieve an absolute majority (in Berlin they polled 34 per cent), but that didn't matter. With the support of his coalition allies, Hitler passed an Enabling Act that gave him dictatorial powers. By summer Germany had been declared a one-party state.

Already ad hoc concentration camps – known as 'brown houses' after the colour of SA uniforms – had sprung up around the city. The SS established itself in Prinz Albrecht Palais, where it was later joined by the secret police, the Gestapo. To the north of Berlin near Oranienburg, the Sachsenhausen concentration camp was set up.

> **'Hitler ordered that the lime trees on Unter den Linden be chopped down to give the boulevard a cleaner, more sanitised form – the first step in Nazi urban planning.'**

Along the Kurfürstendamm squads of SA stormtroopers would go 'Jew baiting', and on 1 April 1933 the first boycott of Jewish shops began. A month later, Goebbels, who became Minister for Propaganda, organised a book-burning, which took place in the courtyard of the university on Unter den Linden. Books by Jews or writers deemed degenerate or traitors were thrown on to a huge bonfire.

With their policy of *Gleichschaltung* ('co-ordination'), the Nazis began to control public life. Party membership became obligatory for doctors, lawyers, professors and journalists. Unemployment was tackled through public works programmes, conscription to an expanding military and by 'encouraging' women to leave the workplace.

During the Night of the Long Knives in July 1934, Hitler settled old scores with opponents within the SA and Nazi Party. At Lichterfelde barracks, officers of the SS shot and killed over 150 SA members. Hitler's predecessor as chancellor, General von Schleicher, was shot with his wife at their Wannsee home.

After the death of President von Hindenburg in August, Hitler had himself named *Führer* ('Leader') and made the armed forces swear an oath of allegiance to him. It had taken the Nazis less than two years to subjugate Germany.

GAMES WITHOUT FRONTIERS

A brief respite came with the Olympic Games in August 1936. To persuade foreign spectators that all was well in the Reich, Goebbels ordered the removal of anti-Semitic slogans from shops. 'Undesirables' were moved out of the city, and the pavement display cases for the racist Nazi newspaper *Der Stürmer* (*The Stormtrooper*) were dismantled.

The Games, centred on the newly built Olympiastadion, were not such a success for the Nazis. Instead of blond Aryans sweeping the field, Hitler had to watch the African-American Jesse Owens clock up medals and records. The Games did work, however, as a public relations exercise. Foreign visitors left with reports of a strident and healthy nation. Few stuck around to observe the reality of Hitler's rule.

As part of a nationwide campaign to cleanse cultural life of what the Nazis considered *Entartete Kunst* ('Degenerate Art'), works of modern art were collected and brought together in a touring exhibition designed to show the depth of depravity in contemporary ('Jewish-dominated') culture. But Nazi hopes that these 'degenerate' works would repulse the German people fell flat. When the exhibition arrived at the Zeughaus in early 1938, thousands queued for admission. People loved the paintings.

After the exhibition, the paintings were auctioned in Switzerland. Those that remained unsold were burnt in the fire station on Köpenicker Strasse. More than 5,000 works were destroyed.

TOTALITARIAN TOWN PLANNING

After taking power, Hitler ordered that the lime trees on Unter den Linden be chopped down to give the boulevard a cleaner, more sanitised form – the first step in Nazi urban planning.

Hitler's plans for the redesign of Berlin reflected the hatred the Nazis felt for the city. Hitler entrusted young architect Albert Speer with the job of creating a metropolis to 'out-trump Paris and Vienna'. The heart of old Berlin was to be demolished, and its small streets replaced by two highways stretching 37 kilometres (23 miles) from north to south and 50 kilometres (30 miles) from east to west.

Each axis would be 90 metres (295 feet) wide. Crowning the northern axis would be a domed Volkshalle ('People's Hall') nearly 300 metres (1,000 feet) high, with space for 150,000 people. Speer and Hitler also had grand plans for a triumphal arch three times the size of the Arc de Triomphe, and a Führer's Palace 150 times bigger than the one occupied by Bismarck. The new city was to be called Germania.

Little of this was built. The new Chancellery, completed in early 1939, went up in under a year – and was demolished after the war. On the proposed east-west axis, a small section around the Siegessäule was widened for Hitler's 50th birthday in April 1939.

A PEOPLE DESTROYED

Of the half a million Jews living in Germany in 1933, over a third were in Berlin. For centuries, the Jewish community had played an important role in Berlin's development, especially in financial, artistic and intellectual circles.

The Nazis wiped all this out in 12 years of persecution and murder. Arrests followed the boycotts and acts of intimidation. From 1933 to 1934, many of Berlin's Jews fled. Those who stayed were subjected to legislation (the 1935 Nuremberg Laws) that banned Jews from public office, forbade them to marry Aryan Germans and stripped them of citizenship. Jewish cemeteries were desecrated and the names of Jews chipped off war memorials.

Berlin businesses that had been owned by Jews – such as the Ullstein newspaper group and Tietz and Wertheim department stores – were 'Aryanised'. The Nazis expropriated them or forced owners to sell at absurdly low prices.

On 9 November 1938 'Kristallnacht', a wave of 'spontaneous' acts of vandalism and violence against Jews, was staged in response to the assassination of a German diplomat in Paris by a young Jewish émigré. Jewish properties across Berlin were stoned, looted and set ablaze. A total of 24 synagogues were set on fire. The Nazis rounded up 12,000 Jews and took them to Sachsenhausen concentration camp.

WORLD WAR II

Since 1935, Berliners had been taking part in air-raid drills, but it was not until the Sudeten crisis of 1938 that the possibility of war became real. At that juncture Hitler was able to get his way and persuade France and Britain to let him take over the German-speaking areas of northern Czechoslovakia.

But a year later, his plans to repeat the exercise in Poland were met with resistance in London and Paris. Following Germany's invasion of Poland on 1 September 1939, Britain and France declared war on the Reich.

Despite the propaganda and early victories, most Berliners were horrified by the war. The first air raids came with the RAF bombing of Pankow and Lichtenberg in early 1940.

In 1941, after the German invasion of the Soviet Union, the 75,000 Jews remaining in Berlin were required to wear a yellow Star of David and the first systematic deportations to concentration camps began. By the end of the war, only 5,000 Jews remained in Berlin.

Notorious assembly points for the deportations were Putlitzstrasse in Wedding, Grosse Hamburger Strasse and Rosenstrasse in Mitte. On 20 January 1942 a meeting of the leaders of the various Nazi security organisations in the suburb of Wannsee agreed on a 'final solution' to the Jewish question. They joked and drank brandy as they sat around discussing mass murder.

The turning point in the war came with the surrender at Stalingrad on 31 January 1943. Looking for a positive spin on this crushing defeat, Goebbels held a rally in the Sportpalast where he announced that Germany was now in a state of 'total war'. By summer, women and children were being evacuated from Berlin; by the end of 1943, over 700,000 people had fled.

The Battle of Berlin, which the RAF launched in November 1943, reduced much of the city centre to rubble. Between then and February 1944, more than 10,000 tonnes of bombs were dropped on the city. Nearly 5,000 people were killed and around 250,000 made homeless.

THE JULY PLOT

On 20 July 1944 a group of officers, civil servants and former trade unionists launched a last-ditch attempt to assassinate Hitler. But Hitler survived the explosion of a bomb placed at his eastern command post in East Prussia by Colonel Count von Stauffenberg.

That evening Stauffenberg was killed by firing squad in the courtyard of army headquarters in Bendlerstrasse, now Stauffenbergstrasse. The other members of the plot were rounded up and put on trial at the People's Court near Kleistpark and subsequently executed at Plötzensee Prison.

In early January 1945 the Red Army launched a major offensive that carried it on to German soil. On 12 February the heaviest bombing raid yet on Berlin killed over 23,000 people in little more than an hour.

'When Bertolt Brecht returned to Berlin in 1948 he found "a pile of rubble next to Potsdam".'

As the Russians moved into Berlin's suburbs, Hitler celebrated his last birthday on 20 April in his bunker behind Wilhelmstrasse. Three days later Neukölln and Tempelhof fell. By 28 April, Alexanderplatz and Hallesches Tor were in the hands of the Red Army.

The next day Hitler called his last war conference. He then married his companion Eva Braun and committed suicide with her the day after. As their bodies were being cremated by SS officers, a few streets away a red flag was raised over the Reichstag. The city officially surrendered on 2 May 1945. Germany's unconditional surrender was signed on 8 May at the Red Army command centre in Karlshorst, now the Museum Berlin-Karlshorst.

DEVASTATION AND DIVISION

When Bertolt Brecht returned to Berlin in 1948 he found 'a pile of rubble next to Potsdam'. Nearly a quarter of all buildings had been destroyed. The human cost of the war was as startling – around 80,000 Berliners had been killed, not including the thousands of Jews who would not return from the concentration camps.

There was no gas or electricity and only the suburbs had running water. Public transport had broken down. In the first weeks after capitulation, Red Army soldiers went on a rampage of looting, murder and rape. Thousands of men were transported to labour camps in the Soviet Union. Food supplies were used up and later the harvest failed in the land around the city. Come winter, the few remaining trees in the Tiergarten and other parks were chopped down for firewood.

Clearing the rubble was to take years of dull, painstaking work. The *Trümmerfrauen* ('rubble women') cleared the streets and created literal mountains of junk – like the Teufelsberg, one of seven hills that now exist as a result.

The Soviets stripped factories across Berlin as part of a programme to dismantle German industry and take it back home. As reparation, whole factories were moved to Russia.

Under the terms of the Yalta Agreement, which divided Germany into four zones of control, Berlin was also split into sectors, with the Soviets in the East and the Americans, British and French in the West. A Kommandatura, made up of each army's commander and based in the building of the People's Court in Kleistpark, dealt with the administration of the city.

Initially, the administration worked well in getting basics such as public transport back in running order. But tensions between the Soviets and the Western Allies began to rise as civilian government of city affairs returned. In the Eastern sector, a merger of the Communist and Social Democratic parties (both refounded in summer 1945) was pushed to form the Socialist Unity Party (SED). In the Western sector, the SPD continued as a separate party.

Events came to a head after elections for a new city government in 1946. The SED failed to get more than 20 per cent of the vote, while the SPD won nearly 50 per cent of all votes cast. The Soviets vetoed the appointment of the SPD's mayoral candidate, Ernst Reuter, a committed anti-Communist.

THE BERLIN AIRLIFT

The situation worsened in spring 1948. In response to the decision by the Western Allies to merge their respective zones in Germany into one administrative entity and introduce a new currency, the Soviets quit the Kommandatura. In late June all transport links to West Berlin were cut off and Soviet forces began a blockade of the city. Three 'air corridors' linking West Berlin with Western Germany became lifelines as Allied aircraft transported food, coal and industrial components to the beleaguered city.

Within Berlin the future division of the city began to take permanent shape as city councillors from the West were drummed out of the town hall. They moved to Rathaus Schöneberg in the West. Fresh elections in the Western sector returned Reuter as mayor. The Freie Universität was set up in response to Communist dominance of the Humboldt-Universität in the East.

'Throughout the 1950s, the two halves of Berlin began to develop separately.'

Having failed to starve West Berlin into submission, the Soviets called off the blockade after 11 months. The blockade also convinced the Western Allies that they should maintain a presence in Berlin and that their sectors of the city should be linked with the Federal Republic, founded in May 1949. The response from the East was the founding of the German Democratic Republic on 7 October. With the birth of the 'first Workers' and Peasants' State on German soil', the formal division of Germany into two states was complete.

THE COLD WAR

During the Cold War, Berlin was the focal point for stand-offs between the United States and the Soviet Union. Far from having any control over its own affairs, the city was wholly at the mercy of geopolitical developments. Throughout the 1950s the 'Berlin Question' remained prominent on the international agenda.

Technically, the city was still under Four-Power control, but since the Soviet departure from the Kommandatura, and the setting up of the German Democratic Republic with its capital in East Berlin (a breach of the wartime agreement on the future of the city), this counted for little in practice.

In principle, the Western Allies adhered to these agreements by retaining ultimate authority in West Berlin, while letting the city integrate into the West German system. (There were exceptions, such as the exemption of West Berliners from conscription, and the barring of city MPs from voting in the West German parliament.) Throughout the 1950s, the two halves of Berlin began to develop separately as the political systems in East and West evolved.

In the East, Communist leader Walter Ulbricht set about creating Moscow's most hardline ally in Eastern Europe. Work began on a Moscow-style boulevard – called Stalinallee – running east from Alexanderplatz. Industry was nationalised and subjected to rigid central planning. Opposition was kept in check by the new Ministry for State Security: the Stasi (see p16 **Truth and spies**).

West Berlin landed the role of 'Last Outpost of the Free World' and, as such, was developed into a showcase. As well as the Marshall Plan, which paid for much of the reconstruction of West Germany, the US poured millions of dollars into West Berlin to maintain it as a counterpoint to communism. The West German government, which at the time refused to recognise East Germany as a legitimate state, demonstrated its commitment to seeing Berlin reinstated as German capital by holding occasional parliamentary sessions in the city. The prominence accorded West Berlin was later reflected in the high profile of its politicians (Willy Brandt, for example) who were received abroad by prime ministers and presidents.

Yet despite the emerging divisions, the two halves of the city continued to co-exist in some abnormal fashion. City planners on both sides of the sectoral boundaries initially drew up plans with the whole city in mind.

The transport system crossed between East and West, with the underground network being controlled by the West and the S-Bahn by the East. Movement between the sectors (despite 'border' checks) was relatively normal, as Westerners went East to watch a Brecht play or buy cheap books. Easterners travelled West to work, shop or see the latest Hollywood films.

The secret services of both sides kept a high presence in the city. Berlin became the espionage capital of the world.

RECOVERY AND RESTRICTIONS

As the effects of US money and the West German 'economic miracle' took hold, West Berlin began to recover. A municipal housing programme meant that by 1963, 200,000 new flats had been built. Unemployment dropped from 30 per cent in 1950 to virtually zero by 1961. The labour force also included about 50,000 East Berliners who commuted over the inter-sector borders.

In the East reconstruction was slower. Until the mid 1950s, East Germany paid reparations to the Soviet Union. To begin with, there seemed to be more acts of wilful destruction than positive construction. The old Stadtschloss, slightly damaged by bombing, was blown up in 1950 to make way for a parade ground, which later evolved into a car park.

In 1952, the East Germans sealed off the border with West Germany. The only way out of the 'zone' was through West Berlin and consequently the number of refugees passing through from the East rose dramatically from 50,000 in 1950 to 300,000 in 1953. Over the decade, one million refugees from the East came through West Berlin.

THE 1953 UPRISING

In June 1953, partly in response to the rapid loss of skilled manpower, the East German government announced a ten per cent increase in working 'norms' – the number of hours and volume of output that workers were required to fulfil each day. In protest, building workers on Stalinallee (now Karl-Marx-Allee) downed tools

Making history

Confronting the past is a big deal in Germany. *Vergangenheitsbewältigung* is the word for it. History resonates throughout the urban landscape, with controversy always ready to erupt around the erection of monuments or the naming of streets, the rebuilding of palaces or the closure of airports. Ignore it or acknowledge it, the past won't go away.

For much of the late 20th century, division meant two official versions of history, and it's perhaps no surprise that it took 19 years for what is now the **Deutsches Historisches Museum** (German Historical Museum; *see p87*) to come up with a permanent exhibition on German history that they deemed morally and historically acceptable. The notion of a national history museum in West Berlin was debated in countless committees before finally being given the go-ahead in 1987. It didn't stop the debate, however. Liberal commentators accused more conservative historians of wanting to sanitise the past and take refuge in the classical history of Hegel and Goethe. Helmut Kohl thought it best to ignore the Nazi era as much as possible.

The result of those 19 years of discussion – from 1987 to 1996 – thankfully paid little heed to politicians. Instead, the DHM aimed to contextualise German history within Europe, but at the same time face Germany's difficult past head on. The exhibition now open in the Zeughaus is super-factual, but the attempt not to make value judgments has created something rather strange in a history museum – at no point in 2,000 years' worth of exhibits does it ever really celebrate history. There has even been criticism in the press that the museum is too objective and correct.

The same could hardly have been said for the previous occupant of the Zeughaus, the DDR-era **Museum für Deutsche Geschicte** (Museum of German History). That version introduced its visitors to national history with a 'pre-Marxist' section, beginning with the Reformation. There followed an entire floor devoted to Marx and Engels. Today, Marx and

Das Kapital are only fleetingly referred to in a box about 19th-century labour movements.

East and West had very different methods for dealing with the past. The DDR exploited history to legitimise the socialist regime. Two traditions of German history were identified, a progressive strand and a reactionary strand, and it's not hard to guess where each one led. While the DDR was the product of the progressive, revolutionary strand, the Federal Republic was the child of Germany's 'feudal', imperial and national socialist past.

In the West, history was ignored more than it was politically exploited. The Federal Republic preferred to draw on the more recent *Wirtschaftswunder* (post-war 'economic miracle') for its legitimisation. Until 1987, only a small exhibition in the Reichstag building, rather timidly entitled Fragen an die Deutsche Geschichte ('Questions on German History') satisfied West German historical curiosity. When history was presented, it too was interpreted through the lens of the Cold War. The Reichstag exhibition focused overwhelmingly on Germany's democratic awakenings. The Revolution of 1848 was celebrated in the West for the formation of the National Assembly, while on the same day in the East everyone had a day off work. Various tools were used to overcome the difficulties of a divided Germany. So as not to forget places of historical significance now in the DDR, West German brochures were created with names such as 'the German States Behind The Iron Curtain' or 'the Countryside of Mid- and Eastern Germany Under Communist Tyranny'. DDR maps of Berlin, meanwhile, simply left the city's western half blank, disdainfully labelling it 'Westberlin', or just 'WB'.

It is no coincidence – and a testament to the political importance of history in Germany – that both former West German chancellor Helmut Kohl and former East German boss Walter Ulbricht were self-appointed historians by profession.

on 16 June and marched to the government offices on Leipziger Strasse. The government refused to relent, and strikes soon broke out across the city. Crowds stormed Communist Party offices and tore red flags from public buildings. By noon the government had lost control of the city and it was left to the Red Army to restore order. Soviet tanks rolled into the centre of East Berlin, where they were met by stones thrown by demonstrators.

By nightfall the uprising was crushed. Officially 23 people died, though other estimates put the figure at over 200. A wave of arrests across East Berlin followed, with more than 4,000 people detained. Most went on to receive stiff prison sentences.

The 17 June uprising only furthered the wave of emigration. And by the end of the 1950s, it seemed likely that East Germany would cease to function as an industrial state through the loss of skilled labour. Estimates put the loss to the East German economy through emigration at some DM100 billion. Ulbricht increased his demands on Moscow to take action.

In 1958, Soviet leader Nikita Khrushchev tried to bully the Allies into relinquishing West Berlin by calling for an end to military occupation and a 'normalisation of the situation in the capital of the DDR (Deutsche Demokratische Republik – German Democratic Republic, or GDR)', by which he meant Berlin as a whole. The ultimatum was rejected and the Allies made clear their commitment to West Berlin. Unwilling to provoke a world war, but needing to prop up his ally, Khrushchev backed down and sanctioned Ulbricht's alternative plan for a solution to the Berlin question.

THE WALL

During the early summer of 1961, rumours spread that Ulbricht intended to seal off West Berlin with a barrier or reinforced border. Emigration had reached a high point as 1,500 East Germans fled to the West each day.

> ## 'For a few tense weeks, American and Soviet tanks squared off at Checkpoint Charlie.'

However, when in the early hours of 13 August units of the People's Police (assisted by Working Class Combat Groups) began to drag bales of barbed wire across Potsdamer Platz, Berlin and the world were caught by surprise.

In a finely planned and executed operation (overseen by Erich Honecker, then Politburo member in charge of security affairs), West Berlin was sealed off within 24 hours. As well

Queuing up at **Checkpoint Charlie**.

as a fence of barbed wire, trenches were dug, the windows of houses straddling the new border were bricked up, and tram and railway lines were interrupted: all this under the watchful eyes of armed guards. Anyone trying to flee west risked being shot; in the 28 years the Wall stood, nearly 80 people died trying to escape. Justifying their actions, the East Germans said they had erected an 'Anti-Fascist Protection Rampart' to prevent a world war.

Days later, the construction of a wall began. When it was completed, the concrete part of the 160-kilometre (100-mile) fortification ran to 112 kilometres (70 miles); 37 kilometres (23 miles) of the Wall ran through the city centre. Previously innocuous streets like Bernauer Strasse (where houses on one side were in the East, on the other in the West) suddenly became the location for one of the world's most deadly borders.

The initial stunned disbelief of Berliners turned into despair as it became clear that (as with the 17 June uprising) the Western Allies could do little more than make a show of strength. President Kennedy dispatched American reinforcements to Berlin, and, for a few tense weeks, American and Soviet tanks squared off at Checkpoint Charlie.

Vice-President Johnson came to show moral support a week after the Wall was built. Two years later Kennedy himself arrived and spoke to a crowd of half a million in front of Rathaus Schöneberg. His speech linked the fate of West Berlin with that of the free world and ended with the now famous statement, 'Ich bin ein Berliner!' (Literally, alas, 'I am a doughnut'.)

In its early years the Wall was the scene of many daring escape attempts. People abseiled off buildings, swam across the Spree, waded through sewers or tried to climb over. But as the fortifications were gradually improved with mines, searchlights and guard dogs, and as the guards were given orders to shoot on sight, escape became nearly impossible. By the time the Wall finally fell in 1989, it had been 'updated' four times to render it more or less completely impermeable.

In 1971, the Four Powers met and signed the Quadrapartite Agreement, which formally recognised the city's divided status. Border posts (such as Checkpoint Charlie) were introduced and designated to particular categories of visitors – one for foreigners, another for West Germans, and so on.

A TALE OF TWO CITIES

During the 1960s, with the Wall an infamous and ugly backdrop, the cityscape of modern Berlin (both East and West) began to take shape. On Tauentzienstrasse in the West the Europa-Center was built, and the bomb-damaged Kaiser-Wilhelm-Gedächtnis-Kirche was given a partner – a new church made up of a glass-clad tower and squat bunker.

Hans Scharoun laid out the Kulturforum in Tiergarten as West Berlin's answer to the Museumsinsel complex in the East. The first building to go up was Scharoun's Philharmonie, completed in 1963. Mies van der Rohe's Neue Nationalgalerie was finished in 1968. In the suburbs, work began on concrete mini-towns, Gropiusstadt and Märkisches Viertel. Conceived as solutions to housing shortages, they would develop into alienating ghettos. Alexanderplatz in the East was rebuilt along totalitarian lines, and the Fernsehturm ('Television Tower') was finished.

The historic core of Berlin was mostly cleared to make way for parks (such as the Marx-Engels Forum) or new office and housing developments. On the eastern outskirts of the city in Marzahn and Hohenschönhausen work started on mass-scale housing projects.

In 1965, the first sit-down was staged on the Kurfürstendamm by students protesting low grants and expensive accommodation. This was followed by several student political demonstrations against the state in general and the Vietnam War in particular. The first communes were set up in Kreuzberg, sowing the seeds of a counterculture that would make the district famous.

The student protest movement came into violent confrontation with the police in 1967 and 1968. One student, Benno Ohnesorg, was shot dead by police at a demonstration against the Shah of Iran, who visited the city in June 1967. A year later the students' leader, Rudi Dutschke, was shot by a right-winger. Demonstrations were held outside the offices of the newspaper group *Springer*, whose papers were blamed for inciting the shooting. It was out of this movement that the murderous Red Army Faction (also known as the Baader-Meinhof Gang) was to emerge. It made headlines often in the 1970s, not least through a series of kidnappings and killings of high-profile city officials.

NORMALISING ABNORMALITY

The signing of the Quadrapartite Agreement confirmed West Berlin's abnormal status and ushered in an era of decline, as the frisson of Cold War excitement and 1960s rebellion petered out. More than ever West Berlin depended on huge subsidies from West Germany to keep it going.

Development schemes and tax breaks were introduced to encourage businesses to move to the city (Berliners also paid less income tax), but still the economy and population declined. At the same time there was growth in the number of *Gastarbeiter* ('guest workers') who arrived from southern Europe and particularly Turkey, to take on menial jobs. Today there are over 120,000 Turks in the city, largely concentrated in Kreuzberg (*see p104* **The Turkish capital**).

By the late 1970s, Berlin was in decline. In the West, the city government was discredited by a number of scandals, mostly connected with property deals. In East Berlin, where Erich Honecker had succeeded Ulbricht in 1971, a regime that began in a mood of reform became repressive. Some of East Germany's best writers and artists, previously supporters of socialism, emigrated. From its headquarters in Normannenstrasse, the Stasi directed its policy of mass observation and permeated every part of East German society (*see p16* **Truth and spies**). Between East and West there were squalid exchanges of political prisoners for hard currency.

The late 1970s and early 1980s saw the rise of the squatter movement (centred in Kreuzberg), which brought violent political protest back on to the streets.

In 1987, Berlin celebrated its 750th birthday and East and West vied to outdo each other's festivities. In the East, the Nikolaiviertel was restored, and Honecker began a programme to do the same for the few remaining historical sites that had survived the ravages of both wartime bombing and post-war planning. The statue of Frederick the Great riding his horse was returned to Unter den Linden.

THE FALL OF THE WALL

Restored monuments were not enough to stem the growing discontent of East Berliners. The arrival of perestroika in the USSR had been ignored by Honecker, who stuck hard to his Stalinist instincts. Protest was strong and only initially beaten back by the police.

By the spring of 1989, the East German state was no longer able to withstand the pressure of a population fed up with communism and closed borders. Throughout the summer thousands fled the city and the country via Hungary, which had opened its borders to the West. Those who stayed began demonstrating for reforms.

By the time Honecker was hosting the celebrations in the *Volkskammer* ('People's Chamber') to mark the 40th anniversary of the DDR on 7 October 1989, crowds were demonstrating outside, chanting 'Gorby! Gorby!' to register their opposition. Honecker was ousted days later.

Honecker's successor, Egon Krenz, could do little to stem the tide of opposition. In a bid to defend through attack, he decided to grant the concession East Germans wanted most: freedom to travel. On 9 November 1989, the Berlin Wall was opened, just over 28 years after it had been built. As thousands of East Berliners raced through to the sound of popping corks, the end of East Germany and the unification of Berlin and Germany had begun.

REUNIFYING BERLIN

With the Wall down, Berlin found itself once again at centre stage. Just as the division of the city defined the split of Europe, so the freedom to move again between East and West marked the dawn of the post-Cold War era.

For a year Berlin was in a state of euphoria. Between November 1989 and October 1990, the city witnessed the collapse of communism and the first free elections (March 1990) in the East for more than 50 years; economic unification, with the swapping of the tinny Ostmark for the Deutschmark (July 1990); and the political merger of East into West, with formal political unification on 3 October 1990. (It was also the year West Germany won its third World Cup. The team may have come from the West, but in a year characterised by outbursts of popular celebration, Easterners cheered too.)

Unification also brought problems, especially for Berlin, where the two halves of the city now had to be welded into one whole. While Western infrastructure in the form of roads, telephones and other amenities was in decent working order, in the East it was falling apart. Challenges also came from the collapse of a command economy where jobs were provided

regardless of cost or productivity. The Deutschmark put hard currency into the wallets of Easterners, but it also exposed the true state of their economy. Within months, thousands of companies cut jobs or closed down altogether.

Responsibility for restructuring Eastern industry was placed with the Treuhandanstalt, a state agency that, for a while, was the world's largest industrial holding company. In Goering's old air ministry on the corner of Leipziger Strasse and Wilhelmstrasse (now the Finance Ministry), the Treuhand gave high-paid employment to thousands of Western yuppies and put hundreds of thousands of Easterners on the dole.

Easterners soon turned on the Treuhand, vilified as the agent of a brutal Western takeover. The situation escalated when Detlev Karsten Rohwedder, a Western industrialist who headed the agency, was assassinated in spring 1991 – probably by members of the Red Army Faction.

'Fast-track gentrification in the east was matched by the decline of West Berlin.'

The killing of another state employee, Hanno Klein, an influential city planner, not always loved by the city's construction sector, drew attention to another dramatic change brought about by unification: the property boom. With the Wall down and – after a 1991 parliamentary decision – the federal government committed to moving from Bonn to Berlin, a wave of construction and investment swept the city.

DRIFTING TO NORMALITY

The giddy excitement of the post-unification years soon gave way to disappointment. The sheer amount of construction work, the scrapping of federal subsidies and tax breaks to West Berlin, rising unemployment and a delay in the arrival of the government all contributed to dampening spirits. In 1994, the last Russian, US, British and French troops left the city. With them went its unique Cold War status. After decades of being different, Berlin was becoming like any other big European capital.

The 1990s were characterised by the regeneration of the East. In the course of the decade the city's centre of gravity shifted towards Mitte. The government and commercial districts were revitalised. On their fringes, especially around Oranienburger Strasse, the Hackesche Höfe and into Prenzlauer Berg, trendy bars, restaurants, galleries and boutiques sprouted in streets that under communism had been grey and crumbling.

Watching the wall. *See p29*

Fast-track gentrification in the East was matched by the decline of West Berlin. Upmarket shops and bars began to desert Charlottenburg and Schöneberg. Kreuzberg, once the inelegantly wasted symbol of a defiant West Berlin, degenerated to near slum-like conditions in places, while a new bohemia developed across the Spree in Friedrichshain.

Westerners did, however, benefit from the reopening of the Berlin hinterland. Tens of thousands of them swapped the city for greener suburbs in the surrounding state of Brandenburg.

THE BERLIN REPUBLIC

Having spent the best part of a decade doing what it had done so often during its turbulent past – regenerating itself out of the wreckage left by history – Berlin ended the 20th century with a flourish. Many of the big, symbolic construction projects had already sprouted: the new Potsdamer Platz, the Reichstag remodelled by Lord (Norman) Foster. Other major landmarks such as Daniel Libeskind's Jüdisches Museum and IM Pei's extension to the Deutsches Historisches Museum on Unter den Linden followed.

The turn of the century also saw Berlin return to its position at the centre of German politics. Parliament, the government and the accompanying baggage of lobbyists and journalists arrived from Bonn. From Chancellor Gerhard Schröder down, everyone sought to mark the transition as the beginning of the 'Berlin Republic' – for which read a peaceful, democratic and, above all, self-confident Germany as opposed to the chaos of the Weimar years or the self-conscious timidity of the Bonn era.

The Kosovo crisis of 1999, the attacks of 11 September 2001 and the wars in Afghanistan and Iraq all saw Germany called upon to play a more active role on the international stage. With this came marked differences from the past. When President George W Bush came to Berlin in May 2002, it was a world away from previous visits by US leaders. Where Kennedy brought a boost in a time of crisis, Reagan a bit of straight talking ('Mr Gorbachev, tear down this wall!') and Bush senior a nod to Germany's emerging importance, George W came to tell the Europeans to fall into line over Iraq. He was soon to be disappointed. Schröder made opposition to military action in Iraq a centrepiece of his September 2002 re-election campaign, which helped the 'Red-Green' coalition of Social Democrats and Greens squeak back into power.

Meanwhile, Berlin's financial problems – brought on by rocketing demands on expenditure, decline in central government handouts and the collapse of traditional industries – grew steadily worse. Matching this was the ineptitude of the city's political establishment, desperate to hang on to old privileges and unwilling to face up to tough, new choices. This was all encapsulated in the collapse of the Bankgesellschaft Berlin, a bank largely owned by the city. In the summer of 2001 it was felled by a raft of dud and corrupt real-estate loans. As well as sparking further deterioration in public finances, the scandal brought down the Senate – a grand coalition of Christian Democrats and SPD that had governed since 1990.

> **'Germany may have failed to scoop the World Cup, but it proved that it knew how to have a good time.'**

The resulting elections went some way towards a new start. Klaus Wowereit, head of the SPD, broke one of the great post-unification taboos and invited the Party of Democratic Socialism – successor party to East Germany's Communists and winners of half the Eastern vote – into a Social Democrat-led coalition.

The hullabaloo all but drowned out Wowereit's other bit of taboo-breaking: his unapologetic homosexuality, which made him the first openly gay politician to be elected to high office.

At national level Schröder's second term was far from happy. A brave attempt at welfare reform saw the chancellor attacked from all sides, including the left of his own

SPD. Defeats in regional polls forced Schröder in May 2005 to make one last bold move: early elections. Schröder entered the bitter campaign trailing his opponent Angela Merkel and the Christian Democrats in the opinion polls, but came within a whisker of winning the September general election.

The result was a mess. Both the main parties – CDU and SPD – lost votes; neither was able to form its preferred coalition. Instead, they were forced into a CDU-led grand coalition with Merkel as chancellor.

BREAKING NEW GROUND

As the first woman and first Easterner to hold the chancellorship, Merkel ensured her place in the history books when she took office in November 2005. Fifteen years after unification, her appointment demonstrated that, for all the difficulties, some progress was being made in bringing East and West together. The election of Matthias Platzeck, another Easterner, to chairmanship of the SPD underscored the point.

It was a development echoed on the ground where the final pieces of Berlin's structural reunification puzzle tumbled into place. The following year was to see the colossal new Berlin Hauptbahnhof take a bow as one of Europe's largest stations, while the renovated Olympiastadion would play host to the World Cup Final. Peter Eisenman's Denkmal für die ermordeten Juden Europas (Memorial to the Murdered Jews of Europe) was unveiled with the usual whiff of controversy. The hexagon of Leipziger Platz took final shape as the city centre's reception room. And after years of argument, demolition of the Palast der Republik finally began. The former communist parliament is eventually to be replaced by a reconstruction of the old Stadtschloss that once stood on the site. But there is still no real idea of where the money will come from, and at press time there wasn't even enough money to complete the demolition.

Initial expectations for the Merkel government were low. Grand coalitions often produce uninspiring compromise, and memories were also aroused of West Germany's grand coalition of the late 1960s, when opposition shifted to the streets and extremist parties prospered.

Defying such predictions, the understated pastor's daughter emerged as a respected international stateswoman. Relations with allies in Washington and London that had been damaged during the Schröder years were rebuilt; Berlin adopted a more sceptical line towards Moscow. And when another interminable round of European Union budget negotiations threatened to fail, it was the German chancellor who came to the rescue with a last-minute injection of funds.

The improvement of Germany's international standing was confirmed by the 2006 FIFA World Cup. Berlin was the centrepiece for what was widely judged to be one of the best-organised and – for the fans – most enjoyable competitions in the competition's history. Key to the success was the bold decision to welcome all fans – ticket-holders or not – to Germany to take part in the wider experience of the event. Hundreds of thousands came and followed the competition at huge open-air gatherings with massive TV screens. Mother of all street parties was Berlin's 'Fanmeile' along the Stasse des 17 Juni, where up to half a million people would gather for big matches. Eliminated by Italy in the semi-finals, Germany may have failed to scoop the cup at the Olympiastadion, but it proved to the world that it knew how to have a good time.

In 2007, Germany took on EU's rotating presidency and the leadership of the G8 group of rich nations. The role brought European leaders to Berlin to sign a 'Berlin Declaration' of ongoing commitment to the 50-year-old union. This was later followed by a Merkel-brokered settlement on a new set of operating rules for the bloc.

On the domestic front the going was heavier. Merkel's relations with the SPD became more strained as the Social Democrats adopted more left-wing positions in a bid to stem a catastrophic collapse in the party's support. Liberalising reforms were put on hold and both parties began to focus more on positioning themselves for federal elections in 2009.

In Berlin the Social Democrats had more to cheer about. Wowereit and his 'Red-Red' senate was returned to office by elections in 2006 that saw the SPD increase its share of the vote while support for the CDU fell. The Left party, which included the PDS, saw its vote slump by more than nine per cent.

Relations between Berlin and the federal government remained strained as the two haggled over who should meet the debt-laden city's 'national' costs. Agreement on some issues was matched by bitter wrangling on others such as the ultimate future of the Tempelhof airport site, which was co-owned by local and national governments. The decision to close the airport – in the face of vocal protest – as part of a consolidation of the city's airports at Schoenefeld was made in 2007, but just what would happen to the landmark site remained unclear.

But everyone could agree on one thing: for all its political coalitions and new city landmarks, Berlin hadn't quite settled down yet.

Berlin Today

Growing into its role as the capital, Berlin has shed Cold War flab and invested in top-notch facial reconstruction.

'Berlin is gradually becoming normal.' Brazen provocation or incongruous wishful thinking? Either way, that five-word phrase was enough both to warm the cockles of conservative hearts longing for a normal country and a normal capital city, and enough to send shivers up spines already braced by Berlin's otherness.

They were the spectacularly mundane words chosen by Thilo Sarrazin, the city's maverick, penny-pinching finance minister, to express his pleasure at the fact that the city was about to balance its budget for the first time in its nearly 60-year history as a federal state. Thankfully, Sarrazine was talking only about money. But his remark made for a bizarre sequel to an earlier remark by Klaus Wowereit, Berlin's flamboyant and openly gay mayor, that Berlin was 'poor but sexy'. A more fitting update might have been 'sexy and solvent'.

This is good news for a city groaning under the burden of post-Reunification reconstruction, and all the security and hospitality expenses that go with its regained status as Germany's capital. In less than two decades, Berlin saw its debt balloon from the equivalent of about €10 billion to a whopping €60 billion, as social welfare costs exploded and tax revenues dried up when hundreds of thousands of manufacturing jobs were lost. Desperate for help from wealthier federal states, the city claimed a budgetary emergency and brought its case to the German constitutional court – only to be told that the problem wasn't how much money it was getting but how much it was spending. Profligacy had become a habit for politicians on both sides of the divide in the heavily subsidised decades of partition.

Berlin finally got a financial break when the federal government agreed to cough up €200

Grounded for good

British architect Lord Norman Foster once described **Flughafen Tempelhof** as the 'mother of all airports'. It was originally designated in 1923, making it the world's second-oldest airport after Sydney, Australia. At least, that's what it was until 31 October 2008, when the last flight departed and Tempelhof closed for good – a victim of Schönefeld's expansion into the new hub of Berlin-Brandenburg International Airport.

After Lufthansa was founded here in 1926, Tempelhof joined London's Croydon and Le Bourget in Paris as one of Europe's three iconic pre-war airports. It was greatly expanded under the Nazis; when it was finished in 1941, Ernst Sagebiel's eagle-shaped building – its wings two giant, curving terraces of hangars – was the largest in Europe. Hitler and Albert Speer conceived Tempelhof as integral to their plans for Germania – Berlin rebuilt as overblown fascist showpiece – and the emphatic link of city and air travel was perhaps the Nazis' major contribution to urban planning. The airport remains Berlin's largest structure and the 20th biggest building on the planet.

When the dust settled in 1945, Tempelhof found itself in the American Sector. During Luftbrücke (Airlift) of 1948-49, blockaded West Berlin was kept alive by supplies flown in on Allied aircraft: at its height, one landed at Tempelhof every 90 seconds. At the main entrance, the Luftbrücke memorial displays the names of the 39 British and 31 American pilots who lost their lives during 'Operation Vittles'; it was unveiled in 1951 and became Berlin's first major post-war monument.

Tempelhof continued as a civil airport until 1973, and was then used exclusively by the US Air Force until civilian traffic resumed in 1990. But its runways were too short for modern airliners, and usage was dwindling long before the decision to axe both it and Tegel in favour of the new Berlin-Brandenburg International at Schönefeld, scheduled to open in 2012. By the end, the airport was losing €10 million a year.

The airport didn't go down without a fight, but a referendum in April 2007 to force a last-minute reconsideration failed on a low turnout. Analysis of the vote turns the kind of confusion that only Berlin can engender: West Berliners and conservatives were broadly in favour, but most East Berliners, with no sentimental connection to the Airlift, didn't even care enough to vote.

The city's problem is a simple one: what to do with this behemoth of a listed building? There are pipe dreams aplenty – a high-tech centre, apartments, movie studios, a Formula 1 track, an aviation museum, a park and entertainment palace – but nothing is close to confirmation; a proposal by cosmetics magnate Ronald Lauder to turn the whole thing into a €350 million fly-in clinic and conference centre has already been firmly nixed. Tempelhof is now in danger of becoming the world's largest white elephant.

million for restoration work on the Staatsoper (*see p248*), and gave extra funding for costs incurred with new capital-city status. To prove its good faith, Berlin shed plenty of weight, cutting the number of city employees from 185,000 to 115,000 since 2001. And today, the local economy is recovering and unemployment has dipped to its lowest rate in more than a decade.

RECONSTRUCTIVE SURGERY

As well as slimming down, Berlin has also undergone some radical plastic surgery. In 1988, for instance, commuting from Schöneberg to northern Mitte was impossible, and it was hardly any easier ten years later. But a further decade on, the journey is less like a ride to work and more of a sightseeing tour. An enormous Cold War wasteland has been plugged with a shimmering chain of architectural mega-projects, from the gargantuan Hauptbahnhof through the none-too-modest Kanzleramt to the vertiginously confident Potsdamer Platz (*see p112* **Berlin revived**). In between is the gigantic yet pragmatic Denkmal für die ermordeten Juden Europas, one of the most living monuments to the dead imaginable.

The redevelopment of nearby Pariser Platz is also as good as finished, with the new US Embassy having opened on 4 July 2008. The building is next door to the Brandenburger Tor, which remains the focus of both history and contemporary politics. Within weeks of the embassy's opening, this symbol of Reunification was once again caught in global ideological struggle when the US Democratic presidential candidate Barack Obama mooted the idea of giving a speech at it. The left-leaning city government gave the green light, but the conservatives in charge of the federal coalition saw red. For once, it didn't take long for all to agree that a candidate was no president, and Barack Obama still no John F Kennedy. Obama accepted the Siegessäule as a substitute venue; 200,000 turned out to hear him speak of the need for US-European reconciliation.

The new city centre has effectively joined West and East Berlin together, yet the city remains a kind of urban archipelago. Its individual neighbourhoods have evolved over centuries, each with their own atmosphere and attitude. Municipal reform merged many eastern and western districts in administrative terms, but the characters of the individual neighbourhood remain. Residents of Kreuzberg, for instance, not only ignore the fact that they're now officially part of Friedrichshain-Kreuzberg, but even still flaunt the borough's 20th-century postal codes, 36 and 61.

NEW ARRIVALS

While Berlin's old-timers cling to their identities, the rest of the population is in flux. In 2007, for the first time in decades, the number of births in Berlin outstripped the number of deaths, a mini-baby boom that some observers put down to the 2006 FIFA World Cup. For four balmy weeks, Berlin let down its collective hair, raised a collective glass and fell head-over-heels in love with itself. Was it a coincidence that local hospitals reported an unusual spike in the number of March births the following year?

However, the World Cup isn't the only reason that the city is growing once more. Number-crunchers also reported 'net inward migration', mainly from the surrounding state of Brandenburg and other parts of eastern Germany. The so-called 'fat-belt' around Berlin is soaking up both city folk and countrysiders, and now accounts for half of Brandenburg's population.

While this internal migration has gone largely unnnoticed, there have been more high-profile arrivals. Knut, a baby polar bear rejected by his mother and hand-raised by a grizzly-looking local zookeeper, became an overnight star. Knut's cause was helped by indignant animal rights groups, who said that nature must take its course and Knut should have been left to die. Outraged Berliners answered with a wave of hysterical sympathy and almost endless queues outside the Zoologischer Garten when Knut was finally introduced to the public. Less cute and cuddly by the day, he remains a popular attraction.

Adolf Hitler came back, too – as a waxwork in the new Madame Tussauds. Despite his depiction as an ageing, weakened man seated behind a desk, and despite a complete ban on any photography, politicians and commentators whipped up a frenzy about whether he should even be on display. On opening day, one of the first visitors lunged for the waxwork and ripped off Hitler's head.

The number of people moving to Berlin from overseas may seem relatively insignificant at fewer than 2,000 each year. Nevertheless, the city still has to deal with plenty of immigration-related issues. Many Germans are still getting used to the fact that millions of guest workers, recruited in the 1950s and 1960s to stoke the Economic Miracle, have put down roots and set up both families and businesses. Commentators have coined the term 'problem districts' in the debate about the apparent ghettoisation of Berlin's ethnic minorities, especially on the lower end of the income scale. Nowhere are these problems more obvious than in the education system, as schools in poorer (read: multi-ethnic) inner-city areas have been finding it hard to deal with the growing challenges and dwindling funds. It's not unusual for ethnic minorities to make up more than half of new pupil enrolments in parts of Kreuzberg, Neukölln and Wedding; some schools have reported that ethnic minorities make up 100 per cent of their new pupils, and have even advised local German kids to try their fortunes elsewhere. The principal of one school in Neukölln asked the authorities to shut it down, saying staff could no longer cope with the violence and chaos. Berliners, native and new, have taken to registering false addresses with the local authorities in order to avoid sending children to certain public schools or be faced with one of the expensive private schools that are popping up all over town.

MULTICULTURAL FLAGS

Still, it's not all doom and gloom on the ethnic interface. Ambivalence can find its expression in positive forms, as relations with the Turkish community, the city's largest minority group, have shown. During the FIFA World Cup Finals in 2006, for which Turkey did not qualify, jerseys, flags and even headscarves in German colours became a familiar sight among the Turkish community.

> **'Berlin's leaders have cast off their dependence on government handouts and are chipping away at the city's mountain of debt.'**

The Euro 2008 football tournament posed a new dilemma: Germany and Turkey were both involved. A new flag culture emerged: many cars flew flags of both countries, and apartment windows were festooned with German tricolours sporting Turkish sickles on the red stripe. Every Turkish victory prompted ecstatic convoys of flag-bearing, horn-tooting fans from Kreuzberg to the Ku'damm. Any time either team scored a goal, fireworks echoed around town.

The love-in climaxed when Germany and Turkey met in the semi-final, and half a million fans from both sides squeezed into the 'Fan Mile' at the Brandenburg gate. When Germany won, securing its place in the final, German fans launched Turkish-style convoys to the Ku'damm. But far from sulking, Turks, many of them second or third generation Berliners, put on another convoy and joined in with the celebrations of their fellow Germans. And it seemed Berlin's 'problem districts' also had a few solutions up their multicultural sleeves (*see p265* **Games without frontiers**).

Berlin has also been experimenting with other ways of resolving its dilemmas, with many issues being put to the vote in local or city-wide referendums. The ballot box has had its say over the future of the iconic Tempelhof airport (*see p34* **Grounded for good**), the development plans for the banks of the river Spree (*see p262* **Brave new World**), and the decision to rename part of Kochstrasse after Rudi Dutschke, the leftist student activist shot by an anti-communist reactionary in 1968 (*see p105*).

One of the main concerns driving locals who launch these petitions are the rising property prices and rents. Interpreters are cleaning up as investors from Britain, Ireland and Scandinavia, many of them ordinary people who can't get a foothold on the real estate ladders at home, turn to the relatively cheap Berlin market. Coupled with major developments bankrolled by big businesses, this state of affairs has forced senior citizens, young families and low earners out of areas where they've lived for all their lives.

BOOMTOWN BERLIN?

So, is Berlin about to turn into a boomtown? It's a bit early to say. Germany's fledgling economic recovery looks decidedly fragile against the backdrop of a stuttering US/global economy, skyrocketing fuel prices and looming food, energy and climate crises, and Berlin's own situation looks equally vulnerable. It's a question of demographics as well as economics: despite the new trend towards petitions and referendums, property developers still threaten to force 'normal' citizens, the life and soul of any town, out towards the suburbs.

On the other hand, Berlin's leaders have finally cast off their dependence on central government handouts and are beginning to chip away at the city's mountain of debt. The incredible amount of reconstruction done in less than two decades has given Berlin a complete facelift. Tourism is thriving and jobs are being created as the city's laid-back pace of life continues to lure artists, designers and other creatives from all over the world.

In terms of a place in the nation, most of the financing disputes with the federal government and federal states have been settled, and Germans are increasingly proud of the image that the city enjoys abroad. Perhaps it's a sign that Berlin, once a 'foreign body' in the German landscape, is finally being accepted and loved as the capital. No wonder: it's lost weight, done some homework and finally stopped begging for more pocket money. Only one terrifying question remains: what if Mr Sarrazin was right?

Neue Wache. See p39.

Architecture

They came, they saw, they built. Then it got torn down.

Berlin is an exhibition of architectural change. After nearly two decades of intense building activity, the city has re-emerged as a metropolis with a mix of contemporary projects and a long history of architectural development and experimentation. During the 1910s and '20s, Berlin was home to some of the century's greatest architects and designers, such as Peter Behrens, Bruno Taut, Ludwig Mies van der Rohe and Walter Gropius. But the path to modernism had been launched a century earlier by Karl Friedrich Schinkel, perhaps Berlin's greatest builder. In addition, fine specimens of nearly every style since the baroque age can be found here, from neo-Renaissance to neo-Rationalism, plus new buildings by just about every famous architect of today.

It wasn't until the late 19th century that Berlin was able to hold its own with grander European capitals, thanks to a construction boom known as the Gründerzeit, triggered by the rapid progress in industry and technology that followed German unification in 1871. The city acquired a massive scale, with wide streets and large blocks. These followed a rudimentary geometry and were filled in with five-storey *Mietskaserne* ('rental barracks') built around

linked internal courtyards. The monotony was partially relieved by a few public parks, while later apartment houses gradually became more humane and eventually got rather splendid. During the 1920s, this method of development was rejected in favour of Bauhaus-influenced slabs and towers, which were used to fill out the peripheral zones at the edge of the forests. The post-war years saw even more radical departures from the earlier tradition in all sectors of the city.

The post-Wall building boom has now deposited a new layer, a mixture of contemporary design and historic emulation. Some of it uses new environmental strategies and much of it attempts to restore a sense of continuity to an urban fabric ruptured by division and heavy-handed reconstruction.

The spirit of historic revival has even taken in the city's most famous landmark, the **Wall** (*see p42*). Speedily dismantled after 1989, it is now commemorated in public art, from the **Gedenkstätte Berliner Mauer** at Bernauer Strasse (*see p123*) to Frank Thiel's portraits of the last Allied soldiers, suspended above **Checkpoint Charlie** (*see p105*). The former line of the Wall is also marked in places by

a cobblestone strip, such as that visible west of the Brandenburg Gate. But with so much new architecture, its memory is fading away.

THE FIRST FEW HUNDRED YEARS

Berlin's long journey to world city status began in Berlin and Cölln, two Wendish/Slavic settlements on the Spree that were colonised by Germans around 1237. Among their oldest surviving buildings are the parish churches **Marienkirche** (*see p96*) and **Nikolaikirche** (*see p96*). The latter was rebuilt in the district known as the Nikolaiviertel, along with other landmarks such as the 1571 pub Zum Nussbaum and the baroque **Ephraim-Palais** (*see p95*). The Nikolaiviertel, between Alexanderplatz and the Spree, is the only part of central Berlin to give any idea of how the medieval city might have felt – except it's a clumsy fake, rebuilt by the East Germans in 1987, just a few decades after they had levelled the district.

Little survives of the massive **Stadtschloss** ('City Palace', 1538-1950; *see p88*), other than recently excavated foundations in front of the almost demolished Palast der Republik. The **Schlossbrücke** crossing to Unter

Architecture

For utopian modernist housing
Bruno Taut's **Hufeisen-Siedlung**. *See p41.*

For Stalinist sightlines
Karl-Marx-Allee. *See p43.*

For Prussian neo-classicism
Schinkel's **Altes Museum**. *See p39.*

For deconstructivist drama
Libeskind's **Jüdisches Museum**. *See p46.*

For imaginative remodelling
Norman Foster's revamped **Reichstag**. *See p46.*

For colourful confidence
Sauerbruch and Hutton's **GSW** headquarters. *See p46.*

For bending the rules
Michael Wilford's **British Embassy**. *See p46.*

For Nazi bombast
Flughafen Tempelhof. *See p42.*

For expressionist whimsy
Mendelsohn's **Einsteinturm**. *See p42.*

Walter Gropius. *See p37.*

den Linden, adorned with sensual figures by Christian Daniel Rauch, and the **Neptunbrunnen** (Neptune Fountain, now relocated south of Marienkirche), were designed on Bernini's Roman fountains, were designed to embellish the palace.

In 1647, the Great Elector Friedrich Wilhelm II (1640-88) hired Dutch engineers to transform the route to the Tiergarten, the royal hunting forest, into the tree-lined boulevard of Unter den Linden. It led west toward **Schloss Charlottenburg** (*see p121*), built in 1695 as a summer retreat for Queen Sophie-Charlotte. Over the next century, the Elector's 'Residenzstadt' expanded to include Berlin and Cölln. Traces of the old stone *Stadtmauer* (city wall) that enclosed them can still be seen on Waisenstrasse in Mitte. Two further districts, Dorotheenstadt (begun 1673) and Friedrichstadt (begun 1688), expanded the street grid north and south of Unter den Linden. Andreas Schlüter built new palace wings for Elector Friedrich Wilhelm III (1688-1713, crowned King Friedrich I of Prussia in 1701) and supervised the building of the Zeughaus (Armoury; Nering and de Bodt, 1695-1706; now home to the **Deutsches Historisches Museum**; *see p87*), whose bellicose ornamentation embodies the Prussian love of militarism.

Wilhelm I, the Soldier King (1713-40), imposed conscription and subjugated the town magistrate to the court and military elite. The economy now catered to an army comprising 20 per cent of the population (a fairly constant percentage until 1918). To spur growth in gridded Friedrichstadt – and to quarter his soldiers cheaply – the King forced people to build new houses, mostly in a stripped-down classical style. He permitted one open square, **Gendarmenmarkt**, where twin churches were built in 1701, one of which now houses the **Hugenotten Museum** (*see p90*).

After the population reached 60,000 in 1710, a new customs wall enclosed four new districts – the Spandauer Vorstadt, Königstadt, Stralauer Vorstadt and Köpenicker Vorstadt; all are now part of Mitte. The 14-kilometre (nine-mile) border remained the city limits until 1860.

Geometric squares later marked three of the 14 city gates in Friedrichstadt. At the square-shaped Pariser Platz, Carl Gotthard Langhans built the **Brandenburger Tor** (Brandenburg Gate) in 1789, a triumphal arch later topped by Johan Gottfried Schadow's **Quadriga** (*see p82*). The stately buildings around the square were levelled after World War II, but have now largely been reconstructed or replaced, including the **Adlon Hotel** (Patzschke, Klotz, 1997; *see p53*), on an expanded version of its original site, and the buildings flanking the gate, **Haus Sommer** and **Haus Liebermann** (Kleihues, 1998).

SCHINKEL AND CO

Even with the army, Berlin's population did not reach 100,000 until well into the reign of Frederick the Great (1740-86). Military success inspired him to embellish Berlin and Potsdam; many of the monuments along Unter den Linden stem from his vision of a 'Forum Fredericianum'. Though never completed, the unique ensemble of neo-classical, baroque and rococo monuments includes the vine-covered **Humboldt-Universität** (Knobelsdorff, Boumann, 1748-53; *see p87*); the **Staatsoper** (Knobelsdorff, Langhans, 1741-43; *see p253*); the Prinzessinnenpalais (1733, now the **Operncafé**; *see p156*) and the **Kronprinzenpalais** (1663, expanded 1732; Unter den Linden 3). Set back from the Linden on Bebelplatz are the **Alte Bibliothek**, reminiscent of the curvy Vienna Hofburg (Unger, 1775-81, part of Humboldt-Universität), and the pantheon-like, copper-domed St Hedwigs-Kathedrale (Legeay and Knobelsdorff, 1747-73; *see p87*).

Not long after the Napoleonic occupation, the prolific Karl Friedrich Schinkel became Berlin's most revered architect under Prince Friedrich Wilhelm IV. Drawing on classical and Italian precedents, his early stage-sets experimented with perspective, while his inspired urban visions served the cultural aspirations of an ascendant German state. His work includes the colonnaded **Altes Museum** (1828; *see p88*), regarded by most architects as his finest work, and the **Neue Wache**

(New Guardhouse, 1818; *see p87*), next to the Zeughaus, whose Roman solidity lent itself well to Tessenow's 1931 conversion into a memorial to the dead of World War I.

'A radical new architecture gave formal expression to long-awaited social and political reforms.'

Other Schinkel masterpieces include the Schauspielhaus (1817-21, now the **Konzerthaus**; *see p252*); the neo-Gothic brick Friedrichwerdersche Kirche (1830, now the **Schinkel-Museum**; *see p87*); and the cubic **Schinkel-Pavillon** (1825; *see p121*) at Schloss Charlottenburg. After his death in 1841, his many disciples continued working. Friedrich August Stüler satisfied the King's desire to complement the Altes Museum with the **Neues Museum** (1841-59; Bodestrasse 1-3, Mitte), mixing new wrought-iron technology with classical architecture. By 1910, Museumsinsel comprised the neo-classical **Alte Nationalgalerie** (also Stüler, 1864; *see p88*) with an open stairway framing an equestrian statue of the King; the triangular **Bode Museum** (von Ihne, 1904; *see p89*); and the sombre grey **Pergamonmuseum** (Messel and Hoffmann, 1906-09; *see p89*). These are a stark contrast to the neo-Renaissance poly-chromy of the

Schinkel-Pavillon.

Martin-Gropius-Bau across town (Gropius and Schmieden, 1881; *see p106*).

WILD ECLECTICISM

As the population boomed after 1865, doubling to 1.5 million by 1890, the city began swallowing up neighbouring towns and villages. Factory complexes and worker housing gradually moved to the outskirts. Many of the new market halls and railway stations used a vernacular brick style with iron trusses, such as **Arminiushalle** in Moabit (Blankenstein, 1892; Bremer Strasse 9) and Franz Schwechten's Romanesque Anhalter Bahnhof (1876-80, now a ruin; Askanischer Platz). Brick was also used for civic buildings, like the neo-Gothic **Rotes Rathaus**

(1861-69; *see p95*), while the orientalism of the gold-roofed **Neue Synagoge** on Oranienburger Strasse (Knoblauch, Stüler, 1859-66; *see p93*) made use of colourful masonry and mosaics.

Restrained historicism gave way to wild eclecticism as the 19th century marched on, in public buildings as well as apartment houses with plain interiors, dark courtyards and overcrowded flats behind decorative façades. This eclectic approach also reflects in the lavish Gründerzeit villas in the fashionable suburbs to the south-west, especially Dahlem and Grunewald. In these areas the modest yellow-brick vernacular of Brandenburg was rejected in favour of stone and elaborate stucco.

Abstract concrete

Next to the railway lines on the Schöneberg/Tempelhof border (General-Pape-Strasse, corner of Dudenstrasse) stands a huge, featureless cylinder of concrete. Built in 1942 as part of the planning for Germania, the Nazi imperial capital that never was, it's a *Grossbelastungskörper* (heavy load testing body) designed to gauge the resilience of Berlin's sandy geology near the site for a proposed triumphal arch.

This artless, seldom-noticed lump is the lone physical trace of the north-south axis whose overblown structures were intended to wow the world. But it's not the only huge hulk of reinforced concrete that the Nazis left behind, and is tiny compared to some of the bunkers, flak towers and air-raid shelters that outlasted the regime they were intended to protect. The question of how to integrate them into the post-war urban landscape has sparked a variety of answers.

Berlin's Zoo flak tower was the biggest bunker in the world when the Royal ngineers began trying to blow it up in July 1947. One year and 66,000 tonnes of explosives later, they finally broke the thing open, causing extensive damage to the zoo. It took many further detonations before the last pieces of the foundations were cleared in 1969-70.

Given the difficulty of demolition, most of these structures have simply been left where they were. On Pallasstrasse in chöneberg, an air-raid shelter, formerly part of the otherwise demolished Sportspalast complex, has been used to support one end of an apartment block that bridges the street.

After the war, two enormous concrete towers in what is now Volkspark Friedrichshain were blown open, then filled in and covered with rubble from the bombed-out city. Result: the park now has two attractively landscaped hills, and only a few visible segments of balustrade hint at what lies beneath.

A little more can be seen of a similarly blasted and buried Nazi flak tower in Wedding's Humboldthain park. Climbers use its north face as a practice peak, several species of bat dwell in its recesses, a viewing platform on the top offers a panorama of the Berlin skyline, and various guided tours of the interior are offered by the Berliner Unterwelten association (www.berlinerunterwelten.de).

There are two other bunkers you can get inside. Kreuzberg's **Gruselkabinett** (*see p105*) is housed in a five-storey concrete hulk, and includes an exhibition about the structure itself, which was once an air-raid shelter for the long-destroyed Anhalter Bahnhof. A bunker on the corner of Reinhardtstrasse and Albrechtstrasse in Mitte, previously a not-very-convenient air-raid shelter for Friedrichstrasse station, was repurposed as a techno club in the early 1990s and today houses the **Sammlung Boros** art collection (*see p217*).

But of Berlin's most famous bunker, the one where Hitler spent his last days, there's no longer any trace. It was demolished in the late 1980s during construction of the apartment blocks along Wilhelmstrasse. An information board on Gertrud-Kolmar-Strasse (opposite the junction with An Der Ministeriumsgarten) is all that marks its former location.

THE NEW METROPOLIS

In anticipation of a new age of rationality and mechanisation, an attempt at greater stylistic clarity was made after 1900, in spite of the bombast of works such as the new **Berliner Dom** (Raschdorff, 1905; *see p89*) and the **Reichstag** (Wallot, 1894; *see p108*). The Wilhelmine era's paradoxical mix of reformism and conservatism yielded an architecture of *Sachlichkeit* ('objectivity') in commercial and public buildings. In some cases, such as Kaufmann's **Hebbel-Theater** (1908; now part of **HAU**; *see p256*), or the **Hackesche Höfe** (Berndt and Endell, 1906-07; Rosenthaler Strasse 40-41, Mitte), *Sachlichkeit* meant a calmer form of art nouveau (or Jugendstil); elsewhere it was more sombre, with heavy, compact forms, vertical ribbing and low-hanging mansard roofs. One of the mostsevere examples is the stripped-down classicism of Alfred Messel's **Pergamonmuseum** (*see above*).

The style goes well with Prussian bureaucracy in the civic architecture of Ludwig Hoffmann, city architect from 1896 to 1924. Though he sometimes used other styles for his many schools, courthouses and city halls, his towering **Altes Stadthaus** in Mitte (1919; Jüdenstrasse, corner of Parochialstrasse) and the **Rudolf-Virchow-Krankenhaus** in Wedding (1906; Augustenburger Platz 1), then innovative for its pavilion system, epitomise Wilhelmine architecture.

Prior to the incorporation of Berlin in 1920, many suburbs had full city charters and sported their own town halls, such as the massive **Rathaus Charlottenburg** (1905; Otto-Suhr-Allee 100) and **Rathaus Neukölln** (1909; Karl-Marx-Strasse 83-85). Neukölln's Reinhold Kiehl also built the Karl-Marx-Strasse Passage (1910, now home of the **Neuköllner Oper**; *see p254*), and the **Stadtbad Neukölln** (1914; *see p270*), with niches and mosaics evoking a Roman atmosphere. Special care was also given to suburban rail stations of the period, such as the **S-Bahnhof Mexikoplatz** in Zehlendorf, set on a garden square with shops and restaurants (Hart and Lesser, 1905), and the **U-Bahnhof Dahlem-Dorf**, whose half-timbered style aims for a countrified look.

WEIMAR'S NEW FORMS

The work of many pioneers brought modern architecture to life in Berlin. One of the most important was Peter Behrens, who reinterpreted the factory with a new monumental language in the façade of the **Turbinenhalle** at Huttenstrasse in Moabit (1909) and several other buildings for the AEG. After 1918, the turbulent birth of the

Neue Synagoge.

Weimar Republic offered a chance for a final aesthetic break with the Wilhelmine style.

A radical new architecture gave formal expression to long-awaited social and political reforms. The *Neues Bauen* ('new buildings') began to exploit the new technologies of glass, steel and concrete, inspired by the early work of Tessenow and Behrens, Dutch modernism, cubism and Russian constructivism.

Berlin architects could explore the new functionalism, using clean lines and a machine aesthetic bare of ornament, thanks to post-war housing demand, and a new social democrat administration that put planner Martin Wagner at the helm after 1925. The city became the builder of a new form of social housing. The *Siedlung* ('housing estate') was developed within the framework of a 'building exhibition' of experimental prototypes – often collaborations among architects such as Luckhardt, Gropius, Häring, Salvisberg and the brothers Taut. Standardised sizes kept costs down and amenities such as tenant gardens, schools, public transport and shopping areas were offered when possible.

Among the best-known 1920s estates are Bruno Taut's **Hufeisen-Siedlung** (1927; Bruno-Taut-Ring, Britz), arranged in a horseshoe shape around a communal garden, and **Onkel-Toms-Hütte** (Haring, Taut, 1928-29; Argentinische Allee, Zehlendorf),

Daimler Building.

with Salvisberg's linear U-Bahn station at its heart. Most *Siedlungen* were housing only, such as the **Ringsiedlung** (Goebelstrasse, Charlottenburg) and **Siemensstadt** (Scharoun et al, 1929-32). Traditional-looking 'counter-proposals' with pitched roofs were made by more conservative designers at **Am Fischtal** (Tessenow, Mebes, Emmerich, Schmitthenner et al, 1929; Zehlendorf).

Larger infrastructure projects and public works were also built by avant-garde architects under Wagner's direction. Among the more interesting are the rounded U-Bahn station at **Krumme Lanke** (Grenander, 1929), the totally rational **Stadtbad Mitte** (1930; *see p270*), the **Messegelände** (Poelzig, Wagner, 1928; Messedamm 22, Charlottenburg), the ceramic-tiled **Haus des Rundfunks** (Poelzig, 1930; Masurenallee 10, Charlottenburg), and the twin office buildings on the southern corner of **Alexanderplatz** (Behrens, 1932).

> **'Post-war architecture is a mixed bag, ranging from the crisp linear brass of 1950s storefronts to concrete 1970s mega-complexes.'**

Beginning with his expressionist **Einsteinturm** in Babelsberg, Erich Mendelsohn distilled his own brand of modernism, characterised by the rounded forms of the Universum Cinema (1928; now the **Schaubühne**; *see p256*) and the elegant corner solution of the **IG Metall** building (1930; Alte Jacobstrasse 148, Kreuzberg).

GRAND DESIGN AND DEMOLITION

In the effort to remake liberal Berlin in their image, the Nazis banned modernist trademarks such as flat roofs and slender columns in favour of traditional architecture. The Bauhaus was closed down and modern architects fled Berlin as Hitler dreamt of refashioning it into the mega-capital 'Germania', designed by Albert Speer. The crowning glory was to be a grand axis with a railway station at its foot and a massive copper dome at its head, some 16 times the size of St Peter's in Rome. Work was halted by the war, but not before demolition was begun in Tiergarten and Schöneberg.

Hitler and Speer's fantasy was that Germania would someday leave picturesque ruins. But ruins came sooner than expected. Up to 90 per cent of the inner city was destroyed by Allied bombing. Mountains of rubble cleared by women survivors rose at the city's edge, such as the **Teufelsberg** (*see p125*) in the West and **Friedrichshain** (*see p100*) in the East. During bombing and reconstruction, many apartment buildings lost their decoration, resulting in the blunted lines characteristic of Berlin today.

Fascism left an invisible legacy of a bunker and tunnel landscape (*see p40* **Abstract concrete**). The more visible fascist rchitecture can be recognised by its stripped-down, abstracted classicism, typically in travertine: in the West, **Flughafen Tempelhof** (Sagebiel, 1941; *see p103 and p286*) and the **Olympiastadion** (March, 1936; *see p122*); in the East, the marble-halled Reichsluftfahrtministerium (now the **Bundesministerium der Finanzen**; Sagebiel, 1936; Wilhelmstrasse 97, Mitte) and the Reichsbank (now the **Auswärtiges Amt**; Wolff, 1938; Werderscher Markt, Mitte).

BERLIN, BERLIN

The Berlin Wall, put up in a single night in 1961, introduced a new and cruel reality. The city's centre of gravity shifted as the Wall cut off the historic centre from the West, suspending the Brandenburger Tor and Potsdamer Platz in no-man's land, while the outer edge followed the 1920 city limits.

Post-war architecture is a mixed bag, ranging from the crisp linear brass of 1950s storefronts to concrete 1970s mega-complexes. Early joint planning efforts led by Hans Scharoun were scrapped, and radical interventions cleared out vast spaces. Among the architectural casualties in the East were Schinkel's Bauakademie and much of Fischerinsel, clearing a sequence of wide spaces from Marx-Engels-Platz to Alexanderplatz. In West Berlin, Anhalter Bahnhof was left to stand in ruins but Schloss Charlottenburg narrowly escaped demolition.

Though architects from East and West shared the same modernist education, their work became the tool of opposing ideologies, and housing was the first battlefield. The DDR adapted Russian socialist realism to Prussian culture in projects built with great effort and amazing speed as a national undertaking. First and foremost was Stalinallee (1951-54; now **Karl-Marx-Allee**, Friedrichshain). The Frankfurter Tor segment of its monumental axis was designed by Herman Henselmann, a Bauhaus modernist who briefly agreed to switch styles. In response, West Berlin called on leading International Style architects such as Gropius, Niemeyer, Aalto and Jacobsen to build the Hansaviertel. A loose arrangement of inventive blocks and pavilions at the edge of the Tiergarten, it was part of the 1957 Interbau Exhibition for the 'city of tomorrow', which included Le Corbusier's Unité d'Habitation in Charlottenburg (**Corbusierhaus**, just south of S-Bahnhof Olympiastadion).

East and West stylistic differences diminished in the 1960s and 1970s, as new *Siedlungen* were built to even greater dimensions. The Gropiusstadt in Britz and Märkisches Viertel in Reinickendorf (1963-74) were mirrored in the East by equally massive (if shoddier) prefab housing estates in Marzahn and Hellersdorf.

To replace cultural institutions then cut off from the West, Dahlem became the site of various museums and of the new Freie Universität (Candilis Woods Schiedhelm, 1967-79; *see p298*). Scharoun conceived a 'Kulturforum' on the site

cleared for Germania, designing two masterful pieces: the **Philharmonie** (1963; *see p252*) and the **Staatsbibliothek** (1976; *see p294*). Other additions were Mies van der Rohe's slick **Neue Nationalgalerie** (1968; *see p115*) and the **Gemäldegalerie** (Hilmer & Sattler, 1992-98; *see p114*).

The US presented Berlin with Hugh Stubbin's Kongresshalle in the Tiergarten (1967, now the **Haus der Kulturen der Welt**; *see p109*), a futuristic work, which embarrassingly required seven years' repair after its roof collapsed in 1980. East German architects brewed their own version of futuristic modernism in the enlarged Alexanderplatz with its **Fernsehturm** (TV Tower, 1969; *see p96*), the nearby **Haus des Lehrers** (Henselmann, 1961-64; Grunerstrasse, corner of Karl-Marx-Allee, Mitte), with its recently restored frieze, and the impressive cinemas, **Kino International** (Kaiser, 1964; Karl-Marx-Allee 33, Mitte) and **Kosmos** (Kaiser, 1962; Karl-Marx-Allee 131, Friedrichshain).

POSTMODERN RENEWAL

Modernist urban renewal gradually gave way to historic preservation after 1970. In the West, largely in response to the squatting movement, the city launched a public-private enterprise within the Internationale Bauausstellung (IBA), to conduct a 'careful renewal' of the *Mietskaserne* and 'critical reconstruction' with infill projects to close the gaps left in areas along the Wall. It is a truly eclectic collection: the irreverent organicism of the prolific Ballers

The impressive golf-ball-on-a-knitting-needle – the **Fernsehturm** (television tower).

(Fraenkelufer, Kreuzberg, 1982-84) contrasts sharply with the neo-rationalist work of Eisenman (Kochstrasse 62-63, Kreuzberg, 1988) and Rossi (Wilhelmstrasse 36-38, Kreuzberg, 1988). A series of projects was also placed along Friedrichstrasse. IBA thus became a proving-ground for contemporary architectural theories.

In the East, urban renewal slowed to a halt when funds for the construction of new housing ran dry; and towards the end of the 1970s, inner-city areas again became politically and economically attractive. Most East-bloc preservation focused on run-down 19th-century buildings on a few streets and squares in Prenzlauer Berg. Some infill buildings were also added on Friedrichstrasse in manipulated grids and pastel colours, so that the postmodern theme set up by IBA architects on the street south of Checkpoint Charlie was continued over the Wall. But progress was slow, and when the Wall fell in 1989 many sites still stood half-finished.

CRITICAL RECONSTRUCTION

Rejoining East and West became the new challenge, requiring work of every kind, from massive infrastructure to commercial and residential projects. There were two key decisions. The first was to eradicate the Wall zone with projects that would link urban structures on either side. The second was to pursue a 'critical reconstruction' of the old city block structure, using a contemporary interpretation of Prussian scale and order.

The historic areas around Pariser Platz, Friedrichstrasse and Unter den Linden were peppered with empty sites and became a primary focus for critical reconstruction. The first major commercial project in Friedrichstrasse stuck with the required city scale but took the game rules lightly. The various buildings of the **Friedrichstadt-Passagen** (1996; Friedrichstrasse 66-75, Mitte), despite their subterranean mall link, offer separate approaches. Pei Cobb Freed and Partner's **Quartier 206** (see p173) is a confection of architectural devices reminiscent of 1920s Berlin, while Jean Nouvel's **Galeries Lafayette** (see p171) is a smooth and rounded glass form. Only the third building, **Quartier 205**, by Oswald Mathias Ungers, uses a current German style, with its sandstone solidity and rigorous square grid. Good examples of the emerging *Berliner Architektur*, based on the solidity of the past but with modern detail and expressive use of materials, are to be found in Thomas van den Valentyn and Matthias Dittmann's monumental **Quartier 108** (1998; Friedrichstrasse, corner of Leipziger Strasse, Mitte) and in the **Kontorhaus Mitte** (1997; Friedrichstrasse 180-190, Mitte) by Josef Paul Kleihues, Vittorio Magnago Lampugnani, Walther Stepp and Klaus Theo Brenner.

On both sides of the city, much historic substance was lost in World War II and the sweeping changes that followed. Today, the rebuilding of the former imperial areas near

The acute angles of **Quartier 206** on Friedrichstrasse.

Hans Scharoun and Edgar Wisniewski's
Staatsbibliothek. *See p43.*

Unter den Linden, the Museumsinsel and Schlossplatz revolve around a choice between critical reconstruction or straightforward replicas of the past. The Kommandenthaus, next to the Staatsoper on Unter den Linden, rebuilt by Thomas van den Valentyn as the **Stiftung Bertelsmann** (2004), is an example of the tendency towards historical replication, as is the mooted reconstruction of Friedrich Schinkel's Bauakademie next door. Thankfully some decisions have been taken in favour of contemporary architecture, particularly the new entrance building to the **Auswärtiges Amt** (Foreign Office; Werdescher Markt 1, 1999) by Thomas Müller and Ivan Reimann, and IM Pei's triangular block for the **Deutsches Historisches Museum** (2003; *see p87* with its curved foyer and cylindrical stair tower.

> **'The "Band des Bundes" resembles a giant paper clip that binds the two halves of the city."**

Berlin's return to capital city status has brought with it a number of interesting new embassies and consulates in and around a revived diplomatic quarter. Notable on Tiergartenstrasse are the solid red stone **Indian Embassy** by Leon Wohlhage Wernik (2001) and the extension of the existing **Japanese Embassy** by Ryohei Amemiya (2000). There are other intriguing examples around the corner in Klingelhöferstrasse: the monumental, louvre-fronted **Mexican**

Embassy by Teodoro Gonzalez de Leon and J Francisco Serrano (2000); and the encircling copper wall of the five Nordic Embassies, containing work by various Scandinavian architects after a plan by Alfred Berger and Tiina Parkkinen (1999).

EAST MEETS WEST

There are four main initiatives intended to link East and West: the area around Potsdamer Platz and Leipziger Platz; the government quarter and the 'Band des Bundes'; the new Berlin Hauptbahnhof; and the reinstatement of the Reichstag and Pariser Platz, the historical formal entrance to the city. These are mostly stand-alone projects outside the discussion on critical reconstruction; their architecture reflects this in a greater freedom of approach.

Potsdamer Platz (*see p110*) was the first of the four, designed as a new urban area based on the old geometries of Potsdamer and Leipziger Platz. This former swathe of no-man's land was redeveloped not only to forge a link between Leipziger Strasse to the East and the Kulturforum to the West, but also to supply Berlin with a new central focus in an area that was formerly neither one side or the other.

The twin squares of Potsdamer Platz and Leipziger Platz have been reinstated and five small quarters radiate to the south and west. Leipziger Platz has risen again as an enclosed octagonal set-piece, with modern terrace buildings. Potsdamer Platz is by contrast once more an open intersection, entrances to the various quarters beyond staked out with major buildings by Hans Kollhoff, Hilmer Sattler and Albrecht, Helmut Jahn, Renzo Piano and

Schweger and Partner (1999-2003). The closed metal and glass block of Helmut Jahn's **Sony Center** (2000) is a singular piece, organised around a lofty central forum with a tented glass and textile roof as its spectacular focus. Offices and apartments look down on to a public space with cinemas, bars, restaurants and the glass-encased remnants of the old Esplanade Hotel.

The Daimler (formerly DaimlerChrysler) area on the other side of Potsdamer Strasse is a network of tree-lined streets with squares and pavement cafés. It's also the work of various architects, though Renzo Piano got all the key pieces, notably the **Arkaden** shopping mall, the **Debis** headquarters, and the **Musicaltheater** and **Spielbank** on Marlene-Dietrich-Platz (all 1999), all in a language of terracotta and glass. The quarter's south-west flank facing on to Tilla-Durieux-Park is a rich architectural mix, with Richard Rogers' two buildings of cylinders, blocks and wedges (1998; Linkstrasse) and Arata Isozaki's concoction of ochre and brown stripes topped with a wavy glass penthouse (Linkstrasse, 1998).

The **'Band des Bundes'**, the linear arrangement of new government buildings north of the Reichstag, is another project linking East and West. The result of a competition won by Axel Schultes and Charlotte Frank, it straddles the Spree and the former border, resembling a paper clip that binds the two halves of the city.

The centrepiece is the **Bundeskanzleramt** (Federal Chancellery; Schlutes and Frank, 2000; Willi-Brandt-Strasse, Tiergarten) flanked by buildings with offices for parliamentary deputies. The arrangement reads like a unity thanks to a common and simple language of concrete and glass.

North of this across the Spree is the new central station, **Berlin Hauptbahnhof** (Von Gerkan Marg, 2006; see p286), now Europe's largest rail intersection. The 321-metre (1,053-feet) east-west overground platforms are covered by a barrel vault of delicately gridded glass. This is crossed in a north-south direction by a station hall 180 metres (590 feet) long and 40 metres (131 feet) wide, that gives access to the trains on each intersecting level and to the shopping centre. Each side of the station hall is framed by buildings spanning the east-west vault. The building stands as a functional and symbolic link between East and West Germany, and as a hub of the whole European rail network.

Finally, there are the historical links. To th^e south of the Bundeskanzleramt is the **Reichstag** (see above), sitting on the old threshold to the East, gutted, remodelled and topped with a new glass dome by Norman Foster (1999) to bring a degree of public access and transparency to a building with a dark past. **Pariser Platz** (see p82) has been almost entirely built to its old proportions. The US Embassy, long delayed but finally unveiled on 4 July 2008 in the south-west corner, completes the set piece. Some of the buildings are a pale blend of modern and historic but there are exceptions such as the **DG Bank** by Frank Gehry (2000; Pariser Platz 3, Mitte) with its witty use of a rational façade in front of the spectacular free forms in its internal court, or Christian de Portzamparc's French Embassy (2002; Pariser Platz 5, Mitte), which plays with classical composition but uses contemporary materials. In the opposite corner is the **Akademie der Künste** (Behnisch and Partner; 2005), an exception to its neighbours with a welcoming and open glass façade. Round the corner Michael Wilford's **British Embassy** (2000; see p291) also came to terms with the city's strict planning limitations by raising a conformist punched stone façade, which he then broke open to expose a rich and colourful set of secondary buildings in the central court.

LESS IS MORE

When the last bits of Leipziger Platz and Pariser Platz are filled in, all the major symbolic linking projects planned in the reunification period will be complete. While they wait for the urban fabric to gel around them, building on a smaller scale continues.

The last decade has also produced work that had nothing to do with reunification. Daniel Libeskind's **Jüdisches Museum** (1999; see p105) in Kreuzberg is a symbolic sculpture in the form of a lightning bolt. Peter Eisenmann's **Denkmal für die ermordeten Juden Europas** (2005; see p84), south of Pariser Platz, is a departure from a traditional memorial, with its open and sunken grid of 2,700 steles.

Nicholas Grimshaw's **Ludwig-Erhard-Haus** for the stock exchange (1998; see p117) breaks with convention by taking the form of a glass and steel armadillo, though a city-required fire wall obscures the structure. On the corner at Kantstrasse 55, Josef Paul Kleihues' **Kant-Dreieck** (1995) extends the sculptural response with its huge metal weather vane. Dominique Perrault's **Velodrom** (1997; see p262) sinks into the landscape in the form of a disc and a flat box of glass, concrete and gleaming steel mesh.

Sauerbruch and Hutton's striking 21-storey headquarters for the **GSW** (1999; Kochstrasse 22A, Kreuzberg), with its translucent sailed top and colourful and constantly changing façade, shows how singular buildings can take the city's urban quality to the next level. Now that the major projects are all finished, it's time to let spontaneity return to the business of filling in the remaining blanks.

Tower of the Hour

Communist icon turned symbol of the resurgent Eastern city, the Fernsehturm towers above Berlin.

Most great cities have their iconic landmarks, the kind of thing film directors work into shot to establish a change of location. Eiffel Tower in the background? Yes, we're in Paris. Big Ben? It's London. Sydney Harbour Bridge? Time for the Australian part of the story. And these days, if the hero's just arrived in Berlin, you'll probably get a shot of the Fernsehturm (television tower).

It was not always so. The Nazis had envisaged a city stuffed with landmarks, with oversized triumphal arches and mountainous meeting halls, but by the late 1940s there was nothing much left to say 'Berlin' save ruins and rubble. In 1950, the East Berlin authorities blew up what was left of the old Prussian Stadtschloss, an act widely regarded as one of cultural barbarism, and started thinking about a new landmark to fill the void at the city's heart. Most of the entries for a 1957 competition concerning the shape of a new socialist capital involved some kind of Stalinist wedding-cake skyscraper, like those in Moscow or Warsaw. But such buildings were going out of fashion even in the Soviet capital, and plans to build one in Berlin were soon shelved as inappropriate.

Meanwhile, there was another problem. The new medium of television demanded that a transmission tower be built in the eastern part of Berlin to provide a service to compete with the powerful signals already emanating from the West. Plans to erect one on the Muggelsberge hills were abandoned when

▶ For access to the Fernsehturm's observation platform, see p96.

it was realised that a tower there would interfere with the flight paths of the planned new Schönefeld airport. The idea of putting a tower in Volkspark Friedrichshain was also dropped; designs produced by the postal service were just too ugly for such a prominent inner-city location.

'At last, the city had a politically neutral but versatile symbol.'

However, a design for a television tower did already exist. In 1958, the architect Herbert Henselmann had come up with a plan for a complete overhaul of Berlin's medieval centre: the now-open area between the Spree and Alexanderplatz. It was mostly low-rise stuff, but part of his vision was for a 'tower of signals'. The inspiration for Henselmann's designs was the new mania for space travel that followed the launch of Sputnik, the first artificial satellite, in October 1957. Henselmann's tower would have a tapering shaft, to represent a rocket soaring into the sky; and at the very top would be a bright, socialist-red sphere to represent a satellite.

The plan was so out of step with the city's requirements in 1958 that it cost Henselmann his job as East Berlin's chief architect. But as

the new spirit of technological optimism became part of the official language of the Soviet system in the 1960s, Henselmann's design looked better and better. It killed two birds with one tower, giving the city a signature structure in politically acceptable form, while solving the TV transmission problem.

Henselmann's plan had placed the tower just across the Spree from the former Stadtschloss. Now it was moved to a more stable location away from the river, while the design was modified by Fritz Dieter and Günter Franke of VEB Industrieprojektierung – a company that specialised in concrete formwork such as chimneys and cooling towers. The final touches were made by Gerhard Kosel, president of the DDR School of Architecture, who divided the tower according to classical rules of proportion.

Construction began in 1965, and the Fernsehturm was finally opened on 7 October 1969 – the 20th anniversary of the founding of the DDR. It marked the very centre of the city in the manner of a medieval church tower, allowed the second DDR TV station to commence broadcasting, and advertised the thrusting virility of socialism in a form visible for miles around, including from all over West Berlin. Equipped with a viewing platform at 203 metres (668 feet) and a revolving restaurant one floor above it (the Telecafe, christened

yogaberlin.de

TICKETS
030 24 749 777
030 25 900 427

www.tanzimaugust.de

TANZ

after a naming competition in the party newspaper, Neues Deutschland), it was also a handy tourist attraction.

Its simple, ball-on-spike shape was also a boon to East Berlin's graphic designers. At last, the city had a politically neutral but versatile symbol that could be used in myriad ways. Soon it was appearing on tourist brochures and party calendars, commemorative stamps and political posters, city maps and menu covers, shopping bags and official invitations. Easily anthropomorphised with a smiley face added to the ball, and often depicted with garlands of flowers, it was also perfect for literature addressed to socialist youth. One way or another, in the heyday of East Berlin, it was as inescapable as a graphic icon as it was as a towering landmark.

ICONIC STRUGGLE

West Berlin had little to compete. The brand-new Fernsehturm made both the Prussian Siegessaüle (Victory Column) in the Tiergarten, and the 1920s Funkturm (Radio Tower) in Charlottenburg look decidedly short and old-fashioned. The Siegessaüle had also become slightly dodgy due to its role as a celebration of Prussian militarism, and it wouldn't acquire a new lease of symbolic life until its 1987 appearance in Wim Wenders' *Wings of Desire*, the ultimate West Berlin movie. Meanwhile, at

the beginning of the Kurfürstendamm, the Kaiser-Wilhelm-Gedächtniskirche had always been the symbol of the city's west end, and had been left as a truncated ruin, with new concrete annex, to continue serving as such. If anything was to be used as an establishing shot for West Berlin, it would be this graphically unfriendly and distinctly unvirile stump. That or a shot of the Wall, of course – undoubtedly the divided city's most famous landmark, Fernsehturm or not.

So West Berlin postcards would feature the Funkturm, Siegessaüle, Kaiser-Wilhelm-Gedächtniskirche and assorted views of the Wall and Checkpoint Charlie, while East Berlin postcards would offer Unter den Linden, the Palast der Republik and every imaginable angle on the Fernsehturm, and ne'er the twain should meet. The ideological struggle of urban icons was also dramatised daily on a West Berlin milk carton, which greeted the city with a colourful 'Guten Morgen Berlin!' among a graphic selection of western landmarks. It wasn't until after Reunification that the Fernsehturm joined them on the breakfast table.

Throughout all this, the Brandenburger Tor had been sitting patiently in no-man's land, just on the eastern side of the Wall. This unfortunate position, and its symbolism as a gateway forcibly blocked, meant it wasn't much use as an icon for either side. East Berlin

Lass Bio in dein Herz!

graphic designers sometimes cautiously paired it with the Fernsehturm, while western propagandists and postcard publishers found uses for its image behind concrete and barbed wire. But it didn't get its big moment until Reunification, becoming the point where the two cities renewed their acquaintance in globally televised celebrations. From then on, the Brandenburger Tor has been the closest thing reunified Berlin has to an official symbol, appearing as the city's jaunty logo on all information materials. See, for example, www.berlin.de.

FERNSEHTURM REDUX

By the time of Reunification, the Fernsehturm was no longer that highly regarded. Its propaganda value had been tarnished by the effect known as the 'Pope's Revenge', whereby sunlight refracts off the sphere in the shape of a cross. Ronald Reagan made a meal of the phenomenon in his 1987 tear-down-this-wall speech before the blocked-off Brandenburger Tor. Meanwhile, most East Berliners would tell you, television towers were all very well, but not much of a substitute for bananas or freedom of speech. Because the tower was so closely associated with the outgoing communist regime, Reunification brought impractical calls to tear it down. But the Fernsehturm remains useful. Still a major tourist draw, it's owned by

Deutsche Telekom, who showed their appreciation of its graphic power by dressing the sphere up as a football for the 2006 FIFA World Cup. Around 40 television and radio stations broadcast from its antenna.

'Berliners have once again learned to love the thing.'

And now that bananas and free speech are sufficiently plentiful, Berliners have once again learned to love the thing. Looming above the junction of Mitte, Friedrichshain and Prenzlauer Berg, it's become an icon not of the old communist city, but of an eastern Berlin resurgent as the heart of the capital's new vitality. Today, the Fernsehturm once more appears everywhere, though its use as a graphic icon has become considerably more playful. The spike spears an apple in publicity for an organic greengrocer. Its shape counterposes that of a stretching human body in an ad for a company offering yoga classes. It dominates a tripped-out Berlin skyline on any number of flyers for rock concerts and techno parties. The revolving restaurant, which originally went round just once an hour, today pirouettes in a giddy 20 minutes, and the tower itself is still the fourth-tallest free-standing structure in Europe. What more could you ask of an icon?

Where to Stay

OSTEL Das DDR Design Hostel.
See p65.

Where to Stay

An increasingly eclectic range of hotels caters to Berlin's exploding demand for tourist beds.

Berlin's word of mouth is good these days. The 2006 World Cup helped dispel some of its darker rep and showcased the city's human face, while tourists have begun to twig that it's a relatively affordable destination as well as a friendly one. And with inter-European travel on the increase, Berlin has been attracting more and more visitors. The *Berliner Morgenpost* estimated that in 2008 the city would see more than 15.9 million of them – that's 25 per cent more than in 2003, and almost 30 per cent fewer than the 20 million expected in 2010.

New hotels are appearing in all categories, shapes and sizes. The 364-room **Meliá** at Friedrichstrasse station, from the Spanish Sol Meliá chain, lends its cool, modern silhouette to the Spree. While it's perhaps not the nicest of façades, it should prove nonetheless to be a popular choice for the stop-over business crowd. Unfortunately for it, however, it sits just across the bridge from the **Artist Riverside Hotel**, completed in 2006 – one of the most affordable and delightfully over-the-top hotels we've ever encountered.

For more majestic fare, the **Hotel de Rome**, a luxurious addition to Unter den Linden, comes courtesy of the Rocco Forte Collection. Plush it certainly is, but it's also surprisingly friendly. An additional 2,000 rooms are now underway at various sites around Alexanderplatz, as well as plans for Berlin-Mitte's first **easyHotel** – a no-frills enterprise of basic beds in pre-fab units (in easyJet's signature orange, and likewise inexpensive.)

And that's just East Berlin. Although Mitte continues to spruce up and expand, attention is once again returning to the West, and rightly so. After an initial defection to the 'new' Berlin, many hotel owners are now focusing back on the old West's tried and trusted charms.

As this guide went to press, the Spanish Silken Group is putting the finishing touches to 205 rooms near the KaDeWe. And up and running since spring 2007 is the **Hotel Ellington** on Nürnberger Strasse. This extraordinarily cool and elegant hotel, perhaps the most important addition to the city skyline, truly – and finally – brings some modern world-class sophistication to Berlin.

Note: since July 2008, smoking is forbidden in all German hotels – both in public spaces and in private rooms.

PRICES

With an average four-star room price of €140 per night, Berlin still ranks down among the least expensive European capitals – compared, at least, to €314 in London, €298 in Paris, €221 in Moscow, €192 in Rome, or even €174 in Amsterdam.

Note, however, that although prices given throughout this chapter were correct as this guide went to press, they should be taken as guidelines, not gospel. Many of the larger hotels now refuse to publish any rates at all, depending instead on direct booking over the Internet (for which many offer a discount), which enables them to vary their prices daily according to need and greed. In addition to hotels' own websites, discount specialists such as expedia.com and hotels.com are worth a look too. It's wise to reserve in advance whenever possible: on any given weekend in Mitte or Prenzlauer Berg many hotels are extremely

The best Hotels

Artist Riverside Hotel & Day Spa
An affordable and delightfully over-the-top hotel experience. *See p59.*

Brandenburger Hof Hotel
The joys of modern luxury. *See p74.*

Ellington Hotel
Cool and sophisticated – just like the Duke. *See p70.*

Hotel-Pension Dittberner
The fine art of the pension. *See p71.*

Miniloftmitte
Pared-down yet cosy apartment digs. *See p59.*

OSTEL Das DDR Design Hostel
Commie chic at its best. *See p61* **Back to the future.**

Art for heart's sake at **Artist Riverside Hotel & Day Spa**. *See p59.*

busy. Be wary of cancellation policies too: it's best to ask before you book.

We've indicated where breakfast is included in the room price. Most hotels offer it as a buffet, which can be as simple as coffee and rolls (called *Schrippen* in Berlin) with cheese and salami, or the full works, complete with smoked meats, muesli with fruit and yoghurt, and even a glass of sparkling wine.

For hotels catering to a predominantly gay clientele, *see p222.*

Berlin Tourismus Marketing
Am Karlsbad 11, 10785 (2647 48801/www.btm.de). U1 Kurfürstenstrasse. Reservations/information (250/025/www.visitBerlin.de).
This privatised tourist service can sort out hotel reservations as well as tickets for shows and travel arrangements to Berlin. It provides a free booklet covering more than 400 hotels – but note that the hotels have paid to be included. It also has lists for campsites, apartments and holiday homes (the latter costs €1.50). Its website is quite comprehensive, although much of it is only in German and there are no phone numbers or direct links to the hotels – you have to book through BTM. This can work to your advantage, however, as it makes deals with hotels and often offers discounts. Allow plenty of time if you visit one of the Berlin BTM branches: the staff here are notoriously inattentive. Booking online or by phone is therefore recommended and also saves you a €3 fee.
Other locations Hauptbahnhof, Neues Kranzler Eck, Brandenburg Gate, Berlin Pavillon at the Reichstag.

Booking.com
Brunnenstrasse 192, 10119 (206 4366/www. booking.com). Toll-free reservations (200 1341/ www.booking.de).
With offices Europe-wide, this service has pre-reserved beds in hotels of all categories, and guest information can be sent directly to the hotel as a confirmed booking. Check for special offers too.

Mitte

The city's historic administrative quarter is alive and well, with an ever-growing number of hotels in all price brackets, and many new beds planned over the next couple of years. While many tourists have started to defect towards less trafficked areas, the faded post-Wall hip of one of the city's oldest quarters is still a hotspot. You may not find much of the historic pension charm of Charlottenburg here, but for shopping and sightseeing it's one of the more exciting parts of Berlin.

Deluxe

Hotel Adlon Kempinski Berlin
Unter den Linden 77, 10117 (226 10/www.hotel-adlon.de). S1, S2 Unter den Linden 77. **Rates** €450

---

❶ Green numbers given in this chapter correspond to the location of each hotel or hostel as marked on the street maps. *See pp316-328.*

---

double; €36 breakfast. **Credit** AmEx, DC, MC, V. **Map** p318/p327 L6 ❶
Not quite the Adlon of yore, which burnt down following World War II, this new, more generic luxury version was rebuilt by the Kempinski Group in 1997 on its original site next to the Brandenburg Gate. Although it's still considered one of Berlin's finest hotels – the Saudi King and his entourage were recent guests, and it's popular with movie stars and anyone keen to make an impression – the 409 rooms (including three bullet-proof presidential suites) are decorated in a generic international-executive style. The staff can be a little frosty if you don't look the part, and the lobby tends to get a bit crowded with gawkers.
Bar. Disabled-adapted rooms (2). Gym. Internet (wireless). Parking (free). Restaurants (3). Room service. Spa. TV.

Hotel de Rome

Behrenstrasse 37, 10117 (460 6090/www.rocco fortecollection.com). U6 Französische Strasse. **Rates** €470 double; €26 breakfast. **Credit** AmEx, DC, MC, V. **Map** p319/p327 N6 ❷
In 2006, this 19th-century manse, which was originally built to house the headquarters of Dresdener Bank, was transformed by Rocco Forte into a pretty sumptuous affair; and yet, despite the intimidating grandeur, the young staff are surprisingly friendly. All 146 rooms are state-of-the-art if somewhat generic plush, with plenty of polished wood, marble and velvet. The former basement vault now houses a pool, spa and fully equipped gym. The lobby restaurant, Parioli, specialises in upscale Mediterranean cuisine, with al fresco dining in the summer, and lighter fare is available in the sleek Bebel Bar & Lounge or the Opera Court, where high tea is served every afternoon.
Bar. Gym. Internet (high-speed). Parking (€20). Restaurant. Room service. Spa. TV.

Sofitel Berlin Gendarmenmarkt

Charlottenstrasse 50-52, 10117 (203 750/www. sofitel.com). U2, U6 Stadtmitte. **Rates** from €190 double; €13-€26 breakfast. **Credit** AmEx, DC, MC, V. **Map** p322/p327 M7 ❸
'Design for the senses' is the motto here. This is a truly lovely hotel, and rooms are often difficult to come by, but it's well worth the fight. So much attention has been paid to detail: from the moment you enter the lobby, with its soothing colour scheme and wonderful lighting, the atmosphere is intimate and elegant. This carries into the rooms, each beautifully styled, with perhaps the best bathrooms in the city. Even the conference rooms are spectacular, and the hotel's 'wellness' area is complete with plunge pools, gym and meditation room. In summer you can wind down on the sun deck high above the rooftops.
Bar. Business centre. Gym. Internet (wireless). Parking (€18). Restaurants (2). Room service. Spa. TV.

Expensive

Dietrich-Bonhoeffer-Haus

Ziegelstrasse 30, 10117 (284 670/www.hotel-dbh. de). U6, S1, S2, S5, S7, S9, S75 Friedrichstrasse or S1, S2 Oranienburger Strasse. **Rates** (incl breakfast) €129 double. **Credit** AmEx, MC, V. **Map** p318/p326 M5 ❹

Ellington Hotel. *See p70.*

Named after the theologian executed by the Nazis for alleged participation in the 1944 Hitler assassination attempt, this hotel sits on the corner of a quiet side street directly behind the Friedrichstadtpalast. It was originally built in 1987 as a meeting place for Christians from East and West; as such, the atmosphere is warm, and the staff helpful – they even post the day's weather forecast in the lift. The rooms are large, the breakfast is pretty good and the location is excellent.

Internet (wireless). Parking (€10). Restaurant. TV.

Hotel Albrechtshof

Albrechtstrasse 8, 10117 (308 860/www.hotel-albrechtshof.de). U6, S1, S2, S5, S7, S9, S75 Friedrichstrasse. **Rates** (incl breakfast) €122-€204 double. **Credit** AmEx, DC, MC, V. **Map** p318/p327 M6 **5**

Located just a stone's throw from the Berliner Ensemble and Friedrichstrasse station, the Albrechtshof is a member of the Verband Christlicher Hotels (Christian Hotels Association). They don't make a song and dance about it, but it has its own chapel, named after former guest Martin Luther King. The rooms are comfy and clean, if not particularly stylish, and the staff are friendly. The restaurant offers local cuisine, and in summer breakfast is served in the courtyard garden.

Bar. Disabled-adapted rooms. Parking (€14). Restaurant. TV.

Hotel Gendarm

Charlottenstrasse 61, 10117 (206 0660/www.hotel-gendarm-berlin.de). U2, U6 Stadtmitte. **Rates** €160 double; €14 breakfast. **Credit** AmEx, DC, MC, V. **Map** p322/p327 M7 **6**

If you fancy a five-star location but don't want to spend a fortune, then this place is just the ticket. Aside from a few pink frills, it doesn't have a lot of extras, but the 21 rooms and six suites are smart and comfortable, and it's close to the restaurants of Gendarmenmarkt, shopping on Friedrichstrasse and the State Opera. At rates around half those at the nearby Sofitel or Hilton, you can't really go wrong – unless you bring a car, that is: parking around here can end up costing as much as your room.

Bar. Gym. TV.

Hotel Hackescher Markt

Grosse Präsidentenstrasse 8, 10178 (280 030/www.loock-hotels.com). S5, S7, S9, S75 Hackescher Markt. **Rates** (incl breakfast) €133-€208 double. **Credit** AmEx, DC, MC, V. **Map** p319/p327 N5 **7**

This elegant hotel in a nicely renovated townhouse avoids the noise of its central Hackescher Markt location by cleverly having many rooms face inwards on to a tranquil green courtyard. Some have balconies, all have their own bath with heated floor, and the suites are spacious and comfortable. The pleasant, helpful staff speaks good English, and, while you don't necessarily get the most atmosphere for the money, you can't beat the address.

Bar. Internet (wireless). Parking (€15). TV.

Hotel Pension Kastanienhof

Kastanienallee 65, 10119 (443 050/www.kastanienhof.biz). U8 Rosenthaler Platz or U2 Senefelderplatz/tram M1, 12. **Rates** (incl breakfast) €103-€138 double. **Credit** AmEx, MC, V. **Map** p319/p328 O4 **8**

Ideally located at the bottom of Kastanienallee – or 'Casting'allee as it's now called, as the cafés on this strip bordering Prenzlauer Berg and Mitte are famous for seeing and being seen at – this is a warm, cosy, old-fashioned hotel. The pastel-coloured rooms are generously proportioned and well equipped, and there are three breakfast rooms and a bar. The English-speaking staff is friendly. It's often booked up on weekends, so it's a good idea to reserve ahead.

Bar. Internet (web TV). Parking (€8). TV.

Lux 11

Rosa-Luxemburg-Strasse 9-13, 10178 (936 2800/www.lux-eleven.de). U2 Rosa Luxemburg-Platz. **Rates** (incl breakfast) €165-€205 apartment. **Credit** AmEx, MC, V. **Map** p319/p326 O5 **9**

A member of the Design Hotels group, this former apartment house for the DDR secret police is a stylish, no-nonsense apartment-hotel with an emphasis on wellbeing. The cool, modern white-walled apartments are elegant and well appointed, with everything from intercom for visiting guests to microwave and dishwasher in the kitchen, and queen-sized beds in between. There's an in-house Aveda salon, and the restaurant, Shiro i Shiro, serves wholefood breakfasts. The location is perfect for the fashionable sites of Mitte, or a night at the Volksbühne. Rates drop dramatically the longer you stay.

Bar. Café. Internet (wireless). Parking (€18). Restaurant. Spa. TV/DVD.

Maritim proArte Hotel Berlin

Friedrichstrasse 151, 10117 (203 35/www.maritim.de). U6, S1, S2, S5, S7, S9, S75 Friedrichstrasse. **Rates** (incl breakfast) from €120 double. **Credit** AmEx, DC, V, MC. **Map** p318/p327 M6 **10**

Despite the fact that its status as one of Berlin's first 'designer hotels' has been overshadowed by newcomers, this is still popular with businessmen and stewardesses, who congregate in the mall-like lobby and like to soak up the posh bar, restaurants and boutiques. The 403 rooms, apartments and suites each have fax and computer connections, air-conditioning and marble bathrooms. The staff is polite and helpful, and it's just a short walk to the shops on Friedrichstrasse or to the Brandenburg Gate.

Bar. Disabled-adapted rooms. Gym. Internet (dataport, wireless in some rooms). Parking (€18). Pool (indoor). Restaurants (3). Room service. TV (pay movies).

Meliá Berlin

Friedrichstrasse 103, 10117 (2060 7900/www.meliaberlin.com). U6, S1, S2, S5, S7, S9, S75 Friedrichstrasse. **Rates** (incl breakfast) €121-€302 double; €20 breakfast. **Credit** AmEx, DC, V, MC. **Map** p318/p327 M6 **11**

Just across the street from Friedrichstrasse station, this new corner building on the banks of the Spree is a huge link in the Spanish Sol Meliá chain. All 364 rooms are similarly and tastefully appointed, many with fine views of the river and Reichstag beyond, but the rich wood units and headboards seem a little incongruous. The rooftop Café Restaurant Madrid offers reasonably priced theatre and business lunch menus, while the tapas bar off the lobby provides lighter fare and entertainment. The helpful staff is pleasant, making this an ideal and convenient stop-over for the harried business traveller, but for simple folk in search of atmosphere, there's better fare for the money elsewhere.
Bar. Internet (wireless). Parking (€20). Restaurant.

Radisson SAS Berlin

*Karl-Liebknecht-Strasse 3, 10178 (238 280/www.
berlin.radissonsas.com). S5, S7, S9, S75 Hackescher
Markt.* **Rates** €149-€340 double; €21 breakfast.
Credit AmEx, DC, MC, V. **Map** p319/p327 N6
With interiors by German designer Yasmine Mahmoudieh (responsible for the cabins of the Airbus A380), the 427 rooms here are fresh, uncluttered and free of the normal blandness typical of big hotel chains. The Radisson's claim to fame, however, is 'the tank' – a 25m- (82ft)- high aquarium with a million litres of salt water housing 2,500 varieties of fish. Many of the bedrooms even have a view of it. If you're tempted to take a dip, though, we suggest the pool in the hotel spa, or dive into a drink in the Aqua Lounge bar.
*Bar. Disabled-adapted rooms. Gym. Internet
(wireless, high-speed). Parking (free). Pool (indoor).
Restaurants (2). Room service. Spa. TV (pay movies).*

Westin Grand

*Friedrichstrasse 158-164, 10117 (202 70/www.
westin.com/berlin). U6 Französische Strasse.* **Rates**
€159-€520 double; €28 breakfast. **Credit** AmEx,
DC, V. **Map** p318/p327 M6
Despite its East German prefabricated exterior, the Westin Grand is pure five-star international posh (the Stones stay here when they're in town). The decor is gratifyingly elegant, with lots of polished crystal and brass and a grandiose foyer and staircase. The rooms are tastefully traditional, and the 35 suites are individually furnished with period decor themed after their names. There's also a garden and patio, plus a bar and restaurant, and the elegant haunts of the Gendarmenmarkt are just outside the door.
*Bar. Business centre. Disabled-adapted rooms (2).
Gym. Internet (dataport, wireless in some rooms).
Pool (indoor). Restaurants (3). Room service. Spa.
TV (pay movies).*

Moderate

Alexander Plaza Berlin

*Rosenstrasse 1, 10178 (240 010/www.alexander-
plaza.com). S5, S7, S9, S75 Hackescher Markt.*
Rates from €100 double; €17 breakfast. **Credit**
AmEx, DC, MC, V. **Map** p319/p326 N6

In a handy location between Hackescher Markt, Alexanderplatz and the Museumsinsel, this attractive building has been renovated as a friendly modern establishment. Despite the hotel's proximity to one of the liveliest parts of Mitte, it stands in an oasis of quiet, and is close to the river. There are 92 rooms, plus features such as a fitness centre and 'wellness landscape'.
*Gym. Internet (wireless). Parking (€15). Restaurant.
Spa. TV (pay movies).*

Arte Luise Kunsthotel

*Luisenstrasse 19, 10117 (284 480/www.arte-
luise.com). U6, S1, S2, S5, S7, S9, S75
Friedrichstrasse.* **Rates** €85-€150 double; €9.50
breakfast. **Credit** MC, V. **Map** p318/p327 L6
Housed in a former neoclassical residential palace just a short walk from the Reichstag and Brandenburger Tor, this 'artist home' is one of the city's more imaginative small hotels, with each of its 50 rooms decorated by a different renowned artist. There's graffiti artist Thomas Baumgärtel's 'Royal Suite', a golden room spray-painted with bananas; and Angela Dwyer's 'Room Like Any Other', whose

Radisson SAS Berlin, complete with tank.

surfaces are covered in stream-of-consciousness scrawlings. Some rooms get a little noise from the S-Bahn trains, but that shouldn't deter you: this is a great place to stay.

Bar. Disabled-adapted rooms. Restaurant.

Artist Riverside Hotel & Day Spa

Friedrichstrasse 106, 10017 (284 900/www. great-hotel.com). U6, S1, S2, S5, S7, S9, S75 Friedrichstrasse. **Rates** €119-€169 double; €9.50 breakfast. **Credit** AmEx, MC, V. **Map** p318/p326/p327 M5 ⓖ

A truly remarkable place, and brilliantly over the top. What was recently a car dealership on the Spree has been converted into a hotel and day spa (Berlin's best, according to a 2007 *Prinz* magazine poll). From the mammoth claw-footed tubs in bronze and whirlpool baths in the rooms to a clamshell flotation tank for two in the spa, this is Vegas-in-Space with health benefits. Owner Uwe Buttgereit, himself a health practitioner, has made each room spectacular, with warm colours and lighting. Therapeutic aromas waft through the halls, and even some of the budget singles have a terrace on the Spree. Artists get a discount. Highly recommended. *Photo p53.*
Internet (shared terminal & wireless in lobby). Parking (€10). Room service. Spa. TV.

Art'otel Berlin Mitte

Wallstrasse 70-73, 10179 (240 620/www.artotels. de). U2 Märkisches Museum. **Rates** €100-€210 double; €16 breakfast. **Credit** AmEx, DC, MC, V. **Map** p323/p327 O7 ⓖ

A real treasure on the Spree. This delightful hotel is a creative fusion of old and new, combining restored rococo reception rooms with ultra-modern bedrooms designed by Nalbach + Nalbach. As well as highlighting the artwork of George Baselitz – originals hang in the corridors and all 109 rooms – the hotel's decor has been meticulously thought out to the smallest detail, from the Philippe Starck bathrooms to the Breuer chairs in the conference rooms. The staff is pleasant, and the views from the top suites across Mitte are stunning.
Bar. Disabled-adapted rooms. Internet (wireless). Parking (€16). Pool (indoor). Restaurant. TV (pay movies).

Flower's Boardinghouse Mitte

Mulackstrasse 1-2, 10119 (2804 5306/www. flowersberlin.de). U8 Weinmeisterstrasse or S5, S7, S9, S75 Hackescher Markt. **Open** 9am-6pm daily. **Rates** (incl breakfast) from €89 apartment. **Credit** AmEx, DC, MC, V. **Map** p319/p326 O5 ⓖ

More for the longer haul than overnight, these small, nicely decorated and fully furnished serviced apartments are under new ownership, and more reasonably priced considering the location, with Hackescher Markt and the Scheunenviertel just outside the door. A complimentary breakfast is served each morning, and there's a wealth of excellent cafés, bars and restaurants nearby if you don't feel like cooking later.
Internet (high-speed). Parking (€7). TV/VCR.

Honigmond Garden Hotel

Invalidenstrasse 122, 10115 (2844 5577/www. honigmond.de). U6 Oranienburger Tor. **Rates** (incl breakfast) €125-€200 double. **Credit** V. **Map** p318/p326 M4 ⓖ

Along with its nearby sister Honigmond Restaurant-Hotel (*see below*), this is one of the most charming hotels in Berlin, and it doesn't cost an arm and a leg. Choose between large bedrooms facing the street, smaller ones overlooking the fish pond and Tuscan-style garden, or spacious apartments on the upper floor. As with all great places, the secret is in the finer detail. The rooms are impeccably styled with polished pine floors, paintings in massive gilt frames, antiques and iron bedsteads. There's also a charming sitting room overlooking the garden. Highly recommended.
Parking (€10). TV.

Honigmond Restaurant-Hotel

Tieckstrasse 12, 10115 (284 4550/www. honigmond.de). U6 Oranienburger Tor. **Rates** (incl breakfast) €89-€199 double. **Credit** V. **Map** p318/p326 M4 ⓖ

The 40 rooms in this beautiful 1899 building are spacious and lovely, and although some of the less expensive ones lack their own shower and toilet, don't let that put you off: this is probably the best and prettiest mid-price hotel east of the Zoo. The reception area has comfy chairs around a gas fireplace, and breakfast is served in the Honigmond restaurant (*see p135*), open since 1920. The friendly staff speaks English, and the hotel is perfectly situated within walking distance of the Scheunenviertel and Hackescher Markt. More affordable luxury would be hard to come by. Highly recommended.
Bar. Parking (€10). Restaurant. TV.

Hotel Am Scheunenviertel

Oranienburger Strasse 38, 10117 (282 2125/2830 8310/www.hotelas.com). U6 Oranienburger Tor or S1, S2 Oranienburger Strasse. **Rates** (incl breakfast) €80 double. **Credit** AmEx, DC, MC, V. **Map** p318/p326 M5 ⓖ

This simple, unpretentious 18-room hotel sits right in the middle of the old Jewish Quarter and the historic heart of town. If just a bit dark, the rooms are clean and comfortable, each with a toilet and good shower. The friendly staff will gladly help you plan your walking tour of the nearby sights. Be sure to request a room in the back if you're a light sleeper, as the bar downstairs can get noisy.
TV.

Miniloftmitte

Hessische Strasse 5, 10115 (847 1090/www. miniloft.de). U6 Zinnowitzer Strasse. **Rates** €100-€140 apartment. **Credit** AmEx, DC, MC, V. **Map** p318 L5 ⓖ

A brilliant alternative to the hotel hustle, these 14 flats – housed in a combined renovated apartment building and award-winning steel-concrete construction – are modern, airy and elegant. Each comes with a queen-sized bed, couch and dining area (the

frosted-glass panels separating bath and kitchen are an interesting touch), with warm-coloured fabrics, organic basics in the kitchen, and lots of space and light. The owners/designers/architects are a young, friendly couple who live and work on the premises. Rates are greatly reduced the longer the stay, and free cleaning is provided weekly for long-term visitors. Highly recommended.
Internet (high-speed wireless). TV.

MitArt Hotel

Linienstrasse 139-140, 10115 (2839 0430/www. mitart.de). U6 Oranienburger Tor. **Rates** (incl breakfast) €110-€160 double. **Credit** AmEx, MC, V. **Map** p318/p326 M5 ㉓
Located off a courtyard in a beautifully restored printing house, this warm, simple and thoroughly unpretentious hotel is perfectly situated for hopping the area's galleries, and – as evidenced by the ever-changing collection of paintings and sculpture that decorate the rooms – the owner is well versed in the scene. The rooms themselves are frill-free, warm and bright, and without TV, so you're pretty much forced to kick back and relax. The breakfast buffet is served each day courtesy of the hotel's organic café, which also serves light snacks and baked goods throughout the day.
Café. Internet (wireless in lobby).

Park Inn Hotel

Alexanderplatz 7, 10178 (238 90/www.parkinn.de). U2, U5, U8, S5, S7, S9, S75 Alexanderplatz. **Rates** €109-€129 double; €18 breakfast. **Credit** AmEx, MC, V. **Map** p319/p327 O5 ㉔
With 1,012 rooms overlooking Alexanderplatz, Berlin's largest (and tallest) hotel is something of a mixed bag. Although the views are spectacular, and most of the rooms have been renovated with extra windows, the vibe is a little cold and impersonal considering the price. There are special package deals – and a casino – for the convention groups that fill the lobby in busloads, and easy access to public transport for a business stopover, but for the traveller in search of warmth and atmosphere, there are better choices nearby.
Bar. Disabled-adapted rooms. Gym. Internet (wireless). Parking (€17). Restaurants (2). TV (pay movies).

Platte Mitte

Rochstrasse 9, 10178 (0177 283 26 02/ dialog@plattemitte.de). S5, S7, S9, S75 Hackescher Markt. **Rates** (per person) from €45 double. **Credit** AmEx, DC, MC, V. **Map** p319/p326/p327 O6 ㉕
Proudly calling itself a 'No Hotel', these three apartments on the 21st floor of a 1967-built *Plattenbau* are airy and well designed, each with spectacular views of the city around Alexanderplatz. Colourfully decorated and eclectic to say the least, the furnishings mix original pieces of the period with artfully fanciful touches such as poster-plastered walls and mannequins by the bed. Babysitting services are available, as well as a personal Pilates trainer. And as most of the neighbours are original tenants, this

is a wonderfully unique way to experience Berlin. The prices listed are for up to two nights only, and are greatly reduced for longer stays. Rates include bedlinen and weekly cleaning.
Internet (wireless). Parking (€9). TV/DVD.

Cheap

Baxpax Downtown Hostel Hotel

Ziegelstrasse 28, 10117 (278 748-80/www.baxpax-downtown.de). U6, S1, S2, S5, S7, S9, S75 Friedrichstrasse. **Rates** from €47 single; from €68 double; from €15 (per person) dorm; €2.50 bedlinen; €4.50 breakfast. **No credit cards.** **Map** p318/p326/p327 M5 ㉓
This new, third addition to the Mittes Backpacker Hostel empire is an excellent place to stay, with a brilliant location. Clean, contemporary and well designed, it has all the usual amenities, from baggage room to darts, with the additional luxury of a fireplace lounge, courtyard and rooftop terrace. There's a dorm just for women, 24-hour reception and keycard access for security, and a friendly, relaxed atmosphere.
Bar. Disabled-adapted rooms. Internet (wireless).

Circus Hostel

Weinbergsweg 1A, 10119 (2839 1433/www.circus-berlin.de). U8 Rosenthaler Patz. **Rates** from €50 single; from €56 double; from €19 (per person) dorm; €2-€5 breakfast. **Credit** MC, V. **Map** p319/p326 N4 ㉗
Almost the standard by which other hostels should be measured, the Circus is a rarity – simple but stylish, warm and comfortable. And the upper-floor apartments have balconies and lovely views. The laid-back staff can help get discount tickets to almost anything, or give directions to the best bars and clubs, of which there are plenty nearby. Deservedly popular, this place is always full, so be sure to book ahead. Just across the Platz, the owners also recently opened the moderately priced Circus Hotel, whose 63 double rooms, each with private bath, surround a central terraced winter garden and café. Reservations and information are available on the above number.
Bar. Café. Disabled-adapted rooms. Internet (wireless in lobby). TV room.

CityStay Hostel

Rosenstrasse 16, 10178 (2362 4031/www.citystay. de). S5, S7, S9, S75 Hackescher Markt. **Rates** (incl breakfast) from €40 single; from €50 double; from €17 (per person) dorm; €2.50 bedlinen. **No credit cards. Map** p327 O6 ㉘
On a small, quiet street, but as central as you can get, this is a great modern hostel for the price. The rooms are clean and simple, and there are showers on every floor. Security is top notch here, with access cards for the video-monitored entrance and floors. The helpful staff is friendly. The breakfast buffet features fresh organic bread, and the kitchen will fix your eggs any way you like 'em.
Café. Internet (shared terminal).

Back to the future

According to a recent poll in *Stern* magazine, one out of every five Germans thinks the country would be better off if the Wall were still in place. Some of Germany's wounds are taking longer to mend than Berlin city planners would care to admit. Superficially at least, unification has simply meant ridding the city of its 'DDR-ness' through demolition or cosmetic overhaul. And mostly for good reason. Apart from the monumental appeal of Karl-Marx Strasse and some other structures, it was a pretty bleak and grey aesthetic. Until the 1970s, that is, when the colour orange suddenly splashed into the standardised vocabulary of the DDR.

Meanwhile, two 'Ossi' (East German) lads, off on a bender, found themselves in an abandoned *Pionierlager* (government-sponsored holiday camp for kids) one night. They grew nostalgic, lying there on the rusty bunks, and a year later, just a stone's throw from the Ostbahnhof, the Ostel – officially the **OSTEL Das DDR Design Hostel** (*see p65*) – was born: a 'Design-Hostel' of absolute 1970s DDR perfection, and retro-suave down to its bathroom scales.

'The "design" in the name is important,' explains Guido Sand, who, with his partner

Daniel Helbig, scoured the whole of Germany for the original wallpaper, dressers, box radios, glass lamps, rugs and official portraits that decorate this six-floor wonder. Only the mattresses and sheets are new. This place is style at its purest. And it's done with such chic – and such cheek – that it's delightful. 'Compared to IKEA, DDR furniture at least looks like something,' Guido points out. Behind him hangs former Cabinet Minister Horst Sindermann, watching over the reception desk. The four clocks on the wall read: Berlin, Moscow, Peking and Havana. 'Only an Ossi could have done this,' he says.

The two partners first met as child performers in the DDR state circus (Sand is now a health practitioner, and Helbig a film editor), yet however glad they are the Wall is down, they want their rooms to inspire memories. Many people, they say, have been moved to recognise a living room lamp or a couch. Others, of course, have been horrified. Yet the boys were in the black within a month of opening, and have had to replace Honecker's portrait so often that it's now being sold as a poster in the lobby. But there's no political message here. This is just brilliant design with (politically incorrect) humour – and (socialist) flair: their Pionierlager dorm sleeps six for only €9 per bed.

By the end of 2008, all 33 rooms will have their own bathroom. For an additional €3.50, guests are given a *Lebensmittelmarke* (food-ration coupon) for breakfast at the Ossi Hof pub out front. And for those who just can't get enough of the stuff, there's a hotel *Konsum* (state-run market), which sells everything from plaster egg cups to chocolate DDR coins. There's even a rare roll of original toilet paper – but it's not for sale.

And now, just a few streets away at Andreasstrasse 20, is the duo's new DDR-Ferienwohnung (holiday apartment), 75 square metres (807 square feet) of classified two-star lodging that sleeps up to six in DDR style with everything from TV to washing machine, great views and a Trabant-driven tour of the city. We're told that a third venue will open in the near future.

So, despite some hard-bitten corners still in the former East Berlin, by mere virtue of its style and humour, the Ostel does something to lighten up the city's healing process. And that – to quote our Mayor – *ist gut so*.

Heart of Gold Hostel Berlin

*Johannisstrasse 11, 10117 (2900 3300/www.
heartofgold-hostel.de). U6, S1, S2, S5, S7, S9,
S75 Friedrichstrasse.* **Rates** (incl bedlinen) €40
single; €50-€60 double; €14 (per person) dorm;
€3 breakfast. **Credit** AmEx, MC, V. **Map**
p318/p326 M5 ㉙

The prime location aside (it's only 50 metres from
Oranienburger Strasse), this member of the
Backpacker Germany Network (www.backpacker-
network.de) is an enjoyable place to stay. The rooms
are bright and cheerful, all newly done with parquet
floors. Lockers are free, and individual bathrooms
and showers and a keycard system guarantee security. The laundry is cheap, as are the €1 shots in the
bar, and with free sens-o-matic sunglasses and
Squornshellous Zeta mattresses to help you recover, what more could a backpacker need?
Bar. Internet (wireless). TV.

Helter Skelter Hostel

*Kalkscheunenstrasse 4, 10117 (2809 7979/www.
helterskelterhostel.com). U6, S1, S2, S5, S7, S9, S75
Friedrichstrasse.* **Rates** (incl bedlinen) €54 double;
€14 (per person) dorm; €3 breakfast. **No credit
cards**. **Map** p318/p326 M5 ㉚

Right behind the Friedrichstadtpalast in the historic
Kalkscheune ('chalk barn') cultural centre, this centrally located hostel is a wonderful, relaxed place to
stay, with an amiable and international English-
speaking staff. There are apartments available for
longer stays, and kitchen facilities in the communal
room. The rooms are curiously decorated, but fun
– one has a pool table on the ceiling. You're within
walking distance of practically everything, and
Friedrichstrasse station is handy for anything that
isn't on the doorstep.
Internet (shared terminal).

Mittes Backpacker Hostel

*Chausseestrasse 102, 10115 (2839 0965/www.
backpacker.de). U6 Zinnowitzer Strasse.* **Rates** €30-
€34 single; €48-€64 double; €18-€19 (per person)
dorm; €2.50 bedlinen (optional); €5.50 breakfast.
Credit AmEx, MC, V. **Map** p318 L4 ㉛

Open since 1994, Mitte's oldest hostel has something
of an antiquated 'student feel' about it, when compared with more contemporary hostels springing up
all over Berlin. But that's somehow part of its charm.
The rooms have a pleasant, old-fashioned vibe, each
with its often less-than-accomplished decor, hand
painted on the walls (and named by the artist/
guest accordingly). The multilingual staff is helpful,
plus there's bike rental, a kitchen and a video room
with English films.
Internet (shared terminal). TV/VCR/DVD room.

Prenzlauer Berg

From the cool of Kastanienallee to the funky
chic of Helmholzplatz, this neighbourhood just
north of Mitte may be charming, but it has a
surprising dearth of decent hotels.

Expensive

Ackselhaus & Bluehome

*Belforter Strasse 21, 10405 (4433 7633/www.
ackselhaus.de). U2 Senefelder Platz.* **Rates**
Ackselhaus from €110 single; €140 double.
Bluehome from €150 single/double. Both €10
breakfast. **No credit cards**. **Map** p319/p328 P4 ㉜

Just doors apart, what ties these two establishments
together – aside from their shared reception desk –
is a wonderfully realised 'modernised colonial' style.
In Ackselhaus each apartment has a bedroom, sitting room, bathroom and kitchenette, with old
wooden floorboards, white walls, antique furniture
and a Mediterranean feel. The blue and white
'Maritime Apartment', with mahogany furniture
and seafaring paintings, is particularly beautiful.
Most rooms have two beds, and one larger apartment is suitable for four to five people. The pricier
Bluehome (at no.24), with its blue façade, and balconies overlooking Belforter Strasse, is home to the
Club del Mar restaurant, which offers a breakfast
buffet and open fireplace. There's also a delightful
balconied garden out back, complete with lawn
chairs in the summer. Recommended, but make sure
you book well ahead.
Internet (wireless). Restaurant. TV.

Moderate

Hotel Greifswald

*Greifswalder Strasse 211, 10405 (442 7888/
www.hotel-greifswald.de). Tram M4 Hufelandstrasse.*
Rates €65-€75 double; €7.50 breakfast. **Credit**
AmEx, DC, MC, V. **Map** p319/p328 Q4 ㉝

A hidden gem for those who want some place
simple, warm and charming to kick their feet up
after a hard day's touring. Tucked away in a quiet
rear courtyard just a short distance from both
Alexanderplatz and Kollwitzplatz (and the nearby
Knaack and Magnet clubs), this is a favourite among
artists and musicians (Mitch Ryder is a regular here).
The rooms are tasteful and cheery without the fluff,
the staff friendly and helpful. But the highlight is
breakfast, which has to be the best buffet in Berlin…
and it's served from 6.30am till noon. During the
summer you can have it al fresco in the back.
Apartments are also available. Note that parking is
limited. Highly recommended. *Photo p64.*
Internet (wireless). Parking (free). TV.

Myer's Hotel

*Metzer Strasse 26, 10405 (440 140/www.
myershotel.de). U2 Senefelderplatz.* **Rates** (incl
breakfast) €99-€199 double. **Credit** AmEx, MC, V.
Map p319 P4 ㉞

This renovated 19th-century townhouse sits on a
tranquil street. There's a garden and a glass-
ceilinged gallery, and the big leather furniture (now
sadly) invites you to light up a cigar. The rooms,
however, seem a bit over-priced. Still, the beautiful
Kollwitzplatz is just around the corner, as are a

No pain at **Hotel Greifswald**. *See p63.*

bunch of decent bars and restaurants, and although the tram stop is just down the street, it's a lovely walk into Mitte.
Bar. Disabled-adapted rooms (3). Internet (dataport). TV.

Cheap

Hotel Transit Loft

Immanuelkirchstrasse 14A, 10405 (4849 3773/ www.transit-loft.de). Tram M4 Hufelandstrasse. **Rates** (incl breakfast) €62 single; €72 double; €21 (per person) dorm. **Credit** AmEx, MC, V. **Map** p319 Q4 ⑤
This loft hotel in a renovated factory is ideal for backpackers and young travellers. The rooms all have en suite bathrooms and there's a private sauna, gym and billiard room with special rates for hotel guests. The staff is friendly and well informed, and there's good wheelchair access too.
Bar. Disabled-adapted rooms. Internet (shared terminal). TV.

Lette'm Sleep Hostel

Lettestrasse 7, 10437 (4473 3623/www.backpackers. de). U2 Eberswalder Strasse. **Rates** €40-€49 double; from €11 (per person) dorm. **Credit** MC, V. **Map** p319/p328 P2 ⑥
Just off the Helmholplatz, this small hostel has new floors and bathrooms, and a beer garden in the back for summer barbecues. There's free tea and coffee but no breakfast, which you can either make yourself in the kitchen or enjoy at one of the many decent cafés around the corner. All rooms have hand-basins and hot showers are always available. The three large apartments can sleep up to ten people each, and there are reduced rates for longer stays.
Disabled-adapted rooms. Internet (shared terminal).

Friedrichshain hasn't quite panned out as the city's new bohemia, but with decent transport connections, a still somewhat 'Eastie' alternative feel, good cafés and lots of nightlife, it continues to be a great area to stay in, especially if you're on a tight budget.

Moderate

East Side City Hotel Berlin

Mühlenstrasse 6, 10243 (293 833/www.eastside hotel.de). U1, S3, S5, S7, S9, S75 Warschauer Strasse. **Rates** (incl breakfast) €70-€100 double. **Credit** AmEx, MC, V. **Map** p324 R8 ⑰
This modest hotel has a certain funky charm, not to mention a fabulous view of one of the last remaining stretches of the Berlin Wall. Get a room in the back if you want peace and quiet, although this will mean missing sunset over the Oberbaumbrücke. Each double room comes with a bathroom and bath, and there's a huge breakfast buffet. There's easy access to public transport, so you're just a short ride away from the main drags in both Friedrichshain and Kreuzberg.
Bar. Internet (shared terminal). Parking (free). Restaurant. TV.

Gold Hotel

Weserstrasse 24, 10247 (293 3410/www.gold-hotel-berlin.de). U5 Samariterstrasse. **Rates** (incl breakfast) from €86 double; 1 child under 10 yrs free. **Credit** MC, V. **Map** p324 T7 ⑱
This is a moderately priced alternative for young travellers who've outgrown the hostel scene but aren't yet ready to splurge on the frills. Perfectly situated just off the main drag on Wismarplatz, this family-run hotel is clean and comfortable with standard rooms and standard decor. Besides the location, however, there's a beautiful winter garden for coffee, and an in-house bar. All of the 35 rooms have showers, toilet and cable TV. It's very German and very OK.
Bar. Disabled-adapted rooms. Parking (€10). TV.

Cheap

A&O Hostel & Hotel Friedrichshain

Boxhagener Strasse 73, 10245 (297 7810/www. aohostel.com). U5 Samariterstrasse or S3, S5, S7, S8, S9, S41, S42, S75, S85 Ostkreuz. **Rates** from €30 single; from €34 double; from €10 (per person) dorm; €3 bedlinen; €6 breakfast. **Credit** MC, V. **Map** p324 U8 ⑲
This branch of the nationwide chain has something of a school camp atmosphere, but the rooms are clean, the pine furniture inoffensive, and there are cooking facilities. There is also the budget 'Easy Dorm': no shower, no booking – just a bed. During the summer, everyone hangs out in the courtyard,

but you can also rent a bicycle and head down the street to the shops and cafés. Single and double rates include bedlinen and breakfast.

Internet (wireless). TV/DVD room.

Other locations A&O Hostel am Zoo, Joachimstaler Strasse 1-3, Tiergarten, 10623 (80947 5300); A&O Hostel Mitte, Köpenicker Strasse 127-129, Kreuzberg, 10179 (80947 5200).

Eastern Comfort

Mühlenstrasse 73-77, 10243 (6676 3806/www. eastern-comfort.com). U1, S3, S5, S7, S9, S75 Warschauer Strasse. **Rates** €46-€60 single; €54-€76 double; €16 (per person) dorm; €5 bedlinen & towel (optional); €4 breakfast. **Credit** MC, V. **Map** p324 R8 ⑩

Berlin's first 'hostel boat' is moored on the Spree by the East Side Hotel, across the river from Kreuzberg. The rooms – or, rather, cabins – are clean and fairly spacious (considering it's a boat), and all have their own shower and toilet. The four-person room can feel a little cramped, but if you need to get up and stretch there are two common rooms, one lounge and three terraces offering beautiful river views. The owners have now done up a second boat, the Western Comfort, which is moored over the river on the Kreuzberg bank.

Internet (wireless in reception). TV room.

Odyssee Globetrotter Hostel

Grünberger Strasse 23, 10243 (2900 0081/www. globetrotterhostel.de). U5 Frankfurter Tor. **Rates** (incl bedlinen) €29-€39 single; €39-€54 double; from €10 (per person) dorm; €3 breakfast. **No credit cards. Map** p324 S7 ⑪

Down a dark wooden corridor and up the backyard stairs, this is the metal and tat version of a good old-fashioned youth hostel. The place has a little edge to it, with a dimly lit reception area and lounge for a change. The rooms are clean, the showers are good and there's billiards and table football, although the neighbourhood also has lots of alternative clubs and bars. There's also a dormitory with its own kitchen, and discounts, for groups and extended stays, as well as a 5% discount for prepaid bookings.

Bar. Internet (shared terminal). TV room.

OSTEL Das DDR Design Hostel

Wriezener Karree 5, 10243 (2576 8660/www. ostel.eu). S1, S2, S5, S7, S9, S75 Ostbahnhof. **Rates** from €59 double; €9 (per person) dorm; €3.50 breakfast. **No credit cards. Map** p324 R7 ⑫ *See p61* **Back to the future.**

Internet (wireless).

Kreuzberg

The former centre of (West) Berlin's alternative scene, Kreuzberg has some of the city's most picturesque streets, liveliest markets, coolest cafés and most interesting alternative venues. Don't miss the post-Mitte renaissance on Schlesiche Strasse.

Expensive

Angleterre Hotel

Friedrichstrasse 31, 10969 (2021 3700/www. gold-inn.de). U6 Kochstrasse. **Rates** €125-€265 double; €15 breakfast. **Credit** AmEx, DC, MC, V. **Map** p322 M8 ⑬

Hotel Transit. *See p67.*

The Berlin hotel group Gold Inn has scrubbed the graffiti off this former squatted building and the original 1871 façade now fronts a warmly furnished mid-range hotel offering a touch of Englishness near Checkpoint Charlie. There's a Speaker's Corner restaurant, and the Commonwealth bar-lounge serves Newcastle Brown Ale. The deluxe rooms have balconies, and the hotel's proximity to the heart of Berlin's major gallery scene also makes it an attractive option.
Bar. Internet (high-speed). Parking (€15). Restaurant. TV.

Hotel Riehmers Hofgarten

Yorckstrasse 83, 10965 (7809 8800/www.hotel-riehmers-hofgarten.de). U6, U7 Mehringdamm. **Rates** (incl breakfast) €129-€169 double. **Credit** AmEx, MC, V. **Map** p322 M10 ④

In a historic building with one of Berlin's prettiest courtyards, this is a wonderful hotel. The 22 exquisitely styled rooms are airy and elegant (the furniture was custom designed), the staff are charming, and Thomas Kurt, chef at the restaurant, e.t.a. hoffmann, was highly praised in 2008's Gault Millau guide. Although the location is somewhat off the beaten track, the neighbourhood has many charms of its own, with Victoria Park and Bergmanstrasse's shops and cafés nearby. If you need to venture further afield, two subway lines stop at the corner. Reasonably priced for what you get, and recommended.
Bar. Disabled-adapted rooms. Internet (wireless). Parking (€9). Restaurant. TV.

Cheap

BaxPax Kreuzberg Hostel

Skalitzer Strasse 104, 10997 (6951 8322/www.baxpax.de). U1 Görlitzer Bahnhof. **Rates** €30-€35 single; €44-€46 double; €12-€17 (per person) dorm; €4.50 breakfast. **Credit** AmEx, MC, V. **Map** p323 Q9 ④

This second hostel by the owners of Mittes Backpacker (*see p63*) has a rather more refined aesthetic than its predecessor, but the English-speaking staff is just as friendly and the party atmosphere still prevails. There's a self-service kitchen and a barbecue balcony, and the rooms are creative, to say the least (one has a bed made from a converted VW). There's also a nearby pool for cooling off in summer. Female-only dorms need to be booked in advance.
Bar. Internet (shared terminal). TV/VCR/DVD room.

Die Fabrik

Schlesische Strasse 18, 10997 (611 7116/www.diefabrik.com). U1 Schlesiches Tor. **Rates** from €38 single; from €52 double; from €18 (per person) dorm; from €3.50 breakfast. **No credit cards.** **Map** p324 R9 ④

Smack bang in the middle of a newly invigorated Schlesiche Strasse, this former telephone factory – hence the name – with turn-of-the-century charm intact, has 50 clean and comfortable no-frills rooms.

No kitchen, no TV and no billiards. Just a bed and a locker. But with the café next door for breakfast, and plenty of restaurants, bars and galleries nearby, you don't need much more. It also produces its own solar-powered heating and hot water, and the bedlinen is free. A child under 12 gets a 50% discount, and a child under 6 can stay for free.
Internet (shared terminal).

Hotel Transit

Hagelberger Strasse 53-54, 10965 (789 0470/www.hotel-transit.de). U6, U7 Mehringdamm. **Rates** (incl breakfast) €62 single; €72 double; from €31 (per person) dorm. **Credit** AmEx, MC, V. **Map** p322 M10 ④

Located in one of the most beautiful parts of Kreuzberg, this former factory is now a bright and airy hotel with 49 basic but clean rooms, each with a shower and toilet. There's a 24-hour bar on the premises, and the staff speaks good English. With Victoria Park around the block and a wealth of bars, cafés and restaurants in the area, it's often full – so it's wise to book ahead. Women-only dorms are also available. *Photo p65.*
Bar. Internet (shared terminal).

Motel One Berlin-Mitte

Prinzenstrasse 40, 10969 (7007 9800/www.motel-one.de). U8 Moritzplatz. **Rates** from €64 double; €6.50 breakfast. **Credit** AmEx, DC, MC, V. **Map** p323 O8 ④

Who'd have thought that such a seemingly anonymous chain could produce such a smart hotel? The 180 rooms, all recently remodelled and refreshed, are basic but done with flair: check out the large dark wood headboards, flat-screen TVs and modern free-standing sinks. Even that appliqué on the curtains and pillows is bearable. Your dog can enjoy it as well for only €2 a night extra. Throw in the bargain rates and top location (in Kreuzberg, despite the name) and you have a winner overall.
Bar. Internet (wireless). Parking (€9.50).

Pension Kreuzberg

Grossbeerenstrasse 64, 10963 (251 1362/www.pension-kreuzberg.de). U6, U7 Mehringdamm. **Rates** (incl breakfast) €42-€61 single; €56-€72 double; €25-€28 (per person) dorm. **No credit cards. Map** p322 M10 ④

Slightly off the beaten track but just a few blocks from various U-Bahn lines, this is a small, friendly 12-room pension in a typical old Berlin apartment house. It's not for the lazy or infirm, as there are four steep flights of stairs up to reception. All the rooms have washbasins, but only half have their own bathrooms (there's also a communal one on each floor). A buffet is served each morning in the breakfast room. There's a cheap, cheerful vibe to the place, and it's definitely worth considering if you're a family travelling on a budget.

Rock 'n' Roll Herberge

Muskauer Strasse 11, 10997 (3061 6236 00/www.rock-n-roll-herberge.de). U Gorlitzer Bahnhof.

Rates (incl breakfast & bedlinen) €29-€34 single; €39-€44 double. **No credit cards**. **Map** p323 Q9 ⑤ Having recently celebrated its first birthday, this is a great place with all the trimmings on a quiet stretch just blocks from the main drags of Kreuzberg. The downstairs rooms are small, but some have bathrooms. The staff is friendly, there's a cocktail party every Wednesday and the bar-restaurant is popular with colourful locals. *Bar. Internet (wireless). Restaurant.*

Tiergarten

Tiergarten is now officially part of Mitte, but don't tell the locals. There are a few notable establishments dotting the edges of the park that gives the district its name, as well as big modern embassies and a complex of cultural institutions by the New National Gallery – and rising like Oz beyond it, the glitz and glare of Potsdamer Platz.

Deluxe

Berlin Marriott Hotel
Inge-Beisheim-Platz 1, 10785 (220 000/www. marriott.com). U2, S1, S2, S9, S26 Potsdamer Platz. **Rates** from €209 double; €28 breakfast. **Credit** AmEx, DC, MC, V. **Map** p322/p327 L7 ⑤
This five-star Marriott is more reasonably priced – and definitely lower-key – than the Ritz-Carlton next door (*see p69*), but it's also quite disappointing. While the 'modern designer'-style decor works well in the huge lobby atrium, with its rotating globe fountain, it leaves the rooms a bit bland and uninspired. The restaurant isn't bad, however, and both the S-Bahn and U-Bahn stations are right across the street, and – this being Potsdamer Platz – there are first-run original-language cinemas if the weather doesn't hold.
Bar. Business centre. Gym. Internet (high-speed). Parking (€28). Pool (indoor). Restaurant. Room service. TV.

Grand Hotel Esplanade
Lützowufer 15, 10785 (254 780/www.esplanade.de). U1, U2, U3, U4 Nollendorfplatz. **Rates** from €139 double; €24 breakfast. **Credit** AmEx, DC, MC, V. **Map** p322 J8 ⑤
With an entry wall of gushing water lit overhead by glittering lights, this is one of Berlin's better luxury hotels, overlooking the Landwehr Canal and close to the Tiergarten. The lobby is equally grand, spacious and beautifully decorated, while the rooms are tasteful and gratifyingly free of frilly decor. There's also a fitness centre and a triangular swimming pool, plus three restaurants to choose from. But just as important is the fact that it's within stumble-back-to-bed distance of Harry's New York Bar on the ground floor.
Bars (2). Disabled-adapted rooms. Internet (wireless). Parking (free). Pool (indoor). Restaurants (3). Spa.

Hotel Askanischer Hof. *See p71.*

Grand Hyatt Berlin
Marlene-Dietrich-Platz 2, 10785 (2553 1234/ www.berlin.grand.hyatt.com). U2, S1, S2, S9, S26 Potsdamer Platz. **Rates** from €244 double; €27 breakfast. **Credit** AmEx, DC, MC, V. **Map** p322/p327 K8 ⑤
This is a classy joint, just far enough off the beaten tourist path to keep its cool. The lobby is all matt black and sleek wood panelling – a refreshing change from the usual five-star marble or country villa look. The rooms, which are decorated without a floral print in sight, are spacious and elegant; the internet TV is also a nice touch. The rooftop spa and gym has a splendid swimming pool with views across the city. The ground-floor restaurant, Tizian, is excellent, offering a choice of international classics and a top wine list.
Bars. Disabled-adapted rooms. Gym. Internet (wireless, web TV). Parking (€24). Pool (indoor). Restaurants (3). Spa. TV.

Hotel Intercontinental
Budapester Strasse 2, 10787 (260 20/www. berlin.intercontinental.com). U2, U9, S3, S5, S7, S9, S75 Zoologischer Garten/bus 200. **Rates** from €220 double. **Credit** AmEx, DC, MC, V. **Map** p321 H8 ⑤
The extremely plush and spacious 'Interconti' exudes luxury. The airy lobby, with its soft leather chairs, is ideal for browsing the papers, and the rooms, overlooking the Zoo and western edges of the new diplomatic quarter, are large and tastefully decorated, right down to the elegant bathrooms.

Thomas Kammeier, Berlin master chef, whips things up in the restaurant, Hugo's (*see p150*), while the huge gym and spa has everything a body could possibly need to exercise off the meal.
Bar. Gym. Internet (high-speed). Parking (€20). Pool (indoor). Room service. Spa. TV.

Mandala Hotel

Potsdamer Strasse 3, 10785 (590 050 000/ www.themandala.de). U2, S1, S2, S9, S26 Potsdamer Platz. **Rates** from €270 studio; €23 breakfast.
Credit AmEx, DC, MC, V. **Map** p322 L7 ⑬
This privately owned addition to the Design Hotels portfolio is, given the address, an oasis of calm, luxury and taste. The 144 rooms and suites, most of which face their glass walls upon an inner courtyard, are perfectly designed for space and light, decorated in warm white and beiges, with big comfortable minimalist furnishings and flat-screen TVs. A sheltered path through the Japanese garden on the fifth floor leads to Facil, the world-cuisine restaurant now vying for its second Michelin star. The Qiu lounge offers lighter fare, and the rooftop wellness centre, windowed from end to end, offers spectacular views of the city. Reduced rates available for longer stays.
Bar. Disabled-adapted rooms. Gym. Internet (wireless). Parking (€29). Restaurant. Room service.

Ritz-Carlton

Potsdamer Platz 3, 10785 (337 777/www.ritz carlton.com). U2, S1, S2, S9, S26 Potsdamer Platz. **Rates** from €245 double; €34 breakfast.
Credit AmEx, DC, MC, V. **Map** p322/p327 L7 ⑯
It's flashy, it's trashy, it's Vegas-meets-Versailles. The Ritz-Carlton is so chock-a-block with black marble, gold taps and taffeta curtains that the rooms seem somewhat stuffy, small and cramped. It's supposedly art deco style but feels more like some upscale shopping mall. Still, the oyster and lobster restaurant is deliciously decadent, and the service is fantastic: the technology butler will sort out the bugs in your computer connection, and the bath butler will run your tub. Bring a fat wallet and get ready to be pampered.
Bars. Disabled-adapted rooms. Gym. Internet (wireless, web TV). Parking (€25). Pool (indoor). Restaurants (2). Room service. TV (pay movies, DVD).

Moderate

Hotel Altberlin

Potsdamer Strasse 67, 10785 (260 670/www. altberlin-hotel.de). U1 Kurfürstenstrasse. **Rates** (incl breakfast) €174 double; free under-12s.
Credit AmEx, DC, MC, V. **Map** p322 K8 ⑰
This 'turn-of-the-century-Berlin' hotel doesn't actually date quite that far back, nor do the seemingly 'retro' furnishings. But the rooms are comfortable, and the restaurant downstairs, as cluttered as a museum, serves up hearty, traditional Berlin food. Right across the street from the Wintergarten

Theatre, and only a short walk to the New National Gallery and Potsdamer Platz, it's a prime location, with easy access to public transport. If you need wireless internet access, ask for a room on the first or second floor.
Bar. Internet (wireless in some rooms). Parking (€8.50). Restaurant. TV.

Cheap

David's Cozy Little Backpacker Hostel

Bredowstrasse 35, 10551 (393 5359/www. david-berlin.de). U9 Birkenstrasse. **Rates** (incl bedlinen) €30 single; €40 double; €10-€18 (per person) dorm; €2 breakfast. **No credit cards.**
Map p317 G4 ⑱
This funky little hostel is ideal for those who prefer a familial atmosphere over the usual anonymity of other digs, especially if you're travelling alone (the preferred clientele here). Groups are discouraged, and a minimum stay of three days is preferred, all to assure the relaxed familiarity. The rooms are slipshod cosy (there's a dorm just for girls as well). David and co are warm, friendly hosts and the vibe is pure 'home away from home'. Just a couple of streets away at Waldenser Strasse 30, their John's Cozy Little Backpacker Hostel (3940 4594) is ready to handle the over-fill.
Internet (shared terminal).

Charlottenburg

This is the smart end of town, with fine dining and elegant shopping, and where five-star luxury hotels sit happily alongside the traditional charms of pensions housed in grand Gründerzeit townhouses.

Deluxe

Hotel Concorde Berlin

Augsburger Strasse 41, 10789 (800 9990/ http://berlin.concorde-hotels.com). U1, U9 Kurfürstendamm. **Rates** (incl breakfast) €180-€570 double. **Credit** AmEx, DC, MC, V.
Map p321/p328 G8 ⑲
Designed by Berlin architect Jan Kleihues, this new French-owned five-star is grandly proportioned with a refreshingly minimalist and contemporary approach. Resembling the bow of an ocean liner, its 311 rooms (including 44 huge suites) are each decorated in warm woods and colour tones, intimate lighting and modern art, to elegant and understated effect. The Restaurant Saint Germain will serve your breakfast, the Brasserie Le Faubourg your French/Med dinner – after cocktails in the Lutèce Bar – and the Club Étoile on the top floors offers a wonderful panorama of the city. The wellness centre may come in handy after all this.
Bar. Internet (wireless). Parking (€18). Restaurants (2). Spa. TV.

Hotel-Pension Dittberner. *See p71.*

Kempinski Hotel Bristol Berlin

*Kurfürstendamm 27, 10719 (884 340/www.
kempinskiberlin.de). U1, U9 Kurfürstendamm.*
Rates from €420 double; €25 breakfast. **Credit**
AmEx, DC, MC, V. **Map** p321/p328 F8 ⑥⓪
Berlin's most famous hotel, and the well-aged
mother of all Kempinskis, was first a celebrated
restaurant before being rebuilt in its present form in
1951. While the rooms aren't as plush as you might
expect at these prices, the generally grand atmosphere, friendly staff, original Berlin artwork and
wonderful pool and saunas make up for it. A new
restaurant, Reinhard's, has added a regional menu
to the proceedings.
*Bar. Business centres (2). Gym. Internet (wireless).
Parking (€21). Pool (indoor). Restaurants (2).
Room service. Spa. TV (pay movies).*

Expensive

Ellington Hotel

*Nürnberger Strasse 50-55, 10789 (6831 50/www.
ellington-hotel.com). U1, U2, U3 Wittenbergplatz or
U1 Augsburger Strasse.* **Rates** €118-€258 double;
€17 breakfast; 1 child under 12 free. **Credit** AmEx,
DC, MC, V. **Map** p321 G9 ⑥①
This new hotel is the classiest, most sophisticated
joint in Berlin. Hidden within the shell of a landmark
art deco dance hall, it combines cool contemporary
elegance with warmth and ease. The rooms, mostly
white with polished wood accents, are brilliantly simple, with modern free-standing fixtures and half-
walls, and absolute calm behind the original double
windows. The staff is helpful and friendly. An ambitious menu is served in the Duke restaurant, and there

are Sunday jazz brunches in the central courtyard. All
this and KaDeWe around the corner... the Duke
would be proud. Highly recommended. *Photo p54.*
*Bar. Business centres (2). Disabled-adapted rooms.
Gym. Internet (wireless). Parking (€15). Restaurant.*

Hecker's Hotel

*Grolmanstrasse 35, 10623 (889 00/www.heckers-
hotel.com). U1 Uhlandstrasse or S5, S7, S9, S75
Savignyplatz.* **Rates** €120-€330 double; €16
breakfast. **Credit** AmEx, DC, MC, V. **Map**
p321/p328 F8 ⑥②
This is a sleek, smart, high-quality hotel; stylish,
with an air of privacy. The rooms are spacious and
comfortable, if not minimally styled, with sparkling
marble in the bathrooms, while the suites come with
air-conditioning and Bang & Olufsen DVD-TVs.
Other highlights include a rooftop terrace and the
Cassambalis restaurant, serving Med cuisine.
*Bar. Disabled-adapted rooms. Internet (wireless).
Parking (€12). Restaurant. TV.*

Hotel Art Nouveau Berlin

*Leibnitzstrasse 59, 10629 (327 7440/7434/
www.hotelartnouveau.de). U7 Adenauerplatz or S5,
S7, S9, S75 Savignyplatz.* **Rates** (incl breakfast)
€126-€176 double. **Credit** AmEx, DC, MC, V.
Map p321/p328 E8 ⑥③
This is one of the most charming small hotels in
Berlin. The rooms are decorated with flair in a mix
of Conran-modern and antique furniture, each with
an enormous black and white photo hung by the
bed. The en suite bathrooms are well integrated into
the rooms without disrupting the elegant townhouse
architecture. Even the TVs are stylish. The breakfast room has a fridge full of goodies, should you feel
peckish in the wee hours, and the folks are sweet.
Internet (dataport). Parking (€4). TV.

Hotel Bleibtreu

*Bleibtreustrasse 31, 10707 (884 740/www.
bleibtreu.com). U1 Uhlandstrasse or S5, S7, S9,
S75 Savignyplatz.* **Rates** €124-€227 double; €17
breakfast. **Credit** AmEx, DC, MC, V. **Map**
p321/p328 E9 ⑥④
The Bleibtreu is a friendly, smart and cosy establishment popular with the media and fashion
crowds. The rooms are on the smaller side, but
they're all very modern, and decorated with environ-
mentally sound materials. The restaurant is famed
for its no-sugar menu, and there's the Deli 31 for a
bagel and coffee. The hotel also offers private yoga
classes, as well as reflexology. A wonderful choice
for the health-conscious, certainly, but good service
with lots of pampering and attention means it
should appeal to anyone.
*Disabled-adapted rooms. Internet (wireless). Parking
(€15). Restaurant. TV.*

Q!

*Knesebeckstrasse 67, 10623 (810 0660/www.
loock-hotels.com). U1 Uhlandstrasse or S5, S7,
S9, S75 Savignyplatz.* **Rates** (incl breakfast)
from €182 double. **Credit** AmEx, DC, MC, V.
Map p321/p328 F8 ⑥⑤

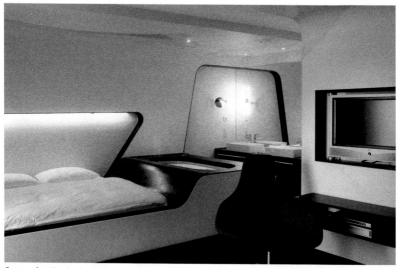

Queue for the bath while lying in bed at **Q**! Surely that's worth an exclamation mark?

This young and friendly hotel is almost worth staying in just for the spa downstairs, complete with Japanese washing room, two saunas, a sand lounge and optional massage. Rooms have their own temperature control, and are ingeniously designed: both bed and bath are part of the same wooden unit, so that you can literally roll into bed after a soak. There's a separate shower and toilet as well. The bar is red from floor to ceiling, with a beautiful gas fireplace. *Bar. Internet (wireless). Restaurant. Spa. TV.*

Savoy Hotel Berlin

Fasanenstrasse 9-10, 10623 (311 030/www.hotel-savoy.com). U2, U9, S3, S5, S7, S9, S75 Zoologischer Garten. **Rates** €146-€277 double; €19 breakfast. **Credit** AmEx, MC, V. **Map** p321/p328 F8 ⑥⑥
Erected in 1929, and a favourite of author Thomas Mann, this is a smart, stylish hotel with lots of low-key flair. The rooms are elegant and understated, but for a little zing in the suites, such as the white Greta Garbo suite and black marble Henry Miller suite. The Weinrot restaurant serves a well-thought-out modern menu. A further bonus is the location, set back just far enough from the hustle and bustle of Zoologischer Garten to be quiet and convenient. *Photo p73.*
Bar. Internet (wireless). Restaurant. Room service. TV (pay movies).

Moderate

Berlin Plaza Hotel

Knesebeckstrasse 62, 10719 (884 130/www.plazahotel.de). U1 Uhlandstrasse. **Rates** (incl breakfast) €70-€180 double; free under-16s. **Credit** AmEx, DC, MC, V. **Map** p321/p328 F9 ⑥⑦

Despite a rather plain minimalist decor and colour scheme in the rooms, there's something posh about the Plaza. All double rooms, and even some singles, have both shower and bath. The restaurant and bar serve regional German specialities, and the breakfast buffet is excellent. Children under 16 can stay with parents for free.
Bar. Internet (wireless). Parking (€12). Restaurant. TV (pay movies).

Hotel Askanischer Hof

Kurfürstendamm 53, 10707 (881 8033/4/ www.askanischer-hof.de). U7 Adenauerplatz or S5, S7, S9, S75 Savignyplatz. **Rates** (incl breakfast) €125-€185 double. **Credit** AmEx, DC, MC, V. **Map** p321/p328 E9 ⑥⑧
Despite being in the middle of one of Berlin's best-known streets, the Askanischer Hof is a well-kept secret, and chock full of atmosphere. Walk down the hall, filled with yellowed drawings, and you can almost see the ghosts of actors and literary types who visited long before World War II. The rooms are a fanciful mix of styles spanning a century of European interiors, from heavy Prussian desks and 1940s wallpaper, to over-stuffed leather chesterfields. The staff is friendly. Recommended. *Photo p68.*
Bar. Internet (wireless). Parking (free). TV.

Hotel-Pension Dittberner

Wielandstrasse 26, 10707 (884 6950/www.hotel-dittberner.de). U7 Adenauerplatz or S5, S7, S9, S75 Savignyplatz. **Rates** (incl breakfast) €97-€133 double. **No credit cards. Map** p321/p328 E9 ⑥⑨
From the ride up the 1911 elevator and into the sitting room, this is a grand place, stylish and eclectic, and an obvious labour of love. It's filled with fine

original artworks, enormous chandeliers and handsome furnishings. From the beautiful breakfast room to the private rooms, each is airy and elegant, and some of the rooms and suites are truly palatial (one has a winter garden around the courtyard, for example). But the main draw here is comfort. Frau Lange, the owner, is friendly and helpful, and goes out of her way to make her guests feel at home. Truly one of the best pensions in the city. *Photo p70.*
Internet (shared terminal). TV.

Hotel-Pension Modena

Wielandstrasse 26, 10707 (885 7010/www.hotel-modena.de). U7 Adenauerplatz or S5, S7, S9, S75 Savignyplatz. **Rates** (incl breakfast) €75-€100 double. **Credit** AmEx, DC, MC, V. **Map** p321/p328 E9 ⑩
Just a floor below the Dittberner (*see p71*), this thoroughly unassuming 19-room pension is charming, sweet and cheap. The staff is very friendly, accommodating and speaks English, and the atmosphere is relaxed. A top choice if you're travelling as part of a group and want to be in the west end. Added bonus: the price gets lower the longer you stay.
Internet (wireless). TV room.

Cheap

Hotel Bogota

Schlüterstrasse 45, 10707 (881 5001/www.bogota. de). S5, S7, S9, S75 Savignyplatz. **Rates** (incl breakfast) €69-€120 double. **Credit** AmEx, DC, MC, V. **Map** p321/p328 E9 ⑪
Though the attractive foyer of this characterful two-star belies rooms more functional than fancy, it's still a wonderful place: terrific value, with a superb atmosphere and friendly staff. The history is remarkable too: there's a bit of ornate parquet near the lobby on which Benny Goodman once tapped his feet at a party. The photographs in the fourth-floor foyer were shot by the fashion photographer Yva, who had her studio on the very spot. Her assistant, Helmut Newton, learned his craft here before fleeing Germany in 1938 (Yva died in the Majdanek concentration camp four years later). Half the doubles have their own showers and all have at least a sink. Good stuff.
TV (TV room, some individual rooms).

Hotel Pension Columbus

Meinekestrasse 5, 10719 (881 5061/www.columbus-berlin.de). U1, U9 Kurfürstendamm or U2, U9, S3, S5, S7, S9, S75 Zoologischer Garten. **Rates** (incl breakfast) €60-€90 double. **Credit** AmEx, MC, V. **Map** p321/p328 F8 ⑫
This pension next to the Ku'damm is a charming and unique place, with children in mind. Kids' drawings line the walls, and there are two larger rooms with an optional adjoining two-bed room, perfect for families. Prices are unbeatable for the area, and the owners are extremely kind and friendly. The breakfast room is a quaint place to enjoy a bowl of home-made yoghurt.
TV.

Hotel-Pension Funk

Fasanenstrasse 69, 10719 (882 7193/www.hotel-pensionfunk.de). U1 Uhlandstrasse. **Rates** (incl breakfast) €52-€99 double. **Credit** AmEx, MC, V. **Map** p321/p328 F9 ⑬
Despite the fancy surroundings, this wonderful pension offers really good value. Built in 1895, this was once the apartment of silent film star Asta Nielsen, and the proprietor does his best to maintain an ambience of graceful pre-war charm. The 14 large, comfortable rooms are furnished to cosy effect with elegant pieces from the 1920s and '30s: satinwood beds and matching wardrobes. The only niggle is that some of the showers are rather antiquated.
Internet (shared terminal). Room service.

Pension-Gudrun

Bleibtreustrasse 17, 10623 (881 6462/www.pension-gudrun-berlin.de). S5, S7, S9, S75 Savignyplatz. **Rates** (incl breakfast) €70-€85 double. **No credit cards. Map** p321/p328 E8 ⑭
This simple, tiny pension has huge rooms and friendly, helpful owners who speak English, French, Arabic and German. The rooms are decorated with

Savoy Hotel Berlin. *See p71.*

Luxury and individuality at the **Brandenburger Hof Hotel**.

lovely turn-of-the-century Berlin furniture, and for families or small groups, it's a marvellous deal. *Room service. TV.*

Pension Kettler

Bleibtreustrasse 19, 10623 (883 4949). U1 Uhlandstrasse or S5, S7, S9, S75 Savignyplatz. **Rates** (incl breakfast) €65-€95 double. **No credit cards**. **Map** p321/p328 E8 🅐
Amid the collection of art that owner Isolde Josipovici has amassed over the past 35 years, she has created the warmest, most eclectic and just plain interesting pension imaginable. Each of the six rooms, five of which have their own shower, is wonderfully decorated as inspired by the historic figure it is named after. There's golden brocade, say, for Goethe. The neighbourhood is fantastic, and public transport is right at hand. Plus breakfast is brought to your room each morning. Highly recommended. *Photo p76.*

Other districts

Wilmersdorf may not be the most interesting of areas, but it does play host to Berlin's most decadent luxury hotel (Schlosshotel im Grunewald Berlin), its most discreet hotel (Brandenburger Hof Hotel), its coolest designer hotel (Ku'Damm 101), its wackiest hotel (Propeller Island) and the world's oldest women-only hotel (Frauenhotel Artemisia).

Deluxe

Brandenburger Hof Hotel

Eislebener Strasse 14, 10789 (214 050/www. brandenburger-hof.com). U3 Augsburger Strasse. **Rates** (incl breakfast) €270-€325 double. **Credit** AmEx, DC, MC, V. **Map** p321/p328 G9 🅐
This discreet, privately owned gem, tucked down a quiet street behind the KaDeWe, is the epitome of modern luxury without the stuffiness. The staff is friendly, and the 72 rooms, all done out in a contemporary-elegant style, are warm and relaxing. There's a beautiful Japanese garden in the middle, surrounded by individually decorated salons available for meetings and special occasions. Chef Bobby Braüer helms the Michelin-starred Quadriga restaurant. For a real treat, however, avail yourself of the hotel's 'Exquisit Program', which includes limousine service from the airport, flowers, afternoon tea and open bar till 6.30pm. Highly recommended.
Bar. Internet (wireless). Parking (€21). Restaurant. Spa. TV/VCR.

Schlosshotel im Grunewald Berlin

Brahmsstrasse 10, 14193 (895 840/www. schlosshotelberlin.com). S7, S9 Grunewald. **Rates** (incl breakfast) €239-€900 double. **Credit** AmEx, DC, MC, V. **Map** p320 A12 🅐
Designed down to the dust ruffles by Karl Lagerfeld, this restored 1914 villa on the edge of Grunewald is

a luxury that mere mortals can only dream of. There are 12 suites and 54 rooms with elegant marble bathrooms, a limousine and butler service, and a well-trained staff to scurry after you. R&R is well covered too, with a swimming pool, a golf course, tennis courts and two restaurants (with summer dining on the lawn, of course). This is a beautiful place, in a beautiful setting, but so exclusive that it might as well be on another planet. It's worth checking the internet for deals, nonetheless.
Bar. Disabled-adapted rooms. Gym. Internet (wireless). Parking (free). Pool (indoors). Restaurants (2). Spa. TV/VCR.

Expensive

Ku'Damm 101

Kurfürstendamm 101, 10711 (520 0550/www. kudamm101.com). U7 Adenauerplatz or S41, S42, S45, S46 Halensee. **Rates** €119-€250 double; €14.50 breakfast. **Credit** AmEx, DC, MC, V. **Map** p320 C9 ⓐ
This hotel is a huge hit with style-conscious travellers. The lobby, created by Berlin designers Vogt and Weizenegger, is enjoyably more funk than functional, while the 170 rooms, with lino floors and Le Corbusier, were designed by the Franziska Kessler, whose mantra is clarity and calm. There's also a breakfast garden terrace, and the Lounge 101 is good for daytime snacks or a late-night cocktail.
Bar. Disabled-adapted rooms. Internet (wireless). Parking (€14). Spa. TV.

Moderate

Frauenhotel Artemisia

Brandenburgische Strasse 18, 10707 (873 8905/ www.frauenhotel-berlin.de). U7 Konstanzer Strasse. **Rates** (incl breakfast) €78-€108 double. **Credit** AmEx, DC, MC, V. **Map** p321 E10 ⓐ
Named for the Italian painter Artemisia Gentileschi, the world's oldest women-only hotel has 12 bedrooms, tucked away on the top two floors of a residential apartment building off the Ku'damm. From tiny to palatial, they're all cheerful, clean and functional and each features the work of a different Berlin-based female artist. There's a roof terrace off the breakfast room, communal fridges in the hallways, and a warm, relaxing atmosphere created by its founders, Manuela Polidori and Renate Bühler. There are no mints on the pillows, perhaps, but the diverse clientele has service, respect and comfort assured.
Internet (wireless). TV.

Hotel-Pension-München

Güntzelstrasse 62, 10717 (8579 120/www.hotel-pension-muenchen-in-berlin.de). U9 Güntzelstrasse. **Rates** (incl breakfast) from €78 double. **Credit** AmEx, MC, V. **Map** p321 G10 ⓐ
This pension is a really charming place. The artist owner has decorated the rooms beautifully and there are original prints all over the clean white walls. Double rooms come with shower and toilet, and single-room facilities are in the hall. It's well located too: a five-minute walk will connect you to the U-Bahn. A welcome change from the average pension.
Parking (€6). TV.

Propeller Island City Lodge

Albrecht Achilles Strasse 58, 10709 (891 9016/ www.propeller-island.com). U7 Adenauerplatz. **Rates** from €84 double; €7 breakfast. **Credit** MC, V. **Map** p320 D9 ⓐ
More than just a hotel, Propeller Island City Lodge is a work of art. Artist-owner Lars Stroschen has created 32 incredible rooms, each themed, and decorated like a jaw-dropping theatre set. The Flying Room, for example, has tilted walls and floors, and a large bed seemingly suspended in air. The Therapy Room, all in white with soft, furry walls, has adjustable coloured lights to change with your mood. While each room has six channels of piped in music, they also have more functional mod cons such as room service and phones. Reservations can only be made by fax (892 8721) or via the website, where you can view each room and choose your favourite three. There's also a gallery next door. Highly recommended.

Camping

If you want to explore the campsites of Berlin or surrounding Brandenburg, ask for a camping map from one of the **BTM** information offices (*see p301*), or download a PDF from its website. The campsites are far out of the city, so check timetables for last buses if you want to enjoy the city's nightlife. Prices don't vary much between sites: for tents, you'll pay about €5; for caravans, €7, plus €5 per person (€4 for 3-14s). More information can be obtained from the **Deutscher Camping Club**.

Landesverband des Deutscher Camping Club

Kladower Damm 213-217, Gatow 14089 (218 6071/2/www.dccberlin.de). **Open** 10.30am-6pm Mon; 8am-4pm Wed; 8am-1pm Fri.

Youth hostels

The three official youth hostels in Berlin – **Jugendgästehaus-International** (261 1097), **Jugendgästehaus am Wannsee** (803 2034) and **Jugendherberge Ernst Reuter** (404 1610) – all have single-sex dormitories. They're crammed most of the year, so reserve in advance.

You can book online or call the hostels directly. You have to be a member of the YHA to stay in them; to obtain a membership card,

Pension Kettler. *See p74.*

go to the Mitgliederservice des DJH Berlin International (also known as the Jugend-Zentrale). Take your passport and a passport-sized photo. Junior membership (under 26s) costs €12.50; family membership is €21. Individual hostels also have a day membership deal – you pay an extra €3.10 per day.

Mitgliederservice des DJH Berlin International

Kluckstrasse 3, 10785 (261 1097/www.djh.de). U1, U7 Möckernbrücke or U1, U2 Gleisdreieck. **Open** 24hrs daily. **Map** p322 L9.

Longer stays

For a longer stay, try calling a *Mitwohnagentur* (flat-seeking agency) to see what it has on offer. The agencies listed below can find you a room in a shared house or furnished flat for anything from a week to a couple of years. Start looking at least a month ahead, especially at holiday times. This is all private accommodation: you will be living in someone's home, often with their furniture and belongings.

If you're staying for a couple of weeks and find something through a *Mitwohnagentur*, you will probably pay €50-€80 a night. For longer stays, agencies charge different rates. Ask for the total figure, including fees, before booking.

Erste Mitwohnzentrale

Sybelstrasse 53, Charlottenburg, 10629 (324 3031/www.mitwohn.com). U7 Adenauerplatz. **Open** 9am-8pm Mon-Fri; 10am-6pm Sat. **No credit cards**. **Map** p321/p328 E8.

Fine + Mine Internationale Wohnagentur

Neue Schönhauser Strasse 20, 10178 (235 5120/ http://fineandmine.de). U8 Weinmeisterstrasse or S5, S7, S9, S75 Hackescher Markt. **Open** 10am-7pm Mon-Fri; 10am-6pm Sat. **Credit** AmEx, MC, V. **Map** p319/p326 O5.

Freiraum

Wiener Strasse 14, Kreuzberg, 10999 (618 2008/ www.frei-raum.com). U1 Görlitzer Bahnhof. **Open** 9am-7pm Mon-Fri; 10am-2pm Sat. **Credit** AmEx, MC, V. **Map** p323 Q9.

HomeCompany

Joachimstalerstrasse 17, Charlottenburg, 10719 (194 45/www.homecompany.de). U1, U9 Kurfürstendamm. **Open** 9am-6pm Mon-Thur; 9am-5pm Fri; 9am-1pm Sat. **Credit** AmEx, V. **Map** p321/p328 G8/G9.

Zeitraum Wohnkonzepte

Immanuelkirchstrasse 8, Prenzlauer Berg, 10405 (441 6622/www.zeit-raum.de). Tram M2 Knaackstrasse. **Open** 10am-1pm, 3-6pm Mon-Thur; noon-6pm Fri; by appointment Sat. **Credit** MC, V. **Map** p319 P4.

Sightseeing

Features

Bode Museum. *See p89.*

Introduction

Berlin's uniquely turbulent history has left plenty behind to see.

Queen Sophie-Charlotte's summer retreat: **Schloss Charlottenburg**. *See p121.*

If you're looking for picturesque sights, you might want to head somewhere else. However, what Berlin lacks in ancient ruins it more than makes up for with modern ones – a turbulent 20th century has left scars and reminders all over town. The city's Prussian past is reflected in a ceremonial centre, while its unified future as the capital is represented by a whole new layer of architectural landmarks, cutting-edge public collections and postmodern memorials.

Most Berlin sights that could properly be described as unmissable, either because you really ought to see them or because you couldn't avoid them if you tried, are in and around the central **Mitte** district. But it's only a small segment of this enormous, sprawling city, carved up by rivers and canals, and fringed with lakes and forest.

After Mitte, **Prenzlauer Berg** and **Friedrichshain** are the two districts of former East Berlin that have changed the most. Prenzlauer Berg retains pockets of radical energy but is now mostly gentrified. Although there are few conventional sights here, it's a relaxed place for a meal or a drink. Friedrichshain, meanwhile, is Berlin's new bohemia, managing both a firm connection with the old East and a forward-looking, youthful scene.

Elsewhere, **Kreuzberg** has correspondingly lost its monopoly on the arty and the anarchic, but it remains fascinatingly diverse and currently seems to be staging a recovery. Neighbouring **Schöneberg** is quiet and mostly residential, but it does contain some great bars and cafés in its northern reaches and is a major hub of the city's gay scene.

North of here, **Tiergarten** is dominated by the park of the same name, and is flanked along its southern fringe by some fine museums, a zoo, the reborn diplomatic quarter and the new Potsdamer Platz. And **Charlottenburg** also has a lot to offer visitors. The shop-rich area around Bahnhof Zoo and the Ku'damm was the centre of old West Berlin; to the west, Schloss Charlottenburg and its surrounding museums are a major draw.

Beyond these central districts, attractions include the Dahlem museums complex, the vast Grunewald woods and the Havel river in the south-west, the proud town of Spandau in the north-west, and the villagey charms of Köpenick and Müggelsee in the south-east.

A 2001 administrative rejig amalgamated many of Berlin's historic districts into larger political units. But just as no Berliner would say that they live in 'Friedrichshain-Kreuzberg', we've used the old district names throughout this guide in the same way as the locals.

For ideas on how to spend your time in the city, *see p81* **Essential Berlin**.

MUSEUMS AND GALLERIES

If you're planning to do a lot of sightseeing and museum-visiting, you may want to invest in a discount card. Many museums and galleries – among them the Pergamonmuseum, the Gemäldegalerie, the Ethnologisches Museum and the Ägyptisches Museum – are administered by the **Staatliche Museen zu Berlin (SMPK)**, which offers both a **one-day card** (€8, €4 reductions) and a **three-day card** (€19, €9.50 reductions) that offers entry to all its museums. You can buy the card from any of the museums it covers; note, though, that the card does not cover entry to temporary exhibitions. Many museums are closed on Mondays but are open until 10pm on Thursdays, when they're free after 6pm.

The **WelcomeCard** combines free public transport with reduced or free entry to selected museums, theatres, attractions, tours and boat trips. For Berlin (transport zones A and B), the card costs €16.50 for 48 hours and €21.50 for 72 hours; for Berlin and Potsdam (transport zones A, B and C), it's €18 for 48 hours and €24.50 for 72 hours. Either way, it's valid for one adult and up to three children under 14. Cards are available from branches of BTM (*see p301*), BVG ticket offices and information centres at larger stations, and at many hotels.

Tours

On foot

If you're pushed for time but want a good overview of the city, go for an **Insider Tour** (692 3149, www.insidertour.com) or try the **Original Berlin Walks** (301 9194,

www.berlinwalks.com), whose three-and-a-half-hour Discover Berlin tour expertly whips through some 700 years of history.

If you've more time and want more detail, the eight-hour walking tour by **Brewer's Best of Berlin** (www.brewersberlintours.com) explores the city's history in depth (there is also a tour of Potsdam). Meanwhile, **Berlin Sightseeing Tours** (7974 5600, www.berlin-sightseeing-tours.de) have come up with an interactive five-kilometre walking tour that takes in all major sights, plus many lesser-known ones.

By bike

Largely flat, Berlin is great for cyclists. **Fat Tire Bike Tours** (2404 7991, www.fatbike toursberlin.com) organise an assortment of tours, including a four- to five-hour tour along the former line of the Wall. **Fahrradstation** (*see p289*) offers themed city tours including 'Cold War Berlin', 'Architecture in Berlin' and a Sunday trip to the countryside. **Insider Tour** (*see above*) offers four-hour bike excursions covering similar ground as their walking tours. **Pedal Power** (5515 3270, www.pedalpower.de) organises tours for two people at a time.

For bike rentals, *see p289*. Remember that you may need to leave some ID as deposit.

By bus

Berolina (8856 8030, www.berolina-berlin. com) offers the works: wraparound windows, commentary in a choice of languages and a handy 'hop-on hop-off' ticketing arrangement. **Top Tour Berlin** is just as flexible but uses open-top buses, while **Zille Bus** operates tours on vintage open-top buses; both are run by the BVG (2562 5556, www.bvg.de). For a cheaper, self-guided alternative, take **bus 100**, a standard public transport route running from Zoo to Prenzlauer Berg that passes many major sights en route.

By boat/ship

Reederei Bruno Winkler (3499 5935, www.reedereiwinkler.de) tours ply the Spree and the Wannsee, and venture as far west as Brandenburg. If you haven't got time for a leisurely cruise, **Stern und Kreisschiffahrt** (536 3600, www.sternundkreis.de) offers a historical city tour that covers a fair few sights in just an hour, including the Reichstag, the remains of the Palast der Republik and the Berliner Dom. **Berliner Wassertaxi-Stadtrundfahrten (BWTS)** (6588 0203, www.berlinerwassertaxi.de) operates tours on Amsterdam-style 'Grachten' boats.

Sightseeing

From Potsdam, Berlin's neighbour, there are more opportunities for sightseeing by boat. **Havel Dampfschiffahrt** (0331 275 9210, www.schiffahrt-in-potsdam.de), for instance, organises 90-minute cruises on the Havel river. *See also p288* and *p120* **Boot trips**.

Specialist tours

Berlin Starting Point (3062 721303, www.berlin-starting-point.de) devises private, customised tours on Berlin in general or on a particular aspect of the city. **Susanne Oschmann** (782 1202, www.schoene-kuenste-exkursionen.de) focuses on the musical history of Berlin. **Milch und Honig** runs tailor-made tours of Jewish Berlin for individuals or groups (6162 5761, www.milch-und-honig.com). **Sta Tours** (3010 5151, www.sta-tours.de) shows you the houses of famous people. And **Berliner Unterwelten** (4991 0517, www.berliner-unterwelten.de) organises tours of subterranean sites.

Essential Berlin

... in one day
The key sights
● Pick a café for breakfast in the **Scheunenviertel** area of Mitte (*see p92*).
● Get your bearings from the top of the **Fernsehturm** on Alexanderplatz (*see p96*).
● Walk across to Museumsinsel and check the architectural treasures at the **Pergamonmuseum** (*see p88*).
● Stroll along Unter den Linden (*see p82*), detouring via the **Gendarmenmarkt** (*see p90*), to the **Brandenburger Tor** (*see p82*).
● Ascend the dome of the **Reichstag** (*see p109*).
● Walk south to **Potsdamer Platz** (*see p110*), taking in the **Denkmal für die ermordeten Juden Europas** (*see p84*).
● Head west, either through **Tiergarten** (*see p108*), ending up at the **Zoo and Aquarium** (*see p115*), or via the **Kulturforum** complex (lovers of Old Masters should take in the **Gemäldegalerie** – *see p114*; modern art fans head for the **Neue Nationalgalerie** (*see p115*).
● Late afternoon shopping on and around the **Ku'damm** (*see p116*)
● U-Bahn to Kreuzberg to see the extraordinary **Jüdisches Museum** (*see p105*).
● Evening: sample the restaurants and bars of **Mitte** (*see chapters* **Restaurants** and **Cafés, Bars & Pubs**).

... in two days
Museums, palaces, greenery and a beach
● Head for **Schloss Charlottenburg** (*see p119*). Apart from the palace and grounds, there are first-rate museums in the area, including the **Bröhan-Museum** (*see p119*), the **Museum Berggruen** (*see p119*) and the **Sammlung Scharf-Gerstenberg** (*see p121*).
● Then, on a fine day, escape to the leafy **Grunewald** (*see p125*) and/or the watery pleasures of the **Wannsee** (*see p126*).

● Evening: experience the laid-back cafés and nightlife of **Prenzlauer Berg**.

... in three days
Great escapes
● If you've had enough of museums, take a boat trip from Mitte through the old East down to the **Müggelsee** (*see p79, p130 and p288*).
● If you want more culture, the museum complex at Dahlem includes the brilliant **Ethnologisches Museum** (*see p125*) and the **Brücke Museum** (*see p126*) and **Allierten Museum** (*see p105*) are nearby.
● Head on to the parks and palaces of Potsdam (*see p272*).
● Evening: try the youthful nightlife of **Friedrichshain** (*see p245*) and **Kreuzberg** (*see p246*).

... in four days
Wartime and Cold War Berlin
● Get the official historical overview at the **Deutsches Historisches Museum** (*see p87*).
● Those interested in Nazi architecture should head for the **Olympiastadion** (*see p122*) or **Flughafen Tempelhof** (*see p42*). For an insight into the Nazi terror machine, check out the **Topographie des Terrors** (*see p106*), the **Gedenkstätte Plötzensee** (*see p122*) or **Sachsenhausen** (*see p278*), a former concentration camp north of Berlin.
● If the Cold War is more alluring, make for the **Gedenkstätte Berliner Mauer** (*see p123*) to see one of the few remaining stretches of Wall, or go to the **Haus am Checkpoint Charlie** (*see p105*). The **Stasi Museum** (*see p129*) and the **Museum Berlin-Karlshorst** (*see p130*) also offer fascinating insights. You'll find the plastic version at the **DDR Museum** (*see p95*).
● Evening: return to your favourite bar – you'll certainly have one by now.

Mitte

Berlin's historic centre has scrubbed up well.

Meaning 'middle', Mitte is the borough where Berlin came to be, on sandy islands in the Spree river, where Museumsinsel is today. The hub of the city before World War II, Mitte was of diminished importance during the Cold War as the off-centre centre of East Berlin – and they still hadn't dealt with all the wartime damage when the Wall came down in 1989. But in the last 20 years, Mitte has regained its position as the centre of the city, culturally, scenically and administratively. With its historic buildings given a facelift, a load of stylish new construction, and an influx of energy from young, moneyed settlers, Mitte is very much back in the middle.

Unter den Linden

Maps p318, p319 & p327

From before the Hohenzollern dynasty through the Weimar Republic, and from the Third Reich to the DDR, the entire history of Berlin can be found on or around this celebrated street.

Originally laid out to connect the town centre with the Tiergarten (*see p108*), Unter den Linden, running east from the Brandenburger Tor to Museumsinsel (*see p88*), got its name from the *Linden* (lime trees) that shaded its central walkway. Hitler, concerned that the trees obscured the view of his parades, had them felled, but they were later replanted.

During the 18th and 19th centuries, the Hohenzollerns erected no-nonsense baroque and neo-classical buildings along their capital's showcase street. The side streets were laid out in a grid by the Great Elector Friedrich Wilhelm for his Friedrichstadt (*see p11*).

Brandenburger Tor & Pariser Platz

The focal point of Unter den Linden's western end is the **Brandenburger Tor** (Brandenburg Gate). Constructed in 1791, and designed by Carl Gotthard Langhans after the Propylaea gateway into ancient Athens, the Gate was built as a triumphal arch celebrating Prussia's capital city. It was initially called the Friedenstor (Gate of Peace) and is the only city gate remaining from Berlin's original 18. (Today, only a few U-Bahn station names recall the other city gates, such as Frankfurter Tor or Schlesisches Tor).

The **Quadriga** statue, a four-horse chariot driven by Victory and designed by Johann Gottfried Schadow, sits on top of the Gate. It has had an eventful life. When Napoleon conquered Berlin in 1806 he carted the Quadriga off to Paris and held it hostage until his defeat in 1814. The Tor was later badly damaged during World War II and, during subsequent renovations, the DDR removed the Prussian Iron Cross and turned the Quadriga around so that the chariot faced west. The current Quadriga is actually a 1958 copy of the 18th-century original, and was stranded in no-man's land for 30 years. The Tor was the scene of much celebration while the Wall came down, and after that there had to be further repairs. The Iron Cross was replaced and the Quadriga was turned back to face into Mitte again.

West of the Gate stretches the vast expanse of the **Tiergarten** (*see p108*), Berlin's central park. Just to the north is the reborn **Reichstag** (*see p109*), while ten minutes' walk south is the even more dramatically reconceived **Potsdamer Platz** complex (*see p110*). Immediately east of the Brandenburger Tor is **Pariser Platz**, which was given its name in 1814 when Prussia and its allies conquered Paris. This square, enclosed by embassies and bank buildings, was once seen as Berlin's *Empfangssaal* – its reception room. Foreign dignitaries would ceremoniously pass through on their way to visit tyrants and dictators in the palaces downtown, and today this remains the area where you'll see enormous limos carting around politicians and diplomats. In 1993, plans were drawn up to revive Pariser Platz, with new buildings on the same scale as the old ones, featuring conservative exteriors and contemporary

Sightseeing

interiors. Some old faces are back on the historical sites they occupied before World War II: the reconstructed **Adlon Hotel** (*see p53*) is now at its old address, as is Michael Wilford's new **British Embassy**, around the corner at Wilhelmstrasse 70-71.

On the south-west corner of the square – the last building to complete the Pariser Platz puzzle – is the recently completed **US Embassy**. Since a return to its old address was announced in 1993, construction was delayed first by budgetary miscalculation, then by various problems attendant on new US State Department regulations stipulating a minimum 30-metre (98-foot) security zone around US embassies. The design was adjusted, streets were moved, and America is now securely back on the block. Meanwhile, Wilhelmstrasse is closed to traffic for a block south of the square because of security provisions for the British Embassy.

While outwardly conforming to aesthetic restrictions, many of the straightforward exteriors front flights of fancy within. Frank Gehry's **DG Bank** at no.3 has a huge, biomorphic interior dome hidden behind its regular façade. The **Dresdner Bank** opposite is virtually hollow, thanks to another interior atrium. Next door, Christian de Portzamparc's **French Embassy** features a space-saving 'vertical garden' on the courtyard wall,and 'french windows' extending over two storeys. Nearby is the **Kennedys** (*see p84*), a museum devoted to the famous US dynasty.

Directly to the south of Pariser Platz is the huge **Denkmal für die ermordeten Juden Europas** (Memorial to the Murdered Jews of Europe). Designed by Peter Eisenmann, it's a city-block-size field of concrete slabs, arranged in rows but sloping in different directions on uneven ground. The project has been mired in controversy since it was conceived in 1993. The winning design of an initial competition was rejected by then Chancellor Kohl, and there was no end of argument over the second competition, including rows over location (the chosen site has no particular link to the Holocaust), function (should such a monument draw a line under history or seek to stimulate debate and discussion?) and content (many feel the memorial should honour all victims of the Holocaust, not only Jewish ones). In the wake of this one, assorted other victim memorials have been built or are planned (*see p84* **Remember, remember**). The first has already appeared on the other side of Ebertstrasse: Elmgreen and Dragset's **Denkmal für die im Nationalsozialismus verfolgten Homosexuellen** (Monument to the Homosexuals Persecuted during National Socialism). It looks like one of the slabs from the Jewish Denkmal, but contains a video installation.

Between the Denkmal and the Leipziger Platz/Potsdamer Platz complex (*see p110*) is an area filled with representations from Germany's various *Länder*. Over on the other side of Wilhelmstrasse is an exhibition about the Stasi, **Stasi: Die Ausstellung** (*see p85*).

Unter den Linden.

Denkmal für die ermordeten Juden Europas

Cora-Berliner-Strasse 1 (2639 4336/www.holocaust-denkmal.de). U2, S1, S2, S26 Potsdamer Platz. **Open** *Field of stelae* 24hrs daily. *Information centre* 10am-8pm daily. **Admission** free. **No credit cards. Map** p322/p327 L7.

After many years of controversy, Peter Eisenmann's 'field of stelae' – 2,711 of them, arranged in undulating rows on 19,704 sq metres (212,000 sq ft) of city block – with its attendant information centre to memorialise the Murdered Jews of Europe, was opened in 2005. Each of the concrete slabs has its own foundation, and they tilt at differing angles. The effect is (no doubt deliberately) reminiscent of the packed headstones in Prague's Old Jewish Cemetery.

There's no vantage point or overview; to engage with the thing you need to walk into it. It's spooky in places, especially on overcast days and near the middle of the monument, where many feel a sense of confinement. The information centre is at the south-east corner of the site, mostly underground. It's like a secular crypt, containing a sombre presentation of facts and figures about the Holocaust's Jewish victims.

Kennedys

Pariser Platz 4A (2065 3570/www.thekennedys.de). S1, S2 Unter den Linden. **Open** 10am-6pm daily. **Admission** €7; €3.50 reductions. **No credit cards. Map** p318/p327 L6.

This small museum celebrates the 'special relationship' between Berlin and the Kennedy family, cemented by John F Kennedy's iconic 'Ich bin ein Berliner'

Remember, remember

Nowhere is the vexed question of Germany's relationship to its past dramatised more intensely than in the startling proliferation of memorials at the heart of Berlin.

The centrepiece, of course, is the memorial to Jewish Holocaust victims – the **Denkmal für die ermordeten Juden Europas** (*see p83*). No debate about the intersection of history, architecture and the form of Berlin's reunified cityscape lumbered on so long or conjured so much controversy as the one that engendered this grid of concrete blocks. The idea of some kind of central memorial had been around since the 1980s opening of the site of the Gestapo headquarters on what is now the **Topographie des Terrors** (*see p106*).

In 1993, the **Neue Wache** (*see p87*), a memorial to the 'victims of fascism and militarism' under the Communists, was recast as one to the 'victims of war and violent rule'. This involved installing an enlarged replica of Käthe Kollwitz's statue, *Mother with Dead Son*. There were immediate protests that this put murdered victims on the same level as dead perpetrators, and memorialised them in a form contrary to Jewish tradition. Chancellor Kohl then promised that a memorial would be erected solely for Jewish victims of the Holocaust.

The winning design of a 1995 competition was a concrete slab the size of two football fields, bearing the names of all 4.2 million identified Holocaust victims. But the cliché

Holocaust Memorial.

Sightseeing

speech in June 1963. With photos and memorabilia, the museum tells the history of the family, beginning with immigration from Ireland in the late 19th century and ending at the deaths of John and Robert Kennedy. It all looks wonderful in a minimalist setting, but that might also be down to the limits of the subject matter. Don't expect to learn anything new.

Stasi: Die Ausstellung

Mauerstrasse 38 (2241 7470/www.bstu.bund.de). *U2 Mohrenstrasse, U6 Französische Strasse.* **Open** 10am-6pm Mon-Sat. **Admission** free. **Map** p322/p327 M7.

A small and unassuming but extremely informative exhibition about the Stasi on the ground floor of the Stasi documentation centre. Ingenious spy equip-ment and rows of jarred 'bodily smells' taken from interrogation chairs illustrate the terrible extent of Stasi surveillance. The exhibition is in German, but if you ring beforehand you can get a very knowledgeable guide in English.

East along Unter den Linden

Heading east along Unter den Linden, passing the 1950s Stalinist wedding cake-style Russian Embassy on your right, and, on the next block, the box office of the **Komische Oper** (*see p252*), you reach the crossroads with Friedrichstrasse, once a café-strewn focus of Weimar Berlin.

On the other side of the junction, on the right, housed in the ground floor of a 1920s building

of equating the enormity of the crime with the enormousness of the memorial was widely criticised. Kohl rejected the design. A second competition in 1998 produced a design by Peter Eisenmann and Richard Serra involving 4,000 columns – what eventually got built is a scaled-down version.

Meanwhile, representatives of groups persecuted as Gypsies, gays, the mentally or physically handicapped, prisoners of war, political prisoners, forced labourers and blacks all pointed to the inadequacy of a memorial for Jewish victims alone. Roma groups argued that the extermination of their people should not be separated from that of the Jews, but then refused to share a memorial with homosexuals.

In May 2008, a memorial to gay victims of the Nazis, designed by Michael Elmgreen and Ingar Dragset, was unveiled on the edge of the Tiergarten. It's a lone concrete slab that looks like it was detached from the Jewish Denkmal over the road, and includes a small window through which a video of two men kissing can be viewed. After criticism by lesbian groups, this will now by rotated every two years with a video of two women.

Disagreements between Roma groups, meanwhile, have delayed construction of a memorial to Gypsy victims of the Nazis. The site that will be home to a fountain designed by Israeli memorial specialist Dani Karavan is on the corner of the Tiergarten closest to the Reichstag, just behind an impromptu memorial to people killed going over the Wall, and not far from the **Sowjetisches Ehrenmal** (Soviet War Memorial; *see p108*). And on another corner of the Tiergarten, in the parking area behind the Philharmonie, a memorial to the mentally and physically disabled victims of the Nazis' T4 euthanasia programme – a kind of lobotomised concrete bus – had just appeared at press time. The construction of Ursula Wilms's €23 million documentation centre at the Topographie des Terrors is, after yet more prolonged debate, also now underway.

And there's more to come. The memorial to the workers' uprising of 17 June 1953 – a huge, weatherproofed documentary photo set in the pavement outside the Finance Ministry on Leipziger Strasse – is a reminder that it wasn't only Nazism that left victims to be memorialised. Currently under discussion are memorials for people who died during the expulsion of Germans from Poland and Czechoslovakia after World War II, and for both people who were persecuted for deserting the German army and people who died while serving in the Bundeswehr. A plaque on the north-eastern corner of the Reichstag thanking Hungary for opening its Western border to DDR citizens in 1989 has inspired Poles to agitate for their own plaque, thanking them for solidarity's role in the downfall of Communism. And conservatives are now asking for a memorial plaque to the victims of 1970s terrorist group, the RAF.

Keen for something positive to stand in this increasingly baleful landscape of segregated victims' memorials, the latest idea is a 'Monument to Germany's Liberty and Unity' – a 'site of joy' that will commemorate the fall of the Wall. The proposal is to locate it 'in the centre of Berlin'. The only question is, where will they find room?

Wanted. Jumpers, coats and people with their knickers in a twist.

From the people who feel moved to bring us their old books and CDs, to the people fed up to the back teeth with our politicians' track record on climate change, Oxfam supporters have one thing in common. They're passionate. If you've got a little fire in your belly, we'd love to hear from you. Visit us at **oxfam.org.uk**

Be Humankind Oxfam

now occupied by Deutsche Bank, is the **Deutsche Guggenheim Berlin** (*see below*), a tiddler compared to its big sisters in New York and Bilbao. Facing the art gallery across Unter den Linden stands the **Staatsbibliotek** (it's open to all, and there's a small café), usually filled with students from the **Humboldt-Universität** (*see p299*). The university's grand old façade has been restored, as have the two statues of the Humboldts (founder Wilhelm and his brother Alexander), between which booksellers set up tables in good weather.

Across the street is **Bebelplatz**, site of the notorious Nazi book-burning, commemorated by Micha Ullmann's monument set into the Platz itself. The glass has become pretty scratched, unfortunately, and it can be hard to see through. Dominating the square's eastern side is the **Staatsoper** (*see p253*), built in neo-classical style by Georg Wenzeslaus von Knobelsdorff in 1741-43. The present building actually dates from 1955 but is faithful to the original. Established as Frederick the Great's Royal Court Opera, it is now one of Berlin's three major opera houses.

Just south of the Staatsoper (and also designed by Knobelsdorff, in 1747) is **Sankt-Hedwigs-Kathedrale** (*see below*), a curious circular Roman Catholic church, inspired by the Pantheon in Rome. A minute's walk east of here brings you to another church, **Friedrichswerdersche-Kirche**, which now contains the **Schinkel-Museum** (*see below*), a homage to the building's architect.

On the west side of Bebelplatz is Rocco Forte's **Hotel de Rome** (*see p54*), occupying what used to be the East German central bank, and the late 18th-century **Alte Bibliotek**. Alongside that, in the centre of Unter den Linden, stands a restored equestrian statue of Frederick the Great.

On the north side of Unter den Linden, the **Neue Wache** (New Guardhouse), constructed by Schinkel in 1816-18, originally served as a guardhouse for the royal residences in the area. Today, it is a hauntingly plain memorial to the 'victims of war and tyranny', with an enlarged reproduction of a Käthe Kollwitz sculpture, *Mother with Dead Son*, at its centre. Beneath this are the remains of an unknown soldier and an unknown concentration camp victim, surrounded by earth from World War II battlefields and concentration camps.

Next to it to the east is the baroque Zeughaus, a former armoury with a deceptively peaceful pink façade. With renovations completed in 2006, the Zeughaus once again houses the **Deutsches Historisches Museum** (*see below*). The new wing by IM Pei hosts changing exhibitions and has a fine café.

This whole last eastern stretch of Unter den Linden is supposed to undergo further heritage restoration, in line with the eventual rebuilding of the nearby Stadtschloss. The road will be narrowed to make the area feel more like a square, and to help revive the idea of the Forum Fredericanum, as this ensemble was historically known, period lampposts and other historical details will be installed.

Deutsche Guggenheim Berlin

Unter den Linden 13-15 (202 0930/www.deutsche-guggenheim.de). U6 Französische Strasse. **Open** 11am-8pm Mon-Wed, Fri-Sun; 11am-10pm Thur. **Admission** €4; €3 reductions; free under-12s. Free to all Mon. **No credit cards. Map** p318/p327 M6.
In partnership with the Deutsche Bank (and housed in one of its buildings), this is the least impressive European branch of the Guggenheim. The modest exhibition space was designed by Richard Gluckman, and in 2009 hosts shows from Anish Kapoor and Julie Mehretu as well as themed exhibitions called Utopian Matters and Picturing America.

Deutsches Historisches Museum

Zeughaus, Unter den Linden 2 (203 040/www.dhm.de). U6 Französische Strasse. **Open** 10am-6pm daily. **Admission** €4; free under-18s. **Credit** MC, V. **Map** p319/p327 N6.
The permanent exhibition in the Zeughaus finally opened in July 2006 and provides an exhaustive blast through German history from 100BC to the present day, divided chronologically into significant eras. The museum originally had trouble raising the funds to buy historical objects, but there's enough here now for the exhibits to work on their own, without the need for an overarching narrative. German nationalism becomes the focus once you enter the 19th century and later on more than one room is dedicated to the Nazi era. The DHM has succeeded admirably in looking the past straight in the eye, although the attempt to be impartial means that it is sometimes factual to the extreme. Temporary exhibitions are housed in the gorgeous new Pei building.

Friedrichswerdersche-Kirche/ Schinkel-Museum

Werderscher Markt (208 1323/www.smb.spk-berlin.de). U2 Hausvogteiplatz. **Open** 10am-6pm Tue-Sun. **Admission** free. **Map** p323/p327 N7.
This brick church, designed by Karl Friedrich Schinkel, was completed in 1831. Its war wounds were repaired in the 1980s and it reopened in 1987 as a homage to its architect. Inside are statues by Schinkel, Schadow and others, bathed in soft light from stained-glass windows. Pictures of Schinkel's works that didn't survive the war are also displayed.

Sankt-Hedwigs-Kathedrale

Hinter der katholischen Kirche 3 (203 4810/www.hedwigs-kathedrale.de). U2 Hausvogteiplatz or U6 Französische Strasse. **Open** 10am-5pm daily. **Admission** free. *Guided tours* €1.50. **Map** p323/p327 N7.

Sightseeing

Constructed in 1747 for Berlin's Catholic minority, this circular Knobelsdorff creation was bombed out during the war and only reconsecrated in 1963. Its modernised interior contains a split-level double altar. The crypt holds the remains of Bernhard Lichtenberg, who preached here against the Nazis, was arrested, and died while being transported to Dachau in 1943.

Museumsinsel

Maps p319 & p327

The eastern end of Unter den Linden abuts the island in the Spree where Berlin was 'born'. The northern part, with its excellent collection of museums and galleries, is known as Museumsinsel (Museum Island), while the southern half (much enlarged by landfill), once a neighbourhood for the city's fishermen (and known as Fischerinsel), is now dominated by a clutch of grim tower blocks.

The five Museumsinsel museums (the Pergamonmuseum, Altes Museum, Alte Nationalgalerie, Bode Museum and Neues Museum) have been undergoing a massive restoration programme for many years; the first four are open, while work remains to be done on the Neues Museum. Such is the importance of the site that it was added to UNESCO's World Cultural Heritage list in 1999.

The **Pergamonmuseum** (*see p89*), one of Berlin's main attractions, is a showcase for three huge and important examples of ancient architecture: the Hellenistic Pergamon Altar (part of a Greek temple complex from what is now western Turkey), the Babylonian Gate of Ishtar and the Roman Market Gate of Miletus. The museum also contains the Museum für Islamische Kunst (Museum of Islamic Art).

Schinkel's superb **Altes Museum** (Old Museum; *see below*), from 1830, has a small permanent collection, hosts some excellent temporary exhibitions, and for now houses the collection of the Ägyptisches Museum (Egyptian Museum). The renovated **Alte Nationalgalerie** (Old National Gallery; *see below*) has once again become home to a wide-ranging collection of 19th-century painting and sculpture.

Currently undergoing major renovation under the direction of British architect David Chipperfield, the **Neues Museum** is due to open again in 2009 as a home to the Ägyptisches Museum and Charlottenburg's **Museum für Vor- und Frühgeschichte** (Primeval and Early History Museum; *see p119*). Instead of rebuilding an exact copy, Chipperfield has created new architecture where the old could not be saved. The resulting collage effect is looking impressive so far.

Dominating the Museumsinsel skyline is the huge, bombastic **Berliner Dom** (*see p89*). It's worth climbing up to the cathedral's dome for fine views over the city. In front of here, bounded on one side by the neo-classical colonnade of the Altes Museum, is the Lustgarten, an elegant green square.

Across the main road bisecting the island, demolition of the poor old **Palast der Republik** was almost complete but stalled at press time. During the Cold War, the Palast contained the main parliamentary chamber of the DDR, but also discos, bars and a bowling alley. It had replaced the remains of the war-ravaged Stadtschloss, residence of the Kaisers, which was heavily damaged in World War II and demolished by the DDR in 1952. Now the Stadtschloss will be rebuilt, although quite what it will house remains a matter of conjecture.

Alte Nationalgalerie

Bodestrasse 1-3 (266 3666/www.alte-nationalgalerie. de). S5, S7, S9, S75 Hackescher Markt. **Open** 10am-6pm Tue, Wed, Fri-Sun; 10am-10pm Thur. **Admission** €8; €4 reductions. **No credit cards.** **Map** p319/p327 N6.

With its ceiling and wall paintings, fabric wallpapers and marble staircase, the Old National Gallery is a sparkling home to one of the largest collections of 19th-century art and sculpture in Germany. Among the 440 paintings and 80 sculptures, which span the period from Goethe to early Modern, German artists such as Adolph Menzel, Caspar David Friedrich, Max Liebermann and Carl Spitzweg are well represented. There are also some first-rank early Impressionist works from Manet, Monet and Rodin. Although it's worth a visit, don't expect to see the definitive German national collection.

Altes Museum

Lustgarten (2090 5245/www.smb.museum). S3, S5, S7, S9, S75 Hackescher Markt. **Open** 10am-6pm Tue, Wed, Fri-Sun; 10am-10pm Thur. **Admission** €8; €4 reductions. **No credit cards.** **Map** p319/p327 N6.

Opened as the Royal Museum in 1830, the Old Museum originally housed all the art treasures on Museumsinsel. It was designed by Schinkel and is considered one of his finest buildings, with a particularly magnificent entrance rotunda, where vast neon letters declare that 'All Art has been Contemporary'. This building currently houses the Ägyptische Museum (Egyptian Museum), whose most celebrated exhibit is the bust of Nefertiti, dating from around 1350 BC. The portrayal of the human face is one of the most compelling aspects of the collection, which includes a series of characterful model faces, and the vivid 'Berlin Green Head'. Another unique treasure is the only known example of Cleopatra's handwriting, and there are mummies and statuary aplenty. The museum's

Bode Museum.

Bode Museum

Monbijoubrücke (266 3666/www.smb.museum).
U6, S1, S2, S5, S7, S9, S75 Friedrichstrasse
or S5,S7,S75,S9 Hackescher Markt. **Open**
10am-6pm Mon-Wed, Fri-Sun; 10am-10pm Thur.
Admission €8; €4 reductions. No credit cards.
Map p319/p327 N6.
Built by Berlin architect Ernst Eberhard von Ihne
in 1904, the Bode Museum reopened after a thorough renovation in 2006. It was originally intended
by Wilhelm von Bode as a home for art from the
beginnings of Christendom, and now contains the
Byzantine Collection, Sculpture Collection and the
Numismatic Collection. The neo-baroque Great
Dome, the Basilica hall and the glorious Cupola
have been carefully restored to keep up with modern curatorial standards, but they retain their mag-
nificence. Most impressively, despite one of the
world's largest sculpture collections and more than
half a million pieces in the coin collection, the
museum somehow retains a totally uncluttered feel
and the sculptures stand free from off-putting glass
cases. In particular, make sure you look out for the
wall-length Apse Mosaic from 545 AD and the
14th-century Mannheim High Altar. Both are well
worth checking out.

Pergamonmuseum

Am Kupfergraben (2090 5566/www.smb.museum).
U6, S1, S2, S5, S7, S9, S75 Friedrichstrasse.
Open 10am-6pm Tue, Wed, Fri-Sun; 10am-10pm
Thur. **Admission €8; €4 reductions. No credit**
cards. Map p319/p327 N6.
One of the world's major archaeological museums,
the Pergamon should not be missed. Its treasures,
comprising the Antikensammlung (Collection of
Classical Antiquities) and the Vorderasiastisches
Museum (Museum of Near Eastern Antiquities),
contain three major draws. The first is the
Hellenistic Pergamon Altar, dating from 170-159
BC; huge as it is, the museum's partial re-creation
represents only one third of its original size. In an
adjoining room, and even more architecturally
impressive, is the towering two-storey Roman
Market Gate of Miletus (29 metres/95 feet wide and
almost 17 metres/56 feet high), erected in AD 120.
This leads through to the third of the big attractions – the extraordinary blue and ochre tiled Gate
of Ishtar and the Babylonian Processional Street,
dating from the reign of King Nebuchadnezzar
(605-562 BC). There are plenty of other gems in the
museum that are also worth seeking out, including
some stunning Assyrian reliefs.

The museum is also now home to the Museum
für Islamische Kunst (Museum of Islamic Art),
which takes up some 14 rooms in the southern
wing. The collection is wide ranging, including
applied arts, crafts, books and architectural details
from the eighth to the 19th century. Entrance is
included in the overall admission price, as is an
excellent audio guide.

Note that the Pergamon is currently undergoing
renovation, which is happening in stages.

normal exhibit has been pared down to make room
for all this, but there are still temporary exhibitions.
When the Egyptian stuff moves to the Neues
Museum in 2009, a vast exhibit on the Etruscans
will take its place.

Berliner Dom

Lustgarten 1 (2026 9133/guided tours 2026
9119/www.berliner-dom.de). S5, S7, S9, S75
Hackescher Markt. **Open** *Apr-Sept* 9am-8pm
Mon-Sat; noon-8pm Sun. *Oct-Mar* 9am-7pm
Mon-Sat; noon-7pm Sun. **Admission €5; €3**
reductions; free under-14s. **No credit cards.**
Map p319/p327 N6.
The dramatic Berlin Cathedral is now finally
healed of its war wounds and celebrated its cente-
nary in 2005. Built in Italian Renaissance style, it
was destroyed during World War II and remained
a ruin until 1973, when extensive restoration work
began. It has always looked fine from the outside,
but now that the internal work is complete, it is
fully restored to its former glory. Crammed with
Victorian detail and containing dozens of statues
of eminent German Protestants, its lush 19th-cen-
tury interior is hardly the perfect acoustic space for
the frequent concerts that are held here, but it's
worth a visit to see the crypt containing around 90
sarcophagi of notables from the Hohenzollern
dynasty, or to clamber up for splendid views from
the cupola. Call to book a guided tour.

Sightseeing

South of Unter den Linden

Maps p322 & p327

What the Kurfürstendamm was in post-war West Berlin, **Friedrichstrasse** had been and is trying to be again: the city's glitziest shopping street. Like Unter den Linden, the north-south street (starting at Mehringplatz in Kreuzberg and ending at Oranienburger Tor in Mitte) was laid out as part of the baroque late 17th-century expansion of the city.

The liveliest, sleekest stretch of the street is that between **Checkpoint Charlie** (see p105) and Friedrichstrasse station. A huge amount of money has been poured into redevelopment here, with office buildings and upmarket shops and malls galore, although opinions differ as to the effectiveness of the architecture.

Look out for the all-glass façade of the modernist-style **Galeries Lafayette** (no.75; see p171), the acute angles of the expressionist **Quartier 206** (nos.71-74; see p173) and the monolithic geometric mass of **Quartier 205** (nos.66-70). Otherwise there are auto showrooms for Rolls-Royce, Bentley, Volkswagen, Audi and Mercedes-Benz, boutiques for Mont Blanc, Cartier and countless other high-class concerns.

Just to the east of this stretch lies the square of **Gendarmenmarkt**, one of the high points of Frederick the Great's vision for the city. Here, two churches, the **Französischer Dom** ('French Cathedral'; home of the **Hugenottenmuseum**; see below) and the **Deutscher Dom** (see below), frame the **Konzerthaus** (see p252), home to the Deutsches Symphonie-Orchester Berlin.

Just west of Friedrichstrasse on Leipziger Strasse is the **Museum für Kommunikation** (see below). There are many other interesting sights close by over the Mitte border with Kreuzberg. For these, see p101.

Deutscher Dom

Gendarmenmarkt, entrance in Markgrafenstrasse (2273 0431). U2, U6 Stadtmitte. **Open** 10am-10pm Tue; 10am-6pm Wed-Sun. Guided tours 11am, 1pm daily. **Admission** free. **Map** p322/p327 M7.

Both this church and the Französischer Dom were built in 1780-85 by Carl von Gontard for Frederick the Great, in imitation of Santa Maria in Montesanto and Santa Maria dei Miracoli in Rome. The Deutscher Dom was intended for Berlin's Lutheran community. Its neo-classical tower is topped by a 7m (23ft) gilded statue representing Virtue. Inside is a permanent exhibition on the history of Germany's parliamentary system, from the 1848 revolution through the suspension of parliamentary politics by the Nazis, right up to the present day. The visitor is encouraged to consider the role of parliaments throughout the modern world, but there are no translations so to get much out of this without a guided tour, your German must be up to scratch.

Grand square – **Gendarmenmarkt**.

Französischer Dom/ Hugenottenmuseum

Gendarmenmarkt (229 1760/www.franzoesischer-dom.de). U2, U6 Stadtmitte. **Open** noon-5pm Tue-Sat; 11am-5pm Sun. **Admission** €2; €1 reductions. **No credit cards. Map** p322/p327 M7.

Built in the early 18th century for Berlin's 6,000-plus-strong French Protestant community, the church was later given a baroque tower, which offers fine views over Mitte. The tower is purely decorative and unconsecrated – and, therefore, not part of the church, which is known as the Französischen Friedrichstadt Kirche (noon-5pm Mon-Sat; after service-5pm Sun).

An exhibition on the history of the French Protestants in France and Berlin-Brandenburg is displayed within the building (the modest church has a separate entrance at the western end). The museum chronicles the religious persecution suffered by Calvinists (note the bust of Calvin on the outside of the church) and their subsequent immigration to Berlin after 1685, at the behest of the Hohenzollerns. The development of the Huguenot community is also detailed with paintings, documents and artefacts. One part of the museum is devoted to the church's history, particularly the effects of World War II – it was bombed during a Sunday service in 1944 and remained a ruin until the mid 1980s.

Museum für Kommunikation

Leipziger Strasse 16 (202 940/www.museum sstiftung.de/berlin). U2 Mohrenstrasse or U2,

U6 Stadtmitte. **Open** 9am-5pm Tue-Fri; 11am-7pm Sat, Sun. **Admission** €3; €1.50 reductions. **Map** p322/p327 M7.

A direct descendant of the world's first postal museum (founded in 1872), this collection covers a bit more than mere stamps. It traces the development of telecommunications up to the internet era, though philatelists might head straight to the basement and the 'Blue Mauritius', one of the world's rarest stamps.

North of Unter den Linden

Maps p318 & p326

The continuation of Friedrichstrasse north of Unter den Linden is less appealing and lively than its southern stretch. Friedrichstrasse station once had an interior notable mostly for its ability to confuse. Its role as the only East-West border crossing point open for all categories of citizen involved a warren of passageways and interior partitions. Today it is open and full of shops.

Following the line of the train tracks east along Georgenstrasse, you come upon the **Berliner Antik & Flohmarkt** (*see p173*) – a succession of antiques stores, bookshops and cafés in the *Bogen* ('arches'), underneath the railway.

The building just to the north of the railway station and behind the tower that is under construction on the rest of the site is known as the **Tränenpalast** ('Palace of Tears'). This was where departing visitors left their Eastern friends and relations who could not follow them through the border. Today, this former checkpoint is a concert and cabaret venue.

Across Friedrichstrasse stands the **Admiralspalast** (*see p250*), a landmark theatre that reopened in 2006 after eight years of darkness. First opened in 1910, a survivor of wartime bombing, the building contains a 1,600-seat theatre used over the decades for everything from Broadway transplants to the Staatsoper. There are also two smaller performance spaces and a restored roman-style bathhouse-turned-21st-century spa.

Crossing the river on the wrought-iron Weidendammer Brücke, a left turn on Schiffbauerdamm brings you to the **Berliner Ensemble** (*see p255*), with its bronze statue of Bertolt Brecht, who directed the company from 1948 to 1956, surrounded by quotations from his works. *Die Dreigroschenoper* (*The Threepenny Opera*) was premiered here on 31 August 1928. There are various congenial bars and restaurants along the riverbank, beyond which this neighbourhood begins to merge into what is now the government quarter.

Back on Friedrichstrasse stands the **Friedrichstadtpalast** (*see p258*), a large

variety venue that was an entertainment hotspot during the DDR days, since it took hard currency; it still pulls the crowds today, albeit mostly grannies from out of town. Further north is the **Brecht-Weigel-Gedenkstätte** (*see below*), home to Bertolt Brecht (until his death in 1956) and his wife Helene Weigel. Both are buried in the Dorotheenstädtische Friedhof (open 8am-dusk daily) next door, along with the architect Schinkel, the author Heinrich Mann and the philosopher Hegel.

Two worthwhile museums are five and ten minutes' walk from here: the **Museum für Naturkunde** (Natural History Museum; *see p92*) and the **Hamburger Bahnhof – Museum für Gegenwart** (Hamburg Station Museum of Contemporary Art; *see below*), which puts on a series of excellent, temporary exhibitions within the atmospheric confines of a former railway station.

Brecht-Weigel-Gedenkstätte

Chausseestrasse 125 (200 571 844). U6 Oranienburger Tor. **Open** *Guided tours* every 30mins 10-11.30am Tue, Wed, Fri; 10am-noon, 5-6.30pm Thur; 9.30am-1.30pm Sat; every hr 11am-6pm Sun. **Admission** €3; €1.50 reductions. **No credit cards**. **Map** p318/p326 M5.

Brecht's home from 1948 until his death in 1953 has been preserved exactly as he left it. Tours of the house (phone in advance for an English one) give interesting insights into the life and reading habits of the playwright. The window at which he worked overlooked the grave of Hegel in the neighbouring cemetery. Brecht's wife, actress Helene Weigel, continued living here until her death in 1971. The Brecht archives are kept upstairs. The Kellerrestaurant near the exit serves Viennese dishes as cooked by Weigel; *see p137*.

Hamburger Bahnhof – Museum für Gegenwart

Invalidenstrasse 50-51 (397 8340/www. hamburgerbahnhof.de). S5, S7, S9, S75 Lehrter Stadtbahnhof. **Open** 10am-6pm Tue, Wed, Fri; 10am-10pm Thur; 11am-8pm Sat; 11am-6pm Sun. **Admission** €8; €4 reductions. **No credit cards**. **Map** p318 K5.

The Hamburg Station Museum of Contemporary Art opened in 1997 within a huge and expensive refurbishment of a former railway station. The exterior features a stunning fluorescent light installation by Dan Flavin. Inside, the biggest draw is currently the gradual unveiling of the Friedrich Christian Flick Collection – a staggering 2,000 works from around 150 artists, mostly of the late 20th century. Flick, from a steel family whose fortune was tainted with Nazi-era controversy, has paid for the refurbishment of the Rieckhalle – an adjacent 300m (984ft) warehouse – to accommodate the works from his collection, many of them large-scale, as they are doled out in temporary, themed exhibitions. There

Sightseeing

are other exhibitions too – work by photographer Wolfgang Tillmans starred for much of 2008 – plus one of Berlin's best art bookshops.

Museum für Naturkunde

Invalidenstrasse 43 (2093 8550/www.museum. hu-berlin.de). U6 Zinnowitzer Strasse. **Open** 9.30am-5pm Tue-Fri; 10am-6pm Sat, Sun. **Admission** €5; €3 reductions. **No credit cards. Map** p318 L4.
Berlin's recently renovated Natural History Museum is a real treasure trove. The biggest draw is the skeleton of a Brachiosaurus dinosaur, which weighed 50 tons at death and is as high as a four-storey house. Restored to its former glory after years in storage, 'Oliver' – as the dinosaur has been nicknamed – is one of the world's largest known land animals and was discovered in the early 1900s. Four renovated exhibition rooms were reopened in 2007, including the new 'Evolution in Action', although unfortunately a lot of information in the old exhibitions is still in German only. The glorious fossil and stone collections downstairs are worth a look.

The Scheunenviertel

If the area south of Friedrichstrasse station is the new upmarket face of Mitte, the Scheunenviertel (stretching around the north bank of the Spree, running east from Friedrichstrasse to Hackescher Markt) is the face of its moneyed bohemia.

This is today Berlin's main nightlife district and art quarter, littered with bars and galleries. Once far enough out of town that it was safe to build the highly flammable hay barns (*Scheunen*) here, this was also historically the centre of Berlin's immigrant community, including many Jews from Eastern Europe. During the 1990s, it again began to attract Jewish immigrants, including both young Americans and Orthodox Jews from the former Soviet Union.

In the 1990s, the Scheunenviertel became a magnet for squatters with access to the list of buildings supposedly wrecked by lazy urban developers, who had ticked them off as 'gone' in order to meet quotas but had actually left them standing. With many other buildings in disrepair, rents were cheap, and the new residents soon learned how to take advantage of city subsidies for opening galleries and other cultural spaces. Result: the Scheunenviertel became Berlin's hottest cultural centre.

The first of these art-squats was **Tacheles**, on Oranienburger Strasse, the spine of the Scheunenviertel. Built in 1907, the building originally housed an early attempt at a shopping mall. It had stood vacant for years when squatted by artists after the Wall came down. It then became a rather arrogant arbiter of hip in the neighbourhood, with studio and performance spaces, a cinema, and several edgy bars and discos. In 1998, it was bought

by a German company, and it now houses various galleries and a dance space (*see p260*).

Across Tucholskystrasse at Oranienburger Strasse 32 is an entrance to the **Heckmann Höfe** (the other is on Auguststrasse), a series of courtyards that have been delightfully restored to accommodate shops and restaurants. The free-standing building with the firm's coat of arms in the pavement in front of it was once the stables.

A little further down the block stands the **Neue Synagoge** (*see p93*), with its gleaming golden Moorish-style dome. Turning into Grosse Hamburger Strasse, you find yourself surrounded by Jewish history. On the right, on the site of a former old people's home, there's a memorial to the thousands of Berlin Jews who were forced to congregate here before being shipped off to concentration camps. Behind the memorial is a park that was once Berlin's oldest Jewish cemetery; the only gravestone left is that of the father of the German Jewish renaissance, Moses Mendelssohn, founder of the city's first Jewish school, next door at no.27. That the school has heavy security fencing and a permanent police presence, even today, only adds to the poignancy of this place.

Across the street at nos.15-16 is the **Missing House**, a memorial by Christian Boltanski, in which the walls of a bombed-out house have the names and occupations of former residents inscribed on the site of their vanished apartments. A little further on, the **Sophienkirche**, from which nearby Sophienstrasse gets its name, is one of Berlin's few remaining baroque churches. It is set back from the street behind wrought-iron fences, and, together with the surrounding ensemble, is one of the prettiest architectural sites in the city. The interior is a little disappointing, however.

At the end of Oranienburger Strasse, at the corner of Rosenthaler Strasse, is the famous **Hackesche Höfe**. Built in 1906-07, these form a complex of nine interlinking Jugendstil courtyards with elegant ceramic façades. The Höfe symbolise Berlin's new Mitte: having miraculously survived two wars, the forgotten, crumbling buildings were restored in the mid-1990s using the old plans. Today, they house an upmarket collection of shops, galleries, theatres, cafés, restaurants and cinemas and are just about Berlin's top tourist attraction. Try to avoid visiting at the weekend.

A few doors up Rosenthaler Strasse is a tumbledown alley alongside the Central cinema, in which a workshop for the blind was located during World War II. Its owner managed to stock it fully with 'blind' Jews, and helped them escape or avoid the camps. Now it houses

Meet under the clock in **Alexanderplatz**. *See p94.*

alternative galleries, bars and shops. Across the street from the Hackesche Höfe, and under the S-Bahn arches, there are further bars, restaurants and shops.

There are still more fashionable bars and shops along Rosenthaler Strasse and around the corner on Neue Schönhauser Strasse, as well as some good sandwich and coffee bars. This area has settled into being Berlin's hip centre with many cool little shops. Most of the original houses have now been renovated and the gaps left by wartime bombing have been filled in by slick new buildings. Even the *Plattenbauten*, the East German prefabs, have been spruced up, although the pavements still have craters.

Leading off Rosenthaler Strasse, **Sophienstrasse** is Mitte's most picturesque street. Built in the 18th century, it was restored in 1987 for the city's 750th anniversary, with craftworkers' ateliers that have replicas of old merchants' metal signs hanging outside them. This pseudo-historicism has now become part of a more interesting mix of handcraft shops. The brick façade of the Handwerker Verein at no.18 is particularly impressive. If you wander into the courtyard (as you can with most courtyards that aren't private), you'll find the **Sophiensaele** (*see p257*), an interesting performing arts space in an old ballroom. The Sophiensaele was also the location of the first German Communist Party HQ.

At nos.20-21 are the **Sophie-Gips Höfe**, which came into being when wealthy art patrons Erika and Rolf Hoffmann were denied permission to build a gallery in Dresden for their collection of contemporary art. Instead, they bought this complex between Sophienstrasse and Gipsstrasse, restored it, and installed the art here, along with their spectacular private residence (*see below*).

Running between the west end of Oranienburger Strasse and Rosenthaler Strasse, **Auguststrasse** was the original core of Berlin's eastern gallery district; it was here that the whole Mitte scene began almost two decades ago, with such important venues as Eigen + Art (*see p214*) and Kunst-Werke (*see p216*), among many others. This became known as Mitte's 'Art Mile', and the street still makes a good afternoon's stroll, although many of the cutting-edge galleries have moved on.

Neue Synagoge

Centrum Judaicum, Oranienburger Strasse 28-30 (8802 8451/www.cjudaicum.de). S1, S2 Oranienburger Strasse. **Open** *Sept-Apr* 10am-6pm Mon-Thur, Sun; 10am-2pm Fri. *May-Aug* 10am-8pm Mon, Sun; 10am-6pm Tue-Thur; 10am-5pm Fri. **Admission** €3; €2 reductions. **No credit cards**. **Map** p319/p326 N5.
Built in 1857-66 as the Berlin Jewish community's showpiece (and inaugurated in the presence of Bismarck), it was the New Synagogue that was attacked during Kristallnacht in 1938, but not too badly damaged – Allied bombs did far more harm in 1945. The façade remained intact and the Moorish dome has been rebuilt. Inside is a permanent exhibition about Jewish life in Berlin and a glassed-in area protecting the ruins of the sanctuary.

Sammlung Hoffman

Sophienstrasse 21 (2849 9121/www.sophie-gips.de). U8 Weinmeisterstrasse. **Open** (by appointment only) 11am-4pm Sat. **Admission** €6. **No credit cards**. **Map** p319/p326 N5.
This is Erika and Rolf Hoffmann's private collection of international contemporary art, including a charming floor installation work by Swiss video artist Pipilotti Rist and work by Douglas Gordon, Felix Gonzalez-Torres and AR Penck. The Hoffmans offer guided tours through their apartment every Saturday by appointment – felt slippers supplied.

Berliner Rathaus.

Alexanderplatz & around

Maps p319 & p327

Visitors who have read Alfred Döblin's *Berlin Alexanderplatz* or seen the television series by Fassbinder may arrive here and wonder what happened. What happened was that in the early 1970s Erich Honecker decided that this historic area should reflect the glories of socialism, and tore it all down. He replaced it with a masterpiece of Commie kitsch: wide boulevards; monotonous white buildings filled with cafés and shops (though to a degree these took their cue from modernist structures dating from the Weimar era, such as the block between the south-west side of the square and the station); and, of course, the impressive golf-ball-on-a-knitting-needle, the **Fernsehturm** (Television Tower; *see p96*). The goofy clock topped with the 1950s-style atom design signals the time in (mostly) former socialist lands; water cascades from the Brunnen der Völkerfreundschaft ('Fountain of the Friendship of Peoples').

There were plans to replace most of Alexanderplatz with a dozen or so skyscrapers, among which the Fernsehturm would remain standing, but it seems unlikely they will ever come to fruition. For now, the Kaufhaus department store on the north-west of the square has been expanded and lost its '70s façade, while the 22,000 square metres of new shopping space going up on the north-east corner at press time have ruined the square's Communist-era sightlines and obscured the view across Grunerstrasse of the domed Kongresshalle

and the Haus des Lehrers with its first-floor frieze – two of Berlin's finest examples of DDR architecture. Beyond them is Alexa (*see p173*), a giant new shopping mall that no one likes.

One of the few survivors from pre-war Alexanderplatz sits in the shadow of the Fernsehturm: the **Marienkirche** (*see p96*), Berlin's oldest parish church, dating from the 13th century. Later 15th-century (the tower) and 18th-century (the upper section) additions enhance the building's harmonious simplicity.

Just south of here stands the extravagant **Neptunbrunnen**, an 1891 statue of the trident-wielding sea god, surrounded by four female figures representing the Elbe, Rhine, Oder and Vistula rivers. It was moved here from the Stadtschloss when the Communists demolished it in 1950. Overlooking Neptune from the south-east is the huge red-brick bulk of the **Berliner Rathaus** (Berlin Town Hall; *see p95*), while to the south-west is the open space of Marx-Engels Forum, one of the few remaining monuments to the old boys – the huge statue of Karl and Fred begs you to take a seat on Marx's lap. On Spandauer Strasse behind the Radisson Hotel, is the entrance to the **AquaDom & Sea Life** (*see p95*), one of Mitte's more eccentric new attractions, and round the corner on the river is the hardly more sensible **DDR Museum** (*see p95*).

For a vague impression of what this part of the city might have looked like before Allied bombers and the DDR did their work, take a stroll around the Nikolaiviertel, just south of Alexanderplatz. This is Berlin's oldest quarter, centred around **Nikolaikirche** (dating from 1220; *see p96*). The DDR's reconstruction involved bringing the few undamaged buildings from this period together into what is essentially a fake assemblage of history. There are a couple of historic residences, including the **Knoblauch-Haus** (*see p96*), and the **Ephraim-Palais** (*see p95*). You'll also find Gottfried Lessing's house, restaurants, cafés (including a reconstruction of Zum Nussbaum, a contender for the oldest bar in Berlin) and overpriced shops. On the southern edge of the district is the **Hanf Museum** (Hemp Museum; *see p96*).

Long before the infamous Wall, Berlin had another one: the medieval **Stadtmauer** (City Wall) of the original 13th-century settlement. There's almost as much left of this wall (a couple of minutes' walk east of the Nikolaiviertel, on Littenstrasse/Waisenstrasse) as there is of the more recent one. Built along the wall by the junction with Parochialstrasse is the extremely old restaurant Zur Letzten Instanz. It takes its name from the neighbouring law court. There has been a restaurant on this site since 1525, Napoleon among its customers.

Just over the Spree from here is the church-like red-brick **Märkisches Museum** (*see p96*), which houses a rambling, but not uninteresting, collection tracing the history of the city, and the small neighbouring **Köllnischer Park**. The park's bearpit is home to Schnute, Maxi and Tilo, Berlin's trio of flesh-and-blood brown bears – and official symbols of the city.

Around the corner on Wallstrasse is the **Museum Kindheit und Jugend** (Museum of Childhood and Youth; *see p96*), with its dry displays of old toys and school life.

AquaDom & Sea Life

Spandauer Strasse 3 (992 800/www.sealife.de). S5, S7, S9, S75 Hackescher Markt. **Open** 10am-6pm daily. **Admission** €13.50; €10-€12.60 reductions. **No credit cards. Map** p319/p327 N6.
Billed as two attractions in one, both involving lots of water and plenty of fish. Sea Life leads you through 13 themed aquaria offering fish in different habitats. The AquaDom is the world's largest free-standing aquarium – a spacey stucture that looks like it might just have landed from some extremely watery planet. You take a lift up through the middle of this giant cylindrical fishtank – a million litres of saltwater that is home to 2,500 colourful creatures, and enfolded by the atrium of the Radisson Hotel (*see p57*).

Berliner Rathaus

Rathausstrasse 15 (902 60/guided tours 9026 2523). U2, U5, U8, S5, S7, S9, S75, Alexanderplatz. **Open** 9am-6pm Mon-Fri. *Guided tours* by appointment. **Admission** free. **Map** p319/p327 O6.
This magnificent building was constructed of terracotta brick during the 1860s. The history of Berlin up to that point is illustrated in a series of 36 reliefs on the façade. During Communist times,

it served as East Berlin's town hall – which made its old nickname, Rotes Rathaus ('Red Town Hall'), after the colour of the façade, doubly fitting. West Berlin's city government workers moved here from their town hall, Rathaus Schöneberg, in 1991. Admission is restricted to small parts of the building; bring some ID.

DDR Museum

Karl Liebknecht Strasse 1 (847 123 731/www.ddr-museum.de). S5, S27, S9, S75 Hackescher Markt. **Open** 10am-8pm Mon-Fri, Sun; 10am-10pm Sat. **Admission** €5; €3 reductions. **Credit** AmEx, MC, V. **Map** p319/p327 O6.
Bright blue neon signage and a Trabant in the window welcome you into 'one of Europe's most interactive museums!' This is 'Ostalgia' in action. Touch screens, sound effects and even the 'DDR Game' mean that the more distasteful aspects of East German life are cheerfully glossed over. The museum is essentially a collection of DDR memorabilia, from travel tickets to Palast der Republik serviettes. Climb inside the Trabi or sit on a DDR couch in a DDR living room where you can watch DDR TV. Information on the Stasi gets the interactive treatment too – you can pretend to be a Stasi officer and listen in on a bugged flat. Take it all with a large pinch of salt.

Ephraim-Palais

Poststrasse 16 (2400 2121/www.stadtmuseum.de). U2, U5, U8, S5, S7, S9, S75 Alexanderplatz. **Open** 10am-6pm Tue-Sun. **Admission** €3; €1.50 reductions; free to all Wed. *Combined ticket (with Knoblauch-Haus & Nikolaikirche)* €5; €3 reductions. **No credit cards. Map** p319/p327 O6.
Built in the 15th century, remodelled in late baroque style in the 18th century, demolished by the Communists, and then rebuilt by them close to its original location for the 750th anniversary of Berlin

DDR Museum.

in 1987, the Ephraim-Palais is today home to temporary exhibitions drawn from the city's collection. Soft, chandelier lighting and parquet floors lend them a refined touch.

Fernsehturm

Panoramastrasse 1A (242 3333/www.berliner fernsehturm.de). U2, U5, U8, S5, S7, S9, S75 Alexanderplatz. **Open** *Mar-Oct* 9am-1am daily. *Nov-Feb* 10am-midnight daily. **Admission** €6.80; €3.50 reductions; free under-3s. **Credit** AmEx, DC, MC, V. **Map** p319/p327 O6.

Built in the late 1960s at a time when relations between East and West Berlin were at their lowest ebb, the 365m (1,198ft) Television Tower – its ball-on-spike shape visible all over the city – was intended as an assertion of Communist dynamism and modernity. A shame, then, that such television towers were a West German invention. A shame, too, that they had to get Swedish engineers to build the thing. Communist authorities were also displeased to note a particular phenomenon: when the sun shines on the tower, reflections on the ball form the shape of a cross. Berliners dubbed this stigmata 'the Pope's revenge'. Nevertheless, the authorities were proud enough of their tower to make it one of the central symbols of the East German capital, and today it is one of Berlin's most popular graphic images (*see p47* **Tower of the Hour**). Take an ear-popping trip in the lift to the observation platform at the top: a great way to orient yourself early on a visit to Berlin. The view is unbeatable by night or day – particularly looking westwards, where you can take in the whole of the Tiergarten and surrounding area. If heights make you hungry, take a twirl in the revolving restaurant, which offers an even better view. There are usually queues to get up there, however.

Hanf Museum

Mühlendamm 5 (242 4827/www.hanfmuseum.de). U2, U5, U8, S5, S7, S9, S75 Alexanderplatz. **Open** 10am-8pm Tue-Fri; noon-8pm Sat, Sun. **Admission** €3; free under-10s. **No credit cards**. **Map** p319/p327 O6.

The world's largest hemp museum aims to teach the visitor about the uses of the plant throughout history, as well as touching on the controversy surrounding it. The café (doubling as a video and reading room) has cakes made with and without hemp.

Knoblauch-Haus

Poststrasse 23 (2345 9991/www.knoblauchhaus.de). U2, U5, U8, S5, S7, S9, S75 Alexanderplatz. **Open** 10am-6pm Tue-Sun. **Admission** *Combined ticket (with Ephraim-Palais & Nikolaikirche)* €5; €3 reductions; free to all Wed. **No credit cards**. **Map** p319/p327 O6.

This neo-classical mid 18th-century townhouse was home to the influential Knoblauch family and contains an exhibition about some of their more prominent members. However, the real draw is the striking haute bourgeoise interior. The first-floor contains an exhibition called 'Domestic Living in the Biedermeier Era'; the second floor hosts temporary exhibitions about 19th-century cultural history.

Marienkirche

Karl-Liebknecht-Strasse 8 (242 4467/www.marienkirche-berlin.de). U2, U5, U8, S5, S7, S9, S75 Alexanderplatz. **Open** *Apr-Oct* 10am-6pm daily. *Nov-Mar* 10am-4pm daily. **Admission** free. **Map** p319/p327 O6.

Begun in 1270, this is one of Berlin's few remaining medieval buildings. Just inside the door is a wonderful Dance of Death fresco dating from 1485, and the 18th-century Walther organ here is considered his masterpiece. Marienkirche hit the headlines in 1989 when the civil rights movement chose it for one of their first sit-ins, since churches were among the few places where people could congregate without state permission. Tours available.

Märkisches Museum

Am Köllnischen Park 5 (3086 6215/www.stadtmuseum.de). U2 Märkisches Museum. **Open** 10am-6pm Tue-Sun. **Admission** €4; €2 reductions; free to all Wed. **Map** p323/p327 O7.

This extensive, curious and somewhat old-fashioned museum traces the history of Berlin through a wide range of historical artefacts. Different sections examine themes such as Berlin as a newspaper city, women in Berlin's history, intellectual Berlin and the military. There are models of the city at different times, and some good paintings, including works by members of the Brücke group. Some sections have captions in English.

Museum Kindheit und Jugend

Wallstrasse 32 (275 0383/www.berlin-kindheitundjugend.de). U2 Märkisches Museum. **Open** 9am-5pm Mon-Fri; 10am-6pm Sat, Sun. **Admission** €2; €1 reductions; €2.50 family; free to all Wed. **No credit cards**. **Map** p323/p327 O7.

The Museum of Childhood and Youth is the place to come if you want to show kids how lucky they are to be going to school today and not 50 years ago. Apart from old toys, it displays artefacts from classrooms during the Weimar Republic, the Nazi era and under Communism. There are also some excellent temporary exhibitions on offer, such as 'DDR Schools in the 1970s'.

Nikolaikirche

Nikolaikirchplatz (2472 4529/www.stadtmuseum.de). U2, U5, U8, S5, S7, S9, S75 Alexanderplatz. **Open** 10am-6pm Tue-Sun. **Admission** €1.50; free to all Wed. *Combined ticket (with Knoblauch-Haus & Ephraim-Palais)* €5; €3 reductions. **No credit cards**. **Map** p319/p327 O6.

Inside Berlin's oldest congregational church is an interesting historical collection chronicling Berlin's development until 1648. Old tiles, tapestries, stone and wood carvings – even old weapons and punishment devices – are on display. The collection includes fascinating photos of wartime damage, plus examples of how the stones melted together in the heat of bombardment.

Prenzlauer Berg & Friedrichshain

Berlin's baby boomtown and its bastion of bohemia.

Abutting Mitte to the north-east and south-east respectively, the districts of Prenzlauer Berg and Friedrichshain present very different faces of East Berlin. The former is largely gentrified, with tree-lined and café-studded streets, evoking something of pre-war Berlin. The latter, stretching out from the Stalinist spine of Karl-Marx-Allee into waterfront and post-industrial quarters, feels more a product of the Communist era. Both districts have lively bar and club scenes; neither offer much in the way of conventional sightseeing.

Prenzlauer Berg

Maps p319 & p328

Once thought of as a grey, depressing working-class district, in the last two decades Prenz'lberg (as the locals call it) has had its façades renovated, its streets cleaned, and its buildings newly inhabited by everyone from Russian artists to West German office workers. Galleries and cafés have sprouted, and century-old buildings have finally had central heating, bathrooms and telephones installed. Hardcore alternative types might now have moved back to Kreuzberg or out to rawer Friedrichshain, feeling the district has lost its edge, but, for many Berliners, there's no cooler part of town.

Prenzlauer Berg is also the district with the highest concentration of babies in all of Berlin. Maybe in all of Europe. The local birth rate has been coming in at a fecund 2.1 kids per woman

of childbearing age, compared to a national average of about 1.36 kids per woman, and an EU average of 1.5. The playgrounds are packed and the streets throng with buggies and prams.

Laid out at the turn of the 20th century, Prenzlauer Berg seems to have had more visionary social planners than other neighbourhoods of the period. It has wider streets and pavements, giving the area a distinctive, open look. Although a few buildings still await restoration, the newly scrubbed and painted streets give the impression of a 19th-century boulevard.

The district's focal point is pretty **Kollwitzplatz**, named after Käthe Kollwitz, the socially minded artist who lived much of her life around here. The square is lined with bars, cafés and restaurants, and hosts an organic market (*see p174*) on Thursday and Saturday.

Statue of **Ernst Thälmann**. *See p100.*

Knaackstrasse, heading south-east from Kollwitzplatz, brings you to one of the district's main landmarks, the **Wasserturm**. This water tower, constructed by English architect Henry Gill in 1852-75, provided running water for the first time in Germany. During the war, the Nazis used its basement as a prison and torture chamber. A plaque commemorates their victims; the tower has been converted into apartments.

Opposite the Wasserturm on Rykestrasse is the **Synagoge Rykestrasse**, a neo-Romanesque turn-of-the-20th-century structure that was badly damaged during Kristallnacht in 1938. After renovation in 1953, it was the only working synagogue in old East Berlin. Now it stands peacefully in gentrified surrounds. Nearby, to the south-west of Kollwitzplatz, is the **Jüdischer Friedhof**

Walk The Wall remembered

Little remains of the Berlin Wall today. Most of it was demolished between June and November 1990. What had become the symbol of the inhumanity of the East German regime was prosaically crushed and re-used for road-fill.

This walk sets out to trace the course of a small stretch of the Wall on the northern border of Mitte. Along the way you can see some of the remnants – including the restored segment at the **Gedenkstätte Berliner Mauer** (see p123) – and gain an impression of how brutally the border carved its way through the city.

The starting point is Berlin's new central station – **Hauptbahnhof-Lehrter Bahnhof** in former West Berlin – one of the final reunifying projects to be completed. Exit the station into Invalidenstrasse, turning right along the street. Continue eastwards, passing on your left a Wilhelmine building, now a regional court, and the railway station turned contemporary art gallery, **Hamburger Bahnhof – Museum für Gegenwart** (see p91).

A little further on is the **Sandkrugbrücke**, located on a former border crossing into East Berlin. A stone by the bridge commemorates Günter Litfin, the first person to be shot dead attempting to escape to West Berlin (in 1961). The Invalidenhaus on the eastern side long predates the Cold War. Built in 1747 to house disabled soldiers, it was used in East German times as a military and government hospital, as well as the state's ministry of health and Supreme Court. Today it houses the **Bundesministerium für Wirtschat und Arbeit** (Federal Ministry of Economics and Labour). Keeping this complex on your right, turn down the canalside promenade, continuing along until you get to the **Invalidenfriedhof**.

The Wall once ran straight through this graveyard – and a section remains. Headstones of the graves in the 'death strip' were removed so as not to impair the sightlines of border guards. The graveyard, more evidence of the area's military links, is a fascinating microcosm of Berlin history. Metres from the splendid 19th-century tombs of Prussian generals, there is a plaque commemorating members of the anti-Hitler resistance. Victims of air raids and the Battle of Berlin are buried in an adjacent mass grave. And it was here in 1962 that West Berlin police shot dead an East Berlin border guard to save a 15-year-old boy who was in the process of escaping.

Just outside the graveyard is a former **watchtower** improbably nestling in front of a new apartment building at the corner of Kieler Strasse. It's closed in winter, and opening times are unpredictable in summer, but sometimes you can look inside the observation post.

Between here and the corner of Chausseestrasse there are few traces left of the Wall, which ran roughly parallel to the canal before veering right, close to the present helipad. At the end of Boyenstrasse, pavement markings indicating the Wall's former course briefly appear before vanishing under the new corner building.

Looking down Chausseestrasse, note the line of powerful street lights indicating the site of another checkpoint. The **Liesenstrasse Friedhof** is the graveyard where 19th-century writer Theodor Fontane is buried. It was also part of East Berlin's border strip. A short section of the Wall appears before the railway bridge at the junction with Gartenstrasse.

The last leg of the walk takes you up Bernauer Strasse. Desperate scenes took place here in August 1961 as people jumped – three of them to their deaths – from the windows of houses that then stood on the street's eastern side. The buildings were in East Berlin, but the pavement before their doors was in the West. The iconic photo of a border guard leaping over barbed wire into the West was snapped days earlier at the

(Jewish Cemetery), Berlin's oldest, and fairly gloomy due to its closely packed stones and canopy of trees. If you want to know more about the district's history, look in at the **Prenzlauer Berg Museum** (*see p100*).

Moving on clockwise to the other side of Kollwitzplatz, Knaackstrasse extends north-west to the vast complex of the **Kulturbrauerei** (*see p237*), an old brewery

that now houses a concert space, galleries, artists' studios, a food market and cinema. South-west from here, the area around Kastanienallee has plenty of good bars, restaurants and funky shops. And to the north-east, the so-called 'LSD' area around Lychener Strasse, Stargarder Strasse and Dunckerstrasse, leading up to Helmholzplatz, is another of Prenzlauer Berg's hot spots.

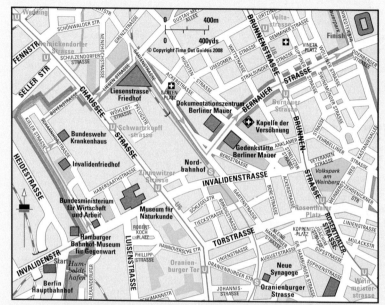

street's northern end. In the 1960s and '70s, a number of tunnels were dug from cellars in this area and dozens escaped this way.

At the **Gedenkstätte Berliner Mauer** you can gain an impression of what the border installation looked like – from below or above. The **Dokumentationszentrum** opposite, an information centre about the Wall, has a viewing platform. The whole thing is undergoing an expansion to be completed in 2011, with a longer piece of wall and an improved information centre.

A little further on is the oval **Kapelle der Versöhnung** (Chapel of Reconciliation), built on the site of an older church that was left stranded in the death strip and finally blown up in 1985 by the East German authorities.

The swathe of former borderland lies largely derelict, despite its prime location. Redevelopment has been slow because of

legal challenges to its appropriation by the Federal Government. The old tarmac patrol road remains in places, as do some of the border illuminations. Note, for instance, the lights on no.20 Swinemünder Strasse. The plasterwork on the building at the corner of Wolliner Strasse also clearly reveals where the eastern side of the Wall abutted existing apartment blocks.

Between Wolliner and Schwedter Strasse, you can still see the turning circle once used by West Berlin buses. On the eastern side, the tram still comes to an abrupt halt in Eberswalder Strasse. Even so, it's hard to believe that this whole area was once part of the world's most heavily fortified border. In the **Mauerpark**, where there is a popular Sunday flea market (*see p173*), you can have one last stroll along the Wall before heading to Eberswalder Strasse U-Bahn.

East of here, over on the other side of Prenzlauer Allee, is **Ernst-Thälmann-Park**, named after the leader of the pre-1933 German Communist Party. In its north-west corner stands the **Zeiss-Grossplanetarium** (*see below*), a fantastic DDR interior space that once celebrated Soviet cosmonauts and still runs programmes on what's up there in space. Over on the Greifswalder Strasse side of the park, just north of the Danziger Strasse corner, is a giant statue of Ernst Thälmann himself, raising a Communist fist – one of Berlin's few remaining socialist-realist monuments.

Prenzlauer Berg Museum

Prenzlauer Allee 227 (902 953 917). U2 Senefelderplatz/M2 Knaackstrasse. **Open** 9am-6pm Mon-Fri. **Admission** free. **Map** p319/p328 P4.
The Prenzlauer Berg Museum is a small but interesting permanent exhibit on the history and culture of the district – lots of old photos – with temporary exhibitions too.

Zeiss-Grossplanetarium

Prenzlauer Allee 80 (4218 4512/www.astw.de). S4, S8, S85 Prenzlauer Allee. **Open** 9am-noon Tue, Thur; 9am-noon, 1.30-3pm Wed; 9am-noon, 7-9pm Fri; 1.30-9pm Sat; 1.30-5pm Sun. **Admission** €5; €4 reductions. **No credit cards.** **Map** p319/p328 Q2.
This vast planetarium was built in the 1980s. Though changing exhibitions are in German only, the shows in the auditorium are entertaining for all.

Stalinist-style architecture.

Friedrichshain

Maps pp323-325

As Prenzlauer Berg and Mitte became gentrified, Berlin's bohemia edged south-east into Friedrichshain. Much of the area remains pretty bleak, dominated as it is by big Communist-era housing blocks – more than half of its buildings were destroyed during World War II – and slashed through by the railway tracks that lead in through Ostbahnhof. Originally known as Stralau, this was historically an industrial district, with Berlin's central wheat and rye mill, its first hospital, and Osthaven, its eastern port. Much of its southern portion bordering the Spree contains the remains of industrial buildings.

The best way to get a feeling for both Friedrichshain and the old DDR is to walk east from Alexanderplatz down Karl-Marx-Allee – a broad boulevard built in Stalinist style. It's from Lichtenberger Strasse onwards that the street truly shows its socialist past, with endless rows of Soviet-style apartment blocks, stretching beyond the twin towers of Frankfurter Tor. The **Internationales Berliner Bierfestival** (*see p198*), held on the street every August, is a good time to see the neighbourhood come out in force.

To the south and east of Frankfurter Tor there is an agglomeration of bars, clubs and restaurants on **Simon-Dach-Strasse** and the surrounding streets, plus a growing number of interesting fashion and second-hand shops. There's also an excellent weekly flea market at **Boxhagener Platz** (*see p173*). This is the lively centre of Berlin's new bohemia, slowly bulging eastwards in the direction of Ostkreuz. North of Frankfurter Allee is another concentration of hangouts in the Rigaer Strasse area.

To the south, on Mühlenstrasse (meaning 'Mill Street; the old mill is at no.8) along the north bank of the Spree is the **East Side Gallery**, a stretch of former Wall given over to international artists. The industrial buildings hereabouts have been renovated and rechristened Oberbaum City, and are now home to loft spaces, offices and studios. Both Universal Music and MTV-Europe have moved their German headquarters here and development of the waterfront continues. This is also now Berlin's main clubbing area, with clubs occupying a variety of post-industrial spaces.

Green relief can be found at the district's far north-west corner in the **Volkspark Friedrichshain**. This huge park is scattered with socialist realist art, and has an open-air stage, a fountain of fairy-tale characters and the popular **Café Schönbrunn** (*see p162*). The graves of fighters who fell in March 1848 in the battle for German unity are also here. It's a popular gay cruising zone too (*see p229*).

Kreuzberg & Schöneberg

Where the Cold War once played out, Berlin's Turkish and gay communities now thrive.

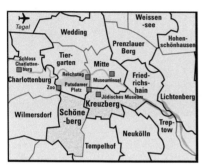

Bordering Mitte to the south is Kreuzberg. Though the area is administratively joined to Friedrichshain across the Spree, it maintains some of the independence of spirit that characterised its Cold War role as the centre of alternative politics and lifestyle. It's also the capital of Turkish Berlin. To its west lies the wealthier, largely residential district of Schöneberg. Much of Berlin's irrepressible gay life is focused in its northern reaches.

Kreuzberg

Maps pp322-323 & p327

The Oberbaumbrücke, renovated in the 1990s by Santiago Calatrava, is the only road bridge crossing the Spree to connect Kreuzberg with Friedrichshain. During the Cold War, it was a more serious crossing place: a border post and spy-exchange venue between East and West Berlin. These days, Kreuzberg is no longer the end of the Free World. And life is even washing back the other way into its increasingly fashionable eastern part.

East Kreuzberg

In the 1970s and '80s, the eastern half of Kreuzberg north of the Landwehrkanal was off at the edge of inner West Berlin. Enclosed on two sides by the Wall, on a third by the canal, and mostly ignored by the rest of the city, its

decaying tenements came to house Berlin's biggest, and most militant, squat community. The area was full of punky left-wing youths on a draft-dodging mission and Turks who came here because the rents were cheap and people mostly left them alone.

No area of West Berlin has changed quite so much since the Wall came down. This once-isolated pocket found itself recast as desirable real estate. Much of the alternative art scene shifted north to Mitte, and even the May Day Riots – long an annual Kreuzberg tradition – began taking place in Prenzlauer Berg. But gentrification was slow to take off in this end of Kreuzberg, unlike in Prenzl'berg, and now the riots have moved back.

Kreuzberg has regained some of its appeal for young bohemia, and enough of the anarchistic old guard stayed behind to ensure that the area retains a distinct atmosphere. It's an earthy kind of place, full of cafés, bars and clubs, dotted with independent cinemas, and is an important nexus for the city's gay community.

And it's still the capital of Turkish Berlin (*see p104* **The Turkish capital**), the world's fifth-largest Turkish city. The scruffy area around Kottbusser Tor bustles with kebab shops and Anatolian travel agents. The open-air **Türkischer Markt** (*see p174*) stretches along the Maybachufer every Tuesday and Friday. Görlitzer Park turns into a huge Turkish barbecue on fine weekends.

Oranienstrasse is the area's main drag, filled with bars and clubs, and the blocks to the north and west are also lively. It's also the location of the quirky **Museum der Dinge**. South across Skalitzer Strasse, Oranienstrasse changes into Wiener Strasse, running alongside the old Görlitzer Bahnhof, where more bars and cafés await. A couple of blocks further south lies Paul-Linke-Ufer, lined with canal-bank cafés.

The U1 line runs overhead through the neighbourhood along the middle of Skalitzer Strasse. The onion-domed Schlesisches Tor station was once the end of the line. These days the train continues one more stop across the Spree to Warschauer Strasse. You can also walk

These are a few of my favourite things: **Museum der Dinge**.

across the Oberbaumbrücke into Friedrichshain and the post-industrial nightlife district around Mühlenstrasse. But traffic is also coming the other way. Courtesy of riverside development on the Spree and of an overspill from Friedrichshain, the area around Schlesisches Tor station and along Schlesische Strasse towards Treptow is Berlin's newest hotspot. Schlesische Strasse leads over the canal and into the borough of Treptow (*see p129*).

Museum der Dinge

Oranienstrasse 25 (9210 6311/www.museum derdinge.de). U1, U8 Kottbusser Tor. **Open** noon-7pm Mon, Fri-Sun. **Admission** €4; €2 reductions. **No credit cards. Map** p323 P9.

On the top floor of a typical Kreuzberg apartment block, the 'Museum of Things' contains every kind of small object you could imagine in modern design from the 19th century onwards – from hairbrushes and fondue sets to beach souvenirs and Nazi memorabilia. It's not a musty collection, but a sleek, minimalist room organised by themes such as 'yellow and black' or 'functional vs kitsch', rather than by era or type, so that the 'things' appear in new contexts. It can get a little confused at times, which is hardly surprising with 20,000 objects, but this is a fascinating diversion and there's a great shop too.

South-west Kreuzberg

The southern and western part of Kreuzberg contains some of the most picturesque corners of West Berlin, including the 'cross hill' ('Kreuzberg') in Viktoriapark after which the borough is named.

Viktoriapark is the natural way to enter the area. In summer it has a cheery, landscaped waterfall cascading down the Kreuzberg, and paths wind their way to the summit, where Schinkel's 1821 monument commemorates victories in the Napoleonic Wars – many of the streets nearby are named after battles and generals of that era. From this commanding view over a mainly flat city, the landmarks of both east and west spread out before you: Friedrichstrasse is dead ahead, the Europa-Center off to the left, the Potsdamer Platz high-rises in between, the Fernsehturm over to the right. The view is clearer in winter, when the trees are bare.

Back on ground level, the streets north of the park lead to one of Berlin's most picturesque courtyard complexes. Riehmers Hofgarten is cobbled, closed to traffic and often used as a film location for its 19th-century feel. It's also home to one of Berlin's nicest small hotels, the **Hotel Riehmers Hofgarten** (*see p67*).

Around the corner on Mehringdamm is the **Schwules Museum** (Gay Museum; *see p103*). Bergmannstrasse, which runs east from here, is the main hub of local activity. Bucking the tendency for everything to move eastwards, this street of cafés, junk shops, bookstores and record shops is livelier than ever by day, although the area is relatively lacklustre at night time. It leads down to Marheinekeplatz, where the old Markthalle has recently been revamped as a sort of small mall full of speciality food stalls. Zossener Strasse, north from here, also bustles.

Schwules Museum

Mehringdamm 61 (6959 9050/www.schwules museum.de). U6, U7 Mehringdamm. **Open** 2-6pm Mon, Wed-Fri, Sun; 2-7pm Sat. **Admission** €5; €3 reductions. **No credit cards**. **Map** p322 M10.

The Gay Museum, opened in 1985, is still the only one in the world dedicated to homosexual life in all its forms. The museum, its library and archives are staffed by volunteers and function thanks to private donations and bequests (such as the archive of DDR sex scientist Rudolf Klimmer). On the ground floor is the actual museum, housing permanent and temporary exhibitions. On the third floor, the library and archives house around 8,000 books (around 500 in English), 3,000 international periodicals, photos, posters, plus TV, film and audio footage, all available for lending.

North-west Kreuzberg

The north-west portion of Kreuzberg, bordering Mitte, is where you will find most of the area's museums and tourist sights. The most prominent is the extraordinary **Jüdisches Museum** (*see p105*) on Lindenstrasse, an example of architecture at its most cerebral, and a powerful sensory experience. West of here, close to the Landwehrkanal, is the enjoyable **Deutsches Technikmuseum Berlin** (German Museum of Technology; *see p105*).

Over the canal to the north is the site of Anhalter Bahnhof, once the city's biggest and busiest railway station. Only a tiny piece of façade remains, preserved in its bombed state near the S-Bahn station that bears its name. The **Gruselkabinett** ('Chamber of Horrors'; *see p105*) occupies an old air-raid shelter on the Schöneberger Strasse side of the area where platforms and tracks once stood.

On Stresemannstrasse, the Bauhaus-designed Europahaus was heavily bombed during World War II, but the lower storeys remain. Nearby, on the north side of the street, Berlin's parliament, the **Abgeordnetenhaus von Berlin** (Berlin House of Representatives), meets in what was formerly the Prussian parliament. Dating from the 1890s, the building was renovated in the early 1990s. Opposite stands the **Martin-Gropius-Bau** (*see p106*), a venue for major art shows. The building was modelled on London's South Kensington museums – the figures of craftspeople on the external reliefs betray its origins as an applied arts museum.

Next to it is a mostly deserted block that once held the Prinz Albrecht Palais, which the Gestapo took over as its headquarters. In the basement's 39 cells, political prisoners were held, interrogated and tortured. The land was flattened after the war. In 1985, during an acrimonious debate over the design of a memorial to be placed here, a group of citizens

Bergmannstrasse continues east past a large cemetery to Südstern. Here is the entrance to the **Volkspark Hasenheide**, the other of the neighbourhood's large parks, with another good view from atop the Rixdorfer Höhe. The streets just south of Bergmannstrasse are like another movie set. Many buildings survived wartime bombing and the area around Chamissoplatz has been immaculately restored. The cobbled streets are lined with houses still sporting their Prussian façades and illuminated by gaslight at night.

South of here, just across the border into the borough of the same name, stands the enormous **Flughafen Tempelhof**. Once the central airport for the city, it opened in the 1920s and was later greatly expanded by the Nazis. It's the largest building in Berlin and one of the largest in the world.

Tempelhof Airport was where Lufthansa started, but its place in the city's affections was cemented during the airlift of 1948-9, when it served as the base for the American and British 'raisin-bombers', which brought supplies to the blockaded city and tossed sweets and raisins to waiting kids. The monument forking towards the sky on Platz der Luftbrücke commemorates those who flew these missions. It has recently ceased operating as an airport.

Across Columbiadamm from the airport are the **Columbiahalle** (*see p235*) and **Columbiaclub** (*see p235*) concert venues. The latter building was constructed by the US Air Force as a cinema for use by their personnel, and is a classic example of 1950s cinema architecture.

Sightseeing

The Turkish capital

Turkish food is a Berlin staple, but few realise that the doner kebab is no Oriental import. It was actually invented here, in Kreuzberg, in 1971, by one Mehmet Aygun, today proprietor of the **Hasir** (*see p148*) restaurant chain.

But Turkish culture stretches further than street food. In Kreuzberg, the mosques now attract more worshippers than the churches. Outside Turkey itself, Berlin is home to the world's largest Turkish community. The hubs are in Kreuzberg and Neukölln, where one in every three residents is of Turkish origin.

The meeting of cultures has had a difficult history. The quick-flow of immigration began in 1961 as a direct consequence of the Berlin Wall. With East German workers cut off from jobs in the West, thousands of *Gastarbeiter* ('guest workers') were recruited from Turkey to provide new cheap labour, and crammed together in purpose-built blocks.

The West German authorities proved ungracious hosts. The 'guest workers' were considered no more than a temporary necessity, and the Nationality Act (or 'Blood Law') of 1913, according to which German citizenship was based on heredity, was rigorously upheld. No person born of Turkish parents could be granted a German passport.

The Turkish community thus remained apart from mainstream society. As recently as 2004, a report found that up to 60 per cent of children in Kreuzberg nursery schools couldn't speak a single word of German. Popular antagonism peaked in 1990, when many feared that large numbers of foreign settlers would destabilise Germany's national identity and hinder a successful reunification. Then-Chancellor Helmut Kohl declared that Germany was 'not a land of immigration' – dissing the nine per cent of the population who had been born abroad.

But attitudes are softening. The basis of nationality on blood has come to be seen as inappropriate for a Germany that wants to transcend the less savoury aspects of its history. Since 2001, a new law grants citizenship to any child born on German soil, provided their parents have been legally resident for at least eight years.

In Kreuzberg, at least, there's a genuine desire for multiculturalism. Turkish families, living side by side with punks and squatters, have developed into a uniquely indigenous community. The sound of *Turkendeutsche*,

the hybrid language of the immigrant population, fills the air around Oranienstrasse, while Turkish-German rappers like Cartel and Azziza-A spit lyrics on bar stereos. The weekly **Turkischer Markt** on the Maybachufer (*see p174*) showcases the settlers' more traditional side, while Turkish gay nights at **SO36** (*see p222*) reveal a corresponding cosmopolitanism. Berlin's Turkish football club, Türkiyemspor (*see p265* **Games without frontiers**), is fêted as a model of integration. And in the run-up to the Turkey-Germany match in Euro 2008, hybrid German-Turkish flags were seen fluttering all over town.

staged a symbolic 'excavation'. To their surprise, they hit the Gestapo's basement, and plans were then made to reclaim the site. Today there is an open-air exhibition while a permanent documentation centre is under construction (*see p106* **Topographie des Terrors**). Along the site's northern boundary is one of the few remaining stretches of the Berlin Wall, pitted and threadbare after thousands of 1990 souvenir-hunters pecked away at it with hammers and chisels.

From here, it's a short walk down Kochstrasse to Friedrichstrasse, where Checkpoint Charlie once stood and where the **Haus am Checkpoint Charlie** (*see below*) documents the history of the Wall. Most of the space where the border post once stood has been claimed by new buildings. The actual site of the borderline is memorialised by Frank Thiel's photographic portraits of an American and a Soviet soldier. The small white building that served as gateway between East and West is now in the **Aliierten Museum** (*see p126*) – the one in the middle of the street is a replica.

In April 2008, Kochstrasse east of Friedrichstrasse – the stretch with the towering headquarters of right-wing media magnate Axel Springer – was renamed Rudi-Dutschke-Strasse in honour of one of Germany's most famous student revolutionaries. Forty years ago, Dutschke was victim of an attempted assassination, shot in the head and chest after various Springer publications had called on their readers to 'eliminate the trouble-makers' and 'stop the terror of the young reds'. He later died of complications arising from the injuries. In April 1968, Dutschke's supporters demonstrated outside the Springer building, claiming the publisher was partially responsible for the shooting. The recent name change – in part the result of vigorous campaigning by the *taz*, the left-wing national daily, which is also headquartered on Rudi-Dutschke-Strasse – was bitterly opposed by Springer and local conservatives. There aren't too many of those in Kreuzberg, though, and when it came to a referendum, Kreuzbergers cheerfully voted in favour of the new name.

Deutsches Technikmuseum Berlin

Trebbiner Strasse 9 (902 540/www.dtmb.de). U1, U7 Möckernbrücke. **Open** 9am-5.30pm Tue-Fri; 10am-6pm Sat, Sun. **Admission** €4.50; €2.50 reductions. **Map** p322 L9.

Opened in 1982 in the former goods depot of the Anhalter Bahnhof, the German Museum of Technology is an eclectic, eccentric collection of new and antique industrial artefacts. The rail exhibits have pride of place, with the station sheds providing an ideal setting for locomotives and rolling stock from 1835 to the present. Other exhibitions focus on

the industrial revolution; street, rail, water and air traffic; computer technology and printing technology. Behind the main complex is an open-air section with two functioning windmills and a smithy. Oddities, such as vacuum cleaners from the 1920s, make this a fun place for implement enthusiasts. The nautical wing has vessels and displays on inland waterways and international shipping, while another wing covers aviation and space travel. There are models and original designs and electronic information points offering commentaries in English on subjects from the international slave trade to the mechanics of a space station. The Spectrum annex, at Möckernstrasse 26, houses over 200 interactive devices and experiments.

Gruselkabinett

Schöneberger Strasse 23A (2655 5546/www. gruselkabinett-berlin.de). S1, S2 Anhalter Bahnhof. **Open** 10am-3pm Mon; 10am-7pm Tue, Thur, Sun; 10am-8pm Fri; noon-8pm Sat. **Admission** €7; €5 reductions. **No credit cards. Map** p322 L8.

This chamber of horrors is housed in the city's only visitable World War II air-raid shelter. Built in 1943, the five-level bunker was part of an underground network connecting various similar concrete structures throughout Berlin, and today houses both the Gruselkabinett and an exhibit on the bunker itself. The 'horrors' begin at ground level with an exhibit on medieval medicine (mechanical figures amputate a leg to the sound of canned screaming). Elsewhere, there's a patented coffin designed to advertise your predicament should you happen to be buried alive. Upstairs is scarier: a musty labyrinth with a simulated cemetery, strange cloaked figures, lots of spooky sounds and a few surprises. Kids love it, but not those under ten.

Haus am Checkpoint Charlie

Friedrichstrasse 43-45 (253 7250/www. mauermuseum.de). U6 Kochstrasse. **Open** 9am-10pm daily. **Admission** €9.50; €5.50 reductions. **No credit cards. Map** p322/p327 M8.

A little tacky, but essential for anyone interested in the Wall and the Cold War. This private museum opened not long after the DDR erected the Berlin Wall in 1961 with the purpose of documenting the events that were taking place. The exhibition charts the history of the Wall, and gives details of the ingenious and hair-raising ways people escaped from the DDR – as well as exhibiting some of the actual contraptions that were used, such as a home-made hot-air balloon.

Jüdisches Museum

Lindenstrasse 9-14 (2599 3300/guided tours 2599 3305/www.juedisches-museum-berlin.de). U1, U6 Hallesches Tor. **Open** 10am-10pm Mon; 10am-8pm Tue-Sun. **Admission** €5; €2.50 reductions; €10 family. **Credit** (over €10) MC, V. **Map** p323 N8.

The idea of a Jewish museum in Berlin was first mooted in 1971, the 300th birthday of the city's Jewish community. In 1975 an association was

Jüdisches Museum. *See p105.*

formed to acquire materials for eventual display; in 1989, a competition was held to design an extension to house them. Daniel Libeskind emerged as the winner, the foundation stone was laid in 1992, the building was completed in 1998, and on 9 September 2001, the permanent exhibition finally opened. The ground plan of Libeskind's remarkable building is in part based on an exploded Star of David, in part on lines drawn between the site and former addresses of figures in Berlin's Jewish history, such as Mies van der Rohe, Arnold Schönberg and Walter Benjamin. The entrance is via a tunnel from the Kollegienhaus next door. The underground geometry is startlingly independent of the above-ground building. One passage leads to the exhibition halls, two others intersect en route to the Holocaust Tower and the ETA Hoffmann Garden, a grid of 49 columns, tilted to disorientate. Throughout, diagonals and parallels carve out surprising spaces, while windows slash through the structure and its zinc cladding like the knife-wounds of history. And then there are the 'voids' cutting through the layout, negative spaces that stand for the emptiness left by the destruction of German Jewish culture.

The permanent exhibition struggles in places with such powerful surroundings. What makes the exhibit engaging is its focus on the personal: it tells the stories of prominent Jews, what they contributed to their community and to the cultural and economic life of Berlin and Germany. After centuries of prejudice and pogroms, the outlook for German Jews seemed to be brightening. Then came the Holocaust. This part of the exhibit is the most harrowing. The emotional impact of countless stories of the eminent and ordinary, and the fate that almost all shared, is hard to convey adequately in print. There are also temporary exhibitions. The museum is a must-see, but expect long queues and big crowds. Last entrance is one hour before closing.

Martin-Gropius-Bau

Niederkirchnerstrasse 7 (254 860/www.gropius bau.de). S1, S2, S26 Anhalter Bahnhof. **Open** 10am-8pm Mon, Wed-Sun. **Admission** varies. **Credit** AmEx, MC, V. **Map** p322/p327 L8.

Cosying up to where the Wall once stood (there is still a short, pitted stretch running along the south side of nearby Niederkirchnerstrasse), the Martin-Gropius-Bau is named after its architect, uncle of the more famous Walter. Built in 1881, it has been renovated and serves as a venue for an assortment of large-scale art exhibitions and themed shows. Summer 2009 is given over to a landmark retrospective commemorating the 90th anniversary of the Bauhaus. It's also a venue for the Berlin Biennale.

Topographie des Terrors

*Niederkirchnerstrasse 8 (2548 6703/www.
topographie.de). S1, S2, S26 Anhalter Bahnhof.*
Open *Oct-Apr* 10am-dusk daily. *May-Sept* 10am-8pm daily. **Admission** free. **Map** p322/p327 M8.
Essentially a piece of waste ground that was once the site of the Prinz Albrecht Palais, headquarters of the Gestapo, and the Hotel Prinz Albrecht, which housed offices of the Reich SS leadership. This was the centre of the Nazi police state apparatus and it was from here that the Holocaust was directed, and the Germanisation of the east dreamt up. Until a documentation centre opens in May 2010, there's not much here except an open-air exhibition about the history of the site and a temporary building where you can buy a catalogue and pick up a free audio guide. A surviving segment of the Wall runs along the site's northern boundary. The main entrance is where that meets the north-east corner of the Martin-Gropius-Bau.

Schöneberg

Maps p321 & p322

Geographically and atmospherically, Schöneberg lies between Kreuzberg and Charlottenburg. It's a diverse and vibrant part of town, mostly built in the late 19th century. Though largely devoid of conventional sights, Schöneberg is rich in reminders of Berlin's recent history.

Schöneberg means 'beautiful hill' – oddly, because the borough is flat. It does have an 'island', though: the triangular **Schöneberger**

Insel, carved out by the two broad railway cuttings that carry S-Bahn line 1 and lines 2 and 26, with an elevated stretch of lines S41, 42 and 45 providing the southern boundary. In the 1930s, the area was known as Rote Insel ('Red Island'), because, socialistically inclined and easy to defend as it was approached mostly over a handful of bridges, it was one of the last bits of Berlin to resist Nazification. There's a fine view from Monumentenbrücke, on the east side of the island going towards Kreuzberg's Viktoriapark. On the north-west edge of the island is **St Matthäus-Kirchhof**, a graveyard and last resting place of the Brothers Grimm.

West along Langenscheidtstrasse leads you towards the Kleistpark. Here, Schöneberg's main street is called Hauptstrasse to the south and Potsdamer Strasse to the north. Hauptstrasse leads south-west in the direction of Potsdam. David Bowie and Iggy Pop once resided at No.155. Further south, **Dominicuskirche** is one of Berlin's few baroque churches.

North-west along Dominicusstrasse is **Rathaus Schöneberg**, outside which John F Kennedy made his famous 'Ich bin ein Berliner' speech. The square now bears his name. This was West Berlin's town hall during the Cold War, and the place where mayor Walter Momper welcomed East Berliners in 1989.

From here, Belziger Strasse leads back in the direction of **Kleistpark**. The entrance to Kleistpark from Potsdamer Strasse is an 18th-century double colonnade, moved here from near Alexanderplatz in 1910. The mansion in the park was originally a law court, and during the Cold War became headquarters for the Allied Control Council. After the 1972 treaty that formalised the separate status of East and West Germany, the building stood virtually unused. But there were occasional Allied Council meetings, before which the Americans, British and French would observe a ritual pause, as if expecting the Soviet representative, who had last attended in 1948, to show up. In 1990 a Soviet finally did wander in and the Allies held a last meeting to formalise their withdrawal from the city in 1994. This may be the place where the Cold War officially ended.

On the north-west corner of Potsdamer Strasse's intersection with Pallasstrasse stood the Sportpalast, site of many Nazi rallies and the scene of Goebbels' famous 'Total War' speech of 18 February 1943. In its place stands a shabby block of flats. One part of the complex straddles Pallasstrasse and rests on the huge concrete hulk of a Nazi air-raid shelter, which planners were unable to destroy.

At the west end of Pallasstrasse stands **St-Matthias-Kirche**. South from here, Goltzstrasse is lined with cafés, bars and interesting shops. To the north of the church is Winterfeldtplatz, site of bustling Wednesday and Saturday morning markets, engendering a lively café life by day that turns into a lively eating-out nexus by night.

Nollendorfplatz to the north is the hub of Schöneberg's nightlife. The theatre on the square has had many incarnations. In the Weimar era it was home to experimental director Erwin Piscator; under the Third Reich Hitler came here to watch Zara Leander shows; in the 1980s it was the infamous Metropol disco. A recent attempt to recast it as an upmarket dine and dance complex quickly failed.

Outside Nollendorfplatz U-Bahn, the small memorial to homosexuals killed in concentration camps is a reminder of the area's history. Christopher Isherwood chronicled Berlin from his rooming house at Nollendorfstrasse 17; Motzstrasse has been a major artery of Berlin's gay life since the 1920s. Gay Schöneberg continues around the corner and straddles Martin-Luther-Strasse along Fuggerstrasse.

Schöneberg's most famous daughter is screen icon Marlene Dietrich, now buried just over the district's southern boundary, in the **Städtische Friedhof III** on Fehlerstrasse in Friedenau, also the last resting place of fellow Berliner Helmut Newton. Nico grew up around here too, and launched her career by hanging around long enough to be 'discovered' outside the **KaDeWe** department store (*see p171*).

Graves of the Brothers Grimm, St Matthäus-Kirchhof.

Tiergarten

A very old park, and a very new frontier.

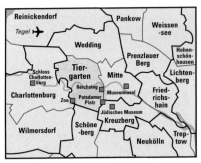

The huge, green Tiergarten – Berlin's central park – dominates, divides and gives its name to this district. The Wall once ran along the park's eastern edge, but now Tiergarten once more links Mitte and Charlottenburg, stretching from the Reichstag in the north-east to the Zoo in the south-west. Along the park's northern boundary meanders the Spree; above here is the drab residential area of Moabit and the new Berlin Hauptbahnhof. And south of the park is a host of cultural, architectural and commercial attractions, including the reborn Potsdamer Platz and the museums of the Kulturforum.

The park & the Reichstag

Maps p318, p321 & p327

A hunting ground for the Prussian electors since the 16th century, **Tiergarten** was opened to the public in the 18th century. It was badly damaged during World War II; in the desperate winter of 1945-46, almost all the surviving trees were cut down for firewood, and it wasn't until 1949 that Tiergarten started to recover. Today, though, joggers, nature lovers, gay cruisers and picnickers pour into the park in fine weather. There's no nicer place from which to appreciate it all than the gardens of the **Café am Neuen See** on Lichtensteinallee.

All roads entering the Tiergarten lead to the park's largest monument, the **Siegessäule** (Victory Column; *see p110*), which celebrates the last wars Germany managed to win. The park's main thoroughfare, Strasse des 17. Juni (the date of the East Berlin workers' strike of 1953), is one of the few pieces of Hitler's plan for 'Germania' that actually got built – a grand

east-west axis, lined with Nazi lampposts and linking Unter den Linden to Neu-Westend. The Siegessäule was moved here from its original position in front of the Reichstag.

Towards the eastern end of Strasse des 17. Juni, just west of the Brandenburger Tor, stands the **Sowjetisches Ehrenmal** (Soviet War Memorial). Once the only piece of Soviet property in West Berlin, it was built in 1945-46 out of granite and marble from the ruins of Hitler's Neue Reichskanzlei but posed a political problem. Standing in the British Zone, it was surrounded by a British military enclosure, which was in turn guarded by Berlin police – all to protect the monument and the two Soviet soldiers who stood guard. The tanks flanking it are said to have been the first two Soviet tanks into Berlin, but this is probably just myth.

At the north-eastern corner of the park stands the **Reichstag**. Described by Kaiser Wilhelm II as the 'Imperial Monkey House', it hasn't had a happy history: the scene of Weimar squabblings, it was then left as a burnt-out ruin during the Third Reich, regarded by the Red Army as its main prize, and then stranded for decades beside the Wall dividing the Deutsches Volk whose representatives it was intended to house. But in 1999, Lord Norman Foster's brilliant refitting of the building was unveiled. His crowning achievement is the glass cupola: a trip to the top should be a must-do on any visitor's agenda.

When the decision was made in 1991 to make Berlin the German capital, the area north of the Reichstag was picked as the central location for new government buildings. Designed by Axel Schultes and Charlotte Frank, the immense Spreebogen complex, also known as the Band des Bundes, is built over a twist in the River Spree (*Bogen* means 'bend'). It crosses the river twice and the old East-West border once, symbolising the reunion of Berlin. The most notable new building is Schultes and Frank's **Bundeskanzleramt** (Federal Chancellery). Across the river to the north, meanwhile, stands the new **Berlin Hauptbahnhof**. Berlin never had a central station before. Now it has the biggest and most futuristic in Europe.

South of the Bundeskanzleramt's western end is the **Haus der Kulturen der Welt** (House of World Cultures), an impressive piece of modern architecture with a reflecting pool

The Reichstag: a trip to the top of Foster's dome is a must.

that contains a Henry Moore sculpture. Formerly known as the Kongresshalle and nicknamed the 'pregnant oyster', the HdKdW opened in 1957 and today hosts exhibits from cultures around the world.

Also on the park's northern boundary stands **Schloss Bellevue**, a minor palace from 1785 that's now the official residence of the German President. Across the river, a serpentine 718-apartment residence for Federal employees, nicknamed 'Die Schlange' (the Snake) winds across land formerly used as a goods yard. West of Schloss Bellevue is the **Englischer Garten**, laid out on the theory that the lack of revolutions in England was due to the abundance of green spaces.

Just north of here, the **Akademie der Künste** (*see p253*) offers a varied programme of arts events and classical concerts. The district between the Akademie and the loop of the Spree is known as the **Hansaviertel**, a post-war housing project designed by a who's who of architects as part of the 1957 Interbau Exhibition for the 'city of tomorrow'. It's of great interest to specialists, but others may see only an assortment of modernist slabs.

Haus der Kulturen der Welt

John-Foster-Dulles-Allee 10 (397 870/www.hkw.de). S5, S7, S9, S75 Bellevue/bus 100. **Open** 10am-9pm Tue-Sun. **Admission** varies. **Credit** AmEx, MC, V. **Map** p318 K6.

Set up in 1989 to promote art from developing countries, the 'House of World Cultures' mounts spectacular large-scale exhibitions on subjects such as contemporary Indian art, Bedouin culture and the Chinese avant-garde. Recent events have included a celebration of electronic music from around the globe, and a festival of new cinema from Africa; the programme also involves readings, lectures, discussions, concerts and dance. Housed in Hugh Stubbins' oyster-like building, erected in 1957 as America's contribution to the Interbau Exhibition, this is a unique Berlin cultural institution. Decent café, too.

Reichstag

Platz der Republik (2270/www.bundestag.de). S1, S2 Unter den Linden/bus 100. **Open** *Dome* 8am-midnight daily; last entry 10pm. **Admission** free. **Map** p318/p327 L6.

The imposing Reichstag was controversial from the beginning. Architect Paul Wallot struggled to find a style that would symbolise German national identity at a time – 1884-94, shortly after Unification – when no such style or identity existed. It was burned on 17 February 1933; the Nazis blamed Dutchman Marius van der Lubbe, and used it as an excuse to suspend basic freedoms. But since its celebrated renovation by Lord Foster, the Reichstag has again housed the Bundestag (the Federal German parliament). Foster conceived it as a 'dialogue between old and new': graffiti scrawled by Russian soldiers in 1945 has been left on view, and there has been no attempt to deny the building's turbulent history.

No dome appeared on Foster's original plans, but the German government insisted upon one. Foster, in turn, insisted that unlike the structure's original dome (damaged in the war and demolished in the 1950s), the new dome must be open to visitors. A lift whisks you to the roof; from here, ramps lead to the top of the dome, which affords fine views of the city. At the centre is a funnel of mirrors, angled so as to shed light on the workings of democracy below but also lending an almost funhouse effect to the dome. A trip to the top of this open, playful and defiantly democratic space is a must, but beware of queues: come first thing or in the evening if possible, and note that the dome is occasionally closed to the public (check the website for details).

Siegessäule

Strasse des 17. Juni (391 2961). S5, S7, S9, S75 Bellevue. **Open** *Summer* 9.30am-6.30pm Mon-Fri; 9.30am-7pm, Sat, Sun. *Winter* 9.30am-5pm Mon-Fri; 9.30am-5.30pm Sat, Sun. **Admission** €2.50; €1.50 reductions. **No credit cards. Map** p321 H7.
Tiergarten's biggest monument was built in 1871-73 to commemorate Prussian campaigns against Denmark (1864), Austria (1866) and France (1870-71). Originally planted in front of the Reichstag, it was moved by Hitler to form a centrepiece for the East-West axis connecting Western Berlin with the palaces and ministries of Mitte. On top of the column is a gilded Goddess of Victory by Friedrich Drake; captured French cannons and cannonballs, sawn in half and gilded, decorate the column itself. It's 285 steps to the viewing platform.

South of the park

Maps p321, p322 & p327

At the south-east corner of the Tiergarten is the reborn **Potsdamer Platz**, intended as the reunified city's new commercial centrepiece. In the 1920s, Potsdamer Platz was reckoned to be one of Europe's busiest squares. The first ever traffic lights stood here (a replica can be seen today on the south side of the square). Then, though, it was bombed flat in World War II; during the Cold War, it became a no-man's land bisected by the Wall. Fierce debate ensued over whether the redevelopment should adopt the typical scale of a 'European' city or go for an 'American' high-rise approach. The result was a compromise: medium-height development except on Potsdamer Platz itself, where high-rises up to 90 metres (295 feet) were allowed.

Opinions are mixed as to the success of the finished article. In the Cold War, the area was neither East nor West, which makes it sound like a good candidate for a unifying space. But it's really an isolated island of redevelopment, not yet quite connected to any area around it and still neither one thing nor the other. Even so, it's beginning to feel worn in, a natural part of a long-disjointed urban landscape.

Helmut Jahn's soaring **Sony Center**, surprisingly light in steel and glass, contains the Forum, an urban entertainment complex that in turn holds the **CineStar** multiplex (*see p209*), the more offbeat **Arsenal** cinema (*see p208*) and the **Filmmuseum Berlin** (*see p114*). (There's another multiplex over the road in the Daimler quarter, the **CinemaxX**.) Served also by a clutch of new five-star hotels, including the **Ritz-Carlton** (*see p69*) and the **Grand Hyatt** (*see p68*), Potsdamer Platz is also now the main venue for the **Berlin International Film Festival** (*see p206*). But there's little to recommend in terms of eating, drinking or shopping. It's all franchise culture.

Siegessäule.

One of only two Potsdamer Platz buildings to survive World War II and the subsequent clearout was once here on the Sony site: the **Kaisersaal Café** from the old Grand Hotel Esplanade, a listed building. When plans for the area solidified, the café was found to be in a bad position, so the whole structure was moved 75 metres (246 feet) to its present location on the building's north side, where it's been integrated into the apartment complex on Bellevuestrasse.

The other major corporate presence at Potsdamer Platz is Daimler (formerly DaimlerChrysler), responsible for most of the development south of the Sony Center. One of the most admired of the area's new buildings is Hans Kollhof's triangular, brick-clad tower at Potsdamer Platz 1, which, together with the curved Deutsche Bahn tower over the road, forms the gateway to the area. It's the tallest building here; the **Panoramapunkt** platform up top (*see p115*) affords fine views.

A few doors down the road at Alte Potsdamer Strasse 5 is **Haus Huth**, the only other building in the area that survives from before World War II. For decades a lonely structure in the middle of overgrown wasteland, it now stands next to the three-storey Arkaden shopping mall. At ground level, Haus Huth hosts **Diekmann's** restaurant (*see p150*); at the top is the **Daimler Contemporary** gallery, which exhibits works from the auto manufacturer's big-name art collection. The company has also positioned various pieces of contemporary sculpture around the quarter, including work by Jeff Koons, Robert Rauschenberg, Keith Haring and Nam June Paik. *See p112* **Walk**.

Immediately west of the Potsdamer Platz development is one of the city's major concentrations of museums, galleries and cultural institutions. Collectively known as the **Kulturforum** and built in anticipation of Reunification, it was based on the designs of Hans Scharoun (1946-57). Scharoun himself designed the **Staatsbibliotek** (State Library) and the gold **Philharmonie** (*see p252*), home to the Berlin Philharmonic. Adjacent is the **Musikinstrumentenmuseum** (Musical Instrument Museum; *see p115*).

One block to the west is a low-rise museum complex. Its biggest draw is the **Gemäldegalerie** (Picture Gallery; *see p114*), but the **Kunstgewerbemuseum** (Museum of Decorative Art; *see p115*) is also worth a peek. Here, too, is the **Kunstbibliotek** (Art Library), and a decent café and shop. Next door stands the **Matthäuskirche** (Matthias Church) and, to the south, the bold glass cube of the **Neue Nationalgalerie** (New National Gallery; *see p115*).

Between the north flank of the Kulturforum and the south flank of Tiergarten runs **Tiergartenstrasse**, the main drag of Berlin's revived diplomatic quarter. Part of Albert Speer's plan for 'Germania', the original embassy buildings of Hitler's Axis allies were designed by German architects. Damaged by bombing, they were largely abandoned, and Tiergartenstrasse became an eerie walk past decaying grandeur. But with the land often still owned by the respective governments, embassies were reconstructed at their old addresses during the diplomatic relocation from Bonn, and this area is now embassy row again.

The **Gedenkstätte Deutscher Widerstand** (Memorial to the German Resistance; *see p114*) lies south on Stauffenburgstrasse, a street named after the leader of the July 1944 plot to kill Hitler. At the corner of Stauffenburgstrasse and Reichpietschufer is **Shell House**, a curvaceous expressionist masterpiece by Emil Fahrenkamp (1932). Five minutes' walk west along the Landwehrkanal sits the gleaming white building of the **Bauhaus Archiv – Museum für Gestaltung** (Museum of Design); a further ten-minute walk leads to the less high-brow attractions of the **Zoologischer Garten & Aquarium** (*see p115*) and the hub of West Berlin around Bahnhof Zoo and the Ku'damm (*see p116*).

Bauhaus Archiv – Museum für Gestaltung

Klingelhöferstrasse 13-14 (254 0020/www.bauhaus. de). Bus 100, 106, 187, M29 Lützowplatz. **Open** 10am-5pm Mon, Wed-Sun. **Admission** *Mon, Sat, Sun* €7; €4 reductions; *Wed-Fri* €6; €3 reductions. **No credit cards. Map** p322 J8.
Walter Gropius, founder of the Bauhaus school, designed the elegant white building that now houses this absorbing design museum. The permanent exhibition presents furniture, ceramics, prints, sculptures, photographs and sketches created in the Bauhaus workshop between 1919 and 1933, when the school was closed down by the Nazis. There are also first-rate temporary exhibitions such as a recent show of multidisciplinary work by Max Bill. An interesting gift shop offers 250 items, including design icons such as the Bauhaus lamp by Wilhelm Wagenfeld. Increasing visitor numbers, and a lack of space to exhibit more than a third of the archive's collection, has made plans to expand the museum, but n' yet been decided.

Daimler Contemporary

Alte Potsdamer Strasse 5 (2594, sammlung.daimler.com). U2, S Platz. **Open** 11am-6pm daily Sat of mth. **Admission** fre' **Map** p322/p327 L8.

Sightseeing

Walk Berlin revived

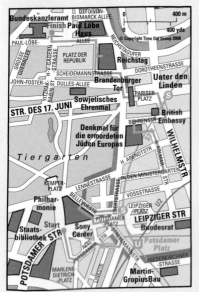

The area around Potsdamer Platz, the Brandenburg Gate and the Reichstag has received special attention in the binding together of the city's two halves. This walk highlights the dramatic changes in what was, until recently, a no-man's land.

The walk begins on the corner of Potsdamer Strasse and Eichhornstrasse, which feels like a border. To the west and south is the 1960s **Kulturforum** (*see p254*), home to a variety of cultural institutions that were placed on the edge of West Berlin in anticipation of Reunification. To the east is a new and much denser commercial quarter. Designed and built in the 1990s, it's generally known as **Potsdamer Platz** (*see p110*), although the ctual Platz is three blocks. Here stands ith Haring's sculpture *The Boxers*, part aimler's collection of art. Comprised of gures in primary blue and red, conjoined onflict, it's appropriate for Berlin al and this corner in particular. vere, walk down Eichhornstrasse, P and Hyatt (*see p68*) to your left. yo the shoulder of a building ahead, apl paceship-like contraption, nning the streets below but

actually another Daimler collection sculpture – Auk de Vries's *gelandet* ('landed'). At the point where this street opens into Marlene-Dietrich-Platz, in front of the Spielbank (casino), there's a third sculpture: Jeff Koons's *Balloon Flower*.

A couple of hundred metres along Alte Potsdamer Strasse on the right is the entrance to the **Arkaden** mall. **Haus Huth** (*see p111*), the old building next to it at No.5, was the only surviving pre-war structure this side of Potsdamer Strasse when Renzo Piano planned the 75,000-square-metre site now known as the Daimler Viertel (quarter) in the early 1990s. Slip through the passage between Haus Huth and the Arkaden, and you'll emerge into Fontaneplatz. The building to the right, with round towers inserted into its corners, is by Richard Rogers. And to the left stands Robert Rauschenberg's *Riding Bikes* – another Daimler-owned sculpture and, like the Haring piece, a symbol of two halves.

Bearing to the left will lead you into Potsdamer Platz itself. The green contraption by the junction is a replica of Europe's first traffic lights, erected here in 1924 when this was supposedly the world's busiest intersection. The borders of the British, American and Soviet occupation zones met at this point, meaning that even among the late 1940s ruins it remained a centre of commerce – no matter which direction the police approached, black market traders were able to escape into another zone. The Wall killed the area for several decades, but with grand new entrances to the sub-surface station and an assortment of high-rises – notably the brick-clad **Kollhoff Tower** and the rounded **Bahn-Tower** that flank Potsdamer Strasse, forming a gateway into Western Berlin – it once more feels like downtown. Ascend to the **Panoramapunkt** (*see p115*) for great views.

Cross Potsdamer Platz and duck left into Helmut Jahn's futuristic **Sony Center** (*see p110*), completely different from the more traditional cityscape of the Daimler Viertel. Taking the exit right of the Café Josty, you'll pass the relocated remains of the 19th-century **Grand Hotel Esplanade** (*see p111*).

The area north of the Sony Center is called the **Lenné Dreieck** (triangle). During the Cold War, this land was politically part of East Berlin but lay west of the Wall, and was left as overgrown wasteland. In 1988, it changed hands as part of an east-west agreement,

Sightseeing

but not before a squatter's camp had occupied it in order to protest against a planned new road. On the day it formally became West Berlin territory, police moved in to evict the squatters, 182 of whom used ladders to flee into the East. It was the single largest escape across the Wall and possibly the only one in an eastwards direction.

Turn right on Bellevuestrasse and left on Ebertstrasse, and you'll see the line of the Wall is marked by a double row of cobblestones. The buildings on the right are embassies of the German Länder, constructed on land once occupied by Hitler's Reichskanzlerei. Turn right down In den Ministergarten and, at the junction with Gertrude-Kolmar-Strasse, you'll find an information board about the Führerbunker, which once lay underground here. Turning left along Gertrude-Kolmar-Strasse brings you to Peter Eisenmann's **Denkmal für die ermordeten Juden Europas** (*see p84*). Get lost among its 2,711 concrete columns, ending up in Behrenstrasse on the other side.

The massive new **US Embassy** is on the corner of Ebertstrasse and Behrenstrasse. Next to it is the anarchistic rear facade of Frank Gehry's **DZ Bank** building. Gehry had to conform to the Pariser Platz conformity rule on the front side, but uses the building's rear quite differently. Before turning left on Wilhelmstrasse, walk 100 metres further down Behrenstrasse behind what's now the **Russian Embassy** to find, on the wall of a former Soviet swimming pool, the city's last image of Lenin.

Michael Wilford's much-lauded **British Embassy** is on a stretch of Wilhelmstrasse currently closed to traffic. Turning left at the end of the block brings you into Pariser Platz, the square before the Brandenburg Gate. Laid out in 1732, from 1850 it was given a uniform, classical style, but was then destroyed in World War II. In 1993 the Berlin Senate decided to recreate it in classical style; on the left side, Günther Behnisch's glass-fronted **Akademie der Künste** defies those rules. And on the other side of the square, the French Embassy rebels against the statutes with slanted window jambs asymmetrically facing the Brandenburger Tor.

Walk through the **Brandenburger Tor** (*see p82*). Ahead in the distance is the Siegessäule and to your right the **Reichstag** (*see p109*). Walk around to the front and queue to visit Norman Foster's wonderful cupola before looking at all the new government buildings hereabouts. Then circumnavigate Platz der Republik to the **Bundeskanzleramt**, admiring the new Hauptbahnhof on the skyline to the north, and the squat Swiss Embassy that has stubbornly survived war and redevelopment. On the east side of Axel Schultes and Charlotte Frank's Kanzleramt is another piece of public art. A sculpture by Basque artist Eduardo Chillida, with two rusty forms reaching out for each other, it's called *Berlin*.

New government buildings.

The **Bauhaus Archiv** – Berlin's famous Museum of Design. *See p111.*

As you'd expect, Daimler's collection is serious stuff. It has stuck to the 20th century, and covers abstract, conceptual and minimal art; its collection numbers around 1,300 works from artists such as Josef Albers, Max Bill, Walter de Maria, Jeff Koons and Andy Warhol. The gallery rotates themed portions of the collection, typically 30-80 works at a time, and often stages joint shows in a spirit of dialogue with other private collections.

Filmmuseum Berlin

Potsdamer Strasse 2 (300 9030/www.filmmuseum-berlin.de). U2, S1, S2, S26 Potsdamer Platz. **Open** 10am-6pm Tue, Wed, Fri-Sun; 10am-8pm Thur. **Admission** €6; reductions €4. **No credit cards.** **Map** p322/p327 L7.

Since 1963, the Deutsche Kinemathek has been amassing a collection of films, memorabilia, documentation and antique film apparatus. In 2000, all this stuff found a home in this roomy, well-designed exhibition space on two floors of the Filmhaus in the Sony Center, chronicling the history of German cinema. Striking exhibits include the two-storey-high video wall of disasters from Fritz Lang's adventure films and a morgue-like space devoted to films from the Third Reich. On a lighter note, there's a collection of clay-mation figures from Ray Harryhausen films, such as *Jason and the Argonauts.* But the main

attraction is the Marlene Dietrich collection – personal effects, home movies and designer clothes. Exhibitions are often linked with film programming at the Arsenal cinema downstairs (*see p208*).

Gedenkstätte Deutscher Widerstand

Stauffenbergstrasse 13-14 (2699 5000/www.gdw-berlin.de). U2, S1, S2, S26 Potsdamer Platz. **Open** 9am-6pm Mon-Wed, Fri; 9am-8pm Thur; 10am-6pm Sat, Sun. *Guided tours* Sat, Sun 3pm. **Admission** free. **Map** p322 K8.

The Memorial to the German Resistance chronicles the German resistance to National Socialism. The building is part of a complex known as the Bendlerblock, owned by the German military from its construction in 1911 until 1945. At the back is a memorial to the conspirators killed during their attempt to assassinate Hitler at this site on 20 July 1944. Regular guided tours are in German only, but you can book an English tour four weeks in advance.

Gemäldegalerie

Stauffenbergstrasse 40 (266 2101/www. smb.museum/gg). U2, S1, S2, S26 Potsdamer Platz. **Open** 10am-6pm Tue, Wed, Fri-Sun; 10am-10pm Thur. **Admission** €8; €4 reductions. **No credit cards.** **Map** p322 K8.

The Picture Gallery's first-rate early European collection features a healthy selection of the biggest names in Western art. Although many fine Italian, Spanish and English works are on display, the highlights are the Dutch and Flemish pieces. Fans of Rembrandt can indulge themselves with around 20 paintings, the best of which include a portrait of preacher and merchant Cornelis Claesz Anslo and his wife, and an electric Samson confronting his father-in-law. Two of Franz Hals' finest works are here – the wild, fluid, almost impressionistic *Malle Babbe* ('Mad Babette') and the detailed portrait of the one-year-old Catharina Hooft and her nurse. Other highlights include a couple of unflinching portraits by Robert Campin (early 15th century), a version of Botticelli's *Venus Rising*, and Corregio's brilliant *Leda with the Swan*. Look out, too, for a pair of Lucas Cranach Venus and Cupid paintings and his *Fountain of Youth*. Pick up the excellent (free) English-language audio guide.

Kunstgewerbemuseum

Kulturforum, Matthäikirchplatz (266 2902/www. smb.museum). U2, S1, S2, S26 Potsdamer Platz. **Open** 10am-6pm Tue-Fri; 11am-6pm Sat, Sun. **Admission** €8; €4 reductions. **No credit cards**. **Map** p322 K7.

The Museum of Decorative Art contains a frustrating collection of European arts and crafts, stretching from the Middle Ages through Renaissance, baroque and rococo to Jugendstil and art deco. There are some lovely pieces on display, particularly furniture and porcelain, but labelling is only in German and the layout of the building is confusing. Recent shows have included a homage to Yves St Laurent and an exhibition of contemporary Italian jewellery. **Other locations** Schloss Köpenick, Schlossinsel, Köpenick (266 3666).

Musikinstrumentenmuseum

Tiergartenstrasse 1 (254 810/www.sim.spk-berlin.de). U2, S1, S2, S26 Potsdamer Platz. **Open** 9am-5pm Tue, Wed, Fri; 9am-10pm Thur; 10am-5pm Sat, Sun. **Admission** €4; €2.50 reductions; free under-12s; free 1st Sun of mth. **No credit cards**. **Map** p322 J7.

More than 2,200 string, keyboard, wind and percussion instruments dating to the 1500s are crammed into the small Musical Instrument Museum next to the Philharmonie. Among them are rococo musical clocks, for which 18th-century princes commissioned jingles from Mozart, Haydn and Beethoven. Museum guides play obsolete instruments such as the Kammerflugel; on Saturdays at 11am, the wonderful Wurlitzer organ – salvaged from an American silent movie house – is cranked into action.

Neue Nationalgalerie

Potsdamer Strasse 50 (266 2651/www.neue-nationalgalerie.de). U2, S1, S2, S26 Potsdamer Platz. **Open** 10am-6pm Tue, Wed; 10am-10pm Thur; 10am-8pm, Fri; 11am-8pm Sat, Sun. **Admission** €8; €4 reductions. *Special exhibitions* varies. **No credit cards**. **Map** p322 K8.

Designed in the 1960s by Mies van der Rohe, the New National Gallery houses German and international paintings from the 20th century. It's strong on expressionism: there are key works by Kirchner, Heckel and Schmidt-Rottluff, as well as pieces by lesser-known expressionist painters such as Ludwig Meidner, whose apocalyptic post-World War I landscapes exert a garish, comic-book power. Cubist pieces cover the likes of Picasso, Gris and Léger. The Neue Sachlichkeit is well represented by paintings from George Grosz and Otto Dix, while the Bauhaus contributes work from Paul Klee and Wassily Kandinsky. Another focus is American Color Field painting, with pieces by Barnett Newman, Morris Louis and Frank Badur. Be warned: the permanent collection is often put into storage to allow for big shows and temporary exhibitions.

Panoramapunkt

Kollhoff Tower, Potsdamer Platz 1, entrance on Alte Potsdamer Strasse (2529 4372/www.panorama punkt.de). U2, S1, S2, S26 Potsdamer Platz. **Open** 11am-8pm daily. **Admission** €3.50; €2.50 reductions. **No credit cards**. **Map** p322/p327 L7.

What's billed as 'the fastest elevator in Europe' shoots up to the 100m (328ft) viewing platform in the Kollhoff Tower. The building's north-east corner is precisely at the point where the borders of Tiergarten, Mitte and Kreuzberg all meet – and also on what was the line of the Wall. From this vantage point, you can peer through railings and the neighbouring postmodern high-rises at the landmarks of new Berlin. There are good views to the south and west; looking north, the DB Tower gets in the way.

Zoologischer Garten & Aquarium

Hardenbergplatz 8 (254 010/www.zoo-berlin.de). U2, U9, S5, S7, S9, S75 Zoologischer Garten. **Open** *Zoo* Summer 9am-6.30pm daily. Winter 9am-5pm daily. *Aquarium* 9am-6pm daily. **Admission** *Zoo* €12; €6-€9 reductions. *Aquarium* €12; €6-€9 reductions. *Combined admission* €18; €9-€14 reductions. **Credit** AmEx, MC, V. **Map** p321 G8.

Germany's oldest zoo was opened in 1841 to designs by Martin Lichtenstein and Peter Joseph Lenné. With almost 14,000 creatures, it's one of the world's largest and most important zoos, with more endangered species in its collection than any in Europe except Antwerp's. It's beautifully landscaped, with lots of architectural oddities, and there are plenty of places for a coffee, beer or snack.

Enter the aquarium from within the zoo or through its own entrance on Olof-Palme-Platz by the Elephant Gate. More than 500 species are arranged over three floors, and it's a good option for a rainy day. On the ground floor are the fish (including some impressive sharks); on the first you'll find reptiles (the crocodile hall is the highlight); while insects and amphibians occupy the second. The dark corridors and liquid ambience, with tanks lit from within and curious aquarian creatures floating by, are as absorbing as an art exhibit. Elsewhere, the baby polar bear Knut has become one of Berlin's major tourist attractions.

Charlottenburg

Culture and the Ku'damm.

Sightseeing

This huge swathe of the city, once the centre of West Berlin, stretches from the Tiergarten to Spandau, from Tegel Airport in the north down to Wilmersdorf to the south. It has two main focal points – the commercial cauldron around Bahnhof Zoo and along the Kurfürstendamm, and the cluster of cultural treasures in and around Schloss Charlottenburg.

Bahnhof Zoo & the Ku'damm

Maps p321 & p328

Hymned by U2 and centrepiece of the film *Christiane F*, **Bahnhof Zoo** (Zoo Station or Bahnhof Zoologischer Garten, to give it its full name) was long the entry point to this part of the city. During the Cold War it was a spooky anomaly – slap in the middle of West Berlin but policed by the East, which controlled the intercity rail system – and a seedy hangout for junkies and winos. In the 1990s, it was spruced up with chain stores and fast-food outlets. Now, since the opening of the new Berlin Hauptbahnhof, it has been downgraded into just another station for local trains: only S-Bahn and RegionalBahn trains stop.

The original building was designed in 1882 by Ernst Dircksen; the modern glass sheds were added in 1934. The surrounding area, with its sleaze and shopping, cinemas and bustling crowds, is the gateway to the Kurfürstendamm, the main shopping street of western Berlin. The discos and bars along Joachimstaler Strasse are best avoided – the opening of the **Beate-Uhse Erotik-Museum** (*see p118*) actually added a touch of class to the area. On the other side of Hardenbergplatz – the square outside Bahnhof

Zoo – is the entrance to the **Zoologischer Garten** itself (*see p115*), which lies over the border in Tiergarten. Fans of photography, in particular Helmut Newton, shouldn't miss the new **Museum für Fotografie** (Museum of Photography; *see p118*) behind Bahnhof Zoo.

The most notable nearby landmark is the fractured spire of the **Kaiser-Wilhelm-Gedächtnis-Kirche** (Kaiser Wilhelm Memorial Church; *see p118*) in Breitscheidplatz. Close by is the 22-storey **Europa-Center**, whose Mercedes star can be seen from much of the rest of the city. It was built in 1965 – and it shows. Intended as the anchor for the development of a new western downtown, it was the first of Berlin's genuinely tall buildings; now it's the grande dame of the city's shopping malls. Its exterior looks best when neon-lit at night. The strange sculpture in front was erected in 1983. It is officially called *Weltenbrunnen* (Fountain of the Worlds), but, like almost everything else in Berlin, it has a nickname: *Der Wasserklops* (Water Meatball).

Running along the south of the Europa-Center, **Tauentzienstrasse** is the westernmost piece of the Generalzug, a sequence of streets laid out by Peter Joseph Lenné to link the west end with Kreuzberg and points east. Constructed around 1860, they're all named after Prussian generals from the Napoleonic wars: Tauentzien, Kleist, Bülow, and so on. The tubular steel sculpture in the central reservation along Tauentzienstrasse was commissioned for the city's 750th anniversary and represents the then-divided city.

The street continues east past **KaDeWe** (*see p171*), the largest department store in continental Europe. Its full title is Das Kaufhaus des Westens (Department Store of the West), and it was founded in 1907 by Adolf Jandorf, acquired by Herman Tietz in 1926 and later 'Aryanised' and expropriated by the Nazis. KaDeWe is the only one of Berlin's famous turn-of-the-century department stores to survive the war intact, and has been extensively modernised over the last decade. Its most famous feature is the sixth-floor food hall.

Tauentzienstrasse ends at Wittenbergplatz. The 1911 neo-classical **U-Bahn station** here (by Alfred Grenander) is a listed building and has been wonderfully restored with wooden kiosks and old ads on the walls. A block further is the huge steel sculpture at An der Urania, with its grim monument to children killed in traffic by Berlin's drivers. This marks the end, or the beginning, of the western 'downtown'.

Leading south-west from the Kaiser-Wilhelm-Gedächtniskirche, the **Kurfürstendamm** (or Ku'damm, as it's universally known), West Berlin's tree-lined shopping boulevard, is named after the Prussian Kurfürst ('Elector') – and for centuries it was nothing but a track leading from the Elector's residence to the royal hunting palace in the Grunewald. In 1881 Bismarck insisted it be widened to 5.3 metres (17 feet).

To the south of the street, many villas were erected, and though few survive today, one sizeable exception contains the **Käthe-Kollwitz-Museum** (*see p118*), the Villa Griesbach auction house and the Literaturhaus Berlin, with its **Wintergarten am Literaturhaus** café (*see p169*) on Fasanenstrasse. The villas soon made way for upmarket tenement buildings with huge apartments. About half of the original buildings were destroyed in the war and replaced by functional offices, but many bombastic old structures remain.

The ground-level Ku'damm soon developed into an elegant shopping boulevard. It remains so today with cinemas (mostly showing dubbed Hollywood fare), restaurants (from classy to burger joints) and upmarket fashion shops: the Ku'damm is dedicated to separating you from your cash. If you tire of shopping, check out the entertaining **Story of Berlin** (*see p119*).

Side streets to the south are quieter but even more upmarket, and Bleibtreustrasse to the north has more shops and a number of outrageous examples of 19th-century Gründerzeit architecture.

At the north-west corner of the intersection of Ku'damm and Joachimstaler Strasse is the **Neues Kranzler-Eck**, a Helmut Jahn-designed ensemble built around the famous old Café Kranzler, with a 16-storey tower and pedestrian courtyards including a habitat for parrots.

Other notable new architecture in the area includes Josef Paul Kleihues' **Kant-Dreieck** (Fasanenstrasse/Kantstrasse), with its large metal 'sail', and Nicholas Grimshaw's **Ludwig-Erhard-Haus** for the Stock Exchange at Fasanenstrasse 83-84. Back towards the Kurfürstendamm end of Fasanenstrasse is the **Jüdisches Gemeindehaus** (Jewish Community House), and, opposite, the **Zille-Hof** flea market.

Kantstrasse runs more or less parallel to the Ku'damm at the Zoo end, and contains the grandiloquent **Theater des Westens** and more shops. Since the opening of the **stilwerk** design centre (*see p192*), the stretch between Fasanenstrasse and Savignyplatz has become

Berlin's grandest boulevard, the **Kurfürstendamm**.

Not to be missed, the new **Museum für Fotografie**.

a centre for designer homeware stores. The environs of leafy **Savignyplatz**, meanwhile, are dotted with chic restaurants, cafés and shops, particularly on Grolmanstrasse and in the Savignypassage. Nearby Knesebeckstrasse includes the excellent **Marga Schoeller Bücherstube** (*see p177*).

Beate-Uhse Erotik-Museum

Joachimstaler Strasse 4 (886 0666/www.beate-uhse-filialen.de). U2, U9, S5, S7, S9, S75 Zoologischer Garten. **Open** 9am-midnight Mon-Sat; 1pm-midnight Sun. **Admission** €6; €5 reductions. **Credit** AmEx, MC, V. **Map** p321/p328 G8.

The three floors of this collection (housed above a flagship Beate-Uhse retail outlet offering the usual videos and sex toys) contain oriental prints; some daft showroom-dummy tableaux; and glass cases containing such delights as early Japanese dildos, Andean penis flutes, 17th-century chastity belts and a giant coconut that looks like an arse. There's a small, drab exhibit on pioneering sex researcher Magnus Hirschfeld, an inadequate item on Heinrich Zille and a corner documenting the career of Frau Uhse herself, who went from Luftwaffe pilot to annual sex-aid sales of €50 million. It's all oddly respectable, given the subject.

Kaiser-Wilhelm-Gedächtnis-Kirche

Breitscheidplatz (218 5023/www.gedaechtnis kirche.com). U2, U9, S5, S7, S9, S75 Zoologischer Garten. **Open** 9am-7pm daily. *Guided tours* 1.15pm, 2pm, 3pm Mon-Sat. **Admission** free. **Map** p321/p328 G8.

The Kaiser Wilhelm Memorial Church is one of Berlin's best-known sights, and one of its most dramatic at night. The neo-Romanesque structure was built in 1891-5 by Franz Schwechten in honour of – you guessed it – Kaiser Wilhelm I. Much of the building was destroyed during an Allied air raid in 1943. These days the church serves as a stark reminder of the damage done by the war, although some might argue it improved what was originally a profoundly ugly building. Inside the rump of the church is a glittering art nouveau-style ceiling mosaic depicting members of the House of Hohenzollern going on pilgrimage towards the cross. Here you'll also find a cross made from the nails from the destroyed cathedral at Coventry, and photos of the church before and after the war. Inside the chapel the wrap-around blue stained-glass in the windows is quite stunning.

Käthe-Kollwitz-Museum

Fasanenstrasse 24, Wilmersdorf (8825210/www.kaethe-kollwitz.de). U1, U9 Kurfürstendamm. **Open** 11am-6pm daily. **Admission** €5; €2.50 reductions. **No credit cards**. **Map** p321/p328 F9.

Käthe Kollwitz's powerful, deeply empathetic work embraces the full spectrum of life, from the joy of motherhood to the pain of death (with rather more emphasis on the latter than the former). The collection includes her famous lithograph *Brot!*, as well as charcoal sketches, woodcuts and sculptures, all displayed to good effect in this grand villa off the Ku'damm. Some labelling is in English.

Museum für Fotografie

Jebenstrasse 2 (266 2188/www.smb.museum/mf). U2, U9, S5, S7, S9, S75 Zoologischer Garten. **Open** 10am-6pm Tue-Sun. **Admission** €6; €3 reductions. **Credit** MC, V. **Map** p321/p328 G8.

Shortly before his death in 2004, Berlin-born Helmut Newton, who served his apprenticeship elsewhere in Charlottenburg at the studio of Yva (now the Hotel Bogota; *see p73*), donated over 1,000 of his nude and fashion photographs to the city and provided funds towards the creation of a new gallery. The new Museum of Photography, doubling as a home for the Helmut Newton Foundation (www. helmutnewton.com), was the result. In a former casino behind Bahnhof Zoo, it's now the largest photographic gallery in the city. The first two floors are given over to Newton's work, which is parcelled up in a series of alternating exhibitions. Six colossal nudes, modelled on Nazi propaganda photos from the 1930s, glare down at you on entering the building, and set the tone for the big, garish, confrontational pieces that dominate the exhibits. Further space is devoted to temporary exhibitions.

Story of Berlin

Kurfürstendamm 207-208 (8872 0100/www.story-of-berlin.de). U1 Uhlandstrasse. **Open** 10am-8pm daily; last entry 6pm. **Admission** €9.80; €8 reductions. **Credit** AmEx, MC, V. **Map** p321/p328 F8.
If you're interested in the city's turbulent history, the Story of Berlin is a novel way of approaching it. The huge floor space is filled with well-designed rooms and multimedia exhibits created by authors, designers and film and stage specialists, telling Berlin's story from its founding in 1237 to the present day. The 20 themed displays are labelled in both German and English. Underneath all this is a massive nuclear shelter. Built by the Allies in the 1970s, the low-ceilinged, oppressive bunker is still fully functional and can hold up to 3,500 people. Guided tours are included in the price of the ticket.

Schloss Charlottenburg & around

Map p316

The palace that gives Charlottenburg its name lies about three kilometres (two miles) north-west of Bahnhof Zoo. In contrast to the commercialism and crush of the latter, this part of the city is quiet, wealthy and serene.
Schloss Charlottenburg (*see p121*) was built in the 17th century as a summer palace for Queen Sophie-Charlotte, wife of Friedrich III (later King Friedrich I), and was intended as Berlin's answer to Versailles. It's not a very convincing answer, but there's plenty of interest in the buildings and grounds of the palace – the apartments of the New Wing and the gardens are the main attractions.
Next to the palace's west wing is the **Museum für Vor- und Frühgeschichte** (Primeval and Early History Museum; *see below*). In front of the Schloss entrance is the **Museum Berggruen** (*see below*) and the art nouveau and art deco collection of the **Bröhan-Museum** (*see below*). The arrival across the street of the

Sammlung Scharf-Gerstenberg (*see p121*), which is mostly concerned with Surrealism, firmly establishes this corner of town as a centre for early 20th-century art.
There are few eating, drinking or shopping opportunities in the immediate vicinity of the palace, but if you head down Schlossstrasse and over Bismarckstrasse, the streets south of here, particularly those named after philosophers (Leibniz, Goethe) have many interesting small shops selling antiques, books and the fashions worn by well-to-do locals.

Bröhan-Museum

Schlossstrasse 1A (3269 0600/www.broehan-museum.de). U2 Sophie-Charlotte-Platz or U7 Richard-Wagner-Platz. **Open** 10am-6pm Tue-Sun. **Admission** €5; €4 reductions. Free 1st Wed of mth. **No credit cards. Map** p316 C6.
This quiet, private museum is made up of three well-laid-out levels of international art nouveau and art deco pieces that businessman Karl Bröhan began collecting in the 1960s and donated to the city of Berlin on his 60th birthday. The wide array of paintings, furniture, porcelain, glass, silver and sculptures dates from 1890 to 1939. Hans Baluschek's paintings of social life in the 1920s and '30s and Willy Jaeckel's series of portraits of women are the pick of the fine art bunch; the furniture is superb too. The third floor hosts special exhibitions, such as a recent one on art deco in Sweden. Labelling is only in German. Good website, though.

Museum Berggruen

Westlicher Stülerbau, Schlossstrasse 1 (3269 5815/www.smb.museum/mb). U2 Sophie-Charlotte-Platz or U7 Richard-Wagner-Platz. **Open** 10am-6pm Tue-Sun. **Admission** €6; €3 reductions. **No credit cards. Map** p316 C6.
Heinz Berggruen was an early dealer in Picassos in Paris, and the subtitle of this museum, Picasso und seine Zeit (Picasso and his Time), sums up this satisfying and important collection. Displayed over an easily digestible three circular floors, it's inevitable that Pablo's works dominate; his astonishingly prolific and diverse output is well represented. The highlight is perhaps the 1942 *Reclining Nude*. There are also works by Braque, Giacometti, Cézanne and Matisse, and most of the second floor is given over to wonderful paintings by Paul Klee.

Museum für Vor- und Frühgeschichte

Langhansbau, Schloss Charlottenburg (3267 4840/ www.smb.museum/mvf). U2 Sophie-Charlotte-Platz or U7 Richard-Wagner-Platz. **Open** 9am-5pm Tue-Fri; 10am-5pm Sat, Sun. **Admission** €3; €1.50 reductions. **Credit** MC, V. **Map** p316 C6.
The Primeval and Early History Museum – spread over six galleries – traces the evolution of Homo sapiens from 1,000,000 BC to the Bronze Age. The highlights are the replicas (and some originals) of Heinrich Schliemann's famous treasure of ancient

Sightseeing

Boot trips

While Berlin's claims to be 'the Prussian Venice' may meet with deserved scepticism, the German capital is still an engagingly watery place. The Spree meanders through the city on its journey from the Czech Republic to the Elbe. Beyond that, the entire city and its surrounding region is a maze of inter-fingering rivers, lakes and canals. For many parts of the city, boats are the ideal form of transport. Indeed, in northwest Berlin, in and around Tegeler See, there are isolated houses on islands that can only be reached by ferry.

Even the regular BVG local transport tickets include ferry services across various lakes. For visitors on a budget, a normal AB zone ticket is enough to get you on the hourly year-round ferry link from Wannsee to Kladow. There's even a decent pub by the pier in a quasi-rural setting on the other side.

A fine range of city centre tours is offered by **Stern und Kreisschiffahrt** (www.sternundkreis. de), **Reederei Winkler** (www.reedereiwinkler. de), **Reederei Riedel** (www.reederei-riedel.de) and **Star-Line** (www.starlineschifffahrt.de). All four operators offer circular tours, usually lasting three to four hours, which take in the Spree and the Landwehrkanal. Passengers can hop on and off at landing stages en route,

and basic food and drink is served on board. For a complete tour, expect to pay around €12 per adult. There are convenient landing stages at the **Schlossbrücke** in Charlottenburg, at the **Haus der Kulturen der Welt** (*see p238*) in Tiergarten, at Märkisches Ufer, at Jannowitzbrücke and in the Nikolaiviertel. Note that many services operate only from mid March to late November.

A short train journey to Wannsee (20 minutes by Regionalbahn from Mitte) opens more opportunities. Stern & Kreis' Seven Lakes Trip (7-Seen-Rundfahrt) gives a chance to ogle some of Berlin's poshest backyards as the cruise slides gently past the handsome mansions surrounding the **Kleiner Wannsee** (*see p126*). The same tour takes in the Glienicker Brücke, cruises the Havel and stops at the **Pfaueninsel** (*see p126*). The service runs daily from late March to mid October with departures at 10.30am and hourly thereafter. Boats leave from piers near Wannsee station. Also with Stern & Kreis, a longer trip from Wannsee (daily in summer, less frequently the rest of the year) runs via Potsdam to quaint Werder, one of the most beautiful of Brandenburg villages, with a cluster of fish restaurants around the quay.

Troy, including works of ceramics and gold, as well as weaponry. Leep an eye out also for the sixth-century BC grave of a girl buried with a gold coin in her mouth. Information is available in English.

Sammlung Scharf-Gerstenberg

*Schlossstrasse 70 (3435 7315/www.smb.
museum/ssg). U2 Sophie-Charlotte-Platz or U7
Richard-Wagner-Platz.* **Open** 10am-6pm Tue-Sat.
Admission €8; €4 reductions. **No credit cards**.
Map p316 C6.

On the verge of opening as we went to press, the Scharf-Gerstenberg Collection is housed in the building used by the Egyptian Museum before it moved back to Museumsinsel. Presented as a three-floor exhibition called 'Surreal Worlds', it concerns the history of Surrealism and its forerunners, traced through artists such as Piranesi, Goya and Redon to Dali, Magritte and Ernst. The original collection was gathered by Otto Gerstenberg around 1910, and added to by his grandsons Walter and Dieter Scharf. In 2000 it was exhibited at the Neue Nationalgalerie, and is now on a ten-year loan to the city.

Schloss Charlottenburg

*Luisenplatz & Spandauer Damm (320 911/
www.spsg.de). U2 Sophie-Charlotte-Platz or U7
Richard-Wagner-Platz.* **Open** *Old Palace* 10am-6pm
Tue-Fri; 10am-5pm Sat, Sun. Last tour 4pm. *New
Wing* (Apr-Oct) 10am-6pm Tue-Sun; (Nov-Mar)
10am-5pm Wed-Sun. *New Pavilion* 10am-6pm Tue-
Sun. *Mausoleum* (Apr-Oct) 10am-6pm Tue-Sun. Last
entry 5.30pm. (Nov-Mar) noon-5pm Tue-Sun. Last
entry 4.30pm. *Belvedere* (Apr-Oct) 10am-6pm Tue-
Sun. (Nov-Mar) noon-5pm Tue-Sun. **Admission**
Day tickets €12; €9 reductions. *Mausoleum* €2;
€1.50 reductions. *Belvedere* €2; €1.50 reductions.
No credit cards. **Map** p316 C6.

Queen Sophie-Charlotte was the impetus behind this sprawling palace and gardens (and gave her name to both the building and the district) – her husband Friedrich III (later King Friedrich I) built it in 1695-9 as a summer home for his queen. Later kings also summered here, tinkering with, and adding to the buildings. It was severely damaged during World War II, but has now been restored, and stands as the largest surviving Hohenzollern palace.

The bafflingly complicated individual opening times and admission prices have many a visitor scratching their heads. The easiest option, therefore, is to go for the combination ticket that allows entrance to all parts of the palace, with the exception of the state and private apartments of King Friedrich I and Queen Sophie-Charlotte in the Altes Schloss (Old Palace), which are only accessible on a guided tour (€8; €5 reductions; in German only). This tour, through more than 20 rooms, some of staggering baroque opulence, has its highlights (particularly the Porcelain Cabinet), but can be skipped – there's plenty of interest elsewhere. The upper apartments in the old palace can be visited without a guided tour, but they are really only of interest to silver and porcelain junkies.

The one must-see is the Neue Flügel (New Wing). Also known as the Knobeldorff Wing (after its architect), the upper floor of the wing contains the State Apartments of Frederick the Great and the Winter Chambers of his successor King Friedrich Wilhelm II. The contrast between the two sections is interesting – Frederick's rooms are all excessive rococo exuberance (the wildly over-the-top Golden Gallery literally drips gilt), while Friedrich Wilhelm's far more modestly proportioned rooms reflect the more restrained classicism of his time. Frederick the Great was a big collector of 18th-century French painting, and some choice canvases hang from the walls, including Watteau's masterpiece *The Embarkation for Cythera*. Also worth a look are the apartments of Friedrich Wilhelm III in the New Wing.

By the east end of the New Wing stands the Neue Pavillon (New Pavilion). Also known as the Schinkel Pavilion, it was built by Schinkel in 1824 for Friedrich Wilhelm III – the King liked it so much that he chose to live here in preference to the grandeur of the main palace.

The huge gardens are one of the palace's main draws. Laid out in 1697 in formal French style, they were reshaped in a more relaxed English style in the 19th century. Within them you'll find the Belvedere, a three-storey structure built in 1788 as a teahouse, now containing a collection of Berlin porcelain. Also in the gardens is the sombre Mausoleum, containing the tombs of Friedrich Wilhelm III, his wife Queen Luise, Kaiser Wilhelm I and his wife. Look out for temporary exhibitions in the Orangery. There's a café and restaurant at the front of the palace. Note: the entire palace is closed on Mondays. *Photo p122*.

Elsewhere in Charlottenburg

Map p316

About three kilometres (two miles) north-east of Schloss Charlottenburg is a reminder of the terror inflicted by the Nazi regime on dissidents, criminals and anybody else they deemed undesirable. The **Gedenkstätte Plötzensee** (Plötzensee Memorial; *see p122*) preserves the execution shed of the former Plötzensee prison, where more than 2,500 people were killed between 1933 and 1945.

A couple of kilometres south-west of Schloss Charlottenburg, at the western end of Neue Kantstrasse, stands the futuristic International Conference Centre (ICC). Built in the 1970s, it is used for pop concerts, political rallies and the like. Next door, the even larger Messe- und Ausstellungsgelände (Trade Fair & Exhibition Area) plays host to trade fairs ranging from electronics to food to aerospace. Within the complex, the **Funkturm** (Radio Tower; *see p122*) offers panoramic views. Nearby, Hans Poelzig's **Haus des Rundfunks** (Masurenallee 9-14) is an expressive example of monumental brick modernism.

Sightseeing

Another couple of kilometres north-west is the **Olympiastadion** (*see below*). One of the few pieces of fascist-era architecture still intact in Berlin, it was extensively renovated to host the 2006 World Cup Final. Immediately south of Olympiastadion S-Bahn station is a huge apartment block designed by Le Corbusier. The **Corbusierhaus**, with its multicoloured paint job, was constructed for the International Building exhibition of 1957. From here, a ten-minute walk along Sensburger Allee brings you to the sculptures of the **Georg-Kolbe-Museum** (*see below*).

Funkturm

Messedamm (3038 1905). U2 Theodor-Heuss-Platz or Kaiserdamm. **Open** *Aug-June* 10am-9pm Mon; 10am-11pm Tue-Sun. **Admission** €4; €2 reductions. **No credit cards. Map** p320 A8/B8.

The 138m (453ft) high Radio Tower was built in 1926 and looks a bit like a smaller version of the Eiffel Tower. The observation deck stands at 126m (413ft); vertigo sufferers should seek solace in the restaurant, only 55m (180ft) from the ground.

Gedenkstätte Plötzensee

Hüttigpfad (344 3226/www.gedenkstaette-ploetzensee.de). Bus 123. **Open** *Mar-Oct* 9am-5pm daily. *Nov-Feb* 9am-4pm daily. **Admission** free. **Map** p317 F3.

This memorial stands on the site where the Nazis executed over 2,500 (largely political) prisoners. In a single night in 1943, 186 people were hanged. In 1952 it was declared a memorial to the victims of fascism, and a commemorative wall was built. There is little to see today, apart from the execution area,

behind the wall, with its meat hooks from which victims were hanged (many were also guillotined), and a small room with an exhibition. Excellent booklets in English are available. The stone urn near the entrance is filled with earth from concentration camps. The rest of the prison is now a juvenile correction centre.

Georg-Kolbe-Museum

Sensburger Allee 25 (304 2144/www.georg-kolbe-museum.de). S5, S75 Heerstrasse/bus X34, X49, 149. **Open** 10am-5pm Tue-Sun. **Admission** €4; €2.50 reductions. *Special exhibitions* €5; €3 reductions. **No credit cards.**

Georg Kolbe's former studio has been transformed into a showcase for his work. The Berlin sculptor, regarded as Germany's best in the 1920s, mainly focused on naturalistic human figures. The Georg-Kolbe-Museum features examples of his earlier, graceful pieces, as well as his later sombre and larger-than-life works that were created in accordance with the ideals of the Nazi regime. One of his most famous pieces, *Figure for Fountain*, is outside in the sculpture garden.

Olympiastadion

Olympischer Platz 3 (3068 8100/www.olympiastadion-berlin.de). U2 Olympia-Stadion or S5 Olympiastadion. **Open** varies. **Admission** varies. **No credit cards.**

Originally designed by Werner March and opened in 1936 for the Olympics, the 74,000-seat stadium underwent a major and long overdue refitting for the 2006 World Cup, including better seats and a roof over the whole lot. Home of Hertha BSC (*see p263*), it also hosts the German Cup Final, plus other sporting events and concerts.

Schloss Charlottenburg. *See p121.*

Other Districts

Part bleak, part bucolic, Berlin's far-flung fringes offer plenty to explore.

The largest city between Paris and Moscow, Berlin sprawls for miles in every direction. If its size should seem daunting, remember that the capital's historical expansion into a hinterland of lakes and forest coincided with the age of railways, and public transport will whisk you to most far-flung neighbourhoods.

North of the centre

Wedding

Maps p317 & p318

The working-class industrial district of Wedding, formerly on the Western side of the Wall, is now politically part of Mitte. Few visitors venture very far into its largely grim fastness. Apart from a couple of low-key attractions – the **Anti-Kriegs-Museum** (Anti-War Museum; *see below*) and the nearby **Zucker Museum** (Sugar Museum; *see below*) – there is also one of the only remaining stretches of the Wall at the **Gedenkstätte Berliner Mauer** (Berlin Wall Memorial; *see below*).

Anti-Kriegs-Museum

Brüsseler Strasse 21 (4549 0110/tours 402 8691/ www.anti-kriegs-museum.de). U9 Amrumer Strasse. **Open** 4-8pm daily. **Admission** free. **Map** p317 H2.
The original Anti-War Museum was founded in 1925 by Ernst Friedrich, author of *War Against War*. In 1933, it was destroyed by the Nazis, and Friedrich fled to Brussels. There he had another museum from 1936 to 1940, when the Nazis again destroyed his work. In 1982, a group of teachers including Tommy Spree, grandson of Ernst Friedrich, re-established this museum in West Berlin. It now hosts films, discussions, lectures and exhibitions, as well as a permanent display including World War I photos and artefacts from the original museum, children's war toys, information on German colonialism in Africa and pieces of anti-Semitic material from the Nazi era. Exhibitions are only in German; however, you can call ahead to arrange a tour in English with Spree. Though admission is free, donations are welcome.

Gedenkstätte Berliner Mauer

Bernauer Strasse 111 (464 1030/www.berliner- mauer-dokumentationszentrum.de). U8 Bernauer Strasse or S1, S2 Nordbahnhof. **Open** *Documentation centre* Nov-Mar 10am-5pm Tue-Sun. Apr-Oct 10am-6pm Tue-Sun. **Admission** free. **Map** p318 M4.

Immediately upon unification, the city bought the stretch of the Wall that's found here to maintain as a memorial, and it was finally dedicated in 1998. Impeccably restored, it is also as sterile a monument as any in Berlin, with a brass plaque decrying the Communist 'reign of terror', which is regularly defaced. The documentation centre, featuring displays on the Wall and a database of escapees, is across the street, and from its roof you can view the Wall and the Kapelle der Versöhnung (Chapel of Reconciliation). *Photo p124.*

Zucker-Museum

Amrumer Strasse 32 (3142 7574/www.dtmb.de/ zucker-museum). U6 Seestrasse or U9 Amrumer Strasse. **Open** 9am-4.30pm Mon-Thur; 11am-6pm Sun. **Admission** free. **No credit cards**. **Map** p317 H2.
A museum that is devoted to the chemistry, history and politics of sugar may not sound like the most entertaining of places to spend an afternoon, but this place, originally opened in 1904, contains a fascinating collection of paraphernalia. Don't miss the slide show on the slave trade.

West of the centre

Spandau

Berlin's western neighbour and eternal rival, Spandau is a little baroque town that seems to contradict everything about the city of which it is now, reluctantly, a part. Spandauers still talk about 'going into Berlin' when they head off to the rest of the city. Berliners, meanwhile, basically consider Spandau to be part of West Germany, though travelling there is easy on the U7, alighting at either Zitadelle or Altstadt Spandau, depending on which sights you want to visit. None are thrilling, but they make for a low-key escape from the city.

The **Zitadelle** (Citadel; *see p124*) contains in one of its museums Spandau's original town charter, which dates from 1232, a fact Spandauers have used ever since to argue their historical primacy over Berlin. Spandau's old town centre is mostly pedestrianised, with 18th-century townhouses interspersed with burger joints and department stores. One of the prettiest is the former Gasthof zum Stern in Carl-Schurz-Strasse; older still are houses in Kinkelstrasse and Ritterstrasse; but perhaps the best-preserved district is north of Am Juliusturm in the area bounded by Hoher

Sightseeing

'Mr Gorbachev, tear down this wall!' **Gedenkstätte Berliner Mauer.** *See p123.*

Steinweg, Kolk and Behnitz. Steinweg contains a fragment of the old town wall from the first half of the 14th century; Kolk has the Alte Marienkirche (1848); and in Behnitz, at no.5, stands the elegant baroque Heinemannsche Haus. At Reformationsplatz, the brick nave of the Nikolaikirche dates from 1410-50; the west tower was added in 1468, and there were later enhancements by Schinkel.

One of the most pleasant times to visit is at Christmas, when the market square houses a life-size Nativity scene with real sheep and the Christmas market is in full swing. The café and bakery on Reformationsplatz are excellent.

Many will know the name Spandau from its association with Rudolf Hess. Hitler's deputy, who flew to Britain in 1940 for reasons that are still disputed, was held in the Allied jail here after the Nuremberg trials, and remained here (alone after 1966) until his suicide at age 93 in 1987. 19th-century brick building at Wilhelmstrasse 21-24 was then demolished to make way for a supermarket for the British forces. Some distance south of Spandau is the **Luftwaffenmuseum der Bundeswehr Berlin-Gatow** (*see below*).

Luftwaffenmuseum der Bundeswehr Berlin-Gatow

Gross-Glienicker Weg, Gatow (811 0769/www. luftwaffenmuseum.de). U7, S9, S75 Rathaus Spandau, then bus 135 to Seekorso. **Open** 10am-6pm Tue-Sun. **Admission** free.

You probably need to be a bit of a plane nut to make the journey here. The museum is on the far western fringes of the city at what was formerly the RAF base in divided Berlin; it is a long journey by public transport followed by a 20-minute walk from the bus stop. Then there's a lot more walking to take in more than 100 aircraft scattered around the airfield plus exhibits in two hangars and the former control tower. The main emphasis is on the history of military aviation in Germany since 1945, although there's also a World War I tri-plane, a restored Handley Page Hastings (as used here in the Airlift) and a whole lot of missiles.

Zitadelle

Am Juliusturm, Spandau (354 9440/tours 334 6270/www.zitadelle-spandau.net). U7 Zitadelle. **Open** 10am-5pm daily. **Admission** €4.50; €2.50 reductions. **No credit cards**.

The oldest structure in the citadel (and the oldest secular building in Berlin) is the Juliusturm, probably dating back to an Ascanian fortress from about 1160. The present tower was home until 1919 to the 120-million Goldmark reparations, stored in 1,200 boxes, which the French paid to Germany in 1874 after the Franco-Prussian War. The bulk of the Zitadelle was designed in 1560-94, in the style of an Italian fort, to dominate the confluence of the Spree and Havel rivers. Since then it has been used as everything from garrison to prison to laboratory. There are two museums within the Zitadelle: one tells the story of the building with models and maps; the other is a museum of local history.

South-west of the centre

Zehlendorf & the Dahlem museums

South-west Berlin contains some of the city's wealthiest suburbs, and in the days of division was the American sector, from which time assorted landmarks survive. One major draw is the museums at Dahlem, including the world-class **Ethnologisches Museum** (Ethnological Museum; *see below*). In the same building are the **Museum für Asiatische Kunst** (Museum of Asian Art) and the **Museum Europäischer Kulturen** (Museum of European Cultures).

Dahlem is also home to the **Freie Universität**, some of whose departments occupy former villas seized by the Nazis from their Jewish owners. North-west of the U-Bahn station, opposite the Friedhof Dahlem-Dorf (cemetery), is the **Domäne Dahlem** working farm (*see below*) – a great place to take kids.

Ten minutes' walk east from Dahlem along Königin-Luise-Strasse brings you to the **Botanischer Garten & Botanisches Museum** (Botanical Garden & Museum; *see below*), while taking the same street for a kilometre or so west of Dahlem brings you to the edge of the **Grunewald** (*see below*).

Botanischer Garten & Botanisches Museum

Königin-Luise-Strasse 6-8 (8385 0100/www. bgbm.fu-berlin.de/BGBM). S1 Botanischer Garten, then 15min walk. **Open** *Botanischer Garten* 9am-dusk daily. *Botanisches Museum* Feb 9am-5pm daily. Mar, Oct 9am-6pm daily. Apr, Aug 9am-8pm daily. May-July 9am-9pm daily. Sept 9am-7pm daily. **Admission** *Combined* €5; €2.50 reductions. *Museum only* €2; €1 reductions. **No credit cards**. The Botanical Garden was landscaped at the beginning of the 20th century. Today, it is home to 18,000 plant species, 16 greenhouses and a museum. The botanical gardens make for a pleasant stroll. The botanical museum, however, is a bit dilapidated and there's no information in English but it's free with a ticket for the gardens and it's the place to come for advice on whether those mushrooms you found in the forest are delectable or deadly.

Domäne Dahlem

Königin-Luise-Strasse 49 (666 3000/www. domaene-dahlem.de). U3 Dahlem-Dorf. **Open** 10am-6pm Mon, Wed-Sun. *Farmer's shop* 10am-6pm Mon-Fri; 8am-1pm Sat. **Admission** *Museum* €2; €1 reductions. Free to all Wed. *Farmer's shop* free. **No credit cards**.
On this organic working farm, children can see how life was lived in the 17th century. Craftspeople preserve and teach their skills. It's best to visit during one of several festivals held during the year, when kids can ride ponies, tractors and hay wagons.

Ethnologisches Museum

Lansstrasse 8 (830 1438/www.smb.spk-berlin.de). U1 Dahlem-Dorf. **Open** 10am-6pm Tue-Fri; 11am-6pm Sat, Sun. **Admission** €6; €3 reductions. **No credit cards**.
The Ethnological Museum is a stunner – extensive, authoritative, beautifully laid out and lit. It encompasses cultures from Oceania to Central America to Africa to the Far East. Only the true ethno-fan should attempt to see it all, but no one should miss the Südsee (South Sea) room. Here you'll find New Guinean masks and effigies, and a remarkable collection of original canoes and boats – some huge and elaborate. The African rooms are also impressive – look out for the superb carvings from Benin and the Congo, and beaded artefacts from Cameroon. An enlightening small exhibit explores the influence of African art on the German expressionists. The museum only has space to exhibit two per cent of its 500,000 items, and is hoping to move to the Stadtschloss in Mitte in 2010.

Two other museums are housed in the same building. The Museum für Asiatische Kunst (Museum of Asian Art) features archaeological objects and works of fine art from India, Japan, China and Korea from the early Stone Age to the present. The Museum Europäischer Kulturen (Museum of European Cultures) contains exhibits about European everyday culture from the 18th century to the present. One highlight is a mechanical model of the nativity, displayed each year in the Advent period. Audio guides in English are available.

Grunewald

The western edge of Zehlendorf is formed by the Havel river and the extensive Grunewald, largest of Berlin's many forests. On a fine Sunday afternoon, its lanes and pathways fill with walkers, runners, cyclists, horse riders and dog walkers. This is because it's so easily accessible by S-Bahn. There are several restaurants next to the station, and on the other side of the motorway at Schmetterlings-platz, open from April to October.

One popular destination is the **Teufelsee**, a tiny lake packed with bathers in summer, reached by heading west from the station along Schildhornweg for 15 minutes. Close by is the mound of the **Teufelsberg**, a product of wartime devastation – a railway was laid from Wittenbergplatz to carry the 12 million cubic metres of rubble that forms it. There are great views from the summit. There has been talk of replacing the abandoned American electronic listening post on the top with some kind of hotel and conference centre. South of the station, at the far end of the **Grunewaldsee**, the 16th-century **Jagdschloss Grunewald** (Grunewald Hunting Lodge) is an example of the kind of building that once maintained the country life

Sightseeing

of the landed gentry, the Prussian Junkers. Here, you can find bathing by the lake in the summer, including a nudist section. The Grunewaldsee is also a favourite promenade for dogs and their owners, who refresh themselves in the deer-horn-bedecked Forsthaus Paulsborn.

A further kilometre south-east through the forest is the **Chalet Suisse**, an over-the-top Swiss-themed restaurant popular with families because of its playground and petting zoo. A further ten-minute walk takes you to the **Alliierten Museum** (Allied Museum; *see below*) on Clayallee. A kilometre north of here is the **Brücke-Museum** (*see below*), housing a collection of expressionist paintings and prints.

Further south, **Krumme Lanke** and **Schlachtensee** are pleasant urban lakes along the south-eastern edge of the Grunewald, perfect for picnicking, swimming or rowing – and each with its own station.

On the west side of the Grunewald, halfway up Havelchaussee, is the **Grunewaldturm**, a tower built in 1897 in memory of Wilhelm I. It has an observation platform 105 metres (344 feet) above the lake, with expansive views as far as Spandau and Potsdam. There is a restaurant at the base, and another over the road, both with garden terraces. A short walk south along Havelufer leads to the ferry to **Lindwerder Insel** (island), which also has a restaurant. To the north, a little way into the forest, the singer Nico, who grew up in Schöneberg, is buried among the trees in the **Friedhof Grunewald-Forst**.

Alliierten Museum

Clayallee 135, corner of Huttenweg (818 1990/ www.alliiertenmuseum.de). U3 Oskar-Helene-Heim/bus 115. **Open** 10am-6pm Mon, Tue, Thur-Sun. **Admission** free.
The Allies arrived as conquerors, kept West Berlin alive during the 1948 Airlift and finally went home in 1994. In what used to be a US Forces cinema, the Allied Museum is mostly about the period of the Blockade and Airlift, documented with photos, tanks, jeeps, planes, weapons and uniforms. Outside is the former guardhouse from Checkpoint Charlie and an RAF Hastings TG 503. Guided tours in English can be booked in advance. It's ten minutes' walk north up Clayallee from the U-Bahn station.

Brücke-Museum

Bussardsteig 9 (831 2029/www.bruecke-museum.de). U3 Oskar-Helene-Heim, then bus 115 to Pücklerstrasse. **Open** 11am-5pm Mon, Wed-Sun. **Admission** €4; €2 reductions. *Temporary exhibitions* €5 **No credit cards.**
This small but satisfying museum is dedicated to the work of Die Brücke ('The Bridge'), a group of expressionist painters that was founded in Dresden in 1905 before later moving to Berlin. A large collection of oils, watercolours, drawings and sculptures

by the main members of the group – Schmidt-Rottluff, Heckel, Kirchner, Mueller and Pechstein – is rotated in temporary exhibitions.

Wannsee & Pfaueninsel

At the south-west edge of the Grunewald, you'll find boats and beaches in summer, and castles and forests all through the year. **Strandbad Wannsee** is the largest inland beach in Europe. Between May and September, there are boats and pedalos and hooded, two-person wicker sunchairs for hire, a playground and a separate section for nudists. Service buildings house showers, toilets, cafés, shops and kiosks.

The waters of the Havel (the Wannsee is an inlet of the river) are extensive and in summer warm enough for comfortable swimming; there is a strong current, so don't stray beyond the floating markers.

A small bridge north of the beach leads to Schwanenwerder, once the exclusive private island retreat of Goebbels and now home to the international think-tank, the Aspen Institute.

The town of Wannsee to the south is clustered around the bay of the Grosser Wannsee and is dominated by the long stretch of promenade, Am Grossen Wannsee, scattered with hotels and fish restaurants. On the west side of the bay is the **Gedenkstätte Haus der Wannsee-Konferenz** (*see p128*). At this elegant Gründerzeit mansion, now a museum, a January 1942 meeting of prominent Nazis laid out plans for the extermination of the Jews.

A short distance from S-Bahn Wannsee along Bismarckstrasse is a little garden where German dramatist Heinrich von Kleist shot himself in 1811; the beautiful view of Kleiner Wannsee was the last thing he wanted to see.

On the other side of the railway tracks is **Düppler Forst**, a forest including a nature reserve at Grosses Fenn at the south-western end. Travelling three S-Bahn stops to Mexikoplatz, then taking the 629 or 211 bus, brings you to the reconstructed 14th-century village at **Museumsdorf Düppel** (*see p128*).

From Wannsee, bus 218 scoots through the forest to a pier on the Havel, and from there it's a brief ferry ride to **Pfaueninsel** (Peacock Island). This 242-acre island was inhabited in prehistoric times, but isn't mentioned in archives until 1683. Two years later, the Grand Elector presented it to Johann Kunckel von Löwenstein, a chemist who experimented with alchemy but instead of gold produced 'ruby glass', examples of which are on view in the castle.

It was only at the start of the Romantic era that the island's windswept charms began to attract more serious interest. In 1793, Friedrich

Beasts of Berlin

Every town has its wildlife, and Berlin is home to all the usual suspects – and more.

The city's symbol is the bear, but outside of the two zoos (*see p115 and p130*), the only place you'll encounter any of those is in the small bearpit in Köllnischer Park near the Märkisches Museum (*see p96*) – home to Schnute, Maxi and Tilo, the official bears of Berlin.

During the Cold War, Berlin was noted for its rabbits, which hopped happily around no-man's land. But one way or another, Reunification seems to have killed off the bunnies. Meanwhile, the number of foxes has increased: they're now often spotted sauntering around the inner city, and scavenging for discarded sandwiches in playground litter bins.

But the biggest increase has been in Berlin's wild boar population. *Wildschwein* often make the news. A man in Dahlem finds a boar under his dining table, which bites him when he tries to shoo it away. Hertha BSC training sessions are disrupted by wild boar tearing up one of the training pitches. They bring in a hunter who studies their habits for a week – and then kills them. A pair of wild boar were even seen in Alexanderplatz, nosing around for food.

These are not shy, retiring creatures. These are undomesticated pigs, typically weighing between 90 to 140 kilos (200-300 pounds), with five-inch tusks and a nasty temper – particularly females with children. If you encounter one, treat it with respect.

Still, many people like them, and leave out food. The abundant supply of eats in the city is one reason for the rise in numbers, along with warmer winters. City hunting consultant Derk Ehlert estimates the total population to be upwards of 8,000, bossing the forests, rooting around city parks, and even making themselves at home on overgrown railway embankments.

Wild boar have been here longer than Berlin, but racoons are a more recent arrival. A bunch of them escaped when a stray Allied bomb hit a racoon farm near Berlin during World War II. Half a century later, these small furry aliens have spread right across Germany.

Racoons have also started leaving their natural habitat near streams or lakes and moving into the city, where food and shelter are easy to find. Unfortunately, shelter often means someone's attic or cellar. Urban racoons shin up drainpipes, jump on to roofs from tree tops, or simply wander in via the cat flap. They can even turn knobs and open latches.

Once racoons have made themselves at home in your garage or gable, it's extremely difficult to get them out again. Studies show that the more of them people trap and kill, the more they breed. Urban racoon experts instead recommend preventative measures: trimming tree branches, covering drainpipes. But whatever does or does not prove effective, there's no escaping the fact that suburban Berliners are on the front line of this furry invasion.

Sowjetisches Ehrenmal (Soviet War Memorial).

Wilhelm II purchased it and built a Schloss for his mistress, but died in 1797 before they had a chance to move in. Its first residents were the happily married couple Friedrich Wilhelm III and Queen Luise, who spent much of their time together on the island, even setting up a working farm there. A royal menagerie was later developed. Most of the animals were moved to the new Tiergarten Zoo in 1842, and only peacocks, pheasants, parrots, goats and sheep remain. Surviving structures include the Jakobsbrunnen (Jacob's Fountain), a copy of a Roman temple; the Kavalierhaus (Cavalier's House), built in 1803 from an original design by Schinkel; and the Swiss cottage, also based on a Schinkel plan. All are linked by winding, informal paths laid out in the English manner by Peter Joseph Lenné. A walk around the island, with its monumental trees, rough meadows and views over the Havel, provides one of the most complete sensations of escape to be had within the borders of Berlin.

Back on the mainland, a short walk south along Nikolskoer Weg is the **Blockhaus Nikolskoe** (805 2914, www.blockhaus-nikolskoe.de), a huge wooden chalet built in 1819 by Friedrich Wilhelm II for his daughter Charlotte, and named after her husband, the future Tsar Nicholas of Russia. There is a magnificent view from the terrace, where you can sit back and enjoy mid-priced Berlin cuisine or coffee and cakes.

Gedenkstätte Haus der Wannsee-Konferenz

Am Grossen Wannsee 56-58 (805 0010/ www.ghwk.de). S1, S7 Wannsee, then bus 114. **Open** 10am-6pm daily. **Admission** free.

On 20 January 1942, a collection of prominent Nazis, chaired by Heydrich, gathered here to draw up plans for the Final Solution, making jokes and sipping brandy as they sorted out the practicalities of genocide. Today, this infamous villa has been converted into the Wannsee Conference Memorial House, a place of remembrance, with a photo exhibit on the conference and its consequences. Call in advance if you want to join an English-language tour otherwise all information is in German.

Museumsdorf Düppel

Clauertstrasse 11 (802 6671/www.dueppel.de). S1 Mexikoplatz, then bus 118, 629. **Open** 3-7pm Thur; 10am-5pm Sun. Last entry 1hr before closing. Closed Nov-Feb. **Admission** €2; €1 reductions. **No credit cards.**

At this 14th-century village, reconstructed around archaeological excavations, workers demonstrate handicrafts, medieval technology and farming techniques. Ox-cart rides for kids. Small snack bar.

Glienicke

West of Wannsee, and only a couple of kilometres from Potsdam, Glienicke was once the south-westernmost tip of West Berlin. The suspension bridge over the Havel here was named **Brücke der Einheit** ('Bridge of Unity')

because it joined Potsdam with Berlin. After the building of the Wall, it was painted different shades of olive green on the East and West sides and used only by Allied soldiers and for top-level prisoner and spy exchanges – Anatoly Scharansky was one of the last in 1986.

The main reason to come here is **Park Glienicke**. Its centrepiece is Schloss Glienicke (which is not open to the public), originally a hunting lodge designed by Schinkel for Prinz Carl von Preussen, who adorned the garden walls with ancient relics collected on his Mediterranean holidays, and decided to simulate a walk from the Alps to Rome in the densely wooded park. The summer houses, fountains and follies are all based on original Italian models, and the woods and fields around them make an ideal place for a Sunday picnic, since this park is little visited.

At the nearby inlet of Moorlake, there's a restaurant in a 1842 hunting lodge.

East & south-east of the centre

Lichtenberg & Treptow

Many of the neighbourhoods in the old East have little to offer the visitor. East of Prenzlauer Berg and Friedrichshain, Lichtenberg isn't very appealing, though it does contain the **Tierpark**

Berlin-Friedrichsfelde (Berlin-Friedrichsfelde Zoo; *see p130*) and both the Stasi Museum, more properly known as the **Forschungs- und Gedenkstätte Normannenstrasse** (*see below*), and the **Gedenkstätte Berlin-Hohenschönhausen** (*see p130*), a former Stasi prison turned chilling exhibit of state oppression. Further south is the **Museum Berlin-Karlshorst** (*see p130*), documenting the somewhat troubled history of Russian-German relations during the last century.

South of Lichtenberg and bordering Neukölln, Treptow is chiefly of note for **Treptower Park**, containing the massive Sowjetisches Ehrenmal (Soviet War Memorial). From here, several boats leave in the summer for trips along the Spree.

The park continues to the south, where it becomes the **Plänterwald** and houses a big amusement park.

Forschungs- und Gedenkstätte Normannenstrasse (Stasi Museum)

Ruschestrasse 103 (553 6854/www.stasimuseum.de). U5, S41, S42, S8, S85 Frankfurter Allee or U5 Magdalenenstrasse. **Open** 11am-6pm Mon-Fri; 2-6pm Sat, Sun. **Admission** €4.50; €2.50 reductions. **No credit cards.**
In what used to be part of the headquarters of the Stasi, you can look around what used to be the offices of secret police chief Erich Mielke – his old uniform still hangs in his wardrobe – and see the

displays of bugging devices and spy cameras concealed in books, plant pots and car doors, all in the service of what was one of the most thoroughgoing police states in history. Documentation is in German, but tours in English can be booked in advance. *See also p16* **Truth and spies.**

Gedenkstätte Berlin-Hohenschönhausen

Gensler Strasse 66 (9860 8230/www.stiftung-hsh.de). M5 Freienwalder Strasse or M6 Gensler Strasse. **Open** *Guided tours* (German) 11am, 1pm Mon-Fri; every hr 10am-4pm Sat, Sun. *Guided tours* (English) 2pm Sat or by request; group tours book in advance. **Admission** €4; free-€2 reductions. Free to all Mon. **No credit cards.**

A sprawling former remand prison run by the Stasi, the building has a dirty history. Originally the site of a canteen for the Nazi social welfare organ, it was turned into 'Special Encampment No.3' by the Soviets and later expanded by the MfS (Ministerium für Staatssicherheit; Stasi). Excellent and highly personal guided tours by ex-prisoners take 90 minutes. The inmates were all political prisoners, from the leaders of the 1953 workers' uprising to critical students. The experience is gut-wrenchingly bleak, but a potent insight into how the Stasi operated. On one interrogator's office wall hangs a painting of a fairytale castle, underneath which prisoners underwent horrifying psychological interrogation.

Museum Berlin-Karlshorst

Zwieseler Strasse 4, corner of Rheinsteinstrasse (5015 0810/www.museum-karlshorst.de). S3 Karlshorst. **Open** 10am-6pm Tue-Sun. **Admission** free.

After the Soviets took Berlin, they commandeered this former German officers' club as HQ for the military administration and it was here, on the night of 8-9 May 1945, that German commanders signed the unconditional surrender, ending the war in Europe. The museum looks at the German-Soviet relationship over 70 years. Divided into 16 rooms, including the one where the Nazis surrendered, it takes us through two world wars and one cold one, plus assorted pacts, victories and capitulations. Exhibits include photos, memorabilia, maps, videos and propaganda posters. Buy a guide in English; exhibits are labelled in German and Russian. English tours can be booked in advance.

Tierpark Berlin-Friedrichsfelde

Am Tierpark 125 (515 310/www.tierpark-berlin.de). U5 Tierpark. **Open** *Jan-late Mar, late Oct-Dec* 9am-4pm daily. *Late Mar-mid Sept* 9am-6pm daily. *Mid Sept-late Oct* 9am-5pm daily. **Admission** €11; €8 reductions; family €18-€29. **No credit cards.**

One of Europe's largest zoos, with plenty of roaming space for herd animals, although others are still kept in small cages. Resident beasts include bears, elephants, big cats and penguins. In the zoo's north-west corner is the baroque Schloss Friedrichsfelde. One of the continent's biggest snake farms is also here.

Köpenick

The name Köpenick is derived from the Slavonic *copanic*, meaning 'place on a river'. The old town, around 15 kilometres (nine miles) south-east of Mitte, stands at the confluence of the Spree and Dahme, and, having escaped bombing, decay and development by the DDR, still maintains much of its 18th-century character. This is one of the most sought-after areas of East Berlin, with handsome shops, cafés and restaurants clustered around the old centre. With its old buildings and extensive riverfront, it's a fine place for a Sunday afternoon wander.

The imposing **Rathaus** (Town Hall) is a good example of Wilhelmine civic architecture. It was here in 1906, two years after the building's completion, that Wilhelm Voigt, an unemployed cobbler who'd spent half his life in jail, dressed up as an army captain and ordered a detachment of soldiers to accompany him into the Treasury, where they emptied the town coffers. He instantly entered popular folklore. Carl Zuckmeyer immortalised him in a play as Der Hauptmann von Köpenick ('Captain of Köpenick') and the Kaiser pardoned him because he had shown how obedient Prussian soldiers were. His theft is re-enacted every June during the Köpenicker summer festival.

Close by is **Schloss Köpenick** (*see below*), with medieval drawbridge, Renaissance gateway and baroque chapel.

Schloss Köpenick

Schlossinsel 1 (6566 1749/www.smb.museum). S47 Spindlersfeld. **Open** 10am-6pm Tue-Sun. **Admission** €4; €2 reductions. **No credit cards.**

Overspill from the Kunstgewerbemuseum is presented as 'RoomArt', with furniture and decorative art from the Renaissance, baroque and rococo eras arranged according to period beneath carefully restored ceiling paintings. There's also an exhibition on the history of the island, plus a riverside café.

Friedrichshagen & the Müggelsee

A couple of kilometres east of Köpenick, the village of **Friedrichshagen** has retained its independent character. The main street, **Bölschestrasse**, is lined with steep-roofed Brandenburg houses, and ends at the shores of a large lake, the **Grösser Müggelsee**.

Friedrichshagen is particularly enjoyable when the **Berliner Burgerbräu** brewery, family-owned since 1869, throws open its gates for its annual summer celebration. Stalls line Bölschestrasse, the brewery lays on music, and people lounge about on the lake shore with cold beer. Boat tours are available, and the restaurant Braustubl, next to the brewery, serves good Berlin cuisine.

Eat, Drink, Shop

Gorki Park. *See p156.*

Restaurants

Traditional dishes may be rudimentary, but there's more to pig out on than pork, cabbage and Currywurst.

As the French would say, 'the cuisine is in the soil'. In Brandenburg, the soil is sandy, and not much good for growing anything but cabbage and potatoes. Along with pork, they're the staples. Berlin's signature dish is *Eisbein* – leathery-skinned and extremely fatty pig's trotter, sometimes marinated, and served with puréed peas – but you'll find this only in the most old-school of places.

So while there are many reasons to visit Berlin, the quality of the food has not traditionally been one of them. Yes, you can dine well here. In fact, with the arrival of the government to stimulate the high end, and an increasingly cosmopolitan population to encourage ethnic variety at street level, you can dine better than ever here. Restaurants tend to be relaxed and roomy and there are interesting options at all price levels. And if you can still

> ❶ Purple numbers given in this chapter correspond to the location of each restaurant as marked on the street maps. *See pp316-328.*

The best Restaurants

Edd's
Top of the Thais. *See p148.*

Grill Royal
See, be seen – and eat steaks. *See p135.*

Konnopke's Imbiss
The *Grossvater* of all sausage stalls. *See p142*

Maxwell
Local ingredients, subtle flavours, super courtyard. *See p137.*

Monsieur Vuong
Perennially popular Vietnamese diner. *See p134.*

Schneeweiss
Inventive Alpine fusion in soothing surrounds. *See p144.*

sense the poverty of any indigenous gastronomic tradition, well, it's not something the English have much right to complain about.

The fact that half the city spent most of the last 50 years cut off from gastronomic trends and deprived of exotic ingredients didn't help eradicate a certain culinary conservatism. The brevity of Germany's colonial experience has meant no deep-rooted link with a foreign cuisine, such as Britain with India's, or Morocco's with France. There's no great ethnic presence here beside the Turks, and they prefer to cook at home while selling snacks to the general public.

But Reunification meant both a more travelled population with a more adventurous palate, and lots of cheap real estate where young restaurateurs could try out their ideas. This has resulted in lighter, healthier and better seasoned eating. It's also improved for vegetarians, as most decent restaurants now include a couple of options on the menu.

On the other hand, there's still plenty missing. Chinese food is rare; good Chinese even rarer. Same for Mexican. Indian restaurants are everywhere, but are of a uniformly mediocre standard. Sushi places have erupted, but it's hard to find any other kind of Japanese food.

For snacking on the hoof, bakeries usually offer a desultory selection of bread rolls filled with cheese or ham. For something more, try an *Imbiss*. The term embraces just about anywhere you get food but not table service, from stand-up street corner stalls to self-service snack bars offering exotic cuisines. Quality varies wildly, but some excellent, cheap food can be found. Turkish places offer the ubiquitous Kebap, Turkish 'pizza', half chickens and salads. The German *Imbisse* will tempt you with various kinds of sausage (*see p153* **The odd history of the Currywurst**).

In restaurants, diners usually add ten per cent to the bill for service, unless it has been awful (not impossible in Berlin). Tips are handed to the server (or you tell staff how much to take) rather than being left on the table. When you hand over the cash, don't say '*danke*' unless you want staff to keep the change.

Note that some restaurants close for their holidays in late July/early August.

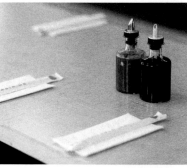

Pan Asia. *See p134.*

Asian

Good Time

Chausseestrasse 1 (2804 6015/www.goodtime-berlin.de). U6 Oranienburger Tor. **Open** noon-midnight daily. **Main courses** €9.50-€19.50. **Credit** AmEx, MC, V. **Map** p318/p326 M5

Indonesian food is rare in Berlin, and this friendly place does it well. The rijstafel, the soup and the rendang (a beef dish) are all excellent. German tastes are catered to with a wide range of noodle dishes and there are Thai specialities too.

Ishin Mitte

Mittelstrasse 24 (2067 4829/www.ishin.de). U6, S1, S2, S5, S7, S9, S75 Friedrichstrasse. **Open** 11am-8pm Mon-Fri; 11am-6pm Sat. **Main courses** €5-€14. **No credit cards. Map** p318/p327 M6 ❷

Roomy but crowded, with a constant stream of happy hour-style discounts (starting at €5.50), this is probably the best money-for-quality sushi deal in Berlin. The fish is fresh, with specials offered daily, and portions are generous: when was the last time you actually received more food than the photos on the menu suggested?

Other locations Galleria Steglitz, Schlossstrasse 101, Steglitz (797 1049); Berlinickestrasse 1A, Steglitz (8182 7071).

Kuchi

Gippsstrasse 3 (2838 6622/www.kuchi.de). U8 Weinmeisterstrasse. **Open** noon-midnight Mon-Sat; 6pm-midnight Sun. **Main courses** €7-€16. **Credit** AmEx, MC, V. **Map** p319/p326 N5 ❸

It's the quality of the ingredients at this Japanese that makes the food special. And it isn't just fish in the sushi rolls: one maki is filled with chicken, mandarin oranges and poppy seeds. Delicate tempura, yakitori chicken hearts or shiitake mushrooms are all excellently served by a young, cool and multinational team. Packed at lunch. The other branch has a takeaway next door that also delivers.

Other locations Kantstrasse 30 (3150 7815/delivery service 3150 7816).

Mirchi

Oranienburger Strasse 50 (2844 4480/www.mirchi.de). U6 Oranienburger Tor. **Open** noon-1am Mon-Thur, Sun; noon-2am Fri, Sat. **Main courses** €7-€14. **Credit** AmEx, MC, V. **Map** p318/p326 M5 ❹

An ambitious 'Singapore fusion' concept sees Indian, Chinese, Thai and Malay ideas mingling on a creative menu. The hearty Thai-Indian soups show the kitchen at its simple, tasty best. Nice entrance, lots of space, useful location.

Monsieur Vuong

Alte Schönhauser Strasse 46 (3087 2643/www.monsieurvuong.de). U8 Weinmeisterstrasse. **Open** noon-midnight Mon-Sat; 2pm-midnight Sun. **Main courses** €7.40. **No credit cards. Map** p319/p326 O5 ❺

River views and glamour: **Grill Royal**.

Something of an institution, serving fresh and tasty Vietnamese soups and noodles. A couple of daily specials supplement a handful of regular dishes. Once you've tried the glass noodle salad, you'll understand why less is more. Chic, cheap and cheery, but often packed to the rafters. If you're too hungry to wait, there is similar fare at Manngo, round the corner at Mulackstrasse 29.

Pan Asia

Rosenthaler Strasse 38 (2790 8811/www.panasia.de). U8 Weinmeisterstrasse or S5, S7, S9, S75 Hackescher Markt. **Open** noon-midnight daily. **Main courses** €6-€14. **Credit** AmEx, DC, MC, V. **Map** p319/p326 N5 ❻

Hidden in a pleasant courtyard off busy Rosenthaler, with tables outside in summer, this is a fashionably minimalist place to see, be seen and eat modern Asian food. Japanese beers and Chinese teas complement excellent wun tun, kimchi salad and a variety of soups and wok dishes. Downsides? Self-conscious crowd, unbelievable bathrooms, inconsistent service.

French

Bandol sur Mer

Torstrasse 167 (6730 2051). U8 Rosenthaler Platz.
Open 6pm-late daily. **Main courses** €19.50-€23.50.
No credit cards. Map p319/p326 N5 **❼**
At last, true French bistro fare in a low-key yet
Gallic-elegant atmosphere. Once a kebab stand, this
teensy restaurant has space for only 22 diners inside,
but Berliners line up for its exquisite entrecôte, innovative seafood (try the swordfish) and an extensive
selection of excellent French and German wines.
Everything comes fresh from the market and the
chefs aren't afraid to add slight twists to the classics, either. The evening's specials are handwritten
in chalk on the wall, and reservations are mandatory
for the two seatings. Even Brad Pitt's a fan.

Entrecôte Fred's

Schutzenstrasse 5 (2016 5496/www.entrecote.de).
U2, U6 Stadtmitte. **Open** 11.30am-midnight Mon-
Fri; 5pm-midnight Sat. **Main courses** €12-€24.
Credit AmEx, DC, MC, V. **Map** p322/p327 M8 **❽**
Steak and frites in a brasserie ambience close to
Checkpoint Charlie. The food is simple but well pre-
pared and Fred's Special Sauce, a mixed herb
remoulade, is excellent. The long wine list encom-
passes all French regions, and there are half bottles
too. Service is very professional.

Margaux

Unter den Linden 78 (2265 2611/www.margaux-
berlin.de). S1, S2 Unter den Linden. **Open** 7-10.30pm
Mon-Sat. **Main courses** €30-€50. **Credit** AmEx,
DC, MC, V. **Map** p318/p327 L6 **❾**
This top-flight place features Michael Hoffman's
slightly avant-garde take on classic French cooking,
such as stewed shoulder of venison seasoned with
coriander, anise and saffron. The spacious interior is
lit by glowing columns of honey-hued onyx, which
reflect in black marble floors. The restaurant is named
for its extraordinary wine list, which includes some
30 vintages of Château Margaux. Service is first-rate.

German, Austrian & Swiss

AlpenStueck

Gartenstrasse 9 (2175 1646/www.alpenstueck.de).
S1, S2, S25 Nordbahnhof. **Open** 6pm-late Tue-Sun.
Main courses €14.50-€17.50. **Credit** AmEx, MC,
V. **Map** p318/p326 M4 **❿**
Ambitious but not over-the-top, artsy but not pretentious, AlpenStueck offers Austrian and south
German classics served in a cool ambience.
Everything from the strudel crust to the bread is
handcrafted; the entrées, including a roast beef
smothered in crispy onions and medallions of pork
with rösti potatoes and endive salad are at the level
where you just can't help talking about flavours and
textures. The pasta, including noodles and peas with
cherry tomatoes as a starter, is especially memo-
rable. Good wine list and desserts too.

Borchardt

Französische Strasse 47 (8188 6262). U6
Französische Strasse. **Open** 11.30am-late daily.
Main courses €16-€22. **Credit** AmEx, MC, V.
Map p322/p327 M7 **⓫**
In the late 19th century, the original Borchardt
opened next door at no.48. It became the place to be
for politicians and society folk, but was destroyed
in World War II. Now Roland Mary and Marina
Richter have reconstructed a highly fashionable,
Maxim's-inspired bistro serving respectable French
food. So why not snarf down a dozen oysters and
tuck into a fillet of pike-perch or beef after a cultural
evening nearby?

Café Nö!

Glinkastrasse 23 (201 0871/www.cafe-noe.de). U6
Französische Strasse. **Open** noon-1am Mon-Fri;
7pm-1am Sat. **Main courses** €4-€12. **Credit**
AmEx. **Map** p322/p327 M7 **⓬**
This unassuming but right-on wine bar with simple
and wholesome meals is owned by a former DDR
rock musician now continuing his family's gastron-
omy tradition, and given the mostly bland or over-
priced restaurants in this neighbourhood, it's a
genuine pearl. Snacks include bruschetta and
marinated plums baked with bacon; Alsatian
flammkuchen and lamb ragout are among the din-
ners. All the food goes well with an intelligent,
international wine list.

Grill Royal

Friedrichstrasse 105B (2887 9288/www.grill
royal.com). U6, S1, S2, S5, S7, S9, S25, S75
Friedrichstrasse. **Open** 6pm-1am daily. **Main**
courses €15-€55. **Credit** AmEx, MC, V.
Map p318/p326 M5 **⓭**
With its entrance on the promenade by the Spree just
down the steps from the north side of
Weidendammer Brücke, this comfortably cavernous
restaurant is more reminiscent of London or Paris
than Berlin, both in scale and colour scheme. In the
beginning it seemed full of what pass for celebrities
in Germany's capital, but has now settled into a
smoothly functioning eaterie for a well-heeled but
more anonymous crowd. They come to enjoy fine
steaks of Irish, French or Argentine provenance,
plus a few other meat and fish dishes, and relax in
river views and a picture window that turns the
kitchen into theatre. Reservations essential.

Honigmond

Borsigstrasse 28 (2844 5512/www.honigmond-
berlin.de). U6 Zinnowitzer Strasse. **Open** 7am-1am
Mon-Fri; 8am-1am Sat, Sun. **Main courses** €8.50-
€15. **Credit** MC, V. **Map** p318/p326 M4 **⓮**
This quiet neighbourhood place serves up traditional
German food alongside an innovative menu that
ranges from kangaroo to fondue. Noteworthy are the
Königsberger Klöpse (east Prussian meatballs in a
creamy caper sauce) and a very good Caesar salad.
Excellent wine list and remarkable home-made
bread (and butter!). It's also a hotel (*see p59*).

YOU KNOW WHO YOU ARE.

BERLIN • MEINEKESTRASSE 21
+49-30-884-620 • HARDROCK.COM

Kellerrestaurant im Brecht-Haus

Chausseestrasse 125 (282 3843/www.brechtkeller.
de). U6 Oranienburger Tor. **Open** 6pm-1am daily.
Main courses €10-€16. **Credit** AmEx, MC.
Map p318/p326 M5 ⓫

Bertholt Brecht got that sleek, well-fed look from
the cooking his partner Helene Weigel learned in
Vienna and Bohemia. This atmospheric place,
crammed with model stage sets and Brecht memorabilia, serves a number of her specialities, including Fleischlabberln (spicy meat patties) and a
mighty Wiener Schnitzel. In summer, the garden
doubles capacity.

Lebensmittel im Mitte

Rochstrasse 2 (2759 6130). U2 Weinmeisterstrasse.
Open 8am-midnight Mon-Fri; 10am-midnight Sat.
Food served 1-11pm Mon-Fri; 5-11pm Sat. **Main
courses** €4-€16. **No credit cards**. **Map** p319/
p326 O5 ⓰

This deli/restaurant, whose name means 'groceries
in Mitte' – is a little journey into the joys of southern German and Austrian cuisine. Up front are fine
cheeses, huge loaves of rustic bread, organic veggies, sausage, even Austrian pumpkin seed oil to
take away. But guests can also stay, settle into long
wooden benches under the antlers on the wall, and
dine on high-fat, carbo-loaded southern German
specialities such as Leberkäse, tongue, rösti and
cheese spätzle, accompanied by a broad selection
of southern German and Austrian wines or authentic Bavarian beer.

Lutter & Wegner

Charlottenstrasse 56 (202 9540/www.lutter-wegner-
gendarmenmarkt.de). U2, U6 Stadtmitte. **Open**
11am-midnight daily. **Main courses** €18-€30.
Credit AmEx, MC, V. **Map** p322/p327 M7 ⓱

This place has it all: history (an early Berlin wine
merchant, its sparkling wine became known as
'Sekt', now the common German term); a lovely
atmosphere in its airy, elegant rooms; great
German/Austrian/French cuisine; and excellent
service. The wine list is justifiably legendary, and
if the prices look high, head for the bistro, where
the same list holds sway along with perfect salads,
cheese and ham plates, plus excellent desserts.

Maxwell

Bergstrasse 22 (280 7121/www.mxwl.de). U8
Rosenthaler Platz or S1, S2, S25 Nordbahnhof.
Open 6pm-midnight daily. **Main courses** €16-€22.
Credit AmEx, MC, V. **Map** p319/p326 N4 ⓲

Set in a beautiful neo-gothic former brewery,
tucked away in a peaceful courtyard with great
summer tables, chef and proprietor Uwe Popall pre-
sides over a relaxed and tasteful atmosphere while
offering a light, eclectic menu. His stress on local,
seasonal ingredients (the spring asparagus menu
is always a sublime treat) and philosophy of colourful simplicity is popular with the art scene and
younger diplomatic crowd. Maxwell is one of our
confirmed favourites too.

Maxwell.

Eat, Drink, Shop

Understanding the menu

GUGELHOF

USEFUL PHRASES
I'd like to reserve a table for...
people. **Ich möchte einen Tisch
für... Personen reservieren.**
Are these places free? **Sind diese Plätze frei?**
The menu, please. **Die Speisekarte, bitte.**
I am a vegetarian. **Ich bin Vegetarier.**
We'd/I'd like to order. **Wir möchten/
Ich möchte bestellen.**
We'd/I'd like to pay. **Bezahlen, bitte.**

BASICS
Frühstück breakfast. **Mittagessen** lunch.
Abendessen dinner. **Imbiss** snack.
Vorspeise appetiser. **Hauptgericht** main
course. **Nachspeise** dessert. **Brot/Brötchen**
bread/rolls. **Butter** butter. **Ei/Eier** egg/eggs.
Spiegeleier fried eggs. **Rühreier** scrambled
eggs. **Käse** cheese. **Nudeln/Teigwaren**
noodles/pasta. **Sosse** sauce. **Salz** salt.
Pfeffer pepper. **gekocht** boiled. **gebraten**
fried/roasted. **paniert** breaded/battered.

SOUPS (SUPPEN)
Bohnensuppe bean soup. **Brühe** broth.
Erbsensuppe pea soup. **Hühnersuppe** chicken
soup. **klare Brühe mit Leberknödeln** clear
broth with liver dumplings. **Kraftbrühe** clear
meat broth. **Linsensuppe** lentil soup.

MEAT, POULTRY AND GAME
(FLEISCH, GEFLÜGEL UND WILD)
Boulette meatball. **Ente** duck. **Gans**
goose. **Hackfleisch** mince. **Hirsch** venison.
Huhn/Hühnerfleisch chicken. **Hähnchen**
chicken (when served in one piece).
Kaninchen rabbit. **Kohlrouladen** cabbage-rolls
stuffed with pork. **Kotelett** chop. **Lamm** lamb.
Leber liver. **Nieren** kidneys. **Rindfleisch** beef.

Nola's am Weinberg
Veteranenstrasse 9 (4404 0766/www.nola.de).
U8 Rosenthaler Platz. **Open** 10am-2am daily.
Main courses €9-€17. **Credit** MC, V. **Map**
p319/p326 N4 ⑲
Swiss food in a former park pavilion, with a quiet
terrace as well as a spacious bar and dining room.
It's hearty fare, such as venison goulash with
mushrooms and spinach noodles, or rösti with
spinach and cheese with fried eggs. The goat's
cheese mousse with rocket starter is big enough for
two and it's worth noting that, with a little thought,
it's possible to eat quite cheaply here.
Other locations Nola's in Tiergarten, Dortmunder
Strasse 9, Tiergarten (399 6969).

Schwarzwaldstuben
Tucholskystrasse 48 (2809 8084). S1, S2
Oranienburger Strasse. **Main courses** €7-€14.50.
Open 9am-11pm Mon-Fri; 9am-midnight Sat, Sun.
No credit cards. Map p318/p326 M5 ⑳
Some of the best German cuisine comes from
Swabia, but Swabian restaurants tend to be filled
with teddy bears and knick-knacks. This place,
however, is a casually chic affair, and wears its
mounted deer head ironically. The food is excel-
lent. The soups are hearty, standout main courses

include the Schäuffele with sauerkraut and potatoes,
and the Flammkuchen (a sort of German pizza) is
good. Rothaus Tannenzapfle beer on tap.

Vau
Jägerstrasse 54-55 (202 9730/www.vau-berlin.de).
U6 Französische Strasse. **Open** noon-2.30pm,
7-10.30pm Mon-Sat. *Set menus* €78-€110. **Credit**
AmEx, DC, MC, V. **Map** p322/p327 M7 ㉑
Love of innovation and inspiration from all corners
of the globe make chef Kolja Kleeberg's menu one
of the best in town. His lobster with mango and
black olives with tapenade, and braised pork belly
with grilled scallops, are complemented by an extensive wine list (bottles from €30). Downstairs, the
fake library bar (the 'books' are bricks of coal) is
great for special occasions. Booking essential.

Weinbar Rutz
Chausseestrasse 8 (2462 8760/www.rutz-weinbar.de).
U6 Zinnowitzer Strasse. **Open** 6.30pm-midnight
Mon-Sat. **Main courses** €29-€34. **Credit** AmEx,
DC, MC, V. **Map** p318/p326 M5 ㉒
The impressive ground-floor bar has a whole wall
showcasing wines from around the globe – not
obscure New World vintages, but the best of the
best. There are no tasting notes on the exhaustive

Eat, Drink, Shop

Sauerbraten marinated roast beef.
Schinken ham. **Schnitzel** thinly pounded
piece of meat, usually breaded and
sautéed. **Schweinebraten** roast pork.
Schweinefleisch pork. **Speck** bacon.
Truthahn turkey. **Wachteln** quail.
Wurst sausage.

FISH (FISCH)
Aal eel. **Forelle** trout. **Garnelen** prawns.
Hummer lobster. **Kabeljau** cod. **Karpfen**
carp. **Krabbe** crab or shrimp. **Lachs** salmon.
Makrele mackerel. **Matjes/Hering** raw
herring. **Miesmuscheln** mussels. **Schellfisch**
haddock. **Scholle** plaice. **Seezunge** sole.
Thunfisch tuna. **Tintenfisch** squid.
Venusmuscheln clams. **Zander** pike-perch.

HERBS AND SPICES (KRÄUTER UND GEWÜRZE)
Basilikum basil. **Kümmel** caraway.
Mohn poppyseed. **Nelken** cloves.
Origanum oregano. **Petersilie** parsley.
Thymian thyme. **Zimt** cinnamon.

VEGETABLES (GEMÜSE)
Blumenkohl cauliflower. **Bohnen**
beans. **Bratkartoffeln** fried potatoes.
Brechbohnen green beans.

Champignons/Pilze mushrooms. **Erbsen**
green peas. **Erdnüsse** peanuts. **grüne**
Zwiebel spring onion. **Gurke** cucumber.
Kartoffel potato. **Knoblauch** garlic.
Kichererbsen chick peas. **Knödel** dumpling.
Kohl cabbage. **Kürbis** pumpkin. **Linsen**
lentils. **Möhren** carrots. **Paprika** peppers.
Pommes chips. **Rosenkohl** Brussels sprouts.
Rösti roast grated potatoes. **rote Bete**
beetroot. **Rotkohl** red cabbage. **Salat**
lettuce. **Salzkartoffeln** boiled potatoes.
Sauerkraut shredded white cabbage.
Spargel asparagus. **Tomaten** tomatoes.
Zucchini courgettes. **Zwiebeln** onions.

FRUIT (OBST)
Ananas pineapple. **Apfel** apple. **Apfelsine**
orange. **Birne** pear. **Erdbeeren** strawberries.
Heidelbeeren blueberries. **Himbeeren**
raspberries. **Kirsch** cherry. **Limette** lime.
Zitrone lemon.

DRINKS (GETRÄNKE)
Bier beer. **dunkles Bier/helles Bier** dark
beer/lager. **Glühwein** mulled wine.
Kaffee coffee. **Mineralwasser** mineral
water. **Orangensaft** orange juice.
Saft juice. **Tee** tea. **Wein** wine.

list, however. The second-floor restaurant serves a
limited nouvelle menu, all of it beautifully presented.
Snacks downstairs. Booking essential.

Imbiss/fast food

Dolores
Rosa-Luxemburg-Strasse 7 (2809 9597/www.
dolores-berlin.de). U2, U5, U8, S5, S7, S9, S75
Alexanderplatz. **Open** 11.30am-11pm Mon-Sat;
1-10pm Sun. **Main courses** €3.90-€5.90.
No credit cards. Map p319/p326 O5 ㉓
For fans of the Northern California-style burrito, this
is a true haven. Black beans and lime rice mix with
fresh greens and a choice of fillings, such as grilled
chicken, marinated beef and tofu. The guacamole is
always fresh and perfectly spicy. Delivery service
too, or you can call in your order and collect.

Der Imbiss W
Kastanienallee 49 (4849 2657). U8 Rosenthaler
Platz. **Open** *Summer* noon-midnight daily. *Winter*
12.30-11.30pm daily. **Main courses** €4-€6.50.
No credit cards. Map p319/p328 O4 ㉔
Owned by 103 (*see p155*), the bar next door, this
vogueish place is named for Gordon W, a minor
celebrity chef from Canada, who devised its wacky

fusion menu of 'naan pizzas', 'rice shells' and international 'dressings'. The food is clever but it's not
always that well executed and the open kitchen can
be a bit much in the small space. Grab an outside
table in summer.

RNBS
Oranienburger Strasse 27 (0179 540 2505/
www.rnbs.de). S1, S2 Oranienburger Strasse.
Open noon-10pm daily. **Main courses** €2.50-
€5.90. **No credit cards. Map** p319/p326 N5 ㉕
Vogueish eau de Nil and orange interior for a New
Agey selection of pan-Asian rice paper rolls, noodles, meat- and fishballs, and soups. Fast food with
no artificial ingredients or flavourings.

Italian

Malatesta
Charlottenstrasse 59 (2094 5071/www.ristorante-
malatesta.de). U2, U6 Stadtmitte. **Open** noon-
midnight daily. **Main courses** €7-€21. **Credit**
AmEx, MC, V. **Map** p322/p327 M7 ㉖
This nicely located, first-rate Italian is spread out
over two floors. Downstairs there's a small bar for
an aperitif or coffee. Starters such as grilled artichoke
hearts and antipasto misto, familiar home-made

Eat, Drink, Shop

pastas, daily fish specialities and meat dishes such as oxtail filled with truffles are among the reasons to linger upstairs. Service is attentive but not intrusive. The third of Piero de Vetis' restaurants (after Osteria No.1, *see p147*, and Sale e Tabacchi, *see p147*) and definitely the best.

Papà Pane di Sorrento

Ackerstrasse 23 (2809 2701/www.papapane.de). U8 Rosenthaler Platz, S1, S2, S25 Nordbahnhof. **Open** noon-midnight daily. **No credit cards. Main courses** €13.50-€16.50. **Map.** p319/p326 N4 ㉗
Streetside windows, an open, high-ceilinged dining room, and lots of Italian-restaurant bustle provide a perfect frame for excellent pizzas and delicious pastas. Papà Pane is a lunchtime favourite for gallerists and creative types working nearby on Brunnenstrasse's back courtyards. At night, the art crowd often convenes here in large groups to see and be seen in a casual, open atmosphere. Also very family-friendly.

Salumeria Culinario

Tucholskystrasse 34 (2809 6767). S1, S2 Oranienburger Strasse. **Open** 10am-11pm Mon-Thur; 11am-midnight Fri-Sun. **Main courses** €8-€19. **No credit cards. Map** p318/p326 M5 ㉘
The daily lunch menu is a great way to recharge after a morning of shopping or gallery hopping. Pick up a bottle of wine, some cheese, olives and salami, or ponder the panettones in the Italian import section, or simply grab a plate to go. There's space for 60 at the busy beer tables on the pavement.

North African & Middle Eastern

Fanous

Brunnenstrasse 3 (4435 2503). U8 Rosenthaler Platz/bus N2, N8. **Open** 11am-1am Mon-Thur, Sun; 11am-3.30am Fri, Sat. **Main courses** €4.50-€6.50. **No credit cards. Map** p319/p326 N4 ㉙
Moroccan snack bar convenient for the Rosenthaler Platz nightlife 'hood. Deep-fried halloumi with salad in pitta, topped with mango or sesame sauce, is the best vegetarian bet. Carnivores should try the merguez (lamb sausages). Also couscous, served warm and as tabouleh salad. Free tea with meals.

Prenzlauer Berg

African

Massai

Lychenerstrasse 12 (4862 5595/www.massai-berlin.de). U2 Eberswalder Strasse. **Open** 4pm-midnight daily. **Main courses** €8.50-€28. **No credit cards. Map** p319/p328 P3 ㉚
A warm and friendly restaurant decked out in traditional Eritrean colours and serving exquisite East African dishes using palm nut oil, peanut sauce, paprika, and berbere sauce made from hot cayenne pepper, sweet paprika and ginger. Highlights include

agbisa (west African aubergines in palm nut sauce with onions and paprika) and kilwa (tender lamb fried in spicy butter). It's all pleasantly light and spicy, and you can also try ostrich and crocodile.

Americas

Bird

Am Falkplatz 5 (5105 3283/www.thebirdinberlin.com). U2, S8, S41, S42, S85 Schönhauser Allee. **Open** 6pm-late Mon-Sat; noon-late Sun. **Main courses** €9.50-€14. **No credit cards. Map** p319/p328 O2 ㉛
The Bird is probably the most authentic American burger and steak joint in Berlin, tucked on a quiet side street across from the Mauerpark. Run by renegades from New York state, it offers freshly ground burgers with a variety of toppings and a plate of hand-cut fries starting at €9.50. There are good steaks and a Caesar salad, and the cheesecake is truly homemade; and although there are some OK cocktails and whiskeys (the name is bar talk for 'Wild Turkey' bourbon), beer in pitchers is the preferred beverage order here.

Marien Burger

Marienburger Strasse 47 (3034 0515/www. marienburger-berlin.de). M2 Marienburger Strasse or M4 Hufelandstrasse. **Open** 11am-10pm Mon-Fri; 2-10pm Sat, Sun. **Main courses** €3-€5. **No credit cards. Map** p319/p328 P4 ㉜
Berlin burger bars tend to suffer from some form of pseudo-Americana theme, so this simple but lively neighbourhood hangout is a welcome relief. Grease out with the traditional variations (cheese, chilli, barbecue) or go even further with the deluxe double Marien Burger. Even the singles are pretty big. An extra 90 cents gets you organic beef, and there are also chicken, fish and vegetarian varieties.

Asian

Chinggis-Khan

Bornholmer Strasse 10 (4471 5604). S1, S2, S8, S25, S85 Bornholmer Strasse/tram 50. **Open** 4.30pm-midnight Mon-Fri; noon-midnight Sat, Sun. **Main courses** €5-€10. **Credit** AmEx, MC. **Map** p319 O1 ㉝
This Mongolian restaurant is off the beaten path but worth seeking out: the ample helpings of rice, fried beef and vegetarian dishes can fuel hordes. One delicacy is the pelmeni-like ravioli filled with meat.

Mao Thai

Wörther Strasse 30 (441 9261/www.maothai.de). U2 Senefelderplatz. **Open** noon-11pm Mon-Thur; noon-11.30pm Fri, Sat. **Main courses** €10-€20. **Credit** AmEx, DC, MC, V. **Map** p319/p328 P3 ㉞
Mao Thai's charming service and excellent food comes with a 'to whom it may concern' framed testimonial from the Thai ambassador, on the stairs down to the lower level. Classics such as tom kai gai, vegetarian spring rolls, green papaya salad with peanuts and sweet vinegar dressing, and

Eat, Drink, Shop

glass noodle salad with minced pork are all spectacular. Comfortable, well established and friendly. **Other locations** Tuans Hütte, Dirkstenstrasse 40, Mitte (283 6940); Sisaket, Mauerstrasse 76 (2065 8186).

Sian

Rykestrasse 36 (4050 5775). U2 Senefelder Platz or M2 Marienburger Strasse. **Open** noon-midnight daily. **Main courses** €5-€7.20. **No credit cards.** Map p319/p328 P3 **③⑤**
You can tell you're approaching the right address because the Asian decor is literally spilling out into the street, as is the hungry crowd at this popular Vietnamese restaurant. The small but varied menu of tasty noodle-based soups and dishes changes twice weekly. The bad news is that when it's crowded, service can be slow. The good news is that it's slow because dishes are made fresh to order.

Sumo Sushi

Kastanienallee 24 (4435 6130). U2 Eberswalder Strasse. **Open** noon-midnight Mon-Fri; 3pm-midnight Sat, Sun. **Main courses** €9-€12. **No credit cards.** Map p319/p328 O3 **③⑥**
Stands out for its sashimi, made with very fresh-tasting tuna or salmon, and California maki, rice rolls with crabmeat and avocado rolled in red caviar. **Other locations** Chausseestrasse 19, Mitte (2404 8910).

German, Austrian & Swiss

Café Oberwasser

Zionskirchstrasse 6 (no phone). U8 Bernauer Strasse/tram M1 Zionskirchplatz. **Main courses** €5-€14.50. **Open** 5pm-late daily. **No credit cards.** Map p319/p328 N4 **③⑦**
This cosy bistro-type restaurant with dim lighting and overstuffed furniture may look a bit second-hand but after a drink or two it starts to look like the attic of some faded aristocrat. The food is a combination of Russian and non-Russian cuisine, freshly prepared to order by a hostess who seems to be the only person on the job. Things go slow, but plan to make an evening of it and you won't be sorry.

Entweder Oder

Oderberger Strasse 15 (448 1382/www.cafe-eo.de). U2 Eberswalder Strasse. **Open** 10am-late daily. **Main courses** €6-€14. **No credit cards.** Map p319/p328 O3 **③⑧**
German food with a light touch: roasts, grilled fish, and the occasional schnitzel cosy up to fresh salads and simple potato side dishes. The menu changes daily and everything is organic. Connected to the underground art scene back in the days of the Wall, this place still rotates new work by local artists.

Gugelhof

Knaackstrasse 37 (442 9229/www.gugelhof.de). U2 Senefelderplatz. **Open** 4pm-1am Mon-Fri; 10am-1am Sat, Sun. **Main courses** €11.50-€20. **Credit** AmEx, MC, V. **Map** p319/p328 P4 **③⑨**
A mature Alsatian restaurant that pioneered the Kollwitzplatz scene in the 1990s. The food is refined but filling, the service formal but friendly, and the furnishings are comfortably worn in. The choucroute contains the best charcuterie in town, and the Backöfe – lamb, pork and beef marinated in riesling and stewed and served in an earthware pot with root vegetables and a bread-crust lid – shows the kitchen at its most characterful. There's also a fine selection of Alsatian tartes flambées. Reservations are very much recommended. Breakfast is served until a leisurely 4pm at weekends.

Imbiss/fast food

Fettnapf

Rykestrasse 48 (321 2464). U2 Senefelder Platz or M2 Marienburger Strasse. **Open** noon-10pm daily. **Main courses** €2.30-€12.80. **Credit** AmEx, V. **Map** p319/p328 P4 **④⓪**
Burgers and fries, bratwurst and fries, chicken and fries, steak and fries – or forget about the other stuff and just get the fries, because that's what it's all about. And none of that frozen stuff – it's all fresh cut daily. The wide assortment of toppings ranges from the usual ketchup or salsa to exotic flavours such as wasabi and truffle mayonnaise.

Konnopke's Imbiss

Under U-Bahn tracks, corner Danziger Strasse/Schönhauser Allee (no phone). U2 Eberswalder Strasse. **Open** 5am-7pm Mon-Sat. **Main courses** €1.25-€3.50. **No credit cards.** Map p319/p328 O3 **④①**
The Currywurst is justly famous at this venerable sausage stand, which has been under the same family management since 1930. *See also p153* **The odd history of the Currywurst.**

Salsabil

Wörther Strasse 16 (4404 6073). U2 Senefelderplatz. **Open** noon-midnight Mon-Fri; noon-1am Sat, Sun. **Main courses** €2.20-€6.50. **No credit cards.** Map p319/p328 P3 **④②**
This Arabic/North African *Imbiss* has all the usual trappings of tabbouleh, falafel, houmous and schwarma, plus lamb sausage, shredded chicken, lots of fried vegetables and some kind of balls made of fried egg and courgette (Eiji). It's all very tasty and reasonably priced to eat here or take out. The assorted platter for two is mammoth. Nice choice of desserts too.

Sezarmeze

Prenzlauer Allee 197 (4403 4280). U2 Eberswalder Strasse. **Open** 11am-2am daily. **Main courses** €1.80-€5. **No credit cards.** Map p319/p328 P3 **④③**
A welcome alternative to the typical Turkish *Imbiss*, featuring home-made snacks. The prerequisite falafel and schwarma are prepared with sheep cheese spreads flavoured with garlic and herbs, as well as freshly grilled vegetables, all wrapped up in durum bread. Meals can be ordered by phone.

Fabulous Italian cuisine and not a flash bulb in sight: **Trattoria Paparazzi**.

Suppen Cult

Prenzlauer Allee 42 (4737 8949/www.suppen-cult.de). M2 Marienburger Strasse or M4 Hufelandstrasse. **Open** 11am-8pm Mon-Fri; noon-4pm Sat. **Main courses** €3-€4.50. **No credit cards.** Map p319/p328 P3 ❹❹

A healthy alternative to fast food for lunch, snacks, or early dinner, this sit-down *Imbiss* offers a wide and tasty assortment of fresh soups and stews to eat in or take out. The menu changes weekly but features the likes of creamed vegetables with ginger and orange or organic lamb stew with coriander and sour cream. Summer brings out chilled soups and various fruit recipes. Also home-made desserts and fresh juices.

Italian

I Due Forni

Schönhauser Allee 12 (4401 7333). U2 Senefelderplatz. **Open** noon-midnight daily. **Main courses** €6-€8.40. **No credit cards.** Map p319/p326 O4 ❹❺

The punky staff at I Due Forni look more likely to throw you out of a club than tease your tastebuds. But in a city of cheap pizzas baked by Turks or Palestinians pretending to be Italian, the stone-oven pizza here is authentic and excellent. A bit pricier than elsewhere, a meal can still run under €10, and there are also daily pasta specials and a salad that's essentially a head of lettuce you have to chop up yourself. Their smaller, sister pizzeria is almost as good.

Other locations Il Casolare, Grimmstrasse 30, Kreuzberg (694 3968).

La Focacceria

Fehrbelliner Strasse 24 (4403 2771). U8 Rosenthaler Platz. **Open** 11am-late daily. **Main courses** €1.50-€8. **No credit cards.** Map p319/p326 N4 ❹❻

Delicious, thin-crust pizzas heated on the spot with fresh toppings such as tuna and rocket, spinach and white cheese, prawns, artichokes and chilli. This bustling *Imbiss* and café is run by old-school Italians who speak little German and pride themselves on classic dishes such as lasagne and a perfect tiramisu.

Trattoria Paparazzi

Husemannstrasse 35 (440 7333). U2 Eberswalder Strasse. **Open** 6pm-1am daily. **Main courses** €8.60-€18.90. **No credit cards.** Map p319/p328 P3 ❹❼

Behind the daft name and ordinary façade is one of Berlin's best Italians. Cornerstone dishes are malfat-ti (pasta rolls seasoned with sage) and strangolapret-ti ('priest stranglers' of pasta, cheese and spinach with slivers of ham), but it's worth paying attention to the daily specials too. Booking essential.

Portuguese

A Cabana

Hufelandstrasse 15 (4004 8508). Tram M4 Hufelandstrasse. **Open** 4pm-late Thur-Sun. **Main courses** €5-€16. **No credit cards.** Map p319 Q4 ❹❽

Eat, Drink, Shop

Schneeweiss.

A bit further east than the fashionable parts of this borough, but convenient for Magnet (*see p155*) and the Knaack Club (*see p237*) this family-run place is great for relaxing over a big bowl of fresh soup, fish or paella. Home-style cooking is the forte, and the menu changes frequently. Occasional live music.

Russian

Pasternak

Knaackstrasse 22-24 (441 3399/www.restaurant-pasternak.de). U2 Senefelderplatz or M2 Knaackstrasse. **Open** 9am-1am daily. **Main courses** €12-€15. **Credit** MC, V. **Map** p319/p328 P4 ❹

Small bar and Russian restaurant that's often crammed, which can be irritating at some tables – try for one in the small side room. The atmosphere is friendly and the food fine and filling. Kick off with borscht or the ample fish plate, then broach the hearty beef stroganoff.

Turkish

Miro

Raumerstrasse 28-29 (4473 3013/www.miro-restaurant.de). S8, S41, S42, S85 Prenzlauer Allee. **Open** 10am-late daily. **Main courses** €8-€17. **Credit** MC, V. **Map** p319/p328 P3 ❺

Named, they say, not after the painter but in honour of a 'Mesopotamian natural philosopher', this cool, roomy place serves excellent Anatolian specialities and well-priced drinks. The menu is long and intriguing, with ample vegetarian possibilities, legions of starters and a good salad selection – all of which arrive in hearty, generous proportions. Friendly service too.

Czech

Prager Hopfenstube

Karl-Marx-Allee 127 (426 7367). U5 Weberwiese. **Open** 11am-midnight daily. **Main courses** €7-€22. **Credit** MC. **Map** p325 S6 ❺

All the favourites from your last Prague holiday appear here: svickova (roast beef), veprova pecene (roast pork), knedliky (dumplings) and the lone vegetarian prospect: smazeny syr or breaded and deep-fried hermelin cheese served with remoulade and fries. Sluice down this heavy fare with mugs of Staropramen beer; afterwards, a Becherovka herbal digestif helps thwart indigestion. Fast and friendly service is a pleasingly inauthentic touch.

Imbiss/fast food

Frittiersalon

Boxhagener Strasse 104 (2593 3906/www.frittier salon.de). U5 Frankfurter Tor. **Open** 6pm-late Mon; noon-late Tue-Fri; 1pm-late Sat, Sun. **Main courses** €2.20-€9. **No credit cards. Map** p324 T7 ❺

Organic burgers, bratwurst and fries are flipped with attitude and served with delicious home-made ketchup, sauces and dips in this 'multikulti' gourmet chip shop. Burgers of the week involve some curious clashes of culture – a Middle-East-influenced 'halloumi burger', for example, where a slab of fried cheese is embellished with yoghurt sauce, sesame dip and salad. For vegetarians there are also soya and camembert burgers, plus a meat-free Currywurst.

Hot Dog Soup

Grünberger Strasse 67 (no phone/www.hot-dog-soup.de). S5, S7, S9, S75, U1 Warschauer Strasse or U5 Frankfurter Tor. **Open** noon-11pm Mon-Fri; noon-midnight Sat; noon-9pm Sun. **Main courses** €1.80-€3. **No credit cards. Map** p324 T7 ⑤
Head here for a quick pick-me-up after scouring the flea market on Boxhagener Platz. Hot Dog Soup serves up a daily changing menu of six tasty soups, including cold ones in summer, and a wide choice of organic Neuland hot dogs in variations such as 'Red Hot Chilli' and 'Hawaii' (with pineapples, chilli sauce and onions). Sausage and soup also come in vegetarian and vegan varieties.

Meyman

Krossener Strasse 11A (0163 806 1636/www.meyman-restaurant.de). U1, S3, S5, S7, S9, S75 Warschauer Strasse or U5 Samariterstrasse. **Open** 11am-2am Mon-Thur, Sun; 11am-4am Fri, Sat. **Main courses** €2.70-€6.80. **No credit cards. Map** p324 T7 ⑤
Moroccan and Arabic specialities plus good fresh fruit shakes and pizza are served in this warm and comfortable *Imbiss*, where there are usually plenty of tables. It's a bit pricier than some comparable places, but the super-fresh ingredients and a wide variety of dishes keep the crowds coming back for more – and few others are open this late.

Nil

Grünberger Strasse 52 (2904 7713). U1, S3, S5, S7, S9, S75 Warschauer Strasse or U5 Frankfurter Tor. **Open** 11am-1am daily. **Main courses** €2-€4.50. **No credit cards. Map** p324 S7 ⑤
Sudanese *Imbiss* offering good-value lamb and chicken dishes and an excellent vegetarian selection, including falafel, halloumi and aubergine salad. Hot peanut sauces are the tasty but sloppy speciality.

Italian

Fliegender Tisch

Mainzer Strasse 10 (297 7648). U5 Samariter Strasse. **Open** noon-midnight Mon-Fri, Sun; 5pm-midnight Sat. **Main courses** €6-€7. **No credit cards. Map** p324 T7 ⑤
A small and unassuming restaurant away from the hubbub of Simon-Dach-Strasse, the 'flying table' nevertheless fills up with locals of an evening. Generous helpings of Italian comfort food, including gnocchi, risotto and, of course, the speciality thin crust pizzas, leave you with a warm, fuzzy feeling and a round belly.

Modern European

Schneeweiss

Simplonstrasse 16 (2904 9704/www.schneeweiss-berlin.de). U1, S3, S5, S7, S9, S75 Warschauer Strasse. **Open** 10am-1am daily. **Main courses** €6-€20. **Credit** AmEx, MC, V. **Map** p324 T8 ⑤
This smart and understated establishment done out in fashionably minimalist white offers modern European dishes they describe as 'Alpine' – essentially a well-presented fusion of Italian, Austrian and south German ideas. There are daily lunch and dinner menus, plus a breakfast selection and snacks, shakes and schnitzels served throughout the day. Although upmarket for the area, it's great quality for the price and deservedly popular, so make sure you book.

North African & Middle Eastern

Shisha

Krossener Strasse 19 (2977 1995). U1, S3, S5, S7, S9, S75 Warschauer Strasse or U5 Samariterstrasse. **Open** 10am-late daily. **Main courses** €6-€13. **No credit cards. Map** p324 T7 ⑤
Arabic restaurant/bar serving exotic vegetarian and meat dishes from Lebanon, Syria and Iraq. Hookahs are the real attraction for the twentysomething crowd: repair to the smoking room and take advantage of the ten flavoured tobaccos at €6 per hookah (€4.50 after 8pm).

Kreuzberg

Asian

Pagode

Bergmannstrasse 88 (691 2640/www.pagode-thaifood.de). U7 Gneisenaustrasse. **Open** noon-midnight daily. **Main courses** €6-€9.50. **No credit cards. Map** p323 N10 ⑤
At Pagode you can watch the gaggle of Thai ladies whipping up your meal behind the counter and ensure that everything is fresh and authentic. Red and green curries here are sensational and the pad thai is heavenly. If the place looks crowded, don't worry: there's extra seating in the basement where you can watch the residents of a huge fish tank.

Sumo

Bergmannstrasse 89 (6900 4963/www.s-u-m-o.com). U7 Gneisenaustrasse. **Open** noon-midnight daily. **Main courses** €8.50-€16. **No credit cards. Map** p322 M10 ⑥
Quick, fresh Japanese food and intense flavours in a well-lit modern interior spread over two floors. The sushi is masterful but you can also enjoy standards such as tempura udon soup, warm bean salad, chicken yakitori and grilled tuna on rice. The feeling is modern Japanese toned down for German tastes.

Eat, Drink, Shop

The **Hopfingerbräu im Hauptbahnhof** opened its doors on 26 May 2006 and offers German and Alpine cuisine. The restaurant comprises over 200 interior seats in addition to 350 outside in the beer garden.

Glass elevators, attractive shopping opportunities and the open and bright atmosphere surrounded by extraordinary architecture make Berlin Hauptbahnhof a tourist attraction in itself. The government quarter, Brandenburg Gate, Reichstag, Potsdamer Platz, and Holocaust Memorial are all within easy reach and attract national and international visitors of the capital.

Our restaurant is open daily from 09:00 to 22:30 (1 April to 30 September) and 11:00 to 22:30 (1 October to 31 March).

We're looking forward to your visit!

Hopfingerbräu im Hauptbahnhof
Europaplatz 1, tel. +49(0)30 - 20 62 46 24

The **Hopfingerbräu im Palais** am Brandenburger Tor opened in June 2008 and is fabulously located between the Reichstag and Berlin's most iconic landmark – the Brandenburg Gate.

Hopfingerbäu seats 270 people on two floors and offers Bavarian, Austrian and Berlin cuisine.
In summer, 120 additional seats are available on the terrace and beer garden.
The restaurant interior speaks a traditional language – wood, glass, granite and cast iron prevail to create a unique atmosphere.

The central location makes it an attraction not only for Berliners, Potsdamers, and Brandenburgers – but also for national and international guests.
At Hopfingerbräu you'll be in the thick of things!

Open daily from 11:00 to 23:00.

Your team from Hopfingerbräu im Palais

Hopfingerbräu im Palais
Ebertstrasse 24, tel. +49(0)30 - 20 45 86 37

German, Austrian & Swiss

Austria

Bergmannstrasse 30, on Marheineke Platz (694 4440). U7 Gneisenaustrasse. **Open** 6pm-1am daily. **Main courses** €13.50-€17.50. **Credit** MC, V. **Map** p323 N10 ⬤

With a collection of antlers, this place does its best to look like a hunting lodge. The meat is organic, and there are also organic wines, Kapsreiter and Zipfer beer on tap, and a famously over-the-top schnitzel. Outdoor seating on a tree-lined square makes it a pleasant warm-weather venue too. Book at weekends and in summer.

Grossbeerenkeller

Grossbeerenstrasse 90 (251 3064). U1, U7 Möckernbrücke. **Open** 4pm-1am Mon-Fri; 6pm-1am Sat. **Main courses** €8-€15. **No credit cards.** **Map** p322 M9 ⬤

In business since 1862, with walls adorned by fading photos of faded theatre stars, Grossbeerenkeller serves good home cooking of a solid Berlinisch bent. A true taste of Alt-Berlin.

Henne

Leuschnerdamm 25 (614 7730/www.henne-berlin.de). U1, U8 Kottbusser Tor. **Open** 7pm-1am Tue-Sun. **Main courses** €3.50-€6.50. **No credit cards.** **Map** p323 P8 ⬤

Only one thing on the menu – half a roast chicken – but Henne's birds are organically raised and milk-roasted. The only decisions required here are whether you want to have cabbage or potato salad, and which beer you fancy washing it all down with (try the Monchshof). Check the letter over the bar from JFK, regretting missing dinner here.

Markthalle

Pücklerstrasse 34 (617 5502/www.weltrestaurant-markthalle.de). U1 Görlitzer Bahnhof. **Open** 9am-2am Mon-Fri; 10am-late Sat, Sun. **Main courses** €9-€14. **Credit** MC, V. **Map** p323 Q8 ⬤

This unpretentious schnitzel restaurant and bar, with chunky tables and wood-panelled walls, has become something of a Kreuzberg institution. Breakfast is served right up until 5pm, salads from noon, and, in the evening, a selection of filling and reasonably priced meals. It's also fun just to sit at the long bar and sample their selection of grappas. After dinner, see what's on downstairs at the Privat Club.

Imbiss/fast food

Bistro Yilmaz Kardesler

Kottbusser Damm 6 (no phone). U8 Schönleinstrasse. **Open** 10am-1am daily. **Main courses** €2.50-€3.50. **No credit cards.** **Map** p323 P10 ⬤

It's crowded, it's nondescript, but this humble *Imbiss* sells one of the best doner kebabs in Berlin. Crammed full of salad and seasoned with a startling array of spices, this is the Turkish fast food icon at its addictive best. And if you're turned off by that great slab of meat slowly sweltering on the spit, there's also a good selection of grilled kebab.

International

Knofi

Bergmannstrasse 11 (6956 4359/www.knofi.de). U7 Gneisenaustrasse. **Open** 7am-8pm daily. **Main courses** €5. **No credit cards.** **Map** p322 M10 ⬤

Connected to the Mediterranean speciality store across the street, Knofi is cosy and not much larger than an *Imbiss*, but it boasts a cheap and delicious speciality in the form of crêpe-like gosses – both vegetarian or filled with schwarma – and generous portions of soup. It's also a top-notch bakery.

Italian

Osteria No.1

Kreuzbergstrasse 71 (786 9162). U6, U7 Mehringdamm. **Open** noon-2am daily. **Main courses** €8-€19. **Credit** AmEx, DC, MC, V. **Map** p322 M10 ⬤

Most of Berlin's best Italian chefs paid their dues at this 1977-founded establishment, learning their lessons from a family of restaurateurs from Lecce. Osteria is run by Fabio Angilè, nephew of the owner of Sale e Tabacchi (*see below*). Excellent three-course lunch menu and, in summer, one of Berlin's loveliest garden courtyards. Staff are super-friendly too. Booking is recommended.

Sale e Tabacchi

Rudi-Dutschke-Strasse 23 (252 1155). U6 Kochstrasse. **Open** 9am-2am Mon-Fri; 10am-2am Sat, Sun. **Main courses** €9-€28. **Credit** MC, V. **Map** p322/p327 M8 ⬤

Well known for fish dishes (tuna and swordfish carpaccio or loup de mer) and for the pretty courgette flowers filled with ricotta and mint, not to mention its large, impressive selection of Italian wines. The interior design is meant to reflect a time when salt (sale) and tobacco (tabacchi) were sold exclusively by the state. In summer, enjoy a leisurely lunch or dinner in the garden under lemon, orange and pomegranate trees.

North African & Middle Eastern

Baraka

Lausitzer Platz 6 (612 6330). U1 Görlitzer Bahnhof. **Open** noon-midnight Mon-Thur, Sun; noon-1am Fri, Sat. **Main courses** €5-€10. **No credit cards.** **Map** p323 Q9 ⬤

North African and Egyptian specialities such as couscous and foul (red beans and chickpeas in sesame sauce) enhance a menu that also includes lots of well-executed standards such as falafel, schwarma and kofte. You can take away your meal or eat in the cavernous restaurant with its cosy seating on embroidered cushions.

Turkish

Hasir

Adalbertstrasse 10 (614 2373/www.hasir.de). U1,
U8 Kottbusser Tor. **Open** 24hrs daily (often closes
2-3hrs early morning). **Main courses** €9.50-€13.50.
No credit cards. Map p323 P9 ⑦

You thought the Turks had been chewing doner
since time immemorial? Sorry, it was invented in
Germany in 1971 by Mehmet Aygun, who eventually opened this highly successful chain of Turkish
restaurants. While you'll get one of the best doners
in Berlin here, you owe it to yourself to check out the
rest of the menu, which involves various other skew-
ered meats in sauce, and some addictive bread rolls.
Other locations throughout the city.

Schöneberg

French

La Cocotte

Vorbergstrasse 10 (7895 7658/www.lacocotte.de).
U7 Eisenacher Strasse. **Open** 6pm-1am daily.
Main courses €9-€20. **No credit cards.**
Map p322 J10 ⑦

Friendly, gay-owned French restaurant where good
cooking is enhanced by a sense of fun and occasional
themed events – such as the Beaujolais nouveau
being welcomed by a 'rustic chic' buffet and a programme of accordion music and 1980s French pop.
Vegetarians aren't forgotten, there's a nice terrace,
and the toilets are absolutely beautiful.

German, Austrian & Swiss

Renger-Patzsch

Wartburgstrasse 54 (784 2059/www.renger-patzsch.
com). U7 Eisenacher Strasse. **Open** 6pm-1am daily.
Main courses €13-€19.50. **No credit cards.**
Map p322 J11 ⑦

The pan-German food – soup and salad starters, a
sausage and sauerkraut platter, plus daily varying
meat and fish dishes – is finely prepared by versatile chef Hannes Behrmann, formerly of the late Le
Cochon Bourgeois. House speciality is Alsatian tarte
flambée: a crisp pastry base baked and served with
toppings in seven variations. Long wooden tables
are shared by different parties and in summer
there's a nice garden on this beautiful corner.

Imbiss/fast food

Habibi

Goltzstrasse 24, on Winterfeldtplatz (215 3332). U1,
U2, U3, U4 Nollendorfplatz. **Open** 11am-3am Mon-
Thur, Sun; 11am-5am Fri, Sat. **Main courses** €4-
€11. **No credit cards. Map** p322 J9 ⑦

Freshly made Middle Eastern specialities including
falafel, kibbeh, tabbouleh and various combination
plates. Wash it down with freshly squeezed orange

or carrot juice, and finish up with a complimentary
tea and one of the wonderful pastries. The premises
are light, bright and well run. Deservedly busy – it
can get very full.
Other locations Akazienstrasse 9, Schöneberg
(787 4428); Körtestrasse 35, Kreuzberg (692 2401);
Oranienstrasse 30, Kreuzberg (6165 8346).

Italian

Petite Europe

Langenscheidtstrasse 1 (781 2964). U7 Kleistpark.
Open 5pm-1am daily. **Main courses** €7-€13.
Credit MC, V. **Map** p322 J10 ⑦

You may have to wait for a table in this popular,
friendly place, but the turnover's fast. Weekly specials are first-rate, as are the pasta dishes. Salads
could be better and none of this is haute cuisine, but
it's all well made, hearty and inexpensive.

Norwegian

Munch's Hus

Bülowstrasse 66 (2101 4086/www.munchshus.
de). U2 Bülowstrasse. **Open** 10am-1am daily.
Main courses €6-€17. **Credit** AmEx, MC, V.
Map p322 K9 ⑦

In a corner of town bereft of good places to eat,
Berlin's only Norwegian restaurant is frequented by
businessmen and artists from the neighbourhood.
Daily specials are reminiscent of the rounded
German meal – potatoes and well-dressed greens
accompany most dishes – but with a twist that usually involves dill. Creamy, fresh soups and delicious
fish dishes are the speciality, but light sandwiches
and salads are also available.

Tiergarten

Asian

Edd's

Lützowstrasse 81 (215 5294). U1 Kurfürstenstrasse.
Open 11.30am-3pm, 6pm-midnight Mon-Fri; 5pm-
midnight Sat; 2pm-midnight Sun. **Main courses**
€14-€21. **No credit cards. Map** p322 J8 ⑦

Known and loved by many, so bookings are pretty
much essential for this comfortable, elegant Thai,
where a husband and wife team please their guests
with well-balanced if somewhat spicy creations. Try
the banana flower and prawn salad or duck no.18,
double cooked and excellent.

Sushi Express

Potsdamer Platz 2, Passerelle (2575 1863/
www.sushiexpress.de).5/1/06 U2, S1, S2, S26
Potsdamer Platz. **Open** 11.30am-9pm Mon-Sat;
3-9pm Sun. **Main courses** €2.50-€17.75. **Credit**
MC, V. **Map** p322/p328 K7 ⑦

Not the easiest place to find, Sushi Express is under
the courtyard of the Sony Center in a passage to the
S-Bahn, accessible from a stairway next to the video

Edd's.

Attempt to infiltrate the arty inner circle at the salon-style **Paris Bar**.

display for the Filmmuseum (*see p113*). But the hunt is worth it for tasty sushi, sashimi and assorted delicacies to be plucked off the conveyor belt cycling past you at the counter. The temptation is to just keep grabbing things, but don't worry, from noon to 6pm Monday to Friday all sushi and rolls are half price. Hot dishes and lunchboxes are also available, as is takeaway.

Australian

Corroboree

Sony Center, Bellevuestrasse 5 (2610 1705/www.corroboree.info). U2, S1, S2, S26 Potsdamer Platz. **Open** 10am-1am daily. **Main courses** €7.30-€19.30. **Credit** MC, V. **Map** p322/p328 L7 ❼❽
Big, noisy and one of the only decent places to eat in the Sony Center. It's hearty stuff, including kangaroo steak as well as burgers and noodle dishes, a small list of Aussie wines, and macadamia nuts with everything. Not too exciting for vegetarians, though.

French

Diekmann im Weinhaus Huth

Alte Potsdamer Strasse 5 (2529 7524/www.j-diekmann.de). U2, S1, S2, S26 Potsdamer Platz. **Open** noon-1am daily. **Main courses** €17.50-€26. **Credit** AmEx, MC, V. **Map** p322/p327 L8 ❼❾
Decent, stylish dining in the only surviving pre-war structure on Potsdamer Platz. The staff are well drilled, there's a small terrace to complement the smart dining room, the wine list has around 120 vintages, and the food is good for the price. A changing menu accommodates various Gallic favourites, such as coq au vin and crêpes suzettes. There aren't many good places round here, so it's always best to book a table in advance.
Other locations Meinekestrasse 7, Charlottenburg (883 3321); Clayallee 99, Dahlem (832 6392); Hauptbahnhof, Tiergarten (2091 1929).

German, Austrian & Swiss

Café Einstein Stammhaus

Kurfürstenstrasse 58 (261 5096/www.cafeeinstein.com). U1, U2, U3, U4 Nollendorfplatz. **Open** 9am-1am daily. **Main courses** €9-€22. **Credit** AmEx, DC, MC, V. **Map** p322 J8 ❽⓪
Red leather banquettes, parquet flooring and the crack of wooden chairs all contribute to the old Viennese café experience at Einstein. Fine Austrian cooking is produced alongside several nouveau cuisine specialities. Alternatively, order Apfelstrudel and coffee and soak up the atmosphere of this elegant 1878 villa. The other branch is more functional and has less charm, but the food is just as good.
Other locations Unter den Linden 42, Mitte (204 3632).

Hugo's

Hotel Intercontinental, Budapester Strasse 2 (2602 1263/www.hugos-restaurant.de). U2, U9, S5, S7, S9, S75 Zoologischer Garten. **Open** 6-10.30pm Mon-Sat. **Main courses** €35-€42. **Credit** AmEx, DC, MC, V. **Map** p321 H8 ❽①
Probably Berlin's best restaurant right now, and with the awards to prove it. Chef Thomas Kammeier juxtaposes classic haute cuisine with an avant-garde

new German style. Dishes such as cheek of ox with beluga lentils and filled calamares, goose liver with mango, and Canadian lobster salad bring out the best of a mature kitchen and well-balanced menu. The beautiful room occupies the entire top floor of the Intercontinental (*see p68*), with absorbing views in all directions.

Weizmann

S-Bahnbogen 390, Lüneberger Strasse (394 2057). S5, S7, S9, S75 Bellevue. **Open** *Winter* 6pm-midnight Mon-Fri, Sun. *Summer* 6pm-midnight daily. **Main courses** €10. **No credit cards.** **Map** p318 J6 **62**

A lovely little place serving the pastas of Swabia, including Spätzle (a dish with Bratwurst, lentils or meatballs), Käsespätzle (with cheese), Maultaschen (like giant ravioli) and Schupfnudeln (a cross between pasta and chips). A dark Berg beer makes the perfect accompaniment. There's a great value €8.50 buffet on Friday evenings that's well worth checking out too.

Italian

Patio

Helgolander Ufer, at Kirchstrasse (4030 1700/ www.patio-berlin.de). S5, S7, S9, S75 Bellevue. **Open** 10am-1am Mon-Fri; 9am-1am Sat, Sun. **Main courses** €9-€19. **Credit** AmEx, MC, V. **Map** p317 H5 **63**

On the banks of the Spree just above the leafy Hansaviertel, this designer barge has a sunny terrace on top and light-filled lounge below, both with extraordinary views of the willows and grand houses on the bank opposite. The menu features pretty good Italian classics including stone-oven pizza (from 6pm), pasta and, unexpectedly, sushi. A well-stocked bar fuels an extensive cocktail menu too. Lunch specials are usually under €7. Reservations recommended.

Charlottenburg & Wilmersdorf

Americas

Julep's

Giesebrechtstrasse 3 (881 8823/www.juleps.de). U7 Adenauerplatz. **Open** 5pm-1am Mon-Thur, Sun; 5pm-2am Fri, Sat. **Main courses** €9-€15. **Credit** MC, V. **Map** p320 D8 **64**

Julep's gets the fusion flavours of contemporary American cuisine just right with an array of imaginative dishes such as duck prosciutto or quesadillas with rhubarb and apple chutney, teriyaki chicken with lemongrass and basmati rice or Cajun-style red snapper. The caesar salad is a real classic, and pleasingly indulgent desserts include chocolate brownies made with Jack Daniels. Happy hour is 5-8pm and all night Sunday.

Asian

Sachiko Sushi

Grolmanstrasse 47 (313 2282/www.sachiko sushi.com). S5, S7, S9, S75 Savignyplatz. **Open** noon-midnight daily. **Main courses** €3.50-€18. **Credit** MC, V. **Map** p321/p328 F8 **65**

This was Berlin's first *kaiten* (conveyor belt) sushi joint. It's invariably packed with upmarket thirtysomethings, plucking the scrummy morsels as they circumnavigate a chrome and black stone bar.

Tai Ji

Uhlandstrasse 194 (313 2881). U2, U9, S5, S7, S9, S75 Zoologischer Garten. **Open** noon-midnight daily. **Main courses** €8.60-€18.60. **Credit** MC, V. **Map** p321/p328 F8 **66**

Fashionable folk cluster at Good Friends around the corner, but the Chinese food is actually far better and more authentic here. The room – a peaceful, semicircular pavilion overlooking a garden courtyard – is showing its age, but starters such as daugoo and button mushrooms and onion, or wun tun in a red chilli sauce, are sensational. Main courses have bizarre names like Meeting on a Magic Bridge or Eight Drunken Immortals Cross the Sea, but don't let that put you off. Note: half the Beijing-Sichuan dishes are vegetarian.

French

First Floor

Hotel Palace, Budapester Strasse 45 (2502 1020/ www.firstfloor.palace.de). U2, U9, S5, S7, S9, S75 Zoologischer Garten. **Open** noon-3pm, 6-10.30pm Mon-Sat. **Main courses** €26-€46. *Set menus* €92-€112. **Credit** AmEx, DC, MC, V. **Map** p321 G8 **67**

Now under the sway of hot young chef Mathias Bucholz, this is the place to come for refined French/European cuisine such as Bresse pigeon served with chanterelles and a ragout of potatoes, venison stuffed with foie gras, or loup de mer and Breton lobster served with saffron and tomato confit. Three set menus are offered daily. One of Berlin's top tables.

Paris Bar

Kantstrasse 152 (313 8052). S5, S7, S9, S75 Savignyplatz. **Open** noon-2am daily. **Main courses** €10-€25. **Credit** AmEx, MC, V. **Map** p321/p328 F8 **68**

Owner Michel Wurthle's friendship with Martin Kippenberger and other artists is obvious from the art hanging on every available inch of wall and ceiling. Paris Bar, with its old-salon appeal, is one of Berlin's tried and true spots. It attracts a crowd of rowdy regulars, and newcomers can feel left out when seated in the rear. The food, it has to be said, isn't nearly as good as the staff pretend. The adjoining Bar du Paris Bar has yet to gain that settled-in feel. To experience the often rude service and pricey food, you'll need to book

Georgian

Genazvale

Windscheidstrasse 14 (4508 6026). S5, S7, S9,
S75 Charlottenburg. **Open** 5pm-midnight daily.
Main courses €8-€21. *Set menu* €28 for 2 people.
No credit cards. Map p320 C8 **89**

A decent, upmarket restaurant that draws a mixed
crowd of Georgian and Russian expats, with a few
Germans and tourists for good measure. Expect
plum sauces, walnuts and coriander as a backdrop
to mega-portions of meat. Georgian kitsch abounds,
but is easily ignored after a vodka or two. Try the
lamb khinkali and expect honey and pomegranates
aplenty. Small range of first-class Georgian wines.

German, Austrian & Swiss

Alt Luxemburg

Windscheidstrasse 31 (323 8730/www.altluxemburg.
de). U2 Sophie-Charlotte-Platz. **Open** 5pm-late Mon-
Sat. **Main courses** €24-€27. *Set menus* €64/€70.
Credit AmEx, DC, V. **Map** p320 D8 **90**

Karl Wannemacher combines classic German and
French flavours with Asian influences in a wonderfully romantic dining room. Sample such wonders
as horseradish terrine with smoked eel, or monkfish
with a succulent saffron sauce and tomato. The wine
list could do with more moderately priced bottles,
but there's 15 per cent off all the food from 5 to 7pm.

Florian

Grolmanstrasse 52 (313 9184/www.restaurant-
florian.de). S5, S7, S9, S75 Savignyplatz. **Open**
6pm-3am daily. **Main courses** €12-€22. **Credit**
MC, V. **Map** p321/p328 F8 **91**

Florian has served fine south German food on this
quietly posh street for a couple of decades now. The
cooking is hearty, the service impeccable. Yes, staff
will put you in Siberia if they don't like your looks,
but they'll also welcome you back if you're good.

Marjellchen

Mommsenstrasse 9 (883 2676/www.marjellchen-
berlin.de). S5, S7, S9, S75 Savignyplatz. **Open**
5pm-midnight daily. **Main courses** €10-€20.
Credit AmEx, DC, MC, V. **Map** p321/p328 E8 **92**

There aren't many places like Marjellchen around
any more. It serves specialities from East Prussia,
Pomerania and Silesia in an atmosphere of old-
fashioned Gemütlichkeit. The beautiful bar and
great service are further draws, and the larger-
than-life owner recites poetry and sometimes sings.

Restaurant 44

Swissôtel, Augsburger Strasse 44 (220 102 288/
www.restaurant44.de). U1, U9 Kurfürstendamm.
Open noon-2.30pm, 6-10.30pm daily. **Main**
courses €32-€36. **Credit** AmEx, DC, MC, V.
Map p321/p328 G8 **93**

New chef Danijel Kresovic offers an international
menu that fuses European ideas with more exotic
flavours in dishes such as monkfish with curry

spices, prawn chiboust and chanterelle ragout, or
halibut with pata negra, pistachios and sweet potatoes. A fine selection of wines by the glass too.

Imbiss/fast food

Ashoka

Grolmanstrasse 51 (3101 5806/www.myashoka.de).
S5, S7, S9, S75 Savignyplatz. **Open** noon-midnight
daily. **Main courses** €2.50-€7. **No credit cards.**
Map p321/p328 F8 **94**

Most Indian restaurants in Berlin seem to offer more
or less the same menu. This one can be forgiven, as
it was the first to open. More than 20 years later, it's
still one of the best, offering well-priced, well-pre-
pared dishes in quiet and tasteful surroundings.
Plenty of vegetarian options and inventive weekly
specials. The branch on Goethestrasse offers vegetarian south Indian cuisine.
Other locations Satyam, Goethestrasse 5
(3180 6111).

Witty's

Wittenbergplatz (no phone). U1, U2, U3
Wittenbergplatz. **Open** 11am-1am daily. **Main**
courses €2.50. **No credit cards. Map** p321 H8 **95**

There are *Imbiss* stands on every corner of
Wittenbergplatz, but this one, on the northwest corner of the square, opposite KaDeWe, is one of the
best in the whole city. It's a friendly and courteous
operation, serves only Neuland organic meat, and
has gorgeous thick-cut chips with a variety of sauces
to choose from (chilli, satay, garlic mayo). Get an
organic Asgard beer to go with it. *See also right* **The**
odd history of the Currywurst.

Italian

XII Apostoli

Savigny Passage, Bleibtreustrasse 49 (312 1433).
S5, S7, S9, S75 Savignyplatz. **Open** 24hrs daily.
Main courses €10-€20. **No credit cards.**
Map p321/p328 F8 **96**

It's overcrowded, cramped and pricey, the service
varies from rushed to rude, the music is irritating –
but the pizzas are excellent and it's always open.
Other locations S-Bahnbogen 177-180,
Georgenstrasse, Mitte (201 0222).

Jewish

Gabriel

Jüdisches Gemeindehaus, Fasanenstrasse 79-80 (882
6138/www.itsgabriel.de). U1, U9 Kurfürstendamm.
Open 10.30am-3.30pm, 6.30-10.30pm daily.
Main courses €14-€22. **No credit cards.**
Map p321/p328 F8 **97**

Enter the Jewish Community Centre through airport-
style security and head one floor up to this excellent
kosher restaurant. Expect a full range of Jewish central and east European specialities, including some of
the best pierogi in Berlin.

The odd history of the Currywurst

Witty's.

Politicians pose with it, pop stars sing songs about it, great cities vie to claim the honour of its invention. The Currywurst is more than just a street snack. It's Germany's premier pop culture item. If Warhol was a Berliner, he would have painted a Bratwurst drenched in lurid red ketchup and liberally sprinkled with curry powder.

Germany is proud of its sausages and boasts more than 1,200 different varieties, all prepared and classified in deeply traditional ways. So how on earth did they get around to putting curry powder on them?

In Hamburg, where the Currywurst is served swimming in a sweet brown sauce, they claim to have invented it in 1947. Germans from the Ruhr area have their own creation myth, in which an Essen sausage seller accidentally drops a can of curry powder into some ketchup. But Berliners know this is nonsense, and there's a commemorative plaque on the corner of Kantstrasse and Kaiser-Friedrich-Strasse in Charlottenburg to prove it.

On the afternoon of 4 September 1949 – a rainy day, by all accounts – 36-year-old Herta Heuwer grew bored with waiting for customers at her humble sausage stand, and began to experiment with spices and seasonings. Some chilli powder in the ketchup... perhaps some worcester sauce, too... pour it all over a skinless pork Bratwurst... scatter curry powder on top... Lo, the Currywurst was born! It was also quickly patented under number 721319.

Sliced up on a paper plate, often served with chips and mayonnaise, and designed to be consumed standing up with a beer, the Currywurst sallied forth in conquest. In the 1950s, *Currywurstbuden* sprang up on every corner, scenting West Berlin with the aroma of hot fat, warm ketchup and Indian spices. By the time the Wall went up in 1961, the Currywurst had already crossed into the East, though to this day it is still often served on that side of town with a skin of pig's intestine, while in western Berlin it is usually skinless. (If you want it without intestine, ask for it '*ohne Darm*').

In East Berlin, the Currywurst held its own through the Communist period, most notably at **Konnopke's Imbiss** (*see p142*), serving sausages since 1930 under the U2 tracks south of Eberswalder Strasse station. In West Berlin, the Currywurst had to fight a war on two fronts against new-fangled Italian pizza slices and that other Berlin street food invention, the doner kebab. Though beaten back for a time, in today's more conservative climate the Currywurst is enjoying something of a comeback, celebrated as classless, authentic and German.

Konnopke's is not the only celebrated Currywurst stand. The sausages at **Ku'damm 195** (Kurfürstendamm 195, Charlottenburg) are pricey but crisp. The perennial queue at **Curry 36** (Mehringdamm 36, Kreuzberg) testifies to the quality of their Wurst. If caught in need of a Currywurst at the opposite end of Kreuzberg, try **Curry 7** (Schlesische Strasse 7). Perhaps our favourite place of all, however, is the organic vendor **Witty's** (*see p152*), serving classic Currywurst and fantastic chips directly opposite KaDeWe,

Eat, Drink, Shop

Cafés, Bars & Pubs

Beer is the mainstay, but cocktails, wine, food and music
add to the 24-hour party.

In Berlin, it's often a blurry line that separates the café from the bar. You can get breakfast, lunch, *Kaffee und Kuchen* (coffee and cakes), dinner and then horribly drunk into the small hours, all in the same place. But then it's also a blurry line that separates the bar from the club – and sometimes the bar/café from the restaurant. Many of the bars in this chapter come equipped with decks and DJs, but if late drinking is your objective, then many more options will be found in the Nightlife section (*see pp240-247*). Many places where you might go out for dinner will also have a decent bar, and there's no law that says you have to eat to have a drink there. And just about anywhere that's open in the morning is going to serve some kind of breakfast – unless it's one of those places where the night before tends to stretch well beyond rush hour of the morning after.

Breakfast is a big ritual in Berlin. At weekends, people will have breakfast parties and invite all their friends around. Many cafés offer a wide variety of ways to start the day, from croissants and jam or a simple selection of rolls, cheeses and cold cuts through to themed extravaganzas that could take all morning to devour. At weekends, all-you-can-eat brunch buffets have become popular (*see p157* **Breakfast time**). Afternoon *Kaffee und Kuchen* also remains a popular tradition, and every café will have at least a modest selection of cakes to choose from.

At the other end of the day, Berliners do like a drink. The capital's changing social composition means that cocktails are on the increase, and there have always been plenty of wine bars, but this is Germany and beer remains the main tipple, even though local brews are a sorry substitute for those of Bavaria and Bohemia. People tend to pay their own way and drink at their own pace – partly because in many places bills are only totted up as you leave – but ceremonial rounds of vodka, Jägermeister or tequila are a feature here.

In Berlin bars can stay open as late as they like. If you're used to a more conservative climate, it might be wise to pace yourself at first. Here no one is going to shout 'time' in your ear, even though the general tendency is for bars to close earlier these days. If you feel like carrying on when the staff finally do get around to putting the chairs up on the tables and pointedly offering to call you a taxi, there's bound to be somewhere else open nearby. Just ask the bar staff – it's probably where they're going.

Smoking is prohibited in places that don't provide a separate room for the purpose. A court decision close to press time, however, ruled that smoking was permitted at the landlord's discretion in places too small to offer a dedicated enclosure. Bars where smoking is permitted should now be advertising the fact with a sign outside.

Mitte

Squatters in Oranienburger Strasse were the first to open cafés after the Wall fell, but these days the Scheunenviertel's main drag mostly

The best Cafés, bars & pubs

Kaufbar
More than just drinks and snacks on sale at the 'Buy-Bar'. *See p163.*

Kim
Art crowd rumpus room. *See p156.*

Le Petit Laboratoire
English-speaking French hangout for Berlin's bohemia. *See p164.*

Prater
Swing-era beerhall backed with traditional beer garden. *See p161.*

Tausend
The height of Berlin exclusivity. *See p159.*

Victoria Bar
Cocktails with class. *See p169.*

caters to the tourist industry. Things are both quieter and funkier up on Auguststrasse, and the corner with Tucholskystrasse bustles of an evening, but Gipstrasse is probably the most happening nexus in this neighbourhood.

Hackescher Markt promises everything and draws a lot of tourists. The restored courtyards across from the S-Bahn station are indeed impressive, but their renovation has chased out the offbeat and left behind rather too many over-designed identikit bars. There are some decent cafés by day, though.

Torstrasse and the Mitte-Nord area beyond it are happier hunting grounds, especially the quarter around Brunnenstrasse, Veteranenstrasse, Rosenthaler Platz and the beginning of Kastanienallee, which is home to an assortment of eccentric establishments.

103

Kastanienallee 49 (4849 2651/www.agentur103.de). U8 Rosenthaler Platz/bus N2, N8, N84. **Open** 9am-2am Mon-Fri; 10am-2am Sat, Sun. **No credit cards.** **Map** p319/p328 O4 ❶

Well lit and airy (for Berlin), this L-shaped bar competes with Schwarzsauer (*see p161*) to be the primary Kastanienallee hangout. The food, an odd mix of Asian and Italian, is generally excellent. But more importantly, it's the perfect summer location to sit outside with a beer and watch well-coiffed local freaks strut their stuff.

Altes Europa

Gipsstrasse 11 (2809 3840/www.alteseuropa.com). U8 Weinmeisterstrasse/bus N2, N5, N8. **Open** noon-1am daily. **No credit cards.** **Map** p319/p326 N5 ❷

The gentle minimalism of the decor – big picture windows, basic furnishings and nothing but a few old maps and prints on the walls – is a relief in an increasingly pretentious neighbourhood, and this spacious place is good for anything from a party to a private conversation. The bar serves light meals, Ukrainian vodka and draught Krusovice in both dark and light varieties to a mixed, youngish crowd. The sounds are cool and the staff have a twinkle in their eye.

Bar 3

Weydingerstrasse 20 (2804 6973). U8 Rosa-Luxemburg-Platz. **Open** 9pm-late Tue-Sat. **No credit cards.** **Map** p319/p326 O5 ❸

Nestled in a cul-de-sac near the Volksbühne, this low-lit bar has wraparound windows, a slick black interior, a spacious U-shaped bar and inexpensive wine and beer. Try the Kölsch brew from Cologne (served in the traditional cylindrical glasses) or small servings of wine that go for €2.50. It's popular with the over-30 art crowd and a great place to both theorise and throw back a few drinks in a sleek but unpretentious atmosphere. They also sell Walkers crisps.

Barcomi's

Sophienstrasse 21, Sophie-Gips-Höfe, 2 Hof (2859 8363/www.barcomi.de). U8 Weinmeisterstrasse.

Open 8v
No cre
Promi
from
serv
me
br
C

40~.
Markt/bu~.
Open *Summer* ~
1am Fri, Sat. *Winter* 11a.
11am-midnight Fri, Sat. **Cren**..
Map p319/p326 N5 ❺

This small and stylish Hackesche Höfe cat~ _
insiders who know that the food here is better – a..
better-priced – than the stuff in the larger places in the first Hof. Expect a mixture of people from the nearby theatres, bars and offices.
Other locations Savignyplatz, S-Bahn Bogen 599, Charlottenburg (3150 9535).

CCCP

Torstrasse 136 (0179 692 913). U8 Rosenthaler Platz. **Open** 6pm-late Tue-Thur; 10pm-late Fri, Sat. **No credit cards.** **Map** p319/p326 N4 ❻

Better red than dead… or, well, maybe the other way round after a long night in this place. CCCP is a celebration of all things Russian. This means copious amounts of vodka – straight or mixed – quaffed by locals and a few other shady characters rubbing shoulders in the small, dark space. A crimson colour scheme, seedy vibe and kitschy decorations complete the picture. The doorman might refuse entry to large groups or anyone who looks too touristy.

Erdbeer

Max-Beer-Strasse 56 (0179 124 7645). U8 Rosa-Luxemburg-Platz/bus N2, N54. **Open** *Summer* 2pm-late daily. *Winter* 6pm-late daily. **No credit cards.** **Map** p319/p326 O5 ❼

The name means strawberry in German, and this dark, spacious (and a bit dingy) bar off Rosa-Luxemburg-Platz has earned a reputation for its powerful and delicious fresh fruit drinks. There are other eccentric mixtures on offer, as well as the usual beers, both bottled and from the Fass. Nightly DJs are of wildly differing styles and quality.

FC Magnet

Veteranenstrasse 26 (0177 291 6707/www. fcmagnet.de). U8 Rosenthaler Platz/bus N2, N8, N84. **Open** 7pm-late daily. **No credit cards.** **Map** p319/p326 N4 ❽

---

❶ Pink numbers in this chapter correspond to the location of each café, bar and pub on the street maps. *See pp313-328.*

began transforming old-
...lubs into fancy new bars.
...urs behind FC Magnet have
..., creating a fashionable foot-
...ith its own team. Though the
...eptional, people pack in at week-
...cker (table football) under a giant
...Franz Beckenbauer.

...sweg 8 (4404 6882/www.galao-berlin.de).
...enthaler Platz/bus N2, N8, N84. **Open**
...-8pm Mon-Fri; 8am-8pm Sat; 9am-7pm Sun.
...credit cards. Map p319/p326 N4 ❾
...rves the best panini in the area, with delicious
...Milchkaffee to accompany. It's small but makes a
virtue of it by tossing a few cushions on to the steps,
transforming what could be a cramped, table-less
restaurant into an outdoor meeting place in summer.

Gorki Park

*Weinbergsweg 25 (448 7286/http://gorki-park.de).
U8 Rosenthaler Platz/bus N2, N8, N84.* **Open**
9.30am-2am Mon-Sat; 10am-2pm Sun. **No credit
cards.** Map p319/p326 N4 ❿
Gorki Park is a tiny Russian-run café with surprisingly tasty and authentic snacks – blini, borscht
and the like. Guests range from students and
loafers to the occasional guitar-toting Ukrainian
and scenesters having a quiet coffee before heading down to pose at more centrally located bars.
The interesting weekend brunch buffet includes a
selection of warm dishes, but the vodka selection
is strangely disappointing.

Greenwich

*Gipsstrasse 5 (2809 5566). U8 Weinmeisterstrasse/
bus N2, N5, N8.* **Open** 8pm-6am daily. **No credit
cards.** Map p319/p326 N4 ⓫
It's not long since East Berlin nightlife was mostly
squats serving cheap beer and industrial vodka. But
when club pioneer Cookie opened this place (which
is still referred to as Cookie's Bar), the city began
its half-hearted romance with glam-flecked exclusivity. Of course, this being Berlin, an Adidas jacket
and an ironed shirt will probably get you in. The
interior looks like a set from *Barbarella*. Increasingly
a yuppie hangout, but the cocktails are top-notch
and the clientele is easy on the eyes.

Kapelle

*Zionskirchplatz 22-24 (4434 1300/www.cafe-
kapelle.de). U8 Rosenthaler Platz/bus N2, N8,
N84.* **Open** 9am-3am daily. **No credit cards.**
Map p319/p328 N4 ⓬
A comfortable, high-ceilinged café-bar across from
the Zionskirch, Kapelle takes its name from Die
Rote Kapelle, 'the Red Orchestra'. This was a clandestine anti-fascist organisation and in the 1930s
and 1940s the Kapelle's basement was a secret
meeting place for the resistance. The regularly
changing menu features organic meat and vegetarian dishes, and the proceeds are donated to local
charities and social organisations.

Kim

*Brunnenstrasse 10 (no phone). U8 Rosenthaler
Platz.* **Open** 9pm-late daily. **No credit cards.**
Map p319/p326 N4 ⓭
Minimal, minimal, minimal! This place perfectly captures that unfinished – and inexplicably sexy – look
with which Berlin's fashionable set is so enamoured.
Kim has been a favourite for twentysomething art-
crowders since it opened in February 2007. The door
is unmarked; just look for an all-glass façade and
crowds of people sporting New Romantic haircuts
and skinny jeans. The dimly lit, white-walled space
is DIY: under a geometric dropped ceiling handmade
by co-owner Oliver Miller are stackable chairs and
tables that guests can arrange as they like. Cheap
drinks and a rotating roster of neighbourhood DJs
add to a don't-give-a-damn aesthetic.

King Kong Klub

*Brunnenstrasse 173 (9120 6860/www.king-kong-
klub.de). U8 Rosenthaler Platz/bus N8, 52.*
Open 9pm-late daily. **No credit cards.**
Map p319/p326 N4 ⓮
King Kong Klub is unpretentious, with pudgy
leather sofas, subdued red lighting and rock 'n' roll
and B-movie paraphernalia scattered about. The
music policy mainly covers rock and electro; live
shows don't happen much here any more, so pick up
one of the monthly flyers to see what's going on.
Popular with student-types and local eccentrics.

Operncafé im Opernpalais

*Unter den Linden 5 (2026 8433/www.opern
palais.de). U6 Französische Strasse/bus N6.*
Open 8am-midnight daily. **Credit** AmEx,
MC, V. Map p319/p327 N6 ⓯
A traditional coffee and cake stop in literally palatial surrounds. Choose from a huge selection of beautifully displayed cakes, then relax over a Milchkaffee
in the elaborate interior, or sit outside in summer and
watch Unter den Linden go by.

Pony Bar

*Alte Schönhauser Strasse 44 (0163 775 6603).
U8 Weinmeisterstrasse/bus N2, N5, N8.* **Open**
noon-late Mon-Sat; 6pm-late Sun. **No credit cards.**
Map p319/p326 O5 ⓰
A good location compensates for some surly staff at
this austere watering hole where affordable cocktails are the principal draw, and wines are best
avoided. It's quiet as the grave by day but often
buzzes deep in the night.

Speakeasy

*Schumannstrasse 16 (4176 5867/www.speakeasy
berlin.de). U6, S1, S2, S5, S7, S9, S25, S75
Friedrichstrasse.* **Open** 6pm-2am daily.
No credit cards. Map p318 L5 ⓱
American goth band Frank the Baptist needed a
hangout from which to explore some unanticipated
success in Europe, and chose a failed Indian restaurant in a subterranean space next to the Deutsches
Theater. Come here late for potentially weird but
friendly conversations with the band members or

Breakfast time

Breakfast is a big thing in Berlin, especially at weekends, when people still have time to make a meal of it. Germans invite each other around for *Fruhstück* ('early piece') the way other cultures hold dinner parties or go out to meet friends and linger over brunch in their favourite café.

Scrambled eggs (*Rühreier*) are often on the à la carte part of the breakfast menu – the **Atlantic** (*see p165*) offers them scrambled in 11 different ways – and some old-school places will offer a Hoppel Poppel (also known as *Bauernfrühstück*), which is a kind of hearty ham and potato omelette. But otherwise a German *Frühstück* has little in common with a British fry-up or an American diner breakfast. The basic deal is cold rather than cooked: an assortment of bread rolls, cold cuts, cheeses, jam or honey, and maybe a soft-boiled egg.

Pretty much any café that's open in the morning will offer something of the sort. At the budget end there is usually a *kleines Frühstück* – a roll or two with jam or honey, what anglophones call a 'continental breakfast'. At the upper end there are grandiose productions involving *Sekt* (sparkling wine) and smoked salmon. At weekends, many places offer elaborate brunch buffets, such as that at **Café 100Wasser** (*see p162*), **Prater** (*see p161*) or **XII Apostoli** (*see p152*). In summer, many places have pavement tables, and at **Café Einstein Stammhaus** (*see p167*) or **Café Schönbrunn** (*see p162*) you can breakfast surrounded by gardens or greenery.

In between, there are variations. A *Käse Frühstück* will offer a selection of cheeses to go with a basket of rolls. A *Fitness Frühstück* will involve yoghurt, muesli and fruit. Breakfasts often take on national themes. A French one will have a croissant or two. An Italian one will feature mozzarella and tomatoes. At **Gorki Park** (*see p156*), you can try a Russian breakfast. **Tim's Canadian Deli** (*see p166*) and **Barcomi's** (*see p155*) offer some kind of North American breakfasting experience. And most of the city's Irish pubs can rustle up a recognisably 'English' breakfast. Other places theme breakfasts according to their name or function. **Potemkin** (*see p166*), for example, does breakfasts themed on the titles of Eisenstein films.

In deference to long Berlin nights, most places that serve breakfast carry on doing so until mid-afternoon or later. And for those whose sense of time becomes totally dislocated by too much clubbing and carousing, the **Schwarzes Café** (*see p169*) serves breakfast 24 hours a day.

Gorki Park.

THE SHORTLIST

WHAT'S NEW | WHAT'S ON | WHAT'S BEST

- **Pocket-sized guides**
- **What's on, month by month**
- **Full colour fold-out maps**

TIME OUT GUIDES
WRITTEN BY
LOCAL EXPERTS
timeout.com/shop

their groupies, or for the frequent toned-down jam with visiting luminaries in the FTB orbit. Don't expect polished service or a full house of people to look at: the name and obscure location don't exactly attract folks off the street, though anyone willing to buy a drink is surely welcome.

Tadschikische Teestube

In the Palais am Festungsgraben, Am Festungsgraben 1 (204 1112). U6, S1, S2, S5, S7, S9, S75 Friedrichstrasse. **Open** 5pm-midnight daily. **No credit cards. Map** p319/p327 N6 **⑱**

An improbable gift from the Soviet Union to the people of the DDR back in the early 1980s, the Tajik Tearoom is an extraordinary throwback. Sip exotic teas while lounging on the floor with samovars, low tables, rugs and cushions. It's a little faded nowadays, but worth the detour. Excellent snacks and light meals, and for less agile guests, there are a few conventional tables. Booking recommended. It's in the same building as the Maxim Gorki theatre (*see p256*).

Tausend

Schiffbauerdamm 11 (4171 5396/www.tausend berlin.com). U6, S5, S7, S9, S75 Friedrichstrasse. **Open** 9pm-late Tue-Sat. **Credit** AmEx, MC, V. **Map** p318/p327 M6 **⑲**

Finally, an elegant bar/lounge in Mitte for 'grown ups' – or at least that's what founder Till Harter (the man behind 103; *see p155*) had in mind for this high-design, upscale establishment. With an unmarked entrance – look for the iron door under the train overpass – and strict entrance policy, it's also as exclusive as Berlin gets. Here's where the well-heeled see and are seen while sipping innovative drinks in a tubular, steel-ceilinged interior lit by eerily eye-like 3D installations. Try a bracing Wasabi cocktail in summer or a malt whisky served with local pine honey in winter. Go late, look sharp.

Prenzlauer Berg

Kollwitzplatz is a leafy square fringed with cafés and bars. There is more of the same around the Wasserturm, at the junction of Rykestrasse and Knaackstrasse. The cafés near Helmholtzplatz (in the so-called 'LSD' neighbourhood, standing for the initial letters of Lychener Strasse, Schliemannstrasse and Dunckerstrasse) stray a bit further downmarket, stay open later and are somewhat more spontaneous. The **Prater** beer garden in nearby Kastanienallee is a pleasant place on a warm summer evening, and a good starting point for crawls down Kastanienallee and into Mitte.

8mm

Schonhauser Allee 177B (4050 0624/www.8mmbar. com). U2 Senefelderplatz/bus N2. **Open** 9pm-late daily. **No credit cards. Map** p319/p326 O4 **⑳**

This purple-walled dive exists to remind travellers that Berlin isn't Stuttgart. The attractive, young and poor go for that fifth nightcap around 6am, and local scenesters rub shoulders with anglophone expats. There seems to be more hard alcohol consumed here than in your average Berlin hangout and, yes, sometimes films are shown, should anyone still be in a fit enough state to watch.

Anna Blume

Kollwitzstrasse 83 (4404 8749/www.cafe-anna-blume.de). U2 Eberswalder Strasse. **Open** 8am-2am daily. **No credit cards. Map** p319/p328 P3 **㉑**

This café and florist rolled into one is named after a poem by Kurt Schwitters. The pastries are expensive but high quality, the terrace is nice in summer, and the interior, not surprisingly, smells of flowers.

Becketts Kopf

Pappelallee 64 (0162 2379 418). U2 Eberswalder Strasse. **Open** 8pm-4am Tue-Sun. **No credit cards. Map** p319/p328 P2 **㉒**

The head of Samuel Beckett stares at you from the window of this red-walled, intimate spot which prides itself on expert cocktails and a variety of scotches and whiskies. Prices are about average for mixed drinks in Berlin but quality is several notches above. Occasional DJs play avant-jazz.

Café Anita Wronski

Knaackstrasse 26-28 (442 8483). U2 Senefelderplatz/bus N2. **Open** 9am-2am daily. **No credit cards. Map** p319/p328 P2 **㉓**

Friendly café on two levels with scrubbed floors, beige walls, hard-working staff and as many tables crammed into the space as the laws of physics allow. Excellent brunches, and plenty of other cafés on this stretch if there's no room here. Quiet in the afternoon and a good spot to sit and read.

Café Galião

Marienburger Strasse 26B (0174 842 2965). M4 Hufelandstrasse. **Open** 8am-8pm Mon-Fri; 10am-7pm Sat; 10am-6pm Sun. **No credit cards. Map** p319/p328 Q4 **㉔**

Café Galião is a comfortable low-key daytime café with a friendly atmosphere. Youngish locals stop by for frequently changing specials such as home-made soups and organic stews, as well as big tasty salads and fresh ciabatta sandwiches. Order one of their fruit shakes and finish it off with a custard mini-tart.

Dr Pong

Eberswalder Strasse 21 (no phone/www.drpong.net). U2 Eberswalder Strasse/bus N42. **Open** 8pm-late Mon-Sat; 2pm-late Sun. **No credit cards. Map** p319/p328 O3 **㉕**

Bring your table tennis bat and prepare for ping-pong madness. The action doesn't start until around midnight, but when it does you can expect 30 or so players – some good, some bad – to surround the table. Beer, soda, tea and juice are available, and sometimes cakes or pastries, but otherwise there's no food. No tables, either. Just a bunch of chairs and two couches in a smoked-out, garage-like room. All in all, it's lots of fun. Note that the opening hours are unreliable.

Razzia in Budapest.

Eckstein

Pappelallee 73 (441 9960/www.cafe-eckstein.de).
U2 Eberswalder Strasse/bus N42. **Open** 9am-1am
Mon-Thur, Sun; 9am-2am Fri, Sat. **No credit cards.**
Map p319/p328 O2 ㉖
This beautiful café, with its broad corner front and
deco-ish look, draws a mixed crowd but maintains
a following among less well-scrubbed locals, adding
a pleasingly bohemian feel to a place that's otherwise clean enough to take your parents.

EKA

Dunckerstrasse 9 (4372 0612/www.eka-leka.de).
U2 Eberswalder Strasse/bus N42. **Open** noon-late
daily. **No credit cards. Map** p319/p328 P3 ㉗
This inexpensive café looks something like a 1940s
American soda shop reimagined as a livery stable.
Berlin always finds a way to sneak beer into an after-
noon of coffee and cake, and EKA is no exception,
serving both Bock and Portuguese brews. Although
in no way set up for it, it also manages to sneak in a
DJ sometimes. The apotheosis of Berlin casual.

Gagarin

Knaackstrasse 22-24 (442 8807). U2
Senefelderplatz/bus N2. **Open** 10am-2am daily.
Credit MC, V. **Map** p319/p328 P4 ㉘
Brought to you by the folks who run Gorki Park (*see*
p156) and Pasternak (*see p144*), adding a bar to their
troika of Russian hospitality. Vogue-ish retro space-
age decor (colourful planets and Yuri's likeness adorn
the walls) and electronic sounds provide the backdrop
for Baltika beer and tasty Russian pub grub.

Hausbar

Rykestrasse 54 (4404 7606). U2 Senefelderplatz/
bus N2. **Open** 7pm-5am daily. **No credit cards.**
Map p319/p328 P4 ㉙
Bright red and gold, with a glorious cherub-filled
sky on the ceiling, this small pocket of fabulous-
ness seats about 15 people at a push. Hausbar is
much more fun than all the wanky cafés with
Russian literary names you'll find around the corner, and it's particularly inviting at three or four in
the morning.

Kakao

Dunckerstrasse 10 (4403 5653/www.intveld.de).
U2 Eberswalder Strasse/bus N42. **Open** noon-late
daily. **No credit cards. Map** p319/p328 P3 ㉚
Kitted in retro orange and brown, floor-lit, and with
a muted soundtrack of the laziest funk and soul,
Kakao serves a glorious selection of cocoas and
other hot drinks. After a mug or two of thick, creamy
chocolate (try it with orange, almonds or cinnamon)
it's hard not to feel that this is the most relaxing
place in Berlin. Attached to the In't Veld chocolate
shop (*see p186* **Chocolate city**).

Klub der Republik

Pappelallee 81 (no phone). U2 Eberswalder
Strasse/bus N42. **Open** 8pm-4am daily.
No credit cards. Map p319/p328 O2 ㉛
Above a music school and accessed via a wobbly
staircase in the courtyard, this spacious bar manages to mix the best of the retro design craze with
the sort of lively revelry associated with the East in

the mid 1990s. The beer selection is gratifyingly big – try the Augustiner, one of Munich's best brews. The DJs are top-notch, playing anything from 1960s soul to jazz fusion to electronica.

Kohlenquelle
Kopenhagener Strasse 16 (no phone). U2, S41, S42 Schönhauserallee. **Open** 9am-late Mon-Fri; 10am-late Sat, Sun. **No credit cards. Map** p319 O2 ③②
All chipped plaster and mismatched junkyard furniture and as comfy as your gran's sitting room, this typical Berlin bar serves relatively cheap drinks as well as food. The daytime crowd verges on the pretentious (everyone seems to be working on a novel) but night-time patrons are much more lively.

November
Husemannstrasse 15 (442 8425/www.cafe-november.de). U2 Eberswalder Strasse/bus N42. **Open** 9am-2am Mon-Sat; 10am-2am Sun. **No credit cards. Map** p319/p328 P3 ③③
Friendly place that's especially nice during the day when light floods in through picture windows, offering views of beautifully restored Husemannstrasse. There's a breakfast buffet until 3pm on Saturdays and 4pm on Sundays.

Prater
Kastanienallee 7-9 (448 5688/www.pratergarten.de). U2 Eberswalder Strasse/bus N42. **Open** 6-11pm Mon-Sat; noon-11pm Sun. **No credit cards. Map** p319/p328 O3 ③④
Almost any evening, this huge and immaculately restored swing-era bar, across the courtyard from the theatre of the same name, attracts a smart, high-volume crowd. The beer-swilling lustiness, big wooden tables, and primeval platefuls of meat and veg can almost make you feel like you've been teleported to Munich. In summer, the shady beer garden makes for an all-day buzz. Brunch is served from 10am-4pm on Saturdays and Sundays.

Rakete
Schönhauser Allee 39A (0160 9763 6247/www. rakete-berlin.de). U2 Eberswalder Strasse/bus N2, N52. **Open** 8pm-late Mon-Sat. **No credit cards. Map** p319/p328 O3 ③⑤
Small, white and bright, with minimalist furnishings and low-key techno in the background, Rakete has become a casual hangout for local music and film scenesters, though it's as likely as not to have only a handful of people inside. No draught beer, but the bartenders know how to mix a drink.

Razzia in Budapest
Oderberger Strasse 38 (4862 3620/www.razzia-in-budapest.eu). U2 Eberswalder Strasse. **Open** 6pm-late daily. **No credit cards. Map** p319/p328 O3 ③⑥
East Berlin not Ost enough? This wood-panelled spot boasts a Hungarian feel that veers from cosy to crazed. There's Böhmisches dark beer on tap, and they pride themselves on their ten house cocktails with names such as 'Sommer in Budapest' and 'Razzia'. Weekend DJs play oldies.

Saphire Bar
Bötzowstrasse 31 (2556 2158/www.saphirebar.de). M10 Answalder Platz or M4 Hufelandstrasse. **Open** 8pm-2am Mon-Thur, 8pm-4am Fri, Sat. **Credit** AmEx, MC, V. **Map** p319 Q4 ③⑦
This sleekly designed bar, a favourite with local creative types, aims for a sophistication more common in cities like New York and Paris. It's worth checking out for the cocktails alone – over 300 of them, with names like Mummies on Ice and the Unbearable Lightness of Being. Add an impressive whisky menu, and it's no wonder Saphire Bar is consistently named in the *Tagesspiegel*'s Top 20 Berlin Bars.

Schwalbe
Stargarder Strasse 10 (4403 6208/www.schwalbe berlin.de). U2, S8, S41, S42, S85 Schönhauser Allee. **Open** 6pm-2am Mon-Fri; 3pm-2am Sat; 2pm-2am Sun. **No credit cards. Map** p319 P2 ③③
Unwilling to endure identikit Irish pubs or brave grumpy local *Eck-Kneipen* (corner pubs)? Schwalbe is about as chi-chi as a football bar gets, offering German and Italian league games in a fashionable café environment where you can grab a coffee and cake instead of a beer. Downstairs there are three strangely crowded Kicker (table football) tables and DJs on a Saturday.

Schwarzsauer
Kastanienallee 13 (448 5633/www.schwarzsauer. com). U2 Eberswalder Strasse/bus N42. **Open** 8am-6am daily. **No credit cards. Map** p319/p328 O3 ③⑨
Possibly the most popular bar on Kastanienallee and currently the main meeting place for those who inhabit the twilight zone between Prenzlauer Berg and Mitte. Odd, then, that its ambience is pretty plain, its staff Berlin surly, and its food and drink of only adequate quality. In summer, the outside tables overflow day and night. In winter, a tolerance for cigarette smoke is helpful.

Wohnzimmer
Lettestrasse 6 (445 5458). U2 Eberswalder Strasse/ bus N42. **Open** 10am-4am daily. **No credit cards. Map** p319/p328 P2 ④⓪
Immediately behind the door of this shabbily elegant 'living room' there's a bar-like structure made from an ensemble of kitchen cabinets. Threadbare divans and artsy bar girls make this the perfect place to discuss Dostoevsky with career students over a tepid borscht. Evening light from candelabra reflects on gold-sprayed walls as students and maudlin poets chase brandies with Hefeweizen. Daytimes can be sluggish.

Friedrichshain

Friedrichshain carries the flag for youthful Berlin bohemia. The area around Simon-Dach-Strasse is full of fun bars, cheap cafés and ethnic takeaways, but on a weekend night don't expect to be the only out-of-towners wandering around. Rigaer Strasse and

Mainzer Strasse were once hubs of the militant squatting scene, and an element of disgruntled radicalism persists. Locals may sneer if you wear your best designer togs or attempt to pay with a credit card.

Meanwhile, the former socialist showcase boulevard that is Karl-Marx-Allee has begun to develop into a nightlife scene, but more as an eastern extension of the Mitte scene than a western annex of the Friedrichshain one.

Café 100Wasser

Simon-Dach-Strasse 39 (2900 1356). U5 Frankfurter Tor or U1, S3, S5, S6, S7, S9, S75 Warschauer Strasse/bus N5, N29. **Open** 9.30am-late daily. **No credit cards. Map** p324 T7 ④
The all-you-can-eat brunch buffet (€7.90 Saturday, €9.50 Sunday) has a cult following among students and other late risers. Take your time and don't panic as the buffet gets plundered. Just when the food seems to be finished, out comes loads of new stuff.

Café Schönbrunn

Am Schwanenteich, Im Volkspark Friedrichshain (4679 3893/www.schoenbrunn.net). Bus 200. **Open** 10am-late daily. **Credit** V. **Map** p319 Q5 ④
Not for those afraid to walk in the park at night, but for everyone else it's a favoured hangout. A couple of years ago, this place by the lake sold coffee and snacks to an elderly crowd. With a change of management, the music and food improved dramatically. The unspectacular concrete front was left as it was, and the (new) lounge furniture is pure 1970s.

On a sunny afternoon, older park-goers take their first afternoon beer on the terrace next to the in-crowd having breakfast. For your first visit come in daytime – just to make sure you can find it.

Chüchliwirtschaft

Grünberger Strasse 68 (no phone). U1, S5, S7, S9, S75 Warschauer Strasse or U5 Frankfurter Tor. **Open** 4-11pm Wed-Fri; 6-11pm Sat; 3-10pm Sun. **No credit cards. Map** p324 T7 ④
It's crêpes galore at this artsy café. Swiss couple Klaus Linder and Roswitha Marie first started selling their sweet and savoury creations from a van on Boxhagener Platz and now they've graduated to a small eatery around the corner. Crêperie doesn't equate to fast food in this case. Wait and you'll be rewarded with beautifully presented pancakes, from sweet classics such as sugar and lemon to the more experimental Ovomaltine cream.

Cupcake

Krossener Strasse 12 (2576 8687/www.cupcake berlin.de). S5, S7, S9, S75, U1 Warschauer Strasse. **Open** noon-7pm Wed-Sun. **No credit cards. Map** p324 T7 ④
Dawn Nelson, an American former make-up artist, makes her cupcakes like they're works of art. Swirls of raspberry cream, a cherry perching on the top and Oreo cookie fillings. Some say the cakes are too sweet, others can't get enough. Americanophiles can get their fix of Rice Krispie cakes and New York cheesecake and there's root beer, cream soda and Dr Pepper as well as the usual teas and coffees to wash it all down with.

Würgeengel. *See p166.*

Ehrenburg

Karl-Marx-Allee 103A (4210 5810). U5 Weberwiese/bus N5. **Open** 10am-late daily. **No credit cards**. **Map** p325 R6 ⁴⁵

Named after Russian-Jewish novelist Ilja Ehrenburg, a dedicated socialist, this café and espresso bar, with its sober, geometric decoration, is one of the few stylish places around Weberwiese U-Bahn station. Although the library looks like it's part of the decorative style, you're free to pick up a book and study the works of Ehrenburg, Lenin, Stalin, Engels or Marx as you enjoy a latte macchiato and other capitalist achievements.

Habermeyer

Gärtnerstrasse 6 (2977 1887/www.habermeyer-bar.de). S3, S5, S7, S75, S9, U1 Warschauer Strasse. **Open** 7pm-late daily. **No credit cards**. **Map** p324 T7 ⁴⁶

Not a dive, but certainly not fancy, Habermeyer is where local hipsters go for low-key drinks, casual conversation, table football, and a marked absence of the teenagers and tourists who nightly flock to Simon-Dach-Strasse. The decor is unobtrusively '70s, the lighting is dim and reddish, and most nights, the music is delivered by a DJ.

Kaufbar

Gärtnerstrasse 4 (2977 8825/www.kaufbar-berlin.de). S5, S7, S9, S75, U1 Warschauer Strasse. **Open** 10am-1am daily. **No credit cards**. **Map** p324 T7 ⁴⁷

A small, stylish bar and café with a neighbourly atmosphere and a gimmick. You can buy the chairs you're sitting on, the table you're eating from, that

fork you're holding, the artwork on the walls – just about everything, in fact – hence the name ('Buy-Bar'). Light organic snacks such as salads and soups are served and in summer there is a pretty garden area.

Kunstliche BEATmung

Simon-Dach-Strasse 20 (7022 0472). U1, S3, S5, S6, S7, S9, S75 Warschauer Strasse/bus N5, N29. **Open** 7pm-2am daily. **No credit cards**. **Map** p324 S7 ⁴⁸

The low-domed ceiling, plastic furniture and coloured neon are like a cross between cocktail bar and space capsule. Around midnight, the beautiful young things start dribbling in and any oddness is soon swallowed in the crush. The main attraction is an elaborate drinks menu, which provides hundreds of lurid opportunities for experimental boozing.

Macondo

Gärtnerstrasse 14 (0151 1073 8829). S5, S7, S9, S75, U1 Warschauer Strasse or U5 Samariter Strasse. **Open** 3pm-late Mon-Fri; 10am-late Sat; 11am-late Sun. **No credit cards**. **Map** p324 T7 ⁴⁹

This café/bar on Boxhagener Platz brands itself a 'Leseplatz' (reading place) and it's perfect for just that. Kitted out, like so many Berlin cafés, with fraying but still trendy vintage furniture, and also offering a good selection of board games, it's more of a chill-out bar than a night-out place. Snacks such as fried yucca and a €5 Latin American brunch on Sundays keep the intellects sated.

Monster Ronson's Ichiban Karaoke

Warschauer Strasse 34 (8975 1327/www.karaokemonster.com). U1, S3, S5, S7, S9, S75, Warschauer

Tim's Canadian Deli: a great choice for breakfast. *See p166.*

Strasse. **Open** 7pm-midnight daily.
No credit cards. Map p324 S8 ❺⓿
In 1999, Monster Ronson – aka Ron Rineck – moved
to Berlin from Salt Lake City with $7,000 in his
pocket. As his savings dwindled, he began sleeping
in his car, bought a second-hand karaoke machine,
and soon was driving to squat houses all over
Europe, throwing karaoke parties and getting paid
to do it. Eventually, he saved up enough to open his
very own karaoke bar and today Monster Ronson's
Ichiban Karaoke is packed with pop star wannabes
most nights of the week, belting out songs in one of
several different karaoke booths, some small and
intimate, others complete with stage area.

Paule's Metal Eck

Krossener Strasse 15 (291 1624/www.paules-metal-
eck.de). U5 Frankfurter Tor or U1, S3, S5, S6, S7,
S9, S75 Warschauer Strasse/bus N5, N29. **Open**
Summer 5pm-late daily. *Winter* 7pm-late daily.
No credit cards. Map p324 S7 ❺❶
Neither a typical heavy metal bar nor remotely typical for this area, the Egyptian-themed Eck attracts
a young crowd with relentless metal videos, a decent
selection of beers and both pool and table football.
Inoperative disco balls, mummy overhead lamps
and formidable dragon busts deck an interior half
designed like a mausoleum, half in gloomy medieval
style. A small menu changes weekly and there's live
Bundesliga football on weekend afternoons.

Le Petit Laboratoire

Grünberger Strasse 87 (0151 5905 0323/www.
myspace.com/lepetitlaboratoire). U5 Samariter
Strasse. **Open** 3pm-late Wed-Sat; noon-late Sun.
No credit cards. Map p324 T7 ❺❷
This French bohemian bar, with lots of sofas,
bright colours and a comfortingly ramshackle feel,
is a new Friedrichshain favourite. The highlight is
a selection of delicious, self-invented cocktails such
as the 'Tiramasu' or the one made with a hot herbal
tea. The bar also works as a gallery space and
plays host to regular concerts. The Gallic propri-
etors haven't got the hang of German yet, so
English is the working language, as a big sign
behind the bar announces.

Supamolly

Jessner Strasse 41 (2900 7294/www.supamolly.de).
U5, S4, S8, S10 Frankfurter Allee/bus N5.
Open 8pm-late Tue-Sat. **No credit cards.**
Map p324 U7 ❺❸
Having opened in the early 1990s as a semi-legal
bolthole fronting a lively squat, Supamolly (or
Supamolli) is a miracle of survival. The frequent live
punk and ska shows in the club behind the bar dictates only some of the clientele; a healthy mix of
young and ageing punks, unemployed activists and
music lovers of all types gather in this dim, mural-
smeared, candlelit watering hole until the early
morning. DJs at weekends.

Kreuzberg

West Berlin's former art and anarchy quarter still offers plenty of alternative life. The fashionable focus is the area around Schlesisches Tor, though the district around Oranienstrasse and Wiener Strasse is also experiencing a revival.

Although well-supplied with cafés and lively during the day, the increasingly upmarket Bergmannstrasse neighbourhood is sadly somnolent after dark, though there is a bit of gay life on Mehringdamm.

Ankerklause

Kottbusser Brücke, corner of Maybachufer, Neukölln (693 5649/www.ankerklause.de). U8 Schönleinstrasse/bus N8. **Open** 4pm-late Mon; 10am-late Tue-Sun. **No credit cards.** **Map** p323 P9 ⓞ

Although it looks over Kreuzberg's Landwehrkanal, the only thing nautical about this 'anchor den' is the midriff-tattooed, punk-meets-portside swank of the bar staff. A slamming jukebox (rock, sleaze, beat), a weathery terrace and good sandwich melts offer ample excuse to dock here from afternoon until whenever they decide to close. Convivial during the week, packed at weekends.

Atlantic

Bergmannstrasse 100 (691 9292). U6, U7 Mehringdamm/bus N19. **Open** *Summer* 9am-2am daily. *Winter* 9am-1.30am daily. **No credit cards.** **Map** p322 M10 ⓞ

On the south side of the street, Atlantic's pavement café thrives in the summer, and a beer as late as 8pm will still have you sitting in a ray of light, if you're lucky enough to get a table. Breakfast, including 11 different ways to have your eggs scrambled, is served until 5pm. There are also daily lunch specials, and dinner is a cheap but decent affair. The staff changes every two days, as does the music.

Barbie Deinhoff's

Schlesische Strasse 16 (no phone/www.barbie deinhoff.de). U1 Schlesisches Tor/bus N29. **Open** 6pm-6am daily. **No credit cards. Map** p324 R9 ⓞ

Run by celebrity drag queen Lena Braun (star of the fashionable documentary *Gender X*), this lively and unusual bar attracts both the more bourgeois members of Berlin's cross-dressing community and the loucher denizens of the Kreuzberg mainstream. The look is pitched somewhere between tacky kitsch and futuristic chic. There are often lectures and art events in the early evening, before the debauchery kicks off. *See also p220.*

Cake

Schlesische Strasse 32 (6162 4610/www.cake-bar.de). U1, U15 Schlesisches Tor/bus N29. **Open** 4pm-late daily. **No credit cards. Map** p324 R9 ⓞ

A diverse crowd in both age and nationality – the hostel across the street lends a youthful international

air – mills about in this lounge that comes with old easy chairs, sofas, art-covered walls and a dark red, musty interior. Music gently hums overhead, providing a great atmosphere for relaxing and chatting. They've even got a vintage jukebox equipped with a variety of oldies. DJs most weekends for free. Happy hour 7-9pm daily.

Haifischbar

Arndtstrasse 25 (691 1352/www.haifischbar-berlin.de). U6, U7 Mehringdamm/bus N19. **Open** 7pm-late daily. **No credit cards.** **Map** p322 M10 ⓞ

Well-run and friendly bar where the staff are expert cocktail-shakers, the music's hip and tasteful in a trancey kind of way, and the back room, equipped with a sushi bar, is a good place to chill out at the end of an evening. Certainly the most happening place in the Bergmannstrasse Kiez, and with some kind of crowd any night of the week.

Luzia

Oranienstrasse 34 (6110 7469/www.luzia.tc). U1, U8 Kottbusser Tor. **Open** 9am-late daily. **No credit cards. Map** p323 P8 ⓞ

This oddly whimsical bar and café, a bit rough around the edges, is the linchpin of Oranienstrasse's renaissance as a hip destination for young Berliners. The simultaneously imposing and welcoming ambience is achieved by a combination of high ceilings, moody lighting, well-worn second-hand furniture and striking walls covered in old wallpaper, gold paint and street art by local talent Chin Chin. There's a small breakfast menu throughout the day, plus a selection of cakes and coffees and a standard range of alcoholic drinks.

Madonna

Wiener Strasse 22 (611 6943). U1 Görlitzer Bahnhof/bus N29, N44. **Open** 3pm-late daily. **No credit cards. Map** p323 Q9 ⓞ

With over a hundred whiskies, and frescoes detailing a lascivious pageant of falling angels and clerical inebriation, this bar and café offers a friendly vantage on the debauched, counterculture erudition of Kreuzberg thirtysomethings. It's particularly interesting as neutral ground for subcultures that, until Berlin's modernisation frenzy gave them common cause, had differing opinions on the proper way to burn a car, squat a building or play a guitar.

Matilda

Graefestrasse 12 (8179 7288/www.myspace.com/ matilda_Berlin). U8 Schönleinstrasse. **Open** 9am-late daily. **No credit cards. Map** p323 P10 ⓞ

The cobbles, tree-lined streets and general peace and quiet make the Graefekiez one of the city's most pleasant neighbourhoods, and Matilda fits in perfectly. It's small and cosy with plenty of retro furniture: tables and chairs in the front room and squidgy sofas in the back. Bar staff are on hand to flip records (mostly 1960s pop and soul) in between serving drinks. Popular with a young, lazy crowd.

Eat, Drink, Shop

Murray's

Erkelenzdamm 49 (615 6917/www.murraysbar.de).
U1 or U8, Kottbusser Tor/bus N8, N29. **Open**
noon-2am Mon-Thur, Sun; noon-4am Fri, Sat.
No credit cards. Map p323 O9 ⓬
Decent all-purpose Irish pub with draught Guinness
and Kilkenny, a big selection of hearty meals, plenty
of TVs for watching British and Irish football and
rugby matches, a pleasant beer garden on the quiet
street outside and a cheerfully rowdy atmosphere.

Mysliwska

*Schlesische Strasse 35 (611 4860). U1 Schlesisches
Tor/bus N29, N65.* **Open** 6pm-late daily. **No credit
cards. Map** p324 R9 ⓭
This small, dark bar draws a mixed local crowd
and doesn't get going until late. The spartan interior boasts old, small, poker-like tables and stiff
wooden chairs. Except for a pistachio dispenser
and a frequently unpopulated, disco-balled side
room, frills are kept to a minimum. There's live
music once or twice a month and DJs play most
weekends (no entrance fee).

Travolta

*Wiener Strasse 14B (0176 2841 8879). U1
Görlitzer Bahnhof/bus N1.* **Open** 7pm-3am daily.
No credit cards. Map p323 Q9 ⓮
Try a shot of Mexicaner – vodka, tequila, tomato
and tabasco for just €1.50. Beer, meanwhile, is
philanthropically priced at €2.80 for the half-litre.
Music runs from punk to funk to Zappa, and the
table football is popular.

Wiener Blut

*Wiener Strasse 14 (618 9023). U1 Görlitzer
Bahnhof/bus N1.* **Open** 6pm-late Mon-Fri, Sun;
3.30pm-late Sat. **No credit cards. Map** p323 Q9 ⓯
A narrow, darkish bar equipped with booths and a
well-abused table football table, Wiener Blut sometimes features DJs who fill the place with wild beats
and wild friends. Otherwise, it's just another red bar.
The tables out front are perfect in summer.

Würgeengel

*Dresdener Strasse 122 (615 5560/www.wuergeengel.
de). U1, U8 Kottbusser Tor/bus N8.* **Open** 7pm-late
daily. **No credit cards. Map** p323 P9 ⓰
Red walls and velvet upholstery convey an atmosphere aching for sin, while well-mixed cocktails and a
fine wine list served by smartly dressed waiting staff
make this a place for the more discerning drinker.
The glass-latticed ceiling and a 1920s chandelier elegantly belie the fairly priced drinks and tapas on
offer. Nice in summer, when a canopy of greenery
curtains the outdoor picnic tables. *Photos pp162-163.*

Schöneberg

This gentrified borough retains a hint of its
more radical past, and, around Motzstrasse
and Fuggerstrasse, contains possibly the
world's oldest – and certainly the city's

largest – gay quarter. You'll find numerous bars
and shops catering to all tastes and fetishes.
   Around Winterfeldtplatz there's a
concentration of lively cafés, and bar life
mingles with the antique shops along
Goltzstrasse to the south.

Green Door

*Winterfeldtstrasse 50 (215 2515/www.greendoor.de).
U1, U2, U3, U4 Nollendorfplatz/bus N2, N5, N19,
N26.* **Open** 6pm-3am Mon-Thur, Sun; 6pm-4am Fri,
Sat. **No credit cards. Map** p322 J9 ⓱
It really does have a green door, and behind it there's
a whole lotta cocktail shaking going on (the drinks
menu is impressively long). There's also a nice long
and curvy bar, perhaps a few too many yuppies and
a good location off Winterfeldtplatz.

Mutter

*Hohenstaufenstrasse 4 (2191 5100). U1, U2,
U3, U4 Nollendorfplatz/bus N2, N5, N19, N26.*
Open 10am-4am daily. **Credit** AmEx, MC, V.
Map p322 J10 ⓲
'Mother' tries to do everything at once: two bars; an
enormous selection of wines, beers and cocktails;
breakfasts until 6pm; a sushi bar from 6pm, plus
other snacks throughout the day. It's a big place, but
it can be difficult to find a seat on weekend nights,
when trancey house plays in the front bar (there are
more sedate sounds in the café area at the back). It's
roomy, the decor is heavy on gold paint and the spectacular corridor to the toilets is worth a visit in itself.

Pinguin Club

*Wartburgstrasse 54 (781 3005/www.pinguin-
club.de). U7 Eisenacher Strasse/bus N4, N48.* **Open**
9pm-4am daily. **No credit cards. Map** p322 J11 ⓳
Though a little past its heyday, this speakeasy-style
bar remains one of Berlin's finest and friendliest
institutions. It's decorated with original 1950s
Americana and rock 'n' roll memorabilia, the owners all have punk roots and good sounds are a feature. Take your pick from 156 spirits, and don't be
surprised if everyone begins to dance to disco or sing
along to Nick Cave tunes.

Potemkin

*Viktoria-Luise-Platz 5 (2196 8181). U4 Viktoria-
Luise-Platz/bus N46.* **Open** 8am-1am Tue-Sun.
No credit cards. Map p321 H9 ⓴
Film stills and the likeness of *Battleship Potemkin*
director Eisenstein adorn the wall, and the red and
black decor has a constructivist feel. Breakfasts also
sport titles of Eisenstein films, from the basic
'Ivan the Terrible' to 'Viva Mexico', with marinated
chicken breast served with pineapple and cheese on
toast. There's also a daily lunch special and snacks
such as mozzarella rolls stuffed with serrano ham.

Tim's Canadian Deli

*Maassenstrasse 14 (2175 6960/www.timinberlin.de).
U1, U2, U3, U4 Nollendorfplatz/bus N2, N5, N19,
N26.* **Open** 8am-1am Mon-Fri; 8am-late Sat; 9am-
1am Sun. **Credit** AmEx, MC, V. **Map** p322 J9 ㉑

Against the odds, this place seems to have conquered the Winterfeldtplatz area, although there's not a café round here that's not full on a market day. Lots of bagels and muffins, egg breakfasts until 4pm and various light meal options. *Photo p164.*

Zoulou Bar

Hauptstrasse 4 (784 6894/www.zouloubar.de).
U7 Kleistpark/bus N4, N48. **Open** 7pm-6am daily.
No credit cards. Map p322 J10

Small bar with a funky vibe and occasional DJs. It can get packed between 10pm and 2am; visit later, when the crowd has thinned.

Tiergarten

The area around Potsdamer Strasse is kind of a northern Schöneberg, its scene overlapping with that of the neighbouring borough. Around Lützowplatz it's rather more upmarket. Alas, we can find little to recommend among all the shiny new franchises of Potsdamer Platz.

Bar am Lützowplatz

Lützowplatz 7 (262 6807/www.baramluetzowplatz.com). U1, U2, U3, U4 Nollendorfplatz/bus N2, N5, N19, N26. **Open** 4pm-4am daily. **Credit** AmEx, MC, V. **Map** p322 J8

Long bar with a long drinks list and classy customers in Chanel suits sipping expensive, well-made cocktails as they compare bank balances.

Café Einstein Stammhaus

Kurfürstenstrasse 58 (261 5096/www.cafeeinstein. com). U1, U2, U3, U4 Nollendorfplatz/bus N2, N5, N19, N26. **Open** 8am-1am daily. **Credit** AmEx, DC, MC, V. **Map** p322 J8

Viennese-style coffeehouse with waiters in bow ties, international papers to read and an Apfelstrudel of legend. In summer you can enjoy a leisurely garden breakfast (served all day). *See also p150.*
Other locations Unter den Linden 42, Mitte (204 3632).

Joseph Roth Diele

Potsdamer Strasse 75 (2636 9884/www.joseph-roth-diele.de). U1 Kurfürstenstrasse. **Open** 10am-midnight Mon-Fri. **No credit cards.**
Map p322 K8

A traditional Berlin book café, just a short stroll south of Potsdamer Platz, which pays homage to the life and work of inter-war Jewish writer Joseph Roth. It's an amiable place in ochre tones and with comfy seating, offering teas, coffees, wines, beers, snacks and stunning value light meals (lunchtime specials from just €3). There's a limited menu on Friday evenings.

Kumpelnest 3000

Lützowstrasse 23 (261 6918/www.kumpelnest3000. com). U1 Kurfürstenstrasse/bus N2, N5, N48. **Open** 5pm-5am Mon-Thur, Sun; 5pm-late Fri, Sat. **No credit cards. Map** p322 K8

Eat, Drink, Shop

Chill out with a cocktail at **Victoria Bar**. *See p169.*

Café im Literaturhaus.

This perennially popular and studiedly tacky establishment is at its best at the end of a long Saturday night, when it's crowded and chaotic and everyone is attempting to dance to disco classics.

Schleusenkrug

Müller-Breslau-Strasse, corner of Unterschleuse (313 9909/www.schleusenkrug.de). S5, S7, S9, S75 Tiergarten/bus N9. **Open** *Summer* 10am-1am daily. *Winter* 10am-6pm daily. **No credit cards.** **Map** p321 G7 ⓱
Bar and beer garden directly on the canal in the Tiergarten, with easy listening, mod and indie pop nights. During the day, Schleusenkrug retains much of its original flavour, hingeing on nautical themes and large glasses of Pils.

Victoria Bar

Potsdamer Strasse 102 (2575 9977/www.victoria bar.de). U1 Kurfürstenstrasse/bus N2, N5, N48. **Open** 6.30pm-3am Mon-Thur, Sun; 6.30pm-4am Fri, Sat. **No credit cards.** **Map** p322 K9 ⓲
Funky, grown-up cocktail bar for a relaxed, mixed crowd. The low-key concept – long bar, subdued lighting, muffled funk and staff who work well together and know what they're mixing – is successful enough for this place to feel like it's been here for ever, though it only opened in 2003. *Photo p167.*

Charlottenburg & Wilmersdorf

There is elegant café life to be enjoyed on the Kurfürstendamm, and around Savignyplatz, Ludwigkirchplatz and Karl-August-Platz, but the last decent nightlife checked out a couple of decades ago, and the bars are no match for neighbouring Schöneberg, let alone Mitte.

Café Hardenberg

Hardenbergstrasse 10 (312 2644/www.cafe-hardenberg.de). U2 Ernst-Reuter-Platz/bus N45. **Open** 9am-1am daily. **Credit** V. **Map** p321/p328 F7 ⓲
Across from the Technical University and usually packed with students drinking coffee. Simple, decent pasta, salads and sandwiches at reasonable prices.

Café im Literaturhaus

Fasanenstrasse 23 (882 5414/www.literaturhaus-berlin.de). U15 Uhlandstrasse/bus N10, N19, N21, N27. **Open** 9.30am-1am daily. **No credit cards.** **Map** p321/p328 F8 ⓴
The café of the Literaturhaus, which has lectures, readings and a bookshop. The greenhouse-like winter garden or salon rooms are great for ducking into a book over breakfast or a snack.

Diener

Grolmanstrasse 47 (881 5329). S3, S5, S7, S9, S75 Savignyplatz/bus N27, N49. **Open** 6pm-2am daily. **Credit** AmEx, MC, V. **Map** p321/p328 F8 ㉛
An authentically old-style Berlin bar, named after famous local boxer Franz Diener. The walls are adorned with faded hunting murals and photos of well-known Germans you won't recognise. You could almost be in 1920s Berlin. Almost.

Galerie Bremer

Fasanenstrasse 37 (881 4908/www.galerie-bremer.de). U1, U9 Spichernstrasse/bus N9. **Open** 8pm-late Mon-Sat. *Gallery* 4-8pm Tue-Fri. **No credit cards.** **Map** p321/p328 F9 ㉜
In the back room of a tiny gallery, this bar has the air of a well-kept secret. The room is painted in deep, rich colours with a beautiful ship-like bar designed by Hans Scharoun, architect of the Philharmonie and Staatsbibliothek. When the assistant barman takes your coat and welcomes you, it's meant to make you feel at home, and it's also the done thing to make a little conversation with the majestically bearded owner – he'll remember you next time you drop in. Then you can sit back, feel privileged and watch the odd member of parliament entering incognito.

Leysieffer

Kurfürstendamm 218, Wilmersdorf (887 2860). U1 Uhlandstrasse. **Open** 9am-7pm Mon-Sat; 11am-5pm Sun. **Credit** AmEx, DC, MC, V. **Map** p321/p328 F8 ㉝
Exquisite tortes and fruit cakes are served upstairs in the high-ceilinged café. Tempting mounds of truffles and bonbons are sold downstairs in the shop.

Schwarzes Café

Kantstrasse 148 (313 8038). S5, S7, S9, S75 Savignyplatz/bus N7, N49. **Open** 24hrs daily (closed 6-10am Tue). **No credit cards.** **Map** p321/p328 F8 ㉞
Open all hours for breakfasts and meals, Schwarzes Café was once all black and anarchistically inclined (hence the name), but the political crowd moved on decades ago and the decor has been brightened. Service can get overstretched when it's crowded, such as early on a weekend morning, when clubbers stop for breakfast on their way home.

Other districts

Club der Visionäre

Am Flutgraben 2, Treptow (6951 8942/www.clubdervisionaere.com). U1 Schlesisches Tor. **Open** 2pm-late Mon-Fri; noon-late Sat, Sun. *Food served* 6pm-1am daily. **No credit cards.** **Map** p324 S9 ㉟
Set on an inlet off the Spree just over the border from Kreuzberg, this popular timbered bar occupies an old boathouse, several floating docks and a decommissioned boat. The totally lo-fi locale is warm and welcoming thanks in no small part to its haphazard, DIY decor. For those in the mood to move their feet, DJs spin minimal techno for the small dancefloor (sometimes it's Ricardo Villalobos at the decks). Most people, however, prefer just to sit under the tree canopy enjoying a casual waterside drink, watching the evening dwindle, or lounging in the Sunday afternoon sun. Later at night, things get more lively.

Eat, Drink, Shop

Shops & Services

Making chaos cool: Berlin's dynamic retail scene blurs boundaries and breaks rules.

High-quality, high prices at **Kunst und Trödel Markt**. *See p173.*

Like everything else in Berlin, the shopping landscape is a jumble of wildly diverse elements unified by a communal nod to innovation, individualism and experimentation. In the German capital, low-brow and high-brow, mainstream and avant-garde, chic and street not only co-exist harmoniously, but interconnect, coming together in interesting unions. A quirky independent bookshop can survive on the same block as a mega chain, and a cheap vintage store selling DDR kitsch can nestle comfortably among some of the city's most expensive boutiques. Even with the influx of big-name international brands and the coming-of-age of the local 1990s avant-garde, Berlin's progressives continue to hatch new schemes for keeping things interesting, while a lively independent shopping scene remains strong.

The best thing to do is just start walking: Berlin has no distinctive shopping centre, and some of its treasures can be found in the least expected places – a hidden inner courtyard, an otherwise empty side street – many popping up for only weeks at a time. Conventional shopping can be found on and around **Tauentzienstrasse** and **Kurfürstendamm** in the west, with luxury brands clustered around **Fasanenstrasse** and household goods in the area between the **Ku'damm** and **Kantstrasse**. In the east, **Friedrichstrasse** offers a similarly up-market selection, but with a hipper, younger edge, while the area around the **Gendarmenmarkt** is home to some cool but pricey concept stores. For cutting-edge local designers, head to the area around **Hackescher Markt**, where many have opened interesting boutiques.

For those seeking more economical options, Berlin offers vintage stores in abundance, with clusters on **Oderberger Strasse** in Prenzlauer Berg and around **Mehringdamm** in Kreuzberg. Frequent flea markets are also a great place to look for second-hand wares. Music and nightlife are an integral part of Berlin, and both the vinyl and streetwear revolutions are palpable across the city. The areas around **Kastanienallee** in Prenzlauer

Berg, **Wühlischstrasse** in Friedrichshain and **Schlesische Strasse**, **Oranienstrasse** and **Bergmannstrasse** in Kreuzberg are particularly resplendent with independent shops selling music, clothes and books, many produced by local artists. Further north, **Brunnenstrasse** is fast developing as a hotspot for idiosyncratic shops stocking everything from silk-screened hoodies to hand-crafted band-aids.

OPENING HOURS

Since the end of 2006, shops can stay open 24 hours on Monday through Saturday and even sometimes on Sundays. Most stores haven't taken full advantage of the new laws, but opening hours are definitely longer than they used to be. Big stores tend to open at 9am and close as late as 10pm, with smaller shops shaving an hour or two at each end. Sunday is still an extremely quiet day, but big department stores and malls are sometimes open. '*Späti*' (late-night delis) can be found all across the city. Internet cafés and filling stations are also open late and stock snacks and drinks.

General

Department stores

There's little to distinguish the four main chains: **Hertie**, **Karstadt**, **Kaufhof** and **Wertheim** all offer decent quality at similar prices.

Dussmann das KulturKaufhaus

Friedrichstrasse 90, Mitte (2025 1111/www. kulturkaufhaus.de). U6, S1, S2, S5, S7, S9, S75 Friedrichstrasse. **Open** 10am-midnight Mon-Sat. **Credit** AmEx, MC, V. **Map** p318/p327 M6.
Intended as a 'cultural department store', this spacious five-floor retailer offers books, CDs, videos, magazines, DVDs and just about everything in between. You can borrow reading glasses (€10 deposit) or a portable CD player (€50 deposit) for the time you're in the store.

Galeries Lafayette

Französische Strasse 23, Mitte (209 480/www. lafayette-berlin.de). U6 Französische Strasse. **Open** 10am-8pm Mon-Sat. **Credit** AmEx, DC, MC, V. **Map** p322/p327 M7.
This elegant glass complex designed by French superstar Jean Nouvel offers great clothes, frequent sales on the upper floors, a good selection of accessories and cosmetics at street level and a basement gourmet food hall where you'll feel transported to Paris. For local flair, check out the store's Labo Mode section, which showcases collections from young, up-and-coming Berlin designers.

KaDeWe

Tauentzienstrasse 21-24, Schöneberg (212 10/ www.kadewe.de). U1, U2, U3 Wittenbergplatz. **Open** 10am-8pm Mon-Wed; 10am-10pm Thur, Fri; 9.30am-8pm Sat. **Credit** AmEx, DC, MC, V. **Map** p321 H9.
The largest department store in continental Europe celebrated its 100th birthday in 2007. It carries name brands in all departments, though the merchandise can be hit or miss. KaDeWe is most famous for its extraordinary food hall, which takes up the entire sixth floor.

Kaufhof

Alexanderplatz 9, Mitte (0180 517 2517/www. galeria-kaufhof.de). U2, U5, U8, S5, S7, S9, S75 Alexanderplatz. **Open** 9.30am-10pm Mon-Sat. **Credit** AmEx, DC, MC, V. **Map** p319/p327 O5.
Once the retail showpiece of communist East Berlin, this busy, utilitarian megastore underwent massive renovation and expansion in 2006. Today, it is the most successful branch of the Kaufhof chain. *Photo p174.*
Other locations Koppenstrasse 8, Friedrichshain (245 400); Frankfurter Allee 115-117, Friedrichshain (408 9980).

Naturkaufhaus

Schlossstrasse 101, Steglitz (797 3716/www. naturkaufhaus-berlin.de). U9 Schlossstrasse. **Open** 10am-8pm Mon-Sat. **Credit** AmEx, MC, V.
Naturkaufhaus is Berlin's first department store for organic goods. It's spread over seven floors of the Galleria mall. The stock ranges from the usual foodstuffs you find in local health food shops to a selection of wine, eco-friendly clothes, shoes, cosmetics and even bedding.

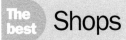

The best Shops

Berlinomat

Looking for local talent? This is the platform for Berlin fashion designers. *See p181.*

Corner Berlin

Berlin's answer to Colette. *See p180.*

KaDeWe

Sixth-floor food hall of the gods. *See above.*

Made in Berlin

A goldmine for second-hand shoppers. *See p185.*

Pro qm

Beautiful books for lovers of all things art and urban. *See p178.*

RSVP

Stationery for the aesthete. *See p194.*

Eat, Drink, Shop

Airline flights are one of the biggest producers of the global warming gas CO_2. But with **The CarbonNeutral Company** you can make your travel a little greener.

Go to **www.carbonneutral.com** to calculate your flight emissions then 'neutralise' them through international projects which save exactly the same amount of carbon dioxide.

Contact us at **shop@carbonneutral.com** or call into the office on **0870 199 99 88** for more details.

CarbonNeutral® flights

Quartier 206

Friedrichstrasse 71, Mitte (2094 6240/www.
quartier206.com). U6 Französische Strasse. **Open**
10.30am-7.30pm Mon-Fri; 10am-6pm Sat. **Credit**
AmEx, DC, MC, V. **Map** p322/p327 M7.
Reminiscent of New York's Takashimaya, this
upmarket store offers not just the most lusted-after
designers, but the definitive items from those labels.
Cult cosmetics and perfumes are on the ground floor;
upstairs is devoted to women's and men's fashion,
lingerie, jewellery and shoes, plus a home-living section stocked with sinfully expensive design items.

Malls

Alexa

Alexanderplatz 4, Mitte (269 3400/www.
alexacentre.com). U2, U5, U8, S5, S7, S9, S75
Alexanderplatz. **Open** 10am-10pm Mon-Sat.
Credit varies. **Map** p319/p327 P6.
This (supposedly) art deco monstrosity may not look
like much from the outside, but inside it's pleasant
enough. And with over 180 stores, it provides some
much-needed shopping convenience in East Berlin.
Includes all the mid-range fashion staples (H&M,
Zara, etc) as well as Europe's largest MediaMarkt.

Potsdamer Platz Arkaden

Alte Potsdamer Strasse 7, Tiergarten (255 9270/
www.potsdamer-platz-arkaden.de). U2, S1, S2, S26
Potsdamer Platz. **Open** 10am-9pm Mon-Sat. **Credit**
varies. **Map** p322/p326 L8.
The glass and steel Arkaden is a modern mall in the
heart of the city. It's a useful address for familiar
names – Benetton, Body Shop, Mango and over 120
others. Don't miss the delicious Italian ice-cream at
Caffé e Gelato on the second floor.

Markets

Flea markets

Berliners love flea markets and just about
every neighbourhood has its own. For a full
list, go to www.berlin.de/orte/shop/kategorie/
wochenmaerkte. From November, the city is
also overrun with Christmas markets, some
tacky, most charming. The loveliest is at
the **Gendarmenmarkt**, while those at
Kollwitzplatz in Prenzlauer Berg and the
Gedächtniskirche in Charlottenburg are
also enchanting. For a complete list, go to www.
berlin-tourist-information.de/kultur/index.en.

Berliner Antik- & Flohmarkt

Bahnhof Friedrichstrasse, S-Bahnbogen 190-203,
Mitte (208 2655/www.antikmarkt-berlin.de). U6, S1,
S2, S5, S7, S9, S25, S75 Friedrichstrasse. **Open**
11am-6pm Mon, Wed-Sun. **Map** p318/p327 M6.
In renovated arches under the S-Bahn tracks, scores
of dealers sell furniture, jewellery, paintings and
vintage clothing. Be warned: it's not cheap.

Flohmarkt am Arkonaplatz

Arkonaplatz, Prenzlauer Berg (0171 710 1662).
U8 Bernauer Strasse. **Open** 10am-4pm Sun.
Map p319/p328 N3.
Flohmarket am Arkonaplatz has a broad array of
retro gear ranging from records to clothing, books
to trinkets, bikes to coffee tables – all at moderate
prices. Best selection in the morning.

Flohmarkt am Boxhagener Platz

Boxhagener Platz, Friedrichshain (0178 476
2242). U1, S3, S5, S7, S9, S75 Warschauer
Strasse or U5 Samariterstrasse. **Open** 10am-
6pm Sun. **Map** p324 T7.
Many local young artists and T-shirt designers set
up stalls at this overflowing market, while punky
types and bohemian mothers shop for vintage sunglasses and unusual crockery. Depending on the
day, you could snatch some great second-hand finds
from students selling their old stuff. This place can
be very cheap if you bargain hard enough.

Flohmarkt am Mauerpark

Bernauer Strasse 63-64, Prenzlauer Berg (0176
2925 0021). U8 Bernauer Strasse. **Open** 7am-5pm
Sun. **Map** p319/p326 N3.
This is one of the biggest and busiest flea markets
in Berlin, retailing everything from cheap Third
World fashion to cardboard boxes of black market
CDs. Students and residents alike sell their things
here at great prices, and you might just find a treasure trove of awesome second-hand clothing,
books, bags and other goods.

Kunst und Nostalgie Markt

Am Zeughaus (0171 710 1662). U6, S1, S2, S5, S7,
S9, S25, S75 Friedrichstrasse. **Open** 11am-5pm Sat,
Sun. **Map** p319/p327 N6.
On the riverbank by the Deutsches Historisches
Museum, Kunst und Nostalgie Markt is one of the
few places in Berlin that you can still find genuine
relics of the DDR, with anything from old signs
advertising coal briquettes to framed pictures of
Honecker. Also paintings, prints, candles, leather-
work, books and CDs.

Kunst und Trödel Markt

Strasse des 17 Juni, Tiergarten (2555 0096/www.
berliner-troedelmarkt.de). U2 Ernst-Reuter-Platz or
S5, S7, S9, S75 Tiergarten. **Open** 11am-5pm Sat,
Sun. **Map** p321 F7.
Kunst und Trödel Markt lies on the stretch west of
the S-Bahn station. Quality, early 20th-century
objects with prices to match, alongside a jumble of
vintage and alternative clothing, old furniture, second-hand records and books. Interesting stuff, but
cramped aisles. *Photo p170.*

General markets

Berlin's many *Wochenmärkte* usually sell
cheaper, fresher produce than regular shops.
For a good list, see www.hungryinberlin.
com/local-market-schedule.

The recently renovated **Kaufhof**. *See p171.*

Farmers' Market at Wittenbergplatz

Wittenbergplatz, Schöneberg (2363 6360). U1, U2, U3 Wittenbergplatz. **Open** 10am-7pm Thur. **Map** p321 H8.

Predominantly organic produce, including cheese, bread, pasta, meat, fruit and veg from local farms. Also non-edible items such as wooden brushes.

Farmers' Market at Zionskirchplatz

Zionskirchplatz, Prenzlauer Berg (394 4073). U2 Senefelderplatz or U8 Rosenthaler Platz. **Open** 11am-6.30pm Thur. **Map** p319/p328 N4.

Regional growers sell fruit and veggies, fresh fish and homemade jams, breads and cheeses. Farmers set up their stands on the cobblestone walkway surrounding one of Berlin's most beautiful churches, making this a truly picturesque market throughout the year.

Organic Market at Kollwitzplatz

Kollwitzplatz, Prenzlauer Berg (no phone). U2 Senefelderplatz. **Open** noon-7pm Thur; 9am-4pm Sat. **Map** p319/p328 P4.

Small, open-air organic market. Steaming punch and wholegrain cinnamon waffles make it *gemütlich* in winter, but it's more lively in summer.

Türkischer Markt

Maybachufer, Neukölln (no phone). U8 Schönleinstrasse. **Open** noon-6.30pm Tue, Fri. **Map** p323 P10.

A crowded market across the canal from Kreuzberg, designed to meet the needs of the local Turkish community. Fresh veg, wonderful spices, great prices.

Winterfeldt Markt

Winterfeldtplatz, Schöneberg (no phone). U1, U2, U3, U4 Nollendorfplatz. **Open** 8am-1pm Wed; 8am-3.30pm Sat. **Map** p322 J9.

On Saturdays, it seems like all of West Berlin is visiting this jam-packed market, full to the brim with vegetables, cheese, wholegrain breads, wurst, meats, flowers, clothes, pet supplies and toys. Many are there for their weekly shopping; others, to meet a friend at one of the many cafés off the square. A Berlin institution worth experiencing first-hand.

Specialist

Antiques

Suarezstrasse in Charlottenburg is lined with over 30 antique shops, offering everything from Victorian furniture to art deco clocks. For 18th- and 19th-century goods, the dealers on Schöneberg's **Keithstrasse** and **Goltzstrasse** are worth a visit, as are the streets around **Fasanenplatz** in Wilmersdorf. Charlottenburg's **Bleibtreustrasse** is also home to a handful of shops. In the east, you'll find several small, unpretentious *Antiquariäten* on **Grünberger Strasse** in Friedrichshain and **Kollwitzstrasse** and **Husemannstrasse** in Prenzlauer Berg. *See also p173* **Flea markets**.

Bleibtreu-Antik

Schlüterstrasse 54, Charlottenburg (883 5212/ www.bleibtreu-antik.de). S5, S7, S9, S75 avignyplatz. **Open** noon-7pm Mon-Fri; 11am-3pm Sat; or by appointment. **Credit** MC, V. **Map** p321/p328 E8.

This shop has been around since the early 1970s, offering collectors and browsers an impressive array of original 19th-century antiques. Fully restored Biedermeier and Jugendstil furniture, glassware, silver and lamps are the main focus, along with an impressive selection of costume jewellery from 1900 to 1960.

Deco Arts

Motzstrasse 6, Schöneberg (215 8672). U1, U2, U3, U4 Nollendorfplatz. **Open** 3-7pm Wed-Fri; noon-5pm Sat. **No credit cards. Map** p321 H9.

Deco Arts stocks shell-shaped 1930s sofas and other deco furniture at fair prices, the odd piece by Marcel Breuer and Carl Jacobs and some 1950s and '60s treasures. If a sofa's too big to get home, pick up a stylish ashtray or vase.

Fingers

Nollendorfstrasse 35, Schöneberg (215 3441). U1, U2, U3, U4 Nollendorfplatz. **Open** 2.30-6.30pm Tue-Fri; 11am-2pm Sat. **No credit cards**. **Map** p322 J9.

Splendid finds from the 1940s, '50s and '60s, including lipstick-shaped cigarette lighters, vintage toasters, weird lighting and eccentric glassware.

Radio Art

Zossener Strasse 2, Kreuzberg (693 9435/www. radio-art.de). U7 Gneisenaustrasse. **Open** noon-6pm Thur, Fri; 10am-1pm Sat. **Credit** AmEx, MC, V. **Map** p323 N10.

A fine collection of antique radios, ranging from big, wooden, 1930s sitting-room centrepieces to tiny '70s transistors in shocking pink plastic.

Books & magazines

Berlin still has a lively independent bookshop scene, with hundreds of small, idiosyncratic booksellers catering to specific neighbourhoods, communities and interests. For gay bookshops, *see p229.*

English-language

Another Country

Riemannstrasse 7, Kreuzberg (6940 1160/www. anothercountry.de). U7 Gneisenaustrasse. **Open** 11am-8pm Mon-Fri; 11am-4pm Sat. **No credit cards**. **Map** p322 M10.

An impressive second-hand bookshop mostly used as a library, Another Country is stocked with about 20,000 English-language titles that can be borrowed

or bought. The spacious, welcoming premises abound with comfortable nooks and crannies for curling up with a book, and the store plays host to a weekly film night, TV night and dinner night.

Books in Berlin

Goethestrasse 69, Charlottenburg (313 1233/ www.booksinberlin.de). S5, S7, S9, S75 Savignyplatz. **Open** noon-8pm Mon-Fri; 10am-4pm Sat. **Credit** V. **Map** p321/p328 E7.

Run by a Bostonian and stocking a dynamic selection of new and existing histories and political tracts, classical and modern fiction and reference and travel books, this is something of a Berlin institution.

East of Eden

Schreinerstrasse 10, Friedrichshain (423 9362/www. east-of-eden.de). U5 Samariterstrasse. **Open** noon-7pm Mon-Fri; noon-4pm Sat. **No credit cards**. **Map** p325 T6.

The owners of this old-school second-hand shop shuttle frequently to London in search of paperback staples and rare editions. Books are also available to borrow at a small fee. Readings and concerts too.

Fair Exchange

Dieffenbachstrasse 58, Kreuzberg (694 4675/ www.fair-exchange.de). U8 Schönleinstrasse. **Open** 11am-7pm Mon-Fri; 10am-6pm Sat. **No credit cards**. **Map** p323 P10.

Big selection of second-hand English-language books, with an emphasis on literature. Cosy atmosphere.

Hugendubel

Tauentzienstrasse 13, Charlottenburg (www.hugen dubel.de). U1, U9 Kurfürstendamm. **Open** 9.30am-10pm Mon-Sat. **No credit cards**. **Map** p321 G8.

Eat, Drink, Shop

Could this be Europe's best bookshop? **Marga Schoeller Bücherstube** *See p177.*

The best guides to enjoying London life

(but don't just take our word for it)

'More than 700 places where you can eat out for less than £20 a head... a mass of useful information in a genuinely pocket–sized guide'

Mail on Sunday

'Armed with a tube map and this guide there is no excuse to find yourself in a duff bar again'

Evening Standard

'I'm always asked how I keep up to date with shopping and services in a city as big as London. This guide is the answer'

Red Magazine

'Get the inside track on the capital's neighbourhoods'

Independent on Sunday

'A treasure trove of treats that lists the best the capital has to offer'

The People

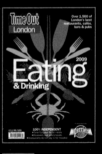

Rated 'Best Restaurant Guide'

Sunday Times

TIME OUT GUIDES WRITTEN BY LOCAL EXPERTS

timeout.com/shop

Time Out London

This large branch of this large chain houses more than 140,000 books, and they have a big English-language section. An in-house café offers drinks and snacks.
Other locations Friedrichstrasse 83, Mitte (0180 148 4484); Potsdamer Platz Arkaden, Alte Potsdamer Strasse 7, Tiergaren (0180 148 4484); Wilmersdorfer Strasse 121, Charlottenburg (0180 148 4484).

König Taschen Berlin

Museum für Fotographie, Jebensstrasse 2, Charlottenburg (3180 8558/www.taschen.com). U2, U9, S5, S7, S9, S75 Zoologischer Garten. **Open** 10am-6pm Tue, Wed, Fri-Sun; 10am-10pm Thur. **Credit** AmEx, MC, V. **Map** p321/p328 G8.
Housed in the Museum für Fotographie, this 'bookstore for photography' is a treasure trove of works printed by art book publisher Taschen. Photography is the store specialty, and catalogues for the foundation's exhibitions are also available.

Marga Schoeller Bücherstube

Knesebeckstrasse 33, Charlottenburg (881 1112). S5, S7, S9, S75 Savignyplatz. **Open** 9.30am-7pm Mon-Wed; 9.30am-8pm Thur, Fri; 9.30am-5pm Sat. **Credit** MC, V. **Map** p321/p328 F8.
Rated among Europe's best independent literary bookshops by *Bookseller* magazine, this excellent establishment, founded in 1930, includes one of Berlin's most interesting English-language sections. *Photo p175.*

Le Matou

Husemannstrasse 29, Prenzlauer Berg (2809 9601/www.le-matou.de). U2 Eberswalder Strasse. **Open** 10am-6.30pm Mon-Fri; 10am-2pm Sat. **No credit cards. Map** p319/p328 P3.
International books for children and young people in close to 30 languages, including English, French, Italian, Spanish, Arabic and Russian. Over 10,000 titles are held in stock.

Saint Georges

Wörther Strasse 27, Prenzlauer Berg (8179 8333/www.saintgeorgesbookshop.com). Tram M2 Marienburger Strasse. **Open** 11am-8pm Mon-Fri; 11am-7pm Sat. **Credit** MC, V. **Map** p319/p328 P3.
Comfortable leather couches are provided for browsing a decent and reasonably priced selection of English-language books, both old and new. Lots of biographies and contemporary lit, plus a good turnover of dog-eared classics.

Storytime Books & Café

Schmargendorfer Strasse 36-37, Friedenau (8596 7004/www.storytime-books.com). U9 Friedrich-Wilhelm-Platz or S1 Friedenau. **Open** 10am-6pm Mon-Fri; 10am-4pm Sat. **Credit** MC, V. **Map** p321 G12.
Owner Diane Pentaleri-Otto specialises in children's books and works hard to make the shop child- and parent-friendly. There are many events for kids, such as a weekly story time in English and sing-alongs in English and German, and coffee and muffins for grown-ups.

General

Artificium

Rosenthaler Strasse 40-41, Mitte (3087 2280/ www.artificium.com). S5, S7, S9, S75 Hackescher Markt. **Open** 10am-9pm Mon-Thur; 10am-11pm Fri. **Credit** AmEx, MC, V. **Map** p319/p326 N5.
Tucked into the Hackesche Höfe, this art bookshop specialises in 20th-century culture, stocking titles on everything from photography to dance, design to film, architecture to theatre.

Berlin Story

Unter den Linden 40, Mitte (2045 3842/www.berlin-story.de). U6 Französische Strasse. **Open** 10am-7pm daily. **Credit** AmEx, MC, V. **Map** p318/p327 M6.
You won't find a better selection of Berlin-related books in German and English: everything from novels with Berlin settings to non-fiction volumes on history and culture. Historical maps, posters, videos, CDs, postcards and souvenirs are also available.

Bildschöne Bücher

Kollwitzstrasse 53, Prenzlauer Berg (4373 5707/ www.bildschoene-buecher.de). U2 Senefelderplatz. **Open** 4-7pm Wed, Fri; 10am-6pm Sat. **Credit** MC, V. **Map** p319/p328 P4.
'Picture Perfect Books' is a publishing house and select shop in one, featuring limited-edition books and box sets that are hard to find elsewhere in Berlin. The varied selection of art, architecture, design and photography books are all high quality.

Bücherbogen

Savignyplatz Stadtbahnbogen 593, Charlottenburg (3186 9511/www.buecherbogen.com). S5, S7, S9, S75 Savignyplatz. **Open** 10am-8pm Mon-Fri; 10am-6pm Sat. **Credit** MC, V. **Map** p321/p328 E8.
The store for all manner of art books. This branch under the Savignyplatz S-Bahn station stocks international magazines and books on painting, sculpture, photography, design and architecture; the branch in the National Gallery specialises in books on 20th-century art, architecture and photography.
Other locations Neue Nationalgalerie, Potsdamer Strasse 50, Tiergarten (261 1090); Schlossstrasse 1, Charlottenburg (3269 5814).

Kohlhaas & Company

Fasanenstrasse 23, Wilmersdorf (882 5044). U1 Uhlandstrasse. **Open** 10am-8pm Mon-Fri; 10am-6pm Sat. **Credit** AmEx, MC, V. **Map** p321/p328 F8.
German literature predominates in this elegant little high-brow bookshop under the Literaturhaus.

Modern Graphics

Oranienstrasse 22, Kreuzberg (615 8810/www. modern-graphics.de). U1, U8 Kottbusser Tor. **Open** 11am-8pm Mon-Fri; 10am-7pm Sat. **Credit** MC, V. **Map** p323 P9.
Large selection of imported and alternative comics. Also T-shirts, graphic novels, anime and calendars.
Other locations Tauentzienstrasse 9-12 in the Europa-Center, Charlottenburg (8599 9054).

Pro qm

Almstadtstrasse 48-50, Mitte (2472 8520/www.pro-qm.de). U2 Rosa-Luxemburg-Platz. **Open** noon-8pm Mon-Sat. **Credit** MC, V. **Map** p319/p326 O5.
The artist owners here offer a well-informed and cosmopolitan selection of new and used books and mags on architecture, art, design, pop culture, urban life and cultural theory. Good selection of English titles.

Used & antiquarian

There are small antiquarian booksellers all over Berlin, and many have at least a shelf or two of English books. The areas around **Knesebeckstrasse** and **Pestalozzistrasse**

in Charlottenburg, **Winterfeldtstrasse** in Schöneberg and **Kollwitzstrasse** and **Husemannstrasse** in Prenzlauer Berg all provide decent literary pickings.

Children

Wooden toys are a German speciality. Puppets from the Dresdener puppet factory and tiny wooden figures from the Erzgebirge region are distinctive. Stuffed toys are also traditional: Steiff and its rival Sigikid offer beautifully made cuddly animals. **Storytime Books** and **Le Matou** (for both *see p177*) are great children's bookshops.

Keep it local

In the 1990s, Berlin's chaotic post-reunification atmosphere gave rise to a vibrant subculture, as artists and bohemians flooded into the city from around Germany and the world. In the melting pot, fashion, photography, architecture, product design, music, parties, clubs and a whole lot of other things became entangled, and Berlin fashion has been an interdisciplinary undertaking ever since.

Though still haphazard, the Berlin fashion world has matured in the past decade, thanks in no small part to the rising reputations of the city's many fashion schools and degree programmes. Today, the rookie mistakes and amateur seamwork of the 1990s have all but disappeared, replaced with high-quality craftsmanship and professionalism. No business better exemplifies this trend than **Butterflysoulfire**, an experimental label that once embodied Berlin grit and now offers perfectly crafted items for purchase on its website, www.btfsf.com.

Though as diverse and ever-changing as the city itself, the local fashion scene is united by some common elements – youth, energy and audaciousness – and some common enemies – indifferent consumerism, conformism and mass production. Individualism is fiercely guarded across the board, and hand-made, limited-edition items highly prized. Between 600 and 800 designers work in Berlin, 200 of which have their own studio shops, mostly in Mitte, Prenzlauer Berg and Kreuzberg.

More established labels include the minimalist, clean-lined **Adddress** (2887 3365, www.adddress.de); **Heartbo**, the girly-with-an-edge label from Danish expat Sarah Heartbo (Oderberger Strasse 20, 4404 5425, www.heartbo.com); *Pulver* (*see p182*), which

sells sleek womenswear out of a shop in Mitte; **c.neeon**, a bold and bright line sold at both Wood Wood (*see p184*) and Konk (Kleine Hamburger Strasse 15, 2809 7839, www.konk-berlin.de); and internationally renowned **Kaviar Gauche**, a top-quality label based on unrefined materials and leather, sold at Konk and Galeries Lafayette (*see p171*). Berlin labels with a more edgy, street look include **starstyling** (*see p183*, stocked at its eponymous shop on Mulackstrasse; **IrieDaily** (*see p184*), which is also sold at streetwear stores such as Eté-clothing (*see p184*); and **mazooka**, sold out of a showroom on Kastanienallee (Kastanienallee 34, 2313 4390, www.mazooka.de).

These and Berlin's other designers are supported by a number of fashion showcases geared specifically towards celebrating local talent. **Berlinomat** (*see p181*), the Labo Mode section of **Galeries Lafayette** (*see p171*) and **Berliner Klamotten** (*see p181*) are just a few of the platforms for Berlin design, where fresh, young talent is given the opportunity to present collections to a large clientele. Meanwhile, **Create Berlin** (www.create-berlin.de), a network linking designers, agencies, companies and institutions from all sectors of design, helps promote Berlin-based labels at both the national and international level. For the past two decades, these and similar initiatives and networks have been helping to convert Berlin's once modest fashion scene into a thriving international powerhouse driven by the city's raw creative energy. Berlin is still not Paris or Milan, nor does it want to be; the German capital is forging its own unique path as a colourful, youthful, unconventional fashion hub.

Fashion

Dollyrocker

Gärtnerstrasse 25, Friedrichshain (5471 9606/
www.dollyrocker.de). U1, S3, S5, S7, S9, S75
Warschauer Strasse or U5 Samariterstrasse.
Open 10am-7pm Tue-Fri; 11am-4pm Sat.
No credit cards. Map p324 T7.
Designers (and mothers) Gabi Hartkopp and Ina
Langenbruch recycle high-quality textiles to create
colourful and adorable clothing and accessories for
kids up to seven years old. Under their sewing
machines, a man's blouse becomes a boy's T-shirt,
women's designer jeans become a girl's dress – each
piece unique. Hand-made leather shoes are also sold.

Emma & Co

Niebuhrstrasse 2, Charlottenburg (8867 6787).
S5, S7, S9, S75 Savignyplatz. **Open** 11am-7pm
Mon-Fri; 11am-4pm Sat. **Credit** MC, V. **Map**
p321/p328 E8.
Melanie Waltje's charming shop offers well-made
but thankfully not overly expensive children's
wear, bedding, toys and gift items such as name
books and terry-cloth teddies.

Toys

Heidi's Spielzeugladen

Kantstrasse 61, Charlottenburg (323 7556). U7
Wilmersdorfer Strasse. **Open** 9.30am-6.30pm Mon-
Fri; 9.30am-4pm Sat. **Credit** MC, V. **Map** p320 D8.
Wooden toys, including cookery utensils and child-
sized kitchens, are the attraction here. Also a good
selection of books, puppets and wall-hangings.

Michas Bahnhof

Nürnberger Strasse 24A, Schöneberg (218 6611/
www.michas-bahnhof.de). U3 Augsburger Strasse.
Open 10am-6.30pm Mon-Fri; 10am-3.30pm Sat.
Credit AmEx, DC, MC, V. **Map** p321 G9.
Small shop packed with model trains, old and new,
and everything that goes with them.

Tam Tam

Knesebeckstrasse 59-61, Charlottenburg (882
1454). S5, S7, S9, S75 Savignyplatz. **Open**
10am-7pm Mon-Fri; 10am-6pm Sat. **Credit** MC, V.
Map p321/p328 F8.
A bright, charming shop filled with stuffed animals
and wooden toys, including building blocks, trains,
trucks, dolls' houses and child-sized wooden stoves.

v.Kloeden

Wielandstrasse 24, Charlottenburg (8871 2512/
www.vonkloeden.de). **Open**
10am-7pm Mon-Fri; 10am-4pm Sat. **Credit** AmEx,
DC, MC, V. **Map** p320 D9.
The oldest and friendliest toy store in town stocks
children's books in English, toys and reading material from the Montessori and Steiner schools, lovely
handmade Käthe Kruse dolls, Erzgebirge wooden
figures and all kinds of modern kids' fare.

Zartholz

Knaackstrasse 54, Prenzlauer Berg (451 4747/
www.zartholz.de). U2 Senefelderplatz. **Open**
10.30am-6pm Mon-Fri; 10am-4pm Sat. **Credit**
MC, V. **Map** p319/p328 P4.
Zartholz is a charming two-storey shop full of traditional German toys, with an emphasis on those
made of wood. Sells all the classics of German
childhood, including a large selection of Käthe
Kruse dolls and wooden items from perennial
Swedish favourite BRIO.

Designer kiosks

This is a hard-to-define category of store that
perfectly reflects the anything-goes, mix-it-all-
up spirit that epitomises Berlin. These shops
are usually run by young, creative types and
sell everything from off-beat knick-knacks
to high-quality art books. In fact, many are
more than just retail outlets, also serving as
platforms for local talent and gathering points
for artists and designers. Most feature a
minimalist, Tokyo pet-architecture aesthetic,
and a stock that can best be described as
pop meets elite.

Kwik Shop

Kastanienallee 44, Mitte (4199 7150/www.
kwikshop.de). U2 Senefelderplatz or U8 Rosenthaler
Platz. **Open** noon-7pm Mon-Sat. **Credit** MC, V.
Map p319/p326 O4.
Originally, this quirky little shop had no door, so
products had to be sold through a kiosk window; the
practice stuck, and today, despite there being a door,
all the goods are displayed in the shop window and
sold through a hatch. The selection features both
wacky gift items and finely crafted household miscellany, much of it self-made by owners Annette
Bruns and Oliver Spies.

Luxus International

Kastanienallee 101, Prenzlauer Berg (4432 4877/
www.luxus-international.de). U2 Eberswalder Strasse.
Open 11am-8pm Mon-Fri; 11am-4pm Sat. **Credit**
AmEx, MC, V. **Map** p319/p326 O3.
For €7.50 a month, this platform for local talent
rents individual shelves to the scores of Berlin
designers who can't afford to open their own shops.
The stock is always changing and usually off-beat,
it includes everything from earrings to ashtrays,
handbags to T-shirts, lamps to notebooks. These
Berlin originals make excellent souvenirs and
fabulous gifts.

Risi-Bisi Popshop

Brunnenstrasse 7, Mitte (6677 3336/www.risi-
bisi.de). U8 Rosenthaler Platz. **Open** noon-8pm Mon-
Fri; 1-6pm Sat. **Credit** AmEx, MC, V. **Map** p319 N4.
A coffee shop meets knick-knack store, this place
offers steaming latté macchiatos alongside a selection of urban clothing, indie CDs, art books, magazines and tons of quirky 'pop items'.

SupaLifeKiosk

Raumerstrasse 40, Prenzlauer Berg (4467 8826/www.supalife.de). U2 Eberswalder Strasse. **Open** noon-7pm Mon-Sat. **Credit** MC, V. **Map** p319/p326 O3.

SupaLifeKiosk is a store, a gallery and design firm all in one. It's a platform for local designers selling handmade and limited-edition objects including silk-screened prints, cards, books, random items and select clothing. Young Berlin-based designers feature heavily, and rotating monthly exhibits keep things interesting.

Über Store

Auguststrasse 26A, Mitte (6677 9095/www.ueber-store.de). U8 Rosenthaler Platz or S1, S2, S26 Oranienburger Strasse. **Open** noon-7pm Tue-Fri; noon-6pm Sat. **Credit** AmEx, MC, V. **Map** p319/p326 N5.

You never know what you'll find at Anja Kantowsky's small boutique, where the assortment of quirky items undergoes a complete overhaul roughly every three months. The stock is chosen according to theme, with past highlights including Wanderlust, Seduction and Melancholy (for the latter, think bittersweet chocolates, self-help books and fake black crows).

Fashion

In the last two decades, the Berlin fashion scene has exploded, with international brands opening flagship stores, local designers selling innovative collections out of studio shops, and guerrilla stores keeping things on the move. High-end department stores and big, mid-market chains are clustered on **Kurfürstendamm** and **Friedrichstrasse**. Traditional luxury brands are focused on **Fasanenstrasse** off the Ku'damm, while fancy, avant-garde boutiques and flagship stores abound in the area around **Hackescher Markt** and on nearby **Münzstrasse** and **Alte Schönhauser Strasse**. Smaller local talents have set up shop on **Kastanienallee** in Prenzlauer Berg, **Wühlischstrasse** in Friedrichshain and **Schlesische Strasse** and **Oranienstrasse** in Kreuzberg.

Designer: international

Acne Jeans

Münzstrasse 23, Mitte (2804 4870/www.acnejeans.com). U8 Weinmeisterstrasse. **Open** noon-8pm Mon-Fri; noon-6pm Sat; 2-6pm Sun. **Credit** MC, V. **Map** p319/p326 O5.

This young Swedish brand has a huge following. Its Berlin flagship store is the first outside of Scandinavia and features the label's complete seasonal collections of men's and women's fashion, shoes, bags, accessories and jewellery.

Apartment

Memhardstrasse 8, Mitte (2804 2251/www.apartmentberlin.de). U2, U5, U8, S5, S7, S9, S75 Alexanderplatz. **Open** noon-8pm Mon-Fri; noon-6pm Sat. **Credit** AmEx, MC, V. **Map** p319/p327 O5.

Unmarked and entirely empty, Apartment's huge white-box storefront is easy to miss. But head down to the basement and you'll find clothing, accessories and shoes from hot local and international designers, from Bernard Wilhelm to Jeremy Scott.

A.P.C.

Mulackstrasse 36, Mitte (2844 9192/www.apc.fr). U2 Rosa-Luxemburg-Platz or U8 Weinmeisterstrasse. **Open** noon-8pm Mon-Fri; noon-6pm Sat. **Credit** AmEx, MC, V. **Map** p319/p326 O5.

Tucked away in a side street, this flagship store from the French cult brand offers mens- and womenswear in classic Paris styles, own-label CDs and gadgets.

Corner Berlin

Französische Strasse 40, Mitte (2067 0940/www.thecornerberlin.de). U6 Französische Strasse. **Open** 10.30am-7.30pm Mon-Fri; 10am-7pm Sat. **Credit** DC, MC, V. **Map** p322/p327 M7.

This impeccably designed store – Berlin's answer to Colette in Paris – offers a select mix of men's and women's fashion, accessories, electronics, books, music, art and even vintage furniture for the stylish set with money to spend. Featured designers include Marc Jacobs and Christian Louboutin and there's an in-house bar and restaurant.

Harvey's

Kurfürstendamm 55-56, Charlottenburg (883 3803/ www.harveys-berlin.de). U7 Adenauerplatz. **Open** 11am-8pm Mon-Fri; 11am-7pm Sat. **Credit** AmEx, DC, MC, V. **Map** p320 D9.

Sigfried Böhnisch has been selling cutting-edge men's labels for over 20 years. He stocks Japanese powerhouses such as Yohji Yamamoto, Issey Miyake and Comme des Garçons, as well as Belgian labels like Martin Margiela and footwear from Canadian shoemaker Paul Harnden.

Lil*Shop

Brunnenstrasse 184, Mitte (2804 5338/www.lil-shop.com). U8 Rosenthaler Platz. **Open** noon-7pm Mon-Fri; noon-6pm Sat. **Credit** AmEx, MC, V. **Map** p319 N4.

Once upon a time, a series of Comme des Garçons guerrilla stores popped up around Berlin and then disappeared, one by one. But the Japanese brand was such a hit here that the women who ran the series decided to open this little (permanent) gem, which carries vintage CDG and Junya Watanabe clothing, accessories and perfumes in addition to the label's current collection.

Mientus

Wilmersdorfer Strasse 73, Charlottenburg (323 9077/ www.mientus.com). U7 Wilmersdorfer Strasse or S5, S7, S9, S75 Charlottenburg. **Open** 10am-7pm Mon-Sat. **Credit** AmEx, DC, MC, V. **Map** p321/p328 E8.

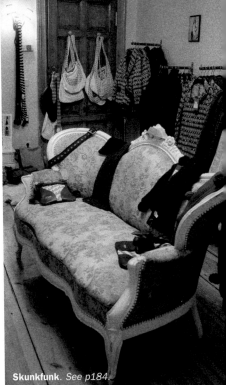

Skunkfunk. *See p184.*

Clean cuts for sharp men from a range of well-known collections including Dsquared, D&G, K Lagerfeld, Miu Miu and Paul Smith.
Other locations Kurfürstendamm 52, Charlottenburg (323 9077).

Veronica Pohle
Kurfürstendamm 64, Charlottenburg (883 3731/ www.veronicapohle.de). U7 Adenauerplatz. **Open** 10.30am-7.30pm Mon-Fri; 11am-6.30pm Sat. **Credit** AmEx, DC, MC, V. **Map** p321 E9.
Large boutique offering womenswear from top international labels such as Anna Sui, Seven, Tocca, Paul Smith, D&G, Lacroix and Paul Smith. This place is also a good place to go star-spotting, with celebs like Kim Fischer and Katharina Witt counting it among their Berlin favourites.

Designer: local

AM1, AM2 & AM3
Münzstrasse 21-23, Mitte (3088 1945/www. andreasmurkudis.net). U8 Weinmeisterstrasse. **Open** noon-8pm Mon-Sat. **Credit** AmEx, MC, V. **Map** p319/p326 O5.
Three concept shops hidden in a courtyard behind the Acne store (*see p180*), AM 1-3 offer a reverently presented selection of cutting-edge, luxury designers,

many of them local. The shop is run by Andreas Murkudis, brother of famous German fashion designer Kostas Murkudis – several of whose items can be found in the stores.

Berliner Klamotten
Rosenthaler Strasse 40-41, Mitte (no phone/www. berlinerklamotten.de). S5, S7, S9, S75 Hackescher Markt. **Open** 11am-8pm Mon-Sat. **No credit cards**. **Map** p319/p310 N5.
Berliner Klamotten is a guerrilla store and internet platform for over 140 local designers. Appearing and disappearing in empty spaces across the city, this arbiter of cutting-edge fashion-cool constantly reinvents itself, but always stocks exclusive clothing, jewellery and accessories from designers stitching and crafting out of Berlin basements and living rooms. Check the website – it may already have reincarnated at a new location.

Berlinomat
Frankfurter Allee 89, Friedrichshain (4208 1445/ www.berlinomat.com). U5, S41, S42, S8, S85 Frankfurter Allee. **Open** 11am-8pm Mon-Fri; 10am-6pm Sat. **Credit** DC, MC, V. **Map** p319 N7.
This is a showroom for local designers off the beaten shopping track at the eastern edge of Friedrichshain. Owners Theresa Meirer and Jörg Wichmann sell fashion, furniture, jewellery and accessories from over 140

Immaculate concepts

No other city can boast as many concept, guerrilla or clandestine stores as Berlin, where the boundaries between shopping, lifestyle, design, fashion, nightlife and art are being constantly questioned, pushed and blurred. Recent years have seen an explosion of intellectually conceived stores that are hard to categorise but easy to recognise – that is, if you know where to go looking for them.

The unmarked, empty storefront of **Apartment** (*see p180*) occupies the entire ground floor of a lifeless DDR concrete high-rise, which is hardly an open invitation to passers-by to come in and explore. But downstairs in the basement, it's full to the brim with designer clothes from the likes of Bernhard Wilhelm, Pulver and Cheap Monday. Further north on Brunnenstrasse, Comme des Garçon's **Lil*Shop** (*see p180*) is easier to spot, but equally minimalistic: an 'anti-concept' concept store purposely situated in an ungentrified, non-commercial area. In the unassuming little shop, the label's clothes and accessories are displayed simply, with reverence but without fanfare. **OONA** (*see p185*) takes this museum-like display of goods one step further, positioning itself sas a 'gallery for jewellery', where the work of innovative, young jewellery artists is displayed and sold. Not far off, Andreas Murkudis's **AM 1-3** (*see p181*) are purposely hard-to-find, and

their super-modern, design-heavy aesthetic only heighten their atmosphere of calculated exclusivity. Other similarly modern stores scattered around Mitte include **ic!** (*see p191*), **Mykita** (*see p191*), **Trippen** (*see p186*) and the **Corner** (*see p180*).

Big brands have muscled in on the action too, although they tend to reject the under-the-radar approach of the smaller stores. Housed on the ground floor of an old, restored building in Mitte, the **Boss Orange** flagship (Max-Beer-Strasse 2-4, Mitte, 8471 07880, www.hugoboss.com) feels self-consciously unfinished. The airy, high-ceilinged, loft-like space is largely undecorated, with raw walls and stark metal racks assuring primacy of visual focus to the clothing itself. Nearby, the Vans **Butchers Block Berlin** store (Alte Schönhauser Strasse 48, Mitte, 2404 7112) is housed in a century-old ex-butcher shop whose interior was left mostly intact.

Another Berlin retail trend is to create designer kiosks that take the form of chameleon stores with constant stock overhauls. To see the concept in action, check out **Über Store** (*see p180*), **Risi-Bisi PopShop** (*see p179*), **Kwik Shop** (*see p179*) and **SupaLifeKiosk** (*see p180*). In Berlin, shopping can be more than just a commercial venture: it can even be an intellectual exercise designed to make you question the nature of consumption.

Berlin labels at prices ranging from €1 to €700. The exciting Young Stars section presents items designed by recent alums from Berlin's seven fashion schools. An in-house café serves coffee and cake.

Claudia Skoda
Alte Schönhauser Strasse 35, Mitte (280 7211/ www.claudiaskoda.com). U8 Weinmeisterstrasse. **Open** noon-8pm Mon-Fri; noon-7pm Sat. **Credit** AmEx, MC, V. **Map** p319/p326 O5.
Berlin's most established womenswear designer has extended her range to include men – items for both sexes are showcased in this loft space. Made with high-tech yarns and innovative knitting techniques, the collections bear her signature combination of stretch fabrics and graceful drape effects.

Flagshipstore
Oderberger Strasse 53, Prenzlauer Berg (4373 5327/ www.flagshipstore-berlin.de). U2 Eberswalder Strasse. **Open** 11am-8pm Mon-Sat. **Credit** MC, V. **Map** p319/p328 O3.
Clothing and accessories for men and women from over 30 up-and-coming designers, mostly based in

Berlin. Some items are unique, others are exclusive to the store, and all are produced on a small scale, in limited amounts. Owner Einat Zinger Feiler also sells his own label, Hazelnut – Street Royalty. Good for hip, young(ish) urbanites.

Heimat
Niederbarnimstrasse 17, Friedrichshain (7469 9914/ www.mein-heimat-laden.de). U5 Samariterstrasse. **Open** 11am-8pm Mon-Fri; 11am-6pm Sat. **Credit** MC, V. **Map** p324 T7.
The clothes, accessories, books, music and knick-knacks that line the shelves of this cosy, friendly, neighbourhood store come almost exclusively from young, local labels such as cuy.cuy, mia., duskworld and froschhimmel. Particular emphasis on silk-screened items (scarves, T-shirts, hoodies) and a good mix of street and chic.

Pulver
Torstrasse 199, Mitte (6792 6496/www.pulver-studio.de). S1, S2, S26 Oranienburger Strasse. **Open** 3-8pm Mon, Thur, Fri; noon-4pm Sat. **Credit** MC, V. **Map** p318/p326 M5.

The three women behind this label focus mainly on detail and clean cuts. They create elegant, young, and whimsical womens' clothing and accessories. Each seasonal collection references historical figures or fictional characters, such as Helen of Troy and Marie Curie.

RespectMen

Neue Schönhauser Strasse 14, Mitte (283 5010/ www.respectmen.de). U8 Weinmeisterstrasse. **Open** noon-8pm Mon-Fri; noon-7pm Sat. **Credit** AmEx, MC, V. **Map** p319/p326 O5.

Dirk Seidel, Karin Warburg and Alfred Warburg's menswear seems traditionally tailored on the rail, yet reveals a body-conscious, contemporary cut when worn. Trousers, jackets, suits and coats can be made to order. Also stocks labels like Drykorn and Franco Ziche.

Starstyling

Mulackstrasse 4, Mitte (9700 5182/www.star styling.net). U2 Rosa-Luxemburg-Platz or U8 Weinmeisterstrasse. **Open** noon-7pm Mon-Fri; noon-6pm Sat. **Credit** AmEx, MC, V. **Map** p319/p326 O5.

Designers Katja Schlegel and Kai Seifried are fixtures in the local creative scene, and their printed and stitched clothing faithfully channels Berlin's quirkiness and dynamism. Irreverent, colourful, fun and off-beat, the well-crafted items are perfect for a night out clubbing.

Fetish

For quality rubber and latex clobber, visit **Black Style** (*see p230*); **Leathers** (*see p231*) produces excellent leather and SM gear.

Schwarze Mode

Uhlandstrasse 171-172, Charlottenburg (8872 9308). U1 Uhlandstrasse. **Open** 11am-8pm Mon-Fri; 10am-6pm Sat. **Credit** AmEx, DC, MC, V. **Map** p321/p328 F8.

Leatherette, rubber and vinyl are among the delicacies stocked here for fetish fashionistas. A selection of erotic and SM books, mags and toys is also sold.

Sports gear

Karstadt

Joachimstaler Strasse 5-6, Charlottenburg (0180 511 4414/www.karstadtsport.de). U2, U9, S5, S7, S9 S75 Zoologischer Garten. **Open** 10am-8pm Mon-Sat. **Credit** AmEx, MC, V. **Map** p321/ p328 G8.

Four-level megastore with a wide selection of both name brands and cheaper alternatives in international sportswear, German football paraphernalia and children's clothes.

MontK

Kastanienallee 83, Prenzlauer Berg (448 2590/ www.mont-k.de). U2 Eberswalder Strasse. **Open** 10am-8pm Mon-Fri; 10am-6pm Sat. **Credit** MC, V. **Map** p319/p328 O3.

If you're a serious camper, skier, canoeist or climber, MontK can outfit you with all the proper equipment, outerwear and footgear.

Niketown Berlin

Tauentzienstrasse 7B-7C, Schöneberg (25 070/ www.nike.com). U1, U2, U3 Wittenbergplatz. **Open** 10am-9pm Mon-Thur; 10am-10pm Fri, Sat. **Credit** AmEx, DC, MC, V. **Map** p321 G8.

The monster outlet for the monster US company is housed in a state-of-the-art glass and neon building, and sells everything bearing the famous swoosh.

Street/clubwear

Despite an influx of some of the biggest names in international streetwear, Berlin has managed to retain an unusually strong contingent of streetwear labels operating independently and under some charmingly idealistic business philosophies, as well as attracting a flood of higher-end urbanwear labels, particularly from Scandinavia and Japan. The streets around **Boxhagener Platz** in Friedrichshain and **Schlesisches Tor** and **Oranienstrasse** in Kreuzberg are particularly good areas for the former, while **Mitte** is the place for the latter.

Best Shop

Alte Schönhauser Strasse 6, Mitte (2463 2482/ www.bestshop-berlin.de). U2 Rosa-Luxemburg-Platz. **Open** noon-8pm Mon-Sat. **Credit** AmEx, MC, V. **Map** p319/p326 O5.

Carries clothing from edgy Scandinavian and Berlin labels such as Henrik Vibskov and Reality Studio as well as records, accessories and general miscellany. In addition to the permanent collections, Best Shop also features two-month Countdown Collections from avant-garde streetwear designers both local and international.

Big Brobot

Kopernikusstrasse 19, Friedrichshain (7407 8388/ www.bigbrobot.com). U5 Frankfurter Tor. **Open** 11am-8pm Mon-Fri; 11am-6pm Sat. **Credit** MC, V. **Map** p324 S7.

The first German home for British label Fenchurch. Big Brobot also stocks Boxfresh, Stüssy and X-Large, among others. There are all sorts of cultish accessories, as well as comics and small-edition publications. The refreshingly unpretentious staff are friendly and helpful.

Cherrybomb

Oranienstrasse 32, Kreuzberg (614 6151). U1 Görlitzer Bahnhof. **Open** 11am-8pm Mon-Fri; 11am-6pm Sat. **Credit** AmEx, MC, V. **Map** p323 P9.

German labels such as Blutsgeschwister, Boogaloo and Berlin's own Volksmarke, plus Holland's King Louis and Colcci from Brazil, rub shoulders in this low-lit storefront. Although popular with women, there's plenty of streetwear for men too. The aesthetic is classic and functional.

Eat, Drink, Shop

Eisdieler

Kastanienallee 12, Prenzlauer Berg (2839 1291/www.eisdieler.de). U2 Eberswalder Strasse. **Open** noon-8pm Mon-Fri; noon-5pm Sat. **Credit** AmEx, MC, V. **Map** p319/p326 O3.

A group of young Berlin designers pooled resources to transform this former ice shop into an urban streetwear collective, and each of them manages a label under the Eisdieler banner – clubwear, second-hand gear, casualwear and street style.

Été-clothing

Bergmannstrasse 18, Kreuzberg (3289 5543/ www.ete-clothing.de). U7 Gneisenaustrasse. **Open** 11am-8pm Mon-Fri; 11am-6pm Sat. **Credit** MC, V. **Map** p322 M10.

Été-clothing stocks a wide range of street fashion – including Billabong, Hurley, Roxy and local label IrieDaily – as well as a good selection of skate- and surfboards. The owners are boarders themselves, so they know what's what.

Firmament

Schröderstrasse 8, Mitte (4980 8674/www.am-firmament.com). S1, S2, S8, S86 Nordbahnhof. **Open** 2-7pm Wed-Fri; noon-6pm Sat; or by appointment. **Credit** MC, V. **Map** p319/p326 M4.

Offering high-end Japanese and local streetwear brands like Visvim, Neighbourhood and Answer, this is also the only shop in Berlin to showcase the entire collection of Munich-based label Acronym. The store's savvy owners are also the driving force behind the online street magazine *Beinghunted* (www.beinghunted.com) and the online shop The-Glade (www.the-glade.com).

IrieDaily

Depot 2, Oranienstrasse 9, Kreuzberg (611 4655/ www.iriedaily.de). U1 Görlitzer Bahnhof. **Open** 11am-8pm Mon-Sat. **Credit** MC, V. **Map** p323 P9.

Eastern earthiness combined with a skater/hip hop aesthetic has made IrieDaily one of the most popular local brands. This is the company's flagship. Girls' tops and trousers are flattering and edgy, the hoodies slinky and cosy; men's cargo pants are classy and velvety. Innovative accessories include belts and bags.

Planet Berlin

Schlüterstrasse 35, Charlottenburg (885 2717). U1 Uhlandstrasse. **Open** 11am-7.30pm Mon-Fri; 11am-6pm Sat. **Credit** MC, V. **Map** p321/p328 F8.

Owners Wera Wonder and Mik Moon have been kitting out Berlin's vibrant club scene since 1985. Their DJ friends pump out deafening music to put you in the right mode, and the shop brims with sparkling spandex shirts, fluffy vests and dance-durable footwear.

Skunkfunk

Kastanienallee 19 & 20, Prenzlauer Berg (4403 3800/www.skunkfunk.com). U2 Eberswalder Strasse. **Open** noon-8pm Mon-Fri; noon-7pm Sat. **Credit** AmEx, MC, V. **Map** p319/p326 O3.

Spanish urban label with adjacent stores housing men's and women's wear in lush cotton, fruity to earthy colours and asymmetric styles. Jackets are streamlined, and the men's jeans baggy and beautifully tailored. The name is on everything, sometimes a little too obviously and sometimes within a charming detail. *Photo p181.*

Wood Wood

Rochstrasse 4, Mitte (2804 7877/www.wood wood.dk). U2, U5, U8, S5, S7, S9, S75 Alexanderplatz. **Open** noon-8pm Mon-Fri; noon-6pm Sat. **Credit** MC, V. **Map** p319 O6.

An avant-garde design collective from Copenhagen, Wood Wood offers beautiful, electric and sometimes outrageous street fashion, sneakers and accessories by higher-end designers such as Cheap Monday, Maharishi and Kim Jones. Almost half the stock is Wood Wood's own, an explosion of prints, stitching and bright colours tempered by clean, classic cuts.

Used & vintage

Take one look at what the locals are wearing, and it's obvious that Berlin has a thriving second-hand shopping culture. You're likely

Whisky & Cigars. *See p188.*

to find some of the best stores by accident, by wandering the untravelled side streets and hidden courtyards. Try getting lost around **Kastanienallee** in Prenzlauer Berg or **Wühlischstrasse** in Friedrichshain, or wandering around **Kreuzberg**, an especially thrift-store-rich neighbourhood. **Wiener Strasse**, **Bergmannstrasse**, **Schlesische Strasse** and the area around **Mehringdamm** are particularly good. Further west, **Mommsenstrasse** in Charlottenburg offers some of the city's best upscale vintage shops – items aren't necessarily cheap, but they're definitely bargains. On the weekend, check out Berlin's busy flea markets, and look out for branches of **Humana**, the super-cheap charity chain whose biggest outpost is at Frankfurter Tor in Friedrichshain.

Calypso

Rosenthaler Strasse 23, Mitte (2854 5415/ www.calypsoshoes.com). U8 Weinmeisterstrasse. **Open** noon-8pm Mon-Sat. **Credit** MC, V. **Map** p319/p326 O5.
Hundreds of stilettos, wedges and platforms in vivid shades and exotic shapes from the 1930s to the '90s, almost all in fine condition.
Other locations Oderberger Strasse 61, Prenzlauer Berg (281 6165).

Colours

Bergmannstrasse 102, Kreuzberg (694 3348). U7 Gneisenaustrasse. **Open** 11am-7pm Mon-Fri; 11am-6pm Sat. **Credit** MC, V. **Map** p322 M10.
Rows of jeans, leather jackets and dresses, including party stunners and fetching Bavarian dirndls, plus the odd gem from the 1950s or '60s.

Garage

Ahornstrasse 2, off Einemstrasse, Schöneberg (211 2760). U1, U2, U3, U4 Nollendorfplatz. **Open** 11am-7pm Mon-Fri; 11am-6pm Sat. **Credit** AmEx, MC, V. **Map** p322 J9.
Garage sells cheap second-hand clothing priced by the kilo. The large selection at this barn-like locale is well-organised, making it easy to root out last-minute party gear.

Made in Berlin

Neue Schönhauser Strasse 19, Mitte (2123 0601). U8 Weinmeisterstrasse. **Open** noon-8pm Mon-Fri; 11am-6pm Sat. **Credit** MC, V. **Map** p319/p326 O5.
Sister store of Garage (*see above*), where the 'better stuff' supposedly goes – vintage Adidas, Burberry and Lacoste, for example. It's still pretty cheap, though, and offers a ton of great no-name 1980s gear.

Sgt. Peppers

Kastanienallee 91-92, Prenzlauer Berg (448 1121/ www.sgt-peppers-berlin.de). U2 Eberswalder Strasse. **Open** 11am-8pm Mon-Fri; 11am-6pm Sat. **Credit** AmEx, MC, V. **Map** p319/p328 O3.
Vivid and colourful gear from the 1960s to the '80s. You'll find some great T-shirts and airline bags.

Sterling Gold

Oranienburger Strasse 32, Mitte (2809 6500/ www.sterlinggold.de). S1, S2 Oranienburger Strasse. **Open** noon-8pm Mon-Fri; noon-6pm Sat. **Credit** AmEx, MC, V. **Map** p319/p326 N5.
Michael Boenke couldn't believe his luck when he was offered a warehouse full of 'prom' dresses during a trip to America. He shipped them to Berlin, and this shop in the Heckmann Höfe was the result. The fabulous ball- and cocktail gowns – in every conceivable shade and fabric from the 1950s to the '80s – are in terrific condition. Prices start at €100, and labels range from big designers to total no-names.

Umsonstladen

Brunnenstrasse 183, Mitte (0176 2569 8582/ www.umsonstladen.info). U8 Rosenthaler Platz. **Open** 3-7pm Tue; 5-7pm Wed; 4-8pm Thur; 2-6pm Fri; 2-4pm Sat. **No credit cards. Map** p319 N4.
No money transactions occur at this 'Free Store', which celebrates sharing and recycling over consuming and wasting. If you see something you like, go ahead and take it. Want to get rid of something you no longer need? Just leave it.

Fashion accessories & services

Jewellery

Heidenreich

Danziger Strasse 17, Prenzlauer Berg (4404 2270/ www.heidenreich-schmuck.de). U2 Eberswalder Strasse. **Open** 11am-7pm Tue-Fri; 11am-2pm Sat. **Credit** AmEx, MC, V. **Map** p319/p328 P3.
Carsten Heidenreich designs beautiful rings, earrings, necklaces and pendants according to personalised taste and specifications – for 'the special moments in life'. His small store also showcases the work of other contemporary designers, with an emphasis on wedding and engagement rings.

OONA

Auguststrasse 26, Mitte (2804 5905/www.oona-galerie.de). S1, S2, S25 Oranienburger Strasse or U8 Rosenthaler Platz. **Open** 2-7pm Tue-Fri; 1-6pm Sat. **Credit** MC, V. **Map** p319/p326 N5.
In addition to its permanent collection, this 'gallery for contemporary jewellery' features the work of innovative young jewellery artists from Europe, Japan and Australia. For these frequent exhibits, the gallery and artists choose a special theme and work together with architects, photographers and interior designers to develop a concept. A mix of precious and non-precious materials means there's a corresponding mix of price tags.

Scuderi

Wörther Strasse 32, Prenzlauer Berg (4737 4240/ www.scuderi-schmuck.de). U2 Senefelderplatz. **Open** 11am-7pm Mon-Fri; 11am-4pm Sat. **Credit** MC, V. **Map** p319/p328 P3.

Eat, Drink, Shop

Bettina Siegmund and Daniela Nagi work magic with gold, silver, pearls, stones and hand-rolled glass, creating lightweight ornaments that make a strong statement.

Bags, hats & buttons

Bag Ground

Gipsstrasse 23B, Mitte (2758 3177). U8 Weinmeisterstrasse. **Open** noon-8pm Mon-Sat. **Credit** MC, V. **Map** p319/p326 N5.
This colourful shop is full of handbags hip and bright, plain or clubby, with prices starting at €35.

Fiona Bennett

Grosse Hamburger Strasse 25, Mitte (2809 6330/ www.fionabennett.com). S5, S7, S9, S75 Hackescher Markt. **Open** 10am-6pm Mon-Wed; noon-8pm Thur, Fri; noon-6pm Sat. **Credit** AmEx, DC, MC, V. **Map** p319/p326 N5.
British-born Bennett turns headgear into a work of art. Though often strange, her hats are always theatrical and evoke a sense of classic beauty.

Knopf Paul

Zossener Strasse 10, Kreuzberg (692 1212/www. paulknopf.de). U7 Gneisenaustrasse. **Open** 9am-6pm Tue, Fri; 2-6pm Wed, Thur. **No credit cards.** **Map** p323 N10.
A Kreuzberg institution stocking thousands of buttons in every shape, colour and style you can think of. Whatever you're seeking, Paul Knopf ('button') will help you find it. His patient and amiable service is remarkable considering most transactions are for tiny sums.

Lingerie

Blush

Rosa-Luxemburg-Strasse 22, Mitte (2809 3580/ www.blush-berlin.com). U2 Rosa-Luxemburg-Platz or U8 Weinmeisterstrasse. **Open** 8pm Mon-Fri; noon-7pm Sat. **Credit** AmEx, MC, V. **Map** p319/p326 O5.
Beautiful lingerie in lace and silk. Imports from France and Italy, as well as German brands.

Les Dessous

Fasanenstrasse 42, Wilmersdorf (883 3632/www.les-dessous.de). U3, U9 Spichernstrasse. **Open** 11am-7pm Mon-Fri; 10am-3pm Sat. **Credit** AmEx, DC, MC, V. **Map** p321/p328 F8.
A beautiful shop featuring lingerie, silk dressing gowns and swimwear by Eres, Dior and La Perla.

Fishbelly

Sophienstrasse 7, Mitte (2804 5180/www. fishbelly.de). U8 Weinmeisterstrasse. **Open** 12.30-7pm Mon-Fri; noon-7pm Sat. **Credit** AmEx, DC, MC, V. **Map** p319/p326 N5.
Often compared to Agent Provocateur, this tiny shop in the Hackeschen Höfe is licensed to thrill with extravagant undergarments by big-name designers and an own-brand line of imaginative lingerie.

Shoes

Bleibgrün

Bleibtreustrasse 29-30, Charlottenburg (882 1689/www.bleibgruen.de). S5, S7, S9, S75 Savignyplatz. **Open** 10.30am-6.30pm Mon-Fri; 10.30am-6pm Sat. **Credit** AmEx, DC, MC, V. **Map** p321/p328 F8.
Some regard this as Berlin's best designer shoe shop, with an anything-but-boring selection from the likes of Lagerfeld, Robert Clergerie and Giuseppe Zanotti.

Budapester Schuhe

Kurfürstendamm 43, Charlottenburg (8862 206/ www.budapester-schuhe.net). U1 Uhlandstrasse. **Open** 10am-7pm Mon-Fri; 10am-6pm Sat. **Credit** AmEx, DC, MC, V. **Map** p321/p328 F8.
This is the largest of four Berlin branches, offering the latest by the likes of Prada, D&G, Sergio Rossi and Miu Miu. At Kurfürstendamm 199, across the street, you'll find a conservative range for men, and at the Bleibtreustrasse branch, prices are slashed by up to 50% for last year's models, remainders and hard-to-sell sizes.
Other locations Bleibtreustrasse 24, Charlottenburg (881 7001); Friedrichstrasse 81, Mitte (2038 8110); Kurfürstendamm 199, Charlottenburg (881 1707).

Massschuhmacherei

Sophienstrasse 28-29, Mitte (4004 2861/www. massschuhmacherei.de). S5, S7, S9, S75 Hackescher Markt. **Open** noon-7pm Wed-Fri; 11am-4pm Sat. **No credit cards.** **Map** p319/p326 N5.
Handmade shoes for men and women in classic, understated designs. Also does repairs.

Solebox

Nürnberger Strasse 16, Charlottenburg (9120 6690/www.solebox.de). U1, U2, U3 Wittenbergplatz. **Open** noon-8pm Mon-Sat. **Credit** MC, V. **Map** p321 G8.
The place for rare and collectable limited-edition Pumas, Nikes or Adidas, Solebox stocks a massive selection of exclusive sneakers as well as a small offering of clothing and gear to wear them with. Friendly and well-informed staff.
Other locations Trainer, Alte Schönhauser Strasse 50, Mitte (9789 4610).

Trippen

Rosenthaler Strasse 40-41, Mitte (2839 1337/ www.trippen.com). S5, S7, S9, S75 Hackescher Markt. **Open** 11am-8pm Mon-Fri; 10am-8pm Sat. **Credit** MC, V. **Map** p319/p326 N5.
In this sunny, minimalist store in the Hackeschen Höfe, Berlin designers Michael Oehler and Angela Spieth present avant-garde shoes and bags in wood, leather and rich colours. Parents will be pleased to know that a children's line is also available at the 'family' branch on Knaackstrasse.
Other locations Alte Schönhauser Strasse 45, Mitte (2463 2284); Knaackstrasse 26, Prenzlauer Berg (4050 0392).

Food & drink

The proliferation of reasonably priced and pleasantly designed organic food shops in Berlin has prodded otherwise complacent supermarket chains such as Kaiser's and Extra into stepping up their game. But those in need of discount groceries will find the omni-present Lidl and Aldi chains unchanged and cheap as ever. Hundreds of speciality stores also abound, ranging from ethnic to gourmet, American to Asian. And there are the great department-store food halls, most notably at the **Galeries Lafayette** and **KaDeWe** (for both *see p171*).

Bonbonmacherei

Oranienburger Strasse 32, Mitte (4405 5243/www.bonbonmacherei.de). S1, S2, S25 Oranienburger Strasse. **Open** noon-8pm Wed-Sat. **No credit cards**. **Map** p319/p326 N5.

Nostalgic candy shop that offers sweet, sour and everything in between. You can watch Katja Kolbe and Hjalmar Stecher produce the sweets in their on-site workshop using vintage equipment and old recipes. High quality at reasonable prices.

Broken English

Körtestrasse 10, Kreuzberg (691 1227/www.broken english.de). U7 Südstern. **Open** 11am-6.30pm Mon-Fri; 11am-4pm Sat. **Credit** MC, V. **Map** p323 O4.

Caters to UK expats with a range of teas, biscuits, crisps, sweets and extras. This is the place to find chocolate digestives, Oxo cubes, Marmite and Heinz Baked Beans. There's also a selection of cheeses and deep-frozen pies, and a gift section. Pricey, though. **Other locations** Leonhardtstrasse 23, Charlottenburg (2859 9402).

Fresh 'n' Friends

Kastanienallee 26, Prenzlauer Berg (4171 7250/www. freshnfriends.com). U2 Eberswalder Strasse. **Open** 24hrs daily. **No credit cards**. **Map** p319/p326 O3.

Chocolate city

Beautifully designed interiors, packaging to savour and, above all, bitter, sweet and surprising chocolate. Berlin may be Germany's rebel city, but when it comes to chocolate, the locals are perfectionists.

Fassbender & Rausch (Charlottenstrasse 60, Mitte, 2045 8443, www.fassbender-rausch.com) specialises in superlatives: 'the most delicious chocolate since 1863', 'the biggest chocolate house in the world' and 'Europe's first chocolate restaurant'. In fact, the two families began separately – Fassbender in 1863 and Rausch seven years later – and only teamed up in 1999. It's hard to avoid the tourist crush in the world's largest chocolate store, but still a joy to see such extravagant celebration of the cocoa bean, with giant edible models of the Brandenburg Gate and other local landmarks. The upstairs restaurant serves wacky seasonal dishes that all contain chocolate, and offers 'chocolate-dinner-shows' with tacky historical themes.

Orthodox chocoholics should make their way to much more self-effacing old-timer, **Erich Hamann Bittere Schokoladen** (Brandenburgische Strasse 17, Wilmersdorf, 873 2085). The shop front looks more like a deserted department store than a revered *confiserie* and retains its original 1928 design by Johannes Itten of the Bauhaus. Inside are stacks of dark, bitter chocolate in the original packaging that make little concession to newfangled chocolate types. In the factory

behind the shop, the third generation of Hamanns are keeping faithful to the recipe.

Erich Hamann bars are sold in most of the newer chocolate shops in the city. **In't veld** (Dunckerstrasse 10, Prenzlauer Berg, 4172 2281; Winterfeldtstrasse 45, Schöneberg, 2362 3256; www.intveld.de) is one of the best. Here is where the experimenting starts, from sea salt chocolate sticks to the goat's milk range with blood orange or mint. Holger in't Veld left his job as a journalist in 2001 to dedicate his life to chocolate, and runs In't veld on the purist principles of the Slow Food movement. Go to the tiny **Nibs** café (Bleibtreustrasse 46, Charlottenburg, 2637 6740, www.nibscacao.de) for Spanish *churros* to dunk in hot chocolate, as well as a good selection of chocolate-related gifts, if at Savignyplatz prices. You can even sign up for a year's chocolate subscription here and get a package of chocolate 'surprises' every month.

Olivia (Wühlischstrasse 30, Friedrichshain, 6050 0368, www.olivia-berlin.de) is a cutesy boutique of a chocolaterie run by an all-woman team and has the best-looking cakes of all. The Chilli Schokoladen Torte is pure chocolate heaven. You can watch the elegant tartes being created nearby on Gärtnerstrasse. Queues stretch out of the tiny shop on market days, so if it's too full, choose from a lengthy list of hot chocolates at the friendly **Karvana** (Gabriel-Max-Strasse 4, 0178 343 3256, www.karvana.de) around the corner.

Eat, Drink, Shop

This store is open 24/7 – practically unheard of in Berlin. What's more, it's actually good. With its offering of fresh, healthy organic foods at standard 'bio-markt' prices, this supermarket-meets-organic-deli is a lifesaver for night owls.

Kadó

Graefestrasse 75, Kreuzberg (6904 1638/www. kado.de). U8 Schönleinstrasse. **Open** 9.30am-6.30pm Tue-Fri; 9.30am-3.30pm Sat. **No credit cards.** **Map** p323 P10.
Mind-boggling selection of liquorice from all over the world, presented beautifully in row after row of glass jars. All shapes, sizes and varieties available.

Königsberger Marzipan

Pestalozzistrasse 54A, Charlottenburg (323 8254). U7 Wilmersdorfer Strasse. **Open** 11am-6pm Mon-Fri; 10am-1pm Sat. **No credit cards.** **Map** p320 D8.
Irmgard Wald and her late husband arrived from Kaliningrad after the war and began their confectionery trade anew. With her smiling American-born granddaughter, Frau Wald still produces fresh, soft, melt-in-your-mouth marzipan.

Leysieffer

Kurfürstendamm 218, Charlottenburg (885 7480/ www.leysieffer.de). U1 Uhlandstrasse. **Open** 9am-7pm Mon-Sat; 10am-5pm Sun. **Credit** AmEx, DC, MC, V. **Map** p321/p328 F8.
The beautifully packaged confitures, teas and handmade chocolates from this German fine food company make perfect gifts.

Vinh-Loi

Ansbacher Strasse 16, Schöneberg (235 0900). U1, U2, U3 Wittenbergplatz. **Open** 9am-7pm Mon-Fri; 9am-4pm Sat. **No credit cards.** **Map** p321 G8.
Asian groceries arrive at this supermarket fresh from the airport two or three times a week. There are teas and tofu, Thai fruit and vegetables, and every kind of noodle, spice mix and bottled sauce. Also woks, rice steamers and Chinese crockery.

Weichardt-Brot

Mehlitzstrasse 7, Wilmersdorf (873 8099/ www.weichardt.de). U7, U9 Berliner Strasse. **Open** 7am-6pm Tue-Fri; 7am-1pm Sat. **No credit cards.** **Map** p321 G11.
Perhaps the best bakery in town, Weichardt-Brot grew out of a Berlin collective from the 1960s. Stoneground organic flour and natural leavens make this a mecca for bread lovers.

Wine & spirits

Absinthe Depot Berlin

Weinmeisterstrasse 4, Mitte (281 6789/ www.erstesabsinthdepotberlin.de). U8 Weinmeisterstrasse. **Open** 2pm-midnight Mon-Fri; 1pm-midnight Sat. **No credit cards.** **Map** p319/p326 O5.
This place stocks the best and most potent absinthes from across the world – including, of

course, the good Czech stuff. If you're lucky the owner might even invite you for a sampling session and history lesson.

Das Blaue Wunder

Seumestrasse 12, Friedrichshain (2576 8900). U5 Samariterstrasse. **Open** 4-8pm Mon-Fri; 10am-4pm Sat. **No credit cards.** **Map** p324 T7.
This neighbourhood treasure stocks organic wines from all over Germany. Owner Klaus Sommer loves to sit you down for a chat and a tasting.

Getränke Hoffmann

Kleiststrasse 23-26, Schöneberg (2147 3096/ www.getraenke-hoffmann.de). U1, U2, U3 Wittenbergplatz. **Open** 9am-8pm Mon-Fri; 8am-8pm Sat. **No credit cards.** **Map** p321 H9.
Branches all over town offer a wide range of everyday booze at everyday prices. Call 0800 440 22 00 to place an order for delivery anywhere in Berlin. **Other locations** throughout the city.

Klemke Wein & Spirituosenhandel

Mommsenstrasse 9, Charlottenburg (8855 1260). S5, S7, S9, S75 Savignyplatz. **Open** 8am-7pm Mon-Fri; 9am-2.30pm Sat. **No credit cards.** **Map** p321/p328 E8.
Respected specialists in French and Italian wines from the tiniest vineyard to the grandest chateau. This mom-and-pop shop offers good wines at good prices, as well as digestifs, whiskies and free delivery in Berlin. *Photo p184.*

Whisky & Cigars

Sophienstrasse 8-9, Mitte (282 0376/www.whisky-cigars.de). S5, S7, S9, S75 Hackescher Markt. **Open** 11am-7pm Mon-Fri; 11am-6pm Sat. **Credit** MC, V. **Map** p319/p326 N5.
Two friends with a love of single malts are behind this shop, which stocks 450 whiskies and cigars from Cuba, Jamaica and Honduras, among others. They hold regular tastings and will deliver. *Photo p184.*

Health & beauty

Hairdressers & barbers

There are plenty of so-called 'no-name salons', where you take a number and wait your turn for a hip, cheap haircut. Many are clustered on and around Kastanienallee, where the local favourite is **Notaufnahme** (Nos. 29-30, 3011 2460, www.notaufnahme-berlin.de, closed Sun). The no-name shop of the moment, however, is in Mitte, on Rosenthaler Strasse near the corner of Torstrasse – you'll know it by the huge 'Je €10' painted on the window.

Beige

Auguststrasse 83, Mitte (2759 4051/www.salon-beige.de). U6 Oranienburger Tor. **Open** noon-9pm Tue-Fri; 3-8pm Sat. **No credit cards.** **Map** p324/p326 M5.

Exclusive salon on the garden level of a private apartment building. The waiting room doubles as a gallery space, and two client rooms are decorated in 1960s and baroque styles. Hair designer Oliver Weidner specialises in modern colours and cuts.

JonnyCut

Yorckstrasse 43, Schöneberg (217 0941/www.jonnycut.de). U7, S1, S2, S26 Yorckstrasse. **Open** 11am-8pm Tue-Fri; 11am-5pm Sat. **Credit** MC, V. **Map** p319/p326 O6.
Jonny Pazo is a versatile stylist who shuttles from magazine shoots and record covers to appointments in his small and pleasingly eccentric salon, decked out with pictures of angels and buddhas.

Salon Sucré

Görlitzer Strasse 32A, Kreuzberg (612 2713/ www.salonsucre.de). U1 Schlesisches Tor. **Open** *Salon* 10am-6pm Wed-Sat. *Pastry shop* 10am-6pm Thur-Sun. **No credit cards. Map** p324 R9.
What happens when a French pâtissier and a Brazilian hairdresser open a shop together? You get Salon Sucré, where good coffee, delicious home-made pastries and quality haircuts are all offered under one roof at reasonable prices.

Shift

Neue Schönhauser Strasse 8, Mitte (2809 9777/ www.shift-friseure.de). U8 Weinmeisterstrasse. **Open** 1-7pm Mon; 10am-8pm Tue, Thur; 2-8pm Wed; 10am-9pm Fri; 10am-7pm Sat. **Credit** AmEx, MC, V. **Map** p319/p326 O5.

Shift is popular with a young, designery crowd who come here for its personalised service. Remember the face of your stylist: you'll probably meet him or her, a few years later, in one of the higher-end salons, locally or internationally.
Other locations Grolmanstrasse 36, Charlottenburg (341 8545).

Udo Walz

Kempinski-Plaza, Uhlandstrasse 181-183, Charlottenburg (882 7457/www.udo-walz.de). U1 Uhlandstrasse. **Open** 9am-6pm Mon-Wed; 9am-7pm Thur, Fri; 9am-3pm Sat. **Credit** AmEx, MC, V. **Map** p321/p328 F8.
Udo Walz is the darling of the Berlin hair brigade, and likes to have his picture taken with the likes of Claudia Schiffer. As you'd expect, his stylists are well-trained and imaginative. Perhaps not so pre-dictable is their friendliness.
Other locations Hohenzollerndamm 92, Wilmersdorf (826 6108); Schlüterstrasse 48, Charlottenburg (8872 7905).

Vokuhila

Kastanienallee 16-17, Prenzlauer Berg (4434 2513/ www.kakoii.de/clients/vokuhila). U2 Eberswalder Strasse. **Open** 10am-8pm Mon, Wed, Fri; 10am-6pm Tue, Sat; 10am-10pm Thur. **No credit cards. Map** p319/p326 O3.
Immerse yourself in Berlin history: this salon is dec-orated entirely in East German kitsch, a homage to the fact that hair has been washed, cut and styled here for over 70 years.

Lovingly crafted pottery and paintings at **Atelier Hinrich Kröger**. *See p191.*

Eat, Drink, Shop

Ruby Designliving. *See p192.*

Opticians

Brille 54

*Friedrichstrasse 71, Mitte (2094 6060/www.
brille54.de). U6 Französische Strasse.* **Open** 10am-
7pm Mon-Fri; 10am-6pm Sat. **Credit** AmEx, MC, V.
Map p322/p327 M7.
Brille 54 is a small but functionally sleek space in
Quartier 206, designed by hot young local architects
Plajer & Franz. All the international names can be
found, including Armani, Gucci and Oliver Peoples.
Other locations Rosenthaler Strasse 36, Mitte
(2804 0818); Kurfürstendamm 54, Charlottenburg
(882 6696).

ic!

*Max-Beer-Strasse 17, Mitte (2472 7200/www.ic-
berlin.de). U8 Weinmeisterstrasse.* **Open** 11am-8pm
Mon-Sat. **Credit** AmEx, DC, MC. **Map** p319/p326 O5.
This is probably the hippest eyewear store for adults
and children, with a diverse range of designer prescription glasses and sunglasses. Friendly staff too.

Lunettes Brillenagentur

*Marienburger Strasse 11, Prenzlauer Berg
(3408 2789/www.lunettes-brillenagentur.de). M2
Marienburger Strasse or M4 Hufelandstrasse.*
Open noon-8pm Mon-Fri; noon-6pm Sat. **Credit**
AmEx, MC, V. **Map** p319/p328 P3.
Owner Uta Geyer has a knack for getting her hands
on hard-to-find vintage frames, ranging from sleek
1920s pieces to rockabilly cateyes, from cool avia-
tors to elegant Jackie Os. Prices range from €20 to
€200, and most items are also available for rental.

Mykita

*Rosa-Luxemburg-Strasse 6, Mitte (2045 6645
/www.mykita.com). U2, U5, U8, S5, S7, S9, S75
Alexanderplatz.* **Open** 11am-8pm Mon-Fri; noon-6pm
Sat. **Credit** MC, V. **Map** p319/p326 O5.
Since 2004, this young Berlin label has been designing and selling top-quality glasses – and winning
praise and acclaim across the world. Creators Philipp
Haffmans and Harald Gottschling present their
handmade prescription frames and sunglasses on
simple, industrial shelves in this beautifully lit, ultra-
minimalist store. A fine selection from other brands
is also available, but beware: this place isn't cheap.

Shops

Belladonna

*Bergmannstrasse 101, Kreuzberg (6904 0333/
www.bella-donna.de). U7 Gneisenaustrasse.* **Open**
10am-7pm Mon-Fri; 10am-6pm Sat. **Credit** AmEx,
MC, V. **Map** p322 M10.
Belladonna stocks all-natural beauty and skin
care products from Lavera, Dr Hauschka and
Weleda, among others, as well as a selection of hair
accessories, aromatherapy products and gift items.
At the in-house cosmetic studio, experienced
aestheticians offer a range of beauty therapies,
including Dr Hauschka treatments.

MAC

*Rosenthaler Str
maccosmetics.*
S9, S75 Hack
Fri; 11am-6p
p319/p326 N
MAC is no
wonderla
graces a
exclusive.
encouraged to try

Spas & salons

Beate Kahlcke

*Rosa-Luxemburg-Strasse 11-13, Mitte (2809 1918/
www.beatekahlcke.de). U2 Rosa-Luxemburg-Platz.*
Open 11am-8pm Mon-Wed; 11am-10pm Thur, Fri;
10am-6pm Sat. **Credit** AmEx, MC, V.
Map p319/p326 O5.
The interior design at Beate Kahlcke is a study in
cool, clean-lined sophistication – perfect for a salon
that operates in conjunction with Aveda and the
design hotel Lux 11 next door (*see p55*). Its internationally trained hairdressers and stylists are person-
able and savvy; therapists offer body wraps,
massage and skin and nail care. What's more, it's all
offered at reasonable prices.

Marie France

*Fasanenstrasse 42, Charlottenburg (881 6555). U1
Uhlandstrasse.* **Open** 9am-6pm Mon-Fri; 9am-2pm
Sat. **No credit cards. Map** p321/p328 F8.
The cosmeticians speak reasonable English and use
luxurious French products at this clean, pleasant
salon, which has been glamming up Berliners for
over 30 years. Hot waxing is a speciality.

House & home

In 2006, UNESCO named Berlin a City of
Design, and it's not hard to tell why. Take a
stroll around any area in the city, and you're
sure to come across several design stores, with
goods ranging from antique to DDR to ultra-
modern, from plastic to ceramic to steel. In
Mitte, **Rosenthaler Strasse** and **Alte** and
Neue Schönhauser Strasse are home to
lots of cool eastern and western items from
the 1950s to 1970s. **Oderberger Strasse** in
Prenzlauer Berg is good for DDR furniture,
and **Grünberger Strasse** in Friedrichshain
features well-kept second-hand goods.

Atelier Hinrich Kröger

*Gipsstrasse 13, Mitte (282 2729/www.galerie-
hinrich-kroeger.de). U8 Weinmeisterstrasse.* **Open**
2-6.30pm Wed-Fri; 2-4pm Sat. **Credit** AmEx, MC, V.
Map p319/p326 N5.
Painter and potter Hinrich Kröger lovingly crafts
vases, decorative wall plates, bowls, cups and other
ceramics and hand paints them with erotic motifs.

...er

...Charlottenburg (882 7373/www.
...m). S5, S7, S9, S75 Savignyplatz.
...m Mon-Fri; 11am-4pm Sat. **Credit**
...ap p321/p328 E8.
...ood balance between Mediterranean and
...burg country style with stripped-down fur-
..., warm lighting and irresistible ornaments.
...lights include natural linens, hand-blown drink-
...g glasses in elegant colours and silk flowers.

DIM

Oranienstrasse 26, Kreuzberg (2850 30121/www.
blindenanstalt.de). U1, U8 Kottbusser Tor. **Open**
10am-7pm Mon-Fri; 11am-4pm Sat. **Credit** AmEx,
DC, MC, V. **Map** p323 P9.
An initiative of Berlin designers Oliver Wogt and
Hermann Weizenegger, the 'Imaginary Factory'
offers witty, high-style brushes and wicker items,
all handmade by blind craftspeople at Berlin's
Institute for the Blind.

Dopo_domani

Kantstrasse 148, Charlottenburg (882 2242/www.
dopo-domani.com). S5, S7, S9, S75 Savignyplatz.
Open 10.30am-7pm Mon-Fri; 10am-6pm Sat.
Credit AmEx, MC, V. **Map** p321/p328 E8.
Dopo–domani is a veritable temple for design afi-
cionados. Combining an interior design practice
with a well-stocked shop, the focus is on Italian out-
fitters, and the presentation creates an environment
you'll dream of calling your own.

KPM

Wegelystrasse 1, Tiergarten (390 090/www.kpm-
berlin.de). S5, S7, S9, S75, Tiergarten. **Open** 10am-
6pm Mon-Sat. **Credit** AmEx, MC, V. **Map** p321 G7.
Founded in 1763 by Frederick the Great to encourage the development of a domestic ceramic industry, the Königliche Porzellan-Manufaktur is still
making high-quality vases, bowls and other porcelain wares today. Beautiful but expensive.

Laden Schönhauser

Neue Schönhauser Strasse 18, Mitte (281 1704/
www.schoenhauser-design.de). U8 Weinmeisterstrasse.
Open noon-8pm Mon-Fri; 11am-8pm Sat. **Credit**
MC, V. **Map** p319 O5.
'Retrofuturism' is the name of the game at this jam-
packed second-hand shop, which offers brightly
coloured plastic 1970s furniture and accessories
alongside classics from the likes of Mies van der
Rohe and Arne Jacobsen.

Ruby Designliving

Oranienburger Strasse 66, Mitte (2838 6030/www.
ruby-designliving.de). S1, S2, S26 Oranienburger
Strasse. **Open** 11am-8pm Mon-Fri; 11am-6pm Sat.
Credit AmEx, MC, V. **Map** p324/p326 N5.
Ruby Designliving is a small shop with an astonishingly large and diverse offering of furniture,
lamps, glass, rugs, fabrics and household goods
from many of the world's most prominent and innovative designers. *Photo p190.*

Stilwerk

Kantstrasse 17, Charlottenburg (315 150/www.
stilwerk.de). S5, S7, S9, S75 Savignyplatz. **Open**
10am-8pm Mon-Sat. **Credit** AmEx, MC, V. **Map**
p321/p328 F8.
This huge, glassy, design marketplace offers high-
end products from an array of retailers, purveying
modern furnishings and kitchens, high-tech lighting
and bathroom fittings, as well as an assortment of
interior items. There's also a fourth-floor showcase
for the work of local craftspeople and designers.

VEB orange

Oderberger Strasse 29, Prenzlauer Berg (9788
6886/www.veborange.de). U2 Eberswalder Strasse.
Open 10am-8pm Mon-Sat. **Credit** AmEx, MC, V.
Map p328/p319 O3.
A wide range of original 1960s and '70s furniture
and decor from the DDR is stocked here.

Music & entertainment

Berlin is a mecca for vinyl collectors and indie
and electronic music junkies. **Kastanienallee**
in Prenzlauer Berg, **Boxhagener Strasse** and
Grünberger Strasse in Friedrichshain, and
Bergmannstrasse and **Zossener Strasse** in
Kreuzberg are the main veins. **Dussmann das**
KulturKaufhaus (*see p171*) also has a good
selection, and the weekend flea markets are
usually full of cheap second-hand records in
good condition. Go to www.platten.net for a
complete guide to every record shop in Berlin.

Asphalt Tango

Ackerstrasse 14-15, Mitte (285 8528/
www.asphalt-tango-shop.de). U8 Rosenthaler Platz.
Open 10am-7pm Mon-Fri. **Credit** AmEx, MC, V.
Map p319/p326 N5.
This label, artist management office and record store
specialises in Gypsy and other music from Poland,
Romania, Serbia, Turkey, Bulgaria and elsewhere.
One of the best places for Balkan music in Berlin.

For unique, classic or designer paper and pens visit **RSVP**. *See p194.*

Da capo

Kastanienallee 96, Prenzlauer Berg (448 1771/www. da-capo-vinyl.de). U2 Eberswalder Strasse. **Open** 11am-7pm Tue-Fri; 11am-4pm Sat. **Credit** MC, V. **Map** p319/p326 O3.

Da capo offers a pricey but wide selection of used vinyl, releases on DDR label Amiga plus rare 1950s 10-inch records and jazz singles. Second-hand books and sheet music are available too.

Gelbe Musik

Schaperstrasse 11, Wilmersdorf (211 3962). U3 Augsburger Strasse. **Open** 1-6pm Tue-Fri; 11am-2pm Sat. **Credit** MC, V. **Map** p321 G9.

One of Europe's most important avant-garde outlets has racks of minimalist, electronic, world, industrial and extreme noise. Rare vinyl and import CDs, music press and sound objects make for absorbing browsing.

Mr Dead & Mrs Free

Bülowstrasse 5, Schöneberg (215 1449/www.dead andfree.com). U1, U2, U3, U4 Nollendorfplatz. **Open** 11am-7pm Mon-Fri; 11am-4pm Sat. **Credit** MC, V. **Map** p322J9.

Long Berlin's leading address for independent and underground rock, Mr Dead & Mrs Free has bucket loads of British, US and Australian imports, a large vinyl section and a staff that knows and loves its music. Small but choice selection of books and magazines as well.

Musikalienhandlung Hans Riedel

Uhlandstrasse 38, Wilmersdorf (882 7394). U1 Uhlandstrasse. **Open** 8am-6.30pm Mon-Fri; 9am-2pm Sat. **Credit** MC, V. **Map** p321/p328 F9.

Probably the best address for classical music in Berlin, this huge, old-fashioned shop has been stocking string and brass instruments since 1910 and has one of the largest selections of sheet music in Europe. A good selection of CDs is also available.

Pigasus – Polish Poster Gallery

Torstrasse 62, Mitte (2849 3697/www.pigasus-gallery.de). U2 Rosa-Luxemburg-Platz. **Open** 2-7pm Mon-Sat. **No credit cards. Map** p319/p326 O5.

A wide range of Polish, Russian and Ukrainian disco and classical music, plus a wonderful selection of old Polish film and propaganda posters.

Space Hall

Zossener Strasse 33, Kreuzberg (694 7664/www.space -hall.de). U7 Gneisenaustrasse. **Open** 11am-8pm Mon-Fri; 11am-7pm Sat. **Credit** MC, V. **Map** p323 N10.

Space Hall holds a huge range of new and second-hand CDs and vinyl. Techno, house and electronica are the emphasis, but there's also lots of hip hop, indie and rock. Prices are competitive, and the employees know their stuff.

Vopo Records

Danziger Strasse 31, Prenzlauer Berg (442 8004/ www.vopo-records.de). U2 Eberswalder Strasse. **Open** noon-8pm Mon-Fri; noon-4pm Sat. **No credit cards. Map** p319/p328 P3.

Vopo stocks every type of rock, from punk to metal, from indie to hardcore, from garage to classic. Selected merchandise, second-hand items and Berlin concert tickets are also available.

Photography

Everyday developing can be done at branches of **Rossmann** (www.rossmann.de) and **Schlecker**; branches of **Saturn** (at Alexanderplatz and Potsdamer Platz, among others; www.saturn.de) also provide processing services.

Fix Foto

Kurfürstendamm 209, Charlottenburg (882 7267/ www.fixfoto.de). U1 Uhlandstrasse. **Open** 9am-8pm Mon-Sat; 11am-7pm Sun. **Credit** MC, V. **Map** p321/p328 F8.

One-hour developing, enlargements, CD-Rom and other fast services performed during unusually generous opening hours. **Other locations** throughout the city.

Fotoimpex

Alte Schönhauser Strasse 32B, Mitte (2859 9081/ www.fotoimpex.de). U8 Weinmeisterstrasse. **Open** noon-8pm Mon-Fri; noon-6pm Sat. **No credit cards.** **Map** p319/p326 O5.

A positive mecca for all things to do with black-and-white, analogue photography, including one-day, by-hand developing and printing. Hundreds of film varieties, high-quality equipment and all manner of cameras and accessories are sold at very reasonable prices. No wonder this is where the local photographers go to stock up.

PPS

Alexanderstrasse 1, Mitte (7001 1640/www.pps-imaging.de). U2, U5, U8, S5, S7, S9, S75 Alexanderplatz. **Open** 9am-7pm Mon-Fri; noon-5pm Sat. **Credit** AmEx, DC, MC, V. **Map** p319 P6.

Professional colour lab providing digital services, black-and-white hand-developed enlargements, scanning, two-hour developing, large-format prints and other services. It's also a good place to rent out high-end equipment.

Souvenirs

Communist relics and alleged Wall chunks are sold at stalls near Checkpoint Charlie and the Museumsinsel. The **Haus am Checkpoint Charlie** (*see p105*) sells key rings, lighters and mouse pads with a 'You Are Leaving The American Sector' theme. Most flea markets (*see p173*) have stalls devoted to old DDR artefacts. **Berlin Story** (*see p177*) has a big selection of toy Trabants, historical maps, mounted Wall chunks and other souvenirs. *See also p179* **Designer kiosks.**

Ampelmann Galerie Shop

Rosenthaler Strasse 40-41, Mitte (4404 8801/ www.ampelmann.de). S5, S7, S9, S75 Hackescher Markt. **Open** 10am-10pm Mon-Sat; 11am-7pm Sun. **Credit** AmEx, MC, V. **Map** p319/p326 N5.

Sells a huge variety of stuff emblazoned with the old East's enduring symbol, the jaunty red and green traffic-light men – these days weirdly proliferating in West Berlin too. **Other locations** Karl-Liebknecht-Strasse 1, in the DomAquarée, Mitte (2758 3238); Alte Potsdamer Strasse 7, in the Potsdamer Platz Arkaden, Tiergarten (2592 5691).

Ausberlin

Karl-Liebknecht-Strasse 17, Mitte (4199 7896/ www.ausberlin.de). U2, U5, U8, S5, S7, S9, S75 Alexanderplatz. **Open** noon-7pm Mon-Sat. **Credit** MC, V. **Map** p319/p327 O5.

Very cool shop for any and everything 'aus Berlin'. Innovative and design-happy like the city itself, this place sells everything from flashy books to Berlin-themed plasters, from postmodern stickers to progressive fashion. All items are made in Berlin, and prices range from €1 to €200.

Berliner Zinnfiguren

Knesebeckstrasse 88, Charlottenburg (315 7000/ www.zinnfigur.com). S5, S7, S9, S75 Savignyplatz. **Open** 10am-6pm Mon-Fri; 10am-3pm Sat. **Credit** AmEx, MC, V. **Map** p321/p328 F8.

Home to armies of handmade tin soldiers, farm animals and historical characters, all painted in incredible detail. You could take home an entire battalion of Prussian Grenadiers, if you should wish to.

Ostkost

Lychener Strasse 54, Prenzlauer Berg (4465 3623). S8, S41, S42, S85 Prenzlauer Allee or U2 Eberswalder Strasse. **Open** 7am-9pm Mon-Fri; 7am-8pm Sat. **Credit** AmEx, MC, V. **Map** p319/p328 P3.

This nostalgic 'Eastern Foods' shop sells almost-forgotten brands from the DDR, once available on every street corner in East Berlin. Othello chocolate biscuits, Spreewald pickles and Werder ketchup are just some of the many products offered alongside more modern fare from today's East.

Stationery & art supplies

Grüne Papeterie

Oranienstrasse 196, Kreuzberg (618 5355). U1 Görlitzer Bahnhof or U1, U8 Kottbusser Tor. **Open** 10am-7pm Mon-Fri; 10am-4pm Sat. **No credit cards.** **Map** p323 P9.

Grüne stocks eco-friendly stationery, wrapping paper, wooden fountain pens and small gifts and toys.

Leporello Papeterie

Rykestrasse 46, Prenzlauer Berg (4435 6912/ www.leporello-berlin.de). U2 Senefelderplatz. **Open** 10am-8pm Mon-Fri; 10am-6pm Sat. **Credit** V. **Map** p319/p328 P4.

Well-presented collection of journals, pens, paper in amazing colours and patterns, bags, plus a wide variety of trinkets, gifts and other stationery items. Good quality, big selection, reasonable prices – a wonderful little shop on a beautiful cobbled street.

Otto Ebeling

Fuggerstrasse 43-45, Schöneberg (211 4627/ www.otto-ebeling.de). U1, U2, U3 Wittenbergplatz. **Open** 8.30am-7pm Mon-Fri; 10am-4pm Sat. **Credit** AmEx, MC, V. **Map** p321 H9.

In business since 1885, this shop offers an excellent selection of art supplies, paper and portfolios.

RSVP

Mulackstrasse 14, Mitte (2809 4644/www.rsvp-berlin.de). U8 Weinmeisterstrasse. **Open** noon-7pm Tue-Fri; noon-6pm Sat. **Credit** AmEx, MC, V. **Map** p319/p326 O5.

Stationery for the aesthete: art deco scissors, exotic erasers, paper from Italy, Polish notebooks, G Lalo boxes and Caran d'Ache pens. *Photo p192.*

Arts & Entertainment

Admiralspalast. *See p250.*

Festivals & Events

From fairytales to riots, there's always a reason to celebrate in Berlin.

Mulled wine and gingerbread galore at Berlin's **Christmas markets**. *See p200.*

See p200.

Berlin hosts an impressive portfolio of themed events, cultural extravaganzas and colourful carnivals. The multicultural **Karneval der Kulturen** and the annual **Christopher Street Day Parade** are summer celebrations of the city's cultural diversity. The **Berlin International Film Festival** brings a welcome bit of glitz. Throughout the year, an assortment of trade fairs such as **ITB Berlin** and **Popkomm** rotate through Messegelände. At the other end of town, the **May Day Riots** are Kreuzberg's rite of spring. Twice annually, the **Lange Nacht der Museen** brings to life the exhibits in Berlin's museums. In summer, the city buzzes with open-air concert programmes. And at Christmas, ice-skating rinks and seasonal markets spring up all over.

Spring

MaerzMusik – Festival für aktuelle Musik

Organisers: Berliner Festspiele, Schaperstrasse 24, Tiergarten (2548 9218/www.berlinerfestspiele.de). **Tickets** vary. **Credit** varies. **Date** 2-3wks in Mar.

A holdover from the more culture-conscious days of the old East Germany, this annual contemporary music festival invites international avant-garde composers and musicians to present new works.

ITB Berlin

Messegelände am Funkturm, Messedamm 22, Charlottenburg (3038 2275/www.itb-berlin.de). U2 Kaiserdamm, S5, S75 Messe Süd or S41, S42, S45, S46 Messe Nord. **Open** 10am-6pm daily. **Tickets** vary. **No credit cards. Map** p320 A8. **Date** 5 days in mid Mar.
Tourism boards, travel agents and hotels satisfy Berliner wanderlust at this major trade fair.

Zeitfenster – Biennale für alte Musik

Konzerthaus, Gendarmenmarkt 2, Mitte (203 090/ www.konzerthaus.de). U2, U6 Stadtmitte. **Tickets** vary. **Credit** AmEx, MC, V. **Map** p322/p327 M7. **Date** 1wk in Apr 2010.
The Biennial Festival of Early Music focuses on works from the 16th and 17th centuries.

Deutschland Pokal-Endspiele

Olympiastadion, Olympischer Platz 3, Charlottenburg (300 633). U2 Olympia-Stadion or S5, S75

Olympiastadion. Information & tickets: Deutscher Fussball-Bund (tickets@dfb.de). **Tickets** vary. **No credit cards. Date** late Apr/early May.
The domestic football cup final has been taking place at the Olympiastadion every year since 1985. It regularly attracts some 65,000 fans and tickets are very hard to come by.

May Day Riots

Around Kottbusser Tor, Kreuzberg. U1, U8 Kottbusser Tor. **Map** p323 P9. **Date** 1 May.
An annual event since 1987, when Autonomen engaged in violent clashes with police. The riots have quietened in recent years, but Kreuzberg is still lively on May Day.

Qatar Telecom German Open

LTTC Rot-Weiss, Gottfried-von-Cramm-Weg 47-55, Grunewald (box office 4430 4430/www. german-open.org). S7, S9 Grunewald. **Tickets** €15-65. **Credit** AmEx, DC, MC, V. **Date** 1st or 2nd wk in May.
The world's fifth largest international women's tennis championship. After match point, the focus switches to a gala ball and other glitzy social affairs. Tickets are hard to come by.

Theatertreffen Berlin

Organisers: Berliner Festspiele, Schaperstrasse 24, Charlottenburg (2548 9100/www.berlinerfest spiele.de). **Tickets** vary. **Credit** AmEx, MC, V. **Date** 3wks in May.
A jury picks out ten of the most innovative and controversial new theatre productions from companies across Germany, Austria and Switzerland, and the winners come to Berlin to perform their pieces in May.

Karneval der Kulturen

Kreuzberg (6097 7022/www.karneval-berlin.de). **Tickets** free. **Date** 4 days in May/June.
Inspired by the Notting Hill Carnival and intended as a celebration of Berlin's ethnic and cultural diversity, the long and popular weekend (always Pentecost) centres on a 'multi-kulti' parade involving dozens of floats, hundreds of musicians and thousands of spectators. The route changes every year: see the website.

Museumsinselfestival

Museumsinsel, Mitte (no phone/www.smb.museum). S5, S7, S9, S75 Hackescher Markt. **Tickets** €5-€25. **Credit** AmEx, MC, V. **Map** p319/p327 N6. **Date** May-Sept.
An open-air season of high-quality rock and classical concerts, readings, plays and film screenings, with events staged not only on Museumsinsel but also at the Kulturforum complex near Potsdamer Platz, and at the Dahlem museums. Previous events have ranged from Serbian Gypsy orchestras through a screening of *Battleship Potemkin* with live soundtrack by the Pet Shop Boys and Dresdner Sinfoniker to shows by the likes of Nigel Kennedy and Patti Smith.

In Transit

Haus der Kulturen der Welt, John-Foster-Dulles-Allee 10, Tiergarten (3978 7175/www.hkw.de). Bus 100. **Tickets** vary. **Credit** DC, MC, V. **Map** p318 K6. **Date** 2wks in May/June.
Dance and performance artists from beyond Europe. Audiences can watch artists prepare their pieces, or wait for the resulting evening performances.

Summer

Yoga-Festival Berlin

Shanti-Park, Alt-Moabit 141, Mitte (3810 8093/ www.yogafestival.de). Hauptbahnhof S5, S7, S75, S9. **Tickets** *Day* €3-€18. *Wknd* €25-€39. **Credit** MC, V. **Map** p318 K6. **Date** wknd in June.
Om-tastic annual event now in its fifth year. A full weekend programme at the Shanti-Park offers practice sessions in the various yoga forms with teachers of note from many different countries. There is also music, a market and special events for children.

Berlin Philharmonie at the Waldbühne

Waldbühne, Am Glockenturm, Charlottenburg (administration 810 750/box office 0180 533 2433/www.berlin-philharmonic.com). S5 Pichelsberg, then shuttle bus. **Tickets** €25-€60. **Credit** AmEx, MC, V. **Date** 1 day in June.
The Philharmonie ends its season with an open-air concert that sells out months in advance. Over 20,000 Berliners light the atmospheric 'forest theatre' with candles once darkness falls.

International Aerospace Exhibition & Conference

Flughafen Schönefeld (3038 2014/www.ila-berlin.de). S9, S45 Flughafen Berlin-Schönefeld. **Tickets** vary. **No credit cards. Date** 8-13 June 2010.
This very popular biennial event, also known as the Berlin Air Show, is held at Schönefeld airport. It features around 1,000 exhibitors from 40 countries, with aircraft of all kinds on display, and a serious focus on space.

Fête de la Musique

Various venues (4171 5289/www.fetedelamusique.de). **Tickets** free. **Date** 21 June.
A regular summer solstice happening since 1995, this music extravaganza of bands and DJs takes place all across the city. The music selection is mixed, with DJs playing everything from heavy metal to Schlager.

Deutsch-Französisches Volksfest

Zentraler Festplatz am Kurt-Schumacher-Damm, Kurt-Schumacher-Damm 207-245, Reinickendorf (213 3290/www.deutsch-franzoesisches-volksfest.de). U6 Kurt-Schumacher-Platz. **Tickets** €1.50. **No credit cards. Date** 4wks in June/July.
A survivor from the days when this area was the French Sector, the German-French Festival offers fairground rides, French music and cuisine, and Bastille Day fireworks.

Arts & Entertainment

Lesbisch-Schwules Stadtfest

*Nollendorfplatz, Schöneberg (2147 3586/
www.regenbogenfonds.de). U1, U2, U3, U4
Nollendorfplatz.* **Tickets** free. **Map** p322 J9.
Date wknd before Christopher Street Day.
The Lesbian & Gay Street Fair takes over Schöneberg
every year, filling several blocks in West Berlin's gay
quarter. Participating bars, clubs, food stands and
musical acts make this a dizzying, non-stop event that
also serves as kick-off for the following week's
Christopher Street Day Parade.

Christopher Street Day Parade

2362 8632/www.csd-berlin.de. **Tickets** free.
Date Sat in late June.
Originally organised to commemorate the 1969 riots
outside the Stonewall Bar on Christopher Street in
New York, the fun and flamboyant parade has
become one of the summer's most enjoyable and
inclusive street parties, attracting straights as well
as gays. In 2008, the parade took a new route, starting on Karl-Liebknecht-Strasse and ending, 4 miles
(6.5km) later, at the Seigessäule.

Classic Open Air

*Gendarmenmarkt, Mitte (Media On-Line 3157
5413/www.classicopenair.de). U6 Französische
Strasse, U2, U6 Stadmitte or U2 Hausvogteiplatz.*
Tickets €30-€97. **Credit** AmEx, MC. **Map**
p322/p327 M7. **Date** 4-7 days in early July.
Big names usually open this concert series held in
one of Berlin's most beautiful squares.

Deutsch-Amerikanisches Volksfest

*Truman Plaza, Hüttenweg, corner of Clayallee,
Zehlendorf (213 3290/www.deutsch-amerikanisches-
volksfest.de). U3 Oskar-Helene-Heim.* **Tickets**
€1.50; free children. **No credit cards**. **Date** 4wks
in July/Aug.
Originally established by the US forces stationed
in West Berlin, the German-American Festival
offers a tacky but popular mix of carnival rides,
cowboys doing lasso tricks, candy floss, hot dogs
and Yankee beer.

Tanz im August

*Organisers: HAU, Hallesches Ufer 32, Kreuzberg
(2590 0427/www.tanzimaugust.de).* **Tickets** vary.
Credit varies. **Date** 2-3wks in Aug.
Tanz im August is Germany's leading modern
dance festival, with big-name participants and an
international reputation. An annual showcase for
global dance trends.

Hanfparade

*Hallesches Tor to Rotes Rathaus (0178 659 4399/
www.hanfparade.de).* **Tickets** free. **Date** 1st Sat
in Aug.
The organisers of the Hemp Parade seek total
legalisation of the use and possession of cannabis.
The route changes every year; in 2008, it started off
from the Fernsehenturm and meandered through to
Potsdamer Platz.

Internationales Berliner Bierfestival

*Karl-Marx-Allee, from Strausberger Platz to
Frankfurter Tor, Friedrichshain (6576 3560/
www.bierfestival-berlin.de). U5 Frankfurter Tor.*
Tickets free. **No credit cards**. **Map** p325 R6/S6.
Date wknd in Aug.
Berlin's International Beer Festival showcases hun-
dreds of beers from over 60 countries, bringing con-
viviality to the city's premier Stalinist boulevard.

Young.euro.classic

*Konzerthaus, Gendarmenmarkt 2, Mitte (1805 568
100/www.young-euro-classic.de). U6 Französische
Strasse.* **Tickets** €12. **No credit cards**. **Map**
p322/p327 M7. **Date** 2wks in Aug.
This annual summer concert programme brings
together youth orchestras from around Europe.

Lange Nacht der Museen

902 699 444/www.lange-nacht-der-museen.de.
Tickets *In advance* €12; €8 reductions. *On the
day* €15; €10 reductions. **Credit** AmEx, MC, V.
Date 1 evening in late Jan & late Aug.
Twice a year, around 100 of Berlin's museums, collections, archives and exhibition halls stay open into
the early hours with special events, concerts, readings, lectures and performances for the 'Long Night
of the Museums'. A ticket gets you free travel on special shuttle buses and regular public transport.

Kreuzberger festliche Tage

*Viktoriapark, Kreuzbergstrasse, Kreuzberg (4340
7905/www.kreuzberger-festliche-tage.de). U6, U7
Mehringdamm.* **Tickets** free. **Map** p322 L10.
Date 2wks in late Aug/early Sept.
This annual late summer festival in characterful
Viktoriapark offers music, games, beer and food.

Musikfest Berlin

*Organisers: Berliner Festspiele, Schaperstrasse 24,
Charlottenburg (254 890/www.berlinerfestspiele.de).*
Tickets vary. **Credit** varies. **Date** 1wk in late
Aug/early Sept.
The Berlin Symphony Orchestra collaborates with
the Berlin Philharmonic and its conductor, Sir Simon
Rattle, in a week of orchestral and chamber music,
plus some musical theatre. Orchestras from London,
New York and around Europe also participate.

Autumn

For the **Berlin Marathon**, *see p264.*

Internationales Literaturfestival Berlin

2787 8620/www.literaturfestival.com. **Tickets** vary.
Credit AmEx, MC, V. **Date** 2wks in Sept/Oct.
Major literary event with readings, symposiums
and discussions attended by both major authors
and rising stars. The 2008 programme included
Maria Warner, Péter Esterházy, Nancy Huston,
Peter Schneider and Jáchym Topol among scores of
established and up-and-coming writers from all
over the world.

Popkomm

Messe Berlin, Messedamm 22, Charlottenburg (3038 3009/www.popkomm.de). U2 Kaiserdamm, S5, S75 Messe Süd or S41, S42, S45, S46 Messe Nord. **Tickets** vary. **Credit** AmEx, MC, V. **Map** p320 A8. **Date** 3 days in Sept.

Europe's largest domestic music industry trade fair takes place in September and brings three days of business schmoozing, and lots of music to go with it. As well as the trade-only conference, the city hosts myriad showcases and live events. *See also below* **Pop goes Berlin**.

Art Forum Berlin

Messegelände am Funkturm, Messedamm 22, Charlottenburg (3038 2076/www.art-forum-berlin.de). U2 Kaiserdamm, S5, S75 Messe Süd or S41, S42, S45, S46 Messe Nord. **Tickets** vary. **Credit** AmEx, MC, V. **Date** 5 days in late Oct/early Nov.

Since 1996, the Art Forum Berlin has sought to bring together gallery-owners and artists for this trade fair of contemporary art. The event attracts many of Europe's leading galleries plus thousands of lay enthusiasts. It also coincides with Berliner

Pop goes Berlin

German industry from out under the shadow of the US and UK. It was also born out of generous subsidy from the state of Nord-Rhein Westfalen – looking, at the time, for ways to compensate for the likely move of government jobs from Bonn to Berlin.

Ironic, then, that Popkomm relocated to Berlin earlier this decade, along with music majors Sony and Universal, as the balance of industry power tipped inexorably from Cologne to Germany's capital of cool. The event makes better sense in Berlin. Since Popkomm began, the business role of music trade fairs has changed. They used to

Just as the Berlin International Film Festival has started to outstrip Cannes not only in terms of glamour and prestige but also for the amount of business that gets done, so has **Popkomm**, Berlin's annual music trade fair, come to rival MIDEM, the opposition in Cannes, as Europe's principal music industry get-together. Thousands of folk, from the smallest creative companies to the most massive of majors, jet into Berlin to make deals, present their artists, and chew over industry issues. And while the trade fair and conference, despite one open day, are essentially for professionals only, Berliners turn out in force for the concerts and special events that appear all over town.

It's not bad going for what began as a domestic music industry conference. Popkomm was a barely significant event on the music business calendar when first launched in Cologne, then the centre of the German music industry, in the late 1980s. It was in part the product of a desire to haul the

be all about buying and selling territorial licenses. Today, now that digital downloading has removed geography from distribution, they're more about promoting and presenting, dealing with media and internet and negotiating music's place in the wider networks of popular culture. As a burgeoning creative hub and true music city, Berlin is just the place.

When autumn comes and the Popkomm bandwagon rolls into town, everyone tries to hitch a ride. Every conceivable venue and club seems to host a related event. Some are official Popkomm concerts, some are showcases sponsored by interest groups or cultural bodies, others are promoted by artists or independent labels hoping to catch the attention of a passing industry cheque book.

And as it does for the Berlinale, the whole town gets involved, tuning in to the media reports, turning out for the concerts and animating what becomes a city-wide event. You'd never get that in Cannes.

Arts & Entertainment

Liste (www.berliner-liste.org) and Preview Berlin (www.previewberlin.de), which feature newer galleries and artists.

Spielzeit'europa

Organisers: Berliner Festspiele, Schaperstrasse 24 (254 890/www.berlinerfestspiele.de). **Tickets** vary. **Credit** AmEx, MC, V. **Date** Oct-Jan.
This forum for theatre and dance from around Europe showcases theatre that incorporates new political and aesthetic ideas from a specifically European perspective. It's supplemented by German co-productions. Shows run on and off for five months.

JazzFest Berlin

Organisers: Berliner Festspiele, Schaperstrasse 24, Charlottenburg (254 890/www.berlinerfestspiele.de). **Tickets** vary. **Credit** AmEx, MC, V. **Date** 4 days late Oct/early Nov.
A wide spectrum of jazz from an array of internationally renowned artists, and a fixture since 1964. The concurrent Fringe Jazz Festival (organised by JazzRadio) showcases less established acts.

Berliner Märchentage

3470 9479/www.berliner-maerchentage.de. **Tickets** vary. **Credit** varies. **Date** 3wks in mid Nov.
The Berlin Fairytale Festival celebrates tales from around the world each year with some 400 storytelling and music events in a carnival atmosphere.

Worldtronics

Haus der Kulturen der Welt, John-Foster-Dulles-Allee 10, Tiergarten (3978 7175/www.hkw.de). Bus 100. **Tickets** vary. **Credit** DC, MC, V. **Map** p318 K6. **Date** 4 days in Nov.
A festival showcasing the world of electronic music in a city that loves the stuff. Guest musicians come from all over (in 2008 from Japan, Chile, Israel and the Democratic Republic of the Congo), while the trade fair covers everything from books, clubs and labels to software and sound laboratories.

Winter

See also p198 **Lange Nacht der Museen.**

Christmas Markets

Kaiser-Wilhelm-Gedächtniskirche, Breitscheidplatz, Charlottenburg (213 3290/www.weihnachtsmarkt-deutschland.de). U2, U9, S3, S5, S7, S9, S75 Zoologischer Garten. **Open** 11am-8pm Mon-Thur, Sun; 11am-10pm Fri, Sat. **Map** p321 G8.
Traditional markets spring up across Berlin during the Christmas season, offering toys, mulled wine and gingerbread. This is one of the biggest. *Photo p196.*

Berliner Silvesterlauf

Grunewald (3012 8820/www.berlin-marathon.com/events/index.php). S5, S75 Messe Süd. **Tickets** free. **Date** 31 Dec.
A local Berlin tradition for decades, the New Year's Eve Run (aka the 'pancake run') starts off in Grunewald at the intersection of Waldschulallee and Harbigstrasse.

Silvester

Date 31 Dec.
With Berliners' enthusiasm for tossing firecrackers and launching rockets from windows, New Year's Eve is always vivid, noisy and hazardous. Thousands celebrate at the Brandenburger Tor. Thousands more trek up to the Teufelsberg at the northern tip of Grunewald or the Viktoriapark in Kreuzberg to watch the fireworks across the city.

Tanztage

Sophiensaele, Sophienstrasse 18, Mitte (283 5266/ www.tanztage.de). U8 Weinmeisterstrasse or S3, S5, S7, S9, S75 Hackescher Markt. **Tickets** €15; €10 reductions. **No credit cards. Map** p319/p326 N5.
Date 2wks in early Jan.
New talent featured in a fortnight of dance events.

Internationale Grüne Woche Berlin

Messegelände am Funkturm, Messedamm 22, Charlottenburg (3038 2267/www.gruenewoche.de). U2 Kaiserdamm, S5, S75 Messe Süd or S41, S42, S45, S46 Messe Nord. **Open** 1-6pm daily. **Tickets** €12. **No credit cards. Map** p320 A8.
Date 10 days in Jan.
An orgy of food and drink from the far corners of Germany and across the planet.

UltraSchall

Organisers: DeutschlandRadio Berlin, Hans-Rosenthal-Platz, Schöneberg (850 30/www.dradio.de/dlr). **Tickets** vary. **Credit** varies. **Date** 10 days in mid Jan.
New music presented in high-profile venues by some of the world's leading specialist ensembles. Concerts are often broadcast live by DeutschlandRadio and Rundfunk Berlin Brandenburg.

Transmediale

Akademie der Künste, Hanseatenweg 10, Tiergarten (2474 9761/www.transmediale.de). S5, S7, S9, S75 Bellevue or U9 Hansaplatz. **Tickets** vary. **Credit** AmEx, MC, V. **Map** p317 H6. **Date** 3-5 days in late Jan/early Feb.
One of the world's largest international festivals for media art and digital culture, with exhibitions and screenings from artists working with video, television, computer animation, internet and other visual media and digital technologies. The satellite event Club Transmediale takes place at Maria am Ostbahnhof and offers performances, discussions and media art about electronic music.

Berlin International Film Festival

Potsdamer Platz, Tiergarten & other venues (259 200/www.berlinale.de). U2, S1, S2, S26 Potsdamer Platz. **Tickets** €7-€16. *Festival pass* €140. **Credit** AmEx, MC, V. **Date** 1-2wks in mid Feb.
Now approaching 60 years old, the Berlinale is one of the world's major cinema festivals, featuring over 300 movies from all five continents. It is centred at the Potsdamer Platz cinemas and attended by international stars, providing this normally glamour-proof city with a bit of glitz in the dead of winter.

Children

The kids are all right, as far as Berlin is concerned.

Domäne Dahlem. *See p204.*

Berlin is a remarkably child-friendly city.
Its many parks nearly all have the usual
swings and roundabouts; some have fantastic
adventure playgrounds. Most of the museums
have decent children's sections, and tickets to
one kids' attraction often include a discount
voucher for another. There are also superb
indoor and outdoor swimming pools (*see p270*)
to cool off in and well-equipped commercial
indoor playgrounds.

Getting around on public transport with
children is relatively hassle-free: kids under six
travel free, the main U- and S-Bahn stations
have lifts, and buses allow easy access for
prams and buggies.

Mitte

There's no problem keeping children busy in
Mitte. **Museumsinsel** (*see p88*), with its
museums and weekend flea market, is a lively
spot to visit. Nearby **Monbijou Park** on
Oranienburger Strasse has playgrounds and,
in summer, a great wading pool, the Kinderbad
Monbijou. For a different perspective, try a
boat tour, many of which operate from the
Museumsinsel and nearby (*see p120* **Boot
Trips**). For a bird's-eye view, scan the city
from the **Fernsehturm** (TV Tower; *see p96*)

on Alexanderplatz. Down below, children cool
off in the **Neptunbrunnen** (*see p94*) during
the summer months.

Children will enjoy the dinosaur skeletons
and new multimedia displays at the **Museum
für Naturkunde** (Museum of Natural History;
see p92), the mummies at the **Ägyptisches
Museum** (currently housed at the Altes
Museum, but due to move to the Neues Museum
in 2009; *see p88*) and the interactive exhibits
at the **Museum für Kommunikation** (*see
p90*). The **Museum Kindheit und Jugend**
(Museum of Childhood and Youth; *see p96*)
has toys and other childhood artefacts from
days of old. For a pricier treat, there's Legoland
in the Sony Center at Potsdamer Platz (*see p203*
Children at work).

AquaDom & Sea Life (*see p95*) has
13 aquaria and plenty of hands-on gadgetry.
Its centrepiece is the mighty AquaDom itself,
a cylindrical saltwater tank with a glass lift
rising through the centre, from which you can
view some of the thousands of exotic fish.

Kindercity in the new Alexa mall near
Alexanderplatz (3087 4390, www.kindercity.
de) offers 'edutainment' for the 21st-century
family. It's a hands-on learning centre with
plenty of wholesome activities such as
'knowledge lanes' and 'factory workshops'

Arts & Entertainment

Alexanderplatz. See p201.

where kids can bake bread, be a car mechanic or learn from insects. There's also a cinema, theatre, restaurant and more on site.

Many restaurants in Mitte have children's menus, but the area around Hackesche Höfe and Rosenthaler Strasse offers the richest pickings, with cafés and restaurants of every type. Or try the potato specialities from around Germany and the world at **Der Kartoffelkeller** (Albrechtstrasse 14B, 282 8548, www.kartoffelkeller.com).

Prenzlauer Berg & Friedrichshain

Prenzlauer Berg has enjoyed something of a baby boom in recent years, although it has few specific attractions for kids. There are, however, plenty of cafés, restaurants, squares and playgrounds, particularly around the Kollwitzplatz area. Friedrichshain is less child-orientated.

Among the restaurants offering children's menus are the Italian **Istoria** (Kollwitzstrasse 64, 4405 0208); **Zander** (Kollwitzstrasse 50, 4405 7678, www.zander-restaurant.de, closed Mon) and **Prater** (Kastanienallee 7; see p160), both serving German food; and the Indian **Maharadscha 2** (Schönhauser Allee 142, 448 5172, www.maharadscha2.de).

Die Schaubude (Greifswalder Strasse 81-84, 423 4314, www.schaubude-berlin.de, closed Mon) is a high-quality puppet theatre used by local and visiting troupes. **Volkspark Friedrichshain** (see p100) has half-pipes

and skater routes, and the Märchenbrunnen ('fairy tale fountain') features figures from stories by the Brothers Grimm.

Kreuzberg

This vibrant borough has lots to offer kids. Older children will enjoy the **Haus am Checkpoint Charlie** (see p105), which displays the old cars and balloons that people used to circumvent the Wall. And they'll love the **Grusel Kabinett** (see p105), a spooky chamber of horrors in an old World War II bunker. For an expensive but novel vertical adventure, there's the Hi-Flyer, a hot-air balloon that, weather permitting, floats 150 metres (492 feet) above ground near Checkpoint Charlie (corner of Wilhelmstrasse & Zimmerstrasse, 226 678 811, www.air-service-berlin.de). The **Deutsches Technikmuseum Berlin** (see p105) has vintage locomotives and cars, computers and gadgets, and a Maritime Wing with boats. Entrance tickets include access to the superb Spectrum and its fantastic hands-on experiments.

Neue City Bowling Hasenheide (see p266) has 12 lanes for children and is open from 10am daily. The Hasenheide park next door has a great adventure playground, a crazy golf course and a small zoo. The little vale in the middle of the park is ideal for tobogganing when it snows.

Leafy **Viktoriapark** (see p102) is a landscaped hill with fine views, and another good place for tobogganing when weather permits. In summer a waterfall cascades down to street level. The park also has playgrounds and a tiny zoo. Stroll down nearby Bergmannstrasse for a choice of international snacks and meals. Close by is the huge supervised indoor playground **Jolo** (Am Tempelhofer Berg 7D, 6120 2796, www.jolo-berlin.de). Facilities include an inflatable mountain, mini bumper cars and a snack bar.

A walk along the south bank of the canal on Carl-Herz-Ufer will take you to the beer garden **Brachvogel** (no.34, 693 0432), which has a crazy golf course and a playground next door. Further east, on the north bank, is **Statthaus Böcklerpark**, Prinzenstrasse 1, with its small petting zoo. It organises a monthly children's flea market as well as other events. Further east again and back on the south side is the child-friendly **Casolare** (Grimmstrasse 30, 6950 6610), which does great pizzas. For dessert, cross the road to **Isabel's Eiscafé** (Böckstrasse 51).

At the east end of the borough is **Görlitzer Park**, with playgrounds and a petting zoo to keep the little ones happy.

Schöneberg

Winterfeldplatz is a pleasant focal point at the northern end of this huge district, with lots of cafés, restaurants and fast food around the square and along Maassenstrasse to the north and Goltzstrasse to the south. There are plenty of parks and playgrounds here.

In the south of the borough, **Natur-Park Schöneberger Südgelände** (www.gruen-berlin.de) is an old railway shunting yard left for nature to reclaim. There's lots for the kids to explore – and no doggy do or crazy cyclists. Nearby is the **Planetarium am Insulaner** (Munsterdamm 90, 790 0930, www.wfs.be. schule.de), which has programmes for children.

The **Volkspark Wilmersdorf** has several good playgrounds (including one with a ski lift ride). Near the park's eastern end is **Stadtbad Schöneberg**, a swimming pool that's ideal for kids (*see p270*).

There are child-friendly restaurants all over Schöneberg. Try hearty pasta at **Petite Europe** (*see p148*) or burgers and bagels at **Tim's Canadian Deli** (*see p166*).

Tiergarten

The major draw in Tiergarten is the park itself, with its playgrounds and open spaces. Paddle and rowing boats can be hired near the **Café am Neuen See**. Meanwhile, along

Children at work

The kids waited patiently as you queued for 45 minutes to get into the Reichstag. And they were absolute angels as the family traipsed around the Bauhaus Archiv looking at chairs. When they've been so good, reward them with the **Legoland Discovery Centre Berlin** at Potsdamer Platz.

The entrance is on ground level behind the giant Lego giraffe outside the Sony Center. The facility itself is in the basement, divided into seven themed areas featuring things to do with Lego bricks, and startling displays that are made from them. It's focused on kids aged three to ten, who can easily spend a few hours here, unwinding from sightseeing and reconnecting to the familiar build-and-dream world that is Lego.

The Discovery Centre is more of an indoor playground than an educational experience. There's a bit of subtle branding going on – kids can 'discover' how Lego bricks are made in a hokey mock-up of an assembly line, for example. But, no matter, the appeal is old-fashioned open space, piles of soft, oversized Lego bricks, well-stocked tables where kids can build, and nobody telling them what to do.

Boys tend to gravitate to a couple of ramps where they can race the Lego vehicles they've put together on the workbenches. Close by is a corner where girls are quietly engineering Lego families to inhabit Lego doll's houses. A concession serves reasonably priced drinks and snacks.

In the Modellbau Workshop, small groups of adults and their children receive step-by-step instructions on how to build customised Lego models. Fascinating how a handful of bricks

can be swiftly ordered into a pretty convincing Brandenburg Gate; frustrating, though, that you can't keep it as a souvenir.

The Dschungel Expedition is a dark grotto and pastiche of the Indiana Jones films, with jaw-snapping alligators and a giant Lego spider with LED eyes. There's a ride called the Drachenberg in which gondolas that look like dragons whisk you on a spooky tour of a castle. Many of the Lego figures here are actually quite scary in an *Alice in Wonderland* kind of way, and the giant red Lego dragon at the end is lost on the very youngest kids, most of whom have already screwed up their eyes in fear.

Upstairs, Miniland is an expansive, animated cityscape of Lego Berlin landmarks, with the towers of Potsdamer Platz, the Victorian brickwork of Hackescher Markt station and the imposing Berliner Dom all built from the bobbly bricks.

In front of the mini Reichstag is a blinking stage where the Berlin reggae band Seed is playing to a spellbound Lego crowd. For adults, the fascination of Miniland is the discovery of a truth our kids knew all along: with a little imagination and a bunch of Lego bricks, there is nothing you cannot build.

Legoland Discovery Centre Berlin

Sony Center, Potsdamer Platz, Tiergarten (3010 4010/www.legolanddiscoverycentre. com/berlin). U2, S1, S2, S25 Potsdamer Platz. **Open** 10am-7pm daily (last entry 5pm). **Admission** €14.75; €11.75 reductions. **No credit cards. Map** p322/p326 K7.

Strasse des 17. Juni, the main road through the park, there's an interesting flea market at weekends (*see p173*).

In the park's south-western corner is Berlin's beautiful **Zoo** (*see p115*), currently booming thanks to the arrival, rejection by his mother and bottle-fed survival of Knut the baby polar bear. But hurry: Knut is growing fast. On rainy days, head for the Zoo's sizeable **Aquarium** (*see p115*). The excellent **Gemäldegalerie** in Matthäikirchplatz (*see p114*) runs Sunday afternoon tours for children.

Charlottenburg

Away from the bustle of Zoologischer Garten and the Ku'damm, the atmosphere is pleasant, with good restaurants, shops and markets. The Saturday market at Karl-August-Platz is a gathering point for families, with a playground, cafés and top-notch ice-cream at **Micha's Eisdiele** (Pestalozzistrasse 85, no phone).

Fifteen minutes' walk west is the pretty **Lietzenseepark**, with a lake, playgrounds, cafés (open Apr-Oct) and sports areas. If the weather's not great, take the kids to **Toka-Tohei** indoor playground (Wintersteinstrasse 22, 3454 0346, www.tokatohei.de).

There are child-friendly restaurants all over Charlottenburg, particularly to the east. The kids will be welcome for Italian food at **La Cantina** (Bleibtreustrasse 17, 883 2156) or **Totò** (corner of Bleibtreustrasse & Pestalozzistrasse, 312 5449, www.trattoria-toto.de). At **Charlottchen** (Droysenstrasse 1, 324 4717, www.charlottchen-berlin.de), parents eat in the dining room (the international food is nothing special) while kids let their hair down in a rumpus room. There are theatre performances on Sundays (11.30am, 3.30pm, €5).

Other districts

The **ufaFabrik** cultural centre in the southern district of Tempelhof (Viktoriastrasse 10-18, 755 030, www.ufafabrik.de) has a farm for kids, several cafés and restaurants, a circus and a variety of courses and workshops. It's right by U-Bahn Ullsteinstrasse (U6).

In the wilds of Neukölln, **Britzer Garten** (www.gruen-berlin.de) is perfect for small children. The immaculately manicured gardens with their once-futuristic architecture look like something out of the *Teletubbies*, and there are farm animals, playgrounds, a narrow-gauge railway, a working 19th-century windmill and plenty of food and drink options.

South-west of the city, the vast **Grunewald** woods (*see p125*) are well suited for long walks, and the Kronprinzessinnenweg, which runs

through the middle, is ideal for rollerblading and cycling. On a breezy day, fly a kite and enjoy the view from the **Teufelsberg** (*see p125*); on a sunny day, take a dip in the **Teufelsee** (*see p125*) or any of the area's numerous lakes. **Strandbad Wannsee** (*see p270*) is Europe's largest inland beach; there's a playground, cafés and pedalos. The 204-step climb up the **Grunewaldturm** (Havelchaussee, 300 0730) is rewarded with a beautiful view of the river Havel and surroundings, and there's a restaurant and beer garden too.

To the east of the Grunewald, **Domäne Dahlem** (*see p125; photo p201*) is a 17th century-style working farm featuring demonstrations by blacksmiths, carpenters, bakers and potters, plus ponies, tractors and hay wagons to ride. **Museumsdorf Düppel** (*see p128*) is a reconstructed 14th-century village around archaeological excavations near the Düppel forest. From April to October, kids can ride ox carts or witness medieval technology, crafts and farming techniques.

To avoid summer crowds on the Havel and Wannsee, try the **Tegeler See** to the north-west of the centre. In bad weather, take refuge at **Jack's Fun World** (Miraustrasse 38, 4190 0242, www.jacks-fun-world.de, closed Mon). Be warned: the extra fees for the best attractions at this indoor playground can add up. North-east of Tegel, in the quaint village of Alt Lübars, is **Jugendfarm Lübars** (415 7027, www.jugend-reinickendorf.de/jugendfarm, closed Oct-Mar, Mon), with farm animals and traditional crafts.

South-east of the centre, the **Mellowpark** in Köpenick (Friedrichshagener Strasse 10-12, 652 603 771, www.mellowpark.de) offers supervised play for older children. Activities, daily from 2pm in summer, include boarding, basketball and BMX on the banks of the Spree.

Also to the east is the **Tierpark Berlin-Friedrichsfelde** (*see p130*), a lovely park and zoo, with playgrounds, a petting zoo and snack stands. Still further east, the **Müggelsee** (*see p270*) is another beautiful sailing and swimming area. There are day trips by boat from Mitte in the summer.

Out in the borough of Marzahn, the **Erholungspark** (Eisenacher Strasse, www.gruen-berlin.de) has oriental gardens, a 'garden of stones' with fountains, ponds, rocks and boulders and a 'rhododendron grove' with statues of characters from Hans-Christian Andersen and the Brothers Grimm. It's also dotted with playgrounds, kiosks and cafés.

Babysitters

There's a good online search engine (in German) for babysitters at www.babysitteragentur.de.

Film

With its prestigious festival, landmark cinemas and brand-new multiplexes, Berlin is ready for its close-up.

Before the arrival of the multiplex, Berlin was a great movie town. You could go to a Lubitsch retrospective with a statue of Lubitsch in the back row; lie on a dilapidated couch in a Hinterhof carriage house and watch a 35mm print of *The Lusty Men*; or have a film show devolve into an all-night party that ends with everyone setting their clothes on fire. Well OK, maybe not every night, but…

Like almost everywhere, the cinema-going experience in Berlin is on its way to extinction. While the city still boasts an amazing screen count of almost 260, you're mostly going to get big blockbuster fodder. Auf Deutsch.

But an alternative film-going scene does still exist and, at least for the time being, the view is not at all bad. Indie mainstays such as **Eiszeit** and **Central** have lately got their groove back, the **Moviemento** has changed hands and seems to be in the process of rebirth, and **Babylon-Mitte** has shaken off its stodgy mindset and spiced up its programming. And all seem to have English programming more in evidence.

For monophones, traditional all-English venues **Odeon** and **Babylon Kreuzberg** are also still there, and the **Cinestar Potsdamer Platz** is all English and eight screens of it.

One surviving Berlin phenomenon is the city's fascination with silent films, often presented with live musical accompaniment, ranging from simple piano to full orchestra with the occasional hardcore band for variety. Favourites include historical hits such as *Metropolis* and *The Cabinet of Dr Caligari*. Babylon-Mitte now has a regular silent film programme and films tend to show up at the **Arsenal**, or any of the outdoor cinemas (*see below*).

Another popular tradition is the outdoor cinema, the Frieluftkino. Almost everything is shown synchronised into German, but original English is in evidence at the **Freiluftkino Kreuzberg** (*see p209*) and the outdoor shows at Central are usually fun. It's a real Berlin thing to do and on a clement night can be very enjoyable. And if you want the outdoor experience but you're feeling a bit perverse, try checking out the **AutoKino Berlin-Mitte** (Kurt Schumacher Damm 207, Reinickendorf). Yes, it's a real drive-in and while the films are just typical Hollywood dubbed into German, it's still a fun, quirky night out.

FESTIVALS

The **Berlin Film Festival**, or Berlinale (*see p200*), is the biggest and most prominent of the international film festivals, but it's far from the only game in town.

The **Fantasy Film Festival** (www. fantasyfilmfest.com) shows the latest in fantasy, splatter, horror and sci-fi from the US, Hong Kong, Japan and Europe. Films are often premieres, with occasional previews, retrospectives and rarities. Most shows are in English or with English subtitles. The festival takes place at the Cinemaxx in Potsdamer Platz around mid August.

Mid August also offers the **Globian World and Culture Documentary Film Festival** (www.globians.com) in Potsdam, a week-long event featuring documentaries from world filmmakers shown in English or with English subtitles. It has a real DIY spirit of sharing movies and information and with an admission price of €3 per show or €30 for the whole week's packed programme, it's definitely worth the haul out to Potsdam.

Along similar lines is the **One World Berlin Festival** (www.oneworld-fest.de) which takes place in November, an extension of an event in Prague. Nominally centred around human rights issues, the festival casts a wide net to include films on politics, religion, theatre, music, art and culture. At least half of the programme is in English or with English subtitles.

New in November is **Rhythm of the Line**, the International Graffiti and Hip Hop Film Festival (www.rotl.de). Films from major players like the US, UK and Brazil mix with surprises from Romania, New Zealand and Russia. Shows are at the Eiszeit.

The **InterFilm Short Film Festival** (www.interfilm.de), also in November, is 23 years old and has grown from a DIY affair into an international event with big buck prizes. It shows over 500 short films from 88 countries, organised into themes such as Miniature Cinema, Love and Insanities, Films by Children, and a programme of midnight movie madness called Eject. Its current home is the Babylon-Mitte with events and parties at the nearby Volksbühne. InterFilm is also responsible for Going Underground, a mini festival of 14 short silent films shown on

Berlin International Film Festival

For nearly 60 years, the **Internationale Filmfestspiele Berlin** (www.berlinale.de) has been the city's biggest cultural event, as well as one of the world's three most prominent film festivals. Born out of the Cold War, it developed from a propaganda showcase, supported by the Allies, into a genuine meeting place – and frequent collision point – for East and West. Whether it was the 1959 French boycott over Stanley Kubrick's indictment of war, *Paths of Glory*, the jury revolt over the pro-Vietnamese film *OK* in 1970 or the 1979 East Bloc walkout over the depiction of Vietnamese people in *The Deer Hunter*, the festival's drama was never confined to the screens. The years following the fall of the Berlin Wall were particularly exciting: the mood and energy of the festival reflected the joy and chaos of the city's changing landscape.

Now settled comfortably into Potsdamer Platz, the festival has taken on more of the glamour and celebrity of its two major rivals, Cannes and Venice. Festival director Dieter Kosslick has concentrated on creating a more open and energetic atmosphere to the proceedings, with various symposia and sidebars, art and performance events (*see below* **Forum**) and an outreach programme for developing filmmakers (*see below* **Talent Campus**). And for those who miss the old landmark theatres (*see p210* **The show must go on**), the Delphi, International, Film Palast, Colosseum and former festival flagship Zoo Palast are still used as venues for repeats and sidebar performances.

What remains the same, however, is the chance to see arguably the widest and most eclectic mix of any film festival anywhere. And unlike Cannes and Venice, Berlin is as much about the audiences as it is about the industry. Every February, it seems like the entire city turns out to see literally hundreds of films, presented in eight sections – the most important of which are listed below.

THE INTERNATIONAL COMPETITION

Recent years have seen a rise in the glamour quotient and more stars attending than ever before. A downside is that the selection is becoming more and more conservative. Concentrating on major, big-budget productions from all over the world, with a heavy (and often heavily criticised) accent on America, these films often make it to general release. Entries compete for the Gold and Silver Bears which are announced at the closing night gala. All shows in the Berlinale Palast come with simultaneous translation over headphones. Repeats are at the **Urania** (An der Urania 17, Schöneberg, 218 9091), **CinemaxX** (Potsdamer Strasse 5, Tiergarten, 2592 2111) and **Kino International** (*see p208*).

THE INTERNATIONAL FORUM OF YOUNG CINEMA

Some devotees claim this is the real Berlin festival, the place where discoveries are made. Born out of the revolt that dissolved the Competition in 1970, the Forum provides challenging and eclectic fare that you wouldn't see elsewhere. Anything can happen here, from the latest American indie film, to African cinema, to midnight shows of Hong Kong action films. A new section, Forum Expanded, curates an accompanying programme of film- and media-related artwork at Kunst-Werke in Mitte (*see p216*), as well as installations and special events in the main Forum lobby by the Arsenal. Shows are at **CineStar** (*see p209*) and the **Arsenal** (*see p208*) with repeats at the **Delphi** (*see p210*), **Colosseum** (*see p210*) and **Cubix** (Rathaus Strasse 1, Mitte, www.cinestar.de).

PANORAMA

Originally intended to showcase films that fell outside the guidelines of the Competition, the Panorama has been giving the Forum a run for its money in terms of innovative programming. But Panorama films are less artistically rigorous than the Forum, with a spotlight on world independent movies, gay and lesbian and political films. Panorama films show in **CineStar** (*see p209*) and **Zoo Palast** (*see p210*) with special premieres at **Kino International** (*see p208*). Repeats are at **CinemaxX** (Potsdamer Strasse 5, Tiergarten, 2592 2111), **CineStar** (*see p209*), **Cubix** (Rathaus Strasse 1, Mitte, www.cinestar.de) and the **Colosseum** (*see p210*). No translation, but most films show with English subtitles.

PERSPEKTIVE DEUTSCHES KINO

Perspektive reflects the festival's increased focus on the latest in German cinema. The newest of the sections, it has emerged as a big audience favourite and all films are shown with English subtitles. If you think German cinema has a bad rep, this is where to break down the stereotypes. Shows take place at **CinemaxX** (Potsdamer Strasse 5, Tiergarten, 2592 2111) and the **Colosseum** (*see p210*).

RETROSPECTIVE

Perhaps the festival's surest bet for sheer movie-going pleasure. While the Retrospective often concentrates on the established mainstream, it's an opportunity to experience classics and rarities on the big screen. Themes have ranged from great directors such as Louis Buñuel, Fritz Lang and William Wyler, to subjects like 1950s Glamour Girls, Production Design, Hollywood Mavericks and even Nazi entertainment films. The main programme often features an *hommage*, a sidebar series celebrating the work of significant film people such as Stanley Kubrick, Arthur Penn or Jeanne Moreau. Programmes are accompanied by an exhibition and daily seminars (often in English) at the nearby **Filmmuseum Berlin** (*see p114*). Films show at **CinemaxX** (Potsdamer Strasse 5, Tiergarten, 2592 2111), **CineStar** (*see p209*) and **Zeughaus Kino** (*see p210*).

TALENT CAMPUS

A platform that offers 350 young filmmakers from all over the world a chance to come together, show and create new work, and learn from world-class professionals. Guest speakers and participants have included Anthony Minghella (*The English Patient, Cold Mountain*), Ken Adam (designer of James Bond films) and Stephen Frears (*The Queen*), and it's usual to find attending guests or jury members making a surprise visit. Selected lectures and masterclasses are open to the public. Tickets available at the usual outlets. Campus HQ is at the **Theater Hebel Am Ufer** (HAU1; *see p256*) with additional classes and events at nearby HAU2 and HAU3, all within walking distance of Potsdamer Platz.

TICKETS

Tickets can be bought up to three days in advance (four days for Competition repeats) at the main ticket office in the **Arkaden am Potsdamer Platz** (Alte Potsdamer Strasse, Tiergarten, 259 2000), as well as several locations around the city. Tickets are also available for online booking. On the day of

performance they must be bought at the theatre box office and last-minute tickets are often available. Queues for advance tickets can be long and online tickets can go fast, so plan ahead. Films in the Competition and Panorama are described in a catalogue which you can pick up for a nominal price at the Arkaden. The Forum has its own programme booklet, available free at every Forum theatre. Daily screening listings and film reviews can be found in industry dailies put out by *Variety*, *Hollywood Reporter* and *Screen International*, available free at most of the surrounding hotels.

Films are usually shown three times. Tickets go on sale three days prior to opening. Ticket prices usually range from €8-€20. Berlinale Palast is cheaper during the day and all films showing on the last day – Berlinale Kinotag – play at reduced prices. From January, check for updates and programme information on the website at www.berlinale.de.

CinemaxX.

Arts & Entertainment

English-language programming is on the up at **Babylon-Mitte**.

those LCD screens on the U-Bahn in the first week of February. They claim to have Berlin's largest attendance – a (captive) audience of over 1.5 million passengers.

In the spring it's **Britspotting**, the British Independent Film Festival (www.brits potting.de), an annual compilation of the freshest new (and occasionally mainstream) cinema from the UK and Ireland. Organised by the British Council, it appears in April/May.

Two festivals spotlight gay and lesbian films. The more elaborate of the two is **Verzaubert: The International Queer Film Festival** (www.verzaubertfilmfest.com), which takes place in April at Kino International (*see p210*). It offers a high-profile survey of gay and lesbian cinema from around the world.

The **Berlin Lesbian Film Festival** (www.lesbenfilmfestival.de) takes place every October at the Arsenal with an international selection of films. Many events are for women only. Also check out the year-round MonGay series at Kino International for weekly Queer Cinema premieres and specials.

Transmediale (www.transmediale.de) is an international five-day programme of digital presentations, installations and performances that currently finds a home at the Haus der Kulturen der Welt and leaves a month-long exhibition in its wake. There are also events and parties at various Berlin clubs.

INFORMATION

Check listings in *tip* and *Zitty*, as well as *(030)*, available free in many bars. An alphabetical overview of the cinemas can be found online at www.berlinien.de/kino/kinoprogramm.html. Watch for the notation OV or OF ('original version' or 'Originalfassung'), OmU ('original with subtitles') or OmE ('original with English subtitles'). But watch out, OmU could just as easily be a French or Chinese movie with German titles. The cinemas listed here are those most likely to be showing films in English. Various combinations of Monday, Tuesday and Wednesday are known as Kinotag, offering reduced admission, and some cinemas offer deals on pre-paid ticket bookings.

Cinemas

Arsenal

Potsdamer Strasse 2, Tiergarten (2695 5100/ www.fdk-berlin.de). U2, S1, S2, S25, S26 Potsdamer Platz. **Tickets** €6; €4 reductions. **No credit cards.** **Map** p322/p316 E4.

Berlin's own cinematheque continues to offer up brazenly eclectic programming, ranging from classic Hollywood to contemporary Middle Eastern cinema, from Russian art films to Italian horror movies, from Third World documentaries to silent films with live accompaniment. Also check out its perpetually cycling series, The History of Film in 365 Films. The Arsenal shows plenty of English-language films and some foreign films with English subtitles. The Arsenal's two state-of-the-art screening rooms in the Sony Center make it a welcome corrective to the great Hollywood beasts of its multiplex neighbours. And together with them, it is one of the core venues for the Berlin International Film Festival (*see p206* **Berlin International Film Festival**).

Babylon Kreuzberg (A&B)

Dresdener Strasse 126, Kreuzberg, 10999 (6160 9693). U1, U8 Kottbusser Tor. **Tickets** *€4.50-€7.* **No credit cards. Map** p323 G4.

Another Berlin perennial, this twin-screen theatre runs a varied programme featuring indie crossover and UK films. Formerly a neighbourhood Turkish cinema, its programme is now almost all English-language and this place offers a homey respite from the multiplex experience.

Babylon-Mitte

Rosa-Luxemburg-Strasse 30, Mitte (242 5076/ www.babylonberlin.de). U2, U5, U8, S3, S5, S7, S75 Alexanderplatz or U2 Rosa-Luxemburg-Platz. **Tickets** *€4.50-€6.50.* **No credit cards. Map** p319/p316 G3.

Housed in a restored landmark building by Hans Poelzig, the former Filmkunsthaus Babylon recently reinvented itself with a much more active programming policy. While it nominally focuses on new German independent cinema, English-language fare is on the up, particularly in its regular Schräge Filme (Weird Films) programme, and its foreign film series tend to have English subtitles. Tuesdays are silent film nights, with live musical accompaniment.

Central

Rosenthaler Strasse 39, Mitte (2859 9973/www.kino-central.de/). U8 Weinmeisterstrasse or S3, S5, S7, S9, S75 Hackescher Markt. **Tickets** *€5.50-€6.50.* **No credit cards. Map** p318/p316 F3.

Still hanging in with a programming attitude that's uniquely its own, this place is worth a look for its various series spotlighting pop/trash culture and all forms of exploitation film. In summer there's an outdoor cinema in the back courtyard.

CineStar Sony Center

Potsdamer Strasse 4, Tiergarten (2606 6400/ www.cinestar.de). U2, S1, S2, S25, S26, Potsdamer Platz. **Tickets** *€4-€7.70; €4.50 reductions.* **No credit cards. Map** p322/p316 E4.

Eight screens showing films exclusively in their original language, mostly English. Despite a few random sparks of creativity, it is basically mainstream fare and all major releases tend to show up here. Counteract the high prices by buying the 5-Star ticket – five films for €30. Also a main venue for the Berlin International Film Festival.

Eiszeit

Zeughofstrasse 20, Kreuzberg (611 6016/www. eiszeit-kino.de/). U1, U15 Görlitzer Bahnhof. **Tickets** *€5-€7; €6.50 reductions.* **No credit cards. Map** p323 H4.

Offering a wide range of alternative cinema – with a recent accent on pop music films – and a goodly amount of English-language programming. It also hosts readings, performances and live music, and is home to a number of small film festivals.

Freiluftkino Kreuzberg

Mariannenplatz 2, courtyard of Haus Bethanien, Kreuzberg (www.eyz-kino.de). U1, U8 Kottbusser Tor or S3, S5, S9, S75 Ostbahnhof. **Tickets** *€5.50.* **No credit cards. Map** p323 G4.

Original English films have made a comeback at this big-screen Dolby Stereo outdoor summer cinema under the trees. Open from June to August, it offers a mix of past cinema hits, as well as some cult films and independent movies. Bring a pillow. And maybe your mack.

FSK

Segitzdamm 2, Kreuzberg (614 2464/www.fsk-kino.de). U1, U8 Kottbusser Tor or U8 Moritzplatz. **Tickets** *€4.50-€6.* **No credit cards. Map** p323 G4.

Named after the state film rating board, this two-screen cinema is deep in the heart of Turkish Kreuzberg. It shows a lot of foreign films, mostly with German subtitles, but occasionally has American or British indie films and documentaries.

Hackesche Höfe Filmtheater

Rosenthaler Strasse 40-41, Mitte (tickets from 2.30pm. 283 4603/www.hackesche-hoefe.org). U8 Weinmeisterstrasse or S3, S5, S9, S75 Hackescher Markt. **Tickets** *€5-€7.50.* **No credit cards. Map** p318/p316 F3.

Being a four-storey walk up hasn't stopped this place from becoming one of the area's most well-attended cinemas. It shows mostly foreign films, with feature-length documentaries and occasional indie features in English.

High End 54 im Kunsthaus Tacheles

Oranienburger Strasse 54-6, Mitte (283 1498). U6 Oranienburger Tor or S1, S2, S25, S26 Oranienburger Strasse. **Tickets** *€4.50-€6.* **No credit cards. Map** p318/p316 F3.

Once the screening room for the GDR State Film Archive, this mini two-screen cinema is part of the multi-purpose Tacheles chain. The programming offers an unpredictable mishmash of independent and off-Hollywood films, as well as some interesting foreign movies. Films in original English or with English subtitles seem to show as often as not.

Moviemento

Kottbusser Damm 22, Kreuzberg (692 4785/ www.moviemento.de). U7, U8 Hermannplatz, U8 Schönleinestrasse. **Tickets** *€4.50-€6.50.* **No credit cards. Map** p323 G5.

This cosy upstairs cinema in Kreuzberg is one of the last bastions of Berlin's original alternative cinema scene. The new management is putting some fresh energy into the programming, and films in English seem to be on the rise.

Odeon

*Hauptstrasse 116, Schöneberg (7870 4019/http://
www.yorck.de/yck/yorck_ie/yorck_kinos/odeon.php).
U4, S45, S46 Innsbrucker Platz, S1, S4 Schöneberg.*
Tickets €5-€7.50; €5 reductions. **No credit cards.**
Map p321 D6.
The Odeon is a last hold-out of the big, old, single-
screen neighbourhood cinema and should be supported just for that. Deep in the heart of Schöneberg,
it's exclusively English-language, providing a reasonably intelligent, though increasingly mainstream, selection of Hollywood and UK fare.

Xenon

*Kolonnenstrasse 5/6, Schöneberg (7800 1530/
www.xenon-kino.de). U7 Kleistpark.* **Tickets** €4-€6;
€3 reductions. **No credit cards. Map** p322 E6.

Only in Berlin would a dedicated gay cinema simultaneously be a multiple award-winner for children's
programming. Those who have come of age can find
gay and lesbian programming, largely but not exclusively from the US and UK.

Zeughaus Kino

*Unter den Linden 2, Mitte (203 0421/tickets 2030
4670/www.dhm.de/kino). U8 Weinmeister Strasse,
S3, S5, S7, S9, S75 Hackescher Markt.* **Tickets** €5.
No credit cards. Map p318/p316 F3.
The Zeughaus Kino, which is at the Deutsches
Historisches Museum, has a variety of interesting
series and often hosts travelling retrospective
shows. It makes a concerted effort to get the original versions of movies and foreign films sometimes
appear with English subtitles.

The show must go on

The first cinema opened in Berlin in 1895
and the city was soon full of movie palaces
such as the Marmorhaus, with its huge white
marble façade; the Lichtburg, which looked
like a futuristic light sculpture; and the
grandest, the Ufa Palast Am Zoo. The latter
had an ever-changing façade, designed to
reflect whatever premiere it was hosting –
sweeping searchlights for Fritz Lang's *Spione*,
illuminated Nazi banners for Leni Riefenstahl's
Olympia; or a spaceship flying across the
starlit exterior for Lang's *Frau Im Mond*.

While few of those survive, part of the joy
of the Berlin Film Festival used to be running
around from one fabulous landmark cinema
to another. Now the festival is focused on
Potsdamer Platz, we forget that some of
those venues remain very much alive.

The **Filmpalast** (Kurfürstendamm 255,
Charlottenburg, 883 8551, www.filmpalast-
berlin.de) dates from 1948 when a café was
converted into a small cinema called the KiKi
(Kino im Kindl) and was later redesigned and
enlarged to become one of West Berlin's
classiest *kinos*. It's still a grand example
of 1950s movie-going luxury with an
illuminated glass ceiling, big comfortable
seats, and a gong to announce the show.

Ufa Palast Am Zoo did not survive the
bombing but its replacement, the **Zoo Palast**
(Hardenbergstrasse 29a, Charlottenburg,
2541 4777), was built to continue the
tradition. Opened as a duplex theatre in
1957, it immediately became the main
venue for the Berlinale. Its main auditorium
seats 1,070 and is still the largest in
Berlin, the great oval ceiling sprinkled
with tiny lights like a starry sky.

The **Delphi** (Kantstrasse 12a,
Charlottenburg, 312 1026) was originally a
popular 1920s dance palace. Bombed out
during the war, it was rebuilt as the Delphi
Filmpalast and became a major Cinemascope
and 70mm venue where films such as *Ben
Hur* and *My Fair Lady* would run for up to a
year. It has a traditional atmosphere and
the city's last working balcony.

In the east, the **Colosseum** (Schönhauser
Allee 123, Prenzlauer Berg, 4401 8180),
built in 1924 from a stable for the horses
that pulled the first trams, was restored by
the Soviets to become the finest cinema in
East Berlin. Although it was turned into a
multiplex in the late 1990s, the original
auditorium is still in use, restored to 1950s
splendour. In the lobby you can see the
original brick walls of the stables, complete
with the rings used to tie up the horses.

The monumental post-Stalinist architecture
of **Kino International** (Karl-Marx-Allee 33,
Mitte, 2475 6011) belies a modest 500-seat
auditorium, but the real reason to go is for
the lobby with its crystal chandeliers and
upholstered seating. A first-class example of
1960s DDR chic, it overtook the Colosseum
as the premier cinema, which in turn made
it the scene of Party functions and socialist
shindigs. Still a top-class venue, it's also the
home of the gay/lesbian Club International.

But the most historic cinema in Berlin
is neither a movie palace nor a landmark.
It's the **Moviemento** (*see p209*), a small
independent cinema in Kreuzberg which
celebrated its 100th birthday in 2007,
making it the oldest continuously running
cinema in Berlin.

Galleries

Berlin's flourishing art scene has finally made the big time, at least in terms of global visibility.

At the opening of 2007's annual **Berlin Art Forum** (www.art-forum-berlin.de) art fair, eminent gallerist Gerd Harry 'Judy' Lybke of **Eigen + Art** proclaimed, 'We are international now.' Indeed. Since early 2006, the number of commercial galleries in the city has boomed from roughly 300 to around 400. And the presence of satellites of established galleries from major art hubs such as New York and London (*see p214* **Global satellites**) has not only added cachet but also attracted a much-needed collector base to the city.

Berlin's increasing art-market savvy has resulted in the annual April 'gallery weekend' shifting from a local art walk into a high-end, increasingly high-heeled parade of foreign buyers strolling through the 30-odd participating galleries. Every autumn, along with Art Forum, satellite fairs such as **Preview** and **Berliner Liste** offer culture vultures a chance to view and purchase art at every price and career level. And there's a new 'minifair' – 50 top local galleries getting together for **Art Berlin Contemporary** – which kicked off in early September 2008. This is all good news in what is still considered a 'city of producers': because of available space and still relatively low rents, the capital remains a place where artists live and work.

The migration isn't just from outside: the art world continues its diaspora within Berlin too. The once-hot western district of Charlottenburg has long quieted into a showplace for established dealers to display and deal pre-1990s art. And while Mitte still holds the city's cards for hot-from-the-studio work, the attraction of the historical gallery strip of Auguststrasse and the surrounding Scheunenviertel has diffused and defused in recent years. Brunnenstrasse is the newest hotbed for emerging art, with a good dozen galleries on its first block alone specialising in it. These include New York imports **Goff + Rosenthal** and **Curators Without Borders**, and **Galerie Birgit Ostermeier** and **Klemm's**, both of which morphed into commercial galleries from artist-run spaces in 2007. And the funky **Artnews Projects** invites foreign galleries to put up shows, offering a splash of outside influence on a rotating basis. Anyone interested in seeing work from the youngest of the city's emerging artists is well advised to take a concentrated stroll starting at Rosenthaler Platz and meandering uphill. And if you catch an evening in which the galleries are co-ordinating their openings, it all turns into a street party.

On the more established end of the scale, the area near Checkpoint Charlie is also expanding. Just a skip away from the five-year-old blue-chip hub on Zimmerstrasse is an even bluer-chip hub on Kochstrasse, where excellent Cologne gallery **Jablonka** as well as **Julius Werner**, **Klara Wallner** and others have set up shop. A brand-new art cluster has also popped up on the Mitte/Kreuzberg border in what was once a department store at Lindenstrasse 34-35. It's now home to Swedish dealer **Claes Nordenhake**'s gallery, along with several others. What will happen in the shadows of the Hauptbahnhof remains to be seen, but an outpost of London and Zurich's **Haunch of Venison** opened in a huge industrial space here, and, in May 2008, six galleries moved into the Hallen am Wasser behind the Hamburger Bahnhof.

And representing the apex of how far Berlin's art world has come is a building that has settled into the last available real estate on the historic Museumsinsel: art collector **Heiner Bastian**'s supersleek commission from British architect David Chipperfield now frames a top-floor space for his own collections as well as a two-storey space for **Contemporary Fine Arts**.

LISTINGS AND INFORMATION

Artery (www.artery-berlin.de) is the most complete art guide for Berlin and environs. It's published every two months and sold at galleries, bookstores and some newsstands. *Berliner Galerien* serves all of Berlin but is more selective, and *Index* lists only galleries in Mitte. Both are free and available at most galleries and museums. *Zitty* and *tip*, the two Berlin listings fortnightlies, cover most current showings throughout the city. Nearly all galleries have English-language websites; if you read German, you should check out **www.art-in-berlin.de** or the Berlin section of **www.artnews.org** for current 'what's on' information.

Kunst-Werke. *See p216.*

Mitte

Alexander Ochs

Sophienstrasse 21 (2839 1387/www.alexanderochs-galleries.de). U8 Weinmeisterstrasse or S5, S7, S9, S75 Hackescher Markt. **Open** 10am-6pm Tue-Fri; 11am-6pm Sat. **No credit cards.** **Map** p319/p326 N5.

Begun in 1997 by Ochs and his partner Janna Prüss as part of a European cultural exchange with China, this gallery, which has a satellite in Beijing, features important young Chinese artists such as Fang Lijun, Yoo Junghyun and Wang Yin.

Arndt + Partner

Zimmerstrasse 90-91 (280 8123/www.arndt-partner.com). U6 Kochstrasse. **Open** 11am-6pm Tue-Sat. **Credit** MC, V. **Map** p322/p327 M8.

One of the city's earliest western German dealers in the post-Wall East, Matthias Arndt runs a tightly professional gallery that shows top international examples of experimental yet somehow accessible work over two sprawling floors. Among his line-up are French star Sophie Calle as well as Thomas Hirschhorn, white-hot Josephine Meckseper and Sue de Beer.

Artnews Projects

Brunnenstrasse 190 (2790 7810/www.artnews.org/projects). U8 Rosenthaler Platz. **Open** noon-6pm Tue-Sat. **No credit cards.** **Map** p319/p326 N4.

Artnews Projects' Vlado Velkov invites gallerists from outside the country to mount single shows in its large street-side space. Brooklyn's Pierogi, Amsterdam's Upstream Gallery and Manhattan's John Connelly have all hosted very well-attended exhibitions here.

BodhiBerlin

Invalidenstrasse 50-51 (3988 7200/www.bodhiart.com). S5, S7, S9, S65 Hauptbahnhof. **Open** 11am-6pm Tue-Sat. **No credit cards.** **Map** p318 L5.

Perhaps the most unusual of the six galleries that moved into former warehouse spaces behind Hamburger Bahnhof in May 2008 is this Indian gallery's first European outpost. On view are primarily artists from India who are making international waves, such as Shilpa Gupta.

BüroFriedrich

Holzmarktstrasse 15-18, S-Bahn arches 53/54 (2016 5115/www.buerofriedrich.org). U8, S5, S7, S9, S75 Jannowitzbrücke. **Open** varies. **No credit cards.** **Map** p323 P7.

Dutch expat Waling Boers began this non-profit venue as a place to house internationally collaborative projects with an interesting cultural studies bent. Opening hours are irregular, so call ahead.

Carlier/Gebauer

Markgrafenstrasse 67 (2400 8630/www.carlier gebauer.com). U6 Kochstrasse. **Open** 8am-5pm

such as Polish artist Agnieszka Kurant's The Unlimited Truth Company show, which featured a mock-up of the *New York Times* from 2020.

Contemporary Fine Arts
Am Kupfergraben 10 (288 7870/www.cfa-berlin. com). U6, S1, S2, S5, S7, S9 S75 Friedrichsstrasse. **Open** 10am-6pm Tue-Fri; 11am-4pm Sat. **No credit cards. Map** p319/p327 N6.
One of the highest-shelf galleries in Berlin recently moved to digs across from famous Museum Island in collector Heiner Bastian's David Chipperfield-designed building. The museum-like space is a slicker-than-slick backdrop for major stars such as Georg Baselitz, YBA luminaries like Cecily Brown, Chris Ofili and Angus Fairhurst, and international enfants terribles Dash Snow and Jonathan Meese.

Curators Without Borders
Brunnenstrasse 5 (4050 0548/www.curators withoutborders.com). U8 Rosenthaler Platz. **Open** 11am-6pm Tue-Sat. **No credit cards. Map** p319/p326 N4.
Manhattan import Sarah Belden opened this multi-roomed space in 2006; since then, it's been a mix of guest-curated shows and high-end commercial activity showcasing young artists such as Jack Warren from New York as well as Via Lewandowski, Christina Dmitriadis and Andreas Templin from Berlin. Rumour has it Belden's moving to Kreuzberg in autumn 2008: check the website for details.

DAADGalerie
Zimmerstrasse 90-91 (261 3640/www.daad-berlin.de). U6 Kochstrasse. **Open** 11am-6pm Mon-Sat. **No credit cards. Map** p322/p327 M8.
A shopfront gallery designed to feature works resulting from the 40-year-old Berlin artists-in-residence programme, which continues to invite important and aspiring artists to Berlin. Rachel Whiteread and Damien Hirst count among the alumni.

Duve Projects
Invalidenstrasse 90 (7790 2302/www.duveberlin. com). U6 Zinnowitzer Strasse, S1, S2 Nordbahnhof. **Open** noon-6pm Tue-Sat. **No credit cards. Map** p318 L5.
The mission of this space, founded by Alexander Duve in September 2007, is to represent artists who've never been repped by a gallery before. Young talents Martin G Schmid and Ali Kepenek produce works that run across all media; the gallerists also host concerts and readings.

Esther Schipper
Linienstrasse 85 (2839 0139/www.estherschipper. com). U8 Rosenthaler Platz. **Open** 11am-6pm Tue-Sat. **No credit cards. Map** p318/p326 N5.
Since beginning her gallery endeavours in the early 1990s with partner Michael Krome, Esther Schipper has always had a penchant for heady projects and cutting-edge greats, and the tradition continues on with shows featuring works by stars Liam Gillick and Carsten Höller, among others.

Mon-Thur; 8am-3pm Fri. **No credit cards. Map** p323/p327 N8.
Now in a brand-new, sprawling location, Ulrich Gebauer and co-director Marie Blanche Carlier present a varied programme of larger-scale installations and work in different media by international and politically minded contemporary artists such as Tracey Emin, Luc Tuymans, Thomas Schütte and Aernout Mik.

C/O Berlin
Corner of Oranienburger Strasse & Tucholsky Strasse (2809 1925/www.co-berlin.com). U6 Oranienburger Tor or S1, S2 Oranienburger Strasse. **Open** 11am-8pm daily. **Admission** €7; €5 reductions. **No credit cards. Map** p318/p326 M5.
Co-founded by photographer Stephan Erfurt, this organisation has exhibited internationally known photographers such as Alfred Eisenstaedt, André Rival, James Nachtwey and Anton Corbijn. In late 2007, it moved into the Postfuhramt, a vast 1870s building that was once a transfer station for the German post system.

COMA
Corner of Leipziger Strasse & Charlottenstrasse (2064 8886/www.coma-berlin.com). U6 Kochstrasse. **Open** 11am-6pm Tue-Sat. **No credit cards. Map** p322/p327 M7.
This new space (whose name is an acronym for 'Centre for Opinions in Music and Art') is run by equally new gallerists and focuses on edgy work,

Feinkost

*Bernauer Strasse 71-72 (2701 5720/www.
galeriefeinkost.com). U8 Bernauer Strasse.*
Open 11am-7pm Wed-Sun. **No credit cards.**
Map p319/p328 N3.
Just six months into his tenure in Berlin, American
expat Aaron Moulton opened this space in what
was once a *Feinkost* (speciality food) store in late
2007. While the focus is on Eastern European art,
another early group show questioned the art world
itself. Clever.

Galerie Birgit Ostermeier

*3rd courtyard, Brunnenstrasse 10 (2757 2140/
www.birgitostermeier.com). U8 Rosenthaler Platz.*
Open 11am-6pm Tue-Sat. **No credit cards.**
Map p319/p326 N4.
Birgit Ostermeier's small, elegant space features a
healthy number of young sculptors from the
Dresden Art Academy, such as André Tempel,
but it has also recently expanded its global scope
to include international artists such as Indonesian-
born Yudi Noor.

Galerie Eigen + Art

*Auguststrasse 26 (280 6605/www.eigen-art.com).
S1, S2 Oranienburger Strasse.* **Open** 11am-6pm
Tue-Sat. **No credit cards.** Map p319/p327 N5.
This small-yet-stalwart anchor gallery of the old
Auguststrasse art strip is where man-about-
town Gerd Harry 'Judy' Lybke continues his long-
standing relationships with New Leipzig School
star painters Neo Rauch and Matthias Weischer. He
also shows thought-provoking works by Christine
Hill, Birgit Brenner and Yehudit Sasportas. A far
cry from Lybke's Leipzig living room gallery in the
early 1980s.

Galerie Max Hetzler

*Zimmerstrasse 90-91 (229 2437/www.maxhetzler.
com). U6 Kochstrasse.* **Open** 11am-6pm Tue-Sat.
No credit cards. Map p322/p327 M8.
With two differently dramatic and versatile spaces,
this wonderful gallery (in business long before its
Berlin days began in 1994) represents an amazing
roster of talent including Christopher Wool, Kara
Walker and Sarah Morris.

Global satellites

At last, Berlin's art world is, well, closer to a
world than it has been in years past. Never
before have so many gallerists from abroad
established new outlets here – or have so
many galleries from other countries set up
a Berlin outpost of their original franchises.

While **Claes Nordenhake**'s eponymous
gallery (*see p218*) opened on Zimmerstrasse
as a second venue (after his original gallery
in Stockholm) in 2000, it has taken several
years for the rest of the world to follow suit.
In late 2006, **Goff + Rosenthal** (*see p215*)
from New York set up its European outpost
on the now-trendy Brunnenstrasse, just
across from the spacious digs used by
Zurich's **Römerapotheke** (Brunnenstrasse
188-190, 2758 2460, www.roemer
apotheke.ch) and nearly adjacent to New
Yorker newcomer Sarah Belden's **Curators
Without Borders** (*see p213*); all three
opened on the same day.

Fast forward a year and lo, there's the
Haunch of Venison (*see p215*), a London
gallery with another outpost in Zurich, in
the area behind the new Hauptbahnhof;
Nice + Fit (Brunnenstrasse 13, 4404
5976, www.niceandfitgallery.com) run by
the Greek-born New York import Helena
Papadoupoulos; and 30-year-old American
expat Aaron Moulton's **Feinkost** (*see p214*)
across the street from former no-man's
land. 'I could never be doing this back

home (Moulton used to work at Gagosian
Gallery in New York),' he says of his
converted space, which will focus largely
on under-exposed Eastern European artists
in a mix of commerce and curatorial
intellectualism. 'Things are simply too
commercial and rents far too expensive.'

The influx shows no sign of slowing. In
autumn 2007, Nordenhake spearheaded the
renovation of a building on Lindenstrasse
for himself and a bevy of other galleries
arriving from places like Slovenia and Poland.
And newest in the mix are the Hallen am
Wasser ('halls on the water'), a row of former
warehouses on an industrial area behind the
Hamburger Bahnhof that opened as galleries
in May 2008. Here's where **BodhiBerlin** (*see
p212*), the first European subsidiary of an
Indian art dealership with other galleries in
New York and Singapore, has put down its
roots, along with one Danish gallery and
four German ones.

'Berlin is about space,' explains Bodhi's
artistic director Shaheen Merali. 'If, in Berlin,
art handlers can drive a truck right up to
the door and install a huge installation or
sculpture by an ambitious artist, why would
anyone set up in a city so packed that this
is impossible, like Paris?' Now that a few
collectors are seeing that Berlin's not such
a bad place to buy art, too, the answer's
pretty clear.

Space to admire at long-standing **Galerie Max Hetzler**.

Galerie Thomas Schulte

Charlottenstrasse 24 (2060 8990/www.galerie thomasschulte.de). U6 Stadtmitte. **Open** noon-6pm Tue-Sat. **No credit cards. Map** p322/p327 M7.
New Yorker Thomas Schulte and Swiss-born Eric Franck opened their doors in 1991, hoping to breathe new life into the art market. They recently moved their upmarket, high-quality offerings to a glassed-in storefront space on the edge of Mitte, where their exhibitions of Gordon Matta-Clark, Katharina Sieverding and others can glitter even more brightly.

Goff + Rosenthal

Brunnenstrasse 3 (4373 5083/www.goffand rosenthal.com). U8 Rosenthaler Platz. **Open** 11am-6pm Tue-Sat. **No credit cards. Map** p319/p326 N4.
The first satellite of a bona fide New York gallery to set up shop in Berlin, G + R shows mostly two-dimensional work by emerging and mid-career artists, notably Melanie Manchot, Simon English and Isca Greenfield-Sanders.

Haunch of Venison

Heidestrasse 46 (3974 3963/www.haunchofvenison. com). S5, S7, S9, S65 Hauptbahnhof. **Open** 11am-6pm Tue-Sat. **No credit cards. Map** p318 K4.
This gargantuan hall in the shadows of the Hauptbahnhof is the third international gallery opened by the London-based outfit. Haunch of Venison exhibits just half a dozen not-necessarily commercial shows each year, often featuring enormous installations by mostly up-and-coming international artists.

Jablonka Galerie

Kochstrasse 60 (2123 6890/www.jablonkagalerie. com). U6 Kochstrasse. **Open** 11am-6pm Tue-Sat. **No credit cards. Map** p322/p327 M8.
Opening with a bang in autumn 2006, this blue-chip satellite of a seminal Cologne gallery shows established international stars like Ron Arad, Alex Katz, Francesco Clemente, David LaChapelle, Richard Prince and Damian Loeb. The jet set presence at openings here makes people feel like they've been teleported to New York or London.

Julius Werner

Kochstrasse 60 (2529 2796/www.juliuswernerberlin. com). U6 Kochstrasse. **Open** 10am-6.30pm Tue-Fri; 11am-6pm Sat. **No credit cards. Map** p322/p327 M8.
Picking up the torch from his father, the legendary gallerist Michael Werner, Julius Werner exhibits top-shelf post-war German art by the likes of Markus Lüpertz in a sprawling space.

Klara Wallner

Courtyard, 2nd floor, Kochstrasse 60 (322 3670/ www.klarawallner.de). U6 Kochstrasse. **Open** 11am-6pm Tue-Sat. **No credit cards. Map** p322/p327 M8.
Klara Wallner pioneered the Brunnenstrasse mini art boom with a small space in 2004, but the energetic former curator quickly moved on to bigger digs on now-bustling Kochstrasse. Her programme features very young but very hot artists such as US expat Hannah Dougherty and Andreas Golder, who's Russian.

Akira Ikeda Gallery Berlin.

Klemm's

Brunnenstrasse 7 (4050 4953/www.klemms-berlin.com). U8 Rosenthaler Platz. **Open** 11am-6pm Tue-Sat. **No credit cards.** **Map** p319/p326 N4.

The recently renamed and revamped space (it was previously an artist-run co-op called Amerika) features Sebastian Klemm's line-up of young photographers and installation artists such as Peggy Buth and Falk Haberkorn, most of whom were trained in East German art academies. Openings here turn into some of the best parties in town.

Klosterfelde

Zimmerstrasse 90-91 (283 5305/www.klosterfelde. de). U6 Kochstrasse. **Open** 11am-6pm Tue-Sat. **No credit cards. Map** p322/p327 M8.

Young, yet from a long line of art world players, gallerist Martin Klosterfelde shows a wide variety of sometimes offbeat art in his courtyard space. Artists range from the überhip Scandinavian duo Elmgreen & Dragset to German star Christian Jankowski. The Linienstrasse location often exhibits editions and works on paper.

Other locations Linienstrasse 160, Mitte (9700 5099).

Kunst-Werke

Auguststrasse 69 (243 4590/www.kw-berlin.de). U6 Oranienburger Tor or S1, S2 Oranienburger Strasse. **Open** noon-6pm Tue-Sun. **No credit cards. Map** p319/p326 N5.

Housed in a former margarine factory and sporting a social event-friendly courtyard designed by Dan Graham, KW has been a major non-profit showcase since the early 1990s. It co-hosts the Berlin Biennale and puts on culturally themed exhibits of contemporary artists – Fassbinder's Berlin Alexanderplatz, for instance. *Photo p212.*

Kunstraum Céline und Heiner Bastian

Am Kupfergraben 10 (2067 3840). U6, S1, S2, S5, S7, S9 S75 Friedrichsstrasse. **Open** 11am-5pm Tue-Fri; 11am-4pm Sat. **Admission** €3. **No credit cards. Map** p319/p327 N6.

Perched atop the sleek David Chipperfield building he built for himself and other art lovers, this brand-new showcase for local collector Heiner Bastian's private collection opened in November 2007 with a stunning show by Damien Hirst. Contemporary Fine Arts (*see p213*) is housed in the same building; the Kunstraum covers the third floor.

MagnusMüller

Weydingerstrasse 10-12 (3903 2040/www.magnus muller.com). U2 Rosa-Luxemburg-Platz. **Open** noon-6pm Tue-Sat. **No credit cards. Map** p319/p327 O5.

In an art deco building near the Volksbühne, Sönke Magnus Müller's corner space features sometimes difficult works by New Yorkers Ellen Harvey and Christoph Draeger and a range of European artists, as well as an increasing number of high-concept shows put together by Berlin's top curators.

Martin Mertens

Courtyard, Brunnenstrasse 185 (4404 3350/ www.martinmertens.com). U8 Rosenthaler Platz. **Open** noon-6pm Tue-Sat. **No credit cards.** **Map** p318/p326 N4.

Martin Mertens moved into this ultra-slick, airy and sociable back courtyard gallery in spring 2008. It's slightly difficult to find, but it's the best space in Brunnenstrasse and features high-concept work by a roster of international artists.

Mehdi Chouakri

Schlegelstrasse 26 (2839 1153/www.mehdi-chouakri.com). U6 Zinnowitzer Strasse. **Open** 11am-6pm Tue-Sat. **No credit cards.** **Map** p318/p326 M4.

Chouakri's sharp eye picks emerging artists and established names like Sylvie Fleury, John M Armleder, Gitte Schäfer and Monica Bonvicini and sets their work into sleek, spacious surroundings.

Neugerriemschneider

Linienstrasse 155 (2887 7277). U6 Oranienburger Tor or S1, S2 Oranienburger Strasse. **Open** 11am-6pm Tue-Sat. **No credit cards.** **Map** p318/p326 M5.

Founded by duo Tim Neuger and Burkhard Riemschneider, this elegant courtyard space showcases international art by blue-chip talent like the brilliant curry-cooking artist Rirkrit Tiravanija and weather man Olafur Eliasson.

Program

Invalidenstrasse 115 (3950 9318/www.program online.de). U6 Zinnowitzer Strasse, S1, S2 Nordbahnhof. **Open** 2-7pm Tue-Fri; 11am-8pm Sat. **No credit cards.** **Map** p318/p326 M4.

Since opening in September 2006, Program has established itself as a non-profit gallery that links art and architectural concepts in cutting-edge inter-disciplinary shows by mostly international artists. Canadian expat Carson Chan and partner Fotini Lazaridou-Hatzigoga also run a small residency pro-gramme, studio spaces and a reading room; the space occasionally hosts concerts too.

Sammlung Boros

Reinhardtstrasse 20 (no phone/www.sammlung-boros.de). U6 Oranienburger Tor. **Open** by appointment only. **No credit cards.** **Map** p318/p327 L5.

More like a museum than a gallery, this concrete World War II bunker has been transformed into 80 stunning spaces totalling over 3,000sq m and con-taining the formidable collection of advertising mogul Christian Boros. Works on view include con-temporary greats such as Olafur Eliasson and Sarah Lucas. Tours are on weekends by appointment only; book well in advance through the website.

Prenzlauer Berg

Aedes Pfefferberg

Christinenstrasse 18-19 (282 7015/www.aedes-arc.de). U2 Senefelderplatz. **Open** 11am-6.30pm Tue-Fri; 1-5pm Sat, Sun. **No credit cards.** Map p319/p326/p328 O4.

Founded in 1980 as Europe's first gallery for archi-tecture, Aedes has a history of showing 'starchitects' such as Zaha Hadid long before they became well known. Recent shows have included local Berlin architecture stars GRAFT. The Aedes Land branch focuses on landscape architecture.

Other locations Aedes Land, Savignyplatz, Else-Ury Bogen 600-601, Charlottenburg (282 7015).

Akira Ikeda Gallery Berlin

Pfefferberg, Schönhauser Allee 176 (4432 8510/ www.akiraikedagallery.com). U2 Senefelderplatz. **Open** 11am-6pm Tue-Sat. **No credit cards.** Map p319/p326 O4.

Akira Ikeda is hidden at the back of the Pfefferberg, a dilapidated 19th-century brewery turned cultural centre. This magnificent third branch of the gallery (other outposts are in Taura, Japan, and New York) specialises in work post-1945.

Kreuzberg

Galerie Berinson

Lindenstrasse 34 (2838 7990/www.berinson.de/ www.berinson.de). U6 Kochstrasse. **Open** 11am-6pm Tue-Sat. **No credit cards.** Map p323 N8.

Hendrik Berinson's gallery is best known for exhibits of fine vintage photography by such 20th-century masters as Weegee and Peter Hujar. Other photographers in his collection include Lee Miller, László Moholy-Nagy and Stanley Kubrick.

Galerie Volker Diehl

Lindenstrasse 35 (2248 7922/www.galerie volkerdiehl.com). U6 Kochstrasse. **Open** 11am-6pm Tue-Sat. **No credit cards.** Map p323/p327 N8.

One of the original organisers of the Berlin Art Forum, Diehl has long been a prominent member of the international art world, concentrating his efforts on young talent such as Janine Gordon and Rina Banerjee. He recently moved into new digs, keeping his old Zimmerstrasse space as a project room.

Other locations Diehl Projects, Zimmerstrasse 88-91, Mitte (2248 7922).

Johann König

Dessauerstrasse 6-7 (2610 3080/www.johannkoenig. de). U2 Gleisdreieck. **Open** 11am-6pm Tue-Sat. **No credit cards.** Map p322 L8.

König (half-brother of New York gallerist Leo and son of museum-man Kaspar, ie veritable German art-world royalty) presents a mixed bag of emerg-ing and mid-career artists and exhibitions in a wide range of media. The line-up includes artists such as Jeppe Hein and Jordan Wolfson, showing works designed to make viewers and collectors think hard.

Arts & Entertainment

Künstlerhaus Bethanien

Mariannenplatz 2 (616 9030/www.bethanien.de). U1, U8 Kottbusser Tor or U1 Görlitzer Bahnhof. **Open** 2-7pm Wed-Sun. **No credit cards. Map** p323 P8.
Housed in a former hospital complex, this Berlin institution began as an art squat in the 1970s and has since developed a major studio residency programme for foreign artists staying in Berlin. With open studios and three full galleries offering frequently 'different' shows, it remains a lively endeavour, despite the threat of budget cuts.

NGBK

Oranienstrasse 25 (616 5130/www.ngbk.de). U1, U8 Kottbusser Tor. **Open** noon-6.30pm daily. **No credit cards. Map** p323 P9.
Begun in the smoky haze of the late 1960s, the NGBK is still confrontational and energetic, continuing its group-based projects with a social conscience. It also runs a public project series on the platform of the U2 at Alexanderplatz. The gallery entrance is through the bookstore.

Nordenhake

Lindenstrasse 34-35 (206 1483/www.nordenhake. com). U6 Kochstrasse. **Open** 11am-6pm Tue-Sat. **No credit cards. Map** p323 N8.
Longtime Swedish gallerist Claes Nordenhake opened his first Berlin gallery on Zimmerstrasse in 2000. Now he has purchased an entire former department store and set up shop there, along with several other galleries. He's known for featuring new artists such as Walter Niedermayr and Esko Männikkö.

Peres Projects

Schlesische Strasse 26 (6162 6962/www.peres projects.com). U1 Schlesisches Tor. **Open** 11am-6pm Tue-Sat. **No credit cards. Map** p324 S9.
Some of the city's most provocative exhibitions are actually from Los Angeles, where Javier Peres's mothership is located (there's another satellite in Athens). In Berlin, Peres has pioneered the Schlesiches Tor area with often over-the-top, downright sexy shows by artists such as Terence Koh.

Tiergarten

Galerie Eva Poll

Lützowplatz 7 (261 7091/www.poll-berlin.de). U1, U2, U3, U4 Nollendorfplatz. **Open** 10am-1pm Mon; 11am-6.30pm Tue-Fri; 11am-3pm Sat. **No credit cards. Map** p322 J8.
Opened in 1968 with her collection of critical realists from the '60s, Eva Poll's beautiful gallery includes, among others, Sabina Grzimek, Peter Sorge and Peter Chevalier. Stiftung Eva Poll exhibits photography. **Other locations** Stiftung Eva Poll, Gipsstrasse 3, Mitte (2849 6250).

Haus am Lützowplatz

Lützowplatz 9 (261 3805/www.hausamluetzowplatz-berlin.de). U1, U2, U3, U4 Nollendorfplatz. **Open** 11am-6pm Tue-Sun. **No credit cards. Map** p322 J8.

Although exhibits were held in this building as early as 1949, the non-profit society that has occupied it since the early 1960s maintains a pledge to present works by both unknown Berlin artists and guests such as Dorothy Iannone, Mario Mertz and Emmett Williams.

Charlottenburg

Camera Work

Kantstrasse 149 (310 0773/www.camerawork.de). S5, S7, S9, S75 Savignyplatz. **Open** 11am-6pm Tue-Sat. **No credit cards. Map** p321/p328 F8.
Named for the magazine started by Alfred Stieglitz, this magnificent courtyard space offers prime viewing of some of the 20th century's most important photographic work, including Irving Penn, Leni Riefenstahl, Peter Beard and Man Ray.

Galerie Anselm Dreher

Pfalzburger Strasse 80 (883 5249/www.galerie-anselm-dreher.com). U1 Hohenzollernplatz. **Open** 2-6.30pm Tue-Fri; 11am-2pm Sat. **No credit cards. Map** p321 F9.
Since opening his gallery in 1967, Anselm Dreher continues the lonely task of championing hardcore minimalist and concrete works by newcomers and old masters such as Dennis Oppenheim, Joseph Kosuth and Carl Andre. He does it wonderfully.

Galerie Georg Nothelfer

Uhlandstrasee 184 (881 4405/www.galerie-nothelfer. de). U1 Uhlandstrasse. **Open** 11am-6.30pm Tue-Fri; 10am-2pm Sat. **Credit** V. **Map** p321/p328 F8.
Long-time doyen Nothelfer quietly and importantly pursues his love of Informel and Tachist work, best exemplified by artists such as Walter Stöhner, Henri Michaux and Jan Voss. **Other locations** Corneliusstrasse 3, Tiergarten (575 9806).

Galerie Springer & Winckler

Fasanenstrasse 13 (315 7220). U2, U9, S5, S7, S9, S75 Zoologischer Garten or U1, U9 Kurfürstendamm. **Open** 10am-6pm Tue-Fri; noon-3pm Sat. **No credit cards. Map** p321/p328 F9.
Originally the gallery of Rudolph Springer (one of post-war Berlin's seminal gallerists), this space is now run by his son and partner Gerald Winckler. The young pair show many of the now-huge artists their father knew well: Georg Baselitz, Sigmar Polke and Gerhard Richter.

Raab Galerie Berlin

Fasanenstrasse 27 (261 9217/www.raab-galerie. de). U1 Uhlandstrasse. **Open** 10am-7pm Mon-Fri; 10am-4pm Sat. **No credit cards. Map** p321/p328 F9.
Since her monumental first show of the Wild Bunch in 1978, Ingrid Raab has been a grand champion of young artists such as Paul Vergier and Christian Sauer as well as stalwarts like Lüpertz, Fetting and the wonderful Odd Nerdrum. Two gallery spaces later, her enthusiasm remains contagious.

Gay & Lesbian

If you're out, you're in: Berlin's queer scene is one of the best in the world.

Back in the 1920s, Berlin became the first city in the world to have what we might recognise as a large gay and lesbian community, frequented by such diverse characters as Marlene Dietrich, Ernst Röhm and Christopher Isherwood. Today, a high tolerance level coupled with a strong and open sense of gay pride means alternative lifestyles in Berlin are considered rather normal. It's even possible to live an exclusively gay or lesbian existence, right down to hiring a pink plumber, if that's what you want. Same-sex couples have the right to a civil registration of their union and though the attached rights don't go as far as some other European countries, more than 2,000 couples in Berlin, 75 per cent of them gay male pairs, have already signed up.

Appropriate, then, that Berlin also has an out gay city mayor, the charismatic Klaus Wowereit or 'Wowi', himself no stranger to the party scene and who, in 2001, before becoming a candidate to be the new mayor of Berlin, winded the tabloid press by openly declaring his homosexuality with a phrase that has entered the local vernacular: 'I am gay, and that's OK!' (*Ich bin schwul, und das ist auch gut so!*').

The capital has a long tradition of open-mindedness. As early as the 18th century, it had the reputation of being extremely tolerant towards people of other faiths and sexual orientation, being the capital of a kingdom whose king himself, Frederick the Great, was rumoured to love 'in the Greek fashion'. In 1897 the first institution in the world with an emancipatory homosexual agenda was founded in Berlin – the Wissenschaftlich-Humanitäres Komitee (Scientific-Humanitarian Committee). Its main aims were legal reform, scientific research into the 'Third Gender' and the publication of emancipatory literature.

After the license of the Weimer years, gays were persecuted by the Nazis and forced to wear a pink triangle in concentration camps. The victims are commemorated on a plaque outside Nollendorfplatz station.

In the late 1960s, Berlin resumed its role as one of the world's homosexual meccas. The gay and lesbian scenes today are big and bold, mostly concentrated in Schöneberg, Kreuzberg, Mitte and Prenzlauer Berg. Summer is the most exciting time of year, when all contingents come together and enjoy themselves. The **Lesbisch-Schwules Stadtfest** (*see p198*) on Nollendorfplatz in mid June is followed by the **Christopher Street Day Parade** (*see p198*), a flamboyant annual event where up to 500,000 gays and lesbians unite in memory of the Stonewall riots.

The scene includes much more than the venues listed here, especially in terms of cultural events: there are plays, drag performances or the Gay Teddy award for the best gay film at the **Berlin International Film Festival** (*see p206*). Queer films can be seen on Mondays at **Kino International** (Karl-Marx-Allee 33, Mitte, 2475 6011). Gay art and history is documented at the **Schwules Museum** (*see p103*), which also has an archive. The successful multi-sport club Vorspiel ('foreplay') celebrated its 20th anniversary in 2006. And of course the Berlin scene offers sex parties for every taste and perversion, in pub darkrooms and dance clubs. There is now also a dance night with darkroom for lesbians (*see p232*).

INFORMATION AND PUBLICATIONS

For gay and lesbian helplines, information and counselling services, *see p291*. *Blu* (www.blu.m) and *Siegessäule* (www.siegessaeule.de) are monthly listings freebies that can be picked up at most venues. Apart from a 'what's on' calendar, both list all gay and lesbian venues and pinpoint them on a map. You can also find pocket-sized Gay City Guides for the districts of Schöneberg and Prenzlauer Berg/Friedrichshain. Siegessäule also publishes *Kompass* (www.siegessaeule-kompass.de), a classified directory of everything gay or lesbian. Comprehensive information in English is available on www.gaymap.info/berlin/index.html. For light relief, English-language monthly *Exberliner* (www.ex-berliner.com) has a funny gay column by Maurice Von Ritz.

Mixed

In West Berlin, gays and lesbians trod separate paths for decades, but in the East things were different. Homosexuals of both genders shared bars and clubs, making common cause under the Communists, a tradition that hasn't

Café Melitta Sundström: a cosy café popular with students.

disappeared despite the emergence of male-only cruise bars in Prenzlauer Berg. That said, the western half of the city has changed. The late 1990s saw an increase in the number of mixed gay and lesbian venues, and lesbians made their voices felt in formerly gay-only organisations and political institutions. One-nighters now usually target both gays and lesbians. Below we list a selection of mixed cafés, bars and clubs.

Cafés & bars

Prenzlauer Berg

Café Amsterdam
Gleimstrasse 24 (448 0792). U2, S8, S41, S42, S85 Schönhauser Allee. **Open** 3pm-4am Mon-Sat; 9am-4am Sun. **Credit** AmEx, MC, V. **Map** p319 G1.
This nice café by day turns at night into a good bar to get wrecked in, with loud house and techno music. It has snacks and salads, a mostly youngish crowd and a central location. Popular.

Schall & Rauch
Gleimstrasse 23 (443 3970/www.schall-und-rauch-berlin.de). U2, S8, S41, S42, S85 Schönhauser Allee. **Open** 9am-3am daily. **No credit cards.** **Map** p319 G1.
Schall & Rauch has a relaxed and friendly atmosphere, serves a good selection of food and has a central location – an ideal place to spend the morning or afternoon, or kick off an evening in Prenzlauer Berg. Wireless internet access available.

Friedrichshain

HT
Kopernicusstrasse 23 (2900 4965). U5 Frankfurter Tor, U1, S3, S5, S9, S75 Warschauer Strasse. **Open** 6pm-2am daily. **No credit cards.** **Map** p324 S7.
A comfortable but quiet café and bar in a popular nightlife district. Good service, friendly staff.

Himmelreich
Simon-Dach-Strasse 36 (2936 9292). U5 Frankfurter Tor, U1, S3, S5, S9, S75 Warschauer Strasse. **Open** 5pm-3am Mon-Fri; 2pm-3am Sat, Sun. **No credit cards.** **Map** p324 S7.
Colourful and comfortable lounge café and bar with snacks. Tuesday is women-only night, although men in drag are accepted.

Kreuzberg

BarbieBar
Mehringdamm 77 (6956 8610/www.barbiebar.de). U6, U7 Mehringdamm. **Open** 2pm-late daily. **No credit cards.** **Map** p322 F5.
Tacky and camp, with lots of dolls and pictures of drag queens adorning the walls, the BarbieBar is also a stylish place, with comfortable easy chairs and quiet music, which makes it good for chatting. Small terrace in summer.

Café Melitta Sundström
Mehringdamm 61 (692 4414). U6, U7 Mehringdamm. **Open** noon-late daily. **No credit cards.** **Map** p322 F5.

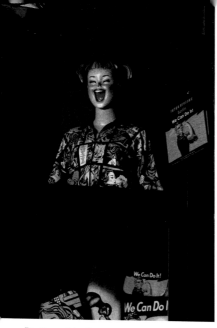

Daytimes, this place serves as a cosy café for students; in the evenings, it's full of gays too lazy to go to Schöneberg and lesbians who wouldn't go to Schöneberg anyway. At weekends, it's the entrance to SchwuZ (*see p225*) and is hectic and fun.

Drama
Mehringdamm 63 (6746 9562/www.dramabar.de). U6, U7 Mehringdamm. **Open** noon-late daily. **No credit cards. Map** p322 M10.
A schizophrenic but stylish café/bar on two floors: the pink palace at street level could only attract the unashamedly camp while rowdy lesbians roll around on leopard-skin cushions amid jungle colours upstairs. Small terrace in summer.

Möbel-Olfe
Reichenberger Strasse 177, corner of Dresdner Strasse (2327 4690/www.moebel-olfe.de). U1, U8 Kottbusser Tor. **Open** 6pm-late Tue-Sun. **No credit cards. Map** p323 G4.
It's an odd location for a gay bar, wedged among Turkish snack bars in a down-at-heel 1960s development at Kottbusser Tor and visible to the world through picture windows on two sides, but this place has been packed since the day it opened, mainly with gay and lesbian beer lovers thanks to a good range on offer. Unpretentious, crowded and fun, with regular DJs nights too.

Roses
Oranienstrasse 187 (615 6570). U1, U8 Kottbusser Tor. **Open** 10pm-5am daily. **No credit cards. Map** p323 G4.
Whatever state you're in (the more of a state, the better), you'll fit in just fine at this boisterous den of glitter. It draws customers from right across the sexual spectrum, who mix and mingle and indulge in excessive drinking amid the plush, kitsch decor. No place for uptights, always full, very Kreuzbergish.

Schöneberg

Neues Ufer
Hauptstrasse 157 (7895 7900). U7 Kleistpark. **Open** 11am-2am daily. **No credit cards. Map** p322 E5.
Established in the early 1970s, this is the city's oldest gay café. The former name Anderes Ufer ('The Other Side') was changed to Neues Ufer ('The New Side'), symbolising a new beginning. Relaxed daytime scene.

Clubs & one-nighters

Mitte

Fate Club
Hochstrasse 46 (0163 303 7372/0172 532 2022/www.fateclub.de). S1, S2, S25 Humboldthain. **Open** from 11pm 1st, 2nd & 3rd Fri of mth; midnight-7am then 7am-6pm Sat/Sun. **Admission** €5-€10. **No credit cards. Map** p318 L2.
Old-school and electro tunes make the Fate Club a worthy alternative to Berghain/Panorama Bar for those looking for something less hectic on a Saturday night. Offering a warmer, more local atmosphere with friendly bar staff, it attracts a mixed gay/lesbian/straight clientele of locals and tourists. The venue is something of a colourful bunker on two floors, with psychedelic lighting, a cage for go-go dancers (professional and impromptu) and a low-lit lounge for snoggers at the back of the dancefloor.

Friedrichshain

Berghain/Panorama Bar
Am Wriezener Bahnhof (no phone/www.berghain.de). U5 Weberwiese, S3, S5, S9, S75 Ostbahnhof. **Open** midnight-late Fri, Sat. **Admission** €10. **No credit cards.**
The hippest and hardest electronic music club in Berlin, if not Europe. The building is a Communist-era power station transformed into a concrete cathedral of techno on two floors, with the mixed Panorama Bar upstairs and Berghain below. Saturday night's Klubnacht sees Berghain awash with pumped-up, shirtless gay men sweating it out on the dancefloor – and in the darkroom at the back. Carrying on well into Sunday afternoon, in summer the garden turns into an outside chill-out area, bar and dancefloor. Once on Am Wriezener Bahnhof, just follow the stream of taxis to reach the door. Cameras are prohibited and taken at the door and returned later. But you won't need photos to remember it.

Haus B
Warschauer Platz 18 (296 0800/www.dashausb.de). U1, S3, S5, S9, S75 Warschauer Strasse.

Arts & Entertainment

Open 10pm-5am Wed; 10pm-7am Fri, Sat.
Admission €3.50-€6. **No credit cards.**
Map p323 H4.

Haus B is an East German relic, formerly known as Die Busche: loud, tacky, mixed and packed, this is one of East Berlin's oldest discos and is full of loutish lesbians, gay teens and their girlfriends. A must for kitsch addicts and mainstream pop/dance fans; definitely a no-go area for guys who like a masculine atmosphere.

Kreuzberg

SO36

Oranienstrasse 190 (6140 1306/www.so36.de).
U1, U8 Kottbusser Tor. **Open** times vary (see below). **Admission** *Parties* €3-€8. *Concerts* €8-€20. **No credit cards. Map** p323 P9.

A key venue for both gays and lesbians. Monday (Verified, from 11pm) is not completely gay, but the hard techno sounds draw a largely male following. Last Saturday in the month is Gay Oriental Night (Gayhane – House of Halay, from 10pm), with belly dancing, transvestites and Turkish hits. Women have a monthly party (Play! Girl; *see p232*), bringing together every imaginable manifestation of womanhood (plus gay friends) to dance to pop and chart music. There is also a female version of Gayhane – Ladyhane – which is held intermittently. Sunday is Café Fatal (7pm-2am May-Sept, 6pm-2am Oct-Apr), where gays and lesbians get into ballroom dancing with a lesson from a professional thrown in at the start of the evening. Every second Tuesday from 7pm, Bingo Bar attracts a colourful mixture of guys and girls, with numbers read by trash-queen announcers.

Gay

You don't need to look for the gay scene in Berlin. It'll find you in about ten minutes. Some areas, however, are gayer than others, especially Schöneberg's Motzstrasse and Fuggerstrasse, and the area around Schönhauser Allee S-Bahn and U-bahn stations in Prenzlauer Berg. Bars, clubs, shops and saunas are so numerous and various it's impossible to take them all in on one visit. The age of consent is 16, same as for everyone else.

Gays making contact in public is rarely of interest to passers-by, but bigots do exist and so does anti-gay violence. In the West it tends to be by gangs of Turkish teenagers, in the East by right-wing skinhead Germans. But violence is rare and, compared to other cities, Berlin is an easy-going place. The scene is always shifting, so places listed here may have changed or new ones might have sprung up by the time you read this. *Siegessäule* and *Blu* are the best sources of current information.

Where to stay

Most hotels know gays are important to the tourist industry and are courteous and helpful. Here are some accommodation options specifically for gay men.

ArtHotel Connection Berlin

Fuggerstrasse 33, Schöneberg (210 218 800/www. arthotel-connection.de). U1, U2, U3 Wittenbergplatz. **Rates** €80 double; extra during gay special event weekends. **Credit** AmEx, MC, V. **Map** p321 D5.

Comfortable and spacious rooms, most en suite and with a sumptuous breakfast included, right in the middle of Schöneberg's gay area. The SM room is fitted with a sling, stocks and a cage.

Bad Boy'z Appartement

Schliemannstrasse 38, Prenzlauer Berg (440 8165/ www.badboyz.de). U2 Eberswalder Strasse. **Rates** (per person) from €15. **Credit** AmEx, MC, V. **Map** p319 P3.

A well-located, fully equipped one-bedroom apartment that sleeps four and has a lounge, kitchenette and bathroom. Prices vary according to time of year.

Eastside

Schönhauser Allee 41, Prenzlauer Berg (4373 5484/ www.eastside-gayllery.de). U2 Eberswalder Strasse. **Rates** from €62 double. **Credit** AmEx, MC, V. **Map** p319 G1.

Quiet guesthouse in the centre of Prenzlauer Berg, convenient for the gay scene. All rooms have TV/VCR and private bath.

Enjoy Bed & Breakfast

Mann-O-Meter, Bülowstrasse 106, Schöneberg (2362 3610/www.ebab.de). U1, U2, U3, U4 Nollendorfplatz. **Rates** (per person) from €20. **No credit cards.** **Map** p321 D5.

This excellent accommodation service caters to both gays and lesbians, and can fix you up with a room in the private apartment of fellow gays.

Lesbian & Gay Hospitality Exchange International

c/o J Wiley, Schönleinstrasse 20, Kreuzberg (691 9537/www.lghei.org).

This LGHEI is a worldwide network of lesbians and gay men who offer each other the gift of short-term hospitality during their travels on the basis of reciprocity. No sex.

Le Moustache

Gartenstrasse 4, Mitte (281 7277/www.lemoustache. de). U8 Rosenthaler Platz, S1, S2, S25 Nordbahnhof. **Rates** from €35 double. **No credit cards.** **Map** p326 M4.

Cosy pension with six rooms on two floors: five double rooms and one single. There's a shared bathroom and toilet on each floor, and one of the doubles has its own washing facilities. The pension is attached to a bar of the same name that is open to all and attracts actors and artists who live in the area.

RoB Leather Apartments Berlin

*c/o RoB, Fuggerstrasse 19, Schöneberg (2196
7400/www.rob-apartments.de). U1, U2, U3
Wittenbergplatz.* **Rates** €79-€144 double. **Credit**
AmEx, MC, V. **Map** p321 D5.

There are two apartments to rent including kitchen,
bathroom, TV, VCR, internet access, own mobile
telephone number – and a playroom.

Schall & Rauch

*Gleimstrasse 23, Mitte (443 3970/www.schall-und-
rauch-berlin.de). U2, S8, S41, S42, S85 Schönhauser
Allee.* **Rates** €83 double. **No credit cards.**
Map p319 G1.

Clean, modern rooms next door to the café of the
same name (*see p220*). All rooms are en suite and
have TVs and telephones. The rate quoted is for one
night, including breakfast; rates are cheaper if you
stay longer.

Tom's House

*Eisenacher Strasse 10, Schöneberg (218 5544/
www.toms-house-alster-berlin.de). U1, U2, U3, U4
Nollendorfplatz.* **Rates** €70-€90 double. **Credit**
AmEx, DC, MC, V. **Map** p321 D5.

Tom's House is an eccentric and unpredictable
establishment located deep in the heart of gay
Schöneberg. Iy hsd seven double rooms, a single one
and serves first-rate buffet brunches.

Cafés, bars & restaurants

Prenzlauer Berg

Flax

*Chodowieckistrasse 41 (4404 6988/www.flax-
berlin.de). S8, S41, S42, S85 Greifswalder Strasse.*
Open 5pm-2am Mon-Sat; 10am-1am Sun. **No credit
cards. Map** p319 H2.

It may be on the edge of the Prenzlauer Berg gay
scene, but the Flax has developed into one of the
most popular café/bars in the East, mainly pulling
a young, mixed crowd. Excellent Sunday brunch
from 10am-5pm for €6.50 per person.

Greifbar

*Wichertstrasse 10 (444 0828/www.greifbar.com). U2
S8, S41, S42, S85 Schönhauser Allee.* **Open** 10pm-
late daily. **No credit cards. Map** p319 G1.

A younger Prenzlauer Berg crowd populates this
cruisy bar looking for adventure and pleasure, either
by picking someone up or by roaming about in the
large darkrooms. There's also a good atmosphere if
you just want to drink.

Stiller Don

*Erich-Weinert-Strasse 67 (0176 5013 3676). U2,
S8, S41, S42, S85 Schönhauser Allee.* **Open** 8pm-
late daily. **No credit cards. Map** p319 G1.

Formerly home to the local avant-garde, now attracting a mixed crowd from all over Berlin, this place is
set up like a cosy café, but it gets high spirited at
weekends and on Mondays.

Kreuzberg

Rauschgold

*Mehringdamm 62 (7895 2668/www.rauschgold-
berlin.de). U6, U7 Mehringdamm.* **Open** 8pm-late
daily. **No credit cards. Map** p322 F5.

This plush and somewhat tacky bar is a good place
for those who feel like prolonging their night into
morning or for taking a first drink on an evening
out. The occasional cabaret performances are generally not to be recommended.

Schöneberg

Café Berio

*Maassenstrasse 7 (216 1946/www.cafe-berio.de).
U1, U2, U3, U4 Nollendorfplatz.* **Open** 8am-
midnight Mon-Thur, Sun; 8am-1am Fri, Sat.
No credit cards. Map p321 D5.

One of the best daytime cafés in Berlin, full of attractive, trendy young men (including the waiters), with
a good people-watching terrace in summer.

Hafen

*Motzstrasse 19 (211 4118/www.hafen-berlin.de). U1,
U2, U3, U4 Nollendorfplatz.* **Open** 8pm-late daily.
No credit cards. Map p321 D5.

A red, plush and vaguely psychedelic bar in the centre of Schöneberg's gay triangle. Popular with the
fashion- and body-conscious, especially at weekends,
when it provides a safe haven from nearby heavy
cruising dens. Usually very crowded, especially for
the pub quiz, Quizz-o-Rama, held in English from
10pm on the first Monday of the month.

Heile Welt

*Motzstrasse 5 (2191 7507). U1, U2, U3, U4
Nollendorfplatz.* **Open** 6pm-4am daily.
No credit cards. Map p321 H9.

A stylish café, lounge and cocktail bar for the fash-
ion-conscious: the front has a '70s disco feel complete with furry wall; the back lounge offers plush
leather seating. It's a good place to kick off an
evening, practise some chat-up lines and decide
whether to go clubbing or not. Packed by 11pm on
Friday and Saturday.

Mutschmanns

*Martin-Luther-Strasse 19 (2191 9640/www.
mutschmanns.de). U1, U2, U3, U4 Nollendorfplatz.*
Open 10pm-late Fri, Sat; 9pm-5am Sun. **Admission**
varies. **No credit cards. Map** p321 D5/6.

This well-frequented hardcore bar, with a large and
hard darkroom in the basement, is suitable for cruising or just hanging out, but with a dress code of
leather, rubber or uniform. Rubber Night is the first
Saturday of the month.

Prinzknecht

*Fuggerstrasse 33 (2362 7444/www.prinzknecht.de).
U1, U2, U3 Wittenbergplatz.* **Open** Apr-Sept 3pm-
3am daily. Oct-Mar 4pm-3am daily. **No credit
cards. Map** p321 D5.

With a large but under-used darkroom out back, this huge, open bar draws in gays from the neighbourhood as well as leather and more hardcore men. The place is somewhat provincial in feel, but nice for a chat and a beer. The crowd moves outside in summer.

Tom's Bar
Motzstrasse 19 (213 4570/www.tomsbar.de). U1, U2, U3, U4 Nollendorfplatz. **Open** 10pm-6am daily. **No credit cards. Map** p321 D5.
Once described by *Der Spiegel* as the climax of the night, Tom's is something of a cruising institution. The front bar is fairly chatty but the closer you get to the steps down to the darkroom the more intense things become. Very popular with men of all ages and styles, especially on Monday when you can get two drinks for the price of one.

Tramps
Eisenacher Strasse 6 (no phone). U1, U2, U3, U4 Nollendorfplatz. **Open** 24 hours daily. **No credit cards. Map** p321 H9.
The name says it all. This back alley of a bar, complete with crazy paving on the walls, is the only gay venue in the district to open its doors 24/7. Expect a random crowd of local soaks, rent boys and horny bucks looking for easy fun in the darkroom at the back.

Clubs & one-nighters

With only a few real discos – **Haus B** (*see p220*), **SchwuZ** (*see p225*) and **Connection** (*see p227*) – one-nighters are all the rage. Some come and go, others run and run. Check *Siegessäule* or *Blu*, or look out for flyers in bars, cafés and shops.

Mitte

GMF
Café Moskau, Karl-Marx-Allee 34 (2809 5396/ www.gmf-berlin.de). U5 Schillingstrasse. **Open** 10pm-late Sun. **Admission** €9. **No credit cards. Map** p319 G3/H3.
For those who want to stick a finger up to Monday mornings, this is the ultimate Sunday tea dance. The venue is the Café Moskau in all of its 1950s glory: the downstairs dancefloor is intense (as is the peacocking) and the cocktail lounge upstairs sociable and buzzing, with a second pop-based dancefloor. Always packed with a stylish, youngish, energetic crowd.

Klub International
Kino International, Karl-Marx-Allee 33 (6904 0780/www.klub-international.com). U5

Schillingstrasse. **Open** 11pm-late 1st Sat of mth. **Admission** €8. **No credit cards. Map** p319 G3.
In a landmark 1950s cinema, this one-nighter is worth a look for the interior alone. It's one of the biggest parties in town, regularly attracting up to 1,500 youngish guests in their tightest T-shirts. There are two dancefloors and DJs play a mix of house and mainstream music.

Prenzlauer Berg

Chantal's House of Shame

Bassy Club, Schönhauser Allee 176A www.myspace.com/chantalshouseofshame). *U2 Senefelderplatz.* **Open** 11pm-7am Thur. **Admission** €7. **No credit cards. Map** p319/p326 O4.
In a new kitsch location, this popular, friendly, electro dance night hosted by well-known local drag queen Chantal has sadly lost some of its underground feel but is still packing in the party set for an early weekend warm-up. Pulls in a cross-section of Berlin's gay scene, including some attractive transvestites.

Irrenhouse

GeburtstagsKlub, Am Friedrichshain 33 (4202 1406). Tram 2, 3, 4 Am Friedrichshain.

Open 11pm-late 3rd Sat of mth. **Admission** €8-€10. **No credit cards. Map** p319 H2.
This popular one-nighter is true to its name: 'Madhouse'. A bizarre mixture of party kids, trashy drag queens and other flotsam of the night party to house and chart music under even more bizarre porn installations. Popular and shrill.

Kreuzberg

SchwuZ

Mehringdamm 61 (693 7025/www.schwuz.de). *U6, U7 Mehringdamm.* **Open** 11pm-late Fri, Sat. **Admission** from €5. **No credit cards. Map** p322 F5.
Saturday is the main disco night at the Schwulen Zentrum ('gay centre'), Berlin's longest-running dance institution. The club attracts a mixed crowd, covering all ages and styles. There are two, sometimes three, dancefloors (one featuring house music) and much mingling between the three bars and Café Melitta Sundström (*see p220*) upstairs. Friday hosts an assortment of one-nighters: first Friday of the month is London Calling, with independent and pop music; second Friday of the month there's FBI Funky Beats Inc, a black music party; third Friday of the month, Search and Destroy Queer Noises offers alternative, punk and rock music, and on

Butcherei Lindinger. *See p230.*

Men from marz

If you're visiting Berlin during a street event or festival, chances are you'll come across a quirky stall selling curious figurines about eight inches (20cm) tall, mounted in glass cases. Your interest may be sparked by the animated designs: macho men in hardcore attire, skinheads and leather boys, and full-bodied women for the ladies. But then you discover that these models have been crafted from marzipan and edible paint. Creator Guenter Frieb insists his figures are intended as art rather than snacks, but adds: 'If you smashed the glass case, took out the model and ate it, it wouldn't poison you.'

The 45-year-old returned to his passion of confectionery after ditching a day job in logistics management. 'I'm a trained confectioner and had always enjoyed making cakes and models out of confectionery for friends, so I decided to turn it into a business. I went to the bank with a business plan and they said yes. My colleagues were all rather surprised.'

The result was his company, **Marzipan meets Art** (2581 8381, www.marzipanmeets art.de), which has been doing pretty well since its foundation in 2006. 'Most of my work is for businesses looking for something special to offer clients as gifts, or for people at trade fairs who want a showpiece work of art, or maybe a unique trophy for a sports competition.' But he also enjoys getting his fingers sticky creating the kind of men he finds attractive in real life.

'Women often complain about the lack of female models. But I do those, too, just not as much.' He recently crafted a buxom pole-dancer in topless corset for a girlfriend's birthday. It has remarkable character and detail – even, rather cruelly, down to the cellulite. He also produces animal figures, and there are some colourful interpretations of Berlin landmarks in his current collection.

Guenter buys the marzipan and paint but makes the models with his own hands. Each takes one to three days to complete and mount. There's no shop or workshop: Guenter works best on his kitchen table at home.

Why choose marzipan? 'It's a question of which material an artist works best with. For some it is glass or wood... for me it's marzipan.' And as an artist, he also has something to say, albeit playfully. The explicit but fun model of the black man penetrating the Latino rimming the white boy is intended to express the egalitarian idea that 'we can all have sex together, regardless of the colour of our skin.'

Frieb is happy to make models to order, with prices from €80; a detailed figure might set you back €130. Postage within Europe costs up to €70 as the cases need careful packaging.

Marzipan Meets Art.

every fourth Friday of the month there is L-Tunes for lesbians and their friends (*see p232*), with music ranging from all-time favourites to electronica. The line-up for Saturdays is Bump!, a night of retro party and disco hits on the first Saturday of the month; Proxi Club on the second Saturday offers electro music and pop, the third Saturday, Repeat, offers a dancefloor of tunes from another country, while Popkicker on the fourth Saturday has a pop/sport mix, with one lounge dedicated to table tennis and table football. A fifth Saturday in the month means Madonnamania, a high-energy party in two rooms playing the best tunes from the artist's 25-year career.

Schöneberg

Connection

Fuggerstrasse 33 (218 1432/www.connection-berlin.com). U1, U2, U3 Wittenbergplatz. **Open** 11pm-late Fri, Sat. **Admission** €7 (incl 1 drink). **Map** p321 D5.

Popular men-only club on Saturdays, with DJs playing mainly electronic sounds. The dancefloor is usually packed, and if you're bored with that you can cruise the vast, flesh dungeons of Connection Garage on two floors below. First Friday of the month is mixed. Also open the night before public holidays.

Propaganda

Goya Club, Nollendorfplatz 5 (419 939 000/www.propaganda-party.de). U1, U2, U3, U4 Nollendorfplatz. **Open** 11pm-late. **Admission** €12. **No credit cards. Map** p322 J9.

New monthly dance night in a legendary 100-year-old location, now revamped with designer décor. Friendly boy-next-door types crowd onto an oval dancefloor beneath chandeliers for a night of feel-good commercial house and dance music that techno/electro fans would probably wish to avoid.

Leather, sex & fetish venues

The hardcore and fetish scene in Berlin is huge. These days, leather gays are outnumbered by a younger hardcore crowd and skinhead-type gays who prefer rubber and uniforms. Places to obtain your preferred garb are plentiful, as are opportunities to show it off, including the eternally crowded Leather Meeting over the Easter holidays, the annual Gay Skinhead Meeting, and various fetish parties and events. Most of the parties are men-only affairs and have a strict dress code.

Mitte

Kit Kat Club

Köpenicker Strasse 76 (7871 8963/www.kitkat club.org). U8 Heinrich-Heine-Strasse. **Open** 11pm-late Fri-Sun. **Admission** €10-€15. **No credit cards. Map** p323 P7.

This legendary mixed/straight sex and techno party club has moved out of Schöneberg to take up residence every weekend at the Sage Club, the nightclub with its own swimming pool. The fourth Friday of the month is Piepshow; Saturday nights feature the club's flagship CarneBall Bizarre, with the Afterhour event to follow. All nights are listed in the gay press. Most parties have a fetish dress code; the least you have to do is take off your shirt. The Kit Kat Club is also the venue for the annual men-only HustlaBall (www.hustlaball.de), a gay dance/sex extravaganza, usually in October, which attracts hungry, hardcore males who strip to next to nothing, if not nothing, for a night of full-on debauchery. The stage shows and cruising areas leave little to the imagination.

Prenzlauer Berg

Blackbox-Bar

Paul-Robeson-Strasse 50 (4437 6720). U2, S8, S41, S42, S85 Schönhauser Allee. **Open** 10pm-6am Mon, Wed; 7pm-6am Tue, Thur; 10pm-8am Fri, Sat; 5pm-6am Sun; **Admission** €6. **Credit** AmEx, MC, V. **Map** p319 G1.

This cruising fetish bar is popular with skinheads and hardcore types. There are sex parties most nights of the week, with Fridays set aside for skins, after-work sex sessions on Tuesdays and Thursdays from 7pm, and a chill-out night on Sunday from 7pm. There are regular happy hours and special parties.

Darkroom

Rodenbergstrasse 23 (444 9321/www.darkroom-berlin.de). U2, S8, S41, S42, S85 Schönhauser Allee. **Open** 10pm-late daily. **Admission** free-€2.50. **No credit cards. Map** p319 G1.

Yes, there is a darkroom in this small bar. In fact, it's more darkroom than bar. And with the help of camouflage netting and urinals, the place pulls in a slightly 'harder' clientele; on less busy nights things can feel a bit desperate, however. The Naked Sex Party on Friday and Saturday's Golden Shower Party are particularly popular. Wednesday has an Underwear Sex Party from 6pm.

Stahlrohr

Greifenhagener Strasse 54 (4473 2747/ www.stahlrohr-bar.de). U2, S8, S41, S42, S85 Schönhauser Allee. **Open** 10pm-late Mon-Sat; 6pm-late Sun. **Admission** €5 incl 1 drink. **No credit cards. Map** p319 G1.

A small, hardcore pub in the front and a large darkroom in the back and downstairs. There are sex parties for every taste, including Fist and Fuck (Sundays), Sneakers and Boots and Slave Market (alternate Fridays), Underwear Naked and Fetish (Mondays and Thursdays), Oben-oder-Unten-Ohne party (Naked Top or Bottom; Wednesdays), There's also a Youngster party for those aged 18-26 (Tuesdays).

Arts & Entertainment

Friedrichshain

Lab.oratory

Am Wriezener Bahnhof (no phone/www.lab-oratory.de). U5 Weberwiese, S3, S5, S9, S75 Ostbahnhof. **Open** 10pm-midnight Thur-Sat; 4-6pm Sun. **Admission** €6-€15. **No credit cards.** **Map** p324 R7.

Housed in the same building as Panorama Bar/Berghain nightclub, this well-decked-out new hardcore sex den – complete with all the props: slings, beds, cages, pissoir etc – takes the sexual perversion on offer in Berlin to another level. In addition to the regular Naked Sex Party on Thursdays and the Friday Fuck 2-4-1 with two drinks for the price of one, the venue also organises Saturday and Sunday night specials ranging from the relatively soft core Office Slut (suits and ties), Gummi (rubber outfits) and Fausthause (oral deep throat) to Yellow Facts (watersports) and Scat. Check the website for dates.

Kreuzberg

Bodies in Emotion

AHA, Mehringdamm 61 (692 3600/www.aha-berlin.de). U6, U7 Mehringdamm. **Open** 9pm-5am 2nd Fri of mth. **Admission** €5. **No credit cards.** **Map** p322 F5.

This sex party is popular with guys under 30 (or who look it – no hairy chests here). What you wear is your business, but most put on shorts, which they then take off in the sex area, where mattresses and slings invite you to have fun.

Club Culture Houze

Görlitzer Strasse 71 (6170 9669/www.club-culture-houze.de). U1 Görlitzer Bahnhof. **Open** 7pm-late Mon, Thur; 8pm-late Wed, Fri, Sun; 10pm-late Sat. **Admission** €7.50. **No credit cards.** **Map** p323 H5.

Diverse sex parties (some of them mixed), ranging from Naked to SM and Fetish. Exclusive gay nights on Monday (Naked Sex), Thursday and Sunday (Naked and Underwear Sex Party), Friday (Fist Factory) and Saturday (Gay Sex Party). Mostly body-conscious night owls visit these kitsch rooms. Mattresses encourage people to lie down, but they do it everywhere.

Quälgeist

4th backyard, ground floor, Mehringdamm 51 (788 5799/www.quaelgeist-berlin.de). U6, U7 Mehringdamm. **Open** varies. **Admission** €8-€15. **No credit cards.** **Map** p322 D5.

First institution established solely to organise SM parties, which include SM for beginners, bondage, slave-market and fist nights. Pick up their flyers at any leather bar. There's usually a dress code.

Triebwerk

Urbanstrasse 64 (6950 5203/www.triebwerk-online.de). U7, U8 Hermannplatz. **Open** 10pm-late Mon, Thur-Sat; 9pm-late Tue, Wed; 4pm-late Sun.

Admission €7.50. **Credit** AmEx, MC, V. **Map** p323 H5.

This small comfortable bar with a huge video screen and a darkroom maze in the basement attracts Kreuzberg gays of every denomination. On Mondays there are two-for-one drinks; Naked & Underwear Parties feature on Tuesdays, Fridays, Saturdays and Sundays; Wednesdays is After Work Sex, and it's Cruising Night on Thursdays.

Schöneberg

Ajpnia

Eisenacher Strasse 23 (2191 8881/www.ajpnia.de). U1, U2, U3, U4 Nollendorfplatz. **Open** 7pm-2am Wed; 9pm-9am Sat. **Admission** €5. **No credit cards.** **Map** p322 D5.

Two-storey, intimate sex club frequented by men of all ages. Every first and third Saturday is Posithiv Verkehr, a party by and for HIV-positives; every second and fourth Saturday is Nachtverkehr (Night Traffic) and Wednesday is Feierabend-verkehr (After Work Traffic). Note that Verkehr also means 'intercourse'.

New Action

Kleiststrasse 35 (211 8256/www.new-action-berlin.de). U1, U2, U3, U4 Nollendorfplatz. **Open** 8pm-late Mon-Fri; 10pm Sat-7am Mon. **No credit cards.** **Map** p321 D5.

In early morning this atmospheric, custom-designed hardcore bar with small darkroom can become quite a gathering of eccentrics who either don't want to go to bed yet or else just got up. Leather, rubber, uniform, jeans, but also the odd woollen pullover creates a casual atmosphere. Don't be sober. Naked Sex Party on Thursday and Sunday from 10pm.

Scheune

Motzstrasse 25 (213 8580/www.scheune-berlin.de). U1, U2, U3, U4 Nollendorfplatz. **Open** 9pm-7am Mon-Thur, Sun; 9pm-9am Fri, Sat. **Admission** varies. **No credit cards.** **Map** p322 D5.

Small and welcoming leather hardcore bar. Action in the cellar is late and heavy. There's a Naked Sex Party Sunday afternoon (entrance 5.30-9pm), plus occasional rubber nights. Very popular.

Other districts

Böse Buben

2nd backyard, Lichtenrader Strasse 32, Neukölln (6270 5610/www.boesebuben-berlin.de). U8 Leinestrasse. **Open** 5pm-4am Wed; 9pm-4am Fri, Sat. **Admission** €6. **No credit cards.** **Map** p323 G6.

Fetish sex party club with imaginatively furnished and decorated rooms. Tiled piss room, sling room, bondage cross and cheap drinks make this quite a grotto of hedonism. Wednesday is the After Work Sex Party; weekends have different parties such as hard SM, fist, bondage and spanking.

Saunas

Saunas are popular and you may have to queue, especially on cheaper days. In-house bills are run up on your locker or cabin number and are settled on leaving. No open cabins, only personal ones.

Apollo Sauna Club Brasil

Kurfürstenstrasse 101, Schöneberg (213 2424/www.gaysaunaclubbrasil.com). U1, U2, U3 Wittenbergplatz. **Open** 1pm-7am Mon-Thur; 1pm Fri-7am Mon. **Admission** €17 per day incl locker; €2-€5 supplement 4-9.30pm Sat & during gay event days. **No credit cards. Map** p322 D5.
Formerly the Apollo Sauna Club Berlin, this huge labyrinth of sin with 250 lockers and 80 cabins has been given a major revamp with a Latin twist. Two floors offer clients a bar, cinema, dry and steam saunas, a massage area, pool, plunge bath and jungle-style cruising area. There are theme nights most nights while a delivery of sand means sex on the beach in summer.

Steam Sauna Club Berlin

Kurfürstenstrasse 113, Tiergarten (218 4060/ www.steam-sauna.de). U1, U2, U3 Wittenbergplatz. **Open** 11am-7am Mon-Thur; 11am Fri-7am Mon. **Admission** €15-€18.50; €6.50/€9 cabin. **No credit cards. Map** p321 D4.
Classic sauna with 180 lockers and 38 cabins plus sauna and steam rooms, whirlpool, bar and TV room showing porn. Sex is plentiful, sometimes hardcore, among clientele of all ages. Clubbers drift in early on Sunday mornings and stay for the day. Steam Night Specials from Monday to Thursday and Sunday from 10.30pm are cheaper.

Treibhaus Sauna

Schönhauser Allee 132, Prenzlauer Berg (448 4503/www.treibhaussauna.de). U2 Eberswalder Strasse. **Open** 1pm-7am Mon-Thur; 1pm Fri-7am Mon. **Admission** €17.50 (incl locker & €6 drink ticket); €5.50 cabin. **No credit cards. Map** p319 G2.
Tucked in the first courtyard (buzz for entry), this has become a big favourite, especially with students and youngsters, and, on Sunday afternoon, those P'bergers who failed to pick up on Saturday night. Facilities include dry sauna, steam room, whirlpool, cycle jet, solarium, a shop stocked with toys and lubricants, and cabins equipped with TV and VCR on a first-come, first-served basis. Internet access, too. During the week, there's a variety of medicinal and therapeutic massage treatments on offer.

Cruising

Cruising is a popular and legal pursuit in Berlin. Most action takes place in the parks, in the daytime often just metres away from the general public, who don't seem to care. And don't panic or jump into a bush when encountering the police – they are actually there to protect you from gay bashers and they never hassle cruisers. One way or another, it's actually very safe to go roaming about at night in Berlin. Summer brings out all of the city's finery and there is no taboo about nudity in parks.

Grunewald

S7 Grunewald.
Go to the woods behind the car park at Pappelplatz. Walk 500m (1,640ft) along Eichkampstrasse until it passes under the Autobahn, then turn to the right into the woods. From there it's about another 50m (164ft) to the car park. This is a popular daytime spot but it's also well frequented at night, when bikers and harder guys mingle among the trees.

Tiergarten

S5, S7, S9, S75 Tiergarten. **Map** p321 D4.
The Löwenbrücke (where the Grosser Weg crosses the Neuer See) is the cruising focal point – but the whole corner south-west of the Siegessäule becomes a bit of a gay theme park in summer, when daytime finds hundreds of gays sunning themselves on the *Tuntenwiese* ('faggot meadow').

Volkspark Friedrichshain

U2, U5, U8 or S3, S5, S7, S9 Alexanderplatz, then Tram 2,3,4 Am Friedrichshain. **Map** p319 H3.
Offering a friendlier, more relaxed feel than Berlin's other hunting grounds, the cruising patch was traditionally the area around and behind the Märchenbrunnen. Recent renovation work to this part of the park means that action has been temporarily dispersed; your best bet is to head up the nearby slopes.

Shops

Books & art

Bruno's

Nollendorfplatz, corner of Bülowstrasse 106, Schöneberg (6150 0385/www.brunos.de). U1, U2, U3, U4 Nollendorfplatz. **Open** 10am-10pm Mon-Sat; 1-9pm Sun. **Credit** AmEx, MC, V. **Map** p321 D4.
Large and rather plush shop offers an extensive selection of reading and viewing material, plus cards, calendars, videos and other paraphernalia. **Other locations** Schönhauser Allee 131, Prenzlauer Berg (6150 0387).

Prinz Eisenherz

Lietzenburger Strasse 9A, Schöneberg (313 9936/www.prinz-eisenherz.com). U1, U2, U3 Wittenbergplatz. **Open** 10am-8pm Mon-Sat. **Credit** MC, V. **Map** p321 D4.
Prinz Eisenherz is one of the finest gay bookshops in Europe, including, among its large English-language stock, many titles unavailable in Britain. There's a good art and photography section, plus magazines, postcards and news of book readings and other events.

Fashion

Boyz 'R' Us
*Maassenstrasse 8, Schöneberg (2363 0640/
www.boyz-r-us.de). U1, U2, U3, U4 Nollendorfplatz.*
Open 11am-8pm Mon-Fri; 10am-8pm Sat. **No credit
cards. Map** p322 J9.
Classy clobber for discerning gays who like to be
noticed and don't mind paying for it. Think G-Star,
Diesel, Calvin Klein. Ladies store Goldelse is
accessed through the back.

Laden 114
*Eisenacher Strasse 114, Schöneberg (2363 9373).
U1, U2, U3, U4 Nollendorfplatz.* **Open** 1-8pm Mon-
Sat. **No credit cards. Map** p321 J9.
Gay designer fashion with a tougher edge, although
there are also second-hand clothing racks with items
from €3 upwards to mix and match.

LadeRaum
*Mehringdamm 55, Kreuzberg (6953 2798).
U7, U8 Mehringdamm.* **Open** noon-8pm Mon-Sat.
No credit cards. Map p322 J9.
Walls full of tight Ts and tops for day and night,
many at bargain prices. If you're still not satisfied,
you can design your own with a print from €6.

Waahnsinn
*Rosenthaler Strasse 17, Mitte (282 0029/www.
waahnsinn-berlin.de). U8 Rosenthaler Platz or*
Weinmeisterstrasse. **Open** noon-8pm Mon-Sat.
Credit AmEx, MC, V. **Map** p319/p326 N5.
Men's sequinned hot pants and tank tops are among
the stand-out new items in this stylish and theatrical 1950s-'70s second-hand clothes shop. Well worth
a look, if only for the novelty factor.

Toys & fetish outfits

Bad Boy'z
*Schliemannstrasse 38, Prenzlauer Berg (440 8165/
www.badboyz.de). U2 Eberswalder Strasse.* **Open**
1pm-1am daily. **Credit** AmEx, MC, V. **Map** p319 P3.
Toys and DVDs and a revamped porn cinema too.
Popular place to buy poppers this side of town.

Black Style
*Seelower Strasse 5, Prenzlauer Berg (4468
8595/www.blackstyle.de). U2, S8, S41, S42, S85
Schönhauser Allee.* **Open** 1-6.30pm Mon-Wed;
1-8pm Thur, Fri; 11am-4pm Sat. **Credit** AmEx,
DC, MC, V. **Map** p319 G1.
From black fashion to butt plugs – if it's made out
of rubber or latex they've got it. High quality, reasonable prices and big variety. Mail order too.

Butcherei Lindinger
*Motzstrasse 18, Schöneberg (2005 1391/
www.butcherei-lindinger.de). U1, U2, U3,
U4 Nollendorfplatz.* **Open** 2-8pm Mon-Sat.
No credit cards. Map p321 G1.

230 Time Out Berlin

Sexclusivitäten. *See p232.*

A smart, new workshop producing tailor-made leather clothing and offering a fantastic range of toys and rubber gear, including some of the biggest dildos on the market.

Connection Garage

Fuggerstrasse 33, Schöneberg (218 1432/www. connection-berlin.com). U1, U2, U3 Wittenbergplatz. **Open** 10am-1am Mon-Sat; 2pm-1am Sun. **Credit** MC, V. **Map** p321 D5.

Connection Garage stocks a huge selection of leather novelties, clothing, SM accessories and magazines. The cruising area comes alive at weekends when it amalgamates with Connection disco (*see p227*).

Jaxx

Motzstrasse 19, Schöneberg (213 8103). U1, U2, U3, U4 Nollendorfplatz. **Open** noon-3am Mon-Sat; 1pm-3am Sun. **Admission** €8; €6 Tue. **Credit** MC, V. **Map** p321 D5.

Jaxx stocks a good selection of toys and videos, plus there are video cabins and a cruising area. It's very popular with younger guys.

Leathers

Schliemannstrasse 38, Prenzlauer Berg (442 7786/ www.leathers.de). U2 Eberswalder Strasse. **Open** noon-7.30pm Mon-Fri; noon-4pm Sat. **Credit** AmEx, MC, V. **Map** p319 G2.

This workshop produces leather and SM articles of the highest quality. There's no smut here – just a range of well-presented products and friendly staff who are happy to help.

Mr B

Motzstrasse 22, Schöneberg (2199 7704/www. misterb.com). U1, U2, U3, U4 Nollendorfplatz. **Open** noon-8pm Mon-Fri; 11am-6pm Sat. **Credit** AmEx, DC, MC, V. **Map** p321 D5.

Everything for the hardcore crowd. This smart place is known particularly for its leather and rubber outfits, metal accessories and toys, SM articles, lubricants and clothing. Mr B also hosts the occasional art exhibition.

Lesbian

Few cities can compete with Berlin's network of lesbian institutions, but there are few lesbian-only bars. For mixed bars and club nights, check *Siegessäule* or *L-mag* (www.L-mag.de), a quarterly free lesbian magazine. There is also a relatively reliable listing at www.youngandlesbian.de/szene.html, part of a support group for young lesbians. Many young lesbians favour mixed venues such as **SchwuZ** (*see p227*), **SO36** (*see p222*) and **Haus B** (*see p220*) although girls now have their own sex night offered free by the usually men-only **Ficken 3000** bar.

Cafés & bars

Mitte

Café Seidenfaden
*Dircksenstrasse 47 (283 2783/www.
frausuchtzukunft.de). U8 Weinmeister Strasse, S5,
S7, S9, S75 Hackescher Markt.* **Open** noon-8pm
Mon-Sat. **No credit cards. Map** p319 G3.
Run by women from a therapy group of former
addicts. There are readings and exhibitions but
absolutely no drugs or alcohol. Packed at lunchtime,
quiet at night.

Friedrichshain

Frieda Frauenzentrum
*Proskauer Strasse 7 (422 4276/www.frieda-
frauenzentrum.de). U5 Samariterstrasse.* **Open**
9am-8pm Tue, Thur; 9am-6pm Wed; 2-8pm Fri;
11am-2pm 4th Sat of mth. **No credit cards.**
Map p325 T6.
Centre for women's wellbeing and interests with a
full programme of lesbian, mother and senior events.

Kreuzberg

Schoko Café
*Mariannenstrasse 6 (615 1561/www.schokofabrik.
de). U1, U8 Kottbusser Tor.* **Open** 5pm-late Mon,
Wed-Sun. **No credit cards. Map** p323 G5.
Part of the Schoko-Fabrik women's centre, mostly
frequented by lesbians. Snacks and occasional parties.

Schöneberg

Begine
*Potsdamer Strasse 139 (215 1414/www.begine.de).
U2 Bülowstrasse.* **Open** 6pm-late Mon-Fri; varies
Sat, Sun. **No credit cards. Map** p322 E5.
This venerable women-only café frequented by les-
bians is part of the 'Meeting point and Culture for
Women' centre.

Charlottenburg

Neue Bar
*Knesebeckstrasse 16 (3150 3062). S5, S7, S9,
S75 Savignyplatz.* **Open** 6pm-late Tue-Sat.
No credit cards. Map p321 C4.
There's a talkative atmosphere at this small pub for
women and lesbians.

Clubs & one-nighters

Prenzlauer Berg

Frauenparty im EWA
*e.V. Frauenzentrum, Prenzlauer Allee 6 (442
5542/www.ewa-frauenzentrum.de). U2 Rosa-*
Luxemburg-Platz. **Open** 9pm-late 1st Fri of mth.
No credit cards. Map p319 G3.
This women's centre hosts a regular Let's Dance
night: check the website and press for these and
other events for further details.

Kreuzberg

L-Tunes
*SchwuZ, Mehringdamm 61 (693 7025/www.
megadyke.de). U6, U7 Mehringdamm.* **Open**
10pm-late 4th Fri of mth. **Admission** €6/€7.
No credit cards. Map p322 F5.
L-Tunes holds dance and electronica nights on two
floors with a chill-out zone every fourth Friday of
the month.

Play! Girl
*SO36, Oranienstrasse 190 (6140 1306/www.
so36.de). U1, U8 Kottbusser Tor.* **Admission**
€5/€7. **No credit cards. Map** p323 G4.
Monthly pop and chart night (dates vary) for girls
and their gay friends. SO36 also organises a
women's version (Ladyhane) of the Gayhane oriental gay dance night, though not on a regular basis –
check their website for details.

Other districts

Frauen 3000
*Ficken 3000, Urbanstrasse 70, Neukölln (6950
7335/www.ficken3000.com). U7, U8 Hermannplatz.*
Open 8pm-late 1st Mon of mth. **Admission** free.
No credit cards. Map p323 P10.
Every first Monday of the month sees a healthy mix
of women taking over this traditionally male-only
sex club for their own bar and dance night, complete
with a downstairs darkroom.

Shops & services

Playstixx
*Waldemarstrasse 24, Kreuzberg (6165 9500/
www.playstixx.de). U1, U8 Kottbusser Tor.*
Open *Women & transvestites* 2-6pm Wed;
2-5pm Fri; noon-4pm every Sat in Feb; noon-3pm
every 2nd & 4th Sat Mar-Jan. *All* 2-6pm Thur.
No credit cards. Map p323 G4.
The dildos on offer at this workshop, run by sculp-
tress Stefanie Dörr, come in the form of bananas,
whales, fists and dolphins rather than phalluses. Most
are made of non-allergenic, highly durable silicon.

Sexclusivitäten
*Laura Mérrit, Fürbringerstrasse 2, Kreuzberg
(693 6666/www.sexclusivitaeten.de). U7
Gneisenaustrasse.* **Open** noon-8pm Fri
by appointment only. **No credit cards.**
Map p322 F5.
Laura Mérrit calls herself a feminist linguist and
'sexpert', offering sex counselling, conflict mediation
and a big selection of sex toys. Shop for a variety of
dildos, vibrators and other items.

Music: Rock, World & Jazz

Tearing down all kinds of walls.

Ausland. *See p235.*

The Berlin music scene long ago abandoned the pretence of having its back against the Wall, but it continues to thrive on a potent cocktail of adversity and diversity. Musically, it's still very much an underground city and it's not about to surrender its secrets too easily. However, the clues aren't that hard to find – parachute behind the lines in Friedrichshain, Mitte, Prenzlauer Berg or Kreuzberg, drop into a likely looking gallery, bar or record store and pick up the flyers or freesheets listing events or happenings, and various networks will begin to open their doors. Once you've cracked one, a domino effect kicks in and they'll topple one after the other, because in Berlin only a very few degrees of separation exists between 'high' and 'low' culture, artists and genres, and the places where things happen.

The most intriguing events might well take place in a gallery, a deconsecrated church or even a living room (various *Wohnzimmer* scenes have periodically thrived in the city, be it for obvious political reasons during the

DDR, or out of a combination of thrift and hospitality, as among the artists clustered around Gudrun Gut's Monika label). Berlin is the place where musicians like To Rococo Rot's Robert Lippok can hymn the virtues of the Helvetica typeface one moment and playfully spar in a duo with electronic songstress Barbara Morgenstern the next.

The best of Berlin might happen just below the radar, but that's not to say it's hard work. On the contrary: the music is nowhere near as confrontational as it was during the 1980s reign of Einstürzende Neubauten and their fellow Geniale Dilletanten; nor is it as unremitting as Berlin techno could get in the 1990s. The scene today is more user-friendly but no less inventive for that. In recent years, Berlin's signature sound has been a minimalist electro take on techno, as exemplified by Ricardo Villalobos (*see p234* **Rhythm of the city**) and Bpitch Control label head Ellen Allien. Yet in Berlin, once a trend starts it tends to stick around. Kreuzberg retains an anarcho-punk aesthetic. Street buskers in Friedrichshain strum Beatles or Nirvana songs. Disco has taken over Mitte in an obvious backlash to the city's hardcore minimalists, while hip hop and goth dominate the suburbs.

Above ground, not many venues in Berlin consistently book top acts but a fair few host some amazing live shows. Even so, it's impossible to recommend a single location. Because booking policies vary so widely, venue loyalty is unheard of. And even though Berlin still offers some of the lowest guarantees in Western Europe, no artist worth their salt can afford to skip this culture capital. Columbiahalle and Postbahnhof are where the likes of Amy Winehouse and Arctic Monkeys stop off, while the Madonnas and Morrisseys play Arena Berlin or Waldbühne, the wooded open-air venue where the Rolling Stones once famously whipped the crowd into such a frenzy that they rioted.

Although that was in 1965, Berlin's audiences are still some of the most enthusiastic in the world. It's not uncommon for normally mild-mannered Berliners to carry on demanding an encore long after the lights have gone up. Every concert has a DJ afterwards and every bartender considers themselves a DJ, even if all they do is slip on Can's *Flow Motion* while they go and smoke a cigarette.

Each September, the city hosts **PopKomm** (*see p199*), an enormous trade show for the German music industry showcasing hundreds of acts at more than 30 venues across Berlin. In

Rhythm of the city

Minimal techno has long been one of Berlin's signature sounds and its principal practitioner, DJ and producer Ricardo Villalobos, has consistently twisted the template beyond the point of no return, leaving listeners happily adrift in some faraway zone.

Born in Chile but raised in Germany, Villalobos has an instinctive multiculturalism that, when combined with his relaxed good humour and tendency to keep playing all night long, makes him admirably well suited to Germany's hip, mixed-up Hauptstadt. The birth of his first child in 2007 might have temporarily put the brakes on his urge to spend not just his working weekends but also his nights off partying for hours at a stretch behind the decks (you'd often find him at, say, Club der Visionäre, keeping the groove going even on a flat Tuesday night) but being at home more only seems to have increased his already prodigious output.

What distinguish Villalobos's most striking tracks of the last few years are his eclectic tastes and his desire to share them. He casts his net wide for his samples, but rather than overly harmonise/homogenise them, he allows his source materials to retain their character as he drops them on to a track, content to let them form random patterns across the underlying rhythm. His sides habitually break the ten-minute mark, gloriously so in the case of his 37-minute 2006 masterpiece 'Fizheuer Zieheuer'. The track is exemplary not only for its length but also for the way Villalobos effortlessly manipulates tension by shifting focus from heavily resonating metal clank through airier beat lattices to the shimmer of Romany brass. A melancholy fragment of melody fleetingly descends over the rhythm, changing the mood without causing a drop in pace.

In 2007, he launched his own Sei Es Drum label with a triple 12-inch that periodically deploys the rolling thunder of Japanese Kodo drummers to shattering effect on the lead-off track 'Andruic', which otherwise foregrounds passages of languidly spoken nonsense; 'Primer Encuentro Latino-Americano' is based on a song by 1970s Chilean protest rock group Los Jaivas; and so on. His second Sei Es Drum release, 'Enfants (Chant)', was even more audacious. It essentially consisted of a loop of children reciting a rhyme in French about Baba Yaga, the sorceress, over a driving piano track lifted from a composition by Christian Vander of 1970s progressive rock juggernauts Magma. Villalobos's minimal but emphatic intervention over its 17-minute stretch suggests he put the record out as a DJ tool, but it is singular and utterly mesmerising in its simplicity, thrilling in its juxtaposition of unlikely elements, defying anyone to recontextualise it further.

Which is all very Berlin, these days, resonating against the combined backdrops of the city's 'multikulti' and experimental traditions. From a city carved in two by the world's most famous border, Berlin has grown into a place where opposites attract and boundaries are crossed, simply because they're there. And Ricardo Villalobos is a model citizen.

July, *Vice* magazine presents an annual festival largely dedicated to dance-rock, while an 80-minute train ride away in Gräfenhainichen, the **Melt! Festival** (www.meltfestival.de) presents indie-rock and electronica. And if you have an unquenchable desire to discover the Berlin backdrop to David Bowie's Low/'Heroes' period or see the bar where Iggy Pop once ended a *Rolling Stone* interview by rolling around on the pavement, the **Fritz Music Tour** (www.musictours-berlin.com) is for you.

Rock

The sports venues **Max-Schmeling-Halle** (*see p261*) and **Velodrom** (*see p262*) also host occasional music events.

Arcanoa

Am Tempelhofer Berg 8, Kreuzberg (691 2564/www. arcanoa.de). U6 Platz der Luftbrücke/Mehringdamm. **Open** 8pm-late daily. **Admission** €3-€5. **No credit cards. Map** p322 M10.

Until it was closed in 1998, the Arcanoa was best known for celebrating art in many eccentric manifestations. Now relocated just around the corner, this venerably quirky venue has rekindled its old spirit through an easygoing booking policy catering to alternative metal and Deutsch-pop types. It also hosts open mic nights.

Arena Berlin

Eichenstrasse 4, Treptow (533 2030/www.arena-berlin.de). S6, S8, S9, S41, S42, S85 Treptower Park. **Open** *Box office* 10am-7.30pm Mon-Fri. **Admission** varies. **No credit cards. Map** p324 S9.

Inside a converted bus garage, Arena Berlin presents A-list artists such as Bob Dylan and Björk. A movable stage means it can also put on smaller acts. The surrounding entertainment complex includes the Badeschiff, a swimming pool anchored in the Spree river, and the party boat MS Hoppetosse.

Ausland

Lychener Strasse 60, Prenzlauer Berg (447 7008/ www.ausland.de). U2 Eberswalder Strasse. **Open** varies. **Admission** €3-€5. **No credit cards. Map** p319/p328 P2.

A small bohemian basement staging free jazz, avant-folk and live electronica as well as films and art installations. Be aware that shows usually begin an hour later than the posted time (on principle, apparently). Nights usually close with guest DJs whose tastes may not always inspire you to move your dancing feet.

Bang Bang Club

Neue Promenade 10, Mitte-Hackescher Markt (6040 5310/www.bangbang-club.de). M1, M4, M5, M6, S5, S9, S7, S75 Hackescher Markt. **Open** 9pm-3am daily. **Admission** varies. **No credit cards. Map** p319/p326 N5.

Located smack bang in touristy Hackescher Markt and decorated with enormous photo prints of 1960s and '70s icons, Bang Bang is small yet inviting. The bleacher seats around the minuscule dancefloor are perfect for watching the crowd dressed in their finest H&M wear. Booking policy veers towards avant-garde or Britpop acts, with soul and Baile-funk DJs often as not completing the bill.

Barbie Deinhoff's

Schlesische Strasse 16, Kreuzberg (no phone/ www.barbiedeinhoff.de). U1 Schlesisches Tor. **Open** 6pm-6am daily. **Admission** varies. **No credit cards. Map** p324 R9.

With its clutter of mirror balls, salvaged airplane and car seats, this bar, alternative art gallery and indie-rock venue embodies some of the most fun aspects of Berlin living. It's especially partial to electro-poppers with names like Sue & the Unicorn, and its discerning DJs are ace.

Bassy Cowboy Club

Schönhauser Allee 176A, Prenzlauer Berg (281 8323/www.bassy-club.de). U2 Senefelderplatz. **Open** 8.30pm-late Tue; 10pm-late Fri, Sat. **Admission** from €3. **No credit cards. Map** p319/p328 O4.

A move from Hackescher Markt to new premises in Schönhauser Allee and a more diverse music programme has done wonders for Bassy's reputation. These days the venue is a champion of local bands of all genres, so expect a bluegrass act one night and electro-rock the next. Readings on Tuesday nights.

Café Zapata in Tacheles

Oranienburgerstrasse 54-56A, Mitte (281 6109/ www.cafe-zapata.de). U6 Oranienburger Tor. **Open** varies. **Admission** varies. **No credit cards. Map** p318/p326 M5.

Although it's part of the squatted Tacheles complex, Café Zapata stands on its own, booking top-flight folk and indie artists like Joanna Newsom, local hero Bruno Adams and Omaha, Nebraska's the Good Life. The small space opens out on to a beer garden in summer.

Columbiaclub

Columbiadamm 9-11, Tempelhof (tickets 6110 1313/ www.columbiaclub.de). U6 Platz der Luftbrücke. **Open** *Box office* 10am-6pm Mon-Fri; 10am-2pm Sat. **Admission** varies. **No credit cards. Map** p323 N11.

Once you get past its old-fashioned box office, this former US Forces cinema is a little characterless. It showcases mid-size acts of every genre, from John Cale to Roni Size. Bigger draws usually play the Columbiahalle next door.

Columbiahalle

Columbiadamm 13-21, Tempelhof (tickets 6110 1313/www.columbiahalle.de). U6 Platz der Luftbrücke. **Open** *Box office* 9am-7pm Mon-Fri; 10am-2pm Sat. **Admission** varies. **No credit cards. Map** p323 N11.

A roomy venue with a reputation for the best sound in town, Columbiahalle promotes larger acts that haven't made it to stadium status, such as

Arts & Entertainment

Check out the attractions at indie fave **Magnet**.

Babyshambles, the White Stripes and Goldfrapp. Drinks are a little expensive, but it's a good-sized place to catch hip hop superstars such as Jay-Z and Eminem, who would most likely be playing amphitheatres in other cities.

Festsaal Kreuzberg

Skalitzer Strasse 130, Kreuzberg (tickets 6110 1313/www.festsaal-kreuzberg.de). U1, U8 Kottbusser Tor. **Open** varies. **Admission** varies. **No credit cards. Map** p323 P9.

It might not be the first place you'd think to go raving, but, thanks to a westward-drifting scene and its eclectic policies, the Festsaal has become one of Kreuzberg's most popular venues, importing indie acts and DJs as different as Detroit noise gods Wolf Eyes and Miss Kittin.

Frannz Club

Schönhauser Allee 36, Prenzlauer Berg (7262 7930/www.frannz.de). U2 Eberswalder Strasse. **Open** from 8.30pm daily. *Parties* from 10pm. **Admission** free-€8. **No credit cards. Map** p319/p328 O3.

A former DDR youth club, Frannz is a black box with decent sound, pricey drinks and unsmiling doormen. Musically, it's heavy on German acts that don't really translate culturally, though it has occasionally booked rockabilly stars such as Wanda Jackson.

Fritzclub im Postbahnhof

Strasse der Pariser Kommune 8, Friedrichshain (698 1280/www.fritzclub.com). S3, S5, S7, S9, S75 Ostbahnhof. **Open** Box office 9am-7pm Mon-Fri; 10am-2pm Sat. **Admission** varies. **No credit cards. Map** p324 R7.

This restored industrial building is relatively young in comparison to other venues, but its association with Radio Fritz gives it the clout to stage the likes of Arcade Fire, Luka Bloom and Fun Lovin' Criminals.

Junction Bar

Gneisenaustrasse 18, Kreuzberg (694 6602/www. junction-bar.de). U6 Gneisenaustrasse. **Open** *Café* noon-8pm daily. *Bar* 8pm-late daily. **Admission** €3-€6. **No credit cards. Map** p323 N10.

Originally opened in 1993, Junction Bar is a Kreuzberg landmark that arranges 365 concerts a year of everything from jazz and swing to rock, with DJs keeping the party going into the early hours.

Kalkscheune

Jannisstrasse 2, Mitte (5900 4340/www. kalkscheune.de). U6 Oranienburger Tor. **Open** *Box office* noon-7pm Mon-Fri. **Admission** varies. **No credit cards. Map** p318/p326 M5.

While it mostly holds Schlager parties and cabaret nights, this elegantly restored 19th-century factory building occasionally presents a few interesting offbeat artists, such as Devendra Banhart and Nouvelle Vague.

Kato Kulturbahnhof Kreuzberg

*In Schlesisches Tor U-Bahn building, Kreuzberg
(611 2339/www.kato-x-berg.de). U1 Schlesisches
Tor.* **Open** 8pm-late daily. **Admission** €4-€22.
No credit cards. Map p324 R9.
The place for ska and reggae lovers but, with a nod
to Kreuzberg's legendary squatter scene, the Kato
Kulturbahnhof also hosts punk and amateur theatre.
Check the website before setting out – Kato can be
overrun with mall rats and goth teenagers.

Knaack

*Greifswalder Strasse 224, Prenzlauer Berg
(concerts 442 7061/club 442 7060/www.knaack-
berlin.de). S8, S41, S42, S85 Greifswalder Strasse.*
Open *Bar* 6pm-late daily. *Club* 8pm-late Wed;
9pm-late Fri, Sat. **Admission** *Club* €1; €5 after
11pm. *Concerts* free-€20. **No credit cards.**
Map p319 Q4.
Follow the Rammstein-ish bar to the back, enter a
narrow hallway and you'll fetch up in a small, dark
club that presents an eclectic array of excellent
acts, from the Rapture to RA The Rugged Man to
Michael Hurley. Knaack also hosts free local band
nights. An upstairs disco provides a little refuge
from rowdy audiences.

Kulturbrauerei

*Schönhauser Allee 35, Prenzlauer Berg (443 150/
www.kesselhaus-berlin.de). U2 Eberswalder Strasse.*
Open *Box office* noon-6pm Mon-Wed, Sun; noon-
8pm Thur-Sat. **Admission** €5-€22. **No credit
cards. Map** p318/p326 O3.
With its assortment of venues, outdoor bars and barbecues, this enormous former brewery can resemble
a cross between a medieval fairground and a school
disco. The three operations linked to the
Kulturbrauerei proper (unlike nbi; *see right*) are
Maschinehaus, Palais and, the largest, Kesselhaus,
where the biggest draws are its reggae concerts. Jazz
and German acts also feature.

Lido

*Cuvrystrasse 7, Kreuzberg (6956 6840/tickets 6110
1313/www.lido-berlin.de). U1 Schlesisches Tor.* **Open**
8pm-late Wed-Sat. **Admission** varies. **No credit
cards. Map** p324 R9.
Built as a cinema in 1951, Lido recently became
Kreuzberg's premier indie-rock and late night dance
party venue. Its excellent outdoor area and feelgood
vibe make it especially popular in summer.

Magnet

*Greifswalder Strasse 212-213, Prenzlauer Berg
(4400 8140/www.magnet-club.de). S8, S41, S42,
S85 Greifswalder Strasse/tram M4.* **Open** 8pm-
late daily. **Admission** €2-€15. **No credit cards.**
Map p319/p328 Q4.
The former jazz club has become one of the biggest
bookers for the kind of up-and-coming indie bands
featured in the *NME* – catch them here before they
hit the stadium circuit. Renovations a while back
improved the sight lines, but it can still be difficult
to see anything when the place fills up.

Maria am Ostbahnhof

*An der Schillingbrücke, Friedrichshain (2123 8190/
www.clubmaria.de). S3, S5, S7, S9, S75 Ostbahnhof.*
Open 8pm-late daily. **Admission** €8-€15. **No
credit cards. Map** p323 Q7.
The premier venue for hipper live acts not quite
ready for Columbiahalle also hosts dance nights
that, although drawing top-notch DJs, don't come off
very glam in Maria's concrete bunker environs. Yet
its stylish post-industrial design is one of its attractions, along with the labyrinth of lounges that swells
or shrinks according to the organisers' whim.

Mudd Club

*Grosse Hamburger Strasse 17, Mitte (4403 6299/
www.muddclub.de). S5, S7, S9, S75 Hackescher
Markt.* **Open** varies. **Admission** varies. **No credit
cards. Map** p319/p326 N5.
NYC Mudd Club founder Steve Mass has rebirthed
his venture in a brick-lined Berlin basement that
resounds to Russendisko rather than No Wave.
Indeed, Mudd self-consciously attempts to ape the
popular Kaffee Burger, hiring DJs with moustaches
and stocking Russian beer. Booking favours lovable
outsiders such as Mark Lanegan or the Dirty Three.

nbi

*Kulturbrauerei, Schönhauser Allee 36, Prenzlauer
Berg (6730 4457/www.neueberlinerinitiative.de).
U2 Eberswalder Strasse.* **Admission** varies. **No credit cards. Map**
p318/p326 O3.
Now at the Kulturbrauerei, the latest home for this
electro club pioneer is a pink box with scattered furniture in the current *Wohnzimmer* style and an
excellent sound system. Labels and promoters such
as Monika and RepeatRepeat take over several
nights a month, encouraging surprise visits by the
likes of Einstürzende Neubauten. The space doesn't
lend itself to dancing, but its programmes remain
interesting, if less electronics-orientated. Sometimes
there's ping-pong.

Oxident Bar

*Frankfurter Allee 53, Friedrichshain (4862 4246/
www.oxident.de). U5 Samariterstrasse.* **Open** 8pm-
late daily. **Admission** €3-€8. **No credit cards.**
Map p324 T7.
The cosy interiors of Oxident host everything from
rock and pop to choral and even polka, while the
rooftop terrace and beer garden also screen matinée
movies and put on DJs. Musicians are encouraged
to participate in occasional after-show jam sessions.

Passionskirche

*Marheinekeplatz 1-2, Kreuzberg (tickets 6959 3624/
6940 1241/www.akanthus.de). U7 Gneisenaustrasse.*
Open varies. **Admission** varies. **No credit cards.**
Map p323 N10.
The likes of Beck, Ryan Adams and Marc Almond
have graced the stage of this deconsecrated church
– the best place to hear artists whose amplifiers don't
go past 4. But get there early, as it's the only church
in Berlin whose pews regularly overflow.

SO36

Oranienstrasse 190, Kreuzberg (tickets 6110 1313/ 6140 1306/www.so36.de). U1, U8 Kottbusser Tor. **Open** 9pm-late daily. *Box office* noon-4pm daily. **Admission** €3-€20. **No credit cards.** **Map** p323 P9.

Berlin's legendary punk club continues to present the heaviest alternative rock, from Bolt Thrower to Killing Joke, as well as pop-rap crossover with attitude from the likes of the Streets. Plus reggae nights, gay parties (*see p222*) and more.

Tempodrom

Möckernstrasse 10, Kreuzberg (747 370/tickets 6953 3885/www.tempodrom.de). S1, S2, S25 Anhalter Bahnhof, U7 Möckernbrücke. **Open** *Box office* noon-6.30pm Mon-Fri; 11am-2pm Sat. **Admission** varies. **No credit cards. Map** p322 L9.

Descendant of the legendary circus tent venue that was pitched in various West Berlin locations, this permanent space in tented form provides a beautiful setting for acts such as Sigur Rós, Pet Shop Boys and Emmylou Harris to perform. Plus there are sports events, comedy, musicals, classical concerts and the Liquidrom.

Volksbühne/Roter Salon

Rosa-Luxemburg-Platz, Mitte (2406 5806/ tickets 240 6577/www.roter-salon.de). U2 Rosa-Luxemburg-Platz. **Open** *Box office* noon-6pm Fri. **Admission** €5-€8. **No credit cards. Map** p319/p326 O5.

Two or three times a month, East Berlin's leading avant-garde theatre presents art music by the likes of Animal Collective and Brazilian dada songster Tom Zé. And sometimes it even turns over its woodpanelled stage to such curator-friendly DJs as Aphex Twin. The same complex contains the hospitable Roter Salon, where you can hear a broad array of DJs and indie acts.

Wabe

Danziger Strasse 101, Prenzlauer Berg (902 953 850/www.wabe-berlin.de). S8, S41, S42, S85 Greifswalder Strasse. **Open** varies. **Admission** varies. **No credit cards. Map** p319 Q3.

A DDR-era community centre in Ernst-Thälmann-Park, Wabe's octagonal space encourages young local groups with 'battle of the bands' contests and MTV co-presentations.

Wild at Heart

Wiener Strasse 20, Kreuzberg (611 9231/www. wildatheartberlin.de). U1 Görlitzer Bahnhof. **Open** 8pm-late daily. **Admission** €3-€12. **No credit cards. Map** p323 Q9.

The only thing possibly louder than the music here are the trinkets scatter-blasted across the walls. Wild at Heart imports artists and DJs from all over Europe to satisfy its enthusiastic tattooed rock, punk, rockabilly and ska regulars. It also has a jukebox to help you down one last shot of whiskey at daybreak while you ponder why your shirt is the only one with sleeves.

World

From indie pop to Brazilian acoustic, Klezmer remix to oriental crossover, the city's palette of worldbeat offerings seems to be simultaneously shrinking and expanding – and as of 1 January 2009, the city's world music station, Radio Multikulti, will no longer be broadcasting. Star performers like Seu Jorge might have made fewer trips to Berlin in 2007, but a profusion of hybrid acts fills the calendar with dizzying diversity. Late spring brings the **Karnival der Kulturen** (*see p197*), a four-day festival of multiculturalism. World music artists also play at the Kesselhaus or Maschinehaus in the **Kulturbrauerei** complex (*see p237*).

Haus der Kulturen der Welt

John-Foster-Dulles Allee 10, Tiergarten (3978 7175/www.hkw.de). S5, S7, S9, S75 Bellevue. **Open** *Box office* 10am-9pm Tue-Sun. **Admission** varies. **No credit cards. Map** p318 K6.

Berlin's largest world music venue is a sort of global cultural centre, housing several auditoriums and exhibition spaces devoted to themed events.

Havanna

Hauptstrasse 30, Schöneberg (784 8565/www. havanna-berlin.de). U7 Eisenacher Strasse. **Open** 9pm-late Wed; 10pm-late Fri, Sat. **Admission** €2.50 Wed; €6.50 Fri; €7 Sat. **No credit cards. Map** p322 J11.

Three dancefloors with salsa, merengue and R&B. It's a popular place with expat South Americans and Cubans. An hour before opening you can pick up a few steps at a salsa class for €4.

El Sur Bar

Pohlstrasse 73, Wilmersdorf (2535 8888/www.el-sur-bar.de). U1 Kurfurstenstrasse. **Open** 7pm-late Mon-Sat. **Admission** free. **No credit cards. Map** p322 K9.

The upbeat El Sur Bar offers Iberian culture à la carte – a decent range of tropical cocktails, tapas and great wines are spiced up with live Spanish and Portuguese sounds.

Werkstatt der Kulturen

Wissmannstrasse 32, Neukölln (609 7700/www. werkstatt-der-kulturen.de). U7, U8 Hermannplatz. **Open** *Box office* 9am-5pm Mon; 9am-6pm Tue-Fri. **Admission** varies. **No credit cards. Map** p323 P11.

This intimate venue presents trad ethnic music or local fusions blending jazz, trance or folk elements.

Jazz

Berlin has never been big on genre purity – and after a post-Wall upswing in activity, many of the city's better jazz folk have since joined forces with their experimental or electronic comrades. A rule of thumb for clubs here is jazz+blues = mouldy; jazz+weird = fun.

Musicians like saxophone colossus Peter Brötzmann and Australian drummer Tony Buck of the Necks make their homes here. November boasts two fantastic overlapping jazz festivals: the larger **Berlin JazzFest** (*see p200*), and the free-rooted **Total Music Meeting** (www.fmp-online.de), which in 2008 celebrated its 40th anniversary. Rather than sticking to the jazz clubs, it's worth searching out galleries, artist-run venues, social clubs and cultural houses. The famed DDR-era **JazzKeller Treptow** (www.jazzkeller69.de) continues to promote interesting shows in a variety of small spaces. Berlin also features Germany's only 24-hour jazz radio (101.9 FM).

A-Trane
Bleibtreustrasse 1, Charlottenburg (313 2550/www. a-trane.de). S5, S7, S9, S75 Savignyplatz. **Open** 9pm-2am Mon-Thur, Sun; 9pm-late Fri, Sat. *Performances* 10pm daily. **Admission** free-€12. **Credit** AmEx, DC, MC. **Map** p321/p328 E8.
A-Trane usually lands at least one top-flight act a month for an extended run. Free entry on Mondays.

B-Flat
Rosenthaler Strasse 13, Mitte (283 3123/www.b-flat-berlin.de). U8 Rosenthaler Platz. **Open** from 9pm daily. **Admission** €4-€12; €4-€8 reductions. **No credit cards. Map** p319/p326 N5.
Maintaining a large piano bar feel, B-Flat pulls in a decent local hero once in a while, but its strongest nights tend to feature singers. Free Wednesday night jam sessions from 9pm.

Quasimodo
Kantstrasse 12A, Charlottenburg (312 8086/www. quasimodo.de). U2, U9, S5, S7, S9, S75 Zoologischer Garten. **Open** *Performances* 10pm Tue-Sun (doors open 1hr before start of performance). **Admission** €5-€25. **No credit cards. Map** p321/p328 F8.
Privileging the 'jazzy' over jazz, this basement spot appears close to irrevocably severing connections to the music for which it was once noted. Yet it still promotes some good homegrown or international acts, such as heroic singer Terry Callier.

Tränenpalast
Reichstagsufer 17, Mitte (206 100/tickets 2061 0011/www.traenenpalast.de). U6, S1, S2, S5, S7, S9, S75 Friedrichstrasse. **Open** *Box office* 6pm-start of performance. **Admission** varies. **No credit cards. Map** p319/p327 M6.
Translating as 'Palace of Tears', this roomy, fascinating location used to be the heavily patrolled DDR border crossing for people entering and leaving East Berlin. It mostly books comedy and cabaret, but sometimes hosts jazz greats such as Pharoah Sanders, Don Byron and Nils Petter Molvaer.

Yorckschlösschen
Yorckstrasse 15, Kreuzberg (215 8070/www. yorckschloesschen.de). U6, U7 Mehringdamm. **Open** 9am-3am Mon-Thur, Sun; 9am-4am Fri, Sat. **Admission** free. **Credit** AmEx, DC, MC, V. **Map** p322 L10.
A century-old *Eck-Kneipe*, Yorckschlösschen offers a faintly ridiculous mix of German Dixieland and vintage beat music. But in its old-world environment, it can get pretty groovy (after a few *Weizenbiers*).

Arts & Entertainment

Jump aboard the **A-Trane** for acts such as Quadro Nuevo.

Nightlife

Nocturnal activities of every nature keep Berlin's feet on the dancefloor.

Culturally speaking, anything goes at **Kaffe Burger**. *See p242.*

There are few cities where the myth of the place is so closely tied to nightlife. Once you've cleared Hitler and the Wall out of the way, most people's clearest image of Berlin is Sally Bowles in some legendarily decadent nightclub. And the good news is, it's all true. Sort of. Every taste is catered for here, all night long, in every kind of venue, from desperate dives in temporary locations to swanky premises where mirror balls make the world go round. There's even a KitKat Club (currently domiciled at Sage), that makes its celluloid namesake seem staid indeed. And while Berlin might no longer star Liza Minnelli, there's certainly no shortage of young Americans imagining that they're in some kind of movie.

As the cityscape continues to change, so the landscape of the night is built on shifting sands. There have been many changes since the last edition of *Time Out Berlin*. Most notably, the incredibly popular Rio managed to go out of business – an unexpected closure that left many partygoers scratching their heads and wondering what to do with their weekends. Yet its demise opened the door for a raft of new locations. Picknick picked up the image-conscious end of the old Rio spectrum while Tape nabbed the more devil-may-care side. The ramshackle Scala is also establishing a reputation as an ultra-cool place to party. Cookies and Tresor have been re-conceptualised and relocated, Bassy has moved house, and White Trash probably now counts more as a restaurant than a club.

Berghain surely needs no more purple prose; it's easy enough to find and the best advice is just to dive in and formulate your own opinion of the city's highest-profile club. But at least it's not content to rest on its reputation. At press time a whole new sound system was being installed – and we thought the old one was pretty damn good. Here techno still rules, and electronic beats of one kind or another remain the dominant sound of the city, but somewhere or other you can find any type of music you like.

Despite the fact that many Berliners seem to coast through the week doing nothing more stressful than wondering where to have brunch, they are madly possessive of their weekends and make the absolute most of them. It's not unusual to head off to a party on Friday night and stumble into bed at some point on Sunday afternoon. While this approach is pretty hardcore, the general attitude to clubbing is incredibly laid-back; no dressing up, no forward planning, no bar crawling. Berliners let themselves go with the flow. It's usual not to head to clubs until 1am at the earliest, so don't make the mistake of hitting the bars at 7pm – not only will there be next to no one there, but you'll more than likely be too wasted by midnight to last the distance.

Just remember that nothing stays the same for very long. These listings were as correct as we could make them at the time of going to press. But before setting out, it's worth checking that places are still in business.

Mitte

Acud

Veteranenstrasse 21 (449 1067/www.acud.de). U8 Rosenthaler Platz or S1, S2, S25 Nordbahnhof/ bus N8, N84. **Open** varies. **Admission** varies. **No credit cards. Map** p319/p326 N4.
A massive complex, containing a cinema, theatre and gallery, operated by a friendly Berlin arts collective. There's also a party floor with a playlist mostly devoted to reggae, breakbeat and drum 'n' bass; the dingy bar is a popular spot for the city's stoners. The cinema programme is interesting, consisting mostly of independent and low-budget films. There's something going on here most nights of the week, and start times and prices vary accordingly. Best to check the website for details first.

Bang Bang

Neue Promenade 10 (6040 5310/www.bangbang-club.de). U8 Weinmeisterstrasse or S5, S9, S75 Hackescher Markt/bus N5. **Open** 9pm-late Tue-Sat. **Admission** €3-€8. **No credit cards. Map** p319/p326 N5.
Bang Bang's decidedly retro decor – all glitter balls and monochrome blow-ups of '60s girl groups – is a little misleading. If you expected this small venue tucked away under the S-Bahn at Hackescher Markt to be all Supremes cover bands and cutesy doo-wop then think again; it's made a name for itself as proud home to weekly indie disco Death By Pop, which has seen lines stretch around the block for guest DJ sets by the likes of Bloc Party and the Klaxons. Berlin indie stalwarts Karrera Klub do give a nod to the past, though – their new weekly party Brit Pop and Beyond is pretty self-explanatory. The occasional live act pops up here too; think Winter Kids and Eight Legs.

Bohannon

Dircksenstrasse 40 (6950 5287/www.bohannon.de). U2, U5, U8, S5, S7, S9, S75 Alexanderplatz or S5, S7, S9, S75 Hackescher Markt/bus N2, N5, N8, N65, N84/tram M4, M5. **Open** 10pm-late Mon, Thur-Sat. **Admission** €7-€10. **No credit cards. Map** p319/p326 O5.
The club's name, a nod to funk legend Hamilton Bohannon, indicates its driving musical principle. Billed as offering 'soulful electronic clubbing', this basement location features two dancefloors and regular sets by the likes of dancehall DJ Barney Millah and excellent Friday night soul parties.

C-Base

Rungestrasse 20 (2859 9300/www.c-base.org). U8, S5, S9, S7, S75 Jannowitzbrücke/bus N40, N65. **Open** varies; usually from 11pm. **Admission** free-€10. **No credit cards. Map** p323 P7.
Taking a walk down Rungestrasse might feel like you're going where no man has gone before, but stick with it: at the end of the street is Berlin's very own spaceship, the arts exhibition space C-Base. This sprawling venue appears to have been constructed by throwing a collection of rooms and industrial rubbish up into the air and seeing where it all lands. It's a quirky mix of tumbledown ceilings, exposed wires, flickering strip lights and retro computer consoles. The spacious upstairs dancefloor opens out onto a riverside drinking area, while the spiral staircase takes you down to the lower deck where there is a smaller club room and chill-out area. Check the website before beaming down, though, as the club was fighting an eviction threat at press time.

Clärchen's Ballhaus

Auguststrasse 24, Mitte (282 9295/www.ballhaus. de), S1, S2 Oranienburger Strasse. **Open** 10am-late daily. **No credit cards. Map** p319/p326 N5. *See p242* **Having a ball.**

Crush

Behrenstrasse 55 (280 8806/www.mycrush.de. Friedrichstrasse 164. U6, S1, S2, S5, S7, S75, S9 Friedrichstrasse. **Open** 11pm-late Tue, Thur, Sat. **Admission** varies. **No credit cards. Map** p318 M6.
This blank canvas of a venue hosts various club nights, including the super-hot Cookies on Tuesdays and Thursdays (accessed via a different entrance at Friedrichstrasse 164; www.cookies-berlin.de), which has been attracting the Beautiful People for years. Aimed squarely at what they call Profiausgänger ('professional clubbers'), Cookies tests the mettle of the most hardcore party people. A catacomb of concrete passageways eventually opens up onto a vast concert room resembling a cross between a school gym and a bingo hall, complete with huge, ostentatious chandeliers. A somewhat understaffed island bar serves all manner of drinks – eventually.

Music can vary but anything with a thumping bass and an electro slant goes. Weekends are occasionally worth a look, with a more diverse selection of parties; Fashion Week after-shows, art exhibitions, hip hop nights… anything goes. The interior is usually completely transformed depending on the theme of the night.

Golden Gate

Dircksenstrasse 77-78 (no phone/www.goldengate-berlin.de). S5, S7, S75, S9 Hackescher Markt. **Open** from 11pm Fri, Sat. **Admission** €5-€8. **No credit cards.** Map p319/p326 O5.

Housed in a ramshackle former bike shop beneath the S-Bahn Arches, Golden Gate's popularity is enjoying something of an upswing these days. Once home to a rather hit-and-miss music policy, with the occasional live show, this grimy little club has now settled firmly on a series of all-weekend techno parties.

The venue is almost a scaled-down version of Berghain (and quite possibly an overflow venue for people turned away from that techno mecca), and boasts a refreshingly intimate atmosphere. People either jam into the small dancefloor room or lounge around the bar or the upstairs toilets. It's an anything goes location with a chilled-out crowd. The backyard garden is nice in summer.

Kaffee Burger

Torstrasse 60 (2804 6495/www.kaffeeburger.de). U2 Rosa-Luxemburg-Platz/bus N2/tram N54. **Open** 8pm-late Mon-Thur; 9pm-late Fri, Sat; 7pm-late Sun. **Admission** €3-€5. **No credit cards.** Map p319/p326 N5.

Best known as home of the popular twice-monthly Russendisko, Kaffee Burger's programme runs the cultural gamut. Early evenings may see readings, lectures, film screenings or live music. Later on, local and expat DJs play anything from old-school country to something called 'sexabilly', as well as Balkan beats, indie-rock, soul and Britpop fare. The club's

Having a ball

For nearly 20 years, Berlin has been famous for its substance-fuelled, all-night techno parties in cavernous raw spaces. But in the heart of Mitte, a decidedly old-school venue is giving the rave a run for its money in terms of popularity and downright fun.

And it's actually nothing new. In 2005, **Clärchen's Ballhaus** (for listings, *see p241*), a dancehall frequented by nimble Berliners since Clara Haberman established it in 1913, reopened after nearly a year of closed doors. Under new management – the rakish duo of David Regehr and Christian Schulz – Clärchen's is more popular than ever.

'People come here to find the love of their lives,' Schulz has said. These people can range from twentysomething hipsters to 75-year-old Ballhaus veterans to celebrities (such as German actress Heike Makatsch, or even Charlotte Rampling) who've stopped in to cut the rug during Berlin film fest parties. Best of all, as the night wears on, these drastically divergent demographics start intermixing. It's not unusual to see a geriatric Fred Astaire teaching a young pink-haired artist how to tango or foxtrot.

The Ballhaus actually has two ballrooms. The vast ground-floor space is lined with silver tinsel streamers. Its spacious dancefloor is ringed by wooden tables bedecked with white tablecloths and candles, while a huge disco ball spins overhead. But upstairs is another room that never fails to elicit gasps of awe from first-time visitors. Smaller but with high ceilings and a fin-de-siècle vibe, the chandeliered Mirror

Salon has huge cracked mirrors, ornate moulding work and candlelight that transport guests straight back to the 1920s.

In fact, very little has really changed since then. When Clärchen's turned over to its new owners, Berliners who'd loved to dance here for decades feared that it would fall prey to the homogenisation that 'renovation' in Berlin often brings. But Schulz and Regehr left the interior almost exactly as it was – both upstairs and downstairs are vintage details, fixtures, even wallpaper... as well as a heady smell of history that's hard to pin down. Is it all DDR, or is it the Weimar era?

Most regulars don't care (after all, more than a few were around during the DDR era). They're here to tango on Tuesdays, learn to swing on Wednesdays, attend the 'pasta opera' nights in the Mirror Salon, or yes, find the love of their lives on weekend nights. Some initially come to have an inexpensive oven-baked pizza inside or in the beautiful front garden. But it never fails: sometime after midnight, both ballrooms teem with all types in a free-for-all that begins with live music and then segues into Michael Jackson, the Beach Boys, old German schlager music, or all of the above. It's more cheesy than chic, but that's part of the charm.

The door policy at the Ballhaus is one of the most democratic in the city. But don't even think about entering on a busy night without checking in your coat, old-school style, with Gunter. The 74-year-old has manned his Garderobe for the better part of 40 years, and has seen it all.

decor has been left intact from GDR days, and the relatively bright lighting facilitates interaction with strangers. To go with the eclectic programming, Burger draws a mixed, international crowd, and drinks are cheap. *Photo p240.*

Picknick

Dorotheenstrasse 90 (no phone/www.myspace.com/ picknickberlin). U6, S1, S2, S5, S7, S75, S9 Friedrichstrasse. **Open** 11pm-late Fri-Sun. **Admission** €6-€8. **No credit cards**. **Map** p318/p327 L6.

Picking up the über-cool baton where Rio dropped it, Picknick was an over-hyped sensation for about five minutes before everyone got over their Rio fixation and realised that it was in fact rubbish. The club itself is split over two floors, neither of which are big enough to swing a cat. In fact most cats would be more discerning than to venture among the depressing gaggle of pretentious, po-faced miseries who hang out listening to the admittedly interesting mixture of fuzzy electro and knowingly kitsch pop soundtrack. An interesting experience for visitors to see that even Berlin sometimes gets it all completely wrong.

Rodeo

Auguststrasse 5A (0163 162 0168/www.rodeo-berlin.de). U6 Oranienburger Tor or S1, S2, S25 Oranienburger Strasse/tram M1. **Open** 7pm-late Fri, Sat. **Admission** €6-€8. **No credit cards**. **Map** p318/p326 M5.

Rodeo is one of Berlin's most stylish venues. Opening around 7pm, the church-like main room, with its stunning domed ceiling and arched windows, acts as a restaurant where guests are seated at long communal tables. Once the meals are over, the tables are cleared away and the DJ takes to the decks. The large hall quickly fills to capacity and while the room's acoustic qualities mean that even the slightest whisper tends to reverberate there are plenty of smaller adjoining spaces to enjoy a quiet drink and a chat. Music policy tends to be electro/rock based.

Sage Club

Köpenicker Strasse 76 (278 9830/www.sage-club.de). U8 Heinrich-Heine-Strasse/bus N8. **Open** 10pm-late Thur; 11pm-late Fri-Sun. **Admission** €6-€12. **No credit cards**. **Map** p323 O7.

A labyrinthine complex of half a dozen or so dancefloors accessed via the north-side entrance to Heinrich-Heine-Strasse U-Bahn station make up Sage Club, which caters to a relatively young, rock-oriented crowd. In addition to Berlin labels occasionally holding release parties here, each night of the week tends to be themed, with Thursday's rock night drawing the biggest crowd. During the week it's a chilled-out, unpretentious place where skinny jeans and leather jackets tend to be the uniform of choice. At weekends you'll have better luck with some fetish gear, as Sage is the current home of the notorious KitKat Club (www.kitkatclub.de).

Tresor.30. *See p244.*

Scala

Friedrichstrasse 112A (0176 8305 3526/
www.myspace.com/scalaberlin). U6 Oranienburger
Tor, S1, S2, S5, S7, S75, S9 Friedrichstrasse or
S1, S2, S25 Oranienburgerstrasse. **Open** 11pm-
late Sat. **Admission** €8. **No credit cards.**
Map p318/p326 M5.

Curious to know what became of those crazy Rio
guys? Well, they've taken up residence in a former
townhouse in the centre of the city. While it doesn't
quite have the same status as its legendary predecessor, Scala does have some of its qualities: to be
specific, a sexy musical line-up and a shambolic, DIY
approach to interior design.

The coolest kids in town can be found here most
weekends, freaking out to a whole host of electro-
themed parties. It's no surprise that hot fashion and
record labels use this location for after-show events.
There's a large dancefloor with a gloomy raised seating area and an assortment of smaller connecting
rooms upstairs. Expect long queues to get to one of
the few toilets.

Sophienclub

Sophienstrasse 6 (282 4552/www.sophienclub-berlin.
de). U8 Weinmeisterstrasse or S5, S7, S9, S75
Hackescher Markt/bus N2, N8, N54, N92/tram
M4, M5. **Open** 10pm-late Tue-Sat. **Admission**
free-€5 Tue-Fri; free-€8 Sat. **No credit cards.**
Map p319/p326 N5.

A survivor from the old East, this space has a reputation for ignoring musical trends. If you are looking for 'ladies night' or what the German's call
'Blackclassics', this is your place. It's not a complete
desert though: the boys from Karrera Klub are now
doing their indie/Britpop thing here on Tuesdays.
Other nights feature disco, house and R&B. All told,
it's good for people looking to dance but not concerned about being fashionable.

Tresor.30

Köpenicker Strasse 70 (no phone/www.tresorberlin.
de). U8 Heinrich-Heine-Strasse or S5, S9, S7,
S75 Jannowitzbrücke. **Open** 11pm-late Wed, Fri,
Sat. **Admission** €5-€12. **No credit cards.**
Map p323 P7.

After a hiatus of some years, it's obvious that this
new incarnation of the original Berlin techno club
was going to take some time to find its feet. Housed
in what was formerly the main central-heating
power station for East Berlin, the colossal location
is breathtaking, and since only a tiny portion of its
28,000sq m (300,000 sq ft) is in use, there's plenty of
room for future development in what is intended to
be not just a club, but a huge centre of alternative
art and culture.

The experience of the basement floor is one you'll
not forget; a black hole occasionally punctuated by
flashing strobes with some of the loudest, hardest
techno you are likely to hear. But with more changes
in the pipeline, only time will tell if Tresor's reinven-
tion proves to be worthy of its near-legendary status on the local scene. *Photo p243.*

Week12End Club

Alexanderplatz 5, 12th floor (2463 1676/
www.week-end-berlin.de). U2, U5, U8 or S5, S7,
S75, S9 Alexanderplatz/bus N5, N8, N65, N92.
Open 11pm-late Thur-Sat. **Admission** €6-€10.
No credit cards. Map p319/p328 O5.

Situated right at the focus point of former East
Berlin, Week12End's home is way up at the top of
one of Alexanderplatz's many Communist-era tower
blocks. While the interior of the club itself is nothing impressive, the roof terrace is a big draw – a perfect summer location combining often excellent
music (2ManyDJs and DFA anyone?) with spectacular cityscape views. It should be awfully pretentious, but somehow it isn't.

White Trash Fast Food

Schönhauser Allee 6-7 (no phone/www.white
trashfastfood.com). U2 Rosa-Luxemburg-Platz/
Senefelderplatz/bus 240/tram M8. **Open** 4pm-late
daily. **Admission** varies. **No credit cards.**
Map p319/p326 O4.

White Trash Fast Food appears set on world domi-
nation, with multiple floors, a *Flintstones*-style cave
in the basement, nightly DJs, gutter-dwelling live
acts and above-average American cuisine (ham-
burgers go for a reasonable €5.50). The enormous
red-draped edifice is usually packed with drunken
expat patrons.

ZMF (ZurMoebelFabrik)

Brunnenstrasse 10 (no phone/www.zurmoebel
fabrik.de). U8 Rosenthaler Platz or S5, S9, S75
Hackescher Markt/tram M1. **Open** 10pm-6am
Fri, Sat. **Admission** €6-€8. **No credit cards.**
Map p319/p326 N4.

The initials stand for 'ZurMoebelFabrik', and a furniture factory is what this building originally
housed before this cosy club took over use of the
basement. It's operated by an arts collective and
while there's often a variety of cultural events taking place, the location is starting to make a name for
itself as a hot party spot. A bare-brick and concrete
dancefloor leads into a spacious lounge with
a liberal supply of comfy beaten-up sofas. A highlight at ZMF is the Neon Raiders party, a monthly
event with a solid queer following and a sexy, open-
minded crowd cutting up the dancefloor to an
impressive line-up of international DJs.

Prenzlauer Berg

Duncker

Dunckerstrasse 64 (445 9509/www.dunckerclub.de).
U2 Eberswalder Strasse or S8, S41, S42, S85
Prenzlauer Allee. **Open** 9pm-late Mon; 10pm-late
Tue, Thur, Sun; 11pm-late Fri, Sat. **Admission**
€1.50-€4; free Thur. **No credit cards.**
Map p319/p326 P2.

Duncker does have a reasonably varied line-up but
definitely operates within a very dark sphere. It's
perfectly located in a neo-Gothic church in a nondescript Prenzlauer Berg side street. While the tail

end of the week focuses mainly on new wave, dark wave and indie, it's the Monday night goth party which is the club's bread and butter. Surprisingly in a city the size of Berlin, venue catering for our friends in black are few and far between, making this a precious gem for fans of the genre.

Icon

Cantianstrasse 15 (4849 2878/www.iconberlin.de).
U2 Eberswalder Strasse/bus N2/tram M10.
Open 11pm-late Tue; 11.30pm-late Fri, Sat.
Admission €3-€10. **No credit cards.**
Map p319/p326 O2.

A tricky-to-locate entrance in the courtyard just north of the junction with Milastrasse leads to an interesting grace cascading down the levels into a long stone cellar. It's a well-ventilated little labyrinth, with an intense dancefloor space, imaginative lighting, good sound and a separate bar. Music here occasionally takes in techno, reggae and hip hop – and it appears to be expanding its tastes by hosting Kitsuné and Ed Banger artists – yet the fact remains that for fans of the genre this is Berlin's premier drum 'n' bass club. Best when the core crowd of locals is augmented by a wider audience for some special event, but this is not usually a spot for the in-crowd.

Roadrunner's Paradise

Saarbrückerstrasse 24 (4849 5755/www.roadrunners-paradise.de). U2 Senefelderplatz/bus N2. **Open** varies. **Admission** €5-€10. **No credit cards.**
Map p319/p326 O4.

Navigate your way through to the third courtyard of the former Koenigstadt brewery and you'll find Roadrunner's tucked away in the corner next to a motorcycle repair shop, a suitably greasy location for this butch venue. On offer is a tasty but irregular mixture of live shows and DJ sets, primarily focusing on garage, blues-rock, rockabilly and surf. The tiny stage may seem a little bit lost in the wide-open concert room but there's plenty of room to dance and the sound system is surprisingly up to scratch. Alternatively pull up a bar stool and marvel at the array of 1950s American kitsch while sinking a cold beer.

Friedrichshain

Berghain/Panorama Bar

Wriezener Karree (no phone/www.berghain.de).
S3, S5, S7, S75, S9 Ostbahnhof/bus N44.
Open 11pm-late Thur; 11pm-late Fri, Sat.
Admission €8-€12. **No credit cards.**
Map p324 R7

A strong contender for best club in the city, if not Europe; words can't really do the place justice. In basic terms, it's a techno club in a former power station, but it has to be experienced to be fully understood. Even non-fans of the genre fall head over heels in love with the relaxed atmosphere, interesting mix of eccentrics, well-thought-out design details, fantastic sound system and sexually liberal attitude.

Tip for newbies: Berghain's anything-goes approach extends only so far as what they don't see you doing. If you're searched at the door, an amnesty box gives you the opportunity to surrender anything illegal you may have before being cleared for entry. The club's reputation for a difficult and random door policy is not entirely undeserved. Panorama, with its smaller dancefloor and Wolfgang Tillmans artwork, is open all weekend; the more intense Berghain part of the venue, complete with darkrooms, is only open on Saturdays.

K17

Pettenkofer Strasse 17 (4208 9300/www.k17.de).
U5, S8, S9, S41, S42, S85 Frankfurter Allee/bus N5. **Open** 10pm-late Tue-Fri. **Admission** free-€15.
No credit cards. Map p325 U6.

Goth, EBM, industrial and metal are undead and well in this three-floor club. Parties have names such as Dark Friday and Schwarzer Donnerstag and the occasional live earaches feature hardcore, nü-metal and crossover bands. There's also a Dark Hostel within the same complex, offering goth-friendly accommodations.

Maria Am Ostbahnhof

An der Schillingbrücke/Stralauer Platz 33 (2123 8190/www.clubmaria.de). S3, S5, S7, S75, S9 Ostbahnhof/bus N44. **Open** 11pm-late Thur; midnight-late Fri, Sat. **Admission** €10. **No credit cards. Map** p323 Q7.

This stalwart of the Berlin club scene seems to have been struggling to hang onto its identity in recent years. Nights here can range from techno to rock to electro, with the occasional record launch or after party thrown into the mix. It's an all-too-confusing recipe and the absence of specific programming means it lacks a solid, regular crowd. The cavernous interior can look awfully lonely sometimes. Nevertheless, it has recently played host to concerts from big names acts such as CSS, Simian Mobile Disco and Alec Empire.

Neighbouring venue Josef is a nicer, more intimate venue and often acts as a VIP area during big parties at Maria. It's also home to new electro party series Cockaigne which has so far rocked crowds with special guests from Kitsuné.

Rosi's

Revalerstrasse 29 (no phone/www.rosis-berlin.de).
S3, S5, S7, S8, S9, S41, S42, S75, S85 Ostkreuz/bus N40, N44. **Open** 9pm-late Thur; 11pm-late Fri, Sat. **Admission** €5. **No credit cards.**
Map p324 T8.

If you were asked to think of the typical Berlin club then something like Rosi's would no doubt spring to mind. It's a tumbledown, DIY affair; all bare bricks and mismatched flea market furniture. The atmosphere is very relaxed and the club tends to attract a young, studenty crowd. Live acts are a regular feature, DJs mainly spin electro and rock, and Karrera Klub hosts parties from time to time. The beer garden is a popular hangout on summer nights.

Arts & Entertainment

Kreuzberg

103 Club
Falckensteinstrasse 47 (6951 5612/www.103club.de).
U1 Schlesisches Tor/bus N1, N65. **Open** 11.30pm-
late Fri, Sat. **Admission** €6-€10. **No credit cards.**
Map p324 R9.

This place has seen plenty of changes recently, the
result of which is a restructured events listing and
new interior layout. Now that this process of rein-
vention has come to an end, the club seems to have
settled on a solid programme of guest DJ sets (the
likes of Feadz, Phono, Digitalism, SMD) and the
occasional live show (artists as diverse as Sam
Sparro and Channel X). The subdued, predominantly red lighting, cosy corners, and generally laid-
back atmosphere make this is a worthy feature on
Berlin's clubbing landscape.

Festsaal Kreuzberg
Skalitzer Strasse 130 (6165 6003/www.festsaal-
kreuzberg.de). U1, U8 Kottbusser Tor. **Open** varies.
Admission varies. **No credit cards. Map** p324 P9.

Festsaal means 'ballroom' and this venue near
Kottbusser Tor has quite a refined edge despite the
shabbiness of the interior, reinforced by a regular
programme of literary and cultural events such as
readings and poetry slams. The big hall and good
sound system are often put to use for gigs or DJ sets.
A special highlight is provided by the two tiny cellar rooms – a great location for small but intense
electro parties such as DJ Emma Eclectic's You're
My Disco.

Lido
Cuvrystrasse 7 (6956 6840/www.lido-berlin.de). U1
Schlesisches Tor/bus M29, N1, N65. **Open** 10pm-
late Fri, Sat. **Admission** €6-€20. **No credit cards.**
Map p324 R9.

Lido is the HQ of famed Berlin indie-rocksters
Karrera Klub, who have been champions of new
music in the city for over ten years now. This former theatre is a suitably spacious location to present
upcoming new live acts and so far artists such as
Raveonettes, MGMT, Shitdisco and You Say Party!
We Say Die! have all graced the stage. Lido has one
of the best sound systems in the city and it has been
put to superb use by MSTRKRFT. What was once
a rear courtyard now has a canopy so even in
inclement weather you can take a break from the
heat of the dancefloor.

Watergate
Falckensteinstrasse 49 (6128 0396/www.water-gate.
de). U1 Schlesisches Tor/bus M29, N1, N65. **Open**
11pm-late Wed, Fri, Sat; check website for occasional
Tue, Thur events. **Admission** €6-€10. **No credit**
cards. Map p324 R9.

This two-floor, riverside club has a slick feel, a great
view of the Spree and a better-than-average sound
system. The two best-known features here are the
panorama windows above the river and the flash,
ceiling-mounted lighting display. Both floors are
open on weekends and usually host two different
sets of acts. Music policy is in the electro, house and
minimal techno area – Ricardo Villalobos and Richie
Hawtin often play – although artists such as Booka
Shade and Digitalism occasionally appear.

Tiergarten

2BE
Heidestrasse 73 (8906 8410/www.2be-club.de). S5,
S7, S9, S75 Hauptbahnhof. **Open** 11pm-late Fri, Sat.
Admission €7.50-€8; women free 11pm-midnight
Sat. **No credit cards. Map** p318 K5.

The roster of in-house DJs at 2BE tends to focus
mainly on hip hop, with the odd reggae and dancehall tune thrown in for good measure, and there's
also usually a live act or two playing each month.
Big name DJs from the genre such as Grandmaster
Flash and LTJ Bukem have been known to put in an
appearance. It's a spacious location with an outside
seating area and several bars. The crowd tends to
be young and enthusiastic if not verging ever so
slightly on chav.

Adagio
Marlene-Dietrich-Platz 1 (2592 9550/www.adagio.
de). U2, S1, S2, S26 Potsdamer Platz/bus N2, N5,
N19. **Open** 7pm-2am Wed, Thur, Sun; 10pm-4am
Fri; 10pm-5am Sat. **Admission** €5-€10. **Credit**
AmEx, V. **Map** p322 K8.

Spin-off of a swanky Zurich disco, its 'medieval'
decor and Renaissance-style frescos are jarringly at
odds with the Renzo Piano-designed theatre whose
basement it occupies. Pricey drinks, abundant mem-
bers-only areas and a music policy of disco, polite
house and oldies cater to fortysomething tourists
and afterwork crowds willing to shell out for an illu-
sion of exclusivity. There's a dress code (no jeans or
sports shoes).

Tape
Heidestrasse 14 (2848 4873/www.tapeberlin.de).
S5, S7, S9, S75 Hauptbahnhof/bus N20, N40.
Open 11pm-late Fri, Sat. **Admission** €8-€20.
No credit cards. Map p318 K4.

You've really got to want to go to Tape. Its location
on a rather desolate industrial estate means it's not
the kind of venue you'd just happen across. That
said, this cavernous warehouse venue has plenty to
make the tiresome trip worthwhile. The huge main
hall has a superior sound and lighting rig making it
the club of choice for multi-media live shows, while
things get sweaty on the smaller, neighbouring
dancefloor. Expect the likes of Modeselektor,
Whomadewho and Santogold to turn up here.

Charlottenburg

Abraxas
Kantstrasse 134 (312 9493). U7 Wilmersdorfer
Strasse or S5, S7, S9, S75 Savignyplatz/bus N49.
Open 10pm-late Tue-Sat. **Admission** free Tue-
Thur; €5 Fri, Sat. **Credit** V. **Map** p320 D8.

Minimal techno and swingin' jazz in the same venue? It's a **Watergate** scandal!

A dusky, relaxed disco where you don't have to dress up to get in and where academics, social workers, bank clerks and midwives populate the floor. Flirtation rules. Dance to funk, soul, Latino and jazz.

Other districts

Glashaus

Eichenstrasse 4, Treptow (5332 0340/www.arena-berlin.de). U1 Schlesisches Tor or S8, S9, S41, S42, S85 Treptower Park/bus 147, 265, N65. **Open** 10pm-late Sat. **Admission** varies. **No credit cards. Map** p324 S9.

Part of the riverside Arena complex (*see p235*). The bare brick walls and sparse lighting of this dingy and intimate location make it look more like a dungeon than a club. It has an adequate sound system

for its size, but does tend to get a bit sleazy towards the early hours. The place also transforms into a theatre, while there are club-type events on the Hoppetosse and Badeschiff, both moored just nearby on the Spree.

Insel

Alt-Treptow 6, Treptow (5360 8020/www.insel-berlin.net). S8, S9, S85 Plänterwald/bus N65. **Open** 7pm-1am Wed; 10pm-late Fri, Sat. **Admission** free Wed; €5-€10 Fri, Sat. **No credit cards.**

Out of the way, but brilliant – like a miniature castle on a tiny Spree island, with several levels and a top-floor balcony. Once a communist youth club, now a live venue/colourful club – with lots of neon and ultra-violet, crusties and hippies, techno and hip hop, punk and metal. Great in summer.

Performing Arts

A world-class classical music scene and some superlative dance talent have helped put Berlin in the spotlight.

Music: Classical & Opera

No city in the world can compete with Berlin when it comes to sheer number of orchestras and opera houses. The former include the Berliner Philharmoniker, Deutsches Symphonie-Orchester Berlin, Rundfunk-Sinfonieorchester Berlin and Konzerthausorchester Berlin, while the latter comprises the Deutsche Oper, Staatsoper Unter den Linden and the Komische Oper. And that's before you get to the smaller companies, not to mention venues.

This cultural richness is not only a legacy of the city's long artistic heritage but also of its Cold War division. After Reunification there was twice the amount of everything, and, as a result, Berlin now boasts enough classical music for any two (maybe three) cities. It's not just quantity, but quality too: the Berlin Philharmonic is arguably the world's finest symphony orchestra, and there are several top-notch performances of one kind or another to choose from here virtually every night of the year.

When it comes to funding, just how much classical music Berlin can afford has become a controversial issue, and during the early years of the millennium many institutions faced belt-tightening subsidy cuts. But the situation for the arts has stabilised somewhat – perhaps partly due to Berlin Mayor Klaus Wowereit taking over the post of culture senator as an additional responsibility, and making music and the arts a central plank of his politics.

The three opera houses are now incorporated into one foundation, the Opernstiftung, headed by Stefan Rosinski, but co-ordination of their programmes is still an issue, as is their simultaneous closure during summer, when visitors fill Berlin. On the plus side, rumours about the imminent shuttering of one of the houses seem to have finally faded away.

A FIGHT AT THE OPERA

The **Deutsche Oper** is still recovering from the death of former long-time intendant Götz Friedrich in 2000. Kirsten Harms, who took over the role in 2004, has been struggling to provide the house with a distinct artistic profile. Luck hasn't always been on her side, however. In summer 2007, the controversy following Danish cartoons about Mohammed brought the international spotlight on to the Deutsche Oper's *Idomeneo*, a production unremarkable save for the appearance of a head of the Prophet. In an unfolding scandal of operatic proportions, the production was cancelled; however, after a national and international protest, *Idomeneo* eventually re-appeared on the programme. This was followed by the unexplained disappearance of the head of Mohammed, the production's essential prop. In the end, several performances took place under unprecedented security measures and international media scrutiny. As if that wasn't enough, the appointment of Italian Renato Palumbo as new musical director came to a premature end after both audiences and critics loudly voiced their discontent. The Scot Donald Runnicles was announced as his successor starting from 2009.

The **Staatsoper Unter den Linden**, meanwhile, seems to go from one success to the next, thanks to the popularity of general music director Daniel Barenboim. Musically, performances are of the highest quality, but often marred by overly spectacular staging. Its orchestra, the Berliner Staatskapelle, founded in 1570, is regarded as Berlin's finest opera orchestra. While comfortably situated in Mitte and enjoying its proximity to German politics, the house itself is in desperate need of renovation – due to start in 2010 and last for at least three years. Early in 2008, a debate erupted about whether to preserve the 1950s rococo-style interior or to provide the Staatsoper with a modern and acoustically advantageous design. At the moment it looks like the plush will prevail. The cost of renovations is estimated at €240 million; in the meantime, the Staatsoper will likely move to the Schiller-Theater.

The **Komische Oper** under intendant Andreas Homoki regularly catches the attention of press and audiences, with controversial productions such as Mozart's *Entführung aus dem Serail*, directed by Catalan Calixto Bieto and full of sex and violence. Even the World Cup got its share of exposure, with a football

Staatsoper Unter den Linden. *See p253*.

oratorio written by Moritz Eggert. Although the Komische Oper makes do with the smallest budget of the three opera houses, it outshone the other two by winning the prestigious Opera House of the Year award in 2007. Popular general music director Kirill Petrenko was succeeded by Carl St Clair in 2008, while Homoki was recently appointed new intendant of the prestigious Zurich Opera House from 2012. His successor in Berlin will be Australian director Barrie Kosky, who recently enjoyed a huge success at the Komische Oper with his broadway musical *Kiss Me Kate*.

For more independent operatic fare, don't neglect the **Neuköllner Oper**, which puts on witty and imaginative productions. Other companies worth checking out are the **Neue Opernbühne**, **Zeitgenössische Oper Berlin** (www.zeitgenoessische-oper.de), the **Berliner Kammeroper** (www.berlinerkammeroper.de) and **Novoflot** (www.novoflot.de), which usually performs at the Sophiensaele. Expect innovative music and theatre of surprising quality despite low budgets.

ORCHESTRAL MANOEUVRES

Berlin's orchestral scene is as vibrant as ever. The **Deutsches Symphonie-Orchester Berlin** (www.dso-berlin.de) still boasts fairly healthy subsidies and remains one of the

finest places in town to hear avant-garde compositions and unusual programmes under chief conductor Ingo Metzmacher.

Groundbreaking 20th-century composers, from Hindemith to Prokofiev and Schönberg to Penderecki, have conducted their own work with the **Rundfunk-Sinfonieorchester Berlin** (www.rsb-online.de). The orchestra, founded in 1923 to provide programming for the new medium of radio, looks set to continue with its tradition of drawing attention to contemporary works under musical director Marek Janowski. The orchestra aims to establish new locations for its concerts, such as the Schlüterhof in the Deutsches Historisches Museum (*see p87*), where a music festival is planned.

Fans of the old masters are still well served by the **Konzerthausorchester Berlin** (www.konzerthausorchester.de), previously known as the Berliner Sinfonie-Orchester, which plays at the splendid Konzerthaus. In 2007, chief conductor Eliahu Inbal was succeeded by Lothar Zagrosek, former general music director of the Staatsoper Stuttgart. The feisty group – founded after the building of the Wall as the East's answer to the Philharmonic – has a loyal following, but one that prefers more familiar works. Lother Zagrosek, widely recognised for his interpretations of contemporary music, has broadened the musical scope and direction of the orchestra to include the genre, and also demonstrated his innovative approach by inviting rapper Saul Williams to his inaugural opening concert.

Berlin's chamber orchestras also offer a steady stream of first-rate concerts. One of the finest groups is **Ensemble Oriol Berlin** (www.ensemble-oriol.de), which has a strong emphasis on contemporary music. The **Kammerorchester Berlin** (www.koberlin.de) remains popular but predictable, with works ranging from Vivaldi to Mozart and back again. Under manager Stefan Fragner, the **Deutsches Kammerorchester Berlin** (www.dko-berlin.de) has acquired an excellent reputation for working with rising star conductors and soloists, and for offering innovative yet audience-friendly programmes.

Last but not least, there's the mighty **Berliner Philharmoniker** (www.berliner-philharmoniker.de), which goes from strength to strength under Sir Simon Rattle, who was joined by intendant Pamela Rosenberg in 2006. Rattle promised to bring adventure to the programme and attract younger audiences, and has introduced an emphasis on contemporary composers such as Thomas Adès and Marc Anthony Turnage. He has also worked with

Arts & Entertainment

Palace of pleasures

The long history of the Admiralspalast entertainment complex began in the 19th century, when a group of workers accidentally stumbled on a natural salt-water spring. The discovery led to the 1873 opening of the Admiralsgartenbad, a luxurious spa. After a later spell as an ice arena, the building was remodelled in 1922 into a 'world variety' theatre, and then mutated into a 24-hour 'amusement palace' with a steam sauna, a bowling alley, a casino, restaurants, ballrooms, cafés, one of Berlin's first cinemas and even a bordello.

Rather miraculously, the Admiralspalast came through World War II intact and reopened in 1955. As the Metropol Theater, it offered operetta programmes all the way through the communist years, until it was closed once more in 1997. Protests and petitions kept the landmark from being demolished, and after a 2003 decision by the Berlin Senate to keep the building as a cultural venue, new owners were found: Falk Walter and Jon Tryggvason, who aimed to renovate the Admiralspalast to its former splendour before marrying its illustrious past with a contemporary programme. As Walter puts it, 'We're deeply impressed by a rich history that has left meaningful traces in every corner of the building. Reflecting on the period of the 1920s, today we want to be a footstone in the Friedrichstrasse, with a rich diversity of art and culture to be experienced under one roof.'

In the Grand Café, the latest influx of construction workers found five ceilings, each from a different era, lying one under the other. Today's taste is for a mix of old and new, so you can now walk through a 1930s foyer to a brand new bar designed to evoke the shape of a violin, while coats are hung in the cloakroom on original Admiralspalast pegs. Other fixtures from the venue's golden age include an immense 490-bulb chandelier hanging in the 1,760-seat theatre.

And after almost a decade of darkness, round-the-clock entertainment is again on the cards. The venue reopened its doors in summer 2006 with a sell-out run of Brecht and Weill's *The Threepenny Opera*, a show first staged just over the river at what is now the Berliner Ensemble, and the 20,000-square-metre complex now presents theatrical productions, concerts and other shows on three separate stages. Foyer 101 hosts cabaret acts, mime troupes, musical ensembles and improv comedy; the Studio has a rotating programme of music and comedy shows, with resident masked theatrical group Familie Flöz; and the main stage presents musicals, concerts and theatre. The opening of the Admiralspalast Klub will be followed in 2009 by the Roman-style baths, tapping the subterranean water source that inspired the opening of the venue more than a century ago. It may never again be quite like the Weimar years. However, you will be able to lounge and relax all day in the spa before choosing from a tantalising variety of entertainments and then dancing the night away – all in the same luxurious facility.

Admiralspalast

Friedrichstrasse 101, Mitte (325 3130/ tickets 4799 7499/www.admiralspalast.de). U6, S1, S2, S5, S7, S9, S75 Friedrichstrasse. **Box office** 11am-7pm Mon-Sat; 11am-5pm Sun; and from one hour before performances. **Tickets** varies. **Credit** AmEx, MC, V. **Map** p316/p325 M6.

Arts & Entertainment

jazz musicians and improvisers. At the same time, Rattle has put the ensemble through more traditional paces. He has also launched a new education programme with projects that aim to integrate youths from different backgrounds and get them hooked on classical music. Right now, he's still flavour of the month.

FESTIVALS

Music festivals pepper Berlin's calendar. **MaerzMusik – Festival für aktuelle Musik** (see p196) takes place in March at various venues, and showcases trends in contemporary music. The **UltraSchall** (see p200) festival of new music, organised by DeutschlandRadio and Rundfunk Berlin-Brandenburg every January, features many of the world's leading specialist ensembles. The biennial **Zeitfenster – Biennale für alte Musik** (see p196) at the Konzerthaus focuses on 17th-century baroque music for one week in April (the next one's in 2010). Popular programmes, orchestras and soloists often kick off the **Classic Open Air** concert series (see p198) on Gendarmenmarkt in July. There's less focus on food, drink and socialising at the **Young.euro.classic** (see p198), which assembles youth orchestras from all over Europe in August.

During the second half of September, 60 talented amateur pianists from around the world take part in the biennial **International Piano Amateur Competition** (www.ipac-berlin.com) at the Philharmonie, which is next held in 2010. The Berliner Festspiele (see p255) organises the annual **Musikfest Berlin** (see p198) in August/September, which brings some of the world's finest orchestras to Berlin.

TICKETS

Getting seats at the Philharmonie can still be difficult, especially when it's for a big-name star or when the Berlin Phil itself is in residence; tickets for concerts by visiting performers are often easier to come by.

Otherwise, it's worth scanning the listings in daily papers or tip and Zitty, and phoning venues or checking their websites to see what's available. If all else fails, try standing outside the venue with a sign reading 'Suche eine Karte' ('seeking a ticket'), or chatting up arriving concert-goers ('Haben Sie vielleicht eine Karte übrig?' means 'Got a spare ticket?'). You may also see people with extras for sale ('Karte(n) zu verkaufen'), but beware of ticket sharks. Some of the former East Berlin venues remain more affordable than their western counterparts, but the days of dirt-cheap tickets are long gone. Standing-room at the top of the Konzerthaus

gives a decent view, but before buying cheap seats for the Staatsoper ask how much of the stage you can see.

Most venues offer student discounts. The **ClassicCard** (www.classiccard.de) is also worth considering: it's €15 if you're under 30, is valid for one year and entitles the holder to excellent seats for a mere €8 for concerts and €10 for opera and ballet. Participating institutions include the Deutsche Oper, Komische Oper, Konzerthaus, Deutsches Symphonie-Orchester Berlin and the Staatsoper Unter den Linden. It can be purchased at these and over the internet.

TICKET AGENCIES

Tickets are sold at concert hall box offices or through ticket agencies, called Theaterkassen. At box offices, seats are generally sold up to one hour before the performance. You can also make reservations by phone, except for concerts by the Berlin Phil. Theaterkassen provides the easiest means of buying a ticket, but commissions can run as high as 17 per cent. **Hekticket** is probably the best bet, or you can try www.ticketonline.de. For the 50 or so other agencies around the city, look in the Gelbe Seiten (Yellow Pages) under 'Theaterkassen'. Note that many places do not accept credit cards.

Hekticket

Hardenbergstrasse 29D, Charlottenburg (230 9930/ www.hekticket.de). U2, U9, S3, S5, S7, S9, S75 Zoologischer Garten. **Open** 10am-8pm Mon-Sat; 2-6pm Sun. **Credit** AmEx, DC, MC, V.
Map p321/p328 G8.
Hekticket offers discounts of up to 50% on theatre and concert tickets. For a small commission, staff will sell you tickets for the same evening's performance. Tickets for Sunday matinées are available on Saturday. You can check ticket availability online, though not everything is listed. The Mitte branch, in a kiosk just south of the S-Bahn bridge, is closed on Sundays.
Other locations Karl-Liebknecht-Strasse 12, Mitte (2431 2431).

Major venues

Deutsche Oper

Bismarckstrasse 35, Charlottenburg (343 8401/ freephone 0800 248 9842/www.deutscheoperberlin. de). U2 Deutsche Oper. **Box office** 11am-30mins before performance Mon-Sat; 10am-2pm Sun.
Tickets €12-€118. **Credit** AmEx, DC, V.
Map p320 D7.
With roots dating back to 1912, the Deutsche Oper built its present 1,900-seat hall in 1961, just in time to carry the operatic torch for West Berlin during the Wall years. Since Reunification it has lost out in profile to the more elegant Staatsoper, but retains a reputation for productions of the classics. Discount tickets available half an hour before performances.

The elaborate 1891 interior of the **Berliner Ensemble**. See p255.

Komische Oper

Behrenstrasse 55-57, Mitte (202 600/tickets 4799
7400/www.komische-oper-berlin.de). S1, S2, S25,
Unter den Linden or U6 Französische Strasse.
Box office *In person* 11am-7pm Mon-Sat. *By phone*
9am-8pm Mon-Sat; 2-8pm Sun. **Tickets** €8-€93.
Credit AmEx, MC, V. **Map** p318/p327 M6.
Despite its name, the Komische Oper puts on a
broader range than just comic works, and, after its
founding in 1947, made its reputation by breaking
with the old operatic tradition of 'costumed concerts'
– singers standing around on stage – and putting an
emphasis on 'opera as theatre', with real acting skill
demanded of its young ensemble. Most of its productions are sung in German. Discounted tickets are
sold immediately before performances.

Konzerthaus

Gendarmenmarkt 2, Mitte (2030 92101/www.
konzerthaus.de). U6 Französische Strasse. **Box**
office noon-7pm Mon-Sat; noon-4pm Sun. **Tickets**
€10-€99; some 25% reductions. **Credit** AmEx, MC,
V. **Map** p322/p327 M7.
Formerly the Schauspielhaus am Gendarmenmarkt,
this 1821 architectural gem by Schinkel was all but
destroyed in the war. Lovingly restored, it was
reopened in 1984 with three main spaces for concerts. Organ recitals in the large concert hall are a
treat, played on the massive Jehmlich organ at the
back of the stage. The Konzerthausorchester (*see*
p249) is based here, presenting a healthy mixture
of the classic, the new and the rediscovered.
The Rundfunk-Sinfonieorchester Berlin and the
Staatskapelle Berlin also play here. There are also
occasional informal concerts in the cosy little Musik
Club in the depths of the building.

Philharmonie

Herbert-von-Karajan Strasse 1, Tiergarten
(254 880/tickets 2548 8999/www.berlin-
philharmonic.com). U2, S1, S2, S25 Potsdamer
Platz. **Box office** 9am-6pm daily. **Tickets**
€7-€138. **Credit** AmEx, MC, V. **Map** p322 K7.
Berlin's most famous concert hall, home to the
world-renowned Berlin Philharmonic Orchestra, is
also its most architecturally daring; a marvellous,
puckish piece of organic modernism. The hall, with
its golden vaulting roof, was designed by Hans
Scharoun and opened in 1963. Its reputation for
superb acoustics is accurate, but it does depend on
where you sit. Behind the orchestra the acoustics
leave plenty to be desired, but in front (where it is
much more expensive) the sound is heavenly. The
structure also incorporates a smaller hall, the
Kammermusiksaal, about which the same acousti-
cal notes apply.
The unique Berliner Philharmoniker (www.
berliner-philharmoniker.de) was founded in 1882 by
54 musicians keen to break away from the penuri-
ous Benjamin Bilse, in whose orchestra they played.
Over the last 120 years, it has been led by some of
the world's greatest conductors, as well as by composers such as Peter Tchaikovsky, Edvard Grieg,
Richard Strauss and Gustav Mahler. Its greatest
fame came under the baton of Herbert von Karajan,
who led the orchestra between 1955 and 1989, and

was succeeded by Claudio Abbado. Since 2002, it has been under the leadership of Simon Rattle. The Berlin Phil gives about 100 performances in the city during its August to June season, and puts on another 20 to 30 concerts around the world. Some tickets are available at a discount immediately before performances.

Staatsoper Unter den Linden

Unter den Linden 5-7, Mitte (203 540/tickets 2035 4555/www.staatsoper-berlin.de). U2 Hausvogteiplatz. **Box office** 10am-8pm Mon-Sat; 2-8pm Sun. **Tickets** €5-€160. **Credit** AmEx, MC, V. **Map** p319/p327 N6.

The Staatsoper was founded as Prussia's Royal Court Opera for Frederick the Great in 1742, and designed along the lines of a Greek temple. Although the present building dates from 1955, the façade faithfully copies that of Knobelsdorff's original, twice destroyed in World War II. The elegant interior gives an immediate sense of the house's past glory, with huge chandeliers and elaborate wall paintings. Chamber music is performed in the small, ornate Apollo Saal, which is housed within the main building and also used for occasional club nights and electronica performances. Unsold tickets are available for €10 half an hour before the performance.

Other venues

Many churches offer organ recitals, as do castles and museums in summer. Phones are often erratically staffed, so check *tip* or *Zitty* for information.

Akademie der Künste

Hanseatenweg 10, Tiergarten (200 572 000/ www.adk.de). U9 Hansaplatz or S3, S5, S7, S9 Bellevue. **Open** 11am-8pm Tue-Sun. **Tickets** €5-€10. **No credit cards. Map** p316 H6.

The Akademie der Künste was founded by Prince Friedrich III in 1696, and is one of the oldest cultural institutions in Berlin. By 1938, however, the Nazis had forced virtually all of its prominent members into exile. It was re-established in West Berlin in 1954, in this fine new building by Werner Duttmann, to serve as 'a community of exceptional artists' from around the world. Apart from performances of 20th-century compositions, its programme offers a variety of other events, from jazz and poetry readings to film screenings and art exhibitions. Although portions of the now-reunified Akademie have moved into a new building at its pre-war address on Pariser Platz, most performances and exhibitions remain here at Hanseatenweg.

Other locations Pariser Platz 4, Mitte (200 570).

Ballhaus Naunynstrasse

Naunynstrasse 27, Kreuzberg (347 459 845/tickets 347 459 844/www.ballhausnaunynstrasse.de). U1, U8 Kottbusser Tor. **Box office** 1hr before performance Mon-Fri. **Tickets** €10; €6 reductions. **Credit** AmEx, MC, V. **Map** p323 P8.

Don't expect to hear anything ordinary at this Kreuzberg cultural centre. A varied assortment of western and oriental music is on the menu, with drinks and snacks in the café out front. The long, rectangular hall, which seats 150, plays host to the excellent Berlin Chamber Opera, among others.

Berliner Dom

Lustgarten 1, Mitte (2026 9136/www.berliner-dom.de). S3, S5, S7, S9, S75 Hackescher Markt. **Box office** *Apr-Sept* 9am-8pm Mon-Sat; noon-8pm Sun. *Oct-Mar* 9am-7pm Mon-Sat. **Tickets** €5-€30. **No credit cards**. **Map** p319/p327 N6.

Berlin's cathedral holds some recommendable concerts, usually of the organ or choral variety.

Meistersaal

Köthener Strasse 38, Kreuzberg (520 0060/www.meistersaal.de). U2, S1, S2, S25, S26 Potsdamer Platz. **Box office** 10am-5pm Mon-Fri. **Tickets** vary. **Credit** MC, V. **Map** p322 L8.

What was once the Hansa recording studio now hosts solo instrumentalists and chamber groups that can't afford to book the Kammermusiksaal of the Philharmonie. But don't let that fool you. Music-making of the highest rank occurs here in this warm and welcoming little salon, which is notable for its superb acoustics. Back when this was a studio, David Bowie and Iggy Pop recorded here during the 1970s.

Musikhochschule Hanns Eisler

Charlottenstrasse 55, Gendarmenmarkt, Mitte (688 305 700/www.hfm-berlin.de). U2, U6 Stadtmitte. **Open** 1.30-3.30pm Mon; 9.30am-noon Tue, Wed; 9.30am-noon, 1.30-3.30pm Thur. **Tickets** vary (usually free). **No credit cards**. **Map** p322/p327 M7.

This musical academy was founded in 1950 and named after the composer of the East German national anthem. It offers students the chance to learn under some of the stars of Berlin's major orchestras and operas. Rehearsals and master classes are often open to the public for free, and student performances, some of them top-notch, are held in the Konzerthaus across the street. Other events are held at the new Krönungskutschensaal in the Marstall, a 300-seat venue with perfect acoustics. **Other locations** Marstall, Schlossplatz 7, Mitte (9026 9700).

Neuköllner Oper

Karl-Marx-Strasse 131-133, Neukölln (6889 0777/www.neukoellneroper.de). U7 Karl-Marx-Strasse. **Box office** 3-7pm Tue-Fri. **Tickets** €12-€21. **Credit** MC, V. **Map** p324 R12.

No grand opera here, but a constantly changing programme of chamber operas and music-theatre works much loved by the Neuköllners who come to see lighter, bubblier, cheaper and much less formal works than those offered by Berlin's big three opera houses. Shame about the acoustics, though.

Radialsystem V

Holzmarktstrasse 33, Friedrichshain (288 788 588/www.radialsystem.de). S3, S5, S7, S9, S75 Ostbahnhof. **Open** noon-7pm Tue-Sun. **No credit cards**. **Tickets** €17.20-€36.40. **Map** p323 Q7.

Radialsystem V is a 'new space for the arts' and a base for Sasha Waltz's dance company is also home to the early music ensemble Akamus (www.akamus.de).

It's a former pumping station by the river, it promotes a variety of one-off performance events, and attracts a well-heeled crowd.

Staatsbibliothek – Otto-Braun Saal

Potsdamer Strasse 33, Tiergarten (2660/www.staatsbibliothek-berlin.de). U2, S1, S2, S25 Potsdamer Platz. **Box office** times vary; call for details. **Tickets** vary. **No credit cards**. **Map** p322 K7.

This smaller ensemble provides the lion's share of the music in this chamber of the state library.

St Matthäus Kirche am Kulturforum

Matthaeikirchplatz, Tiergarten (2035 5311/www.stiftung-stmatthaeus.de). U2, S1, S2, S25 Potsdamer Platz. **Box office** noon-6pm Tue-Sun. **Tickets** vary. **No credit cards**. **Map** p322 K8.

Concerts here might be anything from a free organ recital to a chorus of Russian Orthodox monks. Exquisite acoustics.

Universität der Künste

Hardenbergstrasse 33, corner of Fasanenstrasse, Tiergarten (318 50/www.udk-berlin.de). U2, U9, S3, S5, S7, S9, S75 Zoologischer Garten. **Box office** 3-6.30pm Tue-Fri; 11am-2pm Sat. **Tickets** vary. **No credit cards**. **Map** p321/p328 F7.

This place may be grotesquely ugly, but it is nonetheless a functional hall, hosting both student soloists and orchestras, as well as performances by lesser-known professional groups.

Theatre

In Berlin, the crossover between theatre, dance and performance art has become so complex and enmeshed that it is almost impossible to separate them any more. One of three resident directors at the **Schaubühne**, Thomas Ostermeier, has successfully combined contemporary dance with theatre for several years. Ostermeier now collaborates with choreographer Constanza Macras in productions such as a radical 2007 adaptation of *A Midsummer Night's Dream*. In theatres such as **HAU** and **Sophiensaele**, the work has become an international concoction, and these two venues are continuously reinventing and exploring theatrical possibilities. In more traditional theatre venues, artistic director Armin Petras has injected new life into the **Maxim Gorki Theater**, and under Claus Peymann's direction the **Berliner Ensemble** still presents modern adaptations of classics such as *The Threepenny Opera*. Meanwhile, works from international directors, playwrights, dance companies and performance artists are playing every night of the week.

FESTIVALS

Renowned as a place to be for new artists, Berlin hosts various festivals that feature and promote emerging international talent. **Cut & Paste** in December at the HAU showcases young independent European artists. **100° Berlin – Das Lange Wochenende des Freien Theaters** is a long weekend in February at the Sophiensaele, HAU and Theatre Discounter. It's a chance to overdose on all types of independent productions with mixed artistic media. In mid November, **Sehnsucht – Festival Politik im Freien Theater** (www.politikimfreientheater.de) is a ten-day festival of political fringe theatre. Once a year, one of the most supportive institutions for new drama, the Schaubühne, presents new works from Germany and abroad during its Festival for International New Drama (FIND). The **Berliner Festspiele** (www.berliner festspiele.de) presents two of the most important festivals in the year, including May's Theatertreffen. This festival remains the major festival for German-language work, with an independent jury of critics selecting the ten best productions each year from around 400 plays. Meanwhile, **Spielzeit'europa**, held from October to January, is the Festspiele's biggest theatre festival, featuring influential groups such as DV8 from London.

Civic theatres

Berliner Ensemble

Bertolt-Brecht-Platz 1, Mitte (2840 8155/ www.berliner-ensemble.de). U6, S1, S2, S5, S7, S9, S75 Friedrichstrasse. **Box office** 8am-6pm Mon-Fri; 11am-6pm Sat, Sun. **Tickets** €5-€30; €7 reductions. **Credit** AmEx, DC, MC, V. **Map** p318/p327 M6.

This theatre is best known for its association with Brecht – first during the Weimar period (this was where *The Threepenny Opera* was first staged in 1928) and later under the Communists when Brecht ran the place from 1948 until his death in 1956. Artistic director Claus Peymann focuses on contemporary theatre and original productions as well as directing classics with an updated point of view. Expect a repertoire where modern productions of Brecht rub shoulders with pieces by living artists and directors such as Robert Wilson, whose production of *The Threepenny Opera* is consistently sold out. One of the best ensembles in the city.

Deutsches Theater

Schumannstrasse 13A, Mitte (284 410/tickets 2844 1225/www.deutschestheater.de). U6, S1, S2, S5, S7, S9, S75 Friedrichstrasse. **Box office** 11am-6.30pm Mon-Sat; 3-6.30pm Sun. **Tickets** €5-€43. **Credit** AmEx, MC, V. **Map** p318/p327 L5.

Within the DT's two adjoining buildings are three venues displaying new and experimental work, from

F40. See p257.

one-man shows and concerts to modern interpretations of Gogol, Shakespeare and Büchner. The four in-house directors – Barbara Frey, Dimiter Gotscheff, Jürgen Gosch and Michael Thalheimer – are innovators in the field; Thalheimer in particular has received countless awards and his productions are now touring internationally. Having celebrated its 125th season in 2007-2008, the DT remains an important and relevant institution.

HAU

Main office: HAU2, Hallesches Ufer 32, Kreuzberg (box office 2590 0427/information 259 0040/ www.hebbel-am-ufer.de). U1, U7 Möckernbrücke or U1, U6 Hallesches Tor. **Box office** noon-7pm daily. **Tickets** €11-€18; €7 reductions. **Credit** AmEx, MC, V. **Map** p322 M9.

The most exciting programming in the city is currently coming from the amalgamation of the century-old former Hebbel Theater (HAU1), Theater am Hallesches Ufer (HAU2) and Theater am Ufer (HAU3). Under intendant Matthias Lilienthal this tripartite theatre has become a hotbed of new international work and is one of the leading venues for young, international, experimental and innovative performing arts.
Other locations HAU1, Stresemannstrasse 29, Kreuzberg; HAU3, Tempelhofer Ufer 10, Kreuzberg.

Maxim Gorki Theater

Am Festungsgraben 2, Mitte (box office 2022 1115/ information 2022 1129/www.gorki.de). U6, S1, S2, S5, S7, S9, S75 Friedrichstrasse. **Box office** noon-6.30pm Mon-Sat; 4-6.30pm Sun. **Tickets** €10-€30. **Credit** MC, V. **Map** p319/p327 N6.

This jewel of a theatre is slightly off the beaten tourist track of Unter den Linden. In August 2006, author and director Armin Petras became the Maxim Gorki's intendant, and with a young and new ensemble he has breathed life into this landmark. The programming features new interpretations of classical and modern dramas as well as adaptations from films and novels, with the result that the atmosphere alone is often enough to transcend the language barrier.

Renaissance

Hardenbergstrasse 6, Charlottenburg (312 4202/ www.renaissance-theater.de). U2 Ernst-Reuter-Platz. **Box office** 10am-7pm Mon-Fri; 10am-6pm Sat; 1-6pm Sun. **Tickets** €12-€48. **Credit** AmEx, MC, V. **Map** p321/p328 F8.

If you want famous actors and a classy location, then this is the place. The Renaissance houses some of Germany's best-known performers. The building is one of only two remaining examples of work by Oskar Kaufmann, premier Berlin theatre architect of the early 20th century, and it claims to be Europe's only art deco theatre. It all makes for a great backdrop to the chansons evenings that are served up with a full dinner in the upstairs salon.

Schaubühne am Lehniner Platz

Kurfürstendamm 153, Charlottenburg (890 023/ www.schaubuehne.de). U7 Adenauerplatz or S5, *S7, S9, S75 Charlottenburg.* **Box office** 11am-6.30pm Mon-Sat; 3-6.30pm Sun. **Tickets** €6-€38; €11 reductions. **Credit** AmEx, MC, V. **Map** p320 D9.

The Schaubühne has become one of the most important places for avant-garde theatre and dance in Berlin. The aim of its three resident directors, Thomas Ostermeier, Luk Perceval and Falk Richter, is to highlight dance, experimental contemporary writers and adaptations of classics. The programme also includes some English-language works – plays by Sarah Kane, Nicky Silver, Mark Ravenhill and Caryl Churchill have all been featured. As the theatre is becoming increasingly international, English subtitles are sometimes offered. Considered one of the hotspots for the theatrical in-crowd.

Volksbühne

Linienstrasse 227, Mitte (2406 5777/ www.volksbuehne-berlin.de). U2 Rosa-Luxemburg-Platz. **Box office** noon-6pm daily. **Tickets** €10-€30; €5-€15 reductions. **Credit** (in person only) AmEx, MC, V. **Map** p319/p326 O5.

Established in 1914, this massive landmark theatre was hovering on the brink of closure before Frank Castorf, one of the most talked-about and controversial directors in town, became the artistic director in 1992. His provocative interpretations, four-hour productions and alternative operettas restored the popularity of the 'People's Stage', but his deconstructions and modernisations of Russian novels and American plays have become a bit predictable now. While some are wondering if Castorf has run out of steam, the theatre continues to uphold its tradition, under his direction, of presenting the unexpected. For example, influential American choreographer Meg Stuart and her cross-disciplinary company Damaged Goods, residents in 2006, provoked extreme reactions from audiences. The theatre is also home to a gallery, a small studio theatre (Parasit), and the hip, eclectic Roter and Grüner Salons. Former after-hours hangouts for the East German theatre elite, these two very different halls retain their old-style decor.

Fringe & English-language

Although civic institutions are focusing on presenting new and international talent, the place where Berlin-based artists get their start is in fringe theatre (known in German as *Off-Theater*). The profile of fringe theatre has been growing in recent years, but venues remain dangerously reliant on shrinking public funds. The spaces occupied are often basic and the quality varies considerably, but tickets are affordable, audiences diverse and enthusiastic and it's fun to explore the different productions.

The English-language theatre scene is small but vibrant and has seen a lot of comings and goings. **Platypus Theater** (6140 1920, www.platypus-theater.de), Australian expat actor Peter Scollin's successful youth and children's company, continues to present original, intelligent and sassy shows for youngsters. The only theatre focusing solely on English-language productions is **F40**, which has been producing and hosting quality performances since the early 1990s and is currently upgrading and enlarging its facilities.

Many box offices open one hour before a performance and sell tickets for that performance only. An international student ID card should get you a discount at most venues.

Ballhaus Ost

Pappelallee 15, Prenzlauer Berg (4799 7474/www. ballhausost.de). U2 Eberswalder Strasse. **Open** *By phone* 9am-8pm Mon-Sat; 2-8pm Sun. **Tickets** €13; €8 reductions. **Credit** MC, V. **Map** p319/p328 P2.
This somewhat dilapidated former ballroom offers art, performance art, dance productions and concerts, offering a unique and authentic cultural evening. There's also a lounge and bar populated by a very cool crowd.

Brotfabrik

Caligariplatz, Weissensee (4714 0012/www. brotfabrik.de). Tram M2, M13 Prenzlauer Allee/Ostseestrasse. **Open** *By phone* 9am-8pm Mon-Sat; 4-8pm Sun. **Tickets** €12; €8 reductions. **Credit** MC, V. **Map** p319 Q1.
Far from the centre of town, this former bread factory houses a cinema, gallery, café and a small experimental theatre where productions by visiting companies are performed in a variety of languages. The café has a congenial summer courtyard.

F40

Fidicinstrasse 40, Kreuzberg (box office 691 1211/ information 693 5692/www.etberlin.de). U6 Platz der Luftbrücke. **Box office** 1hr before performance. **Tickets** €7-€15. **No credit cards**. **Map** p322 M11.
Under directors Günther Grosser and Bernd Hoffmeister, F40 (formerly known as Friends of Italian Opera) boasts a high-quality programme. Expect house productions, international guest shows and co-productions with performers from Berlin's lively international theatre scene. Theater Thikwa, one of Europe's most renowned companies working with disabled actors, is also based here.

Orphtheater

Ackerstrasse 169-170, Mitte (441 0009/www. orphtheater.de). U8 Rosenthaler Platz. **Box office** 10am-4pm daily. **Tickets** €12; €8 reductions. **No credit cards**. **Map** p319/p326 N4.
In the back courtyard of the Schoko-Laden, a former squatted house turned cultural centre, lurks a hardcore East German theatre company – one of the few left untarnished by globalisation. Independent, tiny and grungy: a true Berlin experience.

Sophiensaele

Sophienstrasse 18, Mitte (information 2789 0030/tickets 283 5266/www.sophiensaele.com).

U8 Weinmeisterstrasse or S5, S7, S9, S75 Hackescher Markt. **Open** 1hr before performance daily. **Tickets** €15; €10 reductions. **No credit cards**. **Map** p319/p326 N5.
This former club house for craftsmen and DDR theatre workshop now presents a contemporary programme of dance, theatre, music and opera, with up-and-coming groups from around the world. If avant-garde is ever crowd-pleasing, then it's here. The largest of the off-theatres, the Sophiensaele is also the perfect venue for an assortment of theatre and dance festivals.

Theaterdiscounter

Monbijoustrasse 1, Mitte (4404 8561/www. theaterdiscounter.de). S1, S2 Oranienburger Strasse. **Box office** from 7pm until performance daily. **Tickets** €12; €8 reductions. **No credit cards**. **Map** p319/p326 N5.
Opened in 2003 in an old telegraph office, this is where an intense group of ten actors and various directors perform new and experimental work. It's anti-illusion theatre with interactive possibilities – very casual and fresh.

Theater unterm Dach

Kulturhaus im Ernst-Thälmann-Park, Danziger Strasse 101, Prenzlauer Berg (902 953 817/ www.theateruntermdach-berlin.de). S8, S41, S42, S85 Greifswalder Strasse/tram M4, M10. **Open** *By phone* from 7pm until performance daily. **Tickets** €8; €5 reductions. **No credit cards**. **Map** p319 Q3.
In the large attic of a converted factory, situated well off the beaten path, Theater unterm Dach is the place to see new German fringe groups. Productions are always full of energy and can be quite inspiring. Small but surprisingly exciting programme.

Cabaret

Although cabaret in today's Berlin bears little resemblance to the cabaret of the Weimar years, there are some great performers here who can re-create an entire era in one night. The town is teeming with acts that can be more sexually adventurous (or ambiguous) than most other places and still manage to titillate the cool Berlin audiences. Some good acts to watch out for include **Die O-Tonpiraten** (clever drag musical theatre that montages famous film dialogues into irreverent storylines), the charming American entertainer **Gayle Tufts** ('denglish' stand-up comedy with pop) and **Bridge Markland**'s gender-bending dance/poetry.

Don't confuse *Cabaret* with *Varieté*; the l atter is more of a circus-like show, minus the animals but with lots of dancing girls. *Kabarett* is different again – a unique kind of German entertainment with a strong following in Berlin. It's basically political satire sprinkled with songs and sketches, sometimes intellectual and sometimes crass. It can be found at venues such as Stachelschweine, Wühlmäuse, Mehringhof Theatre, Kartoon or Kneifzange (check local listings for details), but most of it will be over your head if you don't have perfect German and a thorough understanding of local politics.

When it comes to *Travestie* – drag revue – Berlin has some of the best on offer, from fabulous to tragic, and in places where you might not expect it. For the more progressive and intelligent drag acts, the **BKA** is a safe bet. Venues come in all sizes and styles, from small and dark to huge and glittery. Remember that the look and price of a venue is not always an indication of the quality of the show.

Varieté & revue

Chamäleon

Hackesche Höfe, Rosenthaler Strasse 40-41, Mitte (tickets 400 0590/www.chamaeleonberlin.de). S5, S7, S9, S75 Hackescher Markt. **Box office** 10.30am-8pm Mon-Fri; 10.30am-10pm Sat; noon-7pm Sun. **Performances** 8.30pm Mon, Wed, Thur; 8.30pm, midnight Fri, Sat; 7pm Sun. **Tickets** €29-€39; €23-€28 reductions. **No credit cards.** **Map** p319/p326 N5.

This beautiful old theatre with a touch of decadence is located in the famous courtyards of the Hackesche Höfe. The focus here is on stunning acrobats combined with music theatre. As Hackesche Höfe becomes increasingly commercialised and touristy, there's a risk this club may become a sort of Wintergarten (*see below*). For now it attracts a diverse audience and is the most comfortable and affordable revue house.

Friedrichstadtpalast

Friedrichstrasse 107, Mitte (2326 2326/www. friedrichstadtpalast.de). U6, S1, S2, S5, S7, S9, S75 Friedrichstrasse. **Open** 6pm-1am daily. *Box office* 10am-6pm Mon, Sun; 10am-7pm Tue-Sat. **Performances** 8pm Tue-Fri; 4pm, 8pm Sat; 4pm Sun. **Tickets** €21-€74. **Credit** AmEx, MC, V. **Map** p319/p326 M5.

An East Berlin institution in a building originally designed to be the opera house in Damascus, this is the city's biggest revue theatre. Since Reunification it has mainly featured big, Las Vegas-style musical revues with Vegas-style prices to match. Mostly packed with coachloads of German tourists.

Wintergarten Varieté

Potsdamer Strasse 96, Tiergarten (250 0880/tickets 2500 8888/www.wintergarten-variete.de). U1 Kurfürstenstrasse. **Box office** 10-11am, noon-6pm Mon-Fri; 1-8pm Sat, Sun. **Performances** 8pm Mon, Tue, Thur, Fri; 4pm, 8pm Wed; 5pm, 9pm Sat; 3pm, 6pm Sun. **Tickets** *Show only* €22-€67. *Show & dinner* €89-€99. **Credit** AmEx, MC, V. **Map** p322 J8.

Prussia meets Disney with shows that are slick and professional and a little boring. Excellent acrobats and magicians, but some questionable comedy acts. Fancy decor and more busloads of tourists.

Cabaret

Bar jeder Vernunft

Spiegelzelt, Schaperstrasse 24, Wilmersdorf (883 1582/www.bar-jeder-vernunft.de). U3, U9 Spichernstrasse. **Box office** noon-7pm Mon-Fri; 3-6pm Sat, Sun. **Performances** daily (usually 7pm or 8pm). **Tickets** €15-€30. **Credit** AmEx, MC, V. **Map** p319/p328 F9.

Some of Berlin's most celebrated entertainers perform in this snazzy circus tent of many mirrors – the

Scheinbar.

programme includes shows, comedy, cabaret, literature and theatre. You can order a €29 menu on top of the ticket price – it's not the cheapest night out in Berlin, but worth it if they revive their much-lauded production of *Cabaret*.

BKA Theater

Mehringdamm 34, Kreuzberg (202 2007/www.bka-luftschloss.de). U6, U7 Mehringdamm. **Box office** 11am-8.30pm Mon-Fri; 2-8.30pm Sat. **Performances** 8pm daily. **Tickets** €9-€24. **Credit** AmEx, MC, V. **Map** p322 M10.

With a long tradition of taboo-breaking acts, BKA still features some of the weirdest and most progressive performers in town: intelligent drag stand-up, freaky chanteuses and power-packin' divas. The theatre is filled with private tables and arena seats overlooking the stage. Fresh performances and good theme parties.

Café Theater Schalotte

Behaimstrasse 22, Charlottenburg (341 1485/www.schalotte.de). U7 Richard-Wagner-Platz. **Box office** varies. **Performances** usually 8.30pm Thur-Sat. **Tickets** €9-€15. **No credit cards**. **Map** p316 D6.

Nice café, dedicated staff and some excellent shows. The O-Tonpiraten, a very clever drag theatre troupe, often plays here. The theatre hosts some brilliant acts in November during its annual international a cappella festival.

Kleine Nachtrevue

Kurfürstenstrasse 116, Schöneberg (218 8950/www.kleine-nachtrevue.de). U1, U2, U3 Wittenbergplatz. **Open** 7pm-3am Tue-Sat. **Performances** 10.45pm Tue-Sat. €15-€25. **Credit** AmEx, DC, MC, V. **Map** p321 H8.

Used as a location for many films, this is as close as it gets to real nostalgic German cabaret – intimate, dark, decadent but very friendly. Nightly shows consist of short song or dance numbers sprinkled with playful nudity and whimsical costumes. Special weekend performances at 9pm vary from erotic opera to a four-course meal to songs sung by the male 'reincarnation' of Marlene Dietrich.

Scheinbar

Monumentenstrasse 9, Schöneberg (784 5539/www.scheinbar.de). U7 Kleistpark. **Box office** from 7.30pm until performance. **Performances** 8.30pm most days. **Tickets** €7-€12. **No credit cards**. **Map** p322 K11.

Experimental, fun-loving cabaret in a tiny club exploding with fresh talent. If you like surprises, try the open-stage nights, where great performers mix with terrible ones, creating a surreal night for all.

Tipi Das Zelt

Grosse Querallee, between the Bundeskanzleramt & Haus der Kulturen der Welt, Tiergarten (0180 327 9358/www.tipi-das-zelt.de). Bus 100, 248 Platz der Republik. **Box office** noon-7pm Mon-Sat; 3-6pm Sun. **Performances** 8.30pm Tue-Sat; 3pm, 8pm Sun. **Tickets** €9.50-€42. **Credit** AmEx, MC, V. **Map** p318 K6.

A circus tent in the Tiergarten, near the Federal Chancellery, with cool international performers presenting various comedy, dance and cabaret shows. Similar fare to Bar jeder Vernunft (*see p258*), except everything's twice the size.

Travestie

Theater im Keller

Weserstrasse 211, Neukölln (623 1452/www.theater-im-keller.de). U7, U8 Hermannplatz. **Box office** 11am-10pm daily. **Performances** 8pm daily. **Tickets** €27. **Credit** AmEx, MC, V. **Map** p323 Q11.

With seating for 43 people, this cosy neighbourhood drag club has a touch of grandma and a passable drag revue.

Dance

In the past decade, Berlin has become home to a dynamic dance scene that cultivates fresh ideas while continuing to nurture the strong traditions of German dance theatre. Throughout the year, the city's theatres are filled with dance events, including international festivals and co-productions for international choreographers; among the latter are Meg Stuart, recently appointed resident director at the Volksbühne. Sasha Waltz is another key figure in European dance, whose fame has essentially put Berlin on the map as a contemporary dance mecca. As a result, the city's dance scene is constantly evolving and expanding, making it an exciting place to witness the art form. Those wanting more accessible entertainment can often find touring productions by DV8 or Pina Bausch here. At the other end of the spectrum, there is a huge amount of highly experimental work on show, often attracting large audiences. In addition to daring programming in major houses, alternative spaces have popped up across the city, offering a more intimate connection with dance.

For information on upcoming performances, pick up a copy of *TanzRaumBerlin* (www.tanzraumberlin.de), Berlin's newspaper specifically about dance.

Venues & festivals

There are many possibilities for young artists to integrate themselves into Berlin's thriving and unconventional dance scene, both by participating in festivals and by making use of the professional training on offer, particularly in Prenzlauer Berg and Kreuzberg. **Dock 11** (www.dock11-berlin.de) is now the city's most recognised dance school, providing training and rehearsal and production space. **Tanzfabrik** (www.tanzfabrik-berlin.de) is another reputable institution that not only houses training and rehearsal space, but also holds international workshops and offers an innovative residency programme for dance makers.

LaborGras, by the canal in Kreuzberg (www.laborgras.com), is a small performance venue offering professional training. It frequently invites well-respected teachers from across the world to teach and perform.

The **Tanz im August** festival, hosted by HAU (*see p256*), is one of Europe's leading dance festivals, attracting people from all over Europe. The three-week festival keeps a keen eye on current trends, showing the most influential and cutting-edge choreography of the season coupled with workshops for the public and lectures from both artists and critics. Its success has allowed it to expand into performance venues around town, including Radialsystem V (*see p254*), Sophiensaele (*see p257*), Ballhaus Naunynstrasse (*see p253*) and Ballhaus Ost (*see p257*).

Since 2004, the Sophiensaele has hosted **Tanztage** (*see p200*), a dance festival held in the first two weeks of January. Here, young local dance artists present their work, in some cases for the first time. The festival is becoming increasingly well recognised across Europe.

The **Lucky Trimmer** dance series (www.luckytrimmer.de) is another mini festival, held at the theatre at the Tacheles arts centre (Oranienburgerstrasse 54-56A, Mitte, 282 6185, www.tacheles.de; *see p92*). Ten short performances are staged in one evening, enabling an easy exchange between artists and their audiences. It has been a roaring success, frequently selling out. Productions tend towards the experimental, although they maintain a light and playful spirit.

The performance venue **Radialsystem V** (*see p254*) was opened in 2006 by Jochen Sandig, the partner of choreographer Sasha Waltz. This warren of rooms in a former pumping station by the river provides an impressive setting for her work, although the programme is generally heavier on music than on dance. Together with high ticket prices, the venue tends to cater to the upper echelons of Berlin society, with programming more conservative than most other dance venues.

Choreographers

Following a similar tradition to her predecessor Pina Bausch, **Sasha Waltz**, Berlin's foremost choreographer, has contributed enormously to the aesthetic continuum of postmodern German dance theatre. Her often heavily dramatic dance works – always visually stunning –

are performed internationally in the biggest theatre houses in Europe and Asia.

The hole left at the Schaubühne after Sasha Waltz departed, meanwhile, has been partially filled by Argentinian choreographer **Constanza Macras**. There are frequent performances of her *Ein Sommernachtstraum*, a collaboration with Thomas Ostermeier, which combines her energetic choreography with his trademark visual flair. You might also catch her new dance theatre piece, *Brickland*.

Less obviously crowd-pleasing than the dance spectacles of Waltz and Macras, but also attracting big audiences, is the work of award-winning choreographer **Meg Stuart**. Since moving to Berlin from Brussels, the American has developed a cult following with her sparse yet rigorous and often provocative productions at the Volksbühne (*see p256*). Her induction into the theatre world has put her at the top of her game, attracting commissions from all over the world.

Other younger and less established choreographers to look out for include **Christoph Winkler**, whose success with *Tales of the Funky B-Boys and Break Girls* and commitment to investigating societal problems and phenomena have made him one of the leaders of the new dance wave.

Thomas Lehmen, another lesser known yet notable figure, produces highly conceptualised dance works that often reflect upon the form itself. His presence in Berlin has been greatly influential on current and future dance makers.

The **Practicable** collective, comprising five French collaborators (Alice Chauchat, Frédéric de Carlo, Frederic Gies, Isabelle Schad and Odile Seitz), is also noteworthy. It recently gained attention for its feminist work, *The Breast Piece*, in which the culturally loaded symbol of the breast is dissected and re-examined. The collective also continues to develop new works and research projects coupled with workshops for the public.

Ballet

In August 2004, three main companies became one, when half of the Deutsche Oper dancers and all but one at the Komische Oper lost their jobs. Those who were left joined the existing Staatsoper Ballet to form the **Staatsballett Berlin** (www.staatsballett-berlin.de). Thankfully, 'dancer of the century' Vladimir Malakhov remained at the helm and, with his roots in the Russian academic tradition, continues to uphold the reputation of Berlin ballet. Malakhov's now 88-member company performs from September to June at the Deutsche Oper and the Staatsoper Unter den Linden.

Sport & Fitness

Berlin offers plenty of ways to sweat, whether you're canoeing the canals or hanging at the hammam.

Velodrom. *See p262.*

Berlin is one big playground. For the serious sportsman or sportswoman, there are countless organisations and clubs. For the more anarchic, there are the parks. In summer, if you take a walk through one of the city's green spaces, you're bound to come across some motley crew playing football, chucking a frisbee about, or testing the patience of a volleyball net. We've even happened upon an unofficial (but utterly sporting) boxing match, complete with gloves and a dozen supporters-cum-commentators-cum-referees.

Spectator sports, meanwhile, are reasonably priced and you can often just show up and pay at the door; only the major events sell out and require booking in advance.

Major stadiums & arenas

See also p262 **Brave new World**.

Max-Schmeling-Halle

Am Falkplatz, Prenzlauer Berg (443 045/tickets 4430 4430/www.max-schmeling-halle.de). U2 Eberswalder Strasse or U2, S4, S8 Schönhauser Allee. **Map** p319/p328 O2.

Named after the German boxer who knocked out the seemingly invincible Joe Louis in 1936 (Louis settled the score two years later in only 124 seconds), this 11,000-capacity indoor arena faces an uncertain future. It was built as part of Berlin's abortive bid for the 2000 Olympics, and its anchor tenants, basketball side ALBA Berlin, have moved to the O$_2$ World. Its main attraction now is the up-and-coming Olympic handball club, Berliner Füchse. With practically no public parking, it's got its back to the wall against the new, bigger kid in town.

Olympiastadion

Olympischer Platz 3, Charlottenburg (3068 8100/ www.olympiastadion-berlin.de). U2 Olympia-Stadion or S5, S75 Olympiastadion.
Designed as the centrepiece for the 1936 Olympics, the Olympiastadion is one of the best surviving examples of Nazi monumentalism. After years of neglect, despite its status as a protected building, the 76,000-seater was given extensive renovations and a new roof before hosting the 2006 FIFA World Cup Final. This huge bowl hosts Berlin's top football club, Hertha BSC (*see p263*), the German football cup final (*see p196*) and the ISTAF annual athletics meeting (*see p262*), as well as rock concerts and sundry other events.

Velodrom

Paul-Heyse-Strasse 26, Prenzlauer Berg (443 045/ tickets 4430 4430/www.velomax.de). S4, S8 Landsberger Allee. **Map** p325 S4.

Opened in 1997, this multifunctional sports and entertainment venue was designed by Dominique Perrault for the annual six-day cycling race, and boasts a cycling track made from Siberian spruce. It also holds equestrian and super-cross events. *Photo p261.*

Spectator sports

Athletics

ISTAF Athletics Meeting

243 1990/www.istaf.de. **Tickets** €8-€69; 10% less for reductions. **Credit** MC, V.

First held in 1937, this international one-day summer meet at the Olympiastadion (*see p261*) is the last of four events in the International Association of Athletics Federations' Golden League. The $1 million prize money is shared between athletes who win their disciplines at all four Golden League meetings. The crowd is often treated to world records.

Basketball

ALBA

300 9050/www.albaberlin.de. **Tickets** €15-€41.50. **Credit** AmEx, MC, V.

Berlin's representatives in German basketball's top flight take their name from their sponsors, a waste disposal and recycling firm. ALBA wiped the floor with the opposition in the late 1990s and early 2000s and are again back to winning ways. They used to pack them into the Max-Schmeling-Halle (*see p261*) but have now moved to the flashier, bigger O$_2$ World (*see below* **Brave new World**).

Brave new World

O$_2$ World, Berlin's latest glitzy multi-purpose arena, and just gearing up to open as we went to press, is part of the city's controversial development plans for the banks of the Spree river. Accordingly, it got the locals' backs up long before the foundation stone was even laid.

Built next to the Ostbahnhof, it has a capacity of 17,000 and state-of-the-art technology that allows it to be converted from sports arena to rock venue in just a few hours. As befits a house of fun on this scale, it has over 60 entertainment, party and conference suites, as well as numerous restaurants, concession stands and shops. It boasts one of the world's largest outdoor LED displays; inside, there's an eight-screen LED video cube and a 360-degree full-colour ticker.

It's the new sporting headquarters of the Eisbären Ice Hockey Team. Bundesliga basketball champions ALBA are setting up shop here too, abandoning the Max-Schmeling-Halle, which now seems dowdy in comparison. At press time, the schedule also included an NBA basketball match, Olympic handball, WWE wrestling, and performances by Elton John, Alicia Keys and the Dalai Lama.

Even the time capsule buried with the foundation stone boasts some big names: the future-bound booty includes a football shirt signed by Jürgen Klinsmann, a tennis ball signed by Boris Becker, a shellac recording of Marlene Dietrich, and a Californian flag signed by Arnold Schwarzenegger.

Government and promoters see the arena as a 'key investment' that will bring jobs and money to a run-down district. Locals, however, are having nightmares about their quaintly dilapidated neighbourhood being invaded by 17,000 strangers. Two thousand parking spaces next to the arena have done nothing to dispel those fears, nor did plans by the development consortium, known as Mediaspree and backed by local government, to build a new bridge across the river.

The Mediaspree controversy came to a head in July 2008 when a citizens' action group forced and won a referendum on the plans. The campaign wants any new bridge to be for cyclists and pedestrians only, a wider reserve for a promenade on both sides of the river, and no new high-rises. The original project foresaw just a narrow walkway along the river, a high-rise office block and a new bridge for buses and trams (which suspicious minds say would soon be opened up to cars and trucks). The referendum was not binding for the local mayor: it remains to be seen whether he stays true to his promise to go back to the drawing board.

Either way, O$_2$ World is here to stay, even if its operators and the neighbours remain forever worlds apart.

O$_2$ World

Muhlenstrasse 12-30, Friedrichshain (2060 7080/tickets 018 059 6900 0111/ www.o2world.de). S3, S5, S7, S9, S75 Ostbahnhof. **Map** p324 R8.

Football

Germany hosted the 2006 FIFA World Cup Finals, wowing visitors and observers with a carnival atmosphere and an uncharacteristically watchable team to boot. The final (featuring Zinedine Zidane's infamous headbutt) was played at Berlin's Olympiastadion (*see p261*). Berlin's biggest club, Hertha BSC, make occasional but usually abortive forays into Europe (*see below*). The only other team even vaguely in the picture is the Eastern club FC Union, although Turkish side Türkiyemspor (*see p265* **Games without frontiers**) have lately been threatening to achieve league status.

Hertha BSC

0180 518 9200/www.herthabsc.de. **Tickets** €12-€48. **Credit** (online bookings only) MC, V.
Berlin's top team have repeatedly been touted as title contenders at the beginning of the season only to disappoint with hot-and-cold performances and mid-table placings in the Bundesliga. In 2008, they launched an advertising campaign, ostensibly to demonstrate their allegiance to the capital but in fact clearly aimed at wooing more supporters from Eastern districts. They play at the Olympiastadion (*see p261*) in the city's far West.

1. FC Union

Stadion An der Alten Försterei 263, Köpenick (6566 880/www.fc-union-berlin.de). S3 Köpenick. **Tickets** €9.50-€23. **No credit cards.**
Having withstood the pressures of communism, 'Iron Union' came close to buckling under the stress and strain of capitalism, slipping to the third division and flirting with bankruptcy. But true to their name, they've stuck it out, and work has begun upgrading the club's cosy stadium to meet the official requirements should they ever get promoted again. No strangers to novel fund-raising efforts, fans also donated hours, days or even weeks of their labour on the construction site.

Horse racing

Galopprennbahn-Hoppegarten

Goetheallee 1, Dahlwitz-Hoppegarten (0334 238 930/tickets 030 780 111/www.hoppegarten-galopp.de). S5 Hoppegarten. **Tickets** €6-€15. **Credit** AmEx, MC, V.
Thoroughbred races are held between April and October. The betting is run along the lines of the British tote system: all money bet on a race goes into a 'pot', which is shared between those who have placed winning bets.

Harness racing (Trotting)

Pferdesportpark

Treskowallee 129, Karlshorst (5001 711/www.psp-sportpark.de). S3 Karlshorst. **Tickets** vary. **No credit cards.**
Trotting events are held all year round.

Trabrennbahn Mariendorf

Mariendorfer Damm 222-298, Mariendorf (740 1212/www.berlintrab.de). U6 Alt-Mariendorf, then bus X76, 176, 179. **Tickets** *Mon-Fri* free. *Sat, Sun* €3. **No credit cards.**

Pferdesportpark.

Meetings take place irregularly (check the website) on Sundays at 1.30pm and Tuesdays at 6pm. Derby Week in August is a major international event.

Ice hockey

Since German ice hockey clubs set up a private national league in 1994, the sport has become big business. For now, Berlin's **Eisbären** ('polar bears'), the old Eastern club, have seen off their Western rivals, the **Capitals**.

EHC Eisbären Berlin
971 8400/tickets 9718 4040/www.eisbaeren.de. **Tickets €17-€30. No credit cards.**
Having survived the hot and cold showers of communism and the ice bath of capitalism, the 2008 all-German champions have moved to the O₂ World.

Olympic handball

This niche sport has been enjoying a renaissance since Germany hosted the 2007 World Championships and the national team got one up on their limelight-hogging football friends by netting gold.

Füchse Berlin
495 6009/tickets 4430 4430/www.fuechse-berlin.de. **Tickets €10-€26. No credit cards.**
The wily Foxes bear testimony to handball's resurgence, and have now taken up residence at the Max-Schmeling-Halle, with occasional high-profile sorties to the O₂ World also planned.

Tennis

The **Qatar Telecom German Open**, as it is now called, is held each May as a warm-up tournament for the French Open and usually attracts most of the big names. *See also p270.*

LTTC Rot-Weiss
Gottfried-von-Cramm-Weg 47-55, Grunewald (tickets 8957 5510/www.rot-weiss-berlin.de). S3, S7 Grunewald. **Open** 8am-5pm Mon-Thur; 8am-noon Fri. **Tickets** €15-€65; €7.50-€10 reductions. **No credit cards.**
Venue for the German Open, played on clay courts.

Active sports & fitness

Berlin is a dream for the DIY athlete. This chapter only covers a fraction of what's on; if you don't find what you're looking for, contact one of the organisations listed. *Verbände* are the umbrella 'associations' that co-ordinate sports.

Landes Sportbund Berlin (LSB)
Jesse-Owens-Allee 2, Charlottenburg (300 020/ www.lsb-berlin.net). U2 Olympia-Stadion or S5 Olympiastadion. **Open** 9am-3pm Mon-Thur; 9am-2pm Fri.

The Berlin Regional Sports Association's central office provides general information and co-ordinates other offices in charge of specific sports. The Landesausschuss Frauensport, Regional Committee for Women's Sport, is at the same address.

Turngemeinde in Berlin 1848
Columbiadamm 111, Neukölln (611 0100/www. tib1848ev.de). U7 Südstern or U8 Boddinstrasse.
The city's oldest sports club is also perhaps its most diverse, with a list of activities almost as long as its history. As the archaic name suggests (it translates as 'Gymnastics Community in Berlin'), it was founded in 1848. It's based beside the Hasenheide park, where Friedrich Ludwig Jahn, the man known as 'the father of German gymnastics', established the country's first physical education facility in 1811. It offers outdoor and indoor tennis courts, badminton courts, beach volleyball and a profusion of other facilities.

Athletics

Berlin Marathon
Organisers: Berlin-Marathon SCC Running Events GmbH, Glockenturmstrasse 23, 14055 Charlottenburg (3012 8810/www.berlin-marathon.com). S9, S75 Pichelsberg. **Entrance fee** €55-€95. **Credit** call for details. **Date** last Sun in Sept.
Almost 60,000 people take part, making it one of the world's biggest marathons. It's spread over two days to accommodate runners, wheelchair athletes and in-line skaters. Because Berlin is flat and the weather moderate in September, world records are often under threat. The less ambitious can try the Berlin Half-Marathon in early April or 'City Night' in August, a 10km (6-mile) trot up and down the Ku'damm. There's also the New Year Fun Run every 1 January, when Berliners work off their hangovers. It starts at the Soviet War Memorial near the Brandenburg Gate.

Badminton

See also p269 **Squash** *and p270* **Tennis**.

Beach volleyball

Land-locked Berlin is, strangely, a major centre for beach volleyball and one of four cities that host a grand slam tournament. The **Volleyball-Verband Berlin** (3199 9933, www.vvb-online.de) is the sport's umbrella organisation. Its website lists all permanent beach volleyball facilities in Berlin.

Beach Mitte
Caroline-Michaelis-Strasse, Mitte (0177 280 6861/ www.beachmitte.de). S1, S2, S86 Nordbahnhof. **Open** 10am-midnight daily. **Rates** €8-€12/hr. **No credit cards. Map** p318 M4.
This new facility boasts outdoor courts and a beach bar atmosphere with cocktails and a bonfire at night.

Games without frontiers

The year 2008 was a busy anniversary for Türkiyemspor, the main football club of Berlin's Turkish community, founded 20 years earlier as modest Kreuzberg Gençler Birliği. First the club were granted an Integration Award from the Deutscher Fussball-Bund (DSB; German football association). DSB president Dr Theo Zwanziger waxed lyrical about the 'commitment and imagination used to set up projects to promote friendly and fair competition within our country', referring to Türkiyemspor's 17 teams (including three for girls) and numerous community initiatives. Türkiyemspor's senior team then won promotion from the NOFV-Oberliga Nord to the Regionalliga Nord, gaining a fourth-division spot for the first time since 1995.

The Türkiyemspor clubhouse was one of many venues in Berlin that hosted public screenings of the Euro 2008 semi final between Germany and Turkey – a match stolen at the death by Germany. Around the Turkish quarter of Kreuzberg and other prominent spots, fans from each community sported hybrid flags – German tricolours with the Turkish star and crescent on the red bit – and T-shirts with each country's flag in joined heart shapes. Despite the intensity and importance of the proceedings, trouble was minimal. A similar dramatic finish by Turkey in the same competition, against Croatia, led to violence and arrests in Mostar, Bosnia, a town whose communities are strictly divided. Berlin – and Türkiyemspor – have come a long way since 1978.

The club began with expats meeting up for park games in Kreuzberg, centre of Berlin's Turkish community. Starting from the tenth and lowest level of the German league pyramid, the club, whose name changed to Izmirspor and then Türkiyemspor, slowly rose through the divisions. By the late 1980s, they were the third biggest club in West Berlin, after Hertha and Tennis Borussia, attracting all sorts of non-Germans along the way. There was even an English player, a certain Mike Sparrow, who is still talked about today.

The participation of foreigners – and then, even German-born Turks had difficulty getting German passports – proved Türkiyemspor's undoing. Within reach of the German second division, whose professionals play for real money, Türkiyemspor were found by the Berlin football authorities to have fielded illegal players and were forced to replay certain matches. The crucial one, against title challengers Tennis Borussia, ended in defeat and was followed by a season-by-season descent back to the lower leagues.

One positive outcome was the so-called 'Lex Türkiyemspor', a ruling by the German FA that allows foreigners to play legally provided they have been at a local club for five years. Türkiyemspor rebuilt, selling their star player and later Turkish international Ümit Karan, and forging commercial links with Turkey. Other Türkiyemspors were formed around Germany and beyond.

Back in Berlin, the club's current revival also has its downside. Too big for their 5,000-capacity Katzbachstadion in Kreuzberg, Türkiyemspor must play 'home' matches across town at the Friedrich-Ludwig-Jahn Sportpark in Prenzlauer Berg. This ex-Prussian Army parade ground is also the occasional home of BFC Dynamo, the former Stasi side with a significant right-wing support.

'Old German clubs benefit from the kind of political and commercial connections we cannot hope to find,' says Harald Aumeier, a Türkiyemspor commercial representative. 'Our players are part-time and only the manager gets paid. All our other staff work for free. We want to show that we are part of the new Germany, a colourful, integrated Germany for everyone to be proud of. That's what we're all working towards.'

For information, visit www.turkiyemspor.net.

City Beach am Friedrichshain

Kniprodestrasse, corner of Danziger Strasse, Prenzlauer Berg (0177 247 6907/www.city-beach-berlin.de). Tram 20 Kniprodestrasse/Danziger Strasse. **Open** call for details. **Rates** *Summer* €10/hr. *Winter* €20-€22/hr. **No credit cards.** **Map** p325 R4.

Nine-court outdoor facility with a beach bar on the Spree in the summer, plus an indoor facility. Call in advance to book a court.

Bowling

BowlingCenter am Alexanderplatz

Rathausstrasse 5, Mitte (242 6657/www.bowling-am-alex.de). U2, U5, U8, S3, S5, S7, S9 Alexanderplatz. **Open** 11am-midnight Mon-Thur; 11am-2am Fri, Sat; 10am-midnight Sun. **Rates** €11.40-€18/hr; €1.60 shoes. **Map** p319/p327 O6.

This DDR relic now boasts all mod cons: 18 lanes, pool tables, darts, pinball machines and a restaurant.

Magic Mountain.

Neue City Bowling Hasenheide

Hasenheide 107-109, Kreuzberg (622 2038/
www.bowling-hasenheide.de). U7, U8 Hermannplatz.
Open 10am-midnight daily. **Rates** €1.60-€3.50/
person/game. **No credit cards**. **Map** p323 P11.
Top international bowling competitions are hosted
at this 28-lane facility, which also has 12 lanes for
children, a bar/restaurant and two rooms reserved
for those who fancy a smoke.

Canoeing & kayaking

Der Bootsladen

Brandensteinweg 8, Spandau (362 5685/www.der-
bootsladen.de). Bus 149. **Open** *Apr-Sept* noon-7pm
Tue-Fri; 9am-7pm Sat, Sun. *Oct-Mar* 1-4pm Fri;
10am-4pm Sat. **Rates** €5.50-€6.50/hr. **Credit** V.
This is a good place for canoe and kayak tours of
the western river and canal system. You'll save
money by booking for a whole day.

Kanu Connection

Köpenicker Strasse 9, Kreuzberg (612 2686/
www.kanu-connection.de). U1 Schlesisches Tor.
Open 10am-7pm Mon-Fri; 9am-1pm Sat. **Rates**
€22-€30/person/day; €49-€65/wknd; €95-€117/wk.
No credit cards. **Map** p324 R8.

Kreuzberg itself is a nice area to paddle through, or
you could head east to the forests. This outfit can
provide you with maps and guides.

Climbing

Climbers can either go to one of the commercial
halls or join a club; the latter offer good-value
introductory courses and access to some
fantastic outdoor venues such as the World
War II-era flak tower in Humboldthain (*see
p40* **Abstract concrete**). The website
www.klettern-in-berlin.de lists official
and unofficial climbing venues in Berlin.

Deutscher Alpenverein

Markgrafenstrasse 11, Kreuzberg (251 0943/
www.alpenverein-berlin.de). U6 Kochstrasse.
Open 2-7pm Mon, Wed; 9am-1pm Fri. **Admission**
Membership €80; €36-€43 reductions. **No credit
cards**. **Map** p323 N8.
The DAV offers information, courses and access to
cool climbing venues.

Magic Mountain

Böttgerstrasse 20-26, Wedding (8871 5790/
www.magicmountain.de). U8, S1 Gesundbrunnen.
Open noon-midnight Mon-Wed, Fri; 10am-midnight

Thur; 11am-10pm Sat, Sun. **Admission** €12-€14; €10-€12 reductions. **Credit** MC, V.
Map p318 L2.
Indoor climbing hall, featuring a range of walls and a 'donut boulder' for experts.

Cricket

It might come as something of a surprise to hear the smack of leather on willow and bellowed 'Howzats!' in Germany, but cricket has been played in Berlin since the mid 19th century. Six teams currently play competitively; in summer there are games starting 11am every Saturday and Sunday at one of the most beautiful grounds in mainland Europe (Körner Platz, Hanns-Braun-Strasse, Charlottenburg; U2 Olympia-Stadion).

If you want to a game yourself, the **Berlin Cricket Club** (8596 1575, www.berlincc.de), nicknamed 'the Refugees', is a multinational, English-speaking team of expats and locals who are always on the lookout for new members. They're also, as you might expect, the best source for general information about cricket in Berlin.

Cycling

Cycling is an ideal method of getting around Berlin, as the city is flat and well supplied with cycle lanes. In fact, it can be a particularly scenic way to see the city, as bike lanes run through parks and alongside canals. Competitive cycling is also popular, and Berlin has produced several internationally renowned riders. The city's level hinterland is also ideal for touring. For bike rental, *see p289.*

Allgemeiner Deutscher Fahrrad-Club

Brunnenstrasse 28, Mitte (448 4724/www.adfc-berlin.de). U8 Bernauer Strasse. **Open** noon-8pm Mon-Fri; 10am-4pm Sat. **Map** p319 N3.
Has an information and meeting point for cyclists and a do-it-yourself repair station. Contact them for a copy of their Berlin cycle path map.

Berliner Radsport Verband

Paul-Heyse-Strasse 29, Prenzlauer Berg (4210 5145/www.bdr-radsport.de/ber). S4 Landsberger Allee. **Open** 9am-1pm Tue, Fri; 2-5pm Thur. **Map** p325 S4.
Information on clubs, races and events. The Tour de Berlin, a five-stage, 600km/375-mile race, is in May.

Arts & Entertainment

Disabled

There are dozens of clubs and organisations for disabled athletes in Berlin. Phone **Behinderten-Sportverband Berlin** (3009 9675) for details or visit its website at www.bsberlin.de.

Fitness centres

There are hundreds of health and fitness clubs in Berlin – everything from sweaty body-building basements to luxurious spa-like penthouses. There are also branches of chains such as Kieser, Swiss Training and Gold's.

Aspria

Karlsruher Strasse 20, Wilmersdorf (890 688 810/ www.aspria.de). S45, S46 Halensee. **Open** 6am-11pm Mon-Fri; 9am-10pm Sat, Sun. **Rates** from €70/mth. **Credit** AmEx, DC, MC, V. **Map** p320 C9.

Luxurious five-floor complex with a health and beauty centre, 25m pool, saunas, steam room, ice room, restaurants, bars, sun terrace with solariums and a view of central Berlin. The club offers massages, beauty treatments, fitness courses and customised workouts.

Club Olympus Spa & Fitness

Grand Hyatt Berlin, Marlene-Dietrich-Platz 2, Tiergarten (2553 1890/www.berlin.grand.hyatt.com). U2, S1, S2, S9, S26 Potsdamer Platz. **Open** 6.30am-10.30pm Mon-Fri; 7.30am-9pm Sat, Sun. **Rates** €60/ day. **Credit** AmEx, DC, MC, V. **Map** p322/p327 K8.

Luxurious, expensive fitness centre on the hotel roof.

Jopp Frauen Fitness

Tauentzienstrasse 13A, Charlottenburg (235 1700/ www.jopp.de). U9 Kurfürstendamm or U1, U2, U3 Wittenbergplatz. **Open** 7am-11pm Mon-Fri; 10am-8pm Sat, Sun. **Rates** from €66/mth. **Map** p321 G8.

This women-only chain has branches across Berlin.

Liquidrom

Möckernstrasse 10, Kreuzberg (258 007 820/www. liquidrom-berlin.de). S1, S2, S25 Anhalter Bahnhof, U7 Möckernbrücke. **Open** 10am-midnight Mon-Thur, Sun; 10am-1am Fri, Sat. **Admission** €17.50/2hrs; €20.50/4hrs; €22.50/day. **No credit cards.** **Map** p322 L9.

Part of the Tempodrom complex, this is a stylish oasis of watery leisure pursuits, with pools, saunas, steam baths, cold dips, an open-air Japanese Onsen pool, massage facilities and a terrace and bar. One of the highlights is 'liquid sound', a domed, circular pool with lighting and underwater speakers. On Friday evenings, it's all candle-lit.

Gay & lesbian sports

The rift in international GLBT sports that led to the creation of the Outgames as well as the Gay Games also affected Berlin's efforts to host a major event. Berlin's gay mayor saw no option but to withdraw official backing for both factions. The Outgames 2009 went to Copenhagen and Cologne got the 2010 Gay Games. Berlin, meanwhile, is out in the cold and the gay sporting community is split. But you can still visit www.vorspiel-berlin.de for details of local sports.

Golf

Global Golf Berlin

Schöneberger Ufer 7, Kreuzberg (2269 7844/www. globalgolf-berlin.net). U2 Mendelssohn-Bartholdy-Park. **Open** 9am-10pm Mon-Sat; 9am-8pm Sun. **Rates** call for details. **Map** p322 L8.

Spectacular inner-city driving range. Facilities for members include computerised swing analysis and automatic teeing, plus chipping and putting greens. Non-members also have a putting green at their disposal. Courses for beginners and the more advanced.

Golfpark Schloss Wilkendorf

Am Weiher 1, OT Wilkendorf, Gielsdorf (0334 133 0960/www.golfpark-schloss-wilkendorf.com). S5 Strausberg Nord, then walk/taxi. **Open** *Nov-Mar* 9am-5pm daily. *Apr-Oct* 9am-6pm. **Rates** *Westside Platz* (18 holes) €35 Mon-Fri; €50 Sat, Sun. *Sandy-Lyle-Platz* (18 holes; members only) €30-€40 Mon-Fri; €60 Sat, Sun. *Public course* (6 holes) €10-€15. **Credit** MC, V.

The only 18-hole course in the area open to non-members: at weekends, you'll need a *Platzreife* (German golf certificate), which is obtainable with any golf membership or by taking a course and/or test. Call for details.

Ice skating

The Christmas market at Alexanderplatz has a small outdoor rink, and you can try your hand at curling in the Sony Center at Potsdamer Platz from late November to early January.

Erika-Hess-Eisstadion-Mitte

Erika-Hess-Stadion, Müllerstrasse 185, Wedding (200 945 550). U6 Reinickendorfer Strasse. **Open** 9am-noon, 3-5.30pm Mon, Tue; 9am-noon, 3-5.30pm, 7.30-9.30pm Wed, Thur; 9am-noon, 3-5.30pm, 7.30-10pm Fri, Sat; 9am-noon, 2-5pm Sun. Closed Apr-Sept. **Admission** €3.30; €1.60 reductions. **No credit cards. Map** p318 K3.

Cheapest public rink in town. The venue also holds important skating competitions.

Horst-Dohm-Eisstadion

Fritz-Wildung-Strasse 9, Wilmersdorf (8973 2734/www.horst-dohm-eisstadion.de). S4 Hohenzollerndamm. **Open** *Oct-mid Mar* 9am-6pm, 7.30-10pm Mon-Fri; 9am-10pm Sat; 10am-6pm Sun. **Rates** €3.30/2hrs; €1.60 reductions. **No credit cards. Map** p320 D11.

Boasts an outer ring for speed skating and an inner field for figure skaters. Skate rental too.

Sailing & motor boating

There's a lot of water around Berlin. The city boasts 50 lakes and a 200-kilometre (125-mile) network of navigable rivers, estuaries and canals. The city is bordered on the west by the Havel river and to the south by the Dahme, while the Spree forms an east-west axis through the centre. The **Berliner Segler-Verband** (3083 9908, www.berlinerseglerverband.de) has information on sailing in and around Berlin.

If you're planning a longer stay, you might join a local sailing club. The **American International Yacht Club Berlin** (8040 3630, www.aiycb.de) has an English website and is a good first port of call. There's also the **German-British Yacht Club** (365 4010, www.dbyc.de). But there are also opportunities for the short-term visitor. The **Wassersportzentrum Berlin** (6418 0140, www.wassersportzentrum.de) runs two sailing/diving/motor boat centres with marinas at the Müggelsee in south-east Berlin. You need a licence for boating and sailing, so if you have one, bring it. Boat rental places may then issue you a charter pass for sailboats or motor boats.

Sauna & Turkish baths

Many of Berlin's public baths have cheapish saunas and massage services. *See below.*

Hamam Turkish Bath

Schoko-Fabrik, Naunynstrasse 72, Kreuzberg (615 1464/www.hamamberlin.de/en). U1, U8 Kottbusser Tor. **Open** 3-11pm Mon; noon-10pm Tue-Sun. **Rates** €14/3 hrs; €21/5 hrs. **No credit cards. Map** p323 P9.
Under the glass cupola of the main hall, women sit in alcoves, soaking in warm water. It's a friendly and laid-back place, attracting a mixed clientele. Enjoy Turkish tea and a reviving massage afterwards. Children are not permitted on Tuesday and Fridays but Thursday is kids' day (women only, but boys up to age of six are allowed in).

Sultan Hamam

Bülowstrasse 57, Schöneberg (2175 3375/www. sultan-hammam.de). U2 Bülowstrasse. **Open** noon-11pm daily. **Rates** €16/3hrs; €13 peel; €18 massage. **No credit cards. Map** p322 J9.
Traditional massages and peelings, as well as more modern cosmetic treatments. Monday is men's day, Sunday is families' day; otherwise it's women only.

Thermen am Europa-Center

Europa-Center, Nürnberger Strasse 7, Charlottenburg (257 5760/www.thermen-berlin.de). U1, U2, U3 Wittenbergplatz. **Open** 10am-midnight Mon-Sat; 10am-9pm Sun. **Rates** €18.80/day; €16.50/3 hrs; €161/10 admissions. **No credit cards. Map** p321 G8.

Big, central, mixed facility offering Finnish saunas, steam baths, hot and cool pools, and a garden (open until October). There is a pool where you can swim outside on to the roof and back, even in the depths of winter. Other facilities include a café, pool-side loungers, table tennis, billiards and massage.

Skateboarding, in-line skating & BMX

Berlin is a skater-friendly city, with small facilities dotted across town, plus several bigger complexes; all are listed at www.skatespots.de. The city's in-line skaters occasionally disrupt street traffic by holding demonstrations for equal rights. Routes vary; check www.berlin parade.de for dates and starting points.

Erlebniswerkstatt des Projektes Erlebnisräume

Sterndamm 82, Treptow (631 0911/www. erlebnisraeume.de). S4, S6, S8, S9, S10 Schäneweide. **Open** call for appointment. **Admission** free.
Trial track with jump ramps, and a good place to connect with what's on. Projekt Erlebnisräume builds and maintains skateboarding, skating and climbing facilities and organises competitions.

Squash

Many tennis clubs have squash courts too (*see p270*).

Sport Oase, Ladyline & Himaxx

Stromstrasse 11-17, Moabit (390 6620/www.sport oase.de). U9 Turmstrasse. **Open** 8am-11.30pm Mon-Thur; 8am-10pm Fri; 10am-8pm Sat; 9am-10pm Sun. **Rates** €11-€19/45 mins; €18-€36/90 mins. **No credit cards. Map** p317 H5.
This impressive complex, housed in a former brewery, has badminton and squash courts, saunas, a mixed fitness room, a women-only fitness centre called Ladyline, and Himaxx, a high-altitude training centre. There's also a pleasant pub/restaurant.

Swimming (indoor)

Every district has an indoor pool. Check the phone book under *Stadtbad* or visit www. berlinerbaederbetriebe.de for the nearest.

SSE Europa-Sportpark

Paul-Heyse-Strasse 26, Prenzlauer Berg (4218 6120). S4, S8, S10 Landsberger Allee. **Open** 6.30am-10.30pm Mon, Tue, Thur; 8am-10.30pm Wed; 9am-10.30pm Fri; noon-7pm Sat; 10am-6pm Sun. **Admission** €4; €2.50 reductions. **No credit cards. Map** p315 S4.
One of the largest swimming pools in Europe, this immense facility next to the Velodrom (*see p262*) often hosts international swimming competitions.

Stadtbad Mitte

Gartenstrasse 5, Mitte (3088 0910). S1, S2 Nordbahnhof/tram 8, 50. **Open** 6.30am-10pm Mon, Wed, Fri; 10am-4pm Tue; 6.30-8am Thur; 2-9pm Sat; 10am-6pm Sun. **Admission** €4; €2.50 reductions. **No credit cards. Map** p318/p326 M4.

This impressive place, which dates from 1928, has a 50m (164ft) pool.

Stadtbad Neukölln

Ganghoferstrasse 3, Neukölln (6824 9812). U7 Rathaus Neukölln. **Open** 2-5pm Mon; 6.45am-6.30pm Tue, Wed; 6.45am-10pm Thur, Fri; 8am-8pm Sat; 8am-2pm Sun. **Admission** €4; €2.50 reductions. **No credit cards. Map** p324 R12.

Described as 'Europe's most beautiful baths' when opened in 1914, the Stadtbad Neuköln survived the 20th century unscathed and beautiful it remains. Built in Greco-Roman style, the complex features two splendid pools flanked by Ionic columns, with original tiling and mosaics, wood panelling and stained-glass windows.

Stadtbad Schöneberg

Hauptstrasse 39, Schöneberg (780 9930). U7 Eisenacher Strasse. **Open** 10am-10pm Mon; 7am-10pm Tue-Fri; 9am-10pm Sat, Sun. **Admission** €4-€5; €3-€4 reductions. **No credit cards. Map** p322 J11.

Great mixture of old and new. Kids can play on the water slide or in the wave pool while you swim laps or recharge batteries in the sauna. Busy at peak times.

Swimming (open-air)

Before setting out to a pool, phone first to make sure it's open (or call the Berlin service hotline on 0180 310 2020) as the city's financial woes affect opening times. Details of all outdoor public pools can be found at www.berliner baederbetriebe.de. There is also plenty of lake swimming in Berlin: **Schlachtensee** and **Krumme Lanke** in the West are clean, set in attractive woodland and easily accessible by public transport.

Most of the following are closed in winter.

Badeschiff Berlin

Eichenstrasse 4, Treptow (533 2030/www.arena-berlin.de). S9, S41, S42 Treptower Park/bus 265. **Open** 8am-midnight daily. **Admission** €3; reductions €1.50. **No credit cards.**

This popular commercial operation features a former barge converted into a heated swimming pool, docked on the banks of the Spree. It belongs to the Arena Berlin (*see p235*) cultural centre, and also boasts two saunas and a bar.

Freibad Müggelsee

Fürstenwalder Damm 838, Rahnsdorf (648 7777). S3 Rahnsdorf. **Open** *May-Sept* 9am-6pm daily. **Admission** €4; €2 reductions. **No credit cards.**

Bathing beach, complete with nudist camp, on the north shore of East Berlin's biggest lake.

Sommerbad Kreuzberg

Prinzenstrasse 113-119, Kreuzberg (616 1080). U1 Prinzenstrasse. **Open** *May-Sept* 7am-8pm daily. **Admission** €4; €2.50 reductions. **No credit cards. Map** p323 O9.

This popular outdoor complex for swimming and sunbathing, known as Prinzenbad, has a 50m (164ft) pool and one for non-swimmers. Disabled access, nudist area and refreshments.

Strandbad Wannsee

Wannseebadweg, Nikolassee (7071 3833). S1, S7 Nikolassee. **Open** *Apr-Sept* 10am-7pm Mon-Fri; 8am-8pm Sat, Sun. **Admission** €4; €2.50 reductions. **No credit cards.**

Strandbad Wannsee is Europe's largest inland beach, with sand, sunbeds, water slides, pedalos, snack stalls and beer garden. The complete seaside experience, only without salty water.

Tennis

An expensive sport in Berlin. The cheapest time is in the mornings and even then it can cost €15-€30 an hour for an indoor court. The **Tennis-Verband Berlin-Brandenburg** (8972 8730, www.tvbb.de) has information about local leagues and clubs.

TC City Sports

Brandenburgische Strasse 53, Wilmersdorf (873 9097/www.citysports-berlin.com). U7 Konstanzer Strasse. **Open** 8am-11pm daily. **Rates** *Tennis* €14-€19/45 mins. *Squash* €12.50-€19.50/45 mins. *Badminton* €10.50-€17.50/45 mins. *Sauna* €7.50. **Credit** V. **Map** p321 E10.

Tennis, squash and badminton courts, plus a sauna, solarium, restaurant and beer garden. Coaching is available for all three sports, along with aerobics and classical dance. If you've been playing a racquet game, the sauna comes free.

Tennis Center Weissensee

Roelckestrasse 106, Weissensee (927 4594/ www.tcwsports.com). S4, S8, S10 Greifswalder Strasse. **Open** 7am-midnight Mon-Fri; 8am-midnight Sat, Sun. **Rates** €14-€20/hr singles; €23-€36/hr doubles. **No credit cards.**

Tennis, badminton and fun ball courts, all indoors. Prices include use of the sauna (10am-10pm).

Windsurfing, water-skiing, wakeboarding & surfing

The **Müggelsee** in the south-east of Berlin is a popular lake for water sports, as are the Wannsee in the south-west and the **Tegeler See** in the north-west. Useful (but German-only) websites are www.fss.berlin.de/ index_content.html (surfing); www.wakeboard-berlin.de (wakeboarding); www.wsev.de/ wsev.jsp (windsurfing) and www.wasser skiclub-berlin.de (water-skiing).

Trips Out of Town

Café Drachenhaus. *See p275.*

Trips Out of Town

Palaces, parks, beaches, Bach – and a whole lot of lakes and forests.

Filmmuseum Potsdam. *See p276.*

Berlin is a city in the middle of nowhere. For miles around, fields, lakes and dense woods are interrupted by a sparse scattering of little-visited towns and villages (*see p275* **Getting nowhere fast**). Indeed, water and greenery crowd into the city from all sides (*see pp123-130*).

By far the most popular day trip is to **Potsdam** (*see below*), which is to Berlin what Versailles is to Paris. There's easily enough there to fill a couple of days. Neighbouring **Babelsberg** (*see p276*) has the old UFA film studios, Germany's answer to Hollywood. Another worthwhile, though more sombre, trip is just north of the city to the former concentration camp **Sachsenhausen** (*see p278*).

The **Spreewald** (*see p278*), a forest cross-hatched with small, navigable streams, is good for a stroll or boat ride, and can be reached in an hour by train. For the seaside, head north to the Baltic coast and the island of **Rügen** (*see p279*), but plan on staying at least one night. Two other good trips are south to the historic cities of Saxony: **Leipzig** (*see p282*) and **Dresden** (*see p280*).

TRAVELLING BY TRAIN

Trains to all destinations depart from the new **Berlin Hauptbahnof**, Europe's biggest and most futuristic train station. Depending on where they're going, trains will also stop at the new

Nordkreuz station (formerly Gesundbrunnen), the new **Südkreuz** station (formerly Papestrasse) and also at **Berlin-Spandau**.

Regionalbahn trains – the red, double-decker ones – serve Berlin's hinterland, including many of the destinations in this chapter. They stop at larger stations such as Zoologischer Garten, Friedrichstrasse, Alexanderplatz and Potsdamer Platz, as well as Hauptbahnof.

Deutsche Bahn has a timetable search facility in English at www.bahn.co.uk.

Around Berlin

Potsdam & Babelsberg

Potsdam is capital of the state of Brandenburg and, just outside the city limits to the south-west, Berlin's most beautiful neighbour. Known for its 18th-century baroque architecture, it's a magnet for tourists. The summer weekend crowds can be overwhelming; visit outside of peak times if you can.

For centuries, Potsdam was the summer residence of the Hohenzollerns, who were attracted by the area's gently rolling landscape, rivers and lakes. Despite the damage wrought during World War II and by East Germany's socialist planners, much remains of the legacy of these Prussian kings. The best-known landmark is **Sanssouci**, the huge landscaped park created by Frederick the Great, one of three royal parks flanking the town.

Potsdam has changed considerably since Reunification. In East German times its associations with the monarchy were regarded with suspicion; the lack of political will and economic means led to much of the town's historic fabric falling into disrepair or being destroyed. In 1990, however, Potsdam was assigned UNESCO World Heritage status and some 80 per cent of the town's historic buildings have since been restored.

The end of East Germany also marked the end of Potsdam's historic role as a garrison town. Until the Soviet withdrawal, some 10,000 troops were stationed here. With their departure, vast barracks and tracts of land to the north of the town were abandoned. The area is currently being redeveloped for civilian use, including the BUGA or Volkspark, with its nature museum, the **Biosphäre**.

THE OLD TOWN

One of the most dominant – if not the prettiest – buildings of historical interest in the old town is the 19th-century **Nikolaikirche**. It's hard to miss the huge dome, inspired by St Paul's in London. Rather more graceful is the mid 18th-century **Altes Rathaus**, diagonally opposite, whose tower was used a prison until 1875. Nowadays, the former town hall is used for exhibitions and lectures. Both the Nikolaikirche and the Altes Rathaus were badly damaged in the war and rebuilt in the 1960s. The two buildings are all that remain of the original Alter Markt, once one of Potsdam's most beautiful squares, and with the Nikolaikirche undergoing renovations until sometime in 2009 and a new bridge going up, it's all a bit of a building site at the moment.

The **Stadtschloss**, in the centre of town, was substantially damaged during the war and the East German authorities demolished the rest of it in 1960. There are plans to rebuild it, but funding problems mean this is unlikely to happen soon. Private sponsors have already paid for the reconstruction of the Fortunaportal, one decorative former entrance to the palace, in the Alter Markt. To get an impression of this square before 1945, take a look at the model in the foyer of the Altes Rathaus.

The area behind the gargantuan Hotel Mercure was once part of the palace gardens. Later, Friedrich Wilhelm I, the Soldier King, turned it into a parade ground. Now it has become a park. If you walk up Breite Strasse, you can see all that is left of the old Stadtschloss.

Nothing to worry about at **Park Sanssouci**.

The low red building that now houses the **Filmmuseum Potsdam** is the former *Marstall*, or royal stables. Dating from 1685 and originally an orangery, it is one of the oldest buildings in the town.

The nearby Neuer Markt survived the war intact. At number 1 is the house where Friedrich Wilhelm II was born. The *Kutschstall*, originally a royal stables, now houses the new **Haus der Brandenburgisch-Preussischen Geschichte**, with its exhibition charting 800 years of Brandenburg history.

THE BAROQUE AND DUTCH QUARTERS

Potsdam's impressive **baroque quarter** is bounded by Schopenhauerstrasse, Hegelallee, Hebbelstrasse and Charlottenstrasse. Some of the best houses can be found in Gutenbergstrasse and Brandenburger Strasse, the city's pedestrianised shopping drag. Note the pitched roofs with space to accommodate troops – the Soldier King built the quarter in the 1730s. Just around the corner is **Gedenkstätte Lindenstrasse**, once the house of a Prussian officer, later a Stasi detention centre (you can now tour the cells).

Three baroque town gates – the **Nauener Tor**, **Jäger Tor** and **Brandenburger Tor** – stand on the northern and western edges of the quarter. On its east, two churches bear witness to Potsdam's cosmopolitan past. The Great Elector's 1685 Edict of Potsdam promised refuge to Protestants suffering from religious persecution in their homelands, sparking waves of immigration. The **Französische Kirche** on Hebbelstrasse was built for the town's

Huguenot community, while **St Peter & Paul's** in Bassinplatz was built for Catholic immigrants who came to this Protestant area in response to the Prussian kings' drive to bring in skilled workers and soldiers.

The **Holländisches Viertel**, or Dutch Quarter, is the most attractive part of Friedrich Wilhelm I's new town extension. As part of a failed strategy to lure skilled Dutch immigrants to the town, the king had Dutch builders construct 134 gable-fronted houses. In the **Jan Bouman Haus** on Mittelstrasse you can see an original interior. Today this area is filled with upmarket boutiques and restaurants.

THE RUSSIAN INFLUENCE

Another Potsdam curiosity is the Russian colony of **Alexandrowka**, 15 minutes' walk north of the town centre. The settlement consists of 13 wooden clad, two-storey dwellings with steeply pitched roofs laid out in the form of a St Andrew's Cross. There's even a Russian orthodox church with an onion dome. Services are still held in the Alexander-Newski-Kapelle.

Alexandrowka was built in 1826 by Friedrich Wilhelm III to commemorate the death of Tsar Alexander I, a friend from the Wars of Liberation against Napoleon. The settlement became home to surviving members of a troupe of Russian musicians given into Prussian service by the Tsar in 1812. Two of the houses are still inhabited by the descendants of these men. Russian specialities are served by waitresses in folkloric costume at the **Teehaus Russische Kolonie** (Alexandrowka 1, 0331 200 6478, closed Mon, mains €8-€17). Nearby is the tiny **Alexandrowka Museum** (Russische Kolonie 2, 0331 817 0203, www.alexandrowka.de, closed Mon) with films and exhibits about the colony.

The area around and to the north of **Alexandrowka** became the focus of a different Russian presence during the Cold War. The late Wilhelmine villas served as offices to the Soviet administration or as officers' homes. Soviet forces took over buildings used by the Prussian army in the 19th century and later by the Nazis. One such is the castle-like **Garde-Ulanen-Kaserne** in Jäger Allee, close to the junction with Reiterweg.

The recently restored **Belvedere**, at the top of the hill to the north of Alexandrowka, is the town's highest observation point. It fell into disuse after the Wall went up in 1961, when people were banned from enjoying views over West Berlin.

POTSDAM'S ROYAL PARKS

Back towards the town centre is Potsdam's biggest tourist magnet, **Park Sanssouci**. It's beautiful, but be warned: its main avenues can become overrun and it is not always easy to get into the palaces (guided tours are compulsory and numbers limited).

The park is a legacy of King Frederick the Great, who was attracted to the area by its fine views. He initially had terraced gardens built here before adding a palace. *Sans souci* means 'without worries' and reflects the king's desire for a sanctuary where he could pursue his philosophical, musical and literary interests. Voltaire was among his guests. His nearby Bildergalerie was the first purpose-built museum in Germany.

After victory in the Seven Years' War, Frederick the Great built the huge **Neues Palais** on the park's western edge. Friedrich II's sumptuous suite, as well as the Grottensaal (Grotto Room), Marmorsaal (Marble Room) and Schlosstheater (Palace Theatre), are worth a visit. Parts of the Palais are being renovated

for Frederick the Great's 300th birthday in 2012, as are portions of the surrounding park.

Attractions in the park include the Orangery; the Spielfestung, or toy fortress, built for Wilhelm II's sons, complete with a toy cannon that can be fired; the Chinesisches Teehaus (Chinese Teahouse), with its collection of Chinese and Meissen porcelain; and the Drachenhaus (Dragonhouse), a pagoda-style café. In the park's south-west corner lies **Schloss Charlottenhof**, with its blue-glazed entrance and copper-plate engraving room, built in the 1830s on the orders of crown prince Friedrich Wilhelm IV. Outside Sanssouci in the Breite Strasse is the Dampfmaschinenhaus that pumped water for Sanssouci's fountains, but was built to look like a mosque.

North-east of the town centre is another large park complex, the **Neuer Garten**, designed on the orders of Frederick the Great's nephew and

Getting nowhere fast

No other European capital is surrounded by such a sparsely populated landscape as Berlin. This is a region of rare and delicate beauty, often ignored by visitors. Flat it may be, but the *Land* of Brandenburg deserves more attention than it gets. Forests and lakes are interspersed with water meadows and low gravelly ridges that speak of glaciers that came this way thousands of years ago.

Speeding along the Autobahn, it might all look a bit dull. But leave the main highways to find empty tree-lined secondary roads that twist and turn through forests and fen to come unexpectedly upon unspoilt villages with neat brick barns, ponds with the statutory quota of ducks and, more often than not, a traditional *Gaststätte* serving beers and improbably large portions of pork with dumplings. At some of the best such hostelries, look for local freshwater fish, notably pike-perch or carp, and off-dry Müller-Thurgau wines from Eastern Germany. Against all odds, decent white wines are produced in the region south-west of Berlin, and though rarely found in the capital, they often pop up in the countryside.

Some of the finest scenery is about 70 kilometres north of the city in an arc from Rheinsberg via Furstenberg to Templin. But travel out of Berlin in any direction to find exquisite unspoilt forests and lakes, and, at the right time of year, storks that preside majestically over a village from a manicured nest on a vantage point. On minor roads, expect ferries rather than

bridges at the major river crossings, and even the odd stretch of gravel or dirt highway too.

Even without a car, it's perfectly feasible to get a flavour of Berlin's hinterland. The **Ostdeutsche Eisenbahn Gesellschaft** (ODEG) (www.odeg.info) runs modern comfortable glass railcars that afford panoramic views from its routes heading out of the city to the east. The OE36 leaves hourly from Berlin-Lichtenberg (U5, S5, S7, S75) and Schöneweide (S8, S9, S45) to Frankfurt-an-der-Oder. The full journey takes two and a half hours, and traverses some of Germany's most unspoilt scenery. Break the trip midway at Wendish-Rietz for a boat excursion (from Easter until the end of October) on the Scharmützelsee (schedules on www.scharmuetzelsee.de/schiffahrt). In Frankfurt there's lots of DDR-era architecture and the pleasure of wandering over the river into Poland. Those with a real appetite for train travel can return to Berlin on ODEG's other main route, OE60, which loops north through the hills of the Oderbruch to rejoin the capital from the north-east. This alternative route runs once every two hours, also takes two and a half hours, and terminates at Berlin-Lichtenberg.

The fares aren't expensive – you can get a day ticket for the whole network for €19, and it's even cheaper with a €26 **Brandenburg-Berlin-Ticket**, which allows up to five people to travel together on the same ticket. Information is at www.vbbonline.de.

successor to the throne, Friedrich Wilhelm II. In the neo-classical **Marmorpalais** the king died a premature death, allegedly as a result of his dissolute lifestyle. At the park's most northern corner is **Schloss Cecilienhof**, the last royal palace to be built in Potsdam. This incongruous, mock-Tudor mansion was built for the Kaiser's son and his wife. Spared wartime damage, in summer 1945 it hosted the Potsdam Conference, where Stalin, Truman and Churchill (later replaced by Clement Attlee) met to discuss Germany's future. Inside, you can see the round table where the settlement was negotiated.

During the conference, the Allied leaders lived across the Havel in one of Babelsberg's secluded 19th-century villa districts. Stalin stayed in Karl-Marx-Strasse 27, Churchill in the Villa Urbig at Virchowstrasse 23, one of Mies van der Rohe's early buildings, and Truman in the Truman-Villa in Karl-Marx-Strasse 2. These buildings can be viewed from the outside only.

Potsdam's third and most recent royal park, **Park Babelsberg**, also makes for a good walk. In East German times this fell into neglect because it lay so close to the border. **Schloss Babelsberg**, a neo-Gothic extravaganza inspired by Windsor Castle, nestles among its wooded slopes. Another architectural curiosity is the Flatowturm, an observation point in mock medieval style close to the Glienicker See.

Also on the east side of the Havel, not too far south of Potsdam's main station, is the Telegraphenberg – once the site of a telegraph station. In 1921, it became the site of Erich Mendelsohn's Expressionist **Einsteinturm**, commissioned to house an observatory that could confirm the General Theory of Relativity. A wonderfully whimsical building, it was one of the first products of the inter-war avant-garde.

On the nearby Brauhausberg, there is one last reminder of Potsdam's complex, multi-layered past. The square tower rising up from the trees is the present seat of Brandenburg's state parliament. In East German days, the building was known as the 'Kremlin' because it served as local Communist party headquarters. Originally, it was the Kriegsschule – 'the war school' – where young men trained to be officers in the German imperial army.

HOLLYWOOD BABELSBERG

The main attraction in Potsdam's eastern neighbour, **Babelsberg**, is the film studio complex, sections of which are open to the public in theme-park form. In the 1920s, this was the world's largest studio outside Hollywood and it was here that Fritz Lang's *Metropolis*, Josef von Sternberg's *The Blue Angel* and other masterpieces of the era were produced. During the Nazi period it churned out

thrillers, light entertainment and propaganda pieces such as Leni Riefenstahl's *Triumph of the Will*. More than 700 feature films were made here in the Communist era.

The studios were privatised after Reunification and now there are modern facilities for all phases of film and TV production, and offices for all manner of media and production companies. The **Filmpark Babelsberg** has an assortment of attractions, ranging from themed restaurants and rides to set tours and stunt displays, but it's all pretty tacky stuff.

Altes Rathaus
Am Alten Markt (0331 289 6336/www.altesrathaus potsdam.de). Tram X98, 90, 92, 93, 96 Alter Markt. **Open** 10am-6pm Tue-Sun. **Admission** €3; €2 reductions. **No credit cards**.

Biosphäre
Georg-Hermann-Allee 99 (0331 550 740/www. biosphaere-potsdam.net). Tram 96 BUGA-Park. **Open** 9am-6pm (last entry 4.30pm) Mon-Fri; 10am-7pm (last entry 5.30pm) Sat, Sun. **Admission** €9.50; €6.50-€8 reductions. **No credit cards**.

Filmmuseum Potsdam
Breitestrasse 1A (0331 271 810/www.filmmuseum-potsdam.de). Tram X98, 90, 92, 93, 96 Alter Markt. **Open** 10am-6pm daily. **Admission** €3.50; €2.50 reductions. *Guided tours* €1. **No credit cards**. The permanent exhibition explores nearly a century of film-making at the Babelsberg studios, focusing on DEFA, East Germany's sole film-making company. The onsite cinema regularly shows films, and guided tours are available in English. *Photo p272*.

Filmpark Babelsberg
entrance on Grossbeerenstrasse (0331 721 2750/ www.filmpark-babelsberg.de). S1, S7 Babelsberg, then bus 601, 619, 690 to Filmpark/RE1 Medienstadt. **Open** 10am-6pm daily. Closed Nov-Mar. **Admission** €19; €13 reductions. **Credit** AmEx, MC, V.

Gedenkstätte Lindenstrasse
Lindenstrasse 54 (0331 289 6136/www.potsdam.de/ potsdam-museum). Tram 91, 94, 96 Dortusstrasse. **Open** 10am-6pm Tue, Thur, Sat. **Admission** €1.50. **No credit cards**. East German secret police interrogated people in this warrenous complex of cells.

Haus der Brandenburgisch-Preussischen Geschichte
Kutschstall, Am Neuen Markt (0331 620 8550/ www.hbpg.de). Tram X98, 90, 92, 93, 96 Alter Markt. **Open** 10am-6pm Tue-Fri; 10am-5pm Sat, Sun. **Admission** €5; €4 reductions. **No credit cards**.

Jan Bouman Haus
Mittelstrasse 8 (0331 280 3773). Tram 90, 92, 95 Nauener Tor. **Open** 1-6pm Mon-Fri; 11am-6pm Sat, Sun. **Admission** €2; €1 reductions. **No credit cards**.

Gedenkstätte Lindenstrasse.

Marmorpalais
Im Neuen Garten (0331 969 4246/www.potsdam.de).
Tram 92, 96/bus 692 Reiterweg/Alleestrasse. **Open**
May-Oct 10am-5.30pm Tue-Sun. *Nov-Apr* as guided
tour only, 10am-4.30pm Sat, Sun. **Admission** €5;
€4 reductions. **No credit cards**.

Nikolaikirche
*Am Alten Markt (0331 291 682/www.nikolaipotsdam.
de). Tram X98, 90, 92, 93, 96 Alter Markt.* **Open**
2-5pm Mon; 10am-5pm Tue-Sun. **Admission** free.

Sanssouci
(0331 969 4202/www.spsg.de). Bus X15, 695. **Open**
Palace & exhibition buildings Apr-Oct 9am-5pm Tue-
Sun. Nov-Mar 9am-4pm daily. *Park* 9am-dusk daily.
Admission *Palace & exhibition buildings* €8; €5
reductions. *Park* free. **Credit** MC, V.
Each of the various palaces and buildings has its
own closing days each month and some are only
open mid May to mid October. Phone or check the
website for full details.

Schloss Cecilienhof
*Im Neuen Garten (0331 969 4244/www.spsg.de).
Bus 692.* **Open** *Apr-Oct* 9am-5.30pm Tue-Sun.
Nov-Mar 9am-4.30pm Tue-Sun. **Admission** €6;
€5 reductions. **Credit** AmEx, MC, V.

Where to eat & drink

B-West (Zeppelinstrasse 146, 0331 951 0798,
mains €5-€10) attracts a lively, young crowd
and serves simple German cuisine. **Café Heider**
(Friedrich-Ebert-Strasse 29, 0331 270 5596,
mains €3-€15) offers excellent coffee and cake,
plus a wide range of main dishes. **Backstoltz**
(Dortusstrasse 59, 0177 326 7253, mains €3-€5)
is a cosy croissanterie, good for a light breakfast
or lunch. **Kinocafé Melodie** (Friedrich-Ebert-
Strasse 12, 0331 620 0699) is a popular watering
hole. **Matschkes Galerie Café** (Alleestrasse
10, 0331 270 1210, mains €4-€8) serves good
simple German and Russian cooking and
has some outdoor seating. There's also an
assortment of cafés, pubs and restaurants along
pedestrianised Brandenburger Strasse, most of
which have tables outside in summer, and on
nearby Lindenstrasse and Dortusstrasse.

Nightlife

Lindenpark (Stahnsdorfer Strasse 76-78, 0331
747 970, www.lindenpark.de) in Babelsberg
offers a range of regular club nights and gigs.
Theaterschiff (Lange Brücke, 0331 280 0100,
www.theaterschiff-potsdam.de), moored close
to the Hans-Otto-Theater, is a vessel hosting
a theatre, cinema, cabaret and discos.
Waschhaus (Schiffbauergasse, 0331 271 560,
www.waschhaus.de), a large club just outside
Potsdam centre, has both DJs and live acts.

Getting there

By train
Both Potsdam and Babelsberg can be reached via
the S7 S-Bahn line. It takes just under an hour from
Mitte and you will need a ticket that covers the
C zone. From some parts of Berlin it's easier to
take the S1 to Wannsee, and change to the S7 there.
There is also a direct, hourly Regionalbahn train
(RE1) to Medienstadt Babelsberg that takes just
20mins from Mitte, and a number Regional trains
to Potsdam Haupbahnhof. The station is across
the river from the centre of town.

Getting around

Potsdam is small compared to Berlin, but it's still
too big and spread out to do everything on foot.
The tram and bus network covers everything,
however, and the routes aren't difficult to figure
out. A **Potsdam Card** (from €9.50), available from
the tourist office, provides free public transport as
well as discounted entry to most attractions.

Tourist information

Potsdam Tourismus Service
*Brandenburger Strasse 3 (0331 275 580/www.
potsdamtourismus.de). Tram 94, 96/bus X15, 695
Luisenplatz.* **Open** *Apr-Oct* 9am-7pm Mon-Fri;
9am-2pm Sat, Sun. *Nov-Mar* 10am-6pm Mon-Fri;
9am-2pm Sat.

Sachsenhausen

Many Nazi concentration camps have been preserved and opened to the public as memorials and museums. Sachsenhausen is the one nearest to Berlin.

Immediately upon coming to power, Hitler set about rounding up and interning his opponents. From 1933 to 1935 an old brewery on this site was used to hold them. The present camp received its first prisoners in July 1936. It was designated with cynical euphemism as a *Schutzhaftlager* ('Protective Custody Camp'). The first *Schutzhaftlagern* were political opponents of the government: communists, social democrats, trade unionists. Soon, the variety of prisoners widened to include anyone guilty of 'anti-social' behaviour, gays and Jews.

About 6,000 Jews were forcibly brought here after Kristallnacht alone. It was here that some of the first experiments in organised mass murder were made: thousands of POWs from the Eastern Front were killed at 'Station Z'.

The SS evacuated the camp in 1945 and began marching 33,000 inmates to the Baltic, where they were to be packed into boats and sunk in the sea. Some 6,000 died during the march before the survivors were rescued by the Allies. Another 3,000 prisoners were found in the camp's hospital when it was captured on 22 April 1945.

But the horror didn't end here. After the German capitulation, the Russian secret police, the MVD, reopened Sachsenhausen as 'Camp 7' for the detention of war criminals; in fact, it was filled with anyone suspected of opposition. Following the fall of the DDR, mass graves were discovered, containing the remains of an estimated 10,000 prisoners. On 23 April 1961, the partially restored camp was opened to the public as a national monument and memorial.

The parade ground, where morning roll-call was taken, and from where inmates were required to witness executions on the gallows, stands before the two remaining barrack blocks. One is now a museum and the other a memorial hall and cinema, where a film about the history of the camp is shown. Next door stands the prison block.

There are another couple of small exhibitions in buildings in the centre of the camp (no English labelling), but perhaps the grimmest site here is the subsiding remains of Station Z, the surprisingly small extermination block. A map traces the path the condemned would follow, depending upon whether they were to be shot (the bullets were retrieved and reused) or gassed. All ended up in the neighbouring ovens.

Note: it's a good idea to hire an audio guide (€3; available in English) at the gate.

KZ Sachsenhausen

Strasse der Nationen 22, Oranienburg (03301 2000/www.gedenkstaette-sachsenhausen.de). **Open** *Apr-Sept* 8.30am-6pm Tue-Sun. *Oct-Mar* 8.30am-4.30pm Tue-Sun. **Admission** free. **No credit cards.** The grounds of the camp are open on Mondays, but the museum is closed.

Getting there

By train

Oranienburg is at the northern end of the S1 S-Bahn line (40mins from Mitte). From the station follow signs to 'Gedenkstätte Sachsenhausen'. It's about 20mins walk.

Further Afield

Spreewald

This filigree network of tiny rivers, streams and canals, dividing patches of deciduous forest and farmland, is one of the loveliest excursions from Berlin. German author Theodor Fontane described the Spreewald as how Venice would have looked 1,500 years ago. It gets crowded in season, particularly at weekends, giving the lie to its claim to be one of the most perfect wilderness areas in Europe. Still, out of season, you can have the area to yourself.

About 100 kilometres (60 miles) south-east of Berlin, the Spree bisects the area into the **Unterspreewald** and Oberspreewald. For the former, Schepzig or Lübben are the best starting points; for the latter, go 15 kilometres (nine miles) further on the train to Lübbenau.

The character of both sections is very similar. The **Oberspreewald** is perhaps better, for its 500 square kilometres (190 square miles) of territory contain more than 300 natural and artificial channels, called *Fliesse*. You can travel around these on punts – rent your own or join a larger group – and also take out kayaks. Motorised boats are forbidden. Here and there in the forest are restaurants and small hotels. The tourist information centre in Lübbenau provides maps and walk routes.

The local population belongs to the Sorbish minority, a Slav people related to Czechs and Slovaks. Their own language is found in street names, newspapers and so on. This adds an air of exoticism, unlike the folk festivals laid on for tourists in the high season.

Where to eat & drink

There are plenty of eating and drinking options in Lübben and Lübbenau, and little to choose between most of them. Follow your nose.

You might find all the sun loungers taken but there's plenty of sand round **Rügen**.

Getting there

By train
There are regular trains to Lübben and Lübbenau. Journey time is around an hour to Lübben and an extra 15mins to Lübbenau. Check www.bahn.co.uk for the timetable.

Tourist information

Tourist websites www.spreewald-info.com and www.spreewald-online.de are good sources of information about the area and allow you to book hotel rooms online.

Haus für Mensch & Natur
Schulstrasse 9, Lübbenau (03542 89210). **Open** 10am-5pm daily. Closed Nov-Mar. **Admission** free. Set in an old schoolhouse, the 'House for Mankind & Nature' is the visitor centre for the Spreewald Biosphere Reservation. It has an exhibition about the environmental importance of the Spreewald.

Spreewald Information
Ehm-Welk-Strasse 15, Lübbenau (035 423 668/ www.spreewald-online.de). **Open** *Apr-Oct* 9am-7pm Mon-Fri; 9am-4pm Sat. *Nov-Mar* 9am-4pm Mon-Fri.

Rügen

The Baltic coast was the favoured holiday destination of the DDR citizen; post-Reunification it is still the most accessible stretch of seaside for Berliners. The coast forms the northern boundary of the modern state of Mecklenburg-Vorpommern. Bismarck famously said of the area: 'When the end of the world comes, I shall go to Mecklenburg, because there everything happens a hundred years later.'

The large island of Rügen is gradually resuming its rivalry with Sylt in the North Sea – both islands claim to be the principal north

German resort. The island is undoubtedly beautiful, with its white chalk cliffs, beechwoods and beaches. Most people stay in the resorts on the east coast, such as Binz (the largest and best known), Sellin and Göhren. In July and August, Rügen can get crowded (don't go without pre-booked accommodation), and the island's handful of restaurants and lack of late-night bars mean visitors are early to bed and early to rise. Go out of season for some peace.

Where to stay & eat

Most accommodation on Rügen is in private houses. Your best bet is to contact the local tourist office (*see below*), which will help you find a room. Camping is very popular on Rügen. Binz offers the best selection of places to eat.

Getting there

By train
There are some direct trains to Bergen on Rügen, but the journey usually involves changing trains at Stralsund. Journey time is between 3 and 4hrs. Check www.bahn.co.uk for timetable.

Tourist information

The head office in Bergen provides information, but cannot book hotel rooms; try the other offices for bookings. Visit www.ruegen.net for general information.

Bergen *Bahnhofstrasse 15 (03838 807 70/ www.ruegen.de).* **Open** *Summer* 8am-6pm Mon-Fri; 9am-3pm Sat. *Winter* 8am-6pm Mon-Fri.
Kurverwaltung Göhren *Postrasse 9 (03830 866 790/www.ostseebad-goehren.de).* **Open** *Summer* 9am-6pm Mon-Fri; 9am-noon Sat. *Winter* 9am-noon, 1-4.30pm Mon, Wed, Thur; 9am-noon, 1-6pm Tue; 9am-noon, 1-3pm Fri.

Semperoper.

Kurverwaltung Sellin *August-Bebel-Strasse 5 (03830 3160/www.ostseebad-sellin.de).* **Open** *Summer* 8.30am-6pm Mon-Fri; 10am-6pm Sat, Sun. *Winter* 8.30am-4.30pm Mon-Fri.
Ostseebad Binz *Heinrich-Heine-Strasse 7 (03839 314 8148/www.ostseebad-binz.de).* **Open** *Summer* 9am-6pm Mon-Fri; 10am-6pm Sat, Sun. *Winter* 9am-4pm Mon-Fri; 11am-4pm Sat, Sun.

Dresden

Destroyed twice and rebuilt one and a half times, the capital of Saxony – 100 kilometres (60 miles) south of Berlin – boasts one of Germany's best art museums and many historic buildings. The most recent wave of rebuilding – including the restoration of the Frauenkirche – was completed in time for the city's 800-year anniversary in 2006.

Modern Dresden is built on the ruins of its past. A fire consumed Altendresden on the bank of the Elbe in 1685, and the city was subsequently reconstructed. On the night of 13 February 1945, one of World War II's largest Allied bombing raids caused huge fire storms that killed between 25,000 and 40,000 people. After the war, Dresden was twinned with Coventry, and Benjamin Britten's *War Requiem* was given its first performance in the Hofkirche by musicians from both towns. Under the DDR, reconstruction was erratic, but a maze of cranes and scaffolding sprang up in the 1990s – Dresden has been making up for lost time.

Its major attractions are the buildings from the reign of Augustus the Strong (1670-1733). The Hofkirche and the Zwinger complex are fine examples of the city's Baroque legacy. Dresden's main draw for art lovers is the **Gemäldegalerie Alte Meister** in the Zwinger. There's usually more art at the **Albertinum**, which is due to reopen after renovation in 2009.

Building was continued by Augustus's successor, Augustus III, who then lost to Prussia in the Seven Years' War (1756-63). Frederick the Great destroyed much of the city during the war, though not the lovely riverside promenade of the Brühlsche Terrasse in the old part of town. A victorious Napoleon ordered the demolition of the city's defences in 1809.

By the Zwinger is the **Semperoper** opera house (1838-41), named after its architect Gottfried Semper. It was fully restored in 1985.

The industrialisation of Dresden heralded a new phase of construction that produced the **Rathaus** (Town Hall, 1905-10) at Dr-Külz-Ring, the **Hauptbahnhof** (1892-95) at the end of Prager Strasse, the **Yenidze cigarette factory** (1912) in Könneritzstrasse, designed to look like a mosque, and the **Landtagsgebäude** (completed to plans by Paul Wallot, designer of Berlin's Reichstag, in 1907) at Heinrich-Zille-Strasse 11. The finest example of inter-war architecture is Wilhelm Kreis' **Deutsches Hygiene-Museum** (1929) at Lingner Platz 1, housing the German Institute of Hygiene.

The **Neue Synagoge** was dedicated in Rathenauplatz in November 2001, 63 years after its predecessor (built by Semper in 1838-40) was destroyed in the Nazi pogroms.

Reconstruction of the domed **Frauenkirche** at Neumarkt was completed and the restored cathedral reconsecrated in October 2005. The Communists had left it as a heap of rubble throughout the Cold War period as a reminder of Allied aggression. In the end its restoration was funded partly by private donations from the UK and US. The golden orb and cross that top the dome were built by goldsmith Alan Smith, son of one of the British pilots who took part in the 1945 bombings.

The **Striezelmarkt**, founded in 1434, is the oldest Christmas market in Germany. It is held on Altstädtermarkt every December and is named after the savoury pretzel you will see everyone eating. Dresden is also home to the best Stollen, the German yuletide cake.

The Neustadt – on the north bank of the Elbe – literally means 'new town', although it is over 300 years old. Having escaped major damage during the war, the Neustadt has much of its original architecture intact. When Augustus the Strong commissioned the rebuilding of Dresden in 1685, he pictured a new Venice. The Neustadt doesn't quite measure up, but the 18th-century townhouses in Hauptstrasse and Königstrasse are charming.

To avoid the tourist spillover from the Altstadt, head north and east of Albertplatz. Recently, a wealth of boutiques, cafés and bars has sprung up here in the cobblestone streets.

Albertinum

Brühlsche Terrasse (0351 491 4622/ www.skd-dresden.de).
Closed for renovation until some time in 2009. In the meantime, the paintings of the Gemäldegalerie and the sculpture collection are at the Gemäldegalerie Alte Meister (*see below*).

Gemäldegalerie Alte Meister

Zwinger, Theaterplatz (0351 4914 2000/www.skd-dresden.de). **Open** 10am-6pm daily. **Admission** €7; €4.50 reductions. **No credit cards**.
A superb collection of Old Masters, particularly Italian Renaissance and Flemish. There is also porcelain from nearby Meissen, and collections of armour, weapons, clocks and scientific equipment.

Semperoper

Tickets: Schinkelwache, Theaterplatz (0351 491 10/www.semperoper.de). **Open** Box office 10am-6pm Mon-Fri; 10am-4pm Sat, Sun; also 1hr before performances. **Tickets** vary. **Credit** AmEx, MC, V.

Where to stay

The **Artotel Dresden** (Ostra-Allee 33, 0351 49220, www.artotel.de, €99-€164 double) is decorated with 600 works by local artist AR Penck. **Bastei/Königstein/Lilienstein** (Prager Strasse, 0351 4856 6388/0351 48560/ 0351 4856 2000, www.ibis-hotel.de, €90-€120 double) are three functional tower-block hotels on Prager Strasse between the rail station and Altstadt. The **Hotel Bayerischer Hof Dresden** (Antonstrasse 33-35, 0351 829370, www.bayerischer-hof-dresden.de, €117-€138 double) has comfy rooms and a personal feel. The **Hotel Taschenbergpalais Kempinski** (Taschenberg 3, 0351 49 120, www.kempinski-dresden.de, €165-€245 double) provides slightly stuck-up luxury in a baroque palace. Over in the Neustadt, the **Hostel Mondpalast** (Katharinenstrasse 11-13, 0351 563 4050, www.mondpalast.de, from €13.50 per person) is a decent budget option. **Hotel Smetana** (Schlüterstrasse 25, 0351 256 080, www.hotel-smetana.de, €97-€117 double) is a pleasant three-star, east of the centre.

Where to eat & drink

Caroussel, Caroussel (Bülow-Residenz, Rähnitzgasse 19, 0351 80030, closed Sun, Mon, mains €30-€40), a contemporary German restaurant, offers fine cooking and has a leafy courtyard that's nice in summer. **Piccola Capri** (Alaunstrasse 93, 0351 801 4848, closed Sun, mains €6.50-€15.50) is one of the best Italians in the Neustadt. In the same part of town, there are plenty of good bars and cafés on and around Alaunstrasse in the area north-east of Albertplatz.

Gorge on the Baroque in **Zwinger**.

Thomaskirche.

Getting there

By train
Regular direct trains take about 2hrs from Berlin.
Check www.bahn.co.uk for the timetable.

Tourist information

Dresden Tourist-Information
*Ostra Allee 11 (0351 491 920/www.dresden-
tourist.de).* **Open** 10am-6pm Mon-Fri; 10am-4pm Sat.
Other locations Schinkelwache, Theaterplatz
(0351 491 920).

Leipzig

One of Germany's most important trade centres
and former second city of the DDR, Leipzig is a
centre of education and culture and the place
where East Germany's mass movement for
political change began. It's also synonymous
with Bach, who lived here for 27 years. The
city, once one of Germany's industrial
strongholds, has also been famed for its fairs
for centuries; trade fairs (*Messen*) are still its
bread and butter. Its pedestrianised, recently
restored old centre is another attraction: with
its Renaissance and baroque churches, narrow
lanes, old street markets and the ancient
university, it's hard to believe that it was
bombed to bits during World War II. The area
is also crammed with enough sights, bars and
restaurants to fill a visit of a day or two.

In Saxony, around 130 kilometres (80 miles)
south-west of Berlin, Leipzig traces its origins
back to a settlement founded by the Sorbs,
a Slavic people who venerated the lime tree,
some time between the seventh and ninth
centuries. They called it *Lipzk* ('place of limes').

Most visitors arrive at **Leipzig
Hauptbahnhof**, the huge, renovated central
train station (largest in Europe before Berlin
Hauptbahnhof was opened). The station stands
on the north-east edge of the compact city
centre, and is surrounded by a ring road that
follows the course of the old city walls. Much
of the ring road is lined with parks; most of the
city's attractions can be found within its limits.

The first place to head is the Leipzig Tourist
Service office, diagonally left across tram-
strewn Willy-Brand-Platz from the front of
the train station. Pick up a guide to the city
in English (which includes a map) and head
for Markt, the old market square, to get your
bearings. The eastern side of the square is
occupied by the lovely Renaissance **Altes
Rathaus** (Old Town Hall), built in 1556-57.
It now houses the **Stadtgeschichtliches
Museum** (Town Museum). On the square's
south side are the huge bay windows of the
Könighaus, once a haunt of Saxony's rulers
when visiting the city (the notoriously rowdy
Peter the Great also once stayed here).

The church off the south-west corner of
Markt is the **Thomaskirche**, where Johan
Sebastian Bach spent 27 years as choirmaster
of the famous St Thomas's Boys Choir; the
composer is buried in the chancel and his
statue stands outside the church. Opposite the
church in the Bosehaus is the Bach-Museum.

South from the Thomaskirche towards the
south-west corner of the ring road is the **Neues
Rathaus** (New Town Hall), whose origins are
16th century, though the current buildings are
only about 100 years old.

Back at the Altes Rathaus, immediately
behind it is the delightful little chocolate box of
the **Alte Börse** (Old Stock Exchange), built in
1687, and fronted by a statue of Goethe, who
studied at Leipzig University. Follow his gaze
towards the entrance to **Mädler Passage**,
Leipzig's finest shopping arcade, within which
is Auerbachs Keller, one of the oldest and most
famous restaurants in Germany. It was in
Auerbachs, where he often used to drink,
that Goethe set a scene in *Faust* – Faust
and Mephistopheles boozing with students
before riding off on a barrel.

North of the Alte Börse is Sachsenplatz,
site of the city's main outdoor market, and
new home of the **Museum der bildenden
Künste** (Museum of Arts Picture Gallery).

Just south-east of here is the **Nikolai**,
Leipzig's proud symbol of its new freedom.
This medieval church, with its baroque interior,
is the place where regular free-speech meetings

Trips Out of Town

started in 1982. These evolved into the 'Swords to Ploughshares' peace movement, which led to the first anti-DDR demonstration on 4 September 1989 in the Nikolaikirchhof.

West of here, on the edge of the ring road, is the **Museum in der 'Runden Ecke'** (Museum in the 'Round Corner', nickname of the building that once housed the local Stasi headquarters and now has an exhibition detailing its nefarious methods). North of here, outside the ring road, is **Leipzig Zoo**. All the usual family favourites are here: lions, tigers, polar bears and hippos.

In the south-east corner of the ring road rises the drab tower block of Leipzig University. Rebuilt in 1970 to resemble an opened book, this modern monstrosity is ironically one of Europe's oldest centres of learning. Alumni, besides Goethe, include Nietzsche, Schumann and Wagner. The university runs the **Äyptisches Museum**; nearby is the **Grassi Museum für Angewandte Kunst**.

The university tower stands at the south-eastern corner of Augustplatz, a project of DDR Communist Party leader Walter Ulbricht, himself a Leipziger. Next door are the brown glass-fronted buildings of the **Gewandhaus**, home of the Leipziger Gewandhaus Orchester, one of the world's finest orchestras. On the square's northern side stands the **Opernhaus Leipzig** (opened in 1960), which also has an excellent reputation. Tours of the building can be booked in advance.

Ägyptisches Museum

Burgstrasse 21 (0341 973 7010/www.uni-leipzig.de/ ~egypt). **Open** 1-5pm Tue-Sat; 10am-1pm Sun. **Admission** €2; €1 reductions. **Credit** AmEx, MC, V.

Bach-Museum

Thomaskirchhof 16 (0341 913 7202/www.bach-leipzig.de). **Open** 10am-5pm daily. **Admission** €6; €4 reductions. **No credit cards.**
Documents, instruments and furniture from Bach's time illustrate the work and influence of the great man. The museum was being renovated at press time and had moved two doors down the road; the main building will reopen in late 2009.

Gewandhaus

Augustusplatz 8 (0341 127 0309/www.gewandhaus. de). **Open** Box office 10am-6pm Mon-Fri; 10am-2pm Sat. **Tickets** vary. **Credit** AmEx, DC, MC.

Grassi Museum für Angewandte Kunst

Neumarkt 20 (0341 973 0770/www.grassimuseum. de). **Open** 10am-6pm Tue-Sun. **Admission** €4; €2 reductions. **No credit cards.**
Leipzig's Museum of Applied Art was founded in 1874. Labelling is in English, and guided tours in English are available by advance booking. Also here

Bach-Museum.

are the Museum für Völkerkunde (Ethnography Museum) and the Museum für Musikinstrumente (Museum of Musical Instruments).

Leipzig Zoo

Pfaffendorfer Strasse 29 (0341 593 3500/ www.zooleipzig.de). **Open** Jan-Mar 9am-5pm daily. *Apr* 9am-6pm Mon-Fri; 9am-7pm Sat, Sun. *May-Sept* 9am-7pm daily. *Oct* 9am-6pm daily. *Nov, Dec* 9am-5pm daily. **Admission** €13; €9-€11 reductions. **No credit cards.**
Photo p284.

Museum der bildenden Künste

Katarienenstrasse 10 (0341 2169 9957/www. mdbk.de). **Open** 10am-6pm Tue, Thur-Sun; noon-8pm Wed. **Admission** €5; €3.50 reductions; free 2nd Wed of mth. *Temporary exhibitions* €8; €5.50 reductions. **No credit cards.**
The Museum of Arts Picture Gallery's 2,200-strong collection stretches from 15th- and 16th-century Dutch, Flemish and German paintings to expressionism and DDR art. Artists featured include Dürer, Rembrandt and Rubens.

Museum in der 'Runden Ecke'

Dittrichring 24 (0341 961 2443/www.runde-ecke-leipzig.de). **Open** 10am-6pm daily. *Guided tours* 3pm daily. **Admission** free. *Guided tours* €3; €2 reductions. **No credit cards.**
An interesting look at the Stasi's frightening yet ridiculous methods – collecting scents of suspected people in jars, say – and a hilarious section on Stasi disguises. There's no English labelling, but it's worth a visit nonetheless.

Nikolaikirche

Nikolaikirchhof 3 (0341 960 5270/www.nikolaikirche-leipzig.de). **Open** 10am-noon Mon, Tue, Thur, Fri; 4-6pm Wed. **Admission** free.

Trips Out of Town

Opernhaus Leipzig

Augustusplatz 12 (0341 12610/www.oper-leipzig.de).
Open *Box office* 10am-8pm Mon-Fri; 10am-4pm
Sat; 1hr before performances Sun. **Tickets** vary.
No credit cards.

Stadtgeschichtliches Museum

*Altes Rathaus, Markt 1 (0341 9651 340/www.
stadtgeschichtliches-museum-leipzig.de).* **Open**
10am-6pm Tue-Sun. **Admission** €2.50; €2
reductions. **No credit cards.**
Special exhibitions are housed in the Neubau, at
nearby Böttchergässchen 3.

Thomaskirche

*Thomaskirchhof 18 (0341 2222 4200/www.thomas
kirche.org).* **Open** 9am-6pm daily. **Admission** free.

Where to stay

The **Precise Hotel Accento Leipzig**
(Taucher Strasse 260, 0341 92620, www.
precisehotels.com, €85 double) has stylish rooms
and polite staff. **Adagio Minotel Leipzig**
(Seeburgstrasse 96, 0341 216 699, www.hotel-
adagio.de, €87 double) features individually
furnished rooms and a central location. For art
nouveau luxury, try the **Seaside Park Hotel**
(Richard-Wagner-Strasse 7, 0341 98520,
www.park-hotel-leipzig.de, €130 double).
 The Leipzig Tourist Service (*see below*)
can help with budget options.

Where to eat

Apels Garten (Kolonnadenstrasse 2, 0341 960
7777, mains €5.50-€17) is a pretty restaurant
with imaginative German cooking. **Auerbachs**

Keller (Mädlerpassage, Grimmaische Strasse
2-4, 0341 216 100, set menus €11-€40), located
in a 1525 beer hall, has a gourmet menu and
a cheaper version: both serve classic Saxon
cuisine (schnitzel, dumplings, pork and
sauerkraut). **Barthels Hof** (Hainstrasse 1,
0341 141 310, mains €13-€22) offers hearty
Saxon cooking in a cosy panelled *Gasthaus*.
El Matador (Friedrich-Ebert-Strasse 108,
0341 980 0876, closed Sun, mains €8-€16)
serves decent Spanish food.

Nightlife

With its major university, Leipzig is a party
town: wander the streets around Markt for late-
night quaffing. For dancing, try **Distillery**
(Kurt-Eisner-Strasse 4, 0341 3559 7400) or
Schauhaus (Bosestrasse 1, 0341 960 0596).
Moritz-Bastei (Universitätsstrasse 9, 0341 702
590) features live jazz and blues. **Velvet Club**
(Körnerstrasse 68, 03442 303 2001) is a gay/
mixed after-hours venue with hip hop and R&B.

Getting there

By train

Regular trains from Berlin Hauptbahnhof take only
an hour to reach Leipzig.

Tourist information

Leipzig Tourist Service

*Richard-Wagner-Strasse 1 (0341 710 4260/4265/
www.leipzig.de).* **Open** *Mar-Oct* 9.30am-6pm Mon-
Fri; 9.30am-4pm Sat; 9.30am-3pm Sun. *Nov-Feb*
10am-6pm Mon-Fri.

Leipzig Zoo. *See p283.*

Directory

Directory

Getting Around

By air

Until the new **Berlin-Brandenburg International Airport** is ready to in late 2011, Berlin is served by two airports: **Tegel** (TXL) and **Schönefeld** (SXF). Information in English on both airports (including live departures and arrivals) can be found at www.berlin-airport.de. Despite campaigns to save it, **Tempelhof** airport closed down at the end of October 2008. Tegel airport is scheduled to close in 2011 when Berlin-Brandenburg-International gets going. There is as yet no official name for the new airport, which will be just south of the existing Schönefeld airport. Willy Brandt, Marlene Dietrich and Albert Einstein are contenders for the honour. Note: most of Berlin's hotels are in Mitte, the revived centre of the united city, or in the area served by Bahnhof Zoo (Zoo Station), pivotal point of the west end.

Flughafen Tegel (TXL)

Airport information (12 cents per minute) 0180 5000 186/ www.berlin-airport.de. **Open** 4am-midnight daily. **Map** p316 C1.
Most scheduled flights use the compact Tegel airport, just 8km (5 miles) north-west of Mitte. The ring-shaped terminal contains tourist information, exchange facilities, shops, restaurants, bars and car rental desks. It's one of Europe's easiest airports. A cab can drop you right by the check-in desk and departure gate.
Buses 109 and X9 (the express version) run via Luisenplatz and the Kurfürstendamm to Zoologischer Garten (also known as Zoo Station, Bahnhof Zoo or just Zoo) in Western Berlin. Tickets cost €2.10 (and can also be used on U-Bahn and S-Bahn

services). Buses run every five to 15 minutes, and take 30-40 minutes to reach Zoo. At Zoo there are rail and tourist information offices (*see p301*), and you can connect to anywhere in the city (same tickets are valid).
You can take bus 109 to Jacob-Kaiser-Platz U-Bahn (U7), or bus 128 to Kurt-Schumacher-Platz U-Bahn (U6), and proceed on the underground from there. One ticket can be used for the combined journey (€2.10).
The JetExpressBusTXL is the direct link to Berlin Hauptbahnhof and Mitte. It runs from Tegel to Alexanderplatz with useful stops at Beusselstrasse S-Bahn (connects with the Ringbahn), Berlin Hauptbahnhof (regional and inter-city train services as well as the S-Bahn), Unter den Linden S-Bahn (north and south trains on the S1 and S2 lines). It costs €2.10, runs every 10 or 20 minutes between 4.30am-12.30am (5.30am-12.30am at weekends), and takes 30-40 minutes.
A taxi to anywhere central will cost around €20-€25, and takes 20-30 minutes, depending on traffic and precise destination.

Flughafen Schönefeld (SXF)

Airport information 0180 5000 186/www.berlin-airport.de.
Open 24hrs daily.
The former airport of East Berlin is 18km (11 miles) south-east of the city centre. It's small, currently working with only one runway, and much of the traffic is to Eastern Europe and the Middle and Far East. But budget airlines from the UK and Ireland also use it – EasyJet flies in from Belfast, Bristol, Gatwick, Glasgow, Liverpool and Luton; Ryanair from Dublin, East Midlands, Edinburgh, Stansted and Shannon.
The usual foreign exchange, shops, snack bars and car hire facilities can be found here, though none in abundance.
Train is the best means of reaching the city centre. S-Bahn Flughafen Schönefeld is a five-minute walk from the terminal (a free S-Bahn shuttle bus runs every ten minutes between 6am-10pm from outside the terminal; at other times, bus 171 also runs to the station). From here, the Airport Express train runs to Mitte

(25 minutes to Alexanderplatz), Berlin Hauptbahnhof (30 minutes) and Zoo (35 minutes) every half hour from 5am-11.30pm.
You can also take S-Bahn line S9, which runs into the centre every 20 minutes (40 minutes to Alexanderplatz, 50 minutes to Zoo) stopping at all stations along the way. The S45 line from Schönefeld connects with the Ringbahn, also running every 20 minutes.
Bus X7, every 10 or 20 minutes from 4.30am-8pm runs non-stop from the airport to Rudow U-Bahn (U7), from where you can connect with the underground. When it's not running, bus 171 takes the same route.
Tickets from the airport to the city cost €2.80, and can be used on any combination of bus, U-Bahn, S-Bahn and tram. There are ticket machines at the airport and at the station.
A taxi to Zoo or Mitte is pricey (€30-€35), and takes around 45 minutes.

Airlines

From outside Germany dial the international access code (usually 00), then 49 for Germany, then the number (omitting any initial zero). All operators speak English.

Air Berlin *0180 573 7800/ www.airberlin.com*
Air France *0180 583 0830/ www.airfrance.de*
Alitalia *0180 507 4747/ www.alitalia.de*
British Airways *0180 526 6522/ www.britishairways.com*
EasyJet *0180 365 4321/ www.easyjet.com*
German Wings *0180 595 5855/ www.germanwings.com*
Iberia *0180 544 2900/ www.iberia.com*
KLM *0180 521 4201/www.klm.de*
Lufthansa *01803 803 803/ www.lufthansa.de*
Ryanair *0190 170 100/ www.ryanair.com*

By rail

Berlin Hauptbahnhof
(11 861/www.bahn.de).
Map p318 K5

The new Berlin Hauptbahnhof, opened in 2006, is the central point of arrival for all long-distance trains, with the exceptions of night trains from Moscow, Warsaw and Kiev, which start and end at Berlin Lichtenberg (S5, S7, S75).

Hauptbahnhof is inconveniently located in a no-man's land north of the government quarter, and is linked to the rest of the city by S-Bahn (S5, S7, S9, S75), but not yet by U-Bahn. The line U55, which will run two stops to Unter den Linden (connecting there with the S-Bahn lines S1, S2, S25), was at press time supposed to open sometime in mid 2009. Eventually the line will extend to connect to the U5 at Alexanderplatz, but work on the second stage has not begun. For now, Berlin has two airports and one central station, none of which connect to its underground system.

The multi-level Hauptbahnhof is huge, with all the facilities you'd expect of a thoroughly modern main station, including left-luggage, currency exchange, tourist information counters, two pharmacies, assorted chain stores, and no fewer than 19 food and drink outlets. Its twin towers and arched central axis also make an impressive dent on the city skyline.

On their way in and out of town, inter-city trains now also stop at Nordkreuz (formerly Gesundbrunnen), Südkreuz (formerly Papestrasse) and Spandau, depending on their destinations.

By bus

Zentraler Omnibus Bahnhof (ZOB)

Masurenallee 4-6, Charlottenburg (Information 301 0380/www.zob-reiseburo.de). **Open** 6am-9pm Mon-Fri; 6am-3pm Sat, Sun. **Map** p320 B8.
Buses arrive in Western Berlin at the Central Bus Station, opposite the Funkturm and the ICC (International Congress Centrum). From here, U-Bahn line U2 runs into the centre. There's also a left luggage office. East Berlin has no bus station.

Getting around

Berlin is served by a comprehensive and interlinked network of buses, trains, trams and ferries. It's efficient and, of course, punctual, but bear in mind that it's not particularly cheap.

With the completion of the inner-city-encircling Ringbahn

in 2002, the former East and West Berlin transport systems were finally sewn back together, though it can still sometimes be complicated travelling between Eastern and Western destinations. Even within one half of the city, journeys can involve several changes of route or mode of transport. But services are usually regular and frequent, timetables can be trusted, and one ticket can be used for two hours on all legs of a journey and all forms of transport.

The Berlin transport authority, the BVG, operates bus, U-Bahn (underground) and tram networks, and a few ferry services on the outlying lakes. The S-Bahn (overground railway) is run by its own authority, but services are integrated within the same three-zone tariff system (*see below* **Fares & tickets**).

Information

The **BVG** website (www. bvg.de) has a wealth of information (in English) on city transport, and there's usually someone who speaks English at the 24-hour **BVG Call Center** (194 49). The S-Bahn has its own website at www.s-bahn-berlin.de.

There are BVG information centres at Tegel airport (6am-10pm daily), Turmstrasse U-Bahn (U9; open 6am-10pm Mon-Fri, 8.45am-4.15pm Sat) and at Zoo Pavillon, Hardenburger Strasse, Bahnhof Zoo (open 6am-10pm daily).

The **Liniennetz**, a map of U-Bahn, S-Bahn, bus and tram routes for Berlin and Potsdam, is available free from info centres and ticket offices. It includes a city centre map. A map of the U- and S-Bahn can also be picked up free at ticket offices or from the grey-uniformed *Zugabfertiger* – passenger assistance personnel – who wander about the larger U-Bahn and S-Bahn stations,

Fares & tickets

The bus, tram, U-Bahn, S-Bahn and ferry services operate on an integrated three-zone system. Zone A covers central Berlin, zone B extends out to the edge of the suburbs and zone C stretches into Brandenburg.

The basic single ticket is the €2.10 *Normaltarif* (zones A and B). Unless going to Potsdam or Flughafen Schönefeld, few visitors are likely to travel beyond zone B, making this in effect a flat-fare system.

Apart from the *Zeitkarten* (longer-term tickets, *see p288*), tickets for Berlin's public transport system can be bought from the yellow or orange machines at U- or S-Bahn stations, and by some bus stops. These take coins and sometimes notes, give change and have a limited explanation of the ticket system in English. Once you've purchased your ticket, validate it in the small red or yellow box next to the machine, which stamps it with the time and date. (Tickets bought on trams or buses are usually already validated.)

There are no ticket turnstiles at stations but if an inspector catches you without a valid ticket, you will be fined €40. Ticket inspections are frequent, and are conducted while vehicles are moving by pairs of plain-clothes personnel.

Single ticket (Normaltarif)

Single tickets cost €2.10 (€1.40 for children between the ages of six and 14) for travel within zones A and B, €2.30 (€1.60) for zones B and C, and €2.80 (€2) for all three zones. A ticket allows use of the BVG network for two hours, with as many changes between bus, tram, U-Bahn and S-Bahn as necessary travelling in one direction.

Short-distance ticket (Kurzstreckentarif)

The *Kurzstreckentarif* (ask for a *Kurzstrecke*) costs €1.30 (€1 concessions) and is valid for three U- or S-Bahn stops, or six stops on the tram or bus. No transfers allowed.

Day ticket (Tageskarte)

A *Tageskarte* for zones A and B costs €6.10 (€4.40 reductions), or €6.50 (€4.80) for all three zones. A day ticket lasts until 3am the morning after validating.

Longer-term tickets (Zeitkarten)

If you're in Berlin for a week, it makes sense to buy a *Sieben-Tage-Karte* ('seven-day ticket') at €26.20 for zones A and B, or €32.30 for all three zones (no concessions).

A stay of a month or more makes it worth buying a *Monatskarte* ('month ticket'), which costs €72 for zones A and B, or €88.50 for all three zones.

U-Bahn

The first stretch of Berlin's U-Bahn was opened in 1902 and the network now consists of nine lines and 170 stations. The first trains run shortly after 4am; the last between midnight and 1am, except on Fridays and Saturdays when trains run all night on lines U1, U2, U5, U6, U7, U8 and U9. The direction of travel is indicated by the name of the last stop on the line.

S-Bahn

Especially useful in Eastern Berlin, the S-Bahn covers long distances faster than the U-Bahn and is a more efficient means of getting to outlying areas. The Ringbahn, which circles central Berlin, was the final piece of the S-Bahn system to be renovated in 2002, though there are still temporary disruptions here and there.

Buses

Berlin has a dense network of 150 bus routes, of which 54 run in the early hours. The day lines run from 4.30am to about 1am the next morning. Enter at the front of the bus and exit in the middle or at the back. The driver sells only individual tickets, but all tickets from machines on the U- or S-Bahn are valid. Most bus stops have clear timetables and route maps.

Trams

There are 21 tram lines (five of which run all night), mainly in the East, though some have been extended a few kilometres into the Western half of the city, mostly in Wedding. Hackescher Markt is the site of the main tram terminus. Tickets are available from machines on the trams, at the termini and in U-Bahn stations.

Other rail services

Berlin is also served by the Regionalbahn ('regional railway'), which once connected East Berlin with Potsdam via the suburbs and small towns left outside the Wall. It still circumnavigates the city. The Regionalbahn is run by Deutsche Bahn and ticket prices vary according to the journey.

For timetable and ticket information (available in English), go to Deutsche Bahn's website at www.bahn.de.

Travelling at night

Berlin has a comprehensive *Nachtliniennetz* ('night-line network') that covers all parts of town via 59 bus and tram routes running every 30 minutes between 12.30am and 4.30am. Before and after these times the regular timetable for bus and tram routes applies.

Night-line network maps and timetables are available from BVG kiosks at stations, and large maps of the night services are found next to the normal BVG map on station platforms. Ticket prices are the same as during the day. Buses and trams that run at night have an 'N' in front of the number.

On lines N11, N35 and N41, the bus will take you to your front door if it's close to the official route. The BVG also operates a *Taxi-Ruf-System* ('taxi calling service') on the U-Bahn for women and people with disabilities from 8pm

every evening until the network closes. Ask the BVG employee in the platform booth to phone, giving your destination and method of payment.

Truncated versions of U-Bahn lines U1, U2, U5, U6, U7, U8, and U9 run all night on Fridays and Saturdays, with trains every 15 minutes. The S-Bahn also runs on weekend nights, with lines S1, S2, S3, S5, S7, S8, S9, S25, S26, S41, S42, S46, S47, S75 in service.

Boat trips

Getting about by water is more of a leisure activity than a practical means of navigating the city, but the BVG network does include a handful of boat services on Berlin's lakes. There are also several private companies offering tours of Berlin's waterways. *See also p120* **Boot trips**.

Reederei Heinz Riedel

Planufer 78, Kreuzberg (693 4646/www.reederei-riedel.de). U8 Schönleinstrasse. **Open** varies, check website for details. **No credit cards. Map** p323 P9.

This company operates excursions that start in the city and pass through industrial suburbs into rural Berlin. A tour through the city's network of rivers and canals costs €4.50-€18.

Stern und Kreisschiffahrt

Puschkinallee 15, Treptow (536 3600/www.sternundkreis.de). S6, S8, S9, S10 Treptower Park. **Open** 21 Mar-5 Oct 9am-6pm Mon-Fri; 9am-2pm Sat. **Credit** Amex, MC, V.

Offers around 25 cruises along the Spree and around the lakes. Times vary. A 3hr 30min tour costs €17.50.

Taxis

Berlin taxis are pricey, efficient and numerous. The starting fee is €3 and thereafter the fare is €1.50 per kilometre (about €3 per mile) for the first seven kilometres, and €1 per kilometre thereafter. The rate remains the same at night. For short journeys ask for a *Kurzstrecke* – up to two kilometres for €3.50, but only available when you've hailed a cab and not from taxi ranks. Taxi stands are numerous, especially in central areas near stations and at major intersections. You can phone for a cab 24 hours daily on 261 026. Most firms can transport people with disabilities, but require advance notice. Cabs accept all credit cards except Diners Club, subject to a €0.50 charge.

Most cabs are Mercedes. If you want an estate car (station wagon), ask for a *combi*. As well as normal taxis, Funk Taxi Berlin operates vans capable of transporting up to seven people (ask for a 'grossraum Taxi'; same rates as for regular taxis) and has two vehicles for people with disabilities. Call 261 026.

Driving

Despite some congestion, driving in Berlin presents few problems. Visitors from the UK and US should bear in mind that, in the absence of signals, drivers must yield to traffic from the right, except at crossings marked by a diamond-shaped yellow sign. Trams always have right of way. An *Einbahnstrasse* is a one-way street.

Breakdown services

The following garage offers 24-hour assistance at a rate of about €65 an hour. But it won't take credit cards.

ADAC
Bundesallee 29-30, Wilmersdorf (0180 222 2222)

Filling stations

Both of the places below are open 24 hours a day.

Aral
Holzmarktstrasse 12, Mitte (2472 0748). Credit AmEx, MC, V. **Map** p323 P7.

Aral
Kurfürstendamm 128, Wilmersdorf (8909 6972). **Credit** AmEx, MC, V. **Map** p320 B9.

Parking

Parking is free in Berlin side streets, but spaces are hard to find. On busier streets you may have to buy a ticket (€1 per hour) from a nearby machine. Without a ticket, or if you park illegally, you risk getting your car clamped or towed.

There are long-term car parks at Schönefeld and Tegel airports (*see p286*). Otherwise there are many *Parkgaragen* and *Parkhäuser* (multi-storey and underground car parks) around the city, open 24 hours, that charge around €2 an hour.

Flughafen Schönefeld Car Park

0180 500 0186. **Rates** *Per day €17-€25. Per week €40-€100.* **Credit** AmEx, MC, V.

Flughafen Tegel Car Park

0180 500 0186. **Rates** *Per day €19-€22. Per week €39-€95.* **Credit** AmEx, MC, V.

Vehicle hire

Car hire in Germany is not expensive and all major companies are represented in Berlin. There are car hire desks at both of the city's airports. Look under *Autovermietung* in the *Gelbe Seiten* (*Yellow Pages*).

Cycling

West Berlin is wonderful for cycling – flat, with lots of cycle paths, parks and canals to cruise beside. East Berlin has fewer cycle paths and more cobblestones and tram lines.

Cycles can be taken on the U-Bahn (except during rush hour, 6-9am and 2-5pm), up to a limit of two at the end of carriages that have a bicycle sign. More may be taken on to S-Bahn carriages, and at any time of

day. In each case an extra ticket (€1.40) must be bought for each bike. The ADFC Fahrradstadtplan, available in bike shops (€6.50), is a good guide to cycle routes.

With a credit card and a mobile, you can rent one of the thousands of DB Call-A-Bikes you'll see in summer parked near stations and major intersections. Call the number on the bike (07000 522 5522) and follow the instructions to register and get the unlocking code. You ride the bike where you want to go, then lock it back up and log off. It costs €0.8 per minute up to a maximum of €15 per 24 hours, and an initial €5 registration fee is taken off your first bill. After the first time, all you have to do is call in your customer number. Details at www.callabike-interaktiv.de

The companies below rent bikes, or see *Fahrradverleih* in the *Yellow Pages*.

Fahrradstation

Dorotheenstr.30, Mitte (2045 4500/www.fahrradstation.de). U6, S1, S2, S5, S7, S9, S75 *Friedrichstrasse.* **Open** 9am-8pm Mon-Fri; 10am-6pm Sat; 10am-4pm Sun. **Rates** Per day from €15; 3 days €35. **Credit** AmEx, MC,V. **Map** p318/p327 M6. **Other locations** Bergmannstrasse 9, Kreuzberg (215 1566); Hackesche Höfe, Mitte (2838 4848).

Pedalpower

Grossbeerenstrasse 53, Kreuzberg (5515 3270/www.pedalpower.de). U1, U7 *Möckernbrücke.* **Open** 10am-6.30pm Mon-Fri; 11am-2pm Sat. **Rates** Per day from €9. **No credit cards. Map** p322 L10. **Other locations** Pfarrstrasse 115, Lichtenberg (5515 3270).

Walking

Berlin is a good walking city, but it's spread out. Mitte is most pleasant on foot, but if you then want to check out Charlottenburg, you'll next need to take a bus or train.

Resources A-Z

Addresses

German convention dictates that the house/building number follows the street name (eg Friedrichstrasse 21), and numbers sometimes run up one side of the street and back down the other side. Strasse (street) is often abbreviated to Str, and is not usually written separately but appended to the street name, as in the example above. Exceptions are when the street name is the adjectival form of a place name (eg Potsdamer Strasse) or the full name of an individual (eg Heinrich-Heine-Strasse).

Within buildings: EG means *Erdgeschoss*, the ground floor; 1. OG (*Obergeschoss*) is the first floor; VH means *Vorderhaus*, or the front part of the building; HH means *Hinterhaus*, the part of the building off the *Hinterhof*, the 'back courtyard'; SF is *Seitenflügel*, stairs that go off to the side from the *Hinterhof*. In big, industrial complexes, stairwells are often numbered or lettered. Treppenhaus B, or sometimes just Haus B, would indicate a particular staircase off the courtyard.

Age restrictions

The legal age for drinking in Germany is 16; for smoking it is 16; for driving it is 18; and the age of consent for both heterosexual and homosexual sex is 16.

Business

Conferences

Messe Berlin
Messedamm 22, Charlottenburg (303 80/www.messe-berlin.de). U2 Theodor-Heuss-Platz. **Open** 10am-6pm Mon-Fri; 10am-2pm Sat. **Map** p320 A8/B8.

The city's official trade fair and conference organisation can advise businesses or individuals on setting up small seminars and congresses, or big trade fairs.

Couriers

A package of up to 5kg delivered within Germany costs about €7; to the UK about €17; and to North America about €32. The post office runs a cheaper express service (*see p297*).

DHL
Linkstrasse 10, Tiergarten (0180 5345 2255/www.dhl.de). U2, S1, S2, S25 Potsdamer Strasse. **Open** 9am-6pm Mon-Fri; 9am-noon Sat. **No credit cards. Map** p322 L8. DHL delivers to 180 countries worldwide.

Office hire

Regus Business Centre
Kurfürstendamm 21, Charlottenburg (887 060/fax 887 061 200/ www.regus.de). U2, U9, S5, S7, S9, S75 Zoologischer Garten. **Open** 8.30am-6pm Mon-Fri. **Credit** AmEx, MC, V. **Map** p321/p328 F8 Part of a worldwide chain, Regus has offices for rent, secretarial services and conference facilities. **Other locations** Friedrichstrasse 50, Mitte.

UPS
Lengeder Strasse 17-19, Reinickendorf (0800 882 6630/www.ups.com). S25 Alt Reinickendorf. **Open** 8am-7pm Mon-Fri. **Credit** AmEx, MC, V. Office hire & secretarial services.

Relocation services

The company listed below offers assistance in looking for homes and schools, and will help deal with residence and work permits.

Hardenberg Concept GmbH
Von-Luck-Strasse 13, Zehlendorf (805-8660/www.hardenberg-relocation.de). S1, S7 Nikolassee. **Open** 10am-4pm Mon-Fri.

Translators & interpreters

See also **Übersetzungen** in the *Gelbe Seiten* (*Yellow Pages*).

K Hilau Übersetzungsdienst
Langenscheidtstrasse 9, Schöneberg (781 7584). U7 Kleistpark. **Open** 1-6pm Mon-Fri. **Map** p322 K10.

Intertext Fremdsprachendienst
Greifswalder Strasse 5, Prenzlauer Berg (4210 1777/ www.intertext.de). Tram 2,3,4 Friedrichshain. **Open** 8am-4.30pm Mon-Fri. **Map** p325 R2.

Useful organisations

American Chamber of Commerce
Charlottenstrasse 42, Mitte (2887 8920/www.amcham.de) U2, U6 Stadtmitte. **Open** 9am-5pm Mon-Fri. **Map** p318/p327 M6.

American Embassy Commercial Dept
Pariser Platz 2, Mitte (238 5174/ www.germany.usembassy.gov). S1, S2 Unter den Linden. **Open** 8.30am-5.30pm Mon-Fri. **Map** p318/p327 L6.

Berlin Chamber of Commerce
Fasanenstrasse 85, Charlottenburg (315 100/www.berlin-partner.de). **Open** 8am-5pm Mon-Thur; 8am-4pm Fri. **Map** p321/p328 F8

British Embassy Commercial Dept
Wilhelmstrasse 70, Mitte (204 570/ www.britischesbotschaft.de). S1, S2 Unter den Linden. **Open** 9-11am, noon-4pm Mon-Fri. **Map** p318/ p327 L6.
The British Embassy's Commercial Department can offer basic advice for British businesses.

Customs

EU nationals over 17 years of age can import limitless goods for personal use, if bought with tax paid on them at

Directory

source. For non-EU citizens and for duty-free goods, the following limits apply:

● 200 cigarettes or 50 cigars or 250 grams of tobacco
● 1 litre of spirits (over 22 per cent alcohol), or 2 litres of fortified wine (under 22 per cent alcohol), or 2 litres of non-sparkling and sparkling wine
● 50 grams of perfume
● 500 grams of coffee
● Other goods to the value of €175 for non-commercial use

Travellers should note that the import of meat, meat products, fruit, plants, flowers and protected animals is restricted and/or forbidden.

Disabled

Only some U- and S-Bahn stations have wheelchair facilities; the map of the transport network (*see p334*; look for the wheelchair symbol) indicates which ones. The BVG is improving things slowly, adding facilities here and there, but it's still a long way from being a wheelchair-friendly system.

Berlin Tourismus Marketing (*see p301*) can give details about which of the city's hotels have disabled access. However, if you require more specific information, try the **Beschäftigungswerk des BBV** or the **Touristik Union International**.

Beschäftigungswerk des BBV

Bizetstrasse 51-5, Weissensee (927 0360/www.bbv-tours-berlin.de). S4, S8, S10 Greifswalder Strasse then bus M4 to Antonplatz. **Open** 9am-8pm Mon-Fri, 10am-6pm Sat. **Map** p325 S2
The Berlin Centre for the Disabled provides legal and social advice, together with a transport service and travel information.

Touristik Union International (TUI)

Unter den Linden 17, Mitte (200 58550/www.tui.com). S1, S2 Unter den Linden. **Open** (by appointment) 9am-9pm Mon-Fri; 10am-6pm Sat. **Map** p318/p327 M6.

The Touristik Union International provides information on accommodation and travel in Germany for the disabled.

Drugs

Berlin is relatively liberal in its attitude towards drugs. In recent years, possession of hash or grass has been effectively decriminalised. Anyone caught with an amount under ten grams is liable to have the stuff confiscated, but can otherwise expect no further retribution. In addition, joint-smoking is tolerated in some of Berlin's younger bars and cafés. A quick sniff will usually tell whether you're in one. Anyone caught with small amounts of hard drugs will net a fine, but is unlikely to be incarcerated.

For *Drogen Notdienst* (Emergency Drug Service), *see p293*.

Electricity

Electricity in Germany runs on 220v. To use British appliances (240v), change the plug or use an adaptor (available at most UK electric shops, and probably at the airport). US appliances (110v) require a converter.

Embassies & Consulates

Australian Embassy

Friedrichstrasse 200, Mitte (880 0880). U6 Französische Strasse. **Open** 8.30am-5pm Mon-Thur; 8.30am-4.15pm Fri. **Map** p322/ p327 M7.

British Embassy

Wilhelmstrasse 70, Mitte (204 570/ www.britischesbotschaft.de). S1, S2 Unter den Linden. **Open** 9-11am, noon-4pm Mon-Fri. **Map** p318/ p327 L6.

Irish Consulate

Friedrichstrasse 200, Mitte (220 720). U2, U6 Stadtmitte. **Open** 9.30am-12.30pm, 2.30-4.45pm Mon-Fri. **Map** p322/p327 M7.

US Consulate

Clayallee 170, Zehlendorf (832 9233/visa enquiries 0190 850 055). U3 Oscar-Helene-Heim. **Open** *Consular enquiries* 8.30am-noon Mon-Fri. *Visa enquiries* 8.30-11.30am Mon-Fri.

US Embassy

Pariser Platz 2, Mitte (238 5174/ www.germany.usembassy.gov). S1, S2 Unter Den Linden. **Open** 8.30am-5.30pm Mon-Fri. **Map** p318/p327 L6.

Emergencies

See also p293 Helplines.

Police
110.

Ambulance/Fire Brigade
112.

Gay & lesbian

Help & information

Lesbenberatung e.V.

Kulmer Strasse 20A, Schöneberg (215 2000/www.lesbenberatung-berlin.de). U7, S1, S2, S26 Yorckstrasse. **Open** 10am-7pm Mon, Tue, Thur; 10am-5pm Wed, Fri. **Map** p322 K10.
The Lesbian Advice Centre offers counselling in all areas of lesbian life as well as self-help groups, courses, cultural events and an 'info-café'.

Mann-O-Meter e.V.

Bülowstrasse 106, Schöneberg (216 8008/www.mann-o-meter.de). U1, U2, U3, U4 Nollendorfplatz. **Open** 5pm-10pm Mon-Fri; 4pm-10pm Sat, Sun. **Map** p322 J9.
Drop-in centre and helpline. Advice about AIDS prevention, jobs, flats, gay contacts, plus cheap stocks of safer sex materials. English spoken.

Schwulenberatung

Mommsenstrasse 45, Charlottenburg (office 2336 9070/counselling 194 46/www.schwulenberatungberlin.de). U7 Adenauerplatz. **Open** 9am-8pm Mon-Fri. **Map** p320 D8.
The Gay Advice Centre provides information and counselling about HIV and AIDS, crisis intervention and advice on all aspects of gay life.

Health

EU countries have reciprocal medical treatment arrangements with Germany.

Travel advice

For current information on travel to a specific country – including the latest news on health issues, safety and security, local laws and customs – contact your home country's government department of foreign affairs. Most have websites with useful advice for would-be travellers.

Australia
www.smartraveller.gov.au

Republic of Ireland
http://foreignaffairs.gov.ie

Canada
www.voyage.gc.ca

UK
www.fco.gov.uk/travel

New Zealand
www.safetravel.govt.nz

USA
http://travel.state.gov

EU citizens will need the **European Health Insurance Card** (EHIC). From the UK, this is available by phoning 0845 606 2030 or online from www.ehic.org.uk. You'll need to provide your name, date of birth and national insurance number. It does not cover all medical costs (for example dental treatment), so private insurance is not a bad idea.

Citizens from non-EU countries should take out private medical insurance. The British Embassy (*see p291*) publishes a list of English-speaking doctors and dentists, as well as lawyers and interpreters.

Should you fall ill in Berlin, you can take your EHIC to any doctor or hospital emergency department and get treatment. All hospitals have a 24-hour emergency ward. Otherwise, patients are admitted to hospital via a physician. Hospitals are listed in the *Gelbe Seiten* (*Yellow Pages*) under Krankenhäuser/ Kliniken.

AOK Auslandsschalter

Karl-Marx-Allee 3, Mitte (253 10/www.aokberlin.de). U2, U5, U8, S5, S7, S9, S75 Alexanderplatz. **Open** 8am-2pm Mon, Wed; 8am-6pm Tue, Thur; 8am-noon Fri. **Map** p319 P6.

Accident & emergency

The following are the most central hospitals. All have 24-hour emergency wards.

Charité

Schumann Strasse 20-21, Mitte (450 50/www.charite.de). U6 Oranienburger Tor. **Map** p323 O10.

Klinikum Am Urban

Dieffenbachstrasse 1, Kreuzberg (6970). U7 Südstern/bus 241, 248. **Map** p323 O10.

St Hedwig Krankenhaus

Grosse Hamburger Strasse 5, Mitte (23110). S5, S7, S9, S75 Hackescher Markt or S1, S2 Oranienburger Strasse. **Map** p319/p327 M5.

Complementary medicine

There is a long tradition of alternative medicine (*Heilpraxis*) in Germany, and your medical insurance will usually cover treatment costs. For a full list of practitioners, look up Heilpraktiker in the *Gelbe Seiten* (*Yellow Pages*). There you'll find a complete list of chiropractors, osteopaths, acupuncturists, homoeopaths and healers of various kinds. However, note that homeopathic medicines

are harder to get hold of and much more expensive than in the UK, and it's generally more difficult to find an osteopath or a chiropractor.

Contraception, abortion & childbirth

Family-planning clinics are thin on the ground in Germany, and generally you have to go to a gynaecologist (*Frauenarzt*).

The abortion law was amended in 1995 to take into account the differing systems that had existed in East and West. East Germany had abortion on demand; in the West, abortion was only allowed in extenuating circumstances, such as when the health of the foetus or mother was at risk.

In a complicated compromise, abortion is still technically illegal, but is not punishable. Women wishing to terminate a pregnancy can do so only after receiving certification from a counsellor. Counselling is offered by state, lay and church bodies.

Feministisches Frauengesund- heitzentrum (FFGZ)

Bamberger Strasse 51, Schöneberg (213 9597/www.ffgz.de). U4, U7 Bayerischer Platz. **Open** 10am-1pm Mon, Tue, Fri; 10am-1pm, 5-7pm Thur. **Map** p321 G10.
Courses and lectures are offered on natural contraception, pregnancy, cancer, abortion, AIDS, migraines and sexuality. Self-help and preventative medicine are stressed. Information on gynaecologists, health institutions and organisations can also be obtained.

ProFamilia

Kalkreuthstrasse 4, Schöneberg (2147 6414/www.profamilia-berlin. de). U1, U2, U3 Wittenbergplatz. **Open** 3-6pm Mon, Tue, Thur; 9am-noon Wed, Sat. **Map** p321 H9.
Free advice about sex, contraception and abortion is offered here. Call for an appointment.

Dentists

Dr Andreas Bothe
*Kurfürstendamm 210,
Charlottenburg (882 6767). U1
Uhlandstrasse.* **Open** 8am-2pm
Mon, Wed, Fri; 2-8pm Tue, Thur.
Map p321/p328 F8.

Mr Pankaj Mehta
*Schlangenbader Strasse 25,
Wilmersdorf (823 3010). U3
Rüdesheimer Platz.* **Open** 9am-noon,
2-6pm Mon, Tue, Thur; 8am-1pm
Wed, Fri.

Doctors

If you don't know of any
doctors in Berlin, or are too
ill to leave your bed, phone
the Emergency Doctor's
Service (*Ärztlicher
Bereitschaftdienst* 310 031).
This service specialises in
dispatching doctors for house
calls. The charges vary
according to the treatment
required by the patient.

The British Embassy (*see
p291*) can provide a list of
English-speaking doctors,
although you'll find that
many if not most doctors can
speak some English. All will
be expensive, however, so
be sure to have either your
EHIC or your private insurance
documents at hand (*see p292*)
if seeking treatment.

If you want to be sure of
communicating clearly, the
doctors listed below all speak
excellent English.

Dr Joseph Francis Aman
*Franzisksus Krankenhaus,
Budapester Strasse 15-19,
Tiergarten (2638 3503/
docaman@gmx.de). U1, U2,
U3 Wittenbergplatz.* **Open** 8am-1pm,
3-6pm Mon, Tue, Thur;
8am-1pm Fri. **Map** p321 H8.
Dr Aman is an American GP with
a practice in the Roman Catholic
hospital that is opposite the
Intercontinental Hotel.

Dr Christine Rommelspacher
*Bochumerstr 12, Tiergarten (392
2075) U9 Turmstrasse.* **Open** 9am-
noon, 3-6pm Mon, Tue, Thur; 9am-
noon Fri. **Map** p317 G5.

Gynaecologist

Dr Lutz Opitz
*Tegeler Weg 4, Charlottenburg
(344 4001). U7 Mierendorffplatz.*
Open 8am-2pm Mon; 4pm-7pm
Tue; 5pm-7pm Thur; 8am-noon Fri.
Map p316 C5.

Pharmacies

Prescription and non-
prescription drugs (including
aspirin) are sold only at
pharmacies (*Apotheken*).
You can recognise these by
a red 'A' outside the front
door. A list of the nearest
pharmacies open on Sundays
and in the evening should be
displayed in the window of
every pharmacy. You can
get a list of Notdienst-
Apotheken (emergency
pharmacies) online at
www.apo110.de.

STDs, HIV & AIDS

For most sexually transmitted
diseases, see a doctor (*see
above*). For specialist AIDS
care and advice, contact the
Berliner Aids-Hilfe.

Berliner Aids-Hilfe (BAH)
*Büro 15, Meinekestrasse 12,
Wilmersdorf (885 6400/advice line
194 11/www.berliner-aidshilfe.de).
U1, U9 Kurfürstendamm.* **Open**
noon-6pm Mon; noon-2.30pm Wed;
noon-3pm Thur, Fri. *Advice line*
10am-midnight daily. **Map**
p321/p328 F9.
Information is given on all aspects
of HIV and AIDS. Free consultations,
condoms and lubricant are also
provided here.

Helplines

Berliner Krisendienst
*Mitte, Friedrichshain, Kreuzberg,
Tiergarten & Wedding (390 6310).
Charlottenburg & Wilmersdorf (390
6320).
Prenzlauer Berg, Weissensee &
Pankow (390 6340).
Schöneberg, Tempelhof, Steglitz (390
6360). www.berlinerkrisendienst.de.*
For most problems, this is the best
service to call. It offers help and/or
counselling on a range of subjects,
and if they can't provide exactly
what you're looking for, they'll put
you in touch with someone who
can. The phone lines, organised by
district, are staffed 24 hours daily.
Counsellors will also come and visit
you in your house if necessary.

Drogen Notdienst
*Ansbacher Strasse 11,
Schöneberg (2191 6010/
www.drogennotdienst.de). U1,
U2, U3 Wittenbergplatz.* **Open**
8.30am-5pm Mon-Thur; 8.30am-3pm
Fri; 2-9.30pm Sat, Sun.
Map p321 G9.
At the 'drug emergency service', no
appointment is necessary if you're
coming in for advice, and the phone
line is staffed 24 hours daily.

Frauenkrisentelefon
615 4243. **Open** 10am-noon Mon,
Thur; 7-9pm Tue, Wed, Fri; 5-7pm
Sat, Sun.
Offers advice and information for
women on anything and everything.

ID

By law you are required to
carry some form of ID, which,
for UK and US citizens, means
a passport. If police catch
you without one, they may
accompany you to wherever
you've left it.

Internet

For internet access, there
are cybercafés all over town.
There is free wireless access
in the Sony Center at
Potsdamer Platz. For long
stays, try www.snafu.de or
www.gmx.de.

For Berlin-related websites,
see p305.

easyInternetCafé
*Dunkin' Donuts, Sony Center,
Tiergarten (www.easyevery
thing.com). U2, S1, S2, S26
Potsdamer Platz.* **Open** 7am-
11pm Mon-Thur, Sun; 7am-midnight
Fri, Sat. **No credit cards.**
Map p322/p327 K7/L7.
Dozens of computers, no staff,
mechanised system to buy time
online, and plenty of doughnuts to
hand. Other branches are similarly
lodged with Dunkin' Donuts.
Other locations: Hardenbergplatz 2,
Charlottenburg; Kurfürstendamm
224, Charlottenburg; Rathaus
Passagen, Rathausstrasse 5, Mitte;
Karl-Marx-Strasse 78, Neukölln;
Schlossstrasse 102, Steglitz.

Internet Café Alpha

*Dunckerstrasse 72, Prenzlauer Berg
(447 9067/www.alpha-internet
cafe.de). U2 Eberswalder Strasse.*
Open noon-1am Mon-Fri; 2pm-
1am Sat, Sun. **No credit cards.**
Map p319/328 P2.
Using one of the 15 computers
costs €2 per hour at this stylish
establishment. Wine, beer and a
range of snacks can fuel your
surfing. Also available: CD
burners, scanners and games.

Left luggage

Airports

There is a left luggage office
at **Tegel** (*see p286*; 0180 5000
186; open 5am-10.30pm daily)
and lockers at **Schönefeld**
(*see p286*; in the Multi Parking
Garage P4).

Rail & bus stations

There are left luggage lockers
at **Bahnhof Zoo,
Friedrichstrasse,
Alexanderplatz,
Potsdamer Platz,
Ostbahnhof** and
Hauptbahnhof. In addition,
**Zentraler Omnibus
Bahnhof** (ZOB; *see p287*)
also provides left-luggage
facilities.

Legal help

If you get into legal difficulties,
contact the British Embassy
(*see p291*): it can provide you
with a list of English-speaking
lawyers in Berlin.

Libraries

Berlin has hundreds of
Bibliotheken/Büchereien
(public libraries). To borrow
books, you will be required
to bring two things: an
Anmeldungsformular
('Certificate of Registration';
see p301) and a passport.

Amerika-Gedenkbibliothek

*Blücherplatz 1, Kreuzberg
(9022 6105/www.zlb.de). U1, U6
Hallesches Tor.* **Open** 10am-8pm

Mon-Fri; 10am-7pm Sat.
Membership Per year €10;
students €5. **Map** p322 M9.
This library only contains a small
collection of English and American
literature, but it has an excellent
collection of English-language
videos and many DVDs.

Staatsbibliothek

*Potsdamer Strasse 33, Tiergarten
(2660/www.staatsbibliothek-
berlin.de). U2, S1, S2, S26
Potsdamer Platz.* **Open** 9am-
9pm Mon-Fri; 9am-7pm Sat.
Map p322 K8.
Books in English on every subject
are available at this branch of the
State Library, which you may
recognise from Wim Wenders'
film *Wings of Desire.*

Staatsbibliothek

*Unter den Linden 8, Mitte
(2660/www.staatsbilbiothek-
berlin.de). U6, S1, S2, S5, S7,
S9, S75 Friedrichstrasse.* **Open**
9am-9pm Mon-Fri; 9am-5pm Sat.
Map p318 M6.
A smaller range of English books
than the branch above, but it's still
worth a visit, not least for its café.

Lost/stolen property

If any of your belongings are
stolen while in Germany, you
should go immediately to the
police station nearest to where
the incident occurred (listed
in the *Gelbe Seiten/Yellow
Pages* under *Polizei*) and report
the theft. There you will be
required to fill in report forms
for insurance purposes. If you
can't speak German, don't
worry: the police will call in
one of their interpreters, a
service that is provided free
of charge.

If you leave something
in a taxi, call the number
that's on your receipt (if you
remembered to ask for one),
and tell them the time of
your journey, the four-digit
Konzessions-Nummer that
will be stamped on the receipt,
a number where you can be
reached, and what you've lost.
They'll pass this information
to the driver, and he or she
will call you if they have
your property.

For information about what
to do concerning lost or stolen
credit cards, *see p297.*

BVG Fundbüro

*Potsdamer Strasse 180-182,
Schöneberg (194 49). U7 Kleistpark.*
Open *Office* 9am-6pm Mon-Thur;
9am-2pm Fri. *Call centre* 24 hrs daily.
Map p322 J10.
You should contact this office if you
have any queries about property lost
on Berlin's public transport system.
If you are robbed on one of their
vehicles, you can ask about the
surveillance video.

Zentrales Fundbüro

*Platz der Luftbrücke 6, Tempelhof
(7560 3101). U6 Platz der
Luftbrücke.* **Open** 7.30am-2pm
Mon; 8.30am-4pm Tue; noon-6.30pm
Wed; 1-7pm Thur; 7.30am-noon Fri.
Map p322 M11.
This is the central police lost
property office.

Media

Foreign press

A wide variety of international
publications are available
at larger railway stations
and Internationale Presse
newsagents around town.
Book retailers **Dussmann**
(*see p171*) and **Hugendubel**
(*see p175*) also carry
international titles. The
monthly *Exberliner* magazine
offers listings as well as
articles on cultural and
political topics in English.

National newspapers

BILD

www.bild.de
The flagship tabloid of the
Axel Springer group. Though its
credibility varies from story to
story, *BILD* leverages the journalistic
resources of the Springer empire and
its four-million circulation to land
regular scoops.

Financial Times Deutschland

www.ftd.de
Since hitting newsstands in 2000, the
FTD's circulation (103,489) has been
steadily increasing, and though it's
not likely to dethrone *Handelsblatt*,
its success proves there's room for
different approaches within the
business trade market.

Directory

Frankfurter Allgemeine Zeitung
www.faz.net
Germany's de facto newspaper of record. Stolid, exhaustive coverage of daily events, plus lots of analysis, particularly on the business pages. The Sunday edition is one of the best-edited papers in the country.

Handelsblatt
www.handelsblatt.com
The closest thing Germany can offer to the Wall Street Journal, the *Handelsblatt* co-operates with that paper's European offshoot. Competition from the *Financial Times Deutschland* has shaken *Handelsblatt* out of its complacency and energised its reporting.

Sueddeutsche Zeitung
www.sueddeutsche.de
Based in Munich, the *Sueddeutsche* blends first-rate journalism with enlightened commentary and uninspired visuals. On Mondays there is an English-language feature supplement called *The New York Times International Weekly*.

die tageszeitung
www.taz.de
Set up in rebellious Kreuzberg in the 1970s, the 'taz' attempts to balance the world view of the mainstream press and give coverage to alternative political and social issues, while the Berlin edition keeps watch on crooks in local government. With a circulation of 123,334, it's still hanging in there.

Die Welt
www.welt.de
Once a lacklustre mouthpiece of conservative, provincial thinking, *Die Welt* has widened its political horizons. But at a circulation of around 17,000 for its Berlin edition, it's not too popular in the capital.

Local newspapers

Berliner Morgenpost
www.morgenpost.de
Fat, fresh and self-conscious, this broadsheet is the favourite of the petty bourgeois. Good local coverage, and it's gained readers in the East through the introduction of neighbourhood editions, but there's no depth on the national and international pages.

Berliner Zeitung
www.berliner-zeitung.de
This East Berlin paper has passed through the hands of a number of owners since it was relaunched in the early 1990s, the latest being a consortium led by Britain's David Montgomery. Though it is profitable and its journalistic ambitions less sullied than of its West Berlin competitor *Der Tagesspiegel*, it remains a local read, with a circulation largely confined to the Eastern districts.

BZ
www.bz-berlin.de
The daily riot of polemic and pictures hasn't let up since it was demonised by the left in the 1970s – but its circulation has. Although still Berlin's largest seller with 189,044 copies daily, *BZ* sales are down substantially since 1991.

Der Tagesspiegel
www.tagesspiegel.de
Owned by the conservative Holzbrinck publishing empire from West Germany, this paper has fallen from the pre-eminent position it once held in West Berlin. The paper has dumbed down to boost circulation, losing the intellectual underpinnings which once attracted well-educated, up-market readers.

Weekly newspapers

Jungle World
www.jungle-world.com
Defiantly left, graphically switched-on and commercially undaunted, this Berlin-based weekly can be relied on to mock the comfortable views of the mainstream press. Born of an ideological dispute with the publishers of *Junge Welt*, a former East Berlin youth title, it lacks sales but packs a punch.

Die Zeit
www.zeit.de
Every major post-war intellectual debate in Germany has been carried out in the pages of *Die Zeit*, the newspaper that proved that a liberal tradition was alive and well in a country best known for excesses of intolerance. The style of its elite authors makes a difficult read.

Freitag
www.freitag.de
'The East-West weekly paper' is a post-1989 relaunch of a GDR intellectual weekly. Worth a look for its political and cultural articles.

Magazines

Focus
www.focus.de
Once, its spare, to-the-point articles, four-colour graphics and service features were a welcome innovation. But the gloss has faded, and *Focus* has established itself as a non-thinking man's *Der Spiegel*, whose answer to the upstart was simply to print more colour pages and become warm and fuzzy by adding bylines.

Der Spiegel
www.spiegel.de
Few journalistic institutions in Germany possess the resources and clout to pursue a major story in the way that *Der Spiegel* can, making it one of the best and most aggressive news weeklies in Europe. After years of firing barbs at ruling Christian Democrats, *Der Spiegel* was caught off guard when the Social Democrats were elected in 1999, but remains a must-read for anyone interested in Germany's power structure. Substantial English content on their website.

Stern
www.stern.de
The heyday of news pictorials may have long gone, but *Stern* still manages to shift around a million copies a week of big colour spreads detailing the horrors of war, the beauties of nature and the curves of the female body. Nevertheless, some say its reputation has never really recovered from the Hitler diaries fiasco in the early 1980s.

Listings magazines

Berlin is awash with listings freebies, notably *[030]* (www.berlin030.de; music, nightlife, film) and *Partysan* (www.partysan.net; a pocket-sized club guide) and their gay cousins *Siegessaeule* (www.siegessaeule.de) and *Blu* (www.blu.fm). These can be picked up in bars and restaurants. Two newsstand fortnightlies, *Zitty* and *tip*, come out on alternate weeks and, at least for cinema information, it pays to get the current title.

Exberliner
www.exberliner.com
Berlin's current English-language monthly is a lively mix of listings, reviews and commentary, mostly written by youngish American expats. It's based on the US 'alternative press' model, apart from the fact that it's not free. And its view is detached, almost self-absorbed, rather than engaged, as one might expect from a magazine put together by outsiders.

Directory

tip

www.tip-berlin.de

A glossier version of *Zitty* in every respect, *tip* gets better marks for its overall presentation and readability, largely due to higher quality paper, full colour throughout and a space-saving TV insert. This makes it more appealing to display advertisers – a double-edged sword depending on why you buy a listings magazine in the first place.

Zitty

www.zitty.de

Having lost some countercultural edge since its foundation in 1977, *Zitty* remains a vital force on the Berlin media scene, providing a fortnightly blend of close-to-the-bone civic journalism, alternative cultural coverage and comprehensive listings. The *Harte Welle* ('hardcore') department of its Lonely Hearts classifieds is legendary.

Television

Germany cabled up in the late 1970s, so there is no shortage of channels. But television has never been viewed as an art form. That means programming revolves around bland, mass market entertainment, except for political talk shows, which are pervasive, but often very good.

At its worst, there are cheesy 'erotic' shows, vapid folk-music programmes with studio audiences that clap in time, and German adaptations of reality TV and casting shows such as *Big Brother* and *Star Search*. Late-night TV, in particular, is chock-a-block with imported action series and European soft porn, interspersed with finger-sucking adverts for telephone sex numbers.

There are two national public networks, **ARD** and **ZDF**, a handful of no-holds-barred commercial channels, and a load of special-interest channels. ARD's daily *Tagesschau* at 8pm is the most authoritative news broadcast nationally.

N-tv is Germany's all-news cable channel, owned partly by CNN, but lacking the satellite

broadcaster's ability to cover a breaking story. **TVBerlin** is the city's experiment with local commercial television but is still catching up with ARD's local affiliate **RBB** (a merger of Berlin and Brandenburg stations SFB and ORB), which covers local news with more insight.

RTL, **Pro 7** and **SAT.1** are privately owned services offering a predictable mix of Hollywood re-runs and imported series, plus their own sensational magazine programmes and sometimes surprisingly good TV movies.

Special interest channels run from **Kinderkanal** for kids to **Eurosport**, **MTV Europe** and its German-language competitors **Viva** and more offbeat **Onyx**, to **Arte**, an enlightened French-German cultural channel with high-quality films and documentaries.

Channels broadcasting regularly in English include **CNN**, **NBC**, **MTV Europe** and **BBC World**. British or American films on ARD or ZDF are sometimes broadcast with a simultaneous soundtrack in English for stereo-equipped TV sets.

Radio

Some 29 stations compete for audiences in Berlin, so even tiny shifts in market share have huge consequences for broadcasters. The race for ratings in the greater metropolitan area is thwarted by a clear split between the urban audience in both East and West and a rural one in the hinterland. The main four stations in the region have their audiences based in either **Berlin (Berliner Rundfunk**, 91.4; **r.s.2**, 94.3) or Brandenburg (**BB Radio**, 107.5; **Antenne Brandenburg**, 99.7). No single station is able to pull in everyone.

Commercial stations **104,6 RTL** (104.6), **Energy 103,4** (103.4) and **Hundert,6** (100.6) offer standard chart pop spiced with news. **RadioEins** (95.8) and **Fritz** (102.6) are a bit more adventurous but still far from cutting-edge. Jazz is round the clock on **Jazz Radio** (101.9). Information-based stations such as **Info Radio** (93.1) are increasing in popularity. The **BBC World Service** (90.2) is available 24 hours a day. **Radio Multikulti** (96.3) broadcasts in 18 languages besides German and serves up global sounds. **US National Public Radio** (87.9) began broadcasting from the former frequency of the American Forces Network and Voice of America.

Money

One euro (€) is made up of 100 cents. There are seven banknotes and eight coins. The notes are of differing colours and sizes (€5 is the smallest, €500 the largest) and each of their designs represent a different period of European architecture. They are: €5 (grey), €10 (red), €20 (blue), €50 (orange), €100 (green), €200 (yellow-brown), €500 (purple).

The eight denominations of coins vary in colour, size and thickness – but not enough to make them easy to tell apart. They share one common side; the other features a country-specific design (all can be used in any participating state). They are: €2, €1, 50 cents, 20 cents, 10 cents, 5 cents, 2 cents, 1 cent. At the time of going to press, the exchange rate was £1 = €1.27 and US$1 = €0.64.

ATMs

ATMs are found throughout the centre of Berlin, and are the most convenient way of obtaining cash. Most major credit cards are accepted, as well as debit cards that are part of the Cirrus, Plus, Star or Maestro systems. You will normally be charged a fee for withdrawing cash.

Banks & bureaux de change

Foreign currency and travellers' cheques can be exchanged in most banks. Wechselstuben (bureaux de change) are open outside normal banking hours and give better rates than banks, where changing money often involves long queues.

Reisebank AG

Zoo Station, Hardenbergplatz, Charlottenburg (881 7117/ www.reisebank.de). U2, U9, S5, S7, S9, S75 Zoologischer Garten. **Open** 7.30am-10pm daily. **Map** p321/p328 G8.
The Wechselstuben of the Reisebank offer good exchange rates, and can be found at the bigger stations.
Other locations: Bahnhof Friedrichstrasse, Mitte (2045 5096); Berlin Hauptbahnhof, Tiergarten (2045 3761); Ostbahnhof, Friedrichshain (296 4393).

Credit cards

Many Berliners prefer to use cash for most transactions, although larger hotels, shops and restaurants often accept major credit cards (American Express, Diners Club, MasterCard, Visa) and many will take Eurocheques with guarantee cards, and travellers' cheques with ID.

In general, German banking and retail systems are less enthusiastic about credit than their UK or US equivalents, though this is gradually changing.

If you want to draw cash on your credit card, some banks will give an advance against Visa and MasterCard cards. However, you may not be able to withdraw less than the equivalent of US$100. A better option is using an ATM.

American Express

Bayreuther Strasse 37, Schöneberg (214 9830). U1, U2, U3 Wittenbergplatz. **Open** 9am-7pm Mon-Fri; 10am-1pm Sat. **Map** p321 H8.
Holders of an American Express card can use the company's facilities here, including the cash advance service.

Lost/stolen cards

If you've lost a credit card, or had one stolen, phone one of the 24-hour emergency numbers listed below.

American Express
0180 523 2377.

Diners Club
069 6616 6123.

MasterCard/Visa
0697 933 1910.

Tax

Non-EU citizens can claim back German value-added tax (*Mehrwertsteuer* or *MwSt*) on goods purchased in the country (it's only worth the hassle on sizeable purchases). Ask to be issued with a Tax-Free Shopping Cheque for the amount of the refund and present this, with the receipt, at the airport's refund office before checking in bags.

Opening hours

Most banks are open 9am to noon Monday to Friday, and 1pm to 3pm or 2pm to 6pm on varied weekdays.

Shops can stay open 6am-10pm, except on Sundays and holidays, though few take full advantage of the fact. Big stores tend to open at 9am and close 8pm-10pm. Most smaller shops will close around 6pm.

An increasing number of all-purpose neighbourhood shops (*Späti*) open around 5pm and close around midnight. Many Turkish shops are open on Saturday afternoons and on Sundays from 1pm to 5pm. Many bakers open to sell cakes on Sundays from 2pm to 4pm

Most 24-hour fuel stations and many internet cafés also sell basic groceries.

The opening times of bars vary, but many are open during the day, and most stay open until at least 1am, if not through until morning.

Most post offices are open 8am to 6pm Monday to Friday and 8am to 1pm on Saturdays.

Police stations

You are unlikely to come in contact with the *Polizei*, unless you commit a crime or are the victim of one. There are few patrols or traffic checks.

The central police HQ can be found at Platz der Luftbrücke 6, Tempelhof (466 40), and there are local stations at: Jägerstrasse 48, Mitte (466 433 2700); Bismarkstrasse 111, Charlottenburg (466 422 7701); Friesenstrasse 16, Kreuzberg (466 455 2700); Hauptstrasse 44, Schöneberg (466 444 2700); Eberswalder Strasse 6-9 (466 411 5700). But police will be dispatched from the appropriate office if you just dial 466 40.

Postal services

Most post offices (simply Post in German) are open from 8am to 6pm Monday to Friday, and 8am to 1pm Saturday.

For non-local mail, use the *Andere Richtungen* ('other destinations') slot in post-boxes. Letters of up to 20 grams (7oz) to anywhere in Germany and the EU need €0.55 in postage. Postcards require €0.45. For anywhere outside the EU, a 20-gram airmail letter costs €1.70, a postcard €1.

Postamt Friedrichstrasse

Georgenstrasse 12, Mitte (0180 233 33). U6, S1, S2, S5, S7, S9, S75 Friedrichstrasse. **Open** 6am-10pm Mon-Fri; 8am-10pm Sat, Sun. **Map** p318 M6.

Berlin has no main post office. However, this branch, which is to be found inside Friedrichstrasse station, keeps the longest opening hours of the Berlin offices.

Poste restante

Poste restante facilities are available at the main post offices of each district. Address them to the recipient 'Postlagernd,' followed by the address of the post office, or collect them from the counter marked Postlagernde Sendungen. Take your passport with you.

Public holidays

On public holidays (*Feiertagen*) it can be difficult to get things done in Berlin. However, most cafés, bars and restaurants stay open – except on the evening of 24 December, when almost everything closes.

Public holidays are: **New Year's Day** (1 Jan); **Good Friday** (Mar/Apr); **Easter Monday** (Mar/Apr); **May/Labour Day** (1 May); **Ascension Day** (May/June; ten days before Whitsun/Pentacost, the 7th Sun after Easter); **Whit/Pentacost Monday** (May/June); **Day of German Unity** (3 Oct); **Day of Prayer and National Repentance** (3rd Wed in Nov); **Christmas Eve** (24 Dec); **Christmas Day** (25 Dec); **Boxing Day** (26 Dec).

Religion

Berlin's not so Godless after all. For places of worship, see **www.berlinfo.com** and click on the link for 'community').

Safety & security

Though crime is increasing, Berlin remains a safe city by Western standards. Even for a woman, it's pretty safe to walk around alone at night in most central areas of the city. However, avoid the Eastern

working-class suburbs if you look gay or non-German. Pickpockets are not unknown around tourist areas. Use some common sense and you're unlikely to get into trouble.

Smoking

Many Berliners smoke, though the habit is in decline. Smoking is banned on public transport, in theatres and many public institutions. Many bars and restaurants have closed-off smoking rooms. Smaller, one-room establishments (under 75 square metres) may allow smoking if they want to, but must post a sign outside denoting a 'Raucher-Kneipe' (smoker pub). There's no problem with smoking at outside tables – which means that even in winter there are now lots of places with outside tables.

Study

Germany's university system is currently in a state of flux. Under the Bologna Process (the EU's initiative to create a unified standard of education throughout Europe), the traditional *Magister* degree – which lasts between nine and 12 terms, during which time students can take a wide variety of courses – is being replaced by the internationally recognised Bachelors and Masters degrees. Confusion reigns among lecturers who have not been trained properly in the new regulations and the gradual changeover has created a two-tiered system, with students on different courses at the same university receiving grossly discrepant levels of education and qualification. Magister students are often favoured by employers because of the length and depth of the degree compared to the three-year Bachelor. A question mark still hangs over the introduction of

tuition fees across the city, while lack of funding has led to increasingly sporadic library opening hours. One thing was laid to rest in 2007 – the Freie Universität was crowned an 'elite university' by the government in October (among nine in Germany), ending months of frenzied competition between Berlin's four universities. Now it's a question of what happens next. Berlin retains its pull on scholars from across the world. There are currently almost 150,000 students in the city – approximately ten per cent of whom are foreigners – divided between four universities and 16 subject-specific colleges.

Language classes

Goethe-Institut

Neue Schönhauser Strasse 20, Mitte (259 063/www.goethe.de). U8 Weinmeisterstrasse or S5, S7, S9, S75 Hackescher Markt. **Map** p319/p326 O5.
Although considerably more expensive than most of its competitors (a four-week course costs €1,040, or €1,470 with accommodation), the Goethe-Institut offers the most systematic and intensive language courses in the city. Enrolled students can benefit from extra-curricular conversation classes, as well as a Cultural Extension Programme that organises regular cinema, theatre and museum visits. Exams can be taken (with certificates awarded) at the end of every course.

Tandem

Lychener Strasse 7, Prenzlauer Berg (441 3003/www.tandem-berlin.de). U2 Eberswalder Strasse. **Map** p319/p328 O3/P3.
For a single payment of €5 Tandem will put you in touch with two German speakers interested in conversation exchange. Formal language classes are also available at €370 a month.

Universities

Freie Universität Berlin

Central administration, Kaiserswerther Strasse 16-18, Dahlem (info 838 700 00/www. FU-Berlin.de). U3 Dahlem-Dorf.

Germany's largest university was founded in 1948, after the Humboldt fell under East German control. Centre of the 1969 student movement, as well as to the quieter radicalism of the Green Party, the FU was for a long time a hotbed of romantic left-wing dissent. A founding constitution ensured that students were represented on the university's governing body and given a vote on all major decisions.

Sadly, though, not much of this idealism remains. The Student Committee still exists, but retains no decision-making powers, and the vast, anonymous campus is embroiled in the same bureaucratic structures as any other modern university. Since the Wall came down the FU lost much of its prestige and influence to its fierce rival, the newly restructured Humboldt, and the vast, anonymous campus is embroiled in the same bureaucratic structures as any other modern (and German) university. The FU got one up on the Humboldt with its new 'elite university' status, won on its strategy for an 'International Network University'. The resulting €21 million a year for proposed new research projects is welcome in the strapped-for-cash capital.

Humboldt-Universität zu Berlin (HUB)

Unter den Linden 6, Mitte (20930/www.hu-berlin.de). U6, S1, S2, S5, S7, S9, S75 Friedrichstrasse. **Map** p318-9/p327 N6/M6
Founded in 1810 by the humanist Willem von Humboldt, the HU was the first university in the world where teachers were expected, as a term of their employment, to further their own research. Hegel and Schopenhauer both taught there, Karl Marx was a student, and other departments have included the likes of Albert Einstein, Werner Heisenberg, Heinrich Heine and Max Planck. The HU entered a dark period in the 1930s, when Professors and students joined enthusiastically in the Nazi book-burning on Bebelplatz. After 1945 the university fell into decline under communism.

Since 1989, the HU has regained much of its former reputation and a variety of new courses are being offered. Together with the FU, it owns the prestigious Charité, one of the largest medical schools in Europe. It lost out in the 'elite universities' competition, but it was a close run thing, with the HU knocked out only in the final round. In August 2007, the university got into the world's press after sociologist Andrej Holm was arrested under anti-terror laws and accused of associating with

a terrorist group, apparently on the basis of his academic work. A protest was mounted and Holm was set free, but remains under investigation.

Technische Universität Berlin (TU)

Strasse des 17. Juni 135, Tiergarten (3140/www.TU-Berlin.de). U2 Ernst-Reuter-Platz. **Map** p321 F7.
The TU began life in 1879 when the former Building and Vocational Academies merged into a single institution. Since 1916 the former Mining Academy has also been included. The university is strong in chemistry, engineering and architecture, and counts Schinkel among its graduates. In the 1930s the emphasis on development, business and construction made the TU a priority for the Nazi government, which allocated it more funds than any other university in the country.

After the war, the TU was reopened under its current name and expanded to include philosophy, psychology and the social sciences. It is now (with some 30,000 students, 19 per cent of whom are foreigners) one of Germany's largest universities. A new library was recently built.

Sprach- und Kulturbörse an der TU Berlin

Raum 1503, Franklinstrasse 29, Charlottenburg (3142 2730/www2.tu-berlin.de/fak1/skb). U2 Ernst-Reuter-Platz. **Open** 3.30-5.30pm Mon; 3.30-6pm Tue; 10.30am-12.30pm Wed; 11am-2pm Thur. Mon, Wed telephone only.
Map p317 F6.
The TU's Language and Cultural Exchange Programme for foreigners, the SKB, is open to students from any university in Berlin. It offers a range of services, including language courses and seminars on international issues.

Universität der Künste Berlin (UdK)

Hardenbergstrasse 33, Charlottenburg (318 50/www.udk-berlin.de). U2, U9, S5, S7, S9, S75 Zoologischer Garten. **Map** p321/p328 F7.
Formerly the Hochschule der Künste (a name most Berliners still use), and founded in 1975 as a single vocational academy comprising the former Colleges of Art, Drama, Music and Printing. The range of subjects has been further broadened over the years, and courses are now offered in everything from Fashion Design to Experimental Film and Media. The eclectic variety of artistic and academic disciplines, along with the appointments of some high-profile

teachers – such as Rebecca Horn, Georg Baselitz and Vivienne Westwood (1992-2005) – have secured the UdK a well-deserved reputation as one of the best establishments of its kind in Europe. About once a month, the student body organises special lectures with modish artists, often in English.

Useful organisations

Studentenwerk Berlin

Hardenbergstrasse 34, Charlottenburg (311 20/info line 311 2317/www.studentenwerk-berlin.de). U2, U9, S5, S7, S9, S75 Zoologischer Garten. **Open** 8am-6pm Mon-Fri. **Map** p321/p328 F7.
The central organisation for students in Berlin will give advice and provide information about accommodation, finance, employment and various other essentials.

Telephones

All phone numbers in this guide are local Berlin numbers (other than those in the chapter Trips Out of Town). However, readers should note that numbers beginning with 0180 have higher tariffs, and numbers beginning 016 or 017 are mobiles. To call a Berlin number from outside the city, *see below*.

Dialling & codes

To phone Berlin from abroad, dial the international access code (00 from the UK, 011 from the US, 0011 from Australia), then 49 (for Germany) and 30 (for Berlin), followed by the local number.

To phone abroad from Germany dial 00, then the appropriate country-code:

Australia 61;
Canada 1;
Ireland 353;
New Zealand 64;
United Kingdom 44;
United States 1.

Then, dial the local area code (minus the initial zero) and the local number.

To call Berlin from elsewhere in Germany, dial 030 and then the local number.

Directory

Making a call

Calls within Berlin between the hours of 9am and 6pm cost €0.10 per minute. Numbers prefixed 0180 are charged at €0.14 per minute.

A call from Berlin to the United Kingdom or Ireland costs €0.13 per minute, to the US and Canada €0.13 per minute and to Australia €0.79 per minute.

Both local and international calls can be a lot cheaper if you simply dial a prefix before the international code. There are various numbers and they change from time to time. Look in local newspapers or visit www.tariftip.de.

Public phones

Most public phones give you the option of cards or coins, and from Telekom phones (the ones with the magenta 'T') you also can send SMSs. Phonecards can be bought at post offices and in newsagents for various sums from €5 to €50.

Operator services

For online directory enquiries, go to www.teleauskunft.de.

Alarm calls/Weckruf
0180 114 1033 (automated, in German).

International directory enquiries
11834.

Operator assistance/German directory enquiries
11833 (11837 in English).

Phone repairs/Störungsannahme
080 0330 2000.

Time (Zeitansage)
090 0100 1191 (automated, in German).

Weather (Wettervorhersage)
0190 116 400 (automated, in German).

Mobile phones

German mobile phones networks operate at 900MHz, so all UK and Australian mobiles should work in Berlin (so long as roaming has been activated in advance). US and Canadian cell phones users (whose phones operate at 1,900MHz) should check whether their phones can switch to 900MHz. If they can't, you can rent a 'Handy', as the Germans call them, via www.edikom-online.com. They'll deliver to your hotel and pick it back up from there when you're going.

Time

Germany is on Central European Time – one hour ahead of Greenwich Mean Time.

When summer time is in effect, London is one hour behind Berlin, New York is six hours behind, San Francisco is nine hours behind, and Sydney is nine hours ahead.

Germany uses a 24-hour system. 8am is '8 Uhr' (usually written 8h), noon is '12 Uhr Mittags' or just '12 Uhr', 5pm is '17 Uhr' and midnight is '12 Uhr Mitternachts' or just "Mitternacht'. 8.15 is '8 Uhr 15' or 'Viertel nach 8'; 8.30 is '8 Uhr 30' or 'halb 9'; and 8.45 is '8 Uhr 45' or 'Viertel vor 9'.

Tipping

A 10 per cent service charge will already be part of your restaurant bill, but it's common to leave a small tip too. In a taxi round up the bill to the nearest euro.

Weather report

	Average max temperature (˚C/˚F)	Average min temperature (˚C/˚F)	Average daily sunshine (hrs/dy)	Average rainfall (mm/in)
Jan	2°C/36°F	-3°C/27°F	2hrs	43mm/0.17in
Feb	3°C/37°F	-2°C/28°F	3hrs	38mm/0.15in
Mar	8°C/46°F	0°C/32°F	5hrs	38mm/0.15in
Apr	13°C/55°F	4°C/39°F	6hrs	43mm/0.17in
May	18°C/64°F	8°C/46°F	8hrs	56mm/0.22in
June	22°C/72°F	11°C/52°F	8hrs	71mm/0.28in
July	23°C/73°F	13°C/55°F	8hrs	53mm/0.21in
Aug	23°C/73°F	12°C/54°F	7hrs	66mm/0.26in
Sept	18°C/64°F	9°C/48°F	6hrs	46mm/0.18in
Oct	13°C/55°F	6°C/43°F	4hrs	36mm/0.14in
Nov	7°C/45°F	2°C/36°F	2hrs	51mm/0.20in
Dec	3°C/37°F	-1°C/30°F	1hr	56mm/0.22in

Directory

Toilets

Coin-operated, self-cleaning 'City Toilets' are becoming the norm. The toilets in main stations are looked after by an attendant and are pretty clean. Restaurants and cafés have to let you use their toilets by law and legally they can't refuse you a glass of water either.

Tourist information

Berlin Tourismus Marketing (BTM)

Europa-Center, Budapester Strasse, Charlottenburg (250 025/www.btm. de). U2, U9, S5, S7, S9, S75, Zoologischer Garten. **Open** 10am-7pm Mon-Fri; 10am-6pm Sat, Sun. **Map** p321 G8.
Berlin's official (if private) tourist organisation. The Brandenburg Gate branch is open 10am-6pm daily.

EurAide

DB Reisezentrum, Hauptbahnhof, Tiergarten (www.euraide.de). S5, S7, S9, S75 Hauptbahnhof. **Open** May-Aug 10am-7pm daily. Sept-Dec 23, Feb 15-Apr 11am-6pm Mon-Fri. **Map** p318 K5.
Staff advise on sights, hostels, tours and transport, and sell rail tickets.

Visas & immigration

A passport valid for three months beyond the length of stay is all that is required for UK, EU, US, Canadian and Australian citizens for a stay in Germany of up to three months. Citizens of EU countries with valid national ID cards need only show their ID cards. Citizens of other countries should check with their local German embassy or consulate whether a visa is required. As with any trip, confirm visa requirements well before you plan to travel.

Residence permits

For stays of longer than three months, you'll need a residence permit. EU citizens, and those of Andorra, Australia, Canada, Cyprus, Israel, Japan, Malta, New Zealand and the US can obtain one by doing the following.

First you need to register at your local *Anmeldungsamt*. There is one in the Bürgeramt of every district. A list can be found at www.berlin.de/buergerberatung. You don't need an appointment, but expect to wait. Bring your passport and proof of a Berlin address. You'll be issued with an *Anmeldungsbestätigung* – a form confirming you have registered at the Anmeldungsamt.

At this point, take your *Anmeldungsbestätigung* to the *Landesamt für Bürger und Ordnungsangelegenheiten Ausländerbehörde* in the Moabit district of Tiergarten. Also bring your passport, two passport photos and something to read. There are always huge queues and it takes forever – people start queuing hours before the office opens – but all you can do is take a number and wait. Eventually you will be issued with an *Aufenthaltserlaubnis* – a residence permit. If you have a work contract, bring it – you may be granted a longer stay.

If unsure about your status, contact the German Embassy in your country of origin, or your own embassy or consulate in Berlin. *See p291* **Embassies & consulates**.

Landesamt für Bürger und Ordnungsangelegenhei ten Ausländerbehörde

Friedrich-Krause-Ufer 24, Tiergarten (info 9026 94000). S41, S42, S45, S46, S47 Westhafen. **Open** 8am-2pm Mon-Fri (telephone only) and then by appointment. **Map** p317 H3

When to go

Berlin has a continental climate, hot in summer and cold in winter. In January and February Berlin often ices over. Spring begins in late March/April. May and June are the most beautiful months.

Women

See also p293 **Helplines** and *p291* **Health**.

Women's centres

EWA Frauenzentrum

Prenzlauer Allee 6, Prenzlauer Berg (442 5542/www.ewa-frauen zentrum.de). U2 Senefelderplatz. **Open** 10am-6pm Mon-Fri; 10pm-11pm Sat. *Café & gallery* 6-11pm Mon-Thur. **Map** p319 P4.

Working in Berlin

The small ads in the magazines *Zitty, tip (see p296)* and *Zweite Hand* are good places to look for work. Teaching English is popular: there is always a demand for native English speakers.

If you're studying in Berlin, try the *Studenten Vermittlung Arbeitsamt* ('Student Job Service'). You'll need your passport, student card and a *Lohnsteuerkarte* ('tax card'), available from your local Finanzamt ('tax office' – listed in the *Yellow Pages*). Tax is reclaimable. Students looking for summer work can contact the Zentralstelle für Arbeitsvermittlung.

The German equivalent of the Job Centre is the Arbeitsamt ('Employment Service'). There are very few private agencies. To find the address of your nearest office in Germany, look in the *Gelbe Seiten* under Arbeitsämter.

EU nationals have the right to live and work in Germany without a work permit.

Studenten Vermittlung Arbeitsamt

Hardenbergstrasse 34, Charlottenburg (311 20/www. studentenwerk-berlin.de). U2 Ernst-Reuter-Platz. **Open** 8am-6pm Mon-Fri. **Map** p321/p328 F7.

Vocabulary

Pronunciation

z – pronounced ts
w – like English v
v – like English f
s – like English z, but softer
r – like a throaty French r
a – as in father
e – sometimes as in bed,
sometimes as in day
i – as in seek
o – as in note
u – as in loot
ch – as in Scottish loch
ä – combination of a and e,
like ai in paid or like e in set
ö – combination of o and e,
as in French eu
ü – combination of u and e,
like true
ai – like pie
au – like house
ie – like free
ee – like hey
ei – like fine
eu – like coil

Useful phrases

hello/good day – guten Tag
goodbye – auf Wiedersehen
goodbye (informal) – tschüss
good morning – guten Morgen
good evening – guten Abend
good night – gute Nacht
yes – ja; (emphatic) jawohl
no – nein, nee
maybe – vielleicht
please – bitte
thank you – danke
thank you very much –
danke schön
excuse me – entschuldigen
Sie mir bitte
sorry! – Verzeihung!
I'm sorry, I don't speak
German – Entschuldigung,
ich spreche kein Deutsch
do you speak English? –
sprechen Sie Englisch?
can you please speak
more slowly? – können
Sie bitte langsamer sprechen?
my name is... – ich heisse...
I would like... – ich möchte...
how much is... ? –
wieviel kostet... ?

can I have a receipt? – darf
ich bitte eine Quittung haben?
how do I get to... ? – wie
komme ich nach... ?
how far is it to... ? – wie
weit ist es nach... ?
where is... ? – wo ist... ?
can you call me a cab? –
können Sie bitte mir
ein Taxi rufen?
open/closed –
geöffnet/geschlossen
with/without – mit/ohne
cheap/expensive –
billig/teuer
big/small – gross/klein
entrance/exit –
Eingang/Ausgang
arrival/departure –
Ankunft/Abfahrt
airport – der Flughafen
railway station – der Bahnhof
ticket – die Fahrkarte,
der Fahrschein
airline ticket – die
Flugkarte, der Flugschein
cashier/ticket office/
box office – die Kasse
currency exchange –
der Geldwechsel
bureau de change –
die Wechselstube
passport – der Reisepass
petrol – das Benzin
lead-free – bleifrei
traffic – der Vehrkehr
left – links
right – rechts
straight ahead – gerade aus
far – weit
near – nah
street – die Strasse
square – der Platz
city map – der Stadtplan
help! – Hilfe!
I feel ill – ich bin krank
doctor – der Arzt
dentist – der Zahnarzt
pharmacy – die Apotheke
hospital – das Krankenhaus
I need a doctor – ich
brauche einen Arzt
please call an ambulance
– rufen Sie bitte ein
Krankenwagen
please call the police –
rufen Sie bitte die Polizei

Numbers

0 null; 1 eins; 2 zwei; 3 drei; 4
vier; 5 fünf; 6 sechs; 7 sieben;
8 acht; 9 neun; 10 zehn; 11
elf; 12 zwölf; 13 dreizehn;
14 vierzehn; 15 fünfzehn;
16 sechszehn; 17 siebzehn;
18 achtzehn; 19 neunzehn; 20
zwanzig; 21 einundzwanzig;
22 zweiundzwanzig; 30
dreissig; 40 vierzig; 50 fünfzig;
60 sechszig; 70 siebzig; 80
achtzig; 90 neunzig; 100
hundert; 101 hunderteins; 110
hundertzehn; 200 zweihundert;
201 zweihunderteins; 1,000
tausend; 2,000 zweitausend

Days & times of day

Monday – der Montag;
Tuesday – der Dienstag;
Wednesday – der Mittwoch;
Thursday – der Donnerstag;
Friday – der Freitag;
Saturday – der Samstag,
der Sonnabend; Sunday –
der Sonntag; Morning –
der Morgen; Noon – der
Mittag; Afternoon – der
Nachmittag; Evening –
der Abend; Night – die Nacht;
Today – Heute; Yesterday
– Gestern; Tomorrow –
Morgen

Everyday idioms

ich verstehe nur Bahnhof
– I understand only station
(I didn't catch a single word)
Schwein/Pech haben –
to have pig/pitch (to be lucky/
unlucky)
bleib auf dem Teppich –
stay on the carpet (keep
your cool)
mein lieber Herr
Gesangsverein! – my
dear Mr Singing Club!
(I am surprised!)
mir ist alles wurst –
it's all sausage to me
(I couldn't care less)

Further Reference

Books

We've chosen for quality and interest as much as availability. Most are in print, but some will only be found in libraries or second-hand. Date is that of first publication in English.

Fiction

Baum, Vicki
Berlin Hotel (London 1946)
Written in 1944, this pulp thriller anticipates the horror of the collapsing Reich via the story of a German resistance fighter trapped in a hotel with a lurid cast of Nazi bigwigs.
Deighton, Len *Berlin Game, Mexico Set, London Match* (London 1983, 1984, 1985)
Epic espionage trilogy with labyrinthine plot set against an accurate picture of 1980s Berlin. The next six books aren't bad either.
Döblin, Alfred
Berlin-Alexanderplatz (London 1975)
Devastating expressionist portrait of the inter-war underworld in the working class quarters of Alexanderplatz.
Eckhart, Gabriele *Hitchhiking* (Lincoln, Nebraska 1992)
Short stories viewing East Berlin through the eyes of street cleaners and a female construction worker.
Grass, Gunther
Local Anaesthetic (New York 1970)
The angst of a schoolboy threatening to burn a dog in the Ku'damm to protest the Vietnam War is firmly satirised, albeit in Grass's irritating schoolmasterly way.
Harris, Robert
Fatherland (London 1992)
Alternative history and detective novel set in a 1964 Berlin as the Nazis might have built it.
Isherwood, Christopher
Mr Norris Changes Trains, Goodbye To Berlin (London 1935, 1939)
Isherwood's two Berlin novels, the basis of the movie Cabaret, offer finely drawn characters and a sharp picture of the city as it tipped over into Nazism.
Johnson, Uwe
Two Views (New York 1966)
Love story across the East-West divide, strong on the mood of Berlin in the late 1950s and early 1960s.
Kaminer, Wladimir
Russian Disco (London 2002)
Best-selling collection of short tales from Russian emigre and DJ.
Kerr, Philip
Berlin Noir (London 1994)
The Bernie Gunther trilogy, about a private detective in Nazi Berlin.
Markstein, George
Ultimate Issue (London 1981)
Stark thriller of political expediency leading to uncomfortable conclusion about why the Wall went up.
McEwan, Ian
The Innocent (London 1990)
Tale of naive young Englishman recruited into Cold War machinations with tragi-comic results.
Nabokov, Vladimir *The Gift* (New York 1963)
Written and set in 1920s Berlin, where impoverished Russian émigré dreams of writing a book very like this one.
Porter, Henry
Brandenburg (London 2005)
Decent fall-of-the-Wall spy thriller, even if the author does get some of the street names wrong.
Regener, Sven *(Berlin Blues* (London 2003)
Irresponsibility and childhood's end in the bars of late 1980s Kreuzberg – a western version of ostalgic thinking.
Ryan, Robert
Dying Day (London, 2007)
Readable espionage thriller with the Berlin Airlift as backdrop.
Schneider, Peter
The Wall Jumper (London 1984)
Somewhere between novel, prose poem and artful reportage, a meditation on the absurdities of the Wall.

Children

Kästner, Erich *Emil and the Detectives* (London 1931)
Classic set mostly around Bahnhof Zoo and Nollendorfplatz.

Biography & memoir

Anonymous *A Woman in Berlin* (New York, 1954)
Extraordinary diary of a woman fighting to survive at the end of World War II in the ruins of Berlin.
Baumann, Bommi
How It All Began (Vancouver 1977)
Frank and funny insider's account of the Berlin origins of West German terrorism.
Bielenberg, Christabel
The Past Is Myself (London 1968)
Fascinating autobiography of an English woman who married a German lawyer and lived through the war in Berlin.
Funder, Anna
Stasiland (London 2003)
Brutal stories of individuals and the East German state, reconstructed through the author's conversations with friends..

Newton, Helmut *Autobiography* (London 2003)
Begins with an absorbing account of growing up Jewish in Weimar Berlin, and Newton's apprenticeship with fashion photographer Yva.
Parker, Peter *Isherwood* (London, 2004)
Enormous biography includes a well-researched section on the author's Berlin trouble.
Rimmer, Dave *Once Upon A Time In The East* (London 1992)
The collapse of communism seen stoned and from street level – tales of games between East and West Berlin and travels through assorted East European revolutions.
Schirer, William L
Berlin Diaries (New York 1941)
Foreign correspondent in Berlin 1931-1941 bears appalled witness to Europe's plunge into Armageddon.

History

Beevor, Antony *Berlin: The Downfall 1945* (London, 2002)
Bestselling narrative history of the Third Reich's final, desperate collapse.
Friedrich, Otto
Before The Deluge (New York, 1972)
Vivid portrait of 1920s Berlin, based on interviews with those who survived what followed.
Gaines, James *Evening in the Palace of Reason* (London 2005)
Fascinating essay on music, politics and the Enlightenment built around the 1747 Potsdam encounter of Bach and Frederick the Great.
Garton Ash, Timothy
We The People (London 1990)
Instant history of the 1989 revolutions by on-the-spot academic.
Kellerhoff, Sven Felix
The Führer Bunker (Berlin 2004)
The bare facts about Hitler's last refuge and what became of it.
Levenson, Thomas
Einstein in Berlin (New York 2003)
Absorbing account of the historical deal between physicist and city.
McElvoy, Anne
The Saddled Cow (London 1992)
Lively history of East Germany by a former Berlin Times correspondent.
Metzger, Rainer
Berlin in the 20s (London 2007)
A wonderful pictorial record – photos, posters, paintings – of Berlin's most creative era.
Read, Anthony and **Fisher, David**
Berlin – The Biography Of A City (London 1994)
Readable, lightweight history.
Richie, Alexandra
Faust's Metropolis (London 1998)
Best one-volume history of Berlin.

Directory

Taylor, Frederick
The Berlin Wall (London 2006)
Now the definitive history of the
notorious border. Taylor's book on
Dresden is well worth a read, too.

Architecture

Ladd, Brian *The Ghosts Of Berlin:
Confronting German History In The
Urban Landscape* (Chicago, 1997)
Erudite and insightful look into the
relationship between architecture,
urbanism and Berlin's violent
political history.

Miscellaneous

Dax, Max and **Defcon, Robert**
*Einstürzende Neubauten: No Beauty
Without Danger* (Berlin 2005)
Engaging oral history of the group
also serves as anilluminating picture
of West Berlin's rock underground
from 1980 through the fall of the Wall.

Film

Cabaret (Bob Fosse, 1972)
Liza Minelli as Sally Bowles, the
very definition of the Berlin myth.
Christiane F. (Uli Edel, 1981)
To hell and back in the housing
estates and heroin scene of late 1970s
West Berlin, with Bowie soundtrack.
A Foreign Affair
(Billy Wilder, 1948)
Marlene Dietrich sings 'Black
Market' among the romantically
rendered ruins of post-war Berlin.
Funeral In Berlin
(Guy Hamilton, 1966)
Adaptation of Len Deighton's novel:
Michael Caine in entertaining,
puzzling Cold War yarn.
Good bye, Lenin!
(Wolfgang Becker, 2003)
Ostalgia, the movie – a comic eulogy
for the GDR, in which socialism gets
a different kind of send-off.
The Good German
(Steven Soderbergh, 2006)
Clooney and Blanchett are old flames
in a black and white pastiche of
Wilder and Reed set in a cynical 1945.
**It's Not The Homosexual
Who Is Perverse But The
Situation In Which He Lives**
(Rosa von Praunheim, 1973)
The best of the flamboyant von
Praunheim's films, a laundry list of
the follies of Berlin's gay population.
The Legend of Paul And Paula
(Heiner Carow, 1974)
Cult GDR love story banned by the
unromantic regime. Soundtrack by
the also legendary Pudhys.
The Lives of Others (Florian
Henckel von Donnersmarck, 2006)
Stasi agent watches writer and
silently changes sides in this
award-winning thriller

M (Fritz Lang, 1931)
Paedophilia and vigilantism as Peter
Lorre's child murderer stalks an
expressionistic Weimar Berlin.
The Man Between
(Carol Reed, 1953)
James Mason stars in the *The
Third Man's* Berlin cousin.
Olympia (Leni Riefenstahl, 1937)
In filming the 1936 Olympics, the
Nazis' favourite director invented the
conventions of modern sportscasting.
One, Two, Three
(Billy Wilder, 1961)
James Cagney is brilliant as the Pepsi
exec whose daughter falls for East
Berlin Communist Horst Buchholz.
Possession (Andrzej Zulawski, 1981)
Sam Neil and Isabel Adjani star in
cult psychosexual horror flick which
uses its West Berlin backdrop to
compellingly weird effect.
**The Spy Who Came In From
The Cold** (Martin Ritt, 1965)
Intense atmosphere, excellent
Richard Burton performance, and
an ending that shatteringly brings
home the obscenity of the Wall.
Westler (Wieland Speck, 1985)
Low-budget gay romance between
West and East Berliners and all you
need know about the Wall in one
checkpoint strip-search scene.
Wings of Desire
(Wim Wenders, 1987)
Bruno Ganz in love, Peter Falk in a
bunker, Nick Cave in concert, and an
angel on the Siegessäule – Wenders
has never surpassed his (double)
vision of the divided city.

Music

AG Geige *Raabe?* (Zensor)
One of the first post-1989 discs
to emerge from the East Berlin
underground came from a bizarre
electronica outfit rooted in The
Residents and Die Tödliche Doris.
Ash Ra Tempel
Join Inn (Temple/Spalax)
The 1972 hippy freakout incarnation
of guitarist Manuel Göttsching,
before he was reborn as techno's
most baffling muse.
Meret Becker *Noctambule* (Ego)
Actress/chanteuse Becker restages
Weimar alongside Berliner Krankheit
classics like Neubauten's Schwarz.
The Birthday Party
Mutiny/The Bad Seed EP (4AD)
Nick Cave and cohorts escaped to
early 1980s Berlin to record their two
most intense EPs, here compressed
into one volatile CD.
David Bowie *Heroes* (EMI)
In which Bowie romanticises the
Wall and captures the atmosphere
of (misspelt) Neuköln.
David Bowie *Low* (EMI)
Begun in France, completed at Hansa
Studios, the album that soundtracked
Bowie's new career in a new town.

Brecht/Weill *Die Dreigroschenoper
Berlin 1930* (Teldec)
Historic shellac transcriptions from
1930 featuring a young and shrill
Lotte Lenya, who also contributes
a brace of Mahagony songs.
Caspar Brötzmann/FM Einheit
Merry Christmas (Blast First/
Rough Trade Deutschland)
Guitarist son Caspar is no less noisy
than père Brötzmann, especially on
this frenzy of feedback and distortion
kicked up with ex-Neubauten man-
mountain FM Einheit on, er, stones.
Peter Brötzmann
No Nothing (FMP)
Uncharacteristically introspective
recording from the sax colossus of
German improvisation for Berlin's
vital Free Music Production label,
which he co-founded 30 years ago.
Ernst Busch *Der Rote Orpheus/Der
Barrikaden Tauber* (BARBArossa)
Two-CD survey of the revolutionary
tenor's 1930s recordings covers
Brecht, Eisler and Weill.
Nick Cave
From Her To Eternity (Mute)
Cave in best Berlinerisch debauched
and desperate mode, with a title track
later featured in Wings of Desire.
Comedian Harmonists
Ihre grossen Erfolge (Laserlight)
Sublime six-part harmonies from
the Weimar sensations whose career
was cut short during the Third Reich.
Crime & The City Solution
Paradise Discotheque (Mute)
Underrated Berlin-Australian group's
finest disc (1990) is an oblique
commentary on the heady 'neo-black
market burnt-out ruins' amorality
of the immediate post-1989 era.
DAF *Kebabträume* (Mute)
Exhilarating German punk satire
of Berlin's Cold War neuroses,
culminating in the coda 'We are
the Turks of tomorrow'.
Marlene Dietrich *On Screen,
Stage And Radio* (Legend)
From 'I Am The Sexy Lola' through
'Ruins Of Berlin', the sultry
Schöneberg songstress embodies
the mood of decadent Berlin.
Einstürzende Neubauten *Berlin
Babylon Soundtrack* (Zomba)
More Neubauten 'Strategies Against
Architecture' accompanying a highly
watchable documentary about the
changes in Berlin's landscape and
the movers and shakers behind them.
Alec Empire *The Geist Of…* (Geist)
Wonderful triple CD compilation of
ATR mainman Empire's less
combative electronica explorations
for Frankfurt brainiac label Force
Inc/Mille Plateaux.
Manuel Göttsching *E2-E4* (Racket)
Great lost waveform guitar album
by ex-Ash Ra Tempel leader.
Die Haut *Head On*
(What's So Funny About)
Avantish Berlin equivalent of The
Ventures lay down Morricone-meets-

Looney-Tunes backdrops for guest singers like Alan Vega, Lydia Lunch, Kim Gordon and Jeffrey Lee Pierce.
Liaisons Dangereuses
Liaisons Dangereuses (Roadrunner) Formed by ex-DAF member Chrislo Haas, their solitary 1982 album of chipped beats and industrial atmospheres is a key influence on Detroit's techno pioneers.
Malaria! *Compiled* (Moabit Musik) With suffocating synth swirls, heavy-stepping beats and songs like 'Passion', 'Jealousy' and 'Death', Malaria! was 80s girl-pop, Berlin-style.
Maurizio *M* (M) Essential CD compilation of Basic Channel mainman Moritz Von Oswald's vinyl releases, which lights up Chicago house with streaming beats diverted from the Berlin-Detroit techno grid.
Modeselektor *Happy Birthday* (Bpitch Con) Out on Berlin techno's leftfield, idiosyncratic duo are joined on second mischievous album by guests such as Thom Yorke and Maximo Park.
Monolake *Hongkong Remastered* (Monolake) Robert Hencke's post-techno pulses in some vast acoustic space, creating a cityscape ambience with urban samples.
Barbara Morgenstern *Vermona ET-61* (Monika) Morgenstern's everywoman voice, simple lyrics and clever accompaniment on a GDR home organ grow after repeated listenings, but the achingly beautiful instrumentals are the true highlights.
Pole *CD1* (Kiff SM) Ex-Basic Channel engineer Stefan Betke defines at the cutting edge of the digidub school of blunted beats and vinyl glitches.
Iggy Pop *The Idiot* (Virgin America) With Bowie in the producer's chair, Iggy begins to absorb the influence of early German electronica and the city of bright, white clubbing.
Iggy Pop *Lust For Life* (Virgin America) Way back in West Berlin, Iggy the passenger cruises through the divided city's ripped-back sides and finds himself full of lust for life.
Rhythm & Sound w/ the artists (Indigo) Techno meets reggae at the mixing desk of Mark Ernestus and Moritz von Oswald. Eight singles (and vocalists) compiled on this and companion b-side CD, the versions.
Spacebow *Big Waves* (Noteworks) Extraordinary reverberating metallic sound sculptures hewn from Berlin-based American expatriate artist Robert Rutman's steel cellos.
Stereo Total *My Melody* (Bungalow) Demented chansons with cheesy lounge backing – Mitte's kitsch aesthetic plus a Francophone spin.

Tangerine Dream *Zeit* (Jive Electro) Where cosmic consciousness and electronic minimalism first met by the Wall.
Ton Steine Scherben *Keine Macht Für Niemand* (David Volksmund) Ernst Busch reincarnated as the early 1970s rock commune which provided Kreuzberg's anarchists with their most enduring anthems.
U2 *Achtung Baby!* (Island) It took Zoo station and post-Wall Berlin to inspire the U2 album for people who don't like U2.
Christian van Dorries *Wagnerkomplex* (Masse und Macht) Spooky examination of 'music and German national identity' carried out in the shell of the Palast der Republik using live and recorded orchestral and techno elements, electronic treatments and the building's acoustics.
Various *Das Beste Aus Der DDR Parts I-III* (Amiga) Three-part DDR rock retrospective, divided into rock, pop and 'Kult', including Ostalgia stalwarts like Puhdys, Silly and Karat plus Sandow's alt anthem 'Born in the GDR' and an early Nina Hagen ditty.
Various *Berlin 1992* (Tresor) On the first of several Tresor compilations, Berlin techno is captured in its early, apocalyptic phase. Includes Love Parade anthem 'Der Klang der Familie' by 3Phase (at that time, Dr Motte & Sven Röhrig).
Various *Berlin Super 80* (Monitorpop) CD/DVD/book set documenting the West Berlin underground 1978-83. Features all the usual musical suspects, plus scratchy Super 8 celluloid from Jörg (Nekromantic) Buttgereit, among many others.
Various *Die Grosse Untergangshow: Festival Genialer Dillentanten* (Vinyl-On-Demand) Double LP/CD and DVD set from the 1981 Tempodrom show that launched the likes of Neubauten, Gudrun Gut, Die Tödliche Doris, Mark Reeder.
Various *Hotel-Stadt-Berlin* (Hausmusik/Kompakt/Indigo) Label showcase bodes well for the future, with local electronica musicians exploring paths off the beaten track of techno and trance.
Various *Pop 2000* (Grönland/Spiegel Edition) Eight-CD companion to TV chronicle of postwar German culture in East and West. 'Ostrock' is under-represented, but otherwise an engaging compilation of the obvious and the obscure.
Various *Russensoul* (Trikont) Wladimir Kaminer and Yuriy Gurzhy's survey of Russian and east European emigré musical activity in Berlin, with the likes of Leonid Soybelman, Vulga Volga and Rotfront, as viewed from their Kaffee Burger DJ console.

Various *Tranceformed From Beyond* (MFS) Compilation that defined Berlin trance. Selection includes Cosmic Baby, Microglobe, Effective Force.
Westbam *A Practising Maniac At Work* (Low Spirit) Effectively summarises the peak of Berlin's best-known DJ, veering from stomping techno to twisted disco.

Websites

Alt-Berliner Stadtplan-Archiv *www.alt-berlin.info* Archive of searchable historic Berlin maps, from 1738 to 1989.
Berlin Info *www.berlin-info.de* Essentially a hotel booking site, but also contains information for visitors and lots of links. Operated by the official tourist board BTM and oriented to upmarket tourism.
Berlin.de *www.berlin.de* Berlin's official site – run by the tourist board (BTM) – is inevitably not its most objective but is nonetheless well written.
BVG *www.bvg.de* Online timetable and public transport information for Berlin/Brandenburg, in English and German. Includes a searchable version of the BVG atlas.
HotelGuide *berlin.hotelguide.net* A commercial site that sends you to the most expensive hotels, but then they're the ones that have online reservation services.
Leo Dictionary *http://dict.leo.org* Simply the best English-German online dictionary.
Ost-Berlin *www.ostberlin.de* Everything you wanted to know about life in the former East Berlin, Hauptstadt der DDR.
SMB *www.smb.museum* Smart bilingual site with detailed information on around 20 major Berlin museums run by the Staatlichen Museen zu Berlin.
Stadtmuseum Berlin *www.stadtmuseum.de* Comprehensive information on Berlin's museums and useful links. In German only.
Stadtplandienst *www.stadtplandienst.de* An interactive map that can pinpoint any address in the city.
Time Out *www.timeout.com/travel/berlin* General information and history, plus shop, restaurant, café, bar and hotel reviews, all written by residents.
Tip *www.tip-berlin.de* Zitty's competition, offering similar German-only listings and search functions.
Zitty *www.zitty.de* The online sister of one of Berlin's two listings fortnightlies. This rather crowded site contains listings and has search functions. In German only.

Index

Advertisers' Index

Please refer to the relevant pages for contact details

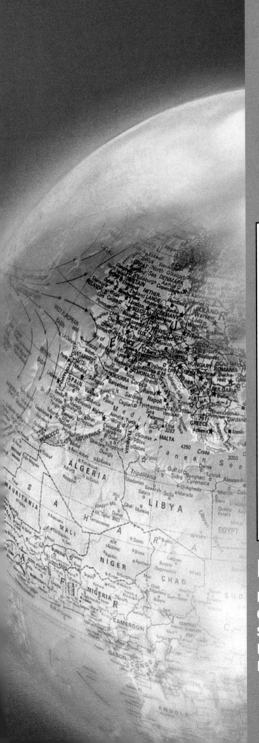

Place of interest and/or entertainment	■
Railway station	■
Park	■
Hospital/university	■
Pedestrian Area	▢
Autobahn	═
Main road	
Airport	✈
Church	✚
S-Bahn Station	Ⓢ
U-Bahn Station	Ⓤ
S-Bahn line	S1
U-Bahn line	U1
District boundary	▬
Course of Wall	▬
Area	MITTE
Hotels	❶
Restaurants	❶
Cafés, Pubs & Bars	❶

Maps

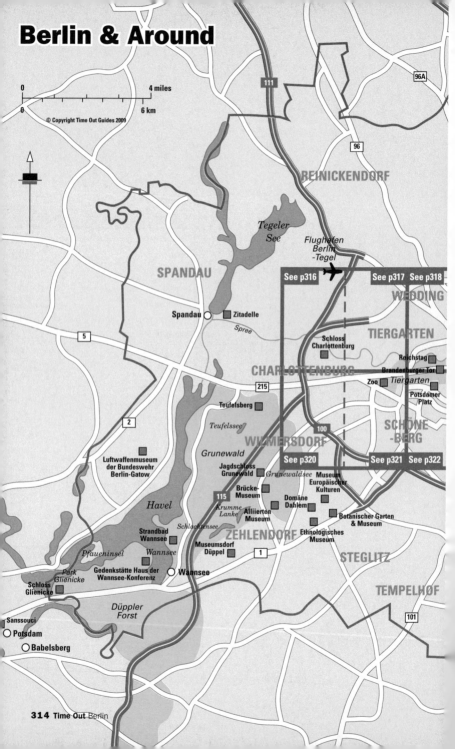

Berlin & Around

0 —————— 4 miles
0 —————— 6 km
© Copyright Time Out Guides 2009

111

96A

REINICKENDORF

Tegeler See

Flughafen Berlin -Tegel

96

See p316   See p317   See p318

WEDDING

SPANDAU

Spandau   ■ Zitadelle

Spree

TIERGARTEN

5

Schloss Charlottenburg

Reichstag
Brandenburger Tor
Zoo   *Tiergarten*

CHARLOTTENBURG

215

Potsdamer /Platz

Teufelsberg ■

Teufelssee

SCHÖNE -BERG

2

Grunewald

WILMERSDORF

100

Jagdschloss Grunewald ■
Brücke- Museum ■

See p320   See p321   See p322

Grunewaldsee   Museum Europäischer Kulturen

Havel

115

Krumme Lanke   Domäne Dahlem ■
Alliierten Museum

Botanischer Garten & Museum ■

Luftwaffenmuseum der Bundeswehr Berlin-Gatow ■

Schlachtensee

ZEHLENDORF

Ethnologisches Museum

Strandbad Wannsee ■

Museumsdorf Düppel ■

1

STEGLITZ

Pfaueninsel   *Wannsee*

Park Glienicke   Gedenkstätte Haus der Wannsee-Konferenz   ○ Wannsee

Schloss Glienicke

TEMPELHOF

Düppler Forst

Sanssouci
○ **Potsdam**

101

○ **Babelsberg**

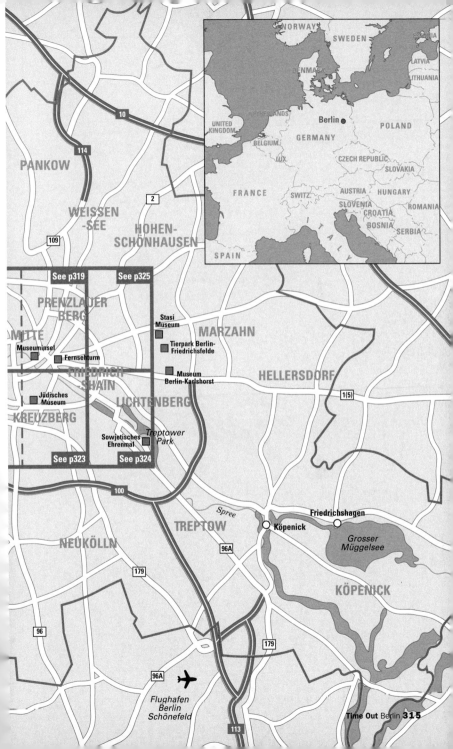

PANKOW

WEISSEN
-SEE

HOHEN-
SCHÖNHAUSEN

PRENZLAUER
BERG

See p319   See p325

MITTE

Museuminsel

Fernsehturm

Stasi
Museum

MARZAHN

Tierpark Berlin-
Friedrichsfelde

FRIEDRICH
SHAIN

Museum
Berlin-Karlshorst

HELLERSDORF

Jüdisches
Museum

LICHTENBERG

KREUZBERG

Sowjetisches
Ehrenmal

Treptower
Park

See p323   See p324

NEUKÖLLN

Spree

TREPTOW

Köpenick

Friedrichshagen

Grosser
Müggelsee

KÖPENICK

Flughafen
Berlin
Schönefeld

NORWAY   SWEDEN

DENMARK

LATVIA

LITHUANIA

UNITED
KINGDOM

NETHERLANDS

Berlin

POLAND

GERMANY

BELGIUM

LUX.

CZECH REPUBLIC

SLOVAKIA

FRANCE

SWITZ.

AUSTRIA   HUNGARY

SLOVENIA

CROATIA

ROMANIA

BOSNIA

SERBIA

SPAIN

ITALY

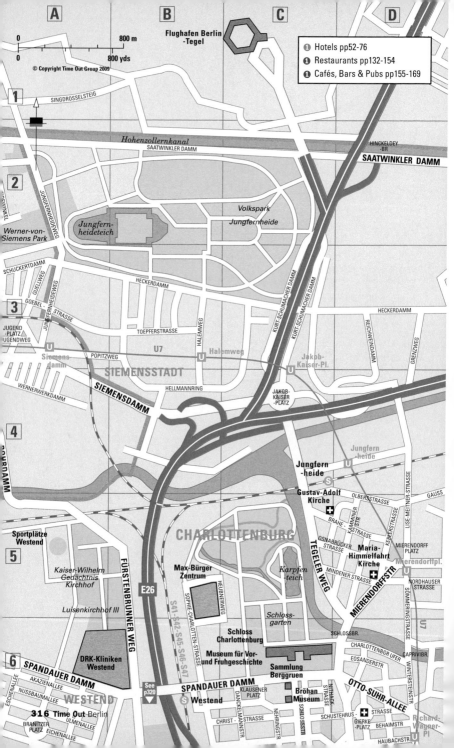

A **B** **C** **D**

0   800 m

0   800 yds

© Copyright Time Out Group 2009

Flughafen Berlin -Tegel

❶ Hotels pp52-76
❶ Restaurants pp132-154
❶ Cafés, Bars & Pubs pp155-169

1

SINGDROSSELSTEIG

Hohenzollernkanal
SAATWINKLER DAMM

HINCKELDEY -BR

SAATWINKLER DAMM

2

JUNGFERNHEIDEWEG

Werner-von- Siemens Park

Jungfern- heideteich

Volkspark Jungfernheide

SCHUCKERTDAMM

QUELLWEG

HECKERDAMM

HECKERDAMM

3

JUGEND -PLATZ UGENDWEG

JUNGFERNHEIDEWEG

GOEBELSTRASSE

TOEPFERSTRASSE

HALEMWEG

KURT-SCHUMACHER DAMM

KURT-SCHUMACHER DAMM

REICHWEINDAMM

GRENZWEG

Siemens damm

POPITZWEG

U7

U Halemweg

Jakob- Kaiser-Pl.

U

SIEMENSSTADT

WERNERWERKDAMM

HELLMANNRING

JAKOB- KAISER -PLATZ

SIEMENSDAMM

4

QUDAMM

Jungfern -heide

U

Jungfern -heide

S

Gustav-Adolf Kirche ✚

OLBERSSTRASSE

LISE-MEITNER-STRASSE

GAUSS

Sportplätze Westend

CHARLOTTENBURG

KAMMIN STR

K STRASSE

BRAHE

KEPERFSTRASSE

5

Kaiser-Wilhelm Gedächtnis Kirchhof

FÜRSTENBRUNNER WEG

Max-Bürger Zentrum

HEILBNWEG

OSNABRÜCKER STRASSE

TEGELER WEG

MINDENER STRASSE

Maria- Himmelfahrt Kirche

MIERENDORFFSTR

MIERENDORFF PLATZ

Mierendorfpl.

U

NORDHAUSER STRASSE

SÖMMERINGSTRASSE

Luisenkirchhof III

E26

SOPHIE-CHARLOTTEN-STRASSE

S41-S42-S45-S46-S47

Karpfen teich

Schloss- garten

SCHLOSSBR.

U7

CHARLOTTENBGR UFER

CAPRIVIBR.

6

SPANDAUER DAMM

DRK-Kliniken Westend

Schloss Charlottenburg

Museum für Vor- und Frühgeschichte

Sammlung Berggruen

Bröhan Museum

EOSANDERSTR

WINTERSTEINSTR

OTTO-SUHR-ALLEE

ESCHENALLEE

AKAZIENALLEE

NUSSBAUMALLEE

WESTEND

See p320 ▼

SPANDAUER DAMM

S Westend

KLAUSENER PLATZ

DANCKELMANNSTR

SCHLOSSSTR

NITHACK STRASSE

Richard- Wagner- Pl.

U

BRANITZER PLATZ

EICHENALLEE

ULMENALLEE

CHRIST- STR

NEHRINGSTR

SCHUSTEHRUS

GIERKE- PLATZ

BEHAIMSTR

HAUBACHSTR

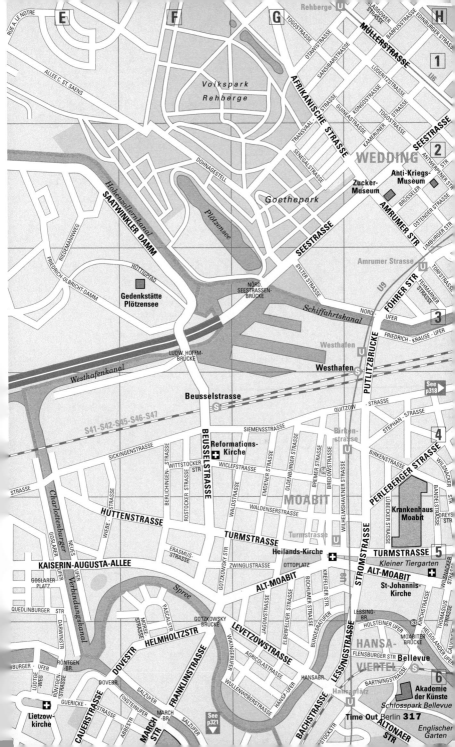

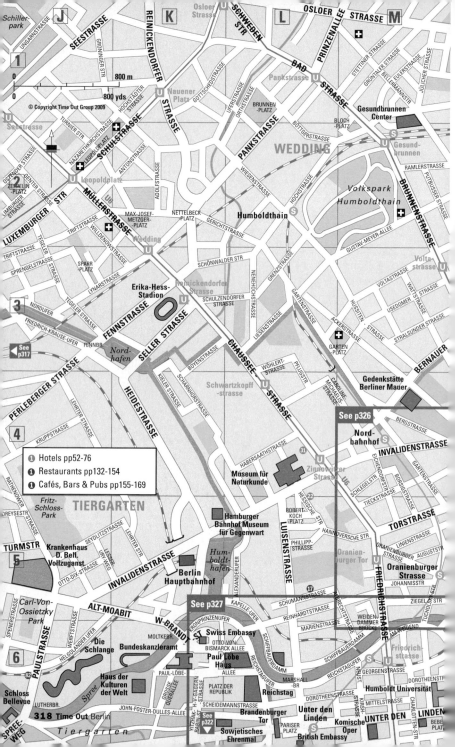

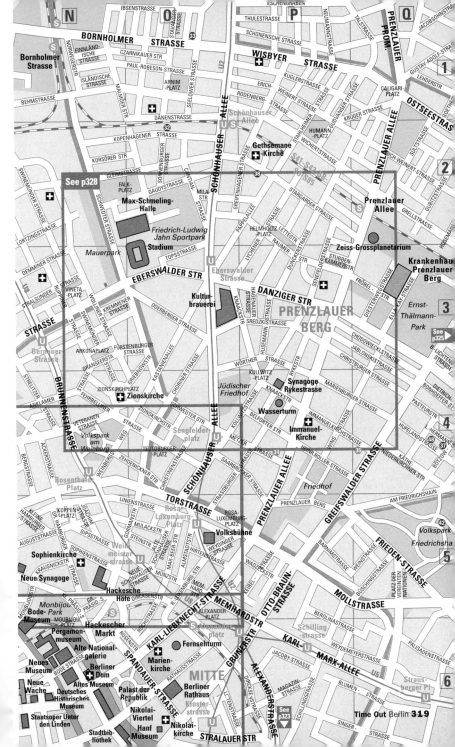

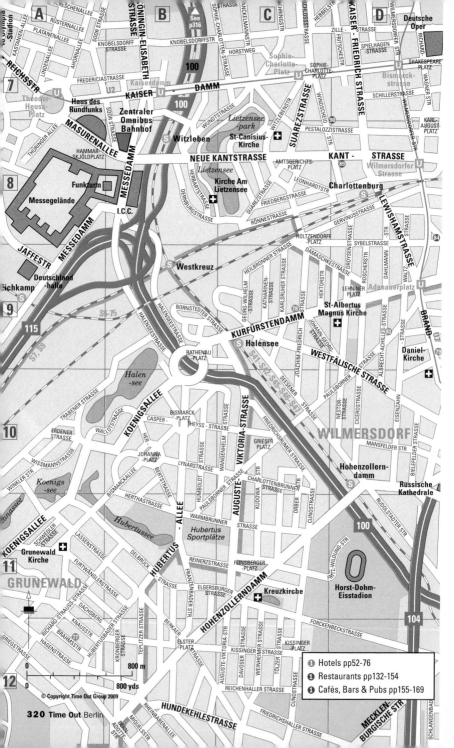

© Copyright Time Out Group 2009

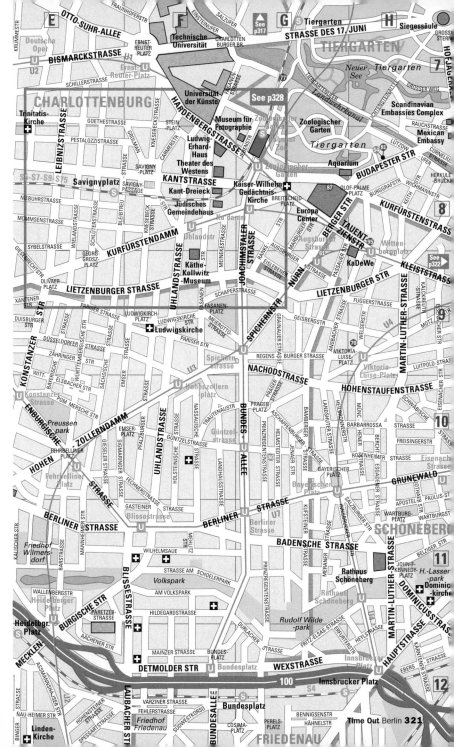

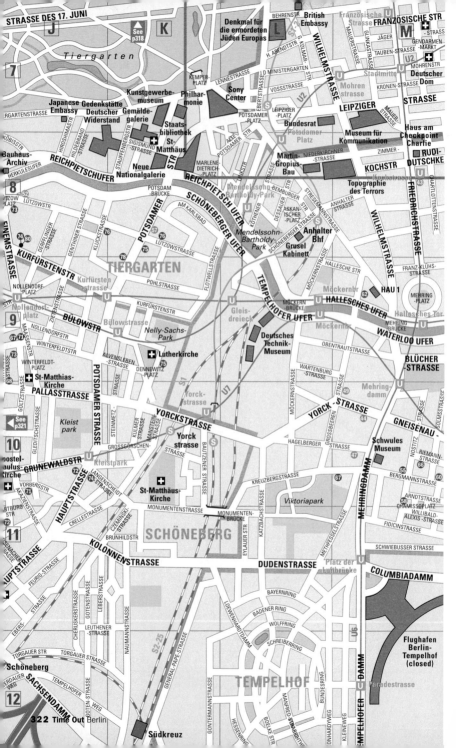

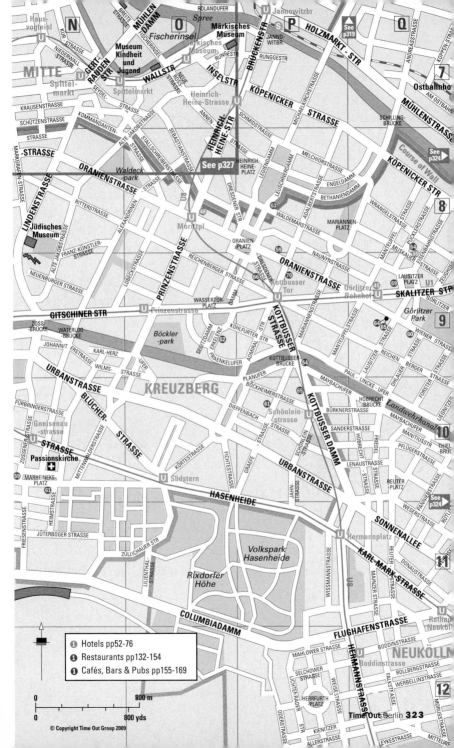

1 Hotels pp52-76
1 Restaurants pp132-154
1 Cafés, Bars & Pubs pp155-169

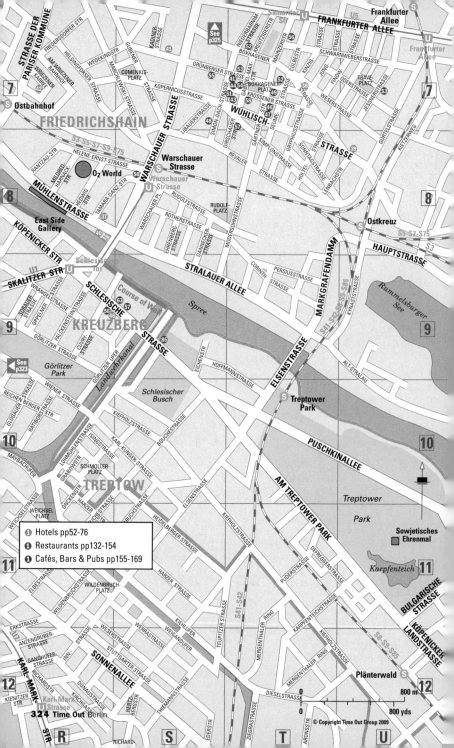

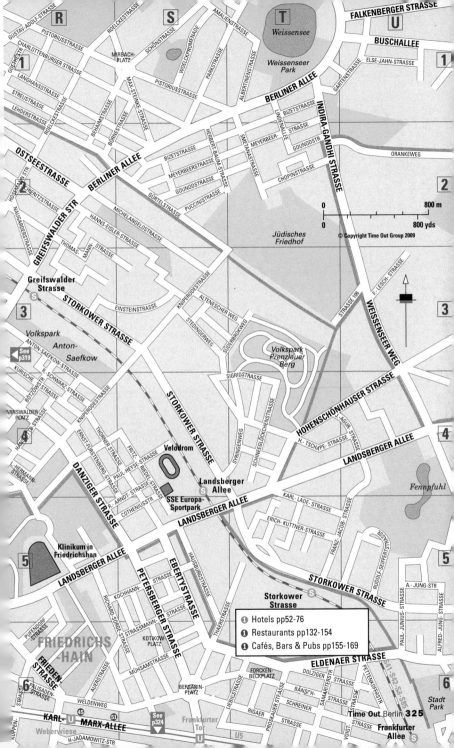

North Mite

Nord-bahnhof Ⓢ

Legend:
- Hotels pp52-76
- Restaurants pp132-154
- Cafés, Bars & Pubs pp155-169

Gedenkstätte Berliner Mauer

Volksbühne

© Copyright Time Out Group 2009

300 m

300 yds

Jüdischer Friedhof

KOLLWITZSTRASSE
METZER STRASSE
SAARBRÜCKER STRASSE
STRASSBURGER STRASSE
TORSTRASSE
SCHÖNHAUSER ALLEE
Senefelder-platz
CHRISTINENSTRASSE
ZIONSKIRCHSTR
FEHRBELLINER STRASSE
ZEHDENICKNER STR
TORSTRASSE
LINIENSTRASSE
GORMANNSTRASSE
MULACKSTRASSE
STEINSTRASSE
ALTE SCHÖNHAUSER STRASSE
Weinmeister-strasse
ROSA-LUXEMBURG-PLATZ
Rosa-Luxemburg-Platz
MAX-BEER-STRASSE
MÜNZSTRASSE
WADZINGER STRASSE
HIRTENSTRASSE
ALMSTADTSTRASSE
R. LUXEMBURG-STRASSE
MEINHARD STR
KARL-LIEBKNECHT-STRASSE
Alexander-platz
Hackescher Markt
ROCHSTRASSE
DIRCKSENSTRASSE
Hackesche Höfe
ROSENTHALER STRASSE
GIPSSTRASSE
JOACHIMSTRASSE
SOPHIENSTRASSE
Sophienkirche
Alter Jüdischer Friedhof
GR. HAMBURGER STRASSE
KOPPEN-PLATZ
ACKERSTRASSE
KLEINE HAMBURGER STRASSE
AUGUSTSTRASSE
KRAUSNICKSTRASSE
Neue Synagoge
NEUE PROMENADE
GR. PRÄSID.-STRASSE
KL. PRÄSID. STRASSE
MOUBIJOU-PLATZ
Monbijou Park
Bode-Museum
MONBIJOUSTRASSE
TUCHOLSKY STR
Volkspark am Weinberg
WEINBERGS-WEG
VETERANENSTRASSE
BRUNNENSTRASSE
Rosenthaler Platz
STRELITZER STRASSE
INVALIDENSTRASSE
BERGSTRASSE
SCHRÖDERSTRASSE
GARTENSTRASSE
BORSIGSTRASSE
TIECKSTRASSE
EICHENDORFSTRASSE
TORSTRASSE
LINIENSTRASSE
Oranienburger Strasse
ORANIENBURGER STRASSE
JOHANNISSTRASSE
KALCKSCHEUNEN-STR
ZIEGEL STRASSE
WEIDEN-DAMMER BRÜCKE
FRIEDRICHSTRASSE
Oranien-burger Tor
Brecht-Weigel-Gedenkstätte
CHAUSSEE-STRASSE
SCHLEGELSTRASSE
HANNOVERSCHE STR
INVALIDENSTRASSE

Mitte

© Copyright Time Out Group 2009

400 m
400 yds

Hotels pp52-76
Restaurants pp132-154
Cafés, Bars & Pubs pp155-169

Prenzlauer Berg

FALKPLATZ
GLEIMSTRASSE
GAUDYSTRASSE
CANTIANSTRASSE
MILA-STR

Max-Schmeling-Halle
Friedrich-Ludwig Jahn Sportpark
Stadium

Mauerpark

SCHWEDTER STRASSE

BERNAUER STRASSE EBERSWALDER STRASSE
Eberswalder Strasse

KREMMENER STRASSE
ODERBERGER STRASSE
TOPSSTRASSE

400 m
400 yds
© Copyright Time Out Group 2009

Kulturbrauerei

SCHÖNHAUSER ALLEE

ARKONAPLATZ
FÜRSTENBERGER STRASSE
SWINEMÜNDER
GRANSEER STR
GRIEBNOWSTR
KASTANIENALLEE
CHORINER STRASSE
SCHWEDTER STR
WÖRTHER

Jüdischer Friedhof

DANZIGER STRASSE
PAPPELALLEE
HELMHOLTZ-PLATZ
LYCHENER STRASSE
RAUMER STRASSE
DUNCKERSTRASSE
SENEFELDERSTRASSE
STUBBEN-KAMMERSTR
HAGENAUER STRASSE
SREDZKISTRASSE
HUSEMANN

KOLLWITZ-PLATZ
Synagoge Rykestrasse
KNAACKSTRASSE

Wasserturm
Prenzlauer Berg Museum

Zionskirche
ZIONSKIRCHSTR
FEHRBELLINER STRASSE
VETERANEN STRASSE
Volkspark am Weinberg

SCHWEDTER STR
ZIONSKIRCHSTRASSE
KOLLWITZSTRASSE
Senefelderplatz
CHRISTINENSTR
METZER STR

Prenzlauer Allee
STARGARDER STRASSE
Zeiss-Grossplanetarium
LETTESTRASSE
DIESTERWEGSTRASSE
FRÖBEL-STR

PRENZLAUER ALLEE
STRASSE
CHRISTBURGER STRASSE
MARIENBURGER STRASSE
WINS STRASSE
IMMANUELKIRCHSTRASSE
GREIFSWALDER STR
Immanuel-Kirche
BELFORTER STRASSE

❶ Hotels pp52-76
❶ Restaurants pp132-154
❶ Cafés, Bars & Pubs pp155-169

Charlottenburg

Universität der Künste
HARDENBERGSTRASSE
Museum für Fotografie
Zoologischer Garten
Bahnhof Zoo

STEIN-PLATZ
KNESEBECKSTRASSE
GROLMANSTRASSE
CARMERSTRASSE
JEBENSTRASSE

Ludwig-Erhard-Haus

Theater des Westens

Zoologischer Garten

400 m
400 yds
© Copyright Time Out Group 2009

❶ Hotels pp48-69
❶ Restaurants pp122-143
❶ Cafés, Bars & Pubs pp144-157

SAVIGNY-PLATZ

KANTSTRASSE

Savignyplatz
SAVIGNY-PASSAGE
BLEIBTREUSTR

Kant-Dreieck

Kaiser-Wilhelm-Gedächtnis-Kirche

LEIBNIZSTR
NIEBUHRSTRASSE
MOMMSENSTRASSE
WIELANDSTRASSE
SCHLÜTERSTRASSE
KNESEBECKSTRASSE
GROLMANSTR
BLEIBTREUSTR

Jüdisches Gemeindehaus

BREITSCHEIDPLATZ
Ku'damm
Uhlandstr
JOACHIMSTHALER STRASSE
AUGSBURGER STRASSE
EISLEBENER STRASSE

KURFÜRSTENDAMM

SYBELSTRASSE
GEORG-GROSZ-PLATZ
UHLANDSTRASSE
FASANENSTRASSE
MEINEKESTRASSE
RANKE-STRASSE
SCHAPERSTRASSE

Käthe-Kollwitz-Museum

OLIVAER PLATZ

PARISER STRASSE
FASANEN-PLATZ

Street Index

Berlin Public Transport

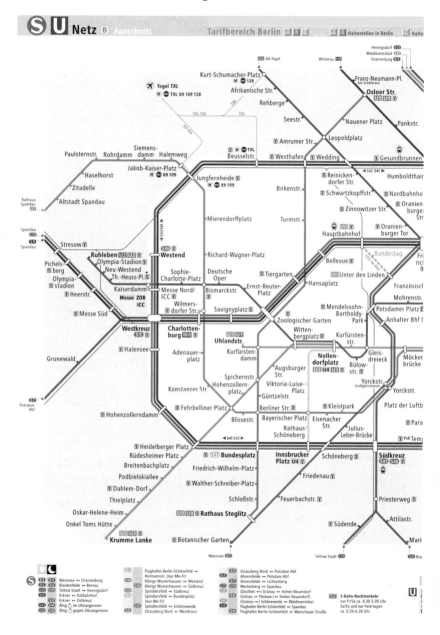

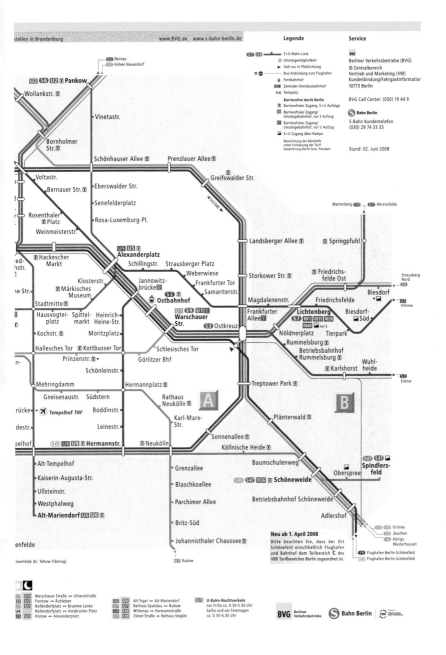

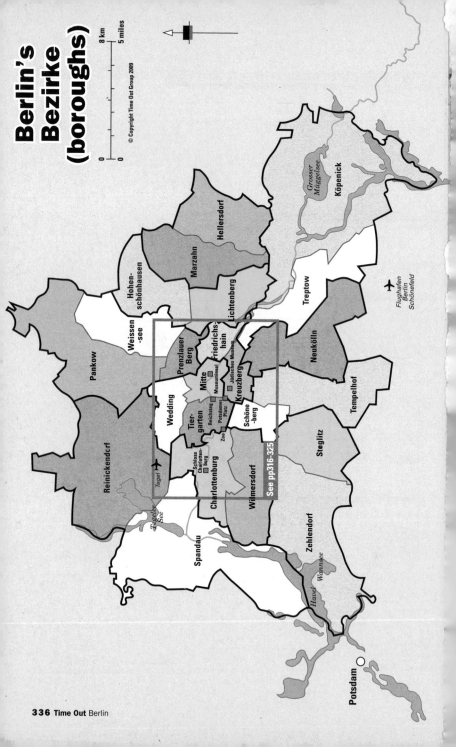

Berlin's Bezirke (boroughs)

0 — 8 km
0 — 5 miles

© Copyright Time Out Group 2009

Köpenick

Grosser Müggelsee

Hellersdorf

Marzahn

Hohen-schönhausen

Lichtenberg

Treptow

Weissen-see

Pankow

Prenzlauer Berg

Friedrichs-hain

Flughafen Berlin Schönefeld

Neukölln

Mitte

Museuminsel

Jüdisches Museum

Reinickendorf

Wedding

Kreuzberg

Tempelhof

Tier-garten

Reichstag

Potsdamer Platz

Schöne-berg

Zoo

Steglitz

Tegel

Schloss Charlotten-burg

See pp316-325

Charlottenburg

Wilmersdorf

Tegeler See

Zehlendorf

Spandau

Wannsee

Havel

Potsdam